For Reference

Not to be taken from this room

NOVELS
for Students

Advisors

Susan Allison: Head Librarian, Lewiston High School, Lewiston, Maine. Standards Committee Chairperson for Maine School Library (MASL) Programs. Board member, Julia Adams Morse Memorial Library, Greene, Maine. Advisor to Lewiston Public Library Planning Process.

Jennifer Hood: Young Adult/Reference Librarian, Cumberland Public Library, Cumberland, Rhode Island. Certified teacher, Rhode Island. Member of the New England Library Association, Rhode Island Library Association, and the Rhode Island Educational Media Association.

Ann Kearney: Head Librarian and Media Specialist, Christopher Columbus High School, Miami, Florida, 1982–2002. Thirty-two years as Librarian in various educational institutions ranging from grade schools through graduate programs. Library positions at Miami-Dade Community College, the University of Miami's Medical School Library, and Carrollton School in Coconut Grove, Florida. B.A. from University of Detroit,

1967 (magna cum laude); M.L.S., University of Missouri–Columbia, l974. Volunteer Project Leader for a school in rural Jamaica; volunteer with Adult Literacy programs.

Laurie St. Laurent: Head of Adult and Children's Services, East Lansing Public Library, East Lansing, Michigan, 1994–. M.L.S. from Western Michigan University. Chair of Michigan Lansing, Michigan, 1994–. M.L.S. from Western Michigan University. Chair of Michigan Library Association's 1998 Michigan Summer Reading Program; Chair of the Children's Services Division in 2000–2001; and Vice-President of the Association in 2002–2003. Board member of several regional early childhood literacy organizations and member of the Library of Michigan Youth Services Advisory Committee.

Heidi Stohs: Heidi Stohs: Instructor in Language Arts, grades 10–12, Solomon High School, Solomon, Kansas. Received B.S. from Kansas State University; M.A. from Fort Hays State University.

NOVELS
for Students

Presenting Analysis, Context, and Criticism
on Commonly Studied Novels

VOLUME 27

GALE
CENGAGE Learning™

Detroit • New York • San Francisco • New Haven, Conn • Waterville, Maine • London

Novels for Students, Volume 27

Project Editor: Ira Mark Milne

Rights Acquisition and Management: Vernon English, Leitha Etheridge-Sims, Aja Perales, Sue Rudolph

Composition: Evi Abou-El-Seoud

Manufacturing: Drew Kalasky

Imaging: Lezlie Light

Product Design: Pamela A. E. Galbreath, Jennifer Wahi

Content Conversion: Civie Green, Katrina Coach

Product Manager: Meggin Condino

For product information and technology assistance, contact us at
Gale Customer Support, 1-800-877-4253.
For permission to use material from this text or product, submit all requests online at **www.cengage.com/permissions.**
Further permissions questions can be emailed to
permissionrequest@cengage.com

Gale
27500 Drake Rd.
Farmington Hills, MI, 48331-3535

ISBN-13: 978-0-7876-8684-0
ISBN-10: 0-7876-8684-0

ISSN 1094-3552

This title is also available as an e-book.
ISBN-13: 978-1-4144-3831-3
ISBN-10: 1-4144-3831-1
Contact your Gale, a part of Cengage Learning sales representative for ordering information.

Printed in the United States of America
1 2 3 4 5 6 7 12 11 10 09 08

Table of Contents

The Informed Dialogue: Interacting with Literature

When we pick up a book, we usually do so with the anticipation of pleasure. We hope that by entering the time and place of the novel and sharing the thoughts and actions of the characters, we will find enjoyment. Unfortunately, this is often not the case; we are disappointed. But we should ask, has the author failed us, or have we failed the author?

We establish a dialogue with the author, the book, and with ourselves when we read. Consciously and unconsciously, we ask questions: "Why did the author write this book?" "Why did the author choose that time, place, or character?" "How did the author achieve that effect?" "Why did the character act that way?" "Would I act in the same way?" The answers we receive depend upon how much information about literature in general and about that book specifically we ourselves bring to our reading.

Young children have limited life and literary experiences. Being young, children frequently do not know how to go about exploring a book, nor sometimes, even know the questions to ask of a book. The books they read help them answer questions, the author often coming right out and *telling* young readers the things they are learning or are expected to learn. The perennial classic, *The Little Engine That Could, tells* its readers that, among other things, it is good to help others and brings happiness:

"Hurray, hurray," cried the funny little clown and all the dolls and toys. "The good little boys and girls in the city will be happy because you helped us, kind, Little Blue Engine."

In picture books, messages are often blatant and simple, the dialogue between the author and reader one-sided. Young children are concerned with the end result of a book—the enjoyment gained, the lesson learned—rather than with how that result was obtained. As we grow older and read further, however, we question more. We come to expect that the world within the book will closely mirror the concerns of our world, and that the author will *show* these through the events, descriptions, and conversations within the story, rather than *telling* of them. We are now expected to do the interpreting, carry on our share of the dialogue with the book and author, and glean not only the author's message, but comprehend how that message and the overall affect of the book were achieved. Sometimes, however, we need help to do these things. *Novels for Students* provides that help.

A novel is made up of many parts interacting to create a coherent whole. In reading a novel, the more obvious features can be easily spotted—theme, characters, plot—but we may overlook the more subtle elements that greatly influence how the novel is perceived by the reader: viewpoint, mood and tone, symbolism, or the use of humor. By focusing on both the obvious and more subtle literary elements within a novel, *Novels for Students* aids readers in both analyzing for message and in determining how and why that message is communicated. In the discussion on Harper Lee's *To Kill a Mockingbird* (Vol. 2), for example, the mockingbird as a symbol of innocence is dealt with, among other things, as is the importance of Lee's use of humor which "enlivens a serious plot, adds depth to the characterization, and creates a sense of familiarity and universality." The reader comes to understand the internal elements of each novel discussed—as well as the external influences that help shape it.

"The desire to write greatly," Harold Bloom of Yale University says, "is the desire to be elsewhere, in a time and place of one's own, in an originality that must compound with inheritance, with an anxiety of influence." A writer seeks to create a unique world within a story, but although it is unique, it is not disconnected from our own world. It speaks to us *because* of what the writer brings to the writing from our world: how he or she was raised and educated; his or her likes and dislikes; the events occurring in the real world at the time of the writing, and while the author was growing up. When we know what an author has brought to his or her work, we gain a greater insight into both the "originality" (the world of the book), and the things that "compound" it. This insight enables us to question that created world and find answers more readily. By informing ourselves, we are able to establish a more effective dialogue with both book and author.

Novels for Students, in addition to providing a plot summary and descriptive list of characters—to remind readers of what they have read—also explores the external influences that shaped each book. Each entry includes a discussion of the author's background, and the historical context in which the novel was written. It is vital to know, for instance, that when Ray Bradbury was writing *Fahrenheit 451* (Vol. 1), the threat of Nazi domination had recently ended in Europe, and the McCarthy hearings were taking place in Washington, D.C. This information goes far in answering the question, "Why did he write a story of oppressive government control and book burning?" Similarly, it is important to know that Harper Lee, author of *To Kill a Mockingbird,* was born and raised in Monroeville, Alabama, and that her father was a lawyer. Readers can now see why she chose the south as a setting for her novel—it is the place with which she was most familiar—and start to comprehend her characters and their actions.

Novels for Students helps readers find the answers they seek when they establish a dialogue with a particular novel. It also aids in the posing of questions by providing the opinions and interpretations of various critics and reviewers, broadening that dialogue. Some reviewers of *To Kill A Mockingbird,* for example, "faulted the novel's climax as melodramatic." This statement leads readers to ask, "Is it, indeed, melodramatic?" "If not, why did some reviewers see it as such?" "If it is, why did Lee choose to make it melodramatic?" "Is melodrama ever justified?" By being spurred to ask these questions, readers not only learn more about the book and its writer, but about the nature of writing itself.

The literature included for discussion in *Novels for Students* has been chosen because it has something vital to say to us. *Of Mice and Men, Catch-22, The Joy Luck Club, My Antonia, A Separate Peace* and the other novels here speak of life and modern sensibility. In addition to their individual, specific messages of prejudice, power, love or hate, living and dying, however, they and all great literature also share a common intent. They force us to *think*—about life, literature, and about others, not just about ourselves. They pry us from the narrow confines of our minds and thrust us outward to confront the world of books and the larger, real world we all share. *Novels for Students* helps us in this confrontation by providing the means of enriching our conversation with literature and the world, by creating an *informed* dialogue, one that brings true pleasure to the personal act of reading.

Sources

Harold Bloom, *The Western Canon, The Books and School of the Ages,* Riverhead Books, 1994.

Watty Piper, *The Little Engine That Could,* Platt & Munk, 1930.

Anne Devereaux Jordan
Senior Editor, TALL (Teaching and Learning Literature)

Introduction

Purpose of the Book

The purpose of *Novels for Students* (*NfS*) is to provide readers with a guide to understanding, enjoying, and studying novels by giving them easy access to information about the work. Part of Gale's "For Students" Literature line, *NfS* is specifically designed to meet the curricular needs of high school and undergraduate college students and their teachers, as well as the interests of general readers and researchers considering specific novels. While each volume contains entries on "classic" novels frequently studied in classrooms, there are also entries containing hard-to-find information on contemporary novels, including works by multicultural, international, and women novelists.

The information covered in each entry includes an introduction to the novel and the novel's author; a plot summary, to help readers unravel and understand the events in a novel; descriptions of important characters, including explanation of a given character's role in the novel as well as discussion about that character's relationship to other characters in the novel; analysis of important themes in the novel; and an explanation of important literary techniques and movements as they are demonstrated in the novel.

In addition to this material, which helps the readers analyze the novel itself, students are also provided with important information on the literary and historical background informing each work. This includes a historical context essay, a box comparing the time or place the novel was written to modern Western culture, a critical essay, and excerpts from critical essays on the novel. A unique feature of *NfS* is a specially commissioned critical essay on each novel, targeted toward the student reader.

To further aid the student in studying and enjoying each novel, information on media adaptations is provided (if available), as well as reading suggestions for works of fiction and nonfiction on similar themes and topics. Classroom aids include ideas for research papers and lists of critical sources that provide additional material on the novel.

Selection Criteria

The titles for each volume of *NfS* were selected by surveying numerous sources on teaching literature and analyzing course curricula for various school districts. Some of the sources surveyed included: literature anthologies; *Reading Lists for College-Bound Students: The Books Most Recommended by America's Top Colleges*; textbooks on teaching the novel; a College Board survey of novels commonly studied in high schools; a National Council of Teachers of English (NCTE) survey of novels commonly studied in high schools; the NCTE's *Teaching Literature in High School: The Novel*; and the Young Adult Library Services Association (YALSA) list of best books for young adults of the past twenty-five years.

Input was also solicited from our advisory board, as well as from educators from various areas. From these discussions, it was determined that each volume should have a mix of "classic" novels (those works commonly taught in literature classes) and contemporary novels for which information is often hard to find. Because of the interest in expanding the canon of literature, an emphasis was also placed on including works by international, multicultural, and women novelists. Our advisory board members—educational professionals—helped pare down the list for each volume. If a work was not selected for the present volume, it was often noted as a possibility for a future volume. As always, the editor welcomes suggestions for titles to be included in future volumes.

How Each Entry Is Organized

Each entry, or chapter, in *NfS* focuses on one novel. Each entry heading lists the full name of the novel, the author's name, and the date of the novel's publication. The following elements are contained in each entry:

Introduction: a brief overview of the novel which provides information about its first appearance, its literary standing, any controversies surrounding the work, and major conflicts or themes within the work.

Author Biography: this section includes basic facts about the author's life, and focuses on events and times in the author's life that inspired the novel in question.

Plot Summary: a factual description of the major events in the novel. Lengthy summaries are broken down with subheads.

Characters: an alphabetical listing of major characters in the novel. Each character name is followed by a brief to an extensive description of the character's role in the novel, as well as discussion of the character's actions, relationships, and possible motivation.

Characters are listed alphabetically by last name. If a character is unnamed—for instance, the narrator in *Invisible Man*—the character is listed as "The Narrator" and alphabetized as "Narrator." If a character's first name is the only one given, the name will appear alphabetically by that name.

Variant names are also included for each character. Thus, the full name "Jean Louise Finch" would head the listing for the narrator of *To Kill a Mockingbird*, but listed in a separate cross-reference would be the nickname "Scout Finch."

Themes: a thorough overview of how the major topics, themes, and issues are addressed within the novel. Each theme discussed appears in a separate subhead and is easily accessed through the boldface entries in the Subject/Theme Index.

Style: this section addresses important style elements of the novel, such as setting, point of view, and narration; important literary devices used, such as imagery, foreshadowing, symbolism; and, if applicable, genres to which the work might have belonged, such as Gothicism or Romanticism. Literary terms are explained within the entry but can also be found in the Glossary.

Historical Context: this section outlines the social, political, and cultural climate *in which the author lived and the novel was created.* This section may include descriptions of related historical events, pertinent aspects of daily life in the culture, and the artistic and literary sensibilities of the time in which the work was written. If the novel is a historical work, information regarding the time in which the novel is set is also included. Each section is broken down with helpful subheads.

Critical Overview: this section provides background on the critical reputation of the novel, including bannings or any other public controversies surrounding the work. For older works, this section includes a history of how the novel was first received and how perceptions of it may have changed over the years; for more recent novels, direct quotes from early reviews may also be included.

Criticism: an essay commissioned by *NfS* which specifically deals with the novel and is written specifically for the student audience, as well as excerpts from previously published criticism on the work (if available).

Sources: an alphabetical list of critical material used in compiling the entry, with full bibliographical information.

Further Reading: an alphabetical list of other critical sources which may prove useful for the student. It includes full bibliographical information and a brief annotation.

In addition, each entry contains the following highlighted sections, set apart from the main text as sidebars:

Media Adaptations: if available, a list of important film and television adaptations of the novel, including source information. The list also includes stage adaptations, audio recordings, musical adaptations, etc.

Topics for Further Study: a list of potential study questions or research topics dealing with the novel. This section includes questions related to other disciplines the student may be studying, such as American history, world history, science, math, government, business, geography, economics, psychology, etc.

Compare and Contrast: an "at-a-glance" comparison of the cultural and historical differences between the author's time and culture and late twentieth century or early twenty-first century Western culture. This box includes pertinent parallels between the major scientific, political, and cultural movements of the time or place the novel was written, the time or place the novel was set (if a historical work), and modern Western culture. Works written after the mid-1970s may not have this box.

What Do I Read Next?: a list of works that might complement the featured novel or serve as a contrast to it. This includes works by the same author and others, works of fiction and nonfiction, and works from various genres, cultures, and eras.

Other Features

NfS includes "The Informed Dialogue: Interacting with Literature," a foreword by Anne Devereaux Jordan, Senior Editor for *Teaching and Learning Literature* (*TALL*), and a founder of the Children's Literature Association. This essay provides an enlightening look at how readers interact with literature and how *Novels for Students* can help teachers show students how to enrich their own reading experiences.

A Cumulative Author/Title Index lists the authors and titles covered in each volume of the *NfS* series.

A Cumulative Nationality/Ethnicity Index breaks down the authors and titles covered in each volume of the *NfS* series by nationality and ethnicity.

A Subject/Theme Index, specific to each volume, provides easy reference for users who may be studying a particular subject or theme rather than a single work. Significant subjects from events to broad themes are included, and the entries pointing to the specific theme discussions in each entry are indicated in **boldface**.

Each entry may include illustrations, including photo of the author, stills from film adaptations, maps, and/or photos of key historical events, if available.

Citing Novels for Students

When writing papers, students who quote directly from any volume of *Novels for Students* may use the following general forms. These examples are based on MLA style; teachers may request that students adhere to a different style, so the following examples may be adapted as needed.

When citing text from *NfS* that is not attributed to a particular author (i.e., the Themes, Style, Historical Context sections, etc.), the following format should be used in the bibliography section:

> *"Night." Novels for Students.* Ed. Marie Rose Napierkowski. Vol. 4. Detroit: Gale, 1998. 234–35.

When quoting the specially commissioned essay from *NfS* (usually the first piece under the "Criticism" subhead), the following format should be used:

> Miller, Tyrus. Critical Essay on *"Winesburg, Ohio." Novels for Students.* Ed. Marie Rose Napierkowski. Vol. 4. Detroit: Gale, 1998. 335–39.

When quoting a journal or newspaper essay that is reprinted in a volume of *NfS,* the following form may be used:

> Malak, Amin. "Margaret Atwood's *The Handmaid's Tale* and the Dystopian Tradition." *Canadian Literature* No. 112 (Spring 1987), 9–16; excerpted and reprinted in *Novels for Students*, Vol. 4, ed. Marie Rose Napierkowski (Detroit: Gale, 1998), pp. 133–36.

When quoting material reprinted from a book that appears in a volume of *NfS,* the following form may be used:

> Adams, Timothy Dow. "Richard Wright: 'Wearing the Mask.'" In *Telling Lies in Modern American Autobiography*. University of North Carolina Press, 1990. 69–83; excerpted and reprinted in *Novels for Students,* Vol. 1, ed. Diane Telgen (Detroit: Gale, 1997), pp. 59–61.

We Welcome Your Suggestions

The editorial staff of *Novels for Students* welcomes your comments and ideas. Readers who wish to suggest novels to appear in future volumes, or who have other suggestions, are cordially invited to contact the editor. You may contact the editor via e-mail at: **ForStudents Editors@ cengage.com.** Or write to the editor at:

Editor, *Novels for Students*
Gale
27500 Drake Road
Farmington Hills, MI 48331-3535

Literary Chronology

1832: Lewis Carroll (pseudonym of Charles Lutwidge Dodgson) is born on January 27 at Daresdury in Cheshire, England.

1871: Lewis Carroll's (Charles Lutwidge Dodgson's) *Through the Looking-Glass* is published at Christmas in an edition of nine thousand copies, with illustrations by Sir John Tenniel (1820–1914).

1874: Gertrude Stein is born on February 3 in Allegheny, Pennsylvania.

1898: Following a colorful career as teacher, writer, and photographer, Lewis Carroll (Charles Lutwidge Dodgson) dies of pneumonia on January 14, while at his sister's home in Guildford, England.

1902: Christina Stead is born on July 17 in Rockdale, Australia.

1914: Bernard Malamud is born on April 26 in Brooklyn, New York.

1919: Doris Lessing is born on October 22 in Kermanshah, Persia (now Iran).

1921: Patricia Highsmith is born Mary Patricia Plangman on January 19 in Fort Worth, Texas.

1922: José Saramago is born on November 16 in Azinhaga, a small village in the province of Ribatejo, Portugal.

1929: Milan Kundera is born on April 1 in Brno, Czechoslovakia.

1931: Alice Munro is born on July 10 in Wingham, Ontario, Canada.

1940: Christina Stead's *The Man Who Loved Children* is published.

1941: Gertrude Stein's *Ida* is published.

1946: Gertrude Stein dies of stomach cancer on July 27 in Neuilly-sur-Seine, outside Paris.

1948: Sue Monk Kidd is born on August 12 in Sylvester, Georgia.

1952: Orhan Pamuk is born on June 7 in Istanbul, Turkey.

1955: Patricia Highsmith's *The Talented Mr. Ripley* is published.

1958: Bernard Malamud's *The Assistant* is published.

1962: Doris Lessing's *The Golden Notebook* is published.

1963: Yann Martel is born on June 25 in Salamanca, Spain.

1971: Alice Munro's *Lives of Girls and Women* is published.

1979: Milan Kundera's *The Book of Laughter and Forgetting* is first published in France.

1983: Christina Stead dies on March 31 in Sydney, Australia.

1986: Bernard Malamud dies of a heart attack on March 18 in New York City.

1995: José Saramago's *Blindness* is first published in Portuguese and will be published in English in 1997.

1995: Patricia Highsmith dies of cancer on February 4 in Locarno, Switzerland.

1998: The Nobel Prize in Literature is awarded to José Saramago "who with parables sustained by imagination, compassion and irony continually enables us once again to apprehend an elusory reality."

2001: Yann Martel's *Life of Pi* is published.

2001: Orhan Pamuk's *My Name Is Red* is first published in an English translation, a year after the original Turkish-language edition

2002: Sue Monk Kidd's *The Secret Life of Bees* is published.

2002: Yann Martel is awarded the Man Booker Prize for *Life of Pi*.

2006: The Nobel Prize for Literature is awarded to Orhan Pamuk "who in the quest for the melancholic soul of his native city has discovered new symbols for the clash and interlacing of cultures."

2007: The Nobel Prize for Literature is awarded to Doris Lessing "that epicist of the female experience, who with scepticism, fire and visionary power has subjected a divided civilisation to scrutiny."

Acknowledgements

The editors wish to thank the copyright holders of the excerpted criticism included in this volume and the permissions managers of many book and magazine publishing companies for assisting us in securing reproduction rights. We are also grateful to the staffs of the Detroit Public Library, the Library of Congress, the University of Detroit Mercy Library, Wayne State University Purdy/ Kresge Library Complex, and the University of Michigan Libraries for making their resources available to us. Following is a list of the copyright holders who have granted us permission to reproduce material in this volume of *NFS*. Every effort has been made to trace copyright, but if omissions have been made, please let us know.

COPYRIGHTED EXCERPTS IN *NFS*, VOLUME 27, WERE REPRODUCED FROM THE FOLLOWING PERIODICALS:

Children's Literature, v. 31, 2003. Copyright © 2003 by Johns Hopkins University Press. All rights reserved. Reproduced by permission.—*Clues: A Journal of Detection*, v. 5, Spring–Summer 1984 for "A Portrait of the Artist: The Novels of Patricia Highsmith," by Erlene Hubly. Copyright © 1984 by Helen Dwight Reid Educational Foundation. Reproduced with permission of the Literary Estate of the author.—*Commentary*, v. 78, October 1984 for "An Open Letter to Milan Kundera," by Norman Podhoretz. Copyright © 1984 by the American Jewish Committee. All rights reserved. Reproduced by permission of the publisher and the author.—*Contemporary Literature*, v. 14.4, Autumn 1973. Copyright © 1973 by the Board of Regents of the University of Wisconsin System. Reproduced by permission.—*Critique*, v. 25, Summer 1984. Copyright © 1984 by Helen Dwight Reid Educational Foundation. Reproduced with permission of the Helen Dwight Reid Educational Foundation, published by Heldref Publications, 1319 18th Street, NW, Washington, DC 20036-1802.—*Dialog: A Journal of Theology*, v. 44, Summer 2005. Copyright © 2005 Basil Blackwell Ltd. Reproduced by permission of Blackwell Publishers.—*The Explicator*, v. 64, Winter, 2006. Copyright © 2006 by Helen Dwight Reid Educational Foundation. Reproduced with permission of the Helen Dwight Reid Educational Foundation, published by Heldref Publications, 1319 18th Street, NW, Washington, DC 20036-1802.—*First Things: A Monthly Journal of Religion and Public Life*, May, 2003. Copyright © 2003 Institute on Religion and Public Life. All rights reserved. Reproduced by permission.—*Midwest Quarterly*, v. XXV, Summer 1984. Copyright © 1984 by *The Midwest Quarterly*, Pittsburgh State University. Reproduced by permission.—*New Criterion*, v. 13, October 1994 for "'A Real Inferno': The Life of Christina Stead," by Brooke Allen. © 1994 The New Criterion. Reproduced by permission of the author.—*New Leader*, v. 84, September 2001. Copyright © 2001 by The American Labor Conference on International Affairs, Inc. All rights reserved.

Reproduced by permission.—*New Republic*, v. 183, December 20, 1980; v. 219, November 31, 1998. Copyright © 1980, 1998 by The New Republic, Inc. Both reproduced by permission of *The New Republic*.—*New Statesman*, v. 130, August 27, 2001. Copyright © 2001 New Statesman, Ltd. Reproduced by permission.—*New York Times Book Review*, September 2, 2001. Copyright © 2001 by The New York Times Company. Reprinted with permission.—*San Francisco Chronicle*, December 9, 2001 for "A Detailed Tapestry of 16th Century Turkey," by Sarah Coleman. Reproduced by permission of the author.— *Studies in Canadian Literature*, v. 7, 1982. Copyright by W.R. Martin./ v. 29, Summer 2004. Copyright 2004 University of New Brunswick. Both reproduced by permission of the editors.— *Studies in the Novel*, v. 38, Summer 2006. Copyright © 2006 by the University of North Texas. Reproduced by permission.—*Twentieth Century Literature*, v. 24, Spring 1978. Copyright 1978, Hofstra University Press. Reproduced by permission.—*Women's Review of Books*, v. 19, April, 2002. Reproduced by permission.

COPYRIGHTED EXCERPTS IN *NFS*, VOLUME 27, WERE REPRODUCED FROM THE FOLLOWING BOOKS:

Cederstrom, Lorelei. From *Fine-Tuning the Feminine Psyche: Jungian Patterns in the Novels of Doris Lessing*. Peter Lang Publishing Inc., 1990. Copyright © 1990 Peter Lang Publishing, Inc., New York. All rights reserved. Reproduced by permission.—Draine, Betsy. From *Substance Under Pressure: Artistic Coherence and Evolving Form in the Novels of Doris Lessing*. University of Wisconsin Press, 1983. Copyright © 1983 by the Board of Regents of the University of Wisconsin System. Reproduced by permission.— Ducharme, Robert. From *Art and Idea in the Novels of Bernard Malamud: Toward the Fixer*. Mouton, 1974. Copyright © 1974 in the Netherlands. Mouton & Co, N.V., Publishers, The Hague. Reproduced by permission of Mouton de Gruyter, a division of Walter de Gruyter & Co.—Helterman, Jeffrey. From *Understanding Bernard Malamud*. University of South Carolina Press, 1985. Copyright © University of South Carolina 1985. Reproduced by permission.— Kegan, Robert. From *The Sweeter Welcome: Voices for a Vision of Affirmation: Bellow, Malamud and Martin Buber*. Humanitas Press, 1976. Copyright © 1976 Humanitas Press. All rights reserved. Reproduced by permission of the author.—Pichova, Hana. From *The Art of Memory in Exile: Vladimir Nabokov and Milan Kundera*. Southern Illinois University Press, 2002. Copyright © 2002 by the Board of Trustees, Southern Illinois University. All rights reserved. Reproduced by permission of the publisher.

Contributors

Susan Andersen: Andersen is an associate professor of literature and composition. Entry on *The Secret Life of Bees*. Original essay on *The Secret Life of Bees*.

Bryan Aubrey: Aubrey holds a Ph.D. in English. Entries on *The Assistant* and *My Name Is Red*. Original essays on *The Assistant* and *My Name Is Red*.

Klay Dyer: Dyer holds a Ph.D. in English literature and has published extensively on fiction, poetry, film, and television. He is also a freelance university teacher, writer, and educational consultant. Entries on *Life of Pi* and *Through the Looking-Glass*. Original essays on *Life of Pi* and *Through the Looking-Glass*.

Joyce Hart: Hart has degrees in English and creative writing, and she is a freelance writer and published author. Entry on *The Golden Notebook*. Original essay on *The Golden Notebook*.

Neil Heims: Heims is a writer and teacher living in Paris. Entry on *Ida*. Original essay on *Ida*.

Diane Andrews Henningfeld: Henningfeld is a professor of English who writes widely on literature and theory. Entry on *The Book of Laughter and Forgetting*. Original essay on *The Book of Laughter and Forgetting*.

Sheri Metzger Karmiol: Karmiol has a doctorate in English Renaissance literature. She teaches literature and drama at the University of New Mexico, where she is a lecturer in the university honors program. Karmiol is also a professional writer and the author of several reference texts on poetry and drama. Entry on *Lives of Girls and Women*. Original essay on *Lives of Girls and Women*.

David Kelly: Kelly is an instructor of creative writing and literature. Entry on *The Man Who Loved Children*. Original essay on *The Man Who Loved Children*.

Lois Kerschen: Kerschen is an educator and freelance writer. Entry on *Blindness*. Original essay on *Blindness*.

Claire Robinson: Robinson has an M.A. in English. She is a former teacher of English literature and creative writing, and is currently a freelance writer and editor. Entry on *The Talented Mr. Ripley*. Original essay on *The Talented Mr. Ripley*.

The Assistant

BERNARD MALAMUD

1958

The Assistant (1958) is American writer Bernard Malamud's second novel and is generally regarded as one of his best. It tells the story of Morris Bober, a poor immigrant Jew who owns a small grocery store in New York in the middle of the twentieth century. Business is bad and he struggles to make ends meet. The core of the novel is the relationship between Bober, an honest man who shows compassion to others, and Frank Alpine, an Italian American drifter who arrives in the neighborhood and ends up working in Morris's store. *The Assistant* paints a detailed and accurate portrait of an impoverished neighborhood in which three very different Jewish immigrant families try to make their living. It touches on issues such as the American dream and what people will or will not do to achieve it. It shows how ethical values, whether conceived in a religious framework or not, potentially offer a person freedom from the oppressive nature of human life. The spiritual journey undergone by Frank Alpine is a moving story of how a man can find hope and renewal in an apparently hopeless situation.

AUTHOR BIOGRAPHY

Bernard Malamud was born in Brooklyn, New York, on April 26, 1914, the son of Bertha and Max Malamud, who were Russian Jewish

Bernard Malamud *(© David Lees / Corbis)*

MEDIA ADAPTATIONS

- An unabridged reading of *The Assistant*, read by George Guidall, was available as of 2007 from Jewish Contemporary Classics. There are six cassettes, lasting a total of nine hours.

immigrants. Malamud's mother died when Bernard was fourteen, and after that he was raised by his father who, like the fictional character Morris Bober in *The Assistant*, owned a small grocery store and worked long hours to keep it solvent. Malamud attended Erasmus Hall High School, and during the Great Depression of the 1930s, he worked in a census office and a factory in order to provide additional income for his impoverished family. He also attended City College of New York, which at the time was a school for poor students. He received a bachelor's degree from that institution in 1936.

In 1942, Malamud received a master's degree in English from Columbia University. He had already begun writing short stories, and some of these were published in magazines during the years of World War II. During this period Malamud supported himself by working odd jobs (rather like Frank Alpine in *The Assistant*), and he also taught evening classes at Erasmus High School and then Harlem High School. In 1949, he joined the English Department of Oregon State College,

where he stayed for twelve years, rising to the rank of associate professor. He married Ann de Chiara in 1945, and they had a son, Paul (born 1947) and a daughter, Janna (born 1952).

In 1952, Malamud published his first novel, *The Natural*, a fable about a baseball player cast in the form of the legend of the Holy Grail. Four years later, in 1956, Malamud received a fellowship in fiction from *Partisan Review*, and he lived in Rome and traveled in Europe. The next year saw the publication of his second novel, *The Assistant*, which in 1958 received the Rosenthal Foundation Award of the National Institute of Arts and Letters and the Daroff Memorial Fiction Award of the Jewish Council of America.

In 1959, Malamud published a collection of short stories, *The Magic Barrel*, which won the National Book Award in 1959. The stories have a mystical flavor and explore moral issues of freedom and responsibility. Most of the characters are Jews. Malamud followed this with a third novel, *A New Life* (1961), which is set in a college and draws on his experiences teaching at Oregon State. In the same year, Malamud moved back to the East to teach creative writing at Bennington College in Vermont.

After *Idiots First* (1963), a second collection of short stories, Malamud published *The Fixer* (1966), a novel about a persecuted Jew in a tsarist Russian prison. The novel was extremely successful and established Malamud's reputation as one of America's leading writers. Malamud received the National Book Award for Fiction and a Pulitzer Prize for this work, which remains his most critically acclaimed and popular novel.

Other works of Malamud include *Rembrandt's Hat* (1973), his third collection of short stories, and the novels, *The Tenants* (1971), *Dublin's Lives* (1979), and *God's Grace* (1982).

Malamud died of a heart attack on March 18, 1986, in New York City.

PLOT SUMMARY

Section 1

The Assistant begins on an early evening in November, in a mostly poor immigrant but mostly non-Jewish area possibly in Brooklyn, New York, although never specifically named. It is some time during the middle of the twentieth century, after World War II. Morris Bober, a sixty-year-old Jew who immigrated to the United States from Russia many years earlier, is working in his grocery store. There are few customers, and the store makes little money. Morris is thinking of selling the store, as his wife Ida wants him to do, but he doubts he will be able to find a buyer. Even if he did manage to sell, he does not know where he would go or what he would do.

Ida is embittered by the poverty they endure. The next day she grumbles at her husband for not doing what their next-door neighbor Julius Karp did. Karp converted his shoe store into a wine and liquor store, which is much more profitable than Morris's grocery store. Their economic situation is getting rapidly worse. Morris stays open seven days a week, sixteen hours a day, but he only just manages to eke out a living. He is close to bankruptcy. The previous year another grocery store opened in the neighborhood and took business away from Morris.

Twenty-three-year-old Helen Bober, who lives with her parents and works at a secretarial job she dislikes, runs into Nat Pearl on the subway. Nat, who is also Jewish, is a law student; he and Helen had been seeing each other during the summer, but she has been avoiding him since and says little to him now. Helen is lonely as she walks home. She hands over her paycheck to her father and after supper goes to her room. She hates living in the five-room flat and hopes that she may be able to go to college one day.

Morris talks with Karp, who tells him he is worried that he will be robbed. He tells Morris to call the police because a suspicious car is parked across the street. Morris does nothing, and it is he, not Karp, who becomes the victim. Two men with handkerchiefs over their faces, one of whom wields a gun, enter Morris's store and demand money. Morris hands over the small amount in the cash register. Thinking that Morris is hiding more money, the man with the gun strikes him across the head. The robbers then ransack the store but find no more money. The man with the gun hits Morris over the head, and he collapses on the floor.

Section 2

Morris lies in bed for a week, recovering, while Ida tends the store. During this time a stranger, Frank Alpine, arrives in the neighborhood. He says he has come from the West and is looking for work. For a while he hangs around Sam Pearl's candy store, then one morning he helps Morris bring in two heavy milk cases. He does the same favor for Morris several days later. Morris invites him into the store, and Frank tells him his story. He is twenty-five years old, an orphan who has yet to find his direction in life. He is restless and keeps moving on from place to place. Frank asks Morris if he may help out at the store, with no wages, so he can learn the grocery business. Morris refuses.

Helen is being courted by Julius Karp's son, Louis Karp, who says he would like to marry her. But Helen says that she does not want to be a storekeeper's wife and insists that they can be no more than friends.

One day, Morris discovers that someone is stealing milk and rolls from him in the mornings. This situation continues for several days, and Morris reluctantly calls the police. Mr. Minogue, a detective who is also investigating the robbery, comes to the store. That night, Morris discovers Frank in the cellar, and Frank confesses to sleeping in the cellar and taking the food because he was hungry. He has been unable to find a job. Morris allows him to sleep in the house.

The next day Morris collapses outside the store. Frank picks him up and brings him in.

Section 3

While Morris is recuperating, Frank works in the store. He turns out to be an efficient and apparently honest worker, even though Ida is suspicious of him. He works longs hours and is content, and the customers like him. Frank is interested in Helen and wants to get to know her, but he finds it difficult to get an opportunity. One day, he tricks her by calling her to the telephone in the store, even though there is no one on the line for her, just so he can find a way of speaking to her.

Business improves at the store, and Frank, who is a good salesman, gets the credit for it. Even Ida begins to respect and trust him, and she and Morris give him a small raise. Frank feels uncomfortable with this because he has been regularly stealing money from the till. He wants to make amends somehow.

Frank goes to a poolroom one night where he meets Ward Minogue, one of the men who robbed Morris. It transpires that the other robber was none other than Frank. Frank wants his gun back from Ward, but Ward wants to recruit him for another robbery, this time of Karp's liquor store. Frank refuses and leaves without his gun.

Frank spies on Helen and through a window catches sight of her naked in the bathroom.

Section 4

After Morris recovers, he decides to keep Frank employed at the store, over Ida's protests. She does not like the way Frank looks at Helen. But Morris and Frank get along well and tell each other stories about their lives. However, Frank continues to steal from the store, trying to justify himself by saying that he has brought the grocer good luck, although he still feels badly about his actions. He also promises himself that he will confess to Morris his part in the robbery, but he can never bring himself to do it. He continues to want to befriend Helen, and after he sees her at the library, he persuades her to walk with him in the park on their way home. She notices that he is dressed better than usual, and she thanks him for the help he has given her father. They talk about the books they have been reading and their desire to attend college. Frank would have to work at nights in order to accomplish his goal. Helen talks about how she dislikes her secretarial job and how she would like to do something more useful, like social work or teaching. He tells her about a girl he knew years ago, who was an acrobat in a carnival. She was killed in a car accident. As Helen goes to sleep that night she is still confused about how she should think about Frank.

Section 5

Business continues to improve during December. Morris is able to pay off outstanding bills, and he allows Helen to keep more of her wages. Helen and Frank continue to get to know each other, walking home together from the library. Helen envies him all the places he has visited, since she has led a more restricted life, traveling seldom. Frank say he plans to start college in the fall, and Helen, excited by this news, recommends some novels she thinks he should read. Frank reads them to please her, but he finds them hard going.

One evening Nat calls Helen, wanting to see her. She puts him off, much to her mother's annoyance. Ida wants Helen to marry and thinks that Nat, who is Jewish and studying law, is a good prospect. Frank buys Helen a gift of a scarf and an edition of Shakespeare's plays, but she refuses to accept them. She likes Frank but does not want to become seriously involved with him, and she tells him to return the gifts to the store for a refund. But Frank just tosses them into the trash. Seeing this, Helen rescues them and eventually agrees to accept one gift, the Shakespeare book. She and Frank remain friends. Ida becomes suspicious and takes to following Frank, and then Helen, at night, convinced there is something going on between them. She tries to persuade her husband to ask Frank to leave, but Morris reminds her they had agreed that he should stay until the summer.

One afternoon, Morris is having his hair cut across the street and sees several customers leaving the grocery store carrying big bags. But when he returns to the store he finds that only a small amount of money has been recorded in the cash register. He wonders if Frank is stealing, and for the next few days watches him closely. But he sees nothing wrong and begins to doubt his suspicions. He concludes that even if Frank has been stealing, it is his, Morris's fault, for paying him so little. So he decides to give Frank another raise, even though Frank protests it is unnecessary.

Section 6

Helen feels that she is falling in love with Frank, even though she has doubts about the wisdom of doing so. They kiss passionately, but she does not fully accept him. Because Frank is not Jewish, she fears that her parents would be devastated if she were to marry him. She postpones making any important decisions. One evening, Frank smuggles Helen up to his room. He wants to make love to her, but she refuses.

Mr. Minogue, the detective investigating the robbery, brings a suspect with him to the store, but Morris says he does not recognize the man. That night, Ward Minogue, the detective's son, visits Frank in his room, but again Frank refuses to take part in another robbery. Ward tries to blackmail him, but Frank replies that if Ward ever says anything about Frank's role in the robbery, he will tell Ward's father, who is looking for him, where he can find him.

Ida follows Helen one night and watches as Helen meets Frank and kisses him. When Helen gets home Ida is angry and upset that her daughter has kissed a "goy," a gentile. She tells Helen she should marry someone with a college education and implores her to give Nat another chance.

Julius Karp visits Morris. They have not spoken for several months, since the robbery. Karp has figured out that Frank is stealing from his employer; he also plans to persuade Morris to get Helen to take a serious interest in his son, Louis. Morris tells Karp that business is good due to Frank, but Karp tries to convince him it is because the rival grocer has been in poor health and his store had been closing for part of each day. Now the rival store has shut down completely, Karp informs Morris, but a new, ultra-modern grocery store will open in its place the following week. Morris dreads that he will soon be put out of business. He also continues to believe that Frank has helped his store by increasing business. Meanwhile, Frank decides that he will replace all the $142 he has stolen. He manages to put six dollars back in the till and feels pleased with himself. He plans to pay it all back within a few months. But then he decides he needs a dollar, because he is seeing Helen that evening. When the next customer comes in, he puts a dollar less in the till than the cost of the item she buys, but Morris catches him red-handed. Frank is forced to confess the truth of Morris's accusation that he has been stealing from him the day he arrived. Morris gives him his week's wages and tells him to leave, which Frank does.

Helen sees Nat but is impatient to be with Frank. But when she goes to the park at night, instead of seeing Frank she is accosted by Ward Minogue. She fights him off, and Frank comes to her rescue. She and Frank kiss and Frank declares his love for her. He then forces himself on her sexually, against her will. She is distressed and curses him.

Section 7

The new grocery is about to open, and Morris is depressed at the prospect. Ida says they must sell the store. Meanwhile, Frank has returned to his room in the house and during the night is full of remorse for his actions. The next day, Helen goes

to work as usual, without telling anyone about the rape. She is full of self-hatred.

Later, the upstairs tenant, Nick, smells gas in the house. Frank drags Morris from his room, saving his life. It transpires that Morris turned on the gas but forgot to light the gas radiator. In the afternoon, Morris develops a fever and is taken to the hospital. Ida lets Frank stay on, but business declines when the new grocery store opens. Frank puts twenty-five dollars in the register as part of his plan to pay back the money he stole. Helen, however, refuses to speak to him. Business declines further, in spite of all Frank's efforts to attract customers.

Helen becomes depressed. She refuses to go to the wedding of her friend Betty Pearl, and she does not sleep well.

Frank tries to get one of Morris's customers, a Swedish painter named Carl, to pay a debt, but when he finds that the painter and his family are poor, he goes back to his room and gets three dollars. On his way back to Carl's, he meets Ward Minogue, who is sick. Ward wants to sell Frank's gun back to him, and Frank gives him the three dollars, which he had intended to give to Carl's family. He then drops the gun into a sewer.

Frank takes a night job at the Coffee Pot, working from ten until six. During the days he runs the grocery, and at the end of the week puts the thirty-five dollars he has earned from his night job into the cash register. This extra money prevents the store from going under. He bitterly regrets losing Helen. To try to win her back, he carves a wooden flower out of a pine board and gives it to her, but she throws it in the garbage.

Section 8

As spring approaches, Morris makes only a slow recovery. Like Helen, he is depressed, and he worries about the business. When he is strong enough to go downstairs to the store, he tells Frank he must leave. Frank confesses to his part in the robbery of Morris's store but claims he is no longer the person he once was. Morris replies that during his convalescence he had put two-and-two together and realized that Frank was one of the robbers. Frank begs to be allowed to stay, but Morris insists that he must leave. He packs his bags and writes an apologetic, farewell note to Helen.

After Frank's departure, business declines even further. The family plans to sell, and Ida visits Karp, inquiring about a potential buyer. The following week, the buyer, a man named Podolsky, arrives, and Morris tries to persuade him to buy the store, but nothing is decided. Despairing, Morris turns to Charlie Sobeloff, an old business partner of his, for help. Charlie owns a large supermarket. Charlie hires Morris as a part-time cashier for a short while, but Morris soon leaves. He goes to two employment agencies in New York City, without any success, and he has no luck either seeking out old friends and customers.

A stranger pays a call on Morris at the store. He proposes an insurance fraud scheme, whereby the man would arrange for the house and store to burn down so they could collect the insurance money. Morris refuses, but the following night, when the house is empty, he deliberately starts a fire. Then he thinks better of it and tries unsuccessfully to beat the flames out. Frank arrives in the nick of time and puts the fire out. Frank asks Morris if he can come back to work at the store, but Morris again tells him to leave.

Ward Minogue's father finds Ward, beats him up, and tells him to stay away from the neighborhood. Ward breaks into Karp's liquor store, gets drunk and accidentally sets fire to the store. He is burned to death in the conflagration. Karp's house and store are burned to the ground. Karp is devastated and wants to buy Morris's house and store so he can continue his business. Morris asks for a higher price than he knows either is worth, but Karp instantly agrees.

Morris shovels snow in cold early spring weather, catches pneumonia, and dies three days later. Frank attends the funeral, where the rabbi lauds Morris as a good Jew. Frank also attends the burial. At one point he loses his balance and falls on top of the coffin.

Julius Karp gets sick and is unable to buy Morris's store. Frank takes over the running of the store, which now belongs to Ida. Frank has some creative ideas that improve business, including offering a wider range of foods, and the rival grocery reduces its opening times. The store begins to prosper and Frank plans to support Helen's college education, even though she still refuses to speak to him. In August he manages to tell her his plans. Her heart softens towards him, but she firmly refuses his offer. He confesses his part in the robbery of Morris's store. She is horrified and runs from him.

Frank continues to work in the store, although he finds it hard to make ends meet. Helen starts seeing Nat again, and Frank is jealous. He starts spying on her in the bathroom and he also starts to cheat his customers. But abruptly he stops both activities. Helen, realizing that it is only because of Frank's ability to keep the store open that she is able to attend college at nights, becomes more friendly to him, rejecting Nat. Frank starts to read the Bible, and dreams of a future with Helen. In April he goes to the hospital for circumcision, and after Passover he converts to Judaism.

CHARACTERS

Frank Alpine

Frank Alpine is a twenty-five-year-old man of Italian extraction. He is described as "tall and not bad looking, except for a nose that had been broken and badly set, unbalancing his face." He has a dark beard and melancholy eyes, and when he first arrives in the neighborhood of Morris's grocery store, he is shabbily dressed.

Frank is a drifter who has had a rough life. His mother died a week after he was born, and he has never even seen a picture of her. His father abandoned him when he was five years old. He was raised in an orphanage, and when he was eight he was sent to live with a tough family. He ran away ten times. He has lived in a lot of places, including California and the East Coast, but he has not had any success in life. As he tells Morris, "sooner or later, everything I think is worth having gets away from me in some way or another," including education, jobs, and women. (A girl he was fond of was killed in a car accident.) Frank blames himself for doing something stupid just when it looks as if he is about to achieve something. He does not know how to make things happen differently; he always ends up with nothing. This pattern repeats itself in his relationship with Helen. He falls in love with her and continues to pursue her in spite of her initial indifference toward him. But when she is finally ready to fall in love with him he forces himself on her sexually and ruins the relationship.

Frank is a man torn between two sides of his nature, the good and the bad. At one point, he conceived the idea that he would make a success of himself through crime. He bought a gun, traveled east and fell in with Ward Minogue in

Brooklyn. Together they rob Morris's store. Then when Frank works at the store, he steals from Morris, a man who has been kind enough to give him a roof over his head. Frank soon regrets his thievery and strives to make amends. His conscience does not let him rest. He wants to behave in an ethical manner, and he makes genuine efforts to pay back the money he stole. He finally confesses to Morris his part in the robbery. Eventually, Frank makes the store a success with his creative ideas and relentless hard work.

Frank's acquaintance with Morris leads him to become interested in Jews—their religion and history. Soon after Morris dies, Frank decides to convert to Judaism.

Helen Bober

Helen Bober is the twenty-three-year-old daughter of Frank and Ida Bober. She is attractive, with brown hair and blue eyes. She took a secretarial job after high school so she could help her parents financially, but she longs to go to college and find more meaningful work. The intelligent Helen reads thick novels and reflects deeply on life. She hates living with her parents in such a restricted environment and at times feels that life is passing her by and she is not accomplishing anything. "I want a larger and better life," she says to Louis Karp. "I want the return of my possibilities." Helen is lonely. Most of her friends from high school are married now, and she has deliberately stopped seeing them. She wants love in her life, and she has been seeing Nat Pearl, but the relationship is not working out. She allowed him to make love to her, but she regrets having done so because she thinks that is all Nat wants. She wants genuine love and refuses to have sex again without love. None of her male admirers seems suitable in her eyes. She has no interest in Louis Pearl, even though he likes her and has money. She takes no notice of Frank Alpine at first, but when he persists in getting to know her, she learns to appreciate his better qualities and even thinks she may be in love with him. But she will not have sex with him. When Frank rescues her from Ward in the park, she falls into his arms, but he responds by raping her, after which she refuses to speak to him for months, rebuffing his persistent attempts to make amends. Eventually, Helen is able to attend college at nights. She is the sort of woman who does not give up on her dreams in spite of adverse circumstances, and

there are hints that she may learn to accept and love Frank after all.

Ida Bober

Ida Bober is Morris Bober's wife. She is fifty-one years old, nine years younger than her husband. She has thick black hair but her face is lined; she has been worn down by the dull, poverty-stricken life they lead. Her life seems bereft of pleasure. She resents the fact that many years ago her husband persuaded her to move from a Jewish neighborhood into the predominantly gentile area where the grocery store is situated. She expresses her resentment by nagging Morris to sell the store, although she also feels guilty because it was she who first persuaded him to become a grocer when he wanted to train as a pharmacist.

Ida keeps telling Morris to get rid of Frank, whom she does not trust, although as Frank proves his worth her attitude toward him softens somewhat. Ida is very protective of her daughter, Helen, and wants her to marry Nat because he has prospects and is Jewish. She cannot bear the thought of her daughter going with a gentile. When she suspects that Helen is seeing Frank, she follows them both at night and is horrified to see them kiss in the park. After Morris's death, which happens in part because he ignored her warnings about shoveling snow, she wails at the funeral that he has deserted her and left her helpless as a child.

Morris Bober

Morris Bober is a sixty-year-old Jew who originally lived in Russia at a time when the Jews were being persecuted. When as a young man Morris was about to be conscripted into the Russian army (this was some time before the Russian Revolution in 1917), his father advised him to escape to the United States. Morris managed to get away on his first day in the army barracks. Once in the United States, he attended night school and wanted to be a pharmacist, but when he met his wife, Ida, he lost patience and did not complete his schooling.

Morris is a sad man who regrets the course his life has taken. He is poor and has always been poor. He sees no possibility that this will ever change and believes himself simply to be unlucky. He contrasts his own miserable fortunes with those of Karp, who always seems to gain advantages without working for them. Morris works hard but just gets poorer and poorer. He is worried that his grocery store, which takes in little enough money as it is, is about to fail completely. He wants to sell the store but has little faith that anyone will buy it.

A crucial event in Morris's life is the death of his young son Ephraim from an ear disease, many years earlier. After that he rarely ventured beyond the corner of the street. It is almost as if he is living in a tomb. Sometimes he thinks regretfully back to his life as a boy when he would spend entire days in the open air.

Although his life has been hard, Morris's redeeming quality is that he is unshakably honest. He is "the soul of honesty—he could not escape his honesty, it was bedrock; to cheat would cause an explosion in him." Although he does not observe all the external requirements of the Jewish faith and does not attend the synagogue, Morris believes he is a good Jew because he follows the basic instruction of Jewish law. According to him, "This means to do what is right, to be honest, to be good."

However, following these precepts does not produce any happiness for him. His life is all about endurance rather than pleasure. Just before his final illness, he is filled with regret. He is ashamed of himself because he has not managed to provide adequately for his family. He worries about the possibility that Helen may never marry. "I gave away my life for nothing," he thinks to himself.

Breitbart

Breitbart is a Jewish acquaintance of Morris Bober. He is in his fifties with white hair, and he walks the neighborhood selling light bulbs for a living. Breitbart has had a hard life. He used to own a good business, but his brother ruined it by gambling, leaving Breitbart with debts. He went bankrupt and lived with his young son in one small room until he learned how to eke out a living carrying two cartons of light bulbs around with him and selling them to local stores.

Nick Fuso

Nick Fuso is a young mechanic who works in a garage in the neighborhood. He is the upstairs tenant in Morris Bober's house. It is Nick who first smells gas in the house, which leads to Frank's dramatic rescue of the grocer.

Tessie Fuso

Tessie Fuso is Nick Fuso's wife. She is described as "a homely Italian girl with a big face."

Carl Johnsen

Carl Johnsen is a Swedish painter and a customer of Morris's. He is in debt to Morris, from the days when Morris used to give credit. When times become hard, Frank visits Carl to try to collect the money, but when he finds that the painter and his family live in poverty, he does not pursue the matter.

Julius Karp

Julius Karp is Morris's Jewish next-door neighbor who runs a prosperous wine and liquor store. He is described as "paunchy . . . with bushy eyebrows and an ambitious mouth" and "short, pompous, a natty dresser in his advanced age." When he was younger, Karp own a shoe store that barely made any money. Then after Prohibition ended in 1933, he acquired a liquor license, converted his business into a wine and liquor store, and became wealthy, buying a big house with a two-car garage. Morris grumbles that Karp is simply lucky and thinks that in spite of Karp's success, he is a foolish man, regarding him as "insensitive and a blunderer." In spite of this they used to get on reasonably well, until Karp, who owns another building in the neighborhood, rents that building out to another grocery, thus taking business away from Morris. After this, the two men do not speak much, and Morris dislikes Karp more and more, thinking him "crass and stupid." Sometimes Karp visits Morris's store, however, and gives him unwanted advice. When Morris's fortunes decline further, Karp, who wants his son Louis to marry Morris's daughter Helen, plans to buy Morris's store. When Karp's liquor store is burned to the ground, he and Morris agree on a price for Morris's store, Karp gets sick and is unable to follow through on their agreement.

Louis Karp

Louis Karp is Julius Karp's son. He works in his father's liquor store and has no ambition to do more. He is able to live off the fruits of his father's prosperity. He knew Helen in high school and is still interested in forming a relationship with her, but he has little confidence in himself, and in any case, Helen has no interest in him. Louis's father and Ida Bober both want Helen and Louis to get married, but nothing ever comes of their plans.

Al Marcus

Al Marcus is a forty-six-year-old man who is dying of cancer. He insists on continuing to work as a salesman of paper products, and Morris is always kind to him.

Mr. Minogue

Mr. Minogue is the "stocky, redfaced" detective who investigates the robbery of Morris's store. He is a widower and the father of Ward Minogue. He was a strict father and beat up his son when Ward was fired from his job for stealing. When he finds Ward in a bar in the neighborhood, he beats him again, telling him that if he ever catches him in the area again, he will murder him.

Ward Minogue

Ward Minogue is one of the men who robs Morris's store. A violent thief, he seems to have no redeeming features. In junior high school he was a "wild boy, always in trouble for manhandling girls." Then he was fired from his job for stealing from the company. Ward tries unsuccessfully to recruit Frank Alpine for another robbery; he also attacks Helen in the park, trying to rape her. Ward dies after he breaks into Karp's store after hours, gets drunk and accidentally sets fire to the place.

Bettie Pearl

Bettie Pearl is Nat Pearl's twenty-seven-year-old sister. She is a friend of Helen's, although they do not see each other very often and Helen finds her rather dull. Bettie marries a man called Shep Hirsch, but Helen does not attend the wedding.

Nat Pearl

Nat Pearl is a Jewish second-year law student. He graduated magna cum laude from Columbia University and is described as "handsome, cleft-chinned, gifted, ambitious." He has excellent prospects and rich friends, although Morris Bober thinks he is a showoff and does not like him. Nat is interested in dating Helen, and they saw each other regularly during the summer, but Helen has taken to avoiding him. She thinks that all he is interested in is sex, when she wants a relationship based on love.

Sam Pearl

Sam Pearl is the father of Nat and Bettie Pearl. He is a former cabdriver, who now owns a corner candy store. Sociable and easy-going, Sam neglects the store, choosing to spend his time betting on horse races. However, he has good luck gambling and has been able to support Nat in college.

Podolsky

Podolsky is a refugee who is a potential buyer of Morris's store. He is a shy, good-natured young man, but nothing ever comes of his interest in the store.

Heinrich Schmitz

Heinrich Schmitz is the German owner of the new grocery store that takes so much business away from Morris. He is an energetic man who dresses like a doctor, in a white jacket. Later he becomes ill and has to close the store.

Charlie Sobeloff

Charlie Sobeloff is an old business partner of Morris's who now owns a thriving supermarket. Morris thinks of Charlie as a "cross-eyed but clever conniver." Many years earlier the two men set up in business together, buying a grocery store. But Charlie, who was in charge of the books, cheated and stole, and the business collapsed. Charlie rebuilt his fortunes, but Morris was unable to do likewise. When his store fails, Morris overcomes his dislike of Charlie and goes to his supermarket to ask him for a job.

Otto Vogel

Otto Vogel is a German who delivers meat to Morris's grocery store. He makes anti-Semitic remarks to Frank Alpine.

THEMES

Redemption through Development of Moral Awareness

When he first appears in the novel, Frank Alpine is a confused man who is merely drifting from one failure to the next. He does not have a clue about how to create a successful life or to live a moral one. Just before the novel begins, he has made his way to Brooklyn with dreams of leading a life of crime, through which he hopes to "live like a prince." He seems like a hopeless case, but his encounter with Morris Bober starts him out on a process that eventually leads to his moral redemption. His very first actions, when he helps Morris in with the milk crates, show that he is not an irretrievably bad character. His instincts are to help others, but he has got trapped in a negative cycle in which one wrong or impulsive action leads inevitably to another. He acknowledges to Morris that there is something missing in him

TOPICS FOR FURTHER STUDY

- Investigate anti-Semitism in the United States. Describe any recent incidents in which anti-Semitism was allegedly involved. Why have Jews not faced the same kind of persecution in the United States that they have in Europe? Make a class presentation with your findings.

- Research the tensions that often exist in families between first and second generation immigrants regarding adherence to cultural traditions. How do immigrants retain their own cultural and ethnic identity while also becoming part of American culture? Should immigrants make it their goal to become Americans or to retain their own distinct language and culture? Write an essay in which you discuss the issues involved.

- Malamud once commented in connection with the prison metaphor that recurs in his works that a man must invent or construct his freedom. Write an essay in which you discuss what he meant by that, and how his comment might apply to *The Assistant*.

- Research the mythical and religious elements in *The Assistant*. Read a synopsis of the medieval story of Parzival and Amfortas and show how it underlies *The Assistant*. Read about the life of St. Francis. Why is Frank attracted to St. Francis? How do the Christian and Jewish elements in the novel interact in the figure of Frank? Make a class presentation in which you explain your findings.

that stops him from accomplishing anything in life. What is missing is a firm moral core to his being that would enable him to favor his good instincts over his bad ones. He makes a bad start by helping to rob Morris's store; then he steals milk and rolls from Morris, and his response to Morris's kindness in feeding him and then taking him in and allowing him to work in the store is to steal money from the cash register.

But Frank learns. Twice he is on hand to save Morris's life, and he does his best to pay back the money he steals. He develops loyalty to the grocer because he recognizes that Morris lives a moral life. Morris may be poor, but he does not compromise his ethics. Not only does he help Frank, he also helps the poor people in this poverty-stricken immigrant neighborhood by extending credit to them at the store, even though he knows he will never see the money. A key moment comes when Morris tells Frank about some of the ways in which grocers he has known trick their customers, but he will not do so himself. He says, "When a man is honest he don't worry when he sleeps. This is more important than to steal a nickel." Although in learning from Morris he has to overcome some of his own anti-Semitic prejudices, Frank eventually learns to listen to the voice of his own conscience, which too often he had ignored or dismissed, and to be more true to the spiritual side of his nature. The process does not happen overnight, but he recognizes that Morris has a self-discipline that he lacks and a deeply embedded moral awareness that recognizes the humanity of others.

This recognition enables Frank to change the direction of his life. He shows an ability to transform himself by self-sacrifice. After Morris's death he toils endlessly, depriving himself of sleep, in order to keep the store open so that Helen can pay her college tuition. He tries to purge himself of guilt by confessing to Helen that he participated in the robbery of the store. Helen eventually has to admit that Frank has changed. His attitude toward her is now quite different from what it was when he first met her. Then he was motivated by lust, as shown when he spies on her in the bathroom. When he first courts her he is frustrated that they meet only in public places, and when he takes her to his room he wants to have sex; then, later, he rapes her in the park. But by the end of the novel, Frank has done his penance for his actions; he is now motivated by a purer form of love that genuinely seeks to promote the welfare of the other person.

The completion of Frank's moral redemption is shown in a symbolic incident that takes place at Morris's gravesite. At the burial he accidentally falls into Morris's grave and jumps out again. This shows symbolically that he is reborn and is ready to become Morris's successor. It prepares the way for his converting to Judaism and continuing to operate the store; he becomes, like Morris, the moral man who runs an ethical business and is an example for others.

Ethical Values Contrasted with Materialism and Selfishness

Although Morris considers himself a failure, this is not the theme of the novel. Rather, the reverse is true. At his funeral, Morris is lauded by the rabbi for his simple humanity, his willingness to suffer and endure, and to sustain hope. The fact that Morris was scrupulously honest, that he wanted for others what he wished for himself, that he worked hard and provided for his family, made him a good Jew in the eyes of the rabbi. "He asked for himself little—nothing, but he wanted for his beloved child a better existence than he had," the rabbi says. It does not matter that Morris did not attend the synagogue and lived and worked among gentiles and sold them pig meat that was forbidden for Jews to eat. To be a Jew, as the rabbi interprets it, is to follow the law that God gave to Moses on Mt. Sinai. Being a Jew is equated with upholding ethical, humanitarian values rather than with any specific religious practice or ritual.

To live an ethical life does not necessarily lead to material success, however. Goodness is its own reward. The novel consistently contrasts the ethical but poor Morris with his neighbor, the prosperous, worldly wise but selfish Julius Karp. Karp does not work hard, but he has the knack of making money and succeeding in the world. However, Karp feels no obligation to his less fortunate neighbor. He allows a grocery store to be set up in the building he owns, even though he knows this could put his neighbor, Morris, out of business. Karp, attuned to the commercial values that dominate society, always seems to have good luck, while Morris meets only ill luck. Morris has a certain wisdom born of suffering and endurance; in contrast, success has come too easily to Karp, and he has gained no wisdom from it, only a crafty understanding of how the world works. He guesses, for example, long before Morris does, that Frank is filching money from the store, because he knows how common such a practice is. He even stole from his employer himself, when he was a young man working for a half-blind shoe wholesaler.

Morris is also contrasted with his former business partner Charlie Sobeloff, whose ethical values are even worse than Karp's. When they were in business together, Sobeloff cheated Morris out of his money and then used his ill-gotten gains to set up in business himself. He has since achieved material success but at the price of

A Jewish immigrant family arrives in New York
(© Bettmann / Corbis)

his personal integrity. There is a deep irony in the situation when Morris, the poor but honest man, is forced to go and work for Sobeloff, the rich but dishonest man. Sobeloff tells him at the end of one day's work that he is short a dollar in the cash register, thus indirectly accusing Morris of theft. Morris instantly makes up the money from his own pocket and then quits the job. He cannot endure such a slur on his character.

STYLE

St. Francis Motif

A motif is a frequently recurring element in a piece of literature. In this novel, Frank Alpine is linked to St. Francis of Assisi (1182–1226). St. Francis was born into a wealthy family but he turned his back on material possessions to devote his life to the care of the poor and the sick. He was reputed to have magical powers over animals and preached to the birds, who it was said, listened without fluttering. In the novel, St. Francis becomes a symbol of Frank's spiritual nature, the better, more moral life to which he aspires. Frank is fascinated by St. Francis. He remembers the stories about the saint that were read to him at the orphanage; he gazes at a picture of St. Francis in a magazine for five minutes and tells Sam Pearl that the saint was "born good." He reads a biography of St. Francis in the library and tells Helen a story about him.

As the months go by, Frank, in his own small way, becomes a little like St. Francis. He helps the poor by keeping the store open and by trying to give money to the Johnsen family; he is on hand to attend to the sick or those who need help. (Twice he saves Morris's life.) When Helen sees Frank in the park, he appears as a St. Francis-like figure as he feeds the birds. Pigeons perch on his shoulders; another bird sits on his hat.

In the penultimate paragraph of the novel, Frank has a thought about St. Francis. He imagines the saint appearing in front of the grocery and plucking from the garbage the wooden rose that Frank had made for Helen and which she had thrown away. In Frank's imagination, the saint turns the wooden rose into a real rose and presents it to Helen, calling it "your little sister the rose." This imaginative image that comes spontaneously into his mind suggests that Frank realizes that following the precepts of St. Francis is helping him to express his true love for Helen and hastening the day when she may accept him for the genuineness of his love. The wooden flower she discards; the real flower, by the grace of St. Francis, is one that perhaps she will accept.

Prison Metaphors

Morris's grocery store is presented metaphorically as a prison or tomb. Early on, Morris thinks back to a time when he would spend whole days out in the open air. Now he almost never gets out: "In a store you were entombed." This is the first occurrence of a cluster of images—tomb, prison, cave—that suggests the nature of Morris's life. "A store is a prison," Morris says to Frank when they first meet. After Morris's death, Helen, who does not entirely share the rabbi's positive evaluation of Morris's life, says of the store, "He buried himself in it; he didn't have the imagination to know what he was missing." It seems that Morris goes from one enclosed box (the store) to another (his coffin). The metaphor may suggest the hardness of human life in general, the lack of freedom people have, perhaps also the necessity of suffering. The point of the metaphor is not only that human life, at least the kind of life

Morris leads, may be compared to a prison, but that what matters is how a person responds to that situation, what kind of moral resources he or she brings to it. Morris shows his worth by his power of endurance and his refusal to act unethically (cheating his customers, for example) to escape his situation. He suffers, but he does not lose his humanity.

In this sense the store/prison serves as a testing ground, an opportunity for moral and spiritual growth. The metaphor is applied also to Frank's life after he begins to work at the store and live in Morris's house. Al Marcus warns him, "This kind of a store is a death tomb," suggesting he is likely to be there forever unless he gets out while he still can. At one point, Frank himself refers to the store as an "overgrown coffin," and in one of his anti-Semitic moments, he thinks that the Jews are "born prisoners." When he finds himself working two jobs to keep the store afloat, Frank "lived in his prison in a climate of regret that he had turned a good thing into a bad," and he longs for escape.

But for Frank, the restricted life he lives at the store comes to resemble a monastic cell, a place where he can grow out of his restlessness and make spiritual progress like his hero St. Francis. The store may be a tomb, but it offers a kind of spiritual rebirth.

HISTORICAL CONTEXT

Jews in America

Over two million Jews fled pogroms in Russia and other countries in Eastern Europe from 1881 to 1924 and came to the safety of the United States. (A pogrom is an organized riot or massacre that targets a particular group, in the nineteenth and twentieth centuries often Jews.) Morris Bober in *The Assistant* took the same route, fleeing Russia probably some time in the 1910s. The high rate of immigration to the United States during this period produced some anti-immigrant sentiment, which resulted in the National Origins Quota of 1924 that drastically restricted immigration from Russia and Eastern Europe.

Although the United States traditionally offered religious tolerance, the new influx of Jewish immigrants faced considerable anti-Semitism during the 1920s and 1930s. Jews were discriminated against in employment, college admissions, and membership of clubs and organizations.

COMPARE
&
CONTRAST

- **1950s:** Three of the greatest of all Jewish American writers are at early stages of their careers. In addition to Malamud, Saul Bellow (1915–2005) publishes *The Adventures of Augie March* (1953), *Seize the Day* (1956), and *Henderson the Rain King* (1959), although Bellow, like Malamud, resists the label Jewish American writer. Both prefer to be known simply as writers, as does Philip Roth, who publishes his first work, *Goodbye, Columbus*, in 1959 and goes on in a stream of later works to examine the experience of second-generation American Jews, many of whom are alienated from their cultural and religious traditions.

   Today: Contemporary Jewish American literature uses more diverse settings than the work of earlier writers, who chose urban settings such as Brooklyn, Manhattan's Lower East Side, and Newark. For example, Steve Stern often explores a Jewish community in Memphis, Tennessee, and Allegra Goodman's *Paradise Park* (2001) is set in Hawaii. This change reflects the dispersal of American Jews over a wider geographical area than formerly. Other contemporary Jewish American writers include Paul Auster (b. 1947), whose works include *Oracle Night* (2004) and *The Brooklyn Follies* (2005); Michael Chabon (b. 1963), whose *The Amazing Adventures of Kavalier & Clay* wins the Pulitzer Prize for Fiction in 2001; and Jonathan Safran Foer (b. 1977), who is best known for his novel *Everything Is Illuminated* (2002).

- **1950s:** Jews in the United States are a tightly knit community. Only about 6 percent of Jews marry non-Jews. Sociologist Will Herberg publishes *Protestant-Catholic-Jew* in 1954, citing surveys showing that Jews seek to retain their distinctive Jewish identity rather than acquire a broader American identity.

   Today: The number of marriages between American Jews and non-Jews is rising. In 2000, the rate of such marriages was about 40 to 50 percent. As a result, many Jews are concerned about how the Jewish community can retain its distinct Jewish identity in the twenty-first century. Jewish leaders emphasize the importance of continuity within American Jewry.

- **1950s:** The U.S. Jewish community is growing in number. Anti-Semitism is in decline, partly in response to the Holocaust, the establishment of Israel in 1948, and Israel's alliance with the United States. Increasingly prosperous, American Jews migrate from cities to suburbs. Jewish populations increase substantially in Los Angeles and Miami.

   Today: According to the World Jewish Population Survey of 2002, there are 5,914,682 Jews in the United States, which is about 2 percent of the U.S. population, but 40.5 percent of the worldwide population of Jews. Jews occupy a slightly smaller percentage of the total population of the United States than they did in the 1920s. The Jewish community has not grown appreciably in size since 1960. The metropolitan area with the highest Jewish population is New York City.

Anti-Semitic activists propagated vicious stereotypes of the Jewish character, presenting them as atheists and communists who controlled the press and the financial centers and were therefore a threat to Christianity and the United States. The white supremacist organization, the Ku Klux Klan, was virulently anti-Semitic, as were the writings of Henry Ford, the head of the Ford Motor Company. Anti-Semitism was also disseminated in the radio broadcasts of Father Charles Coughlin, a Catholic priest, in the 1930s. Coughlin expressed sympathy for Adolf Hitler's policies in Nazi Germany and blamed the Depression on a conspiracy of Jewish bankers. His anti-Semitism became so extreme that in the late 1930s, some radio stations in New York and Chicago refused to air his programs unless they were allowed to approve the script in advance. At the height of his popularity, Coughlin's broadcasts were heard by millions of Americans. However, anti-Semitism in the United States never approached the levels it attained in Europe during this period. In Europe, anti-Semitism reached its terrible climax during the years of the Nazi regime in Germany (1933–1945) that resulted in the Holocaust in which six million Jews were murdered.

After World War II and the extermination of European Jewry, the United States became the home of the largest and wealthiest Jewish community in the world. Anti-Semitism declined and increasing numbers of Jews were able to make lasting contributions to U.S. society and culture in all fields of endeavor. During the 1950s and 1960s, there was a sense of optimism among American Jews. The determination and high educational achievements of many second-generation Jewish immigrants ensured their success. (In *The Assistant*, Nat Pearl, the law student, is an example of a young Jew who is eager to live the American dream and become a prosperous professional.) However, as *The Assistant* shows, anti-Semitic sentiments were not entirely eliminated. Anti-Semitism is apparent in the attitude of the Polish immigrant woman who shops at Morris's grocery: "She had come with it from the old country, a different kind of anti-Semitism from in America." Otto Vogel, the German, says to Frank: "Don't work for a Yid, kiddo. They will steal your ass while you are sitting on it." Frank Alpine also has some anti-Semitic thoughts, and Morris thinks for some time that one of the reasons business has improved since Frank arrived is that people in the largely gentile neighborhood are more willing to shop at his store if they do not have to deal with a Jew.

Although the novel makes no direct mention of the Holocaust, that event is hinted at in Morris's attitude to Vogel. Morris always pays cash for the supplies Vogel brings, because "from a German he wanted no favors." Significantly also, when Morris is being gassed in his own home due to his carelessness, in his dreams he sees the two Norwegian grocers who are his rivals "gabbing in German" while he speaks in "gibbering Yiddish." Norwegians of course would speak Norwegian, not German, and it is notable also that Morris has this dream of "Germans" invading and stealing from his store while he is being gassed, since millions of Jews met their deaths in the gas chambers of the Nazis.

CRITICAL OVERVIEW

The Assistant is generally regarded as one of Malamud's three major novels, along with *A New Life* and *The Fixer*. Critics have often noted that the novel represents a significant advance on Malamud's first novel, *The Natural* (1952), in that the author has learned how to integrate symbolic and mythic elements into a realistic narrative. In this respect, Jeffrey Helterman comments that Malamud "settles brilliantly into the mode that will inform most of his best fiction. The world of the grocery store is real, and its characters are flesh and blood." But Helterman points out that these characters have mythic dimensions also, and he discusses the underlying importance of the medieval story of Parzival and the Fisher King. Parzival (Frank) is the pure spirit who heals the wound of Amfortas (Morris). At yet another level, Helterman suggests Frank is St. Francis, and Morris is Christ.

Another critic, Sheldon J. Hershinow, has pointed out the importance of fathers and sons in *The Assistant*. He writes, "The archetypal core of the novel is a variation of the biblical story of the Prodigal Son, in which the father demonstrates unwavering love for his wayward son." Hershinow comments further on the merits of what he calls a "brilliant" novel: "Malamud weaves an intricate plot, and in taking the reader through unexpected but believable twists and reverses, he proves himself a master of both dramatic and ironic effect." When this is combined with an accurately observed setting and use of Yiddish speech rhythms, the novel becomes an "expression of simple dignity that presents a vision of the life of all men, not just Jews."

For Robert Kegan, *The Assistant* is not so much a realistic novel as a mystical one that creates in the relationship between the characters Morris and Frank the "I-thou" relationship described by the Jewish existentialist philosopher, Martin Buber in his book *I and Thou*. According to Kegan, "*The Assistant* mixes the flavor of the Hasidic folktale with the fervor of the twentieth-century quest."

WHAT DO I READ NEXT?

- Malamud's short story, "The First Seven Years," written in 1950, has some interesting similarities to *The Assistant*. It is about a Jewish shoemaker in New York who takes on a Jewish refugee as an assistant. Malamud was drawn to the character type of the apprentice who is trying to change his life, and in *The Assistant*, Frank Alpine fulfills the same role. "The First Seven Years" was published in Malamud's collection of short stories *The Magic Barrel* (1958).

- Saul Bellow's novel *Herzog* (1964) tells the story of Moses E. Herzog, a Jewish intellectual who is plunged into a personal crisis after his second marriage breaks up and he contemplates the failure of his life. He responds by sending out letters to all kinds of people; the letters reveal his experience growing up Jewish in the United States in the mid-twentieth century. Herzog is very different from Morris Bober in *The Assistant*; he presents another strand of the complex tapestry of the Jewish-American experience.

- One of Philip Roth's earliest and best-known novels is the satire *Portnoy's Complaint* (1969). Its portrayal of the domineering Jewish mother and her repressed but libidinous son Alexander Portnoy is extremely funny, and it gives a picture of what it was like growing up Jewish in the United States in the 1940s and 1950s.

- Henry Roth's *Call It Sleep* (1934) is one of the finest novels ever written about the immigrant experience in the United States. Set in the slums of New York City's Lower East Side and beginning in 1911, it presents three years in the life of David, a sensitive young Jewish boy. Roth records the effect on the boy of growing up in a harsh environment in a difficult family. The novel perfectly captures the language used by the Jewish immigrants, including Yiddish and Hebrew. Roth's technique and achievement has been compared to that of James Joyce.

CRITICISM

Bryan Aubrey

Aubrey holds a Ph.D. in English. In the following essay, he discusses The Assistant *in terms of father-son relationships.*

Bernard Malamud's *The Assistant* is a somber novel which suggests that the human lot is to suffer and to endure and through that to learn how to behave in a moral way, recognizing the needs of others even when one's own life is hard. The novel is at once tragic, since Morris Bober dies unfulfilled and poor, and redemptive, since Frank Alpine, learning from Morris, finds a way of patterning his own life after a moral ideal that had formerly eluded him.

Although the main characters are Morris and Frank, the minor characters all contribute to the structural pattern of the novel. *The Assistant* is in fact a novel about fathers and sons. There are four pairs of fathers and sons: Julius Karp and his son Louis; Sam Pearl and his son Nat; Detective Minogue and his son Ward; and Morris and his, in effect, adopted son Frank. The sons might be described respectively as the lazy, unambitious son; the successful but materialistic son; the bad son; and the good and the spiritual son. All of these young men seek Helen, the out-of-reach fertility goddess figure in the novel, but they go about it in very different ways.

The first son to appear is Louis Karp. He is the "slightly popeyed son and heir," a generally unimpressive figure, unambitious, lacking in self-confidence, content to make "a relaxed living letting the fruit of his father's investment fall into his lap." Louis cannot see beyond his narrow, conventional horizons. He is too timid to

""

WHEREAS BEFORE, FRANK WAS HOMELESS
AND RESTLESS, WITHOUT A PURPOSE IN LIFE, HE NOW
BEGINS TO SEE, ALTHOUGH IT TAKES A WHILE BEFORE
HE CAN ACKNOWLEDGE IT TO HIMSELF, THE
STEADFASTNESS AND THE WORTH OF THE MAN WHO IN
THE EYES OF THE WORLD IS WORTH ALMOST
NOTHING."

court Helen seriously himself. As his father knows, if Louis is rebuffed he will retreat into a corner and bite his nails. Julius Karp has to concoct a scheme that he thinks will help his son win Helen's favor, but Helen, who has a vision of what her life might be if she could get a college education and meet the right man, does not take Louis seriously as a suitor, even though they spent a lot of time together when they were both in high school. Louis's great fault is that he does not change. The only change Helen ever observed in him was when, in high school, he saw a photograph of a movie actor and decided to part his hair in the same way that the star did. Louis is limited because all he wants is more of what he already has; he can only think in terms of what already exists; he cannot conceive a new way of thinking or acting. In this respect, he is his father's son, but without the ambition and cunning. All that can be said in favor of Louis Karp is that he will inherit some money, but he will never have the ability to ruthlessly examine his own life in the way that Frank Alpine does. Things have come too easily to him.

Nat Pearl is a stark contrast to Louis Karp. While it would be hard to imagine Louis ever having the ambition or drive to surpass his father, Nat has these qualities in abundance and is set to dwarf his father's very modest accomplishments. Sam Pearl, the candy store owner, is an amiable man who lets his wife run the store; he augments their income by successfully betting on horses. Unlike Julius Karp, however, he does not expect Nat merely to follow in his footsteps, but financially supports his son through college. Nat is described as "gifted, ambitious." He is in his second year of law school, has rich friends and is

certain to be materially successful. He is a typical second-generation Jewish immigrant in the 1950s, eager to achieve the American dream and quite willing to pay the price of assimilation to achieve it. While Morris thinks of fulfilling the Jewish law, Nat is busy studying U.S. law. He is the type of young man who looks out for himself. His desires come first in his eyes, and he is accustomed to using his charm to make sure his desires are fulfilled. He wants Helen, for example, because he thinks she is available for sex. He seduced her during the summer, much to her regret, and he cannot understand why she has since frozen him out. Like Louis, Nat is not exactly a deep thinker, his academic brilliance notwithstanding. He wants what he can get out of life, rather than what he can give to others. Ultimately Helen rejects him because of this narrow, self-centered approach to life, in spite of the fact that her mother regards Nat as the most suitable candidate for her because he is or soon will be a professional and because he is Jewish. There is a sub-theme here about the tension between first- and second-generation immigrants that is common to many immigrants to the United States, Jewish or otherwise. Ida is desperate for her daughter not to associate with a "goy" (gentile), in order to maintain the family's Jewish identity, while Helen, although aware of her Jewishness, is also attuned to American values and does not use Jewishness as the sole factor in her search for a husband. The problem with Nat, as with Louis, is that he is not likely to change, not likely to re-examine his life and the principles on which it is based. When Helen starts tentatively seeing him again, she finds him "unchanged after all the months she hadn't been with him."

The third father-son relationship is between the non-Jews, Detective Minogue and Ward. Although it is only lightly sketched by Malamud, this relationship is the saddest of all the father-son relationships shown in the novel. Ward is a violent predator. He has been in trouble since junior high school, where he assaulted girls. He cannot hold down a job and has become a violent predator. He thinks nothing of hitting an old man over the head during a robbery, and he assaults Helen in the park with the intention of raping her. His father's response to all Ward's transgressions, going back to junior high, is to beat him up. Detective Minogue is not a man to whom a son might look for compassionate understanding, and the two have become enemies. It is a cruel inversion of the ideal father-son relationship. They are so estranged from each other that the father does not even know where his son is and has to search for him in the neighborhood. When he does find him, he beats him up yet again. The situation would be funny, like something out of a cartoon, if it were not so tragic. This is a natural relationship turned inside out; instead of closeness and nurturing there is distance and violence, a mutual incomprehension that can never be overcome. Ward's ludicrous death, when on a drunken raid on Karp's liquor store he accidentally sets fire to the place, is all too predictable. If Nat Pearl is too well attuned to the world and its materialistic values, Ward Minogue is so out of touch with what it takes to survive that his death seems almost merciful.

The final relationship, between Morris and Frank, is quite different from all of these. Morris once had a son, Ephraim, who died as a boy of an ear disease. After that tragedy, life closed down for Morris. Before, he would sometimes on holidays take his family out to see a Yiddish play or go visiting. Now, he hardly ever goes out. Morris still thinks of Ephraim; the loss of his son has left a hole in his life that has never been filled. Frank, for his part, is an orphan. His mother died giving birth to him, and his father left him when he was only five years old. Given their personal histories, it is perhaps natural that Morris and Frank are drawn to each other in the cramped prison of the grocery store. They are ready to serve a need in the other, whether that need is consciously acknowledged or not. Morris, for all his complaints about his life, possesses wisdom born of suffering; Frank, who is probably about the age Ephraim would have been, is an ignorant man badly in need of a guiding hand. Unlike the other fathers in the novel, Morris is uniquely capable of giving Frank such a helping hand. His adherence to a moral law that he identifies as Jewish law ensures that he regards others not as objects to be manipulated or exploited for his own gain, but as suffering individuals from whom he is not, in his own humanity, separate. Morris may not like to admit it, but poverty is a great teacher. Suffering and deprivation sensitize a man to the pain that others endure and to their essential helplessness in the face of their tragic fates: "The world suffers. *He* felt every schmerz." Because of his natural gift of empathy, Morris consistently helps those who need it. For example, he continues to offer credit to the customer who is identified only as "Drunk Woman." He once ran two blocks in the snow to give back to a poor woman a nickel she had left on the counter. He is kind to Al Marcus, who is dying of cancer but continues to do his rounds selling paper products in order to give himself a sense of worth. Even though Morris knows Al does not really need any money, "No matter how bad business was, Morris tried to have some kind of little order waiting for him." To give to others when you have almost nothing yourself is quite an achievement. Morris's quiet but empathic response to Frank the stranger is remarkable. He invites him in for coffee because he "knew a poor man when he saw one." He allows Frank to talk, accepting the younger man's need to unburden himself, and he is moved by Frank's story. "Poor boy," he says.

During his months working at the store, as Frank struggles with his wayward desires and nurses his ambition to better himself, he gradually finds himself absorbing Morris's instinctive moral bearings. Whereas before, Frank was homeless and restless, without a purpose in life, he now begins to see, although it takes a while before he can acknowledge it to himself, the steadfastness and the worth of the man who in the eyes of the world is worth almost nothing. He quietly adopts Morris as his substitute father, and Morris, although he never openly acknowledges it, guides Frank by example, the way a true father should. Nothing in this novel of poverty and suffering is ideal, but the fact that Frank can change so profoundly under Morris's influence offers hope that even within the prison of life, a measure of freedom can be found. This is the legacy that the good father gives to his adopted son.

Source: Bryan Aubrey, Critical Essay on *The Assistant*, in *Novels for Students*, Gale, Cengage Learning, 2008.

Jeffrey Helterman

In the following excerpt, Helterman presents the novel as a retelling of medieval myth in a modern setting. Frank Alpine plays St. Francis to the Christ of Morris Bober. There are also elements of the Parzival Myth.

In *The Natural*, the characters are mythic at both levels: the literal story of the baseball season and the archetypal level of the Grail myth. Even though sometimes based on real people and no matter how fascinating or how sharply drawn, these are characters who never were. They are literary characters who have never dwelt beyond the covers of a book. This is not true of Malamud's second novel, *The Assistant* (1957),

"

LIKE PARZIVAL, HIS INTENTIONS ARE GOOD, BUT HE IS NOT READY TO ASSUME THE PLACE OF THE KING AND IS THROWN OUT WHEN HE MAKES A FOOLISH MISTAKE."

in which the novelist settles brilliantly into the mode that will inform most of his best fiction. The world of the grocery store is real, and its characters are flesh and blood. Malamud knows this world well. His father ran a grocery store not unlike Bober's, and Malamud's first published story in high school was an account of his own life "behind the counter."

The characters live and breathe the small lives of the most ordinary men, but what is extraordinary is that Malamud has also invested them with the mythic stature he had given his baseball players. This is partially because these characters have very carefully worked out mythic antecedents, but more because Malamud has made their every act meaningful. They are capable of deeds of courage and cowardice, hard-heartedness and compassion, worthy of the greatest of heroes.

In *The Assistant*, Malamud again retells medieval myth in a modern setting. This time, however, he counterpoints the Wasteland myth found in *The Natural* against the history of St. Francis of Assisi. Both medieval archetypes center around a pair of characters: Parzival and the Fisher King, Amfortas, in the first, and Francis and Christ in the second. The novel's principal characters, Frank Alpine and Morris Bober, find themselves in a set of antithetical relationships. Frank Alpine, a man who comes from San Francisco, whose favorite book is *The Little Flowers* (a medieval collection of vignettes of St. Francis), who is first seen feeding birds in the park (the saint loved birds so much he preached to them), will become St. Francis to Morris Bober's Christ. In this relationship, the morally weak Frank will learn from Bober's spiritual strength. In the Wasteland myth, however, Bober, is Amfortas, the maimed Fisher King who is waiting to be restored by Frank's Parzival. On this level, the despondent Bober will be cured by the energetic Frank.

St. Francis, the son of a wealthy cloth merchant, turned his back on his father's material possessions to enter the monastic life where he embraced poverty so completely that his followers were called Pauvres Frères ("impoverished brothers"). In giving up worldly wealth, he turned his back on the flesh and its pleasures, particularly, food and women. He was known for his fasts and would go off for weeks with a minimal amount of bread and water and return with half his supplies intact. In giving up the wealth of world, he was following literally Christ's admonition to "sell all you have and follow me." In all he did, Francis's aim was the imitation of Christ. His ultimate reward was the appearance of the stigmata, the five wounds of Christ, on his body. The stigmata signified that he had learned to suffer like Christ for mankind. In the novel, Morris is wounded in the robbery staged by Frank and the detective's son, Ward Minogue. This wound doubles as the Fisher King's wound and the original stigmata of Christ. Frank first appears to have stigmata when he scratches his hands with his nails in his frustrated desire for Helen, but the ultimate stigmata occur at the end of the novel when he is circumcised, making him a Jew like Bober.

When Frank first appears in Bober's grocery, he is filled with the same worldly appetites that Francis had to give up. Frank steals food, and even looks upon Bober's daughter Helen with "hungry eyes." Little by little, Frank learns to govern and then give up his appetites. This restraint is not a negative or limiting attitude, but is converted into a positive activity, feeding the poor, which he learns from the example of Bober. At the very beginning of the novel, Bober, standing under his No Trust (no credit) sign gives food on credit to a drunken woman he knows will never repay him. Later, Frank performs the same duty when he goes to collect a bad debt from Carl, the Swedish painter. Seeing the man's poverty, he forgives the debt just as Bober would do, though he still has much to learn about the extent of Bober's powers of forgiveness. Eventually, Frank feeds the hungry day and night by turning the grocery into an all-night restaurant and working in a diner by day to help pay Bober's bills. By this time, he, like the saint, has almost stopped eating entirely.

Frank also learns to restrain his sexual appetites. When St. Francis was wondering about his decision to become a friar, he built himself a snow woman and snow children and declared that they were all the family he needed because he was going to put the flesh behind him. Frank tells Helen this story, but she takes it in a self-centered way and begins to think of herself as an idealized snow woman whose chastity is her only valuable possession. After Frank forces himself upon Helen the night he rescues her from attempted rape, Helen wraps herself in the snow woman's mantle and looks on Frank with an icy face while Frank dreams of looking at her through a frozen window. From this stage of self-revulsion on his side and rejection on hers, Frank's love for Helen changes from appetitive lust to a love that is more responsibility than anything else.

As the maimed Fisher King in the Parzival legend, Morris Bober laments the fact that he cannot even feed his family, just as the king of the Wasteland cannot feed his people. Like Pop Fisher in *The Natural*, Morris attributes his failure to bad luck. Though his luck is bad, the real reason he fails is that he is too honest to take advantage of anyone. He continues to give credit to the poor and refuses to cheat his customers.

In his honesty and bad luck, Morris is contrasted with a neighboring shopkeeper, Julius Karp, a liquor store owner, who seems always to have good luck. Morris never realizes that most of Karp's luck is manufactured by his selfishness. In the robbery that opens the novel's action, Karp, who is afraid his liquor store is about to be robbed, goes to Bober to let him know he might want to use his telephone (Karp, the richer man, is too cheap to have a telephone) to call the police. The obligation to remain open in case Karp returns freezes Bober in the store, while Karp runs off and leaves Bober as the robbers' only victim.

Karp also keeps renting an empty storefront to rival grocers on Bober's block, even though he knows the neighborhood cannot support two groceries. Though Karp pleads financial hardship, he makes it clear he would leave the store empty if his son Louis married Helen. Only self-interest can make Karp charitable. The wonder of their relationship is that Karp appreciates Bober's virtue more than Bober does himself, and often finds ways to spend time with Bober, if only to be in the presence of such goodness. This contact with goodness does not, however, change Karp at all.

Bober, on the other hand, never takes advantage of anyone. When a poor immigrant is about to buy his wretched store, Bober cannot keep his mouth shut, and by telling him the truth about the store's meager earnings frightens off the potential buyer. Not only does Morris refuse to cheat the poor, he doesn't even feel jealous of the success of his ex-partner, Charlie Sobeloff, who has bilked him out of four thousand dollars and used the money to start a successful supermarket.

Morris's despair comes from the fact that he does not appreciate the value of his own virtue and charity. Though he despises the values of Karp, the worldly wise man, who makes his living selling brain-destroying alcohol rather than life-giving milk, Bober still measures his own success by Karp's standards, and seen on those terms, the little grocery is a wasteland as barren as Amfortas's.

The Wasteland can only be restored if a pure, but foolish, knight comes to the Grail feast where he must ask the right question. The question is different in different versions of the myth, but usually has to do with the nature of the king's wound or the meaning of the feast. In the legend, Parzival finds Amfortas, is too overwhelmed by decorum to ask the question, and is sent away after being told he has failed his quest forever. Parzival, too "foolish" to accept this judgment, finds the Fisher King again, asks the question, heals the Fisher King, takes his place, and the land is restored.

Frank makes much the same mistakes as Parzival. His mindless eating in the store is the same as Parzival's presence at the initial Grail feast. Frank does ask the questions, "What is a Jew?" and "Why do you suffer?" but he is not wise enough to understand the apparently simple answers, "a Jew is a good man" and "I suffer for you." Like Parzival, his intentions are good, but he is not ready to assume the place of the king and is thrown out when he makes a foolish mistake. Frank begins his virtuous life by putting back some of the money he has stolen from Morris. Morris catches Frank stealing Frank's own money, but doesn't realize it. He fires his assistant just at the moment that Frank has begun his reformation. This is the fate of men like Frank: every time he tries to do a good deed, it turns out wrong. He has yet to learn that the nature of the deed is more important than its result.

Frank's virtue, instead of easing Morris's despair, therefore, increases it, because Morris feels he has lost the "son" he thought he had found in Frank. At the same time, new rival grocers have driven Morris's business down to nothing, and he turns on the gas and "accidentally" forgets to light it. Frank rescues Morris and resumes his job while Morris recuperates. The gas-filled store becomes Morris's self-created gas chamber as he dreams the rival Norwegian grocers are speaking German. Between the apparent betrayal of Frank, his daughter's indiscretions with the assistant, and Karp's renting to the Norwegians, Morris becomes convinced of man's infinite inhumanity to man. Since he might as well have become a victim of the Nazis, he allows the gas to destroy his spirit, his breath of life.

Though Frank has saved his life, Bober has hardened his heart against him and refuses to let him stay, even after Frank confesses his part in the holdup. Bober already knew this, and it is not the original crime that makes him refuse the assistant. Bober wants Frank to stay, but is not yet Christlike enough to turn the other cheek. He had accepted the robbery that occurred when Frank was a stranger and desperate. He cannot accept the subsequent petty theft in the store (even though it is finished) because this time Frank had asked to be trusted. For Morris, the breakdown of trust is the breakdown of one man's responsibility for another.

When Frank finds out that Bober had known for a long time that he was one of the robbers, he begins to understand what Bober means by saying, "I suffer for you." In fact, Frank understands Bober better than Bober understands himself. By knowing about Frank's crimes without revealing them or using them for moral leverage, Bober has taken responsibility for Frank's life and suffer for him the way Christ suffered for mankind. Since Christ was crucified for our sins, the pain of his crucifixion is increased every time man sins. When Frank realizes this, he knows that he must take up Morris's burden in the store as Morris had taken up his burden of sin. In doing this, he learns what St. Francis had learned about taking up the burdens of Christ.

Source: Jeffrey Helterman, "*The Assistant*," in *Understanding Bernard Malamud*, University of South Carolina Press, 1985, pp. 37–44.

Robert Kegan

In the following essay, Kegan shows that the novel mixes elements of the Hasidic folktale with the modern mystical quest. He analyzes the key moments in terms of Malamud's mysticism that occurs within a Hasidic context. The emphasis is on the relationship between Morris Bober and Frank Alpine.

> THE ULTIMATE ACT OF ALPINE'S CONVERSION, THE COMPLETE COMING TOGETHER, IS A STORY PAINTED WITH THE COLOR AND STROKE OF THE HASIDIC FOLKTALE."

The Assistant mixes the flavor of the Hasidic folktale with the fervor of the twentieth-century quest. The result is startling. Malamud, a *macher* indeed, fashions Identity itself, alive and dancing, and in so doing, brings to life the very rhythm of the *I-Thou* relationship—a self-transcending communication. Mystery abounds, redounds to the reader: life is renewed, creation continuous. *The Assistant* is, in greatest part, of a cool or stern mysticism—as characteristic of Malamud's mystery as heat and explosion are proper to Bellow—of a stern mysticism, to be likened to the Hasidic stance of *aboda*, of service or devotion, of "collecting oneself and becoming at one." Akin to this is the notion of the *yihud*, the unity of the transcendent—that a man produces or creates the unity of the transcendent through the unity of his own becoming. The man of becoming, this Frank Alpine, comes out of nowhere, the American man, belonging to nothing, lastly himself, rightly defined by what he is not ("a goy after all"), a man wholly disjoint. "what am I," *aboda* asks, "and what is my life?"

Alpine's identity is the central concern of even our first meeting with him when he comes into the store. It is our concern: he is masked, a white handkerchief over his face. It is his concern: "A cracked mirror hung behind him on the wall above the sink and every so often he turned to stare into it." And it is Morris's concern: the grocer's "frightened eyes sought the man's but he was looking elsewhere."

Looking elsewhere or not, the grocer and the robber, at this first meeting, experience an oddly primal sort of communication as the two men take water from the same cup; and so, in this folktale fashion of his, Malamud introduces the spirit of the *yihud* through the act of meeting, the act of union; Malamud lets us know that whoever this man is he is going to relate to Morris in a way that runs deep, to the core, to the beginning.

Through the flavor of folktale Malamud manages—without any damage to the story—to pull across every page the continuing question, "Who is this Frank Alpine?" We know at the start, from the intensity of their unity, that the answer lies in Morris Bober; and Alpine himself—as in need of the answer as the rest of us, the man of becoming, of *aboda*, mystically attached to Morris—repeatedly emerges as the grocer's savior. *Aboda* is service: "all action bound in one and the infinite carried into every action: this is *aboda*." Frank's repeated saving of Morris has about it the mystery of something bigger than persons. It is that which exists *between* persons: it is relationship. It is here, say Buber and Malamud—each in his own way—it is here that the sacred resides.

Saving the grocer the first time wins Alpine legitimate entry to the house where he at is once a stranger—this disciple of St. Francis, this "Italyener," this man who when eating a Jewish roll says, "Jesus, this is hard bread"—and at once a familiar—"Morris knew a poor man when he saw one", being a poor man himself. Alpine evokes in the grocer a sense of repulsion—"He shifted in his chair, fearing to catch some illness", and a sense of affinity—"I am sixty, he talks like me", and throughout this first face-to-meeting the two men continue to communicate on an order as primal and pure as the sharing of water:

Why don't he go home, Morris thought.
"I'm going," Frank said.

But *The Assistant* is not a folktale or a myth. It is not, like Malamud's first novel, *The Natural*, a story of magic through and through. Instead Malamud waits until the reader is drawn into a real frame before he begins without warning to distort that frame. Malamud creates a real frame by giving us perfectly plausible motives for Frank's appearance and desire to remain in the store: at first we see this as guilt at his thievery and pity for Morris; and then, when this wears thin, the author introduces the attraction to Helen, Morris's daughter. Malamud draws us into the frame by duping us twice over: by the promise of superior knowledge, and by a pretense to gimmickry. We think we know more than Morris and Helen. But this is of course a deception. The reason Frank stays *is* because of

Morris and Helen, but only initially for the reasons we suppose. There is a force growing here, about which we have no knowledge whatever, and when we do begin finally to sense that this is so, when the frame of reality begins to give way, it is too late. We are caught.

We know before anyone, for example, that Frank is the man who robbed the store. Thus Helen's feeling that Frank "had done something—had committed himself in a way she couldn't guess" is quickly understood by us to refer to the robbery. It is only later that—duped into thinking we know all the dynamics—thoroughly drawn into the store and the story—we discover the exact nature of Frank's commitment: to learn self, to learn relation. In the same way, Malamud is careful to inform the reader that Frank's touching self-explorations before the grocer are little more than theater. When Frank says to Morris, "Something is missing in me," Malamud follows this with "Frank felt he had all he wanted from him at the moment." This is, at the moment, convincing enough for us. We feel we understand the man and his motives.

Dwelling in what we think is a completely real world we see Frank's move toward Jewishness as the author's device to indicate the development of Frank's relationship to Helen and Morris. We think of the emerging identity as significant in terms of its sameness to that of Helen and Morris. In other words, if we are thinking about it, we think of it as a gimmick. In fact, however, as we come to learn in what is the essential experience of the story, the move toward Jewishness is the very definition of these relationships. For example, in the beginning, when we see Alpine dressed in the grocer's clothes, then stripped of them, then in them again more firmly than before, we feel that with the subtlety of a small hammer Malamud is saying, "Look, Frank is becoming like Morris." Exposed to this kind of surface work, we feel we are simply being *told* he is getting more Jewish rather than being *shown* what it *is* to be Jewish and so we think of Jewishness as an indicator, a device.

Unthreatened by obvious device, made comfortable by prior knowledge, we are relaxed in a situation we are convinced we understand. There seems to be nothing going on that is beyond our control: a reader likes this feeling of sitting on high, looking down and deciding it's all very interesting. And Malamud makes certain we stay convinced of our superiority. If we were thinking some deeper attraction might be involved, and had begun to ask ourselves, "What exactly can Frank get from Morris?", Malamud quiets this thought in Bober's line that, swallowed here, becomes difficult to digest later on: "What can you learn here? Only one thing—heartache." If and when we are no longer satisfied that Alpine remains at the store simply out of guilt or pity, when we are on the verge of discovering with what kind of energies we are really dealing, Malamud feeds us a little more line by introducing the second motive—the attraction to Helen. Fine. This we understand. The fish stays and the hook is set.

Now that he has us Malamud spares us nothing. The mere wearing of the Jew's apron, and "the clean clothes Morris had sent down [for Alpine] that fitted him after Ida lengthened and pressed the cuffs"—all of this easy role-playing, this telling, gives way to internal wrenching, internal lengthening and pressing. Guilt at his deed, lust for the daughter—hah!—this is just the sort of tolerable anguish to pull Frank and the reader into the house. What is he doing there? He answers the question—significantly enough—with a question of his own: "What is the Jew," he asks, "to me?" And what are we doing there? Why, we hardly know. Only a moment before everything seemed so clear. The story was being told to us, and now—now it's hard to explain, things have a new shape, or rather no shape at all. And there we are, with Frank, in the middle of things, looking for something we can recognize. It is the most difficult task of all for a twentieth-century American author to bring his reader to transcendent mystery. Yet this is, as he has told me, Malamud's very goal. "My job" he has said, "is to create mystery. Exemplification of mystery is the creation of mystery." And if it can only be done by a trick, then at least it can still be done. Saul Bellow, as we will see, accomplished the end through the American voice in *Augie March* and through myth in *Henderson the Rain King*. Malamud, in *The Fixer*, pretends to historical perspective. In *The Assistant* he dupes us by setting up a frame of reality that we can objectify, and then distorting that reality, disturbing our peace, toppling us into the story itself, never telling us anything again, passing all of it on through relation:

> What kind of a man did you have to be to shut yourself up in an overgrown coffin? You had to be a Jew. They were born prisoners. Deadly patience, endurance. That's what they live for, Frank thought, to suffer. And the one that has got the biggest pain in the gut and can hold onto it the longest without running to the toilet is the best Jew. No wonder they got on his nerves!

Patience and endurance get on his nerves. Yet he is drawn, violently, desperately, to the two people who represent these qualities to him. For Helen, too, repeatedly alarms him with her "determination" and her "seriousness." Their relationship, like that with Morris, is clearly shaped by Alpine's drive to find some shape of his own.

And though there is an important distinction, which we will discuss later, it is as much through Helen as Morris that we see the identity emerging. Through Helen, too, we are in the presence of *aboda*, of a special service whose purpose is to answer the question "Who am I and what is my life?" As their relationship tightens Alpine grows enough for Helen to sense, if only subconsciously, that her confusion—"something evasive about him, something hidden. ... He sometimes appeared to be more than he was, sometimes less"—that this confusion has a name: "Don't forget," she blurts uncontrollably, "I'm Jewish." He replies, "So what?" and thinks of himself as crashing through a wall. A commitment is made and it is followed by the desire for instruction. "What do Jews believe in?" he asks Morris. And though he has not yet grown enough to appreciate how profound is his instructor, he is faced with the most essential definition of Jewishness Malamud or Hasidism are able to impart:

> "Why do they suffer so much? It seems they like to suffer."
> "They suffer because they are Jews."
> "More than they have to?"
> "If you live you suffer."
> "What do you suffer for, Morris?"
> "For you."
> "What do you mean?"
> "I mean you suffer for me."

Here is the core of the novel. It is to this moment that all action real and mystical has led; and it is from this moment that all action real and mystical proceeds. We have learned by this time that Frank's metamorphosis is something more than a gimmick, that we are involved with definition; but not until this moment are we given that definition. We have seen the mystery of *aboda* and *yihud* in the repeated rescuing of Morris, in the strange way the two men are drawn together; and we will see it again in Frank's later "discipline," in the "unity of becoming" that is the story's climax—but the essential Hasidic mystery, the mystery the Hasidim saved from Judaism, and that Buber consecrated into the *I-Thou* relationship, is the mystery to be found in these lines:

> "What do you suffer for, Morris?"
> "For you."
> "What do you mean?"
> "I mean you suffer for me."

The first words of Hasidism, the spoken tale, which Buber says "developed out of a simple necessity to create a verbal expression adequate to an overpowering objective reality," which have, "at their base ... the stammering of inspired witnesses" record the mystery Malamud exhumes in the dialogue above. The Hasidim tell the story of Rabbi Aaron of Karlin, who, desiring to greet a friend a long way from his home, set out one day to reach him. After a long trip he found his door, knocked on it, and heard a voice say, "Who is it?" Rabbi Aaron answered, "I," and was refused admission. Returning to his home, Rabbi Aaron spent a year grieving and considering what had passed. At the end of this time he set out again for the home of his friend. Again he knocked on the door, and again he heard a voice within say, "Who is it?" This time Rabbi Aaron answered, "Thou" and was admitted.

But inasmuch as Frank does not understand Morris, is not at this stage ready to understand, let us ourselves grow with him into the shape of this mystery. Frank has some distance to travel. While there is certainly truth to his repeated phrase "I am not the same guy I was," he has only glimpsed the significance of what Malamud chooses to call "discipline." That he has none himself he demonstrates twice over by trying to rob what he needs to complete himself from the two people he knows to possess it. But what he needs from the grocer is not money, nor from the daughter, sex. What he needs are not things. He emerges at this stage a Jew only to the undiscerning eye of Ward Minogue ("You stinking k——"), whose misperception is grotesquely underscored by the donation of his identity to Alpine himself, a man that night as far from the covenant as any man might be—"Dog, uncircumcised dog," Helen yells at him after he violates her. "The span of a man's life lies between seeking and finding," Buber says of *aboda*. "Yea, a thousand-fold backsliding of the weak and wandering soul."

Frank is a man in search of fulfillment. He is in need. In robbing Morris of his money, Helen of her virginity, he seeks perversely to satisfy that need, demonstrating its intensity. "He spoke of his starved and passionate love, and all the endless heartbreaking waiting. Even as he spoke he thought of her as beyond his reach ..." But Frank is the man of *aboda*, of service, the assistant. This is his way to fulfillment. In the language of neo-Hasidism, it is only through achieving the relationship of an *I* to a *Thou* with Morris and Helen, rather than treating them as things, or uses, that he will reach such fulfillment. Although the relationship to Helen is different from the one with Morris—the first within the frame of reality, the second, allegorical, and beyond it—Frank serves each, is devoted to each, and his fate rests upon what he can learn from the first to apply to the second.

Only now, wallowing in self-disgust, does Frank learn that he has with him the muscle for discipline, for self-initiated devotion, for *aboda*: "He discovered that all the while he was acting like he wasn't he was really a man of stern morality." Once again he saves the grocer, who this time has nearly asphyxiated himself; but this kind of service we have seen before. It is part of the mystical wave that washes over the story. Frank must do it himself, unassisted either by Nick, the other tenant, or forces beyond himself: "He would do it all on his own will, nobody pushing him but himself."

Now Frank's service becomes mysterious. Though bound ever more intensely to the grocer he becomes himself the object of his assistance, and to more than either of them, it is to an ultimate focus—the relationship *between*, the holy sparks seeking redemption—that he is drawn. We have wondered throughout at Frank's *intentions*; now suddenly the matter is transformed, suffused by Forster's "bar of light." Frank's intentions have become "*kavanas*," the mystery of the intending soul directed to redemption, goalful, but without purpose. *Kavana* is not will," Buber writes:

> It does not think of transplanting an image into the world of actual things, of making fast a dream as an object so that it may be at hand, to be experienced at one's convenience in satiating recurrence. Nor does it desire to throw the stone of action into the well of happening that its waters may for a while become troubled

and astonished, only to return then to the deep command of their existence ... not this is *kavana*'s meaning, that the horses pulling the great wagon should feel one impulse more or that one building more should be erected beneath the awe-full gaze of the stars. *Kavana* does not mean purpose but goal.

But this is difficult for the purposeful assistant to learn. In his frenzied rededication to fulfill himself he reads a history of the Jews, "trying to figure out why they are the Chosen People"; but he cannot. "But," Buber writes of *kavana*,

> the liberation [of the holy sparks, the redemption from the exile within] does not take place through formulae of exorcism or through any kind of prescribed and special action. All this grows out of the ground of otherness, which is not the ground of *kavana*. No leap from the everyday into the miraculous is required. ... It is not the matter of the action, but only its dedication that is decisive. Just that which you do in the uniformity of recurrence or in the disposition of events, just this answer of the acting person to the manifold demands of the hour—an answer acquired through practice or won through inspiration—just this continuity of the living stream, when accomplished in dedication, leads to redemption.

Frank works. He works twenty hours a day, giving all of his money, all of himself, to the Bober family. He cleans the store, repaints the walls, varnishes the shelves. He suffers, he repents, he waits, and keeps serving: "All action bound in one," doing it, "with discipline and with love." It is a period of ultimate service: "Frank felt he would promise anything to stay there." There is in his devotion, in *aboda* with *kavana*, the quality of prayer, of prayer as the Hasidim understand it: "Men think they pray before God, but it is not so, for prayer itself is divinity."

In Frank's final rescue of Morris from the fire, Frank is able himself, beyond the mystical wave that seems to keep bringing them together, to see the necessity of their union, of their meeting. His language indicates that he does not yet understand exactly how the union is effected; still he says it: "For Christ's sake, Morris, take me back here." "Each act becomes divine service and divine work when it is directed toward the union."

But that union is not finally consummated—cannot be consummated—until Morris dies, dies as he lived, brushing away a little snow, which, before his body is cold, returns to fill in the little space he cleared. As the relationship between Morris and Frank has been carried out beyond the reality frame, as they are, in relation, not so much persons as the personification of the *I-Thou* relationship itself, Frank's at-one-ment becomes a celebrative collecting of Morris.

The ultimate act of Alpine's conversion, the complete coming together, is a story painted with the color and stroke of the Hasidic folktale. In its brightness and fancy, joy and sadness it most vividly calls to mind the work of Marc Chagall. Pushed by the wave that moves over the entire story, Alpine falls into his teacher's grave, "flailing his arms, landing feet first," "dancing," as Helen and Ida see it, "on the grocer's coffin." In this moment Alpine receives the one gift the grocer has to give—his identity—as the *I-Thou* relationship is literally consummated. Here the transcendent is most powerfully present through the metaphorical acting out of the notion of the *yihud:* one produces or creates the unity of God through the unity of his own becoming.

In fulfillment *aboda* is transcended and replaced by ecstasy: "Hitlahabut is as far from *aboda* as fulfillment is from longing. And yet *hitlahabut* streams out of *aboda* as the finding of God from the seeking of God ... As *aboda* flows out to *hitlahabut*, the basic principle of Hasidic life, so here too *kavana* flows into *hitlahabut* ... He who serves in perfection ... [brings] ... *hitlahabut* into the heart of *aboda*. He who has ascended from *aboda* to *hitlahabut* has submerged his will in service, and receives his deed from it alone, having risen above every separate service. In this moment Frank Alpine is prayer. Of *hitlahabut*, Buber has written: "At times it reveals itself in some action which it consecrates and fills with holy significance. The purest manifestation is in *dance*. In this the whole body becomes subservient to the ecstatic soul. Out of a thousand waves of movement it evokes in a kindred and visible form an image of the many fluctuations of elation and dejection of the enraptured soul. 'Among all who saw his holy dancing, there was not one in whom a divine conversion did not take place.' ..."

This is the moment of Alpine's conversion, the complete unification: "all walls have fallen, all boundary stones are uprooted, all separation is destroyed," as Buber says it. Only a moment before dancing in the grave, while sitting in the synagogue, he was not a Jew. He thought then, "Suffering to them is like a piece of goods. I bet the Jews could make a suit of clothes out of it." But a moment after having left the grave, suffering is not to him a thing, something to be worn or traded. But instead it is something within which one effects the most essential sort of communication: "He felt pity on the world for harboring him." He expresses his suffering for himself in terms of his suffering for that which is beyond himself. Woven into his expression of feeling for another is the apprehension of the other's feeling for him. He both eliminates himself and increases himself as he himself becomes no part and all part of relationship.

He is the Jew. He is Morris. The women in the family think of him not as the clerk but as "the grocer." His hair, like Morris's has grown thick. He is attached, with the same irony, to the Yiddish newspaper *The Forward*. And keenest of all, for no reason he has to explain, he finds himself awaking to get the Polisheh her three cents' worth of rolls. Of that practice he had said earlier, "Who but a Jew?"

"What do you suffer for, Morris?"
"For you."
"What do you mean?"
"I mean you suffer for me."

Within the Hasidic context Malamud brings to life the mystery of two men relating so perfectly that one person becomes that other person to whom he relates. The pure and perfect communication that takes place in the beginning of the book, when the two men share water, finds its mystically mature expression in Frank's actual assumption of Morris's identity.

But Malamud's mysticism has been carefully confined to Alpine's relationship with the grocer. The lesson we learn here—in a world removed from our own—is important only as we see it can be applied to the world we understand; only Frank is person as well as metaphor. The author is careful to screen the relationship with Helen from any of these flights from the frame of reality. It is here, in the real-life situation, that the lesson is applied. "Love," Buber tells us, "is the responsibility of an *I* for a *Thou*." We have learned through the personification of an idea that the essence of the relationship is a responsibility—an ability to respond—that results in one person becoming the other. Is there a sense in which we see this to happen in realistic terms between Frank and Helen? Both Frank and Helen want a college education more than anything else, yet at the book's end each expresses this desire in terms of providing the college education for the other.

Nonetheless, in characteristic fashion, Malamud gives us only a hopeful indication that the young people will be able to achieve such a relationship. Moses, Morris, the book itself—they wander through the desert and die with salvation still left to be written ... by the reader.

What Malamud has written for us is the wandering, the moving to the edge. And he has written it in the form of a painstakingly slow moment-by-moment account of one person relating to another man. Who is the other? He is a man who has been in the desert all his life. When he tells Morris of his life (and Morris tells him of the Old Country) he tells tales of "wandering" and "long periods of travel." He is the man born in the wilderness: "Now all of the people that came out were circumcised; but all the people that were born in the wilderness by the way as they came forth out of Egypt, them they had not circumcised" (Joshua 5:3). Both in this country of Italian origin, an orphan for as long as he can remember—cut loose from father and fatherland—he is from every part of the United States and from no part. He is the American.

Malamud really carries one step further Joyce's story of Leopold Bloom, the wandering Jew of the modern world. Having lost his son while still a child, left only with a daughter, Bloom is reunited at the end of his day to the father-son relationship, as he and Stephen—so promising yet so in need of father and friend—share cocoa in the early hours of the morning. In effect, what Malamud has done with Morris and Frank is to nurture the seed that seems to have been planted amidst the fertile energy of Molly Bloom's closing soliloquy. Rudy has returned. As Buber has said: "Every man can say *Thou* and is then *I*, every man can say Father and is then Son."

Source: Robert Kegan, "*The Assistant*'s Service," in *The Sweeter Welcome: Voices for a Vision of Affirmation: Bellow, Malamud, and Martin Buber*, Humanitas Press, 1976, pp. 37–48.

Robert Ducharme

In the following essay, Ducharme discusses the pervasive irony in the novel, in both situation and language, and its thematic functions. Through the use of irony, Malamud juxtaposes the fantastic and the real and achieves a balance between hope and despair.

My strictures against *The Natural* may have left the impression that I think mixing of comic and serious modes is fatal to the novel. While it is

MARC RATNER HAS ARGUED THAT MALAMUD'S PECULIAR BRAND OF IRONY 'IS OFTEN ACHIEVED BY JUXTAPOSING REALISTIC DESCRIPTION WITH FANTASTIC INCIDENTS, OR POETIC IMAGERY WITH ORDINARY OCCURRENCES.'"

true that the mixing of modes has been unfortunate in some novels—as, for instance, the clash of the romantic with the satiric in Evelyn Waugh's *Brideshead Revisited*—there have been, nevertheless, modern novels remarkable for the success with which they combine the comic with tragic. Keith Waterhouse's *Jubb* is a brilliant example. But we do not have to go any further than Malamud's *The Assistant* to find a novel that successfully combines the realistic with the symbolic, the serious with the comic.

If, as Harold Kaplan suggests, irony is a device by which "an omniscience entertains itself, but also it is the way in which it proves itself", Malamud entertained himself with *The Natural* and proved himself with *The Assistant*. The materials and themes of this novel have been used in earlier stories of Malamud collected in *The Magic Barrel*. In "Take Pity" Eva, a poor widow, refuses the pity and help of Rosen because to accept it is to accept her own defeat. This is analogous to the resistance Helen offers to the repentant love of Frank Alpine in *The Assistant* because to accept it means to give up her dreams of escaping from the tedium of a life like Ida's and Morris's. In "The Mourners" we have in Kessler a repentant reprobate like Frank Alpine, while in "The Prison" the setting of a neighbourhood store becomes a symbolic ands real prison for the proprietor Tommy Catelli just as the grocery operates for Morris Bober as a confining cell. *The Assistant*'s old lightbulb salesman Breitbart appeared in the earlier, uncollected story "An Apology" where he was an equally pitiable figure. Finally "The High Cost of Living" and "The Bill" worked with the theme of economic depression in the Thirties and the suffering it caused Jewish shopkeepers; Malamud uses the same social materials for *The Assistant*.

The irony in *The Assistant* begins with the title. It initially refers to Frank Alpine as the helper in Morris Bober's grocery store, but Frank also assist Helen to move away from her selfish ambition for success in the world. Ironically, Frank also assist Morris to his grave at the same time that Morris is assisting Frank to discover a set of principles that will give his suffering value. There is a great deal of irony too in the situation of the novel. The three Jewish families (Karp, Pearl, and Bober) live isolated within a gentile neighbourhood, a kind of microcosm of the ghetto within a modern urban setting. Yet it is to these isolated Jewish families that the Italian Frank Alpine, who was brought up in a Catholic orphanage, comes in search not only of economic survival but of a home as well. Furthermore, as Ben Siegel has remarked, Frank's conversion to Judaism reverses "the familiar assimilation story." Morris and Frank, however, reverse not only a cultural pattern, but a religious one as well. Naim Kattan, a French Canadian critic, has noted that Frank Alpine, as an ironically wandering Christian "reverse les roles assignés habituellement aux Juifs et aux Chrétiens." Thus, the Jew Morris Bober is the apologist for the Christian virtues of charity and compassion. This role reversal then issues in the reversal of the American cultural pattern of assimilation of foreigners, for "c'est le Chrétien qui se convertit, c'est le Judaisme qui est assimilateur."

Like Leopold Bloom, Morris "dotes on the memory of a dead son in infancy, and Frank, his heir, is Stephen Deadalus." But ironically, because Morris does not see Frank as a replacement for the dead son Ephraim, he never really accepts Frank once he has discovered his petty thievery and his role in the initial robbery of the store. Just as Morris yearns for a son but turns out the son who comes to him, Frank is also in quest of a father; but here, too, there is irony in the displacement pattern, for Frank finds a father in Morris only to replace him through death, and he finds a girl to love in Helen only to assume a selfless, essentially paternal, role toward her as provider for her education. Morris refuses to forgive Frank's thievery, but Julius Karp overlooks his son Louis' pilfering from the cash register, though he occasionally complains loudly about it. Karp's forbearance, however, ironically issues from no attitude of forgiveness; rather, he looks upon Louis' pilfering as inevitable, a sign of his shrewdness, a mark of the same business acumen that has been largely responsible for his own financial success.

One central event on which much of *The Assistant*'s plot turns is Frank's unfortunate rape of Helen in the park. Just before this, Morris has discovered Frank's petty thievery from the till and fired him. Ironically Morris discovers Frank removing one of six dollars he has just put into the cash register to pay back part of what he has been pilfering. While Helen awaits Frank in the park, she admits to herself for the first time, and she is ready to admit to Frank, that she is in love with him. Frank's fortunes with Morris are low at this point, though not irreparable; his prospects for winning Helen, however, could not be better. Frank's rescue of Helen from the lascivious arms of Ward Minogue can only enhance his position in her eyes. Though just a little while earlier Helen's idea of discipline had seized him with an unexpected attraction, Frank is nevertheless, overwhelmed by his own passion and he takes Helen by force, ironically destroying thereby his best chance for winning her permanently.

There is irony too in the language in which Morris Bober describes his own plight; it arises from a bleakly comic perspective that is dark, but not bitter, in the tradition if Yiddish humorists. Morris interposes this wry point of view between himself and his difficult life in order to wrench, if possible, a smile from his circumstance, a guffaw to forestall a terrible howl of grief. This is consistent with Malamud's attempt to show us men who are good, though highly flawed, men who manage, as Frank says, to be "better than they are." "The affectionate insult and the wry self-deprecation are parts of the same ironic vision which values one's self and mankind as both less and more than they seem to be worth, at one and the same time."

Helen Bober expects Frank to become better than he is when she meets him, so she gives him books to read. But, as Frank remarks, "Those books you once gave me to read, did you understand them yourself?" It is clear that Helen has learned no life-lessons from her reading. She gave Frank *Crime and Punishment* to read; but she herself learned from Dostoyevky's novel neither compassion nor forgiveness, and she apparently missed entirely its theme of redemption through suffering endured out of love. Her own dreams are the tawdry dreams of success cast in the clichéd mold of the Jew who seeks status and wealth through education. Frank, on the other hand, is extremely limited in his own self-knowledge. When he read *Crime and Punishment*, Frank "had this crazy sensation that he was reading about himself." But the discovery is not illuminating; it only depresses him. Finally, when Frank's transformation is radically effected, he does not realize either what has happened to him or why. "Then one day, for no reason he could give, though the reason felt familiar, he stopped climbing up the air shaft to peek at Helen, and he was honest in the store." Though a dramatic change has taken place within Frank, he has no understanding of it except that he is a better man now than he was. Frank could no more explain the Jewish religion he assumes (outside of repeating Morris's very unorthodox catechism) than he was able to read a book of Jewish history.

The ironic nature of the location of Morris within a gentile neighbourhood (which I referred to earlier) has a thematic function in the novel. Morris Bober is "representative of the traditions of the older Jewish community" within the "more competitive and fluid urban community." His poverty is a symbol of a larger moral and economic trap, for he represents an ethic of honesty and intense responsibility, a feeling that is an ironic anachronism in modern competitive society. Frank's assumption of these values, though it is the mark of his moral redemption, severely limits his chances of economic success. Though Frank may have envisioned his future in the clichéd terms of the American dream, the irony of the novel is that his displacement of Morris is an acceptance of old world values and a rejection of tawdry values of the American dream of success. These new values prevent Frank from achieving the success he envisioned when he came to New York looking for a better life. Frank's only triumph will be the moral victory of the loving man Morris Bober—a failure in the eyes of the world. What Frank has learned from Morris is a regimen of pain; the pain of circumcision is the ritual acceptance of Morris's views and values and it seals Frank's doom to a life of privation and frustration as a suffering Jew in love with humanity. Just as Morris's life has been a "holding operation on the edge of dissolution" so we cannot expect that Frank's will be much different. The irony of Frank's climbing out of one grave (Morris's grave in the cemetery) only to accept life in another (the tomb of Morris's store) is summed up in Frank's circumcision which both enrages and inspires him, which liberates him from selfishness and commits him to service.

The ambiguity of the novel's ending arises from the juxtaposition of Frank's dream of St. Francis, transforming his wooden rose into a real one and giving it to Helen, with the reporting of the fact of Frank's painful circumcision. This ambiguity has troubled several critics. Sanford Pinsker finds the irony here monstrous.

> That Frankie misinterprets the significance of Bober's life [Pinker feels it is a tragedy and a waste]; that he converts to a Judaism he does not understand; that he will (presumably) marry Helen and keep the grocery store running in Morris's memory—all these strike me as monstrous ironies resulting from Frankie's attempt to achieve a moral transformation.

This is certainly an extreme and minority view that depends on seeing Frank's and Morris's lives in terms other than those indicated by the achetypes of Christ and St. Francis. Measured by the moral standard of the love ethic, Frank and Morris approximate the ethical quality of their prototypes to an amazing and admirable degree. I do not wish, however, to deny the ambiguity of the novel's ending, though I think it obvious that the Christ/St. Francis parallel to Morris/Frank Alpine is not functioning ironically in the novel. The juxtaposition of Frank's fantasy of St. Francis and the painful reality of circumcision is, however, characteristic of Malamud's ironic technique. Marc Ratner has argued that Malamud's peculiar brand of irony "is often achieved by juxtaposing realistic description with fantastic incidents, or poetic imagery with ordinary occurrences." The ambiguity involved in such an ironic technique reveals a simultaneous optimism and pessimism in the author, his balance of hope and despair. Ruth Mandel has called this Malamud's distinctive brand of ironic affirmation in *The Assistant*:

> It is the disparity between hopes, dreams, and aspirations of the characters in the novel and the horrible reality that is insisted upon over and over again as it denies the fulfillment of their dreams that produces the overwhelming pathos. This shocking and repeated juxtaposition of hope and reality is an essential part of the ironic technique in *The Assistant*.

Certainly there is pathos in the novel, though I think Miss Mandel overstates the case a bit; certainly the reality of Frank's life—like all lives—will be much less than what he dreams and hopes for. Though Frank's quest for a better

life has landed him in a kind of prison, a man can be free anywhere. It is Malamud's object to show "how an imprisoned man can forge a new self in his reaction to the imprisoning forces."

Charles Hoyt has characterized Malamud's vision as a new kind of romanticism, one that consists in his creation of characters whose approach to their own suffering transcends logic, who endure past all sense, who look beyond the absurdity and wrest a meaning from it. Such a romanticism, though embodying an attitude toward suffering that may be construed as mystical, is grounded on a realistic acceptance of the inescapable pain of life. Combining the mystical with the realistic, Malamud's moral romanticism is aptly conveyed in his ironic technique that juxtaposes the fantastic and the real to achieve a balance between hope and despair.

Source: Robert Ducharme, "The Ironic Perspective," in *Art and Idea in the Novels of Bernard Malamud: Toward "The Fixer,"* Mouton Publishers, The Hague, 1974, pp. 36–42.

SOURCES

Helterman, Jeffrey, *Understanding Bernard Malamud*, University of South Carolina Press, 1985, p. 37.

Hershinow, Sheldon J., *Bernard Malamud*, Frederick Ungar, 1980, p. 46.

Kegan, Robert, *The Sweeter Welcome: Voices for a Vision of Affirmation: Bellow, Malamud and Martin Buber*, Humanitas Press, 1976, p. 37.

Malamud, Bernard, *The Assistant*, in *Two Novels: "The Natural" and "The Assistant,"* Modern Library, 1957, pp. 209–438.

FURTHER READING

Abramson, Edward A., *Bernard Malamud Revisited*, Twayne Publishers, 1993, pp. 25–42.
    Abramson surveys many aspects of the novel, including how it presents Jewishness and its motifs of imprisonment, suffering, and redemption. Abramson also discusses how the novel's realism interacts with its metaphoric and symbolic quality, as well as Malamud's style, language, and use of humor.

Cohen, Sandy, *Bernard Malamud and the Trial by Love*, Rodopi N.V., 1974, pp. 37–55.
    Cohen argues that the development of character in the novel is of more importance than its

mythic background of a fertility cycle. He traces the growth of Frank's character, from liar and thief to saint.

Handy, W. J., "The Malamud Hero: A Quest for Existence," in *The Fiction of Bernard Malamud*, edited by Richard Astro and Jackson J. Benson, Oregon State University Press, 1977, pp. 65–86.
Handy examines the nature of the hero in Malamud's three major novels, *A New Life*, *The Assistant*, and *The Fixer*. Malamud's heroes are not victims; rather, they all seek to discover a new life, beginning with a search for self. They succeed in their quests, but not in the terms they first envision.

Hays, Peter L., "The Complex Pattern of Redemption in *The Assistant*," in *Centennial Review*, Vol. 13, 1959, pp. 200–14.
Hays discusses the parallels between the work of the Jewish philosopher Martin Buber and the beliefs espoused by the character Morris Bober. It is Morris's love that guides Frank from despair to hope and redemption.

Blindness

JOSÉ SARAMAGO
1995

José Saramago has been a bestselling author of plays, short stories, novels, poems, and other works in Portugal for many years. Some of his works have been translated into more than twenty languages. A well-known atheist and communist, Saramago wrote religious or political satires. He published several critically acclaimed novels before 1991 when his highly controversial *The Gospel According to Jesus Christ* was banned as blasphemous in a number of countries. Yet, in 1998, he was awarded the Nobel Prize in Literature for *Blindness*, an allegorical novel. The Portuguese edition, *Ensaio sobre a cegueira* (Essay on Blindness), was published in 1995 and translated into English in 1997. *Blindness* raises questions about the frailty of social structures and the strengths and weaknesses of human nature. The central question is: What would happen if everyone suddenly went blind? To imagine an answer to this question, Saramago writes a story about an epidemic that creates chaos in the capital city of an unknown country in the late twentieth century. It is a worst case scenario of government and social failure in which the best and worst in humankind is portrayed. This tale has no specific setting, no names for the characters, and no chapter titles. It is written in Saramago's unique style that uses little punctuation, long sentences that can continue for a paragraph, and paragraphs that can run for pages. Since 1995, Saramago has continued to publish extensively, including a sequel to *Blindness* published in English in 2006 as *Seeing*.

José Saramago (*AP Images*)

AUTHOR BIOGRAPHY

José Saramago was born on November 16, 1922, in Azinhaga, a small village in the province of Ribatejo, Portugal. His parents were landless peasants, José de Sousa and Maria da Piedade. His name would have been José de Sousa as well, but a registrar took it upon himself to give the newborn the name of a wild radish that was also the family's nickname within the village: Saramago. In 1924, the family moved to Lisbon; shortly thereafter Saramago's older brother Francisco died. Although Saramago did well in school, he had to withdraw at the age of twelve because his parents could not afford the expense. He then enrolled in a technical school where he spent five years learning to be a mechanic. The school also offered courses in French and literature, and Saramago developed a keen interest in the written word, spending many hours in the local public library. After graduation, he worked for two years as a car mechanic then as an administrative civil servant.

In 1947, Saramago published his first novel, *The Land of Sin*, but he did not publish a novel again until 1976.

In the interim years, Saramago worked as a publishing production manager, a translator, a literary critic, and as a newspaper editor until he was fired for his communist views. During his subsequent unemployment he decided to devote his time to writing. He published poetry, newspaper articles, short stories, plays, and novels. Saramago married Ilda Reis in 1944. They had one child, Violante, born in 1947, but the couple divorced in 1970. He then married Pilar del Rio, a Spanish journalist, in 1988. That same year, Saramago gained worldwide attention with the translation of *Baltasar and Blimunda*, a 1982 novel written in the style of magical realism. In 1991, that attention turned to notoriety with the publication of *The Gospel According to Jesus Christ*. The Portuguese clergy and Vatican protested what they perceived as its blasphemous storyline, and the following year the undersecretary of the Ministry of Culture refused to allow the novel's entry into a European competition. Disgusted by this treatment, Saramago left Portugal and moved to the Canary Islands.

Saramago has written a number of highly acclaimed novels, but perhaps his best known work is *Blindness*, published in Portuguese in 1995 and in English in 1997. The sequel, *Seeing*, was published in English in 2006 and has the same setting as *Blindness*, but is actually on a very different topic. Saramago has received honorary doctorates from the University of Turin and the University of Sevilla, as well as numerous other national and European awards, culminating in the Nobel Prize for Literature in 1998. He was the first Portuguese author to win a Nobel Prize.

PLOT SUMMARY

Chapter 1

Waiting at a stop light, a man suddenly goes blind with a white blindness. A stranger drives him home, but the blind man turns down the stranger's offer to stay with him until his wife comes home because the blind man fears having a stranger in his house. When his wife arrives, she calls an ophthalmologist, and they are able to get in for an examination right away, but they discover that the stranger has stolen their car.

The doctor is unable to determine the cause of the blindness.

Chapter 2

The stranger who stole the car leaves it to contemplate his actions only moments before he, too, goes blind. Meanwhile, the ophthalmologist ponders the mysterious case of sudden white blindness and plans his course of research on the subject. That evening, however, he goes blind as well. At the same time, one of his patients from the afternoon, a prostitute who leaves wearing sunglasses to ease her mild conjunctivitis, goes to meet a client and soon thereafter goes blind.

Chapter 3

A policeman takes the car thief home, and another policeman removes the panicked girl in the dark glasses from her hotel and takes her home to her parents. The doctor spends the night thinking about his situation. He finally tells his wife the next morning and then realizes that if the blindness is contagious, he could infect her, but she remains calm. When the doctor tries to talk to an official at the Ministry of Health about a possible contagion, the doctor runs into bureaucratic roadblocks, so he calls the director of his hospital who wants to be cautious to avoid starting a panic. As the day goes by, however, and more cases are reported, the ministry calls the doctor to find out if all the cases are his patients then tells him that he needs to be quarantined. When he gets in the ambulance, his wife gets in with him declaring that she, too, has gone blind.

Chapter 4

The Commission on Logistics and Security, after debating several options, decides to use an empty mental hospital to quarantine the newly blind on one wing and those infected in another. By the end of the second day, all the blind have been rounded up and placed under armed guard at the asylum. The doctor and his wife arrive first. She is not really blind, so she inspects the facility. Then the first blind man, the one who stole his car, the girl with the dark glasses, and the boy with a squint who had also been the doctor's patient all arrive. The boy keeps crying for his mother. They all make an attempt to get acquainted. Then the loudspeaker announces the rules of their quarantine and the process for receiving food rations. The six internees decide to organize with the doctor as their leader. One man starts to blame the doctor for being their link to blindness, and the first blind man realizes he is with the man who stole his car. They scuffle but are separated. The doctor's wife leads the group single file to the lavatories. The thief tries to fondle the girl, so she kicks him with a stiletto heel. The doctor and his wife have to try to bandage the wound. Upon returning, they count the beds to learn their places.

Chapter 5

The next morning, the thief has a bad fever from the wound. More people arrive, and when introductions are made, the first blind man discovers his wife, and other connections are made. The girl with dark glasses asks the thief for forgiveness, and he apologizes, too. When the doctor and his wife go to get the group's food, they try to ask for assistance for the wounded man but are brutally rebuffed. They are receiving rations for only five when there are ten, then three more arrive from the infected ward. Shortly thereafter, a crowd of blind people arrives from the city, the ward is filled, and some go to the other empty ward. The doctor realizes how difficult sanitation will be. The thief tells the doctor's wife that he knows she can see. That night, he crawls out of the ward, hoping to convince the guard to send him to a hospital; instead, he is shot, and the others are told to come drag away the body.

Chapter 6

The doctor and his wife have to negotiate with the guards for a spade. Digging the grave is very difficult, and no breakfast rations come. When the soldiers finally deliver some food, they are so startled by the internees who had come to the front to wait that the soldiers open fire, killing a number of people. The infected, too afraid of contamination to move around the dead to get to the food, watch as the blind come, remove the bodies to the yard, and carry away the containers. The people from the second ward cannot be coaxed into burying their dead. The doctor discovers that there is no more toilet paper in the lavatories. His wife helps to clean him, then she too worries about the sanitation problems and when she will go blind. As most sleep, some couple has sex, and the sounds disgust those who are awake.

Chapter 7

The doctor's wife's watch stops because she forgot to wind it, and the further disorientation of the loss of time causes her to sob uncontrollably. The girl in the dark glasses consoles her. While waiting for the food to arrive, some people from the two wards talk to each other testily. The guards are so afraid of contagion that they make the internees come out into the yard to get their food, and the people have to crawl around to find where it is placed. One man becomes so lost that he has to be guided back by the shouts of the group. Taking advantage of this distraction, someone steals some of the food containers. After this incident, the wards decide to set up a committee to oversee distributing the food equally. However, a large group of people arrives, and there is panic and shoving as they try to find their way into the building. A man with a black patch waits outside until the chaos subsides then finds his way to the first ward where happenstance provides him the last remaining bed there.

Chapter 8

The crowded conditions convince the second ward to bury their dead and try to police their garbage as the first ward has been doing. The man with the black patch turns out to be a cataract patient of the ophthalmologist, and he was in the waiting room that first day of the epidemic. He has brought a radio, which the group agrees to use only for news to preserve the batteries. However, as they search for news, they hear some music, and it causes them to cry about what they are missing. The doctor's wife is able to get the correct time and restart her watch. The man with the black patch is able to tell the group what has been happening on the outside since they were interned, which amounts to the inability of the government to meet the demands of the situation since the blindness struck everywhere with great rapidity. Each member of the ward recalls what they were seeing when they went blind, and people realize that the girl with the dark glasses is a prostitute. The news claims that there will soon be a unified government and help for all.

Chapter 9

The extent of the filth and sewage in the hallways becomes a severe problem. The doctor's wife contemplates telling the others that she can see but realizes that too many demands would be made of her. The men from the third ward arm themselves with sticks and metal rods and take all the food, telling the others that they will have to pay for rations. The inmates ask for help from the soldiers but are once again rebuffed because the soldiers have been told to let the inmates kill each other so there will be fewer of them. The head of the third ward gang reveals that he has a gun and demands payment in the form of jewelry and other valuables. The two other wards decide that they have no choice but to comply. While looking for valuables, the doctor's wife discovers that she packed a pair of scissors. The doctor and the first blind man turn in the valuables and realize that one of the hoodlums is a man who is experienced at being blind and has a Braille machine with which he is keeping inventory. The leader puts his gun against the doctor's head, and the doctor considers trying to grab it but does not.

Chapter 10

Listening to the radio, the old man with the black eye patch hears the news station go silent as the people who are broadcasting are all struck blind. The doctor's wife decides to go outside while the others sleep to sit and think. She observes the other inmates as she walks by their beds, including a couple making love, and she cries to see that there is still tenderness amid the terror. Her wandering ends at the third ward, where she counts the hoodlums and sees that they are not distributing all the food containers but stockpiling them.

Chapter 11

Conditions in the asylum become worse as the lack of proper nutrition and the spread of influenza create greater misery. When a group tries to protest to the hoodlums, their ward is given no provisions for three days in punishment. The hoodlums then demand further valuables, so the wards scrounge to find anything that might be left and turn that over. A week later, the hoodlums demand women. After much arguing, the seven women of the first ward decide they can pay the price so that all may eat. The girl with the dark glasses has already been taking care of some of the men sexually, even the old man with the dark patch. One night, the doctor, too, crawls into her bed, not knowing that his wife is watching. The doctor's wife, however, sits on their bed and assures them that she understands. She then tells the girl with the dark glasses that she can see. The next day the women go to the third ward where they are brutally and repeatedly raped. As they leave, one of the women collapses from her injuries and dies. The doctor's wife brings water in plastic bags to the ward so the women can clean themselves and the body of the dead woman.

Chapter 12

Four days later, the thugs come for the women in the second ward. The doctor's wife slips in line with them carrying her scissors and, unnoticed, goes to the leader's bed where she thrusts the scissors into his throat. When the woman he is molesting feels the spurting blood, she screams, and pandemonium ensues as the death of the leader is discovered. The accountant grabs the gun, but the women make their way out of the ward. The doctor's wife stabs another hoodlum to death, and another woman strangles a man. The doctor's wife shouts threats at the men, and the accountant says that he will kill her the next time he hears her voice. The hunger that follows, though, is due more to the fact that the deliveries of food have stopped. The men finally decide to try to overtake the hoodlums, and the doctor's wife says the women should go, too, to take out their bitter feelings. The woman she saved from the hoodlum leader has come to their ward to listen and she says, "Wherever you go, I shall go." That night, the power goes out. The next day, the assault on the hoodlums results in two from the other wards being killed by gunshots. In the aftermath, the doctor's wife tells her group that she can see. Everyone returns to their wards, but the woman who said "Wherever you go, I shall go" is energized by the effort and searches for a lighter she has hidden that she uses to set fire to the hoodlums' barricade. She dies, but so do all the hoodlums. The fire and smoke drive the inmates out into the yard where they discover that there are no soldiers and that they are free.

Chapter 13

Most of the inmates wait in the yard for daytime in the vain hope that the soldiers or the Red Cross will bring food. The doctor, the doctor's wife, the girl with the dark glasses, the boy with the squint, the first blind man and his wife, and the old man with the black eye patch huddle together planning their route to their various homes. What they find is a city in which everyone has gone blind. The doctor's wife finds out that the soldiers went blind last and that people have left their homes in search of food with little hope of finding their houses again. Even if they do, someone else has probably taken it over. The streets are littered with trash and excrement. The

doctor's wife leaves her group in an appliance shop while she hunts for food. She finally finds a supermarket and figures that there must be a storage unit that the blind could not find. She finds a basement filled with foodstuffs and carries out as many bags as she can, but some in the outside crowd can smell the food, and she hurries away. She gets lost and sits down to cry. A dog comes up and licks away her tears. She embraces him then sees signs set up for tourists directing them to various areas. She and the dog find their way back to the group and all eat and then sleep.

Chapter 14

The group finds new clothes and shoes then makes its way to the flat of the girl with the dark glasses. There are bodies in the streets from those who left hospitals after there was no more care, from those who have died of starvation or violence or accident in their blindness. At the girl's flat, neither her parents nor their neighbors are home except for an old woman who has been living off the chickens and rabbits in her yard, eating them raw since she could not cook. The group spends the night in the girl's flat which is clean and comfortable. However, the lavatories are unusable, and they must all defecate in the yard. They make plans about staying together and where they will live. The old man with the black eye patch tells them he has only a room and no family. They make their way to the fifth floor flat of the doctor and his wife, going past dogs eating a corpse, and sights of disarray that the old man with the black eye patch is able to explain, such as runs on the banks, that he remembers from before entering the asylum.

Chapter 15

The flat of the doctor and his wife is intact. The doctor's wife finds clean clothes for everyone. She also finds bottled water, which they drink as if it were rare wine. The next morning it is raining, so the men and women take turns on the balcony, cleaning their clothes, shoes, and themselves with soap as if in a shower. The old man with the black eye patch, however, asks to wash in a tub, and the girl with the dark glasses slips into the bathroom and scrubs his back for him. The first blind man, his wife, and the doctor's wife leave to look for food and to go to the first blind man's flat. There they find a writer who moved in when his own flat was taken from him. The writer is very polite, and it is decided that he and his family should stay there. They all exchange news about the asylum and life on the outside. The writer has been keeping notes, even though no one may ever read them. That night the doctor's wife reads to the group.

Chapter 16

Two days later, the doctor wants to visit his office. He and his wife and the girl with the blind glasses find everything undisturbed. They go to the girl's flat and find the old woman dead and half devoured by animals. They bury the body in the back yard and leave a lock of the girl's hair on the doorknob for her parents to find. That night the doctor's wife reads to them again. The girl and the old man with the black eye patch talk of love and living together when they are finally able to go off on their own. In effect, they become engaged.

Chapter 17

The next day the doctor and his wife and the dog go back to the supermarket where they discover that people found the basement but fell to their deaths because they could not manage the treacherous stairs. The doctor's wife is so sickened by stench and guilt that they take refuge in a church, but there is no room until the dog growls and a place opens up. She faints, but upon opening her eyes, she sees that all the sacred images in the church have had their eyes covered with cloth or paint. When the doctor's wife tells her husband, others hear and are frightened enough by this bizarre occurrence to go running out of the church, many leaving their belongings behind. So the doctor's wife goes through things and finds enough food to fill their bags half full. That night, the first blind man suddenly regains his sight. The excitement that ensues causes all of them to stay awake all night waiting for their sight to return. The next to regain sight is the girl in the dark glasses who assures the old man with the eye patch that she still wants him even after seeing how he looks. The doctor gets his sight back the next dawn. The girl wants to go to her flat to leave a note for her parents and the old man goes with her. The first blind man and his wife go to their flat to find out if the writer has regained his sight, too. They all can hear people shouting in the street that they can see. The doctor's wife says that she does not think that any of them went blind but were already blind people who could see, but do not see.

CHARACTERS

The Boy with the Squint

Separated from his mother, the boy with the squint has no one to take care of him in the asylum. At first, he cries continuously for this mother, so the girl with the dark glasses comforts him. Only a small boy, he is scared and sometimes wets his pants. Adopted by the girl with the dark glasses, he is taken into the core group; the group cares for and protects him and takes him wherever they go.

The Car Thief

At first seeming to be a kind stranger who helps the first blind man to get home, the car thief is actually sleazy and opportunistic. He steals the first blind man's car and tries to fondle the girl with the dark glasses. Her forceful reaction results in a severe wound that becomes infected. His only moments of remorse and sincere feeling come when he apologizes to her for his actions and thanks the doctor's wife for her care. He also figures out that the doctor's wife can see, but he does not tell anyone except her. Seeking medical assistance, the car thief accidentally gets too close to the internment camp's gates and, in their panic, the guards shoot him. He is the first blind internee to die.

The Doctor

As an ophthalmologist, the doctor is supposed to know how to treat eyes and help people see, so the epidemic not only strips him of his sight but also his purpose. Without his sight, he cannot so much as bandage a wound. Yet he is not one "to surrender helplessly to despair." He is thoroughly devoted to his wife, and they consult each other on everything, but he also has a moment of weakness when he seeks sexual comfort from the girl in the dark glasses who can more completely understand his situation. Even though he can do nothing for their eyes, the doctor is still seen as an authority figure and is chosen as a leader by the other blind internees in the ward. He takes his position as leader seriously and shows courage when asked to stand up for his fellow inmates. He actively works to make their situation better, even though he is often unsuccessful in getting what they need. The doctor is a thoughtful and kind man who, strengthened by his wife's courage, tries to make the best of a horrible situation.

The Doctor's Wife

The doctor's wife makes a decision that demonstrates her remarkable generosity and simultaneously propels her into a horrifying journey. As her husband is being taken away to be quarantined, she claims that she is also blind so she can accompany him. However, she is not blind, and as the only person left who can still see, she alone fully experiences the horror that eventually surrounds them. She learns that she is not necessarily lucky to have escaped the blindness because she is witness to the rapid disintegration of society and the fragility of human decency. She is extremely "close to her husband in everything" but does not become angry or jealous when her husband sleeps with the girl with the dark glasses because she knows it will bring both of them comfort. The doctor's wife does as much as she can to help all those around her instead of using her sight to take advantage of or control anyone. Yet the doctor's wife is not immune to the character changes that their situation creates, and, after she is brutally raped by the hoodlums, she develops the militancy needed to use her hidden scissors to murder the hoodlums' leader. It pains her terribly to realize that even good actions can lead to bad when she learns that a number of blind people fell to their deaths because they followed the scent of the food she had found in the grocery basement. The doctor's wife does everything she can to hold on to her own humanity and that of the others in her care, and this struggle makes her the unforgettable heroine of the story.

The Dog of Tears

Although he does not appear until late in the story, the dog of tears acts as a companion to the doctor's wife in a way the others cannot. He, too, can see the chaos that has overwhelmed the city, and he becomes unfalteringly loyal to the woman who shares his pain. He licks the tears of the doctor's wife in an effort to comfort her; she embraces him and cries even harder because she has found someone who understands. Their providential meeting allows the doctor's wife to gather the strength to keep moving forward. In addition, the dog of tears offers protection to the group of seven for he is a "gruff, ill-tempered animal when he does not have to dry someone's tears."

The First Blind Man

The first blind man suddenly sees nothing but white while waiting at a stop light. Then all those with whom he comes in contact, the car thief who helps him get home, his wife, the ophthalmologist he consults, and all the people in the doctor's waiting room, become blind as well. Thus begins the epidemic. Once in the internment camp, he and his wife join forces with the doctor and the doctor's wife in trying to maintain order and civility. The first blind man shows courage when he accompanies the doctor to deliver the ward's valuables to the hoodlums, and he tries to protect his wife when they are told that the hoodlums want the women. The first blind man, though initially frightened by his sudden disability, shows great resilience and loyalty.

The First Blind Man's Wife

The first blind man's wife insists on seeking medical help when he goes blind, thus bringing them to the ophthalmologist's office and making the contacts that lead to the start of the epidemic and the core group that evolves from there. The first blind man's wife is separated form her husband when she is sent to the ward for those who have been contaminated and he is sent to the ward for the blind. After she too falls blind, they are reunited and are inseparable for the rest of the ordeal. She is normally "docile and respectful towards her husband," but when she is told that the women are wanted by the hoodlums, she refuses to be protected by her husband. She says she is "no different from the others." Horrific though it is, she has an opportunity to provide food for her husband and the group, and so she does it. She shows great courage in sacrificing herself for others.

The Girl with the Dark Glasses

Before the epidemic, the girl with the dark glasses is a prostitute used and discarded by strangers; however, as a blind internee, she becomes a compassionate caretaker who is embraced by strangers. When the boy with the squint cries for his lost mother, it is the girl with the dark glasses who becomes his surrogate parent. When the doctor is looking for comfort, she allows him into her bed. She is a tough woman, but she is more concerned about the welfare of her family and new friends than many of the others in her same situation. She is truly grieved that her reaction to the car thief's groping caused his fatal wound and asks his forgiveness. Although she acts mature, she is actually young, and her search for her family reveals that she is just a girl who misses her family and needs someone to take care of her just as much as she takes care of others. Perhaps for this reason, she becomes close to the old man with the black eye patch, and his gentleness and paternal attention bring her comfort. Even though they seem like an odd match, they become a couple.

The Hoodlums

As soon as they arrive at the internment camp, the hoodlums smell an opportunity to take advantage of others. They have no morals and try to grab whatever they can for themselves in the moment with no consideration for others or the consequences of their actions. Although they are just as blind as the rest of the inmates, the ringleader has a gun and the hoodlums make bludgeons which they use to terrorize the other inmates. The hoodlums gain control of all the food and use their cache to cruelly extort valuables from the other blind people and demand sex from the women. One of them, an accountant, was already blind before the epidemic, so he knows how to function in blindness and use a Braille machine to keep track of the bounty from their extortion. The hoodlums are parasites who make an already dire situation much worse. In the end, justice is served when the other inmates finally revolt, and all the hoodlums die in a massive fire.

The Old Man with the Black Eye Patch

Kindly and resilient, the old man with the black eye patch is more willing than others, perhaps because of his age, to confront and resist the forces that are trying to destroy his humanity. He appreciates art and in fact went blind while in a museum looking at a painting. Since he is the last of the doctor's patients to go blind, he is able to tell the first ward what has been happening outside in the city since their quarantine. Also, he has brought a radio, which gives them a little news and a moment of beauty as they listen to music. The old man with the black eye patch is patient and tries to come up with games to distract the other internees from their situation. He slowly builds a connection with the girl with the dark glasses, even though he cannot imagine what she sees in an old man like him. He does not think he has much to offer a young girl like

her, but their bond brings comfort and hope to them both. Their relationship is a step towards regaining their humanity and a sense of normalcy.

The Old Woman

The ultimate survivor, the old woman is another example of what happens when society collapses and a person's humanity is slowly stripped away. She has holed up in her apartment and eats the rabbits and chickens that live in her back yard. Since she cannot cook, she eats them raw, and her apartment is a den of filth and rotting carcasses. Her animal instincts are in charge; she is territorial and suspicious, in many ways like the dog of tears. "Hard of heart," she winds up dying alone.

The Pharmacist's Assistant

The pharmacist's assistant insults the girl with the dark glasses when they first get acquainted and is chagrined later that she goes to the beds of other men, but never comes to him. He is usually active in the affairs of the first ward and is killed in the attempt to attack the hoodlums.

The Woman Who Said "Wherever You Go, I Go"

The woman who said "Wherever you go, I go" is in the process of being raped by the hoodlums' leader when the doctor's wife drives her scissors into his throat. In gratitude, she tells the doctor's wife, "Wherever you go, I go." She devotes herself to the one who saved her life and saved her, too, from a life that is unbearable to live. It is in this devotion that she finds her power. When all the other plans to overthrow the hoodlums fail, the woman who said "Wherever you go, I go" realizes she has the ability to do something. She has a lighter, and she uses it to start a fire that kills not only the hoodlums but also herself.

The Writer

The first blind man and his wife find the writer living in their flat when they return. The writer has been displaced from his own flat and sought shelter with his family in whatever other safe place he could find. Like the doctor, the writer feels that his purpose has been lost in the blindness because there is no one to read what he writes. Nonetheless, he keeps writing with a pen and paper, making a record of the catastrophe. The first blind man and his wife allow the writer to stay in their place since they want to remain with their group from the asylum.

THEMES

Response to Crisis

Albert Camus wrote *The Plague* about a deadly disease that causes survivors to question how they are to go on when so many around them have died. Similarly, Saramago was inspired to write *Blindness* by an initial hypothetical question: What would happen if a highly contagious, debilitating, and non-lethal disease struck a community? Saramago examines how people might react if a non-lethal disease disabled everyone to the point that the basic social system and support services in their way of life were no longer functioning. Choosing blindness as his disability, he paints the bleakest possible picture of the social devastation that would result. The point may be to remind people that struggle is a part of the human condition, and sometimes extreme difficulties can arise which test beliefs about oneself and one's society. Thus beside the hypothetical question Saramago attempts to answer, there are important questions the text presents to readers: What would people do in a crisis? Are people sufficiently prepared to handle a crisis? Are people sufficiently committed to their personal values to know for sure that they would react ethically and with courage? *Blindness* serves as a reminder to each individual to establish ethical foundations for the times when they are needed the most. There is also a cautionary reminder here: During crisis people do what they must to survive; even the unthinkable is possible. This reminder may give readers heightened compassion for disabled others and for whole communities that are fragmented by a widespread disaster, for example, the ravages of a communicable disease or war.

Worst and Best in Human Nature

In this depiction of how people may react in a community exposed to a highly contagious and disabling disease, Saramago includes examples of the worst and the best behavior under stress. An early example of the worst is with the seemingly kind man who assists the first blind man but who then turns around and steals the blind man's car.

The worst kind of response continues when the government moves in quickly to order the affected people into quarantine at a former asylum. The government does not provide medical attention or insure adequate facilities. It shows no humane consideration to the people who are

TOPICS FOR FURTHER STUDY

- Why do you think Saramago did not name his characters, the city, or the chapters? Discuss as a class.

- Individually choose any page from *Blindness* and examine the sentence and paragraph structure. How many lines of text do the sentences occupy? How many paragraphs are there on the page? Compare with others in the class and discuss the difficulties readers find in Saramago's lack of punctuation and unusually long sentences.

- In reality, if an epidemic like that in *Blindness* occurred, the World Health Organization, the Red Cross/Red Crescent, and other agencies would step in to help. Research emergency preparedness as represented by these organizations or your local city and create an outline showing what they would do in a sudden medical crisis.

- Write an essay about the "dog of tears." What is his role in the book? Does he symbolize something? What is his relationship with the doctor's wife? You may want to include in your report the healing uses of dogs in various physical therapy treatments, in hospitals, and in prisoner rehabilitation systems.

- *Oedipus the King*, *Lord of the Flies*, and *Endgame* are three works that have similarities to *Blindness*. Go to an online bookseller such as Amazon.com or Barnes and Noble and find these titles. Check to see what other books are suggested by these booksellers. Make an annotated list of these other books, pointing out the elements that these works have in common with *Blindness*.

in desperate need of assistance. Many individuals give up in despair, are unable to cooperate, and become hostile and lawless. The very worst is shown by the third ward men who have a gun and use it to confiscate all the food and then use the rations to extort valuables and sexual access to the women in the other wards.

The best behavior is shown by the ophthalmologist's wife who is willing to give totally of herself for others. Further examples of good come from the people in her group who cooperate with each other, try to maintain civilized conduct, and take care of each other. The writer remains civil. The internalized civility of these people suggests that once the epidemic is over, the social fabric will be restored and the city will be reestablished.

Saramago presents so dark a picture that readers may be surprised by the happy ending. The conclusion suggests that there is hope that the best may triumph over the worst in human nature.

Social Disintegration

The theme of how crisis brings out the worst and best in people is connected to the theme of how social disintegration is the result of the worst traits in human nature. As vice rages unfettered by law, social order disintegrates. The message of this theme is about how fragile the social structure is that sustains civic order. Saramago advises readers to appreciate the qualities of everyday life that they take for granted, which were not easily established and which are vulnerable when catastrophe hits. In established societies, the ongoing government and peace are handed down from previous generations. Those who do not struggle to achieve social order need to be reminded of its vulnerability. Saramago provides in *Blindness* a picture of social breakdown: no health services; no government protection from lawless predators; no electricity, gas, water, or garbage collection services; no legal recourse for damages or rights violations. The society that enjoys these social structures and services is obligated to uphold and maintain them with vigilance and conviction. Otherwise, as *Blindness* warns, catastrophe can disrupt the longstanding social order and structure.

STYLE

Absence of Proper Nouns

Saramago does not use proper nouns in this novel. The characters are not given names; rather they are distinguished by a particular action or physical trait, the epithet standing in

for a name. Perhaps Saramago provides an explanation for the namelessness of his characters in a comment given by the writer: "Blind people do not need a name, I am my voice, nothing else matters." No quotation marks set off dialogue, although the start of a new speaker is signaled by capitalization. However, there is no space break when a new speaker is introduced and sometimes no identification of the speaker. The result is a text that can be confusing and daunting to new readers. Saramago's choice here perfectly suits his subject matter. His intention is to create a drama that has universal application, one that is not true just of certain individuals in a particular place and time and facing a particular crisis. Rather he wants to show the basic verities of human instinct and interaction under extreme circumstances. The incremental chaos that engulfs the world of the novel could occur in any country among any group of people trying to cope with sudden disability and fraying social structure. Using this strategy, Saramago drives home the point that the distinction between those who are afflicted and those who are spared is only superficial; in essence, human nature is universally the same.

Allegory

An allegory is a symbolic representation of abstract ideas or principles. Characters and objects may personify these concepts while the action of a plot may state something about the concept. In short, the elements of an allegory represent one thing in the guise of another. While the allegorical story makes sense on its own, it is almost like a parallel universe to that which it represents in real life. The purpose is to convey indirectly a statement about human conduct or experience. The writer may use allegory to deliver a politically or socially challenging statement without directly naming anyone or citing any actual situation. In the case of *Blindness*, Saramago's allegory serves as a warning that even in modern times social disintegration can occur swiftly, and each person must have the integrity to display the best of human traits under worst circumstances. Blindness, treated literally in this story, is a metaphor for widespread denial and resistance that prompt people to ignore or reject the basic truths about base human nature and the fragility of any social structure.

HISTORICAL CONTEXT

The Literary Tradition in Allegory

Allegory as a genre includes fables and parables. Examples of allegories are Aesop's *Fables*, Book VII of Plato's *Republic*, William Langland's fourteenth-century *Piers Plowman*, Dante's *The Divine Comedy*, the medieval morality play *Everyman*, Edmund Spenser's 1596 poem *The Faerie Queen*, John Bunyan's 1675 narrative *Pilgrim's Progress*, Jonathan Swift's *A Tale of the Tub*, and Edgar Allen Poe's *The Masque of the Red Death*.

Among modern writers, the two allegorical novels most commonly compared to Saramago's *Blindness* are Albert Camus' *The Plague* (1948) and William Golding's *Lord of the Flies* (1958). Set fifty years earlier than *Blindness*, *The Plague* also asks what might happen to a society when an epidemic strikes. As the title indicates, the disease is a deadly one, so the problem is not as much one of coping with life with the disease as coping with being alive when almost everyone else is suddenly dead. Despite differences, both authors explore basic human nature as it copes with adversity.

In *Lord of the Flies*, a group of English school boys, marooned on a deserted island, create their own society. The boys are unable to achieve cooperation and their lives disintegrate into barbarism like that of the men in the third ward of the asylum in *Blindness*. Although Saramago provides a hopeful ending, Golding does not. Still, Golding and Saramago make similar points about how easily social order can disintegrate into chaos.

A famous modern allegorical play that can be compared to *Blindness* is Samuel Beckett's 1958 play, *Endgame*. This drama uses a bizarre situation to convey Beckett's message, just as *Blindness* does for Saramago. Beckett's plot is set up as a chess game in a time that appears to be in a post-nuclear war setting. Beckett suggests the aftermath of a disaster, but his play conveys a sense of existential hopelessness, of going in circles because all action is meaningless and futile. The only progress is toward nothingness. There is here an implied eternal torment that Saramago's characters fear, but from which they are spared by the author's optimistic plot resolution.

Modern Portuguese Literature

Dating from the establishment of the republic in 1910, Portuguese literature of the early twentieth century expressed a longing for the imagined glories of the Portuguese past, a movement called Suadonismo. The greatest Portuguese poet since the sixteenth century, Fernando Pessoa, wrote in the early twentieth century.

In 1972, readers of Portuguese literature were surprised by the publication of the erotic feminist work of novelists Maria Velho da Costa and Maria Isabel Barreno and poet Maria Teresa Horta. Banned at first by the government, the book was eventually published in the United States as *The Three Marias: New Portuguese Letters*. After 1974, Portuguese literature showed the influence of French literary theory that emphasizes the language techniques and technical elements of a story. In addition, there was an explosion of talent with numerous high-quality fiction writers appearing on the Portuguese scene. Saramago's contemporaries among Portuguese novelists include Vergilio Ferreira, Agustina Bessa-Luis, Antonio Lobo Antunes, and Jose Cardoso Pires. Their counterparts in poetry are Eugenio de Andrade and Antonio Ramos Rosa.

Included in Portuguese literature is the work of writers from Portuguese-speaking countries other than Portugal itself. In the late 1990s, novelists Agostino Neto and Laudino Vieira of Angola, Luis Bernardo Howana of Mozambique, and Manuel Lopes, Orlanda Amarilis, and Manuel Ferreira of Care Verde gained recognition.

Just as the formation of the republic in 1910 spawned a melancholy nostalgia among Portuguese writers, the revolution of 1974 inspired a search for a national identity that eschewed myths of the past. Works were celebrated by writers in Portuguese from other nations and by female writers such as novelist Olga Goncalves who is known for her portrayal of returning emigrants after the 1974 revolution, for example in her book *A Florist in Bremerhaven*. Besides Saramago's being awarded the Nobel Prize, Jose de Almeida Faria's trilogy about the 1970s and 1980s marks a high point in twentieth-century Portuguese literature.

CRITICAL OVERVIEW

Since Saramago won the Nobel Prize for Literature within a few years of writing *Blindness*, and many critics feel that this novel was a major factor in his winning that award, one would expect that there is much praise and little negative criticism for the book. Indeed, there is much praise.

However, George Snedeker, a sociology professor at the State University of New York, expresses a note of concern given this age of increased sensitivity in referring to disabilities. Snedeker points out in his article for the *Journal of Visual Impairment & Blindness* that none of the critics seems to have given any thought to the possibility "that the use of blindness as a metaphor might pose a problem to the real blind community." While Snedeker admits that "the analogy between 'seeing' and 'understanding' is one of the oldest in Western philosophy," he thinks that "Saramago is more interested in probing the human capacity to understand social reality than in the philosophical concept of absolute truth." Snedeker concludes, "I wish he had chosen a better way of representing this quest."

Other than this consideration, the reviews provide a string of superlatives in describing this unique novel. Philip Landon, writing for the *Review of Contemporary Fiction*, thinks that Saramago has written "a parable for the millennium." Landon makes mention of the traditional symbolism associated with blindness. He notes that previous classics "have used the figure of the blind man to dramatize the vulnerability of the individual buffeted by the forces of existence." Landon further explains that *Blindness* "extends and challenges this tradition" of depicting "the cosmic alienation felt by a social outcast or an everyman figure." Landon concludes that Saramago's "self-reflexive fiction" has a positive conclusion that "turns away from the quicksands of philosophical despair and affirms instead the redeeming structures of civilization."

Writing a novel with classic themes about blindness, social degradation, and the strength of the human spirit is daunting enough because of the inevitable comparisons, but writing the novel in language that is unique in its use of punctuation, sentence structure, and paragraphing is a real risk. However, *Publishers Weekly* editor Drenka Willen states that "Saramago has never shied away from big game." Further, in an age when mass violence is a part of world culture to the extent that people are becoming almost shock-proof and seem numb to the horror, Willen asserts that "this most sophisticated fiction retains its peculiar power to move and persuade."

A *Library Journal* reviewer, Lisa Rohrbaugh, states that Saramago's work is "written in a concise, haunting prose" that complements the "unsettling" nature of the novel. Kevin Grandfield, writing for *Booklist,* adds that the novel is an "inspired characterization of human nature" that deftly shows "how vulnerable humans are, how connected and how blind."

In summary, Saramago apparently did well to revisit a classic theme. As judged by literary critics and the Nobel Prize committee, his originality of treatment and presentation was a masterpiece of fiction.

CRITICISM

Lois Kerschen

Kerschen is an educator and freelance writer. In the following essay, she discusses the reality check that, for the average reader, Saramago's Blindness *requires.*

In reading literature, there is a practice called the suspension of disbelief, which means that the reader is willing to go along with the implausible or unrealistic elements in a work of art in order to appreciate the worldview and story the work presents. Inconsistencies in the author's proposal or that violate common sense, however, may break this temporary suspension of incredulity on the reader's part and lead to criticism of the work of art. In *Blindness*, Saramago does not violate his agreement with his readers. He is consistent with his request that the reader believe in the possibility of a white blindness epidemic and all that he says that epidemic entails. The problem is, though, that he surrounds his imaginary epidemic with circumstances that are so contrary to reality and common sense that it is difficult for some readers to enjoy the novel.

It may seem impudent to criticize a winner of the Nobel Prize in Literature, but many readers do not have the literary expertise of the Nobel committee and, therefore, do not see the finer points that make a work a masterpiece to the trained eye. The situation is similar to that of modern art: It may show stunning technique to those in the field who are knowledgeable about artistic techniques, but to the average viewer, modern art can be bizarre, meaningless, confusing, if not downright unattractive. Similarly, a literary work of art may be difficult to understand.

WHAT DO I READ NEXT?

- The sequel to *Blindness* was published in English in 2006 as *Seeing*. The setting is the same nameless city, but this time the story is a witty satire of European politics and the media built around an election in which 70 percent of the public casts blank ballots.

- *Blindness* is often compared to Albert Camus's *The Plague*, an existential novel about epidemic and death set in Oran, Algeria. The story, first published in 1947, chronicles the efforts of several people to cope individually and collectively with fear, loneliness, and suffering.

- William Golding's *Lord of the Flies* (1959) is similar to *Blindness* in that it portrays the increasing barbarism among a group of English schoolboys who are marooned on an island and must try to cooperate to survive.

- Saramago's *Baltasar and Blimunda* (1988), set in eighteenth-century Portugal, is a dark, surrealistic story about a genius priest who is aided by a soldier and a clairvoyant in making a flying machine.

- *The Stand* is Stephen King's 1978 allegorical novel that has a very similar premise to that of *The Plague*. A virus kills over 99 percent of the people on Earth, leaving those remaining to struggle with preserving sanity and civilized society while maintaining hope in the fight between good and evil.

- For an understanding of the crisis surrounding an actual epidemic, there is *America's Forgotten Pandemic: The Influenza of 1918* (2003), by Alfred W. Crosby. This book is a comprehensive account of the flu epidemic in the United States at a time when 25 million people died from the disease worldwide.

- The idea of a devastating plague such as described allegorically by Camus and Saramago probably comes from their knowledge of the Black Plague that killed a third of the European population in the middle of the fourteenth century. This catastrophe is described in John Kelly's *The Great Mortality: An Intimate History of the Black Death, the Most Devastating Plague of All Time* (2005).

In *Blindness*, a mysterious and highly contagious white blindness strikes the population of the unnamed capital city of an unknown country. The lack of specificity about the setting is acceptable to readers because they understand that this story takes place no where in particular; it could happen anywhere. Concerning the disease, only the wife of a local ophthalmologist remains unaffected. While she often questions why she has been spared, there is no answer given. In regards to this mystery, the reader is probably willing to accept her exception for the sake of the story, understanding that having one person with sight in this world of blindness is a necessary device for providing an eyewitness who experiences unique difficulties in this context. Besides, believing that one person is not

infected with the white blindness is not too much of a stretch of the reader's credulity.

It is the rest of the story that violates common sense, or rather, common knowledge. Although specifics are not given regarding the name of the city or the time period, the story evidently takes place in modern times because there are automobiles, telephones, medical specialties, radio stations, electricity, and so on. Since the author is Portuguese, one might assume that the city is in Portugal, but there is no proof of that, and Saramago may have intended for the city to represent any city. Nonetheless, it is not a city in a third world country; it is not a city without government or resources. It is a modern city and, as such, should have all the emergency preparedness procedures of any modern city. Readers expect an organized response to the crisis situation that is presented.

In the event of hurricanes, tsunamis, earthquakes, or the outbreak of a dangerous contagious disease, any reasonably informed person knows that government rescue teams can soon be in place to help the afflicted. In the United States, the Center for Disease Control has a lengthy manual explaining step by step how to handle even the most potentially lethal situations with contagious diseases. Anyone who has ever seen a disaster movie knows how teams of medical experts come to the scene, even in cases in which wearing protective gear and setting up isolation areas are required. The response and treatment is humane and based on established modern medical procedures and precautions. To believe, as readers are asked to do in *Blindness*, that the government would not respond with medical assistance and a safe, clean place with adequate facilities for those who have become ill is ludicrous. If something like what Saramago describes ever actually happened, the World Health Organization and the Red Cross/Red Crescent would be there as soon as possible with medical experts and assistance from a number of other countries. These aid organizations would at least air drop supplies if they could do nothing else. At one point, just after the internees leave the asylum, Saramago even mentions that some wait in the yard hoping that the Red Cross "might bring them food and the other basic comforts." The reader has to wonder why Saramago bothered to mention the Red Cross that late in the novel. If response by the Red Cross were possible in this fictive world, then it would have been on site long before this reference to it occurs.

In addition, it is incredible that the ophthalmologist and his wife, even with the supplies she brings from the supermarket basement, have only enough in their pantry to feed their group for a few days. Yes, there are seven people, and yes, it could be a tiny kitchen, but it seems that they ought to be able to go a little longer. The girl's apartment is intact. Could they not have gotten food from her parents' stores? Or is this a culture in which people shop daily at the market and do not keep much at home? There is mention of grocery stores and supermarkets, so there should have been some stocking in pantries. Yet, "In the larder there were some jars of preserves, some dried fruit, sugar, some left-over

> WHETHER THE ALLEGORY BORDERS ON FANTASY, MAGICAL REALISM LIKE THAT OF GABRIEL GARCÍA MÁRQUEZ, SCIENCE FICTION, OR HORROR, EACH STORY HAS TO BE READ ACCORDING TO ITS OWN PREMISE."

biscuits, some dry toast" and that is all. Further, it seems like people in this city would have barbecue grills or hibachi that might be used on the back porch for cooking. It seems just as likely that people would have gas stoves instead of electric ones. Of course, Saramago is trying to make the situation as difficult as possible, so there is no gas stove, no hibachi, and little food. Meanwhile, some readers may think these people are surprisingly unprepared.

Readers of Franz Kafka's "Metamorphosis" are only asked to believe the protagonist turns into a bug. Once readers accept this impossibility as a given, the rest of the story works in a logical pattern. Everything in the allegory falls into place concerning a person who is different—the adjustments that have to be made, the shame and embarrassment, and the search for a new place in life. In *Blindness*, however, there are multiple unrealistic elements that the reader is asked to accept in addition to the epidemic of white blindness, and those elements test the reader's willingness to suspend disbelief.

At this point, the reader is asked to understand illusory reality. An article on a website devoted to author biographies (www.kirjasto. sci.fi/saramago.htm) quotes Saramago as saying: "The possibility of the impossible, dreams and illusions, are the subject of my novels." In this literary framework, nothing has to be like reality at all. The story is sustained by the imagination of the readers. Whether the allegory borders on fantasy, magical realism like that of Gabriel García Márquez, science fiction, or horror, each story has to be read according to its own premise. The improbable occurrence is designed to explore certain human emotions and interactions, whatever deviations of the expected route that might take.

In *Blindness* Saramago imagines what would happen if there were an epidemic of blindness.

He also imagines what would happen if the local government and international aid organizations failed to respond. These additional hypotheses taken together make it difficult for the reader to believe in the story. The reader is being asked to go along for the sake of the story and the message that will result from it. The critics agree this novel deserves the reader's suspension of disbelief. Readers are advised to relax, ignore logic and reason, and then enjoy the benefits that reading *Blindness* provides.

Source: Lois Kerschen, Critical Essay on *Blindness*, in *Novels for Students*, Gale, Cengage Learning, 2008.

Kevin Cole

In the following essay, Cole explains the significant role that dogs play in the novel Blindness, *especially the "dog of tears" that becomes an actual character. Although he appears late in the novel, the dog of tears serves as a savior and companion to the ophthalmologist's wife, who is one of the few not afflicted with the blindness and is a symbol of those who can truly see.*

Dogs play a significant role in José Saramago's 1995 novel *Blindness*. One in particular, the dog of tears, becomes a full-fledged character. The narrator describes the dog of tears as "an animal of the human type." But the dog is more than humanlike; it is humane. Among the group of nameless protagonists, only two figures are sighted throughout most of the novel, the doctor's wife and the dog of tears. Each acts as a heroic guide for the protagonists as they endure episodes of hellish events. In its role as savior and protector, the dog of tears is a seeing-eye dog in every sense of the term: it recognizes and responds to human suffering. A few examples will illustrate.

He appears late in the novel, in the thirteenth chapter (Saramago does not number the chapters), after the protagonists escape the insane asylum where the government has quarantined them. During the internment, however, everyone in the nameless city goes blind. Although free of the miseries of the asylum, the protagonists now contend with the apocalyptic misery of a modern city in anarchy.

Both in and out of the asylum, the doctor's wife bears responsibility for the group and experiences unspeakable suffering. After they escape, she first finds shelter for them and then braves the streets to search for food. She finds food but gets lost, and, in the midst of a rainstorm,

> SARAMAGO MAKES CLEAR IN THE FINAL SCENE OF THIS ALLEGORICAL NOVEL THE PRIMARY DIFFERENCE BETWEEN HUMANS AND THE DOG OF TEARS: IT TRULY SEES."

succumbs to monumental despair. It is then that she encounters her savior:

> The dogs gathered around her, sniffed at the bags, but without much conviction, as if their hour for eating had passed, one of them licks her face, perhaps it had been used to drying tears ever since it was a puppy. The woman strokes its head, runs her hand down its drenched back, and she weeps the rest of her tears embracing the dog. When she finally raised her eyes, the god of crossroads be praised a thousand times, she saw a great map before her.

The wife sees a city map—a map for tourists—and finds her way back. Unlike other feral dogs that terrorize the city, the dog of tears acts as a savior. Saramago leads readers to this "holy" interpretation. When the wife and dog return with food, the dog shakes the water from his pelt, baptizing the protagonists: "Holy water of the most efficacious variety, descended directly from heaven, the splashes helped the stones to transform themselves into persons [. . .]" The dog restores their dignity, and the doctor's wife reciprocates, giving him food. The dog then immediately assumes his role as protector, "barking furiously when anyone outside shook the door hard" and "blocking the entrance" because "he is a gruff, ill-tempered animal when he does not have to dry someone's tears."

On the one hand, the dog's selfish instincts draw him to the sighted wife: he knows he has a better chance of surviving with her. On the other, he is like all humans in their selfish quest to survive. Moreover, he does not need them to survive:

> The dog of tears did not mix with his former companions in the pack and the hunt, his choice is made, but he does not wait to be fed, he is already chewing heaven knows what, these mountains of rubbish hide unimaginable treasures, it is all a matter of searching, scratching and finding.

Thus, although survival in *Blindness* requires brutish selfishness, the dog of tears acts selflessly, recognizing and responding to the suffering of humans.

For instance, when the wife finds her old apartment, she feeds her charges, helps them bathe, then washes their clothes. Exhausted and full of sadness, she goes to the balcony to survey the misery of the city. The dog responds to her despair, even though there are no tears to lick: "The dog of tears appeared on the balcony, it was restless, but now there were no tears to lick up, the despair was all inside her, eyes were dry."

The dog of tears howls incessantly in the presence of all human suffering, not just the wife's suffering. During a harrowing excursion to restore rations, they encounter a rotting body, as they frequently do. Whereas other dogs will eat the body, the dog of tears mourns over it:

> The dog of tears moves closer, but death frightens it, it still takes two steps forward, suddenly its fur stands on end, a piercing howl escapes from its throat, the trouble with this dog is that it has grown too close to human beings, it will suffer as they do.

The wife relies on this aspect of the dog's universal empathy:

> [I]n her confusion and anguish she had to depend on a dog to console her, the same dog who is here snarling at the packs of other dogs who are coming too close, as if it were telling them, You don't fool me, keep away from here.

When they reach the store where the wife previously found food, the dog recognizes before she does that something horrific has transpired (many have died after being trapped in the basement). His hair stands on end, he whines, and he howls. The wife shortly joins the dog in the physical reaction to and expression of suffering. She vomits while "The dog of tears gave a very long howl, it let out a wail that seemed never-ending, a lament which resounded through the corridor like the last voice of the dead down in the basement." On their way home, they encounter a church. The wife wants to enter to find solace but cannot because it is full of people seeking shelter. The dog of tears makes a space for her "with two growls and a couple of charges, all without malice." He does so "without malice" because he is loyal to the wife but also empathetic to all human suffering.

Near the end, one protagonist suddenly regains his sight, suggesting to the wife that the epidemic and her nightmare are drawing to a close. She is overwhelmed by cathartic emotions, and again the dog of tears responds to her grief:

> The dog of tears went up to her, it always knows when it is needed, that's why the doctor's wife clung to him [...] at that moment her feeling of loneliness was so intense, so unbearable, that it seemed to her that it could be overcome only by the strange thirst with which the dog drank her tears.

As each protagonist gains his or her sight, the dog of tears responds to their cathartic emotions as well, so much so that he "did not know whose tears it should attend to first."

The dog of tears appears in the final scene: "stretched out with his muzzle on its forepaws, [it] opened and closed its eyes from time to time to show that it was still watchful [...]." Here, the wife articulates the prominent theme of the novel: "I don't think we did go blind, I think we are blind, Blind but seeing, Blind people who can see, but do not see." Saramago makes clear in the final scene of this allegorical novel the primary difference between humans and the dog of tears: it truly sees.

Source: Kevin Cole, "Saramago's *Blindness*," in *Explicator*, Vol. 64, No. 2, Winter 2006, pp. 119–21.

James Woods

In the following essay, Woods examines the themes running through several of Saramago's works in comparison to their use in Blindness. *He concludes that* Blindness *is an "anguished essay on the necessity of relations."*

In *If It Die*, his account of his childhood, André Gide writes of hearing that Mouton, a little friend from Luxembourg, was going blind. The young Gide went to his room and wept: "For several days I would keep my eyes shut for long periods and move around without opening them, attempting to feel what Mouton must have been feeling." This resonant suggestion might serve for us as a whisper to awaken not only *Blindness*, Jose Saramago's new novel, but his entire body of work. For within Gide's little crystal of anecdote, different meanings move: the boy with his eyes fiercely shut is trying to join in sympathetic concord with another human, and this could be an emblem not only of necessary human ethics, but also of the task of the novelist, who must concentrate artistically on the distribution of sympathy.

ONLY BY RELATION DO WE CONSTITUTE

OURSELVES."

Yet if Gide links himself with Mouton, he also dissolves himself in the process. It is the paradox of all imaginative identification. And this paradox is intensified, in Gide's case, by the act of closing one's eyes, because in doing so we lose our visible relations with the rest of life. When we close our eyes—it is the little nightly crisis of sleep—we darkly falter, in the gloom of self-cancellation: perhaps we no longer exist. Being ourselves involves seeing ourselves; and yet seeing ourselves, curiously, is not about looking inward but about looking outward, at others. It is seeing others that makes us visible to ourselves, that reminds us that we exist. Although imaginative identification with others threatens to dissolve oneself, it also constitutes oneself.

The shadowiness of the self is Saramago's great theme, which he partly inherits from the poetry of Fernando Pessoa, his Portuguese predecessor, the Pessoa whom Saramago quotes at the beginning of his great novel *The Year of the Death of Ricardo Reis*, which appeared in 1984: "If they tell me that it is absurd to speak thus of someone who never existed, I should reply that I have no proof that Lisbon ever existed, or I who am writing, or any other thing wherever it might be." His new novel, which is an allegorical fantasy in which an entire people is struck by an epidemic of blindness, merely allegorizes what is already symbolic in the rest of Saramago's work.

In an unnamed country, citizens are suddenly afflicted by loss of sight. Quickly, society begins to break down: there is no electricity or running water, no food beyond that which can be scavenged, no law beyond the simple throbbing of need. We follow a small group of unfortunates, led by a doctor (an ophthalmologist, in the days when he had eyesight) and his wife, who has miraculously not lost her sight and appears to be the only sighted person in the land. In the streets, the blind crawl on all fours and defecate anywhere. It is not just the contingency of

institutions that is exposed, but the contingency of verification: the blind "go around like ghosts, this must be what it means to be a ghost, being certain that life exists, because your four senses say so, and yet unable to see it."

Pressed into precis, the story sounds primitive, or merely conceptual; but it lives in the spread of its particulars, and in the conviction of its allegory. The *Inferno* and *The Plague* are obvious models for this fall into hell. Reviewing Saramago's novel *Baltasar and Blimunda* in 1987. Irving Howe wrote that "I think I hear in his prose echoes of Enlightenment sensibility, caustic and shrewd." Yet Saramago, in his skepticism and in his healthy, delightfully literal approach toward the supernatural and the fantastic, more recalls the Greeks—both Greek tragedy and Greek satire.

In Lucian's *Menippus*, for instance, the hero descends into Hades to find that death has undone all the fragile hierarchies of life: Philip of Macedon is stitching sandals to earn money, Xerxes is begging, and so on. But Lucian's lesson is made earlier, when Menippus tells us that on earth things have already become sadly inverted: "On observation I found people practicing the very opposite of what they preached. I saw those who advocated despising money clinging to it tooth and nail...and those who would have us reject fame doing and saying everything for just that, and again pretty well all of them speaking out against pleasure, but in private clinging to it alone." In this light, Hades corrects the sad inversions of the world by reinverting them.

Thomas More, who translated Lucian from Greek into Latin, borrowed this idea for his beautifully literal and logical satire *Utopia*. The island of Utopia does not represent the ideal society so much as a comic one—it is the comic inversion of the uncomic inversion of rectitude that we practice in life. More did not intend us to live in Utopia, but to be logically mocked by it. (The Shakespearean Fool is a near-equivalent of this mode.) Saramago has said that "I cannot save anything but what I can do is write about what I think and feel and the anguish of seeing a world that could already have resolved a large portion of its humanitarian problems, but which not only has not solved any, but which, in fact, aggravates many of them. ... The Romans used to say that man is the wolf of mankind. What would they say were they alive today?" Saramago is a Communist, even now, but he has something in common with the implicit communitarianism of Lucian and More.

And he has something in common, too, with the ancient idea of magical inversion. In his novel *The History of the Siege of Lisbon* (1989), a proofreader decides to insert the word "not" into history of Portugal that he is checking. Suddenly, the history book asserts, against the evidence, that the crusaders did not help the Portuguese to conquer Lisbon in the twelfth century. This apparently tiny inversion causes havoc with Portugal's official sense of itself, and it allows Saramago to unwind an exquisitely sly satire on the contingency of national history.

Likewise, in his greatest book, *The Gospel According to Jesus Christ*, which appeared in 1991, Saramago secularizes the Gospel narrative with the simplest inversions. In this book God is fallible, and Jesus is not the son of God but the son of Joseph. Thus every time Jesus uses the word "Father," a little spark of blasphemy is struck. When Jesus is told by God how much suffering and bloodshed will flow in history as a result of his crucifixion, he tries to abdicate his duty: "Father, take from me this cup." As he dies on the cross, he inverts Jesus's penultimate words, "Father, forgive them, for they know not what they do," and cries out "Men, forgive Him, for He knows not what he has done."

In *Blindness*, similarly, so great are the horrors witnessed by the doctor's sighted wife that the simple privilege of sight over blindness begins to seem the worst privilege, begins to seem its inversion. Sight "had exposed her to greater horror than she could ever have imagined, it had convinced her that she would rather be blind, nothing else." In the country of the suddenly blind, the one-eyed man is not, in fact, king. He is the slave of all the blind, and the most unhappy one of all, because he sees their degradation.

Yet Saramago is most like the Greeks—and like then Renaissance heirs, such as Montaigne—in the manner in which he keeps in balance both skepticism and realism, or uncertainty and health. Indeed, he is a kind of Pyrrhonist in reverse, who wriggles through a skeptical tunnel only to emerge into a climate of truth, a climate slightly thinned and rarified of certainty, but still certainly extant. His work plays with, but ethically thickens, Pessoa's hallucinatory sense of reality. It might be said that Saramago is epistemologically

skeptical (he uses his fiction to knock away at our foundations) but metaphysically faithful.

If Saramago is skeptical about foundations, it is because he is skeptical of these foundations, not all foundations. This paradox can be tasted in an apparently small technical triumph, from which, in fact, the deepest concerns of his fiction flow. This is his use of what Barthes called "the reference code," whereby a writer confidently refers to the general consensus by means of such locutions as "as is usual" or "as everyone knows" or "as people always do in such circumstances." Showing his roots in the *nouveau roman*, Barthes wanted to finger it as the spoiled child of nineteenth-century realism (such realism being the enemy of the *nouveau romanciers*). Yet this realism has always existed in imaginative writing. Tolstoy, when he used it with the greatest beauty and simplicity, was merely being Homeric. When Ivan Ilyich's colleagues hear of his death, Tolstoy writes that "the mere fact of the death of an intimate associate aroused, as is usual, in all who heard of it a complacent feeling that 'it is he who is dead, and not I.'"

Very few writers can ever reach Tolstoy's great median, and in our age most writers eschew the reference code, or flutter self-consciously around it. Its obsolescence has to do with a larger nervousness about omniscient narration, which is for some writers ideologically too little. The reference code is the most obvious flower of the authorial omniscience. But Saramago, characteristically, uses the reference code both to affirm and to question.

Omniscient narration generally affirms how much we know, how much we have in common, but Saramago uses it to illuminate how little we know. This is partly because he narrates his novels as if he were someone both wise and ignorant. His novels are all told by someone who has Saramago's powers of narration, but who is not Saramago—the tone is skeptical, a little saucy, a little prejudiced (the narrator always has a firm view about women's proper role), even a little garrulous and foolish at times. The sentences loiter, without punctuation or paragraph breaks or quotation punctuation marks for speech. It is as if Saramago's books were tales told by a stubborn old Portuguese man sitting on a bench, endlessly smoking and flicking the ash of surly speculation all over his clothes. Occasionally he spits out a truth onto the ground, examines it curiously, and then rubs it sarcastically with his shoe.

Sometimes this narrator uses the reference code to affirm the most banal truths, thereby parodying the mode by exhausting it—but exhausting the mode of truth-telling, not the truth, which remains anciently immovable: "Everyone knows that men like to fight each other." More often, he does it by misdirecting the reference code, by pointing it at shared questions, or at the unanswerable, rather than at shared answers. And he uses his curious, unpunctuated nudging of syntax to do this. At the beginning of *The Year of the Death of Ricardo Reis*, for instance, Ricardo Reis arrives at the harbor in Lisbon, on a boat from Brazil. A tone of strange mockery—but also, strange respect—is established when Ricardo hails a taxi, and is initially flummoxed by the taxi driver's question. "Where to?" Ricardo has not really thought this far ahead; he does not even have a hotel in mind. Saramago's narrator speculates that Ricardo was befuddled "perhaps because he has been asked one of the two fatal questions, Where to. The other question, and much worse, is Why."

Similarly, in *The Gospel According to Jesus Christ*, Saramago's narrator questions everything, but uses a tone of certainty—the reference code—in order to encourage uncertainty. "For in truth, there are things God Himself does not understand, even though He created them." In this book, the narrator is a sly old Portuguese peasant, who knows everything and nothing. "The rest of the journey to Jerusalem was not so easy. In the first place, there are Samaritans and there are Samaritans, which means that even in those days one swallow was not enough to make a summer. ... " Saramago uses the habits of certainty to pick away at the fabric of certainty; and yet the result is not the cheap vacuum of postmodernism's usual excavations, but a strangely refreshed respect for mystery. During Passover, crowds wander through Jerusalem, "exclaiming, Alleluia, Hosanna, Amen, or saying none of these things, feeling it was inappropriate to walk around shouting Hallelujah or Hip hip hurrah, because there is really not much difference between the two expressions, we use them enthusiastically until with the passage of time and by dint of repetition we finally ask ourselves. What does it mean, only to find no answer."

The Vatican complained about *The Gospel According to Jesus Christ* (and complained again when Saramago won the Nobel Prize), but it is right that this novel is "testimony of a substantial antireligious sentiment." Still, there is also a kind of healthy secularism of ignorance in evidence, which often blooms, in Saramago's work, into the enunciation of the old, simple, weary truths. And to announce them, Saramago is able to use a now-cleansed reference code, because he has torn it out of the domain of consensus, and let it go to work in the domain of discovery. He makes omniscient narration a process; and because narration is not settled for Saramago, his stories can speak truths without complacency. He earns the right of authority by dissolving it. Near the end of *The Year of the Death of Ricardo Reis*:

> They say time stops for no man, that time marches on, commonplaces that are still repeated, yet there are people who chafe at the slowness with which it passes. Twenty-four hours to make a day, and at the end of the day you discover that it was not worthwhile, and the following day is the same all over again, if only we could leap over all the futile weeks in order to live one hour of fulfillment, one moment of splendor, if splendor can last that long.

Saramago is both a literalist and a fantasist, as he is both a realist and a skeptic. All his phantasmagorias gain their strength from the straightforward, unsentimental literalism of their magical elements. In *Baltasar and Blimunda*, Saramago makes it seem the most natural idea in the world that these two eighteenth-century renegades would want to escape the Portuguese Inquisition and fly to heaven in a flying-machine. *Blindness* is written up like a medical report. Likewise, *The Gospel According to Jesus Christ* is powerful, in part, because Saramago tells his blasphemous story while making the most simple and direct use of supernatural elements—Satan, an angel, a pillar of flame, walking on water, and so on. Indeed, it is by making these elements absolutely literal that Saramago holds them up to the light of reason, and peers through them.

In that book, Jesus is the natural son of Joseph, but is called upon by God to lay down his life for man. By tampering with the Gospel stories in a delicately subversive manner, Saramago creates his own dark parable. Early in the book, Joseph overhears two soldiers discussing King Herod's plan to murder all the newly born children in Bethlehem. He runs home, and flees Bethlehem with Mary and the infant Jesus. He saves his child, but he is haunted by the guilty idea that he could have warned the parents of Bethlehem about Herod's plan, and did not. He suffers terrible nightmares, in which he is one of the soldiers marching to kill his own son.

Joseph, writes Saramago, is condemned by God for his sin of omission, and his guilt will pass to Jesus. "God does not forgive the sins He makes us commit," is Saramago's bitter comment. Sure enough, Joseph is mistakenly arrested in Jerusalem by Roman soldiers who are rounding up Jewish rebels, and is crucified on a hill. He is thirty-three years old. When Jesus is older, he asks his mother about the nightmare that made his father cry out in his sleep, and she tells him about Herod's murder of the innocents. Jesus is horrified, and says: "Father murdered the children of Bethlehem." Jesus leaves home, and never really returns. He sees not Satan, but God in the wilderness. When he asks God why he must die, God replies that "you will be the spoon I dip into humanity and bring out filled with people who believe in the new god I intend to become."

Saramago's novel is an extraordinarily eloquent heretical text, filled with deep compassion for humanity's suffering. When Jesus asks God what the future will be like once Jesus has died, God falters, and then describes the establishment of the Church, the persecution of the martyrs, the bloodiness of the Crusades, the horrors of the Inquisition, the abrasions of schism, the barbs of fundamentalism, the cruelties of exclusion. Jesus asks God to spare him from his sentence, and thus prevent the unfolding of this terrible future, but God refuses. Jesus cannot be spared, because he has been condemned. Saramago's novel flows with a relentlessly inverting logic from one simple Gnostic premise: that God is either wicked, false, or fallible.

The story winds outward from Herod's massacre of the children. God, the supposed Father, did not save the little children. Joseph, Jesus's father, did not save them either. God condemns Joseph to death for this sin, and the sins of the fathers pass to Jesus, who is crucified like his father. Thus, in Saramago's reading, Jesus went to the cross not as our savior but as one of us, condemned by a form of Original Sin. We are Jesus's inheritors, condemned like him to crucify each other, generation after generation. We are the victims of an original sin, and our sentence is to be human. But "Father murdered the children

of Bethlehem," says Jesus, and Saramago, of course, intends us to note the irony. It was God, the original Father, who killed the children, and therefore God must have condemned himself, and therefore God is not only the inventor of original sin, but its first practitioner, and thus its first victim. The sins of the fathers are in fact the sins of the Father's. God is condemned by the evil that He Himself allows. As Satan cannily tells Jesus, "your God is the only warden of a prison where the only prisoner is your God."

Saramago, adds almost nothing to the Gospel story. What he does, rather like Milton but more emphatically, is activate the ancient heretical cruxes, above all the familiar one that a God who originates evil must Himself be evil. In addition, he turns on its head the New Testament idea of Jesus as the sacrificial lamb, slaughtered to cleanse humans of their sin. No, says Saramago. Jesus was slaughtered for his Father's sins, both Joseph's and God's. Here Saramago is the splendid heir, in force and in idea, of Nietzsche in *The Anti-Christ*, who rails against the "paganism" of Jesus's "sacrifice." And Saramago makes resonant the implicit blasphemy at the heart of the incarnation. For if Jesus was truly human, then he inherited Adam's sin; but if he was also truly divine, then the sin he inherited was not Adam's but God's—not his father's, but his Father's.

At one point in the novel, Jesus speaks with God, who appears as a pillar of smoke, and Saramago writes that "it grieved him to be sent away in this manner, after having met God, for to the best of his knowledge there was not a single man in all Israel who could boast of having seen God and lived." Saramago's narrator continues:

> It is true that Jesus did not exactly see Him, but if a cloud appears in the desert in the form of a pillar of smoke and says, I am the Lord, and then holds a conversation that is not only logical and sensible but so compelling that it can only be divine, then to have even the slightest doubt is unpardonable.

This is characteristic of the tone of all of Saramago's fiction, and it is what makes him so attractive and sinuous a writer. His narrators always hover somewhere between belief and doubt, giving with one hand and taking with the other.

Saramago, who is an atheist, is wittily casting doubt on the idea of God's appearing—by asserting that he believes that God appeared! Or rather, he believes that a cloud appeared and said, "I am the Lord." There is a way in which Saramago uses literalism to affirm *and* to subvert. The passage above might, after all, be a theory of fiction. If a cloud appears in a novel and says "I am the Lord," and if the spectacle is done with enough reality, then it would be wrong to doubt it. Likewise for Jesus in the desert. All of Saramago's fiction is full of magical occurrences which are described in the most touchingly literal fashion, as if they were merely one of the ordinary working days in realism's week. Yet, equally, all literalism tends toward skepticism, because it makes us scrutinize literal appearances. Can a pillar of cloud exist? Can God exist as a pillar of cloud? *The Gospel According to Jesus Christ* is so powerful because Saramago's fictional skepticism spills so naturally into a deeper skepticism about belief.

Thus a theory of fiction becomes, in effect, an anti-theology. Saramago suggests that we can only be literal about belief (the cloud appeared; it was God), but that as soon as we are literal about belief we infect it with the virus of parody, because we see it, precisely, as belief and nothing more. This tidal movement reaches a particular black force in *The Gospel According to Jesus Christ* and in *Blindness*, and a particular skittering, intermittent beauty in *The Year of the Death of Ricardo Reis* (which is Saramago's own favorite among his novels).

Ricardo Reis, a doctor from Brazil, is an aloof, conservative aesthete who has decided to return to his native Portugal. It is the end of 1935, and the great poet Fernando Pessoa has just died. Reis is himself a poet and mourns Pessoa's departure. He is not sure what to do. He has saved some money, and for a while he lives in a hotel, where he has an affair with a chambermaid. He writes several beautiful lyrics, and is visited by the now-ghostly Pessoa, with whom he converses. As usual, Saramago describes these conversations in a frankly literal and direct manner, quite without the satiny shimmer that we have come to expect from certain American practitioners of magical realism.

Reis wanders the streets of Lisbon, as 1935 curdles into 1936. He reads the newspapers, and is increasingly alarmed by the baying of Europe's dogs: in Spain civil war and the rise of Franco, in Germany Hitler, in Italy Mussolini, and in Portugal the fascist dictatorship of Salazar. He would like to retreat from this bad news. He reflects

fondly on the story of the 97-year-old John D. Rockefeller, who has a specially doctored version of *The New York Times* delivered every day, altered to contain only good news. "The world's threats are universal, like the sun, but Ricardo Reis takes shelter under his own shadow."

But Ricardo Reis is not a "real" fictional character, whatever that means. He is one of the four names which the actual Pessoa—the poet who worked and lived in Lisbon and died in 1935—assumed, and in whose persona he wrote poetry. The special flicker of this book, the tint and the delicacy that make it seem hallucinatory, derive from the solidity with which Saramago invests a character who is a fictional character twice over: first Pessoa's, then Saramago's. This enables Saramago to tease us with something that we already know, namely that Ricardo Reis is fictional. Saramago makes something deep and moving of this because Ricardo also feels himself to be somewhat fictional, at best a shadowy spectator, a man on the margins of things. And when Ricardo reflects thus, we feel a strange tenderness for him, aware of something that he does not know, that he is not real.

Is there a way in which all of us are fictional characters, parented by life and written by ourselves? This is something like Saramago's question; but it is worth noting that he reaches his question by travelling in the opposite direction of those postmodernist novelists who like to remind us of the fictionality of all things. A writer such as William Gass is always lecturing us: "Remember, this character is just a character. I invented him." By starting with an invented character, however, Saramago is able to pass through the same skepticism, but in the opposite direction, toward reality, toward the deepest questions. Saramago asks, in effect: But what is just a character? And Saramago's uncertainty is more real than Gass's skepticism, for no one ever says "I don't exist." We say, rather, "I believe I exist," exactly as Ricardo does.

In Saramago's novels, the self may cast only a shadow, like Ricardo Reis, but this shadow implies not the non-existence of the self, but only its difficult visibility, its near-invisibility, rather as the shadow cast by the sun warns us that we cannot look directly at it. The self is blindingly real in Saramago's work. This is touched on, with lovely tugging indirections, in both *The Year of the Death of Ricardo Reis* and *Blindness*. Ricardo Reis is aloof, ghostly. He does not want to get pulled into real relationships, including the real relationships of politics. Europe is scrambling for war, but Ricardo luxuriously sits around wondering if he exists. He writes a poem that begins "We count for nothing, we are less than futile." Another poem begins: "Walk empty-handed, for wise is the man who contents himself with the spectacle of the world."

Yet the novel suggests that perhaps there is something culpable about being content with the spectacle of the world if the world's spectacle is horrifying. Near the end of the book, Ricardo reads in the newspaper that some Hitler Youth students from Hamburg were guests of honor at a Teacher Training College in Lisbon, and that they wrote in the guest book: "We are nobody." Saramago comments: "This meant, as the clerk on duty hastened to explain, that the people are indeed nobody if not guided by the elite, the cream, the flower, the chosen few of our society." To be a "nobody" may be to surrender oneself to dictatorship. And the reader is suddenly jerked back two hundred pages, to Ricardo's poem, that began. "We count for nothing, we are less than futile." Ricardo's ghostliness of relations may have a fascist element, and Saramago intends us to reflect on the fascism implicit in modernism's spectatorial shadowiness. The question of this book, and by extension of all Saramago's work, is not the trivial fictional game-playing of "Does Ricardo Reis exist?" It is the much more poignant question. "Do we exist if we refuse to relate to anyone?" If we read only a special version of *The New York Times*, like John D. Rockefeller, are we alive? Only by relation do we constitute ourselves.

Blindness is an anguished essay on the necessity of relations. In despair, the doctor's sighted wife cries out that without anyone to see her, her eyesight is useless: "I shall become more and more blind because I shall have no one to see me." Her eyesight is constituted by everyone else's eyesight. Earlier in the novel, she laments: "Dear God, how we miss having our sight, to be able to see, to see, even if they were only faint shadows, to stand before the mirror, see a dark diffused patch and be able to say, That's my face, anything that has light does not belong to me." We may be only a shadow on the mirror, but this is everything, and if it is everything. Saramago's work seems to suggest, then we must not take shelter under our own shadow, as Ricardo Reis

does. We must attend to all the other shadows that brush the earth. I may not know if I exist, but I know if other people exist. And if other people exist, then I exist. It is a kind of primary deduction. We are all like little André Gide, confirming ourselves by closing our eyes and thinking of each other.

Source: James Woods, "The Seeing I," in *New Republic*, Vol. 219, No. 4, November 30, 1998, pp. 48–56.

SOURCES

Grandfield, Kevin, Review of *Blindness*, in *Booklist*, Vol. 94, No. 22, September 1998, p. 1969.

"José Saramago," in *Books and Writers*, www.kirjasto. sci.fi/saramago.htm (accessed November 2, 2006).

Landon, Philip, Review of *Blindness*, in *Review of Contemporary Fiction*, Vol. 19, No. 1, Spring 1999, p. 179.

Rohrbaugh, Lisa, Review of *Blindness*, in *Library Journal*, Vol. 123, No. 13, August 1, 1998, p. 134.

Saramago, José, *Blindness*, translated by Giovanni Pontiero, Harcourt Brace, 1997.

Snedeker, George, "Blindness as Metaphor," in *Journal of Visual Impairment & Blindness*, Vol. 93, No. 6, June 1999, p. 382.

Willen, Drenka, "A Review of *Blindness*," in *Publishers Weekly*, Vol. 245, No. 28, July 13, 1998, p. 62.

FURTHER READING

Bloom, Harold, *José Saramago*, Chelsea House Publications, 2005.

   As part of Bloom's series, Modern Critical Views, this book is a collection of criticism on the works of Saramago but does not include commentary on *Blindness*.

Cole, Kevin, "Saramago's *Blindness*," in *Explicator*, Vol. 64, No. 2, Winter 2006, p. 109.

   For those who are intrigued about the role of the dog of tears in *Blindness*, this is a wonderful explanation of the purpose and symbolism of this unique character.

Driscoll, Kevin, "A Nobelist's Allegorical Analysis of the Human Condition," in *Washington Times*, October 18, 1998, p. 8.

   Longer than a typical review, this penetrating newspaper article covers many majors issues with the novel.

Frier, David, *The Novels of José Saramago*, University of Wales Press, 2007.

   Frier, a senior lecturer in Portuguese Studies at

the University of Leeds, provides a comprehensive overview of Saramago's writings, including ideological concerns and information about Portuguese literary and cultural traditions.

Quilligan, Maureen, *The Language of Allegory: Defining the Genre*, Cornell University Press, 1992.
    The nature of both medieval and modern allegory is examined, with emphasis on *The Faerie Queen* and *Piers Plowman*, but this study also

contains criticism on the allegories of Hawthorne, Melville, Nabokov, and Pynchon.

Stanley, Sandra Kumamoto, "The Excremental Gaze: Saramago's *Blindness* and the Disintegration of the Panoptic Vision," in *Critique*, Vol. 45, No. 3, Spring 2004, pp. 293–308.
    Despite its difficult title, this article is an in-depth analysis of *Blindness* that is quite easy to read and provides a thorough yet reasonably brief look at the various elements of the novel.

The Book of Laughter and Forgetting

MILAN KUNDERA

1979

In 1978, while exiled in France, the Czechoslovakian writer Milan Kundera wrote a novel destined to become an international success. Forbidden to be published in his homeland, Kundera's *The Book of Laughter and Forgetting* was written in Czech but first published in French as *Le livre du rire et de l'oublie* in 1979. It was subsequently translated into English and published in the United States in 1980.

Although the book is generally classified as a novel, it does not have the traditional structure of beginning, middle, and end. Rather, the seven parts of the book have individual characters and different plot lines. Yet *The Book of Laughter and Forgetting* is more than a collection of connected short stories. Indeed, the separate sections do not even correspond to the traditional notions regarding short stories. Rather, they are snippets of a story interspersed with historical commentary interspersed with philosophical meditation interspersed with autobiographical detail. What holds the entire work together is the compellingly controlled voice of the narrator, a voice that remains consistent throughout the text. This voice, Kundera himself (or a character playing the part of "Milan Kundera"), gradually reveals to the reader the themes and variations that comprise the novel.

The historical context of *The Book of Laughter and Forgetting* is important for any reader approaching the text. From an exile's perspective, Kundera writes of his nation's descent from a

Milan Kundera (AFP | Getty Images)

republic to a Communist dictatorship, its brief resurgence as an open society during the Prague Spring of 1968, and the country's return to a totalitarian police state, after Soviet tanks rolled into Prague in August 1968, reestablishing Czechoslovakia as a Communist Eastern-bloc nation.

The Book of Laughter and Forgetting explores the ways that governments and people both create and extinguish memories, how laughter can be both angelic and demonic, and what is required to remain human in the face of crushingly dehumanizing circumstances.

A recent edition of the novel, translated from French by Aaron Asher, was published by Perennial Classics in 1996.

AUTHOR BIOGRAPHY

Milan Kundera was born on April 1, 1929, in Brno, Czechoslovakia (now the Czech Republic). His parents were Ludvik and Milada Kunderová.

His father was a well-known musician who studied with the famous Czech composer, Leos Janácek. Indeed, his father's musical influence can be seen in many of Kundera's later works.

In 1948, Kundera completed secondary school and enrolled in Charles University in Prague. He began his studies in literature, later changing his emphasis to film and directing. He joined the Communist Party in 1948 as an idealistic youth; he quickly became disillusioned, however, as the Party quickly established a police state. An outspoken critic of the Party, he was expelled in 1950. Kundera joined the faculty of the Film Academy in 1952.

Kundera published his first collection of poems in 1953, while working as a translator and playwright. By 1956, Kundera was readmitted to the Communist Party. By this time, he had become a well-known literary celebrity in Czechoslovakia. In 1960, he wrote *Umení romáu: Cesta Vladislava Vancury za velkou epikou* (*The Art of the Novel: Vladislav Vancura's Journey to the Great Epic*, 1960) The book was a work of Marxist criticism, a type of criticism that considers class, economics, and the flow of power in a culture; it was well received by Czechoslovakian critics and scholars, although Kundera later renounced the work. In 1988, however, he wrote a different book under the same title.

Kundera began writing his first novel, *Zert*, in 1962, although it was not published in Czechoslovakia until 1967 due to censorship. The book is a satire of totalitarianism in Czechoslovakia, and was first published in English as *The Joke* in 1969.

In 1968, for a brief period, restrictions on writers and artists lifted slightly in what became known as the "Prague Spring." The Soviet Union, however, was fearful that the freedom enjoyed by the Czech people could spill over into a revolution throughout the nearby Communist bloc countries. In August, 1968, Soviet tanks entered Prague, and a new repressive government was installed by the Soviets; this government ruled Czechoslovakia for twenty-one years. As a leader of the Prague Spring movement, Kundera found himself blacklisted: he could not publish any writing in Czechoslovakia and he lost his job at the university.

In 1975, Kundera received permission from the government to move to France. There he began *The Book of Laughter and Forgetting*, his most important work to date. Written first in Czech, the novel was then translated into French as *Le livre du rire et de l'oublie* and was published in 1979. Soon thereafter, the book was translated into English and was published in 1980. In 1996, Kundera, working with translator Aaron Asher, issued a new English edition of the novel.

Since the publication of *The Book of Laughter and Forgetting*, Kundera has written many well-known novels, plays, short stories, and essays, including *The Unbearable Lightness of Being* (1984) and, more recently, *Ignorance* (2000). Kundera has been honored with a host of international prizes for his fiction, and critics consider him to be one of the finest writers of the twentieth century.

An intensely private person, Kundera lives in Paris with his wife, Vera Hrabankova.

PLOT SUMMARY

Part One: Lost Letters

The Book of Laughter and Forgetting is comprised of seven sections. Although the stories in

each section resonate with the other stories, the book does not have an overarching plot. Rather, each section functions as a variation on a theme, in much the same way the various parts of a musical symphony interact. In addition, Kundera frequently interrupts the story he is telling in each section with autobiographical remarks, essays on Czechoslovakian history, philosophical musings, or additional stories. Consequently, the plot does not function as it might in a more traditional novel.

The Book of Laughter and Forgetting opens with an important anecdote about Communist leader Klement Gottwald. The leader is standing on a balcony in Prague with his comrade Vladimir Clementis at an important public gathering. Because it is cold and windy, and because Gottwald has no hat, Clementis puts his own fur hat on Gottwald's head. The moment is captured in photographs displayed throughout the country. However, four years later, Clementis is hanged for treason, and carefully airbrushed out of the picture. All that remains of him in Czech memory is his hat. The fur hat as a metaphor of public memory resonates throughout the rest of the text. While Gottwald and Clementis were historical figures, it is likely that the anecdote about the hat is fictional.

The story then turns to Mirek, a man who meticulously writes down everything that he and his friends discuss in a diary, in spite of the fact that his papers might be confiscated. He decides he will put his journals in a safe place, but first, he wants to retrieve old love letters from Zdena, a woman he had an affair with twenty-five years earlier. The only reason he wants the letters, Kundera surmises, is that she is ugly, and he does not want it to be known that he had an affair with an ugly woman. He notices as he drives to Zdena's that two men are following him. Zdena refuses to give him the letters and he realizes after he leaves her apartment that it is now too late to remove the incriminating documents from his own house. Mirek is convinced that Zdena has betrayed him to the police; however, she has not done so, and Kundera reveals that she loves Mirek. By the time he returns home, the police are already there. He is sentenced to six years in prison, his son is sentenced to two years, and ten of his friends are sentenced for one to six years, depending on the severity of their transgressions. The significance of the section title becomes apparent: although the letters still exist, they are lost to Mirek. In addition, Mirek has overestimated the importance of the letters held by Zdena and underestimated the incriminating nature of the letters left at his house.

Part Two: Mama

In this part, readers meet Marketa, her husband Karel, his mother Mama, and their friend Eva. Marketa has never liked her mother-in-law, but as the story takes place, her feelings soften somewhat. Karel and Marketa invite Mama to stay with them for a week. Mama, however, has confused the day she is supposed to return to her home. This is unfortunate because Eva, a woman with whom the couple has sexual relations, arrives before Mama has left. In a comic scene, Mama comes into the sitting room to say goodnight to the three young people, just as Eva comes in scantily clad, and Marketa approaches the room with nothing on but a necklace. Marketa hastily retreats before Mama notices her.

Later, readers learn that Marketa has been one of Karel's mistresses, and that the two of them arrange for her to meet Eva. Eva never realizes that her new best friend has been intimate with her husband before the three of them begin their mutual affair.

Many things happen at once in this story: Karel and Marketa's marriage seems troubled, Marketa falls in love with Eva, and Karel comes to an understanding of his mother and has warmer feelings toward her. Love, it seems, heals several of the characters.

Part Three: The Angels

Part Three opens with the story of two American girls, Gabrielle and Michelle, who are studying in Europe under the tutelage of Madame Raphael. They are reading a play by Eugene Ionesco, *The Rhinoceros*, and they do not really understand it. The narrator (presumably Kundera) interrupts this story to interject a meditation on the subject of laughter, then to tell the story of how he wrote an astrology column under an assumed name after he lost his job in 1968. He next turns to a discussion of two kinds of laughter: that of the angels and that of the devil. The angels' laughter, he asserts, is secondary to the devil's, and is an imitation. The devil's laugh is in response to the meaninglessness of the world, while the angels' laugh rejoices in the orderliness of the world. Kundera then returns to the story of the young Americans,

who completely miss the subversive nature of the play they are studying. Next he returns to the story of the young woman who gave him the job writing horoscopes and who lost her own job as a consequence. He closes the section by revealing that he knows he must not live among the people he loves any longer, and he decides to leave his homeland.

Part Four: Lost Letters

Kundera introduces readers to Tamina in Part Four. She is a thirty-two-year-old Czech exile, living somewhere in Western Europe, and working as a waitress. She came to this unspecified location with her husband several years earlier, but he has since died. She struggles to retain her memories of their life together. As time goes on, she becomes obsessed with recovering a set of notebooks and letters that she gave to her mother-in-law for safe keeping when she and her husband fled Czechoslovakia. In these notebooks, she recorded the details of her life. Now, in order to keep her memories from fading, she feels she needs to retrieve the notebooks and letters. However, it is not safe for her to return to Czechoslovakia. Various people promise her that they will retrieve the notebooks for her, but in turn, each withdraws their offer. Tamina is so desperate that she even sleeps with a man who promises to get them for her. Finally, her brother agrees to retrieve them. When he arrives at Tamina's mother-in-law's home, he discovers that the package has been opened and the notebooks have been read (but it is not clear who has read them). At the same time, Hugo, the man Tamina has been sleeping with, decides he cannot go to Czechoslovakia because he has published an article that he believes will cause him problems with Czech authorities. These revelations disturb Tamina greatly, and she feels a terrible revulsion for Hugo. Even worse, she realizes that her affair with Hugo has erased all memory of the sexual relations she once shared with her beloved husband.

That Kundera titles two sections of his book "Lost Letters" reveals the importance he places on written records. Through these sections, he explores the consequences of lost letters as a substitute for lost memories.

Part Five: Litost

Part Five is a meditation on a word that Kundera claims only has meaning in Czechoslovakian. The closest he can come to a definition is "a state of torment created by the sudden sight of one's own misery." This misery is nearly always followed by a desire for revenge, to make another person feel as miserable as the person experiencing *litost*. In a story that illustrates the concept, a young student invites a butcher's wife named Kristyna (who is from a small town he has visited) to meet with him in Prague. The young student expects to sleep with her. However, he is given a last-minute invitation to a gathering of famous poets on the same evening his guest is supposed to arrive. He tells her of his dilemma, and she urges him to go, so long as he will bring her an autographed copy of a book of poems. He agrees.

Kundera gives each of the famous Czech poets names of other literary figures from the past such as Voltaire, Petrarch, and Boccacio (these are the names of actual writers, none of whom are Czech). He uses the occasion of their gathering to parody all such gatherings and to parody self-important writers.

The student returns home after the drunken evening, and attempts to have sex with Kristyna. She refuses, saying that it will kill her to have sex. He believes that her love for him is so great that she cannot bear the thought of living without him if they have sex. In the morning, however, he discovers that her fear of pregnancy caused her to refuse; giving birth, not her love for the student, would kill her. The emotion the student then feels, Kundera explains, is *litost*.

Part Six: The Angels

Kundera opens this section (which has the same title as Part Three) with a retelling of the story of Klement Gottwald and Clementis, this time inserting the detail that Franz Kafka attended school in the building where the two men stood on the balcony. In Kafka's novel, *The Trial*, Kundera writes, "Prague is a city without memory." This opening passage is crucial for the entire book: Kundera again addresses how the public state has erased private memory by reiterating the Gottwald Clementis story. He is suggesting that Kafka, writing many years before the Communist takeover, predicted that in the modern age, Prague would be a city where people could simply disappear, the memory of their existence obliterated by the state.

Next, Kundera turns to the story of his father's last years. A famous musicologist, the elder Kundera suffers from aphasia during the last ten years of his life, and the condition causes him to gradually lose all memory of words. Kundera uses this as the backdrop for the tale he begins to tell, returning once more to Tamina's story.

Tamina is deeply saddened by the loss of her husband, and is unhappy with her life. One day, a young man comes into the restaurant where she works and offers to take her away, to a place where she can forget that she has forgotten much of her life with her husband. She agrees to go with the man. What follows is a long dreamlike sequence in which Tamina is taken by boat to an island inhabited by children who have no memories. She is the only adult there, and must learn to play their games. The children begin to fondle her, and finally they rape her. The sexual games they play out while using her cause friction among the children, who begin to quarrel and become hostile. When Tamina is finally able to put a stop to the sexual abuse, the children mistreat her in other ways. Although Tamina has now forgotten Prague and her husband, she is terribly unhappy. Trying to escape the island, she dives into the water and begins to swim. She swims all night, only to find in the morning that the children have rowed a boat out to meet her and are watching her. She struggles, then slips beneath the water and drowns.

Part Seven: The Border

The final section of *The Book of Laughter and Forgetting* tells the story of a man named Jan and his sexual encounters at orgies or with a variety of women, most notably Edwige, who is also his friend. One of Jan's friends, Passer, is dying of cancer. In the midst of this, Jan attends an orgy at a house owned by a woman named Barbara. Throughout, he finds himself preoccupied with the idea of the border. Jan spends a good deal of time thinking about the various kinds of borders that exist in the world, of the lines that separate one thing from another. On the one hand, the border is what separates men and women. By the end of the chapter however, it is also the border that separates the living and the dead. When Passer dies, all the characters gather for his funeral. Papa Clevis, an older man who is usually very self-possessed and serious, loses his hat. The man who is to give the funeral oration does not notice, however. All the mourners can think about is the hat, and how it has toppled into the grave on top of the coffin.

Although people struggle to control themselves, they are overcome with laughter.

In the last scene of the chapter, Jan goes with Edwige to a nude beach. The scene serves to demonstrate how two people, lovers for many years, are not able to fully communicate with each other. Edwige comments on how beautiful all the nude bodies are; Jan, however, is reminded of the nakedness of the Jews as they were herded into extermination chambers during the Holocaust. Kundera writes, "They never understood each other, Edwige and he, yet they always agreed. Each interpreted the other's words in his or her own way, and there was wonderful harmony between them. Wonderful solidarity based on lack of understanding." The final image is of a group of naked people standing together; a man lectures them while "their bare genitals stared stupidly and sadly at the yellow sand."

CHARACTERS

Boccacio

Boccacio is the name Kundera gives to a famous Czech poet who appears in Part Five. In reality, Boccacio is the name of a famous medieval Italian poet who wrote popular, funny stories. Kundera uses this name to characterize the Czech writer's literature.

The Children

The Children on the island are nameless and largely featureless. They exist as a group, and as a group, they brutalize Tamina. Kundera uses them to represent the mass mentality of the Communist state. Indeed, the scenes on the island are reminiscent of the camps to which children in Communist countries were sent to be indoctrinated.

Edwige

Edwige is a young woman having an affair with Jan in Part Seven. She functions as an illustration of companionship based on misunderstanding, ignorance, or meaninglessness.

Eva

Eva appears in Part Two. Eva is a young woman who has had an affair with a married man, Karel. Karel arranges for Eva to meet his wife, Marketa. The women become very close friends

and decide to have sex with Karel at the same time. Eva ultimately asks Marketa to visit her house, presumably for sex with her and with her husband, but Eva actually intends to sleep with Marketa alone.

Gabrielle

Gabrielle is a young American girl studying in Europe with her friend Michelle. She appears in Part Three, and she serves as an illustration of ignorance and also as a means to segue into a discussion of angelic and demonic laughter.

Hugo

Hugo is a young writer who is infatuated with Tamina. He has sour breath, and is very unappealing to Tamina, although he thinks highly of himself. After Tamina goes to bed with him on the understanding that he will retrieve her lost notebooks for her by going to Prague, he breaks his word, saying that it would be too dangerous for him to do so.

Jan

Jan is the protagonist of the final section of the book. He is a forty-five year old man who is suffering from a perceived meaninglessness in his life. He has had many affairs, but believes that a new chapter of his life has opened after he begins an affair with Edwige. His friends invite him to orgies, which he attends, and he visits a nude beach with Edwige. At the beach, he realizes that the reason he and Edwige get along so well is that they generally misunderstand each other. This scene, and these characters, reveal Kundera's notion that people can never really know each other.

Karel

Karel appears in Part Two. Karel is married to Marketa, and has affairs with several women. His mother is a widow and she has come for a visit at an awkward time. Indeed, Karel, Eva, and Marketa had planned to sleep together during her visit. At the end of Part Two, both he and his wife find their feelings toward his mother to be warmer than they had been earlier.

Kristyna

Kristyna's story is related in Part Five of the novel. She is a young, married woman who lives in a small town, and she works in her husband's butcher shop. She meets a student who is traveling through the town and begins to meet him secretly. They agree that she should come to Prague to visit him once he returns there. Kristyna does so, but does not permit the student to have sex with her as he had hoped.

Milan Kundera

While it might seem strange to list the author of *The Book of Laughter and Forgetting* as one of the characters in the book, he is perhaps the most important character in the novel. Kundera frequently interrupts his stories to speak directly to the reader. Throughout the novel, Kundera gives his personal opinions on history, philosophy, and human nature. While one would usually ascribe these functions to a generic narrator, the autobiographical details related in the book make this distinction somewhat unnecessary. Furthermore, aside from these autobiographical details, Kundera inserts stories where he plays a major role. This intrusive narrator becomes the reader's guide throughout *The Book of Laughter and Forgetting* and all of the stories in the novel are filtered through his interpretations of them.

Lermentov

Lermentov is the name Kundera gives to a famous poet appearing in Part Five. Historically, Lermentov was a Russian writer and Kundera uses his name to comment on the work by his character.

Mama

Mama is Karel's mother. She appears only in Part Two. At a key moment in this section, she clearly remembers an event from her past, but she cannot accurately remember when the event took place. In addition, she walks in on Marketa, Karel, and Eva as they are beginning their threesome.

Marketa

Marketa is married to Karel. She has overlooked her husband's womanizing in the past, but finds it increasingly difficult. She has never liked her mother-in-law, although she has softened toward her. During the story, Marketa finds herself falling in love with her friend Eva, who is also Karel's mistress.

Michelle

Michelle is a young American girl studying in Europe for the summer. She appears in Part Three. Like her cohort, Gabrielle, she serves as an illustration of ignorance and also as a means to segue into a discussion of angelic and demonic laughter.

Mirek

Mirek is a middle-aged man who, although well educated, has been assigned by the government to work as the foreman of a construction crew. He keeps records about his daily life and conversations, and becomes obsessed with recovering the letters he sent to a former lover whom he now considers to be ugly. While he is attempting to recover the letters he sent to her, the police raid his apartment and take his private papers. Within these papers Mirek has incriminated his friends and family and all of them are sentenced to prison.

Petrarch

Petrarch is the name Kundera gives to a famous Czech poet who appears in Part Five. In actuality, Petrarch is the name of the Italian Renaissance poet who first developed the sonnet. Petrarch's ideas about love were highly stylized. Kundera uses this name to comment on the work of his character, the Czech poet.

Madame Raphael

Madame Raphael appears in Part Three, and she teaches Michelle and Gabrielle. The three women together bear the names of the primary archangels in the Bible. This is noteworthy because Kundera later discusses the difference between angelic and demonic laughter in Part Three of the book.

Tamina

After Kundera himself, Tamina is the most important character in *The Book of Laughter and Forgetting*. In many ways, she is a stand in for Kundera himself: she is an exile, she is deeply concerned about the power of memories and the pain of forgetting, and she understands the power of language to both preserve and destroy the past. Kundera writes in Part Six, "It is a novel about Tamina, and whenever Tamina goes offstage, it is a novel for Tamina. She is its principal character and its principal audience, and all the other stories are variations on her own story and meet with her life as in a mirror." Tamina is in her early thirties; she and her husband moved to the country (where she now lives illegally) three years before the story opens. Her husband then dies (again, this occurs before the

TOPICS FOR FURTHER STUDY

- Research Czechoslovakia and its history over the course of the twentieth century, then create an illustrated timeline that traces the important political and historical events that occurred. Add lines taken from *The Book of Laughter and Forgetting* that are appropriate to the events described in your timeline.

- Research Franz Kafka's life and read his book *The Trial*. In what ways does Kafka's novel predict the circumstances in Czechoslovakia under Communist rule? In what ways is Kafka an important influence on Kundera? Write an essay discussing your findings.

- Read George Orwell's *1984*. Lead a class discussion comparing and contrasting Orwell's and Kundera's ideas about state censorship and public memory.

- Listen to a symphony by Ludwig von Beethoven, and try to identify major themes and variations. Read several analyses of the symphony to better understand the idea of themes and variations. Now use this knowledge to write an essay about the structure of *The Book of Laughter and Forgetting*. How does Kundera use the ideas of themes and variations in his novel?

story opens), and she finds herself alone, working as a waitress and trying to recover her memories of her husband. Tamina believes that she would have a clearer memory of him if she could recover the notebooks in which she detailed her eleven years of marriage. At the end of Part Four, Tamina has given everything she has, even her own celibacy, to try to recover the notebooks, but she is unsuccessful. Later, Tamina finds herself on an island inhabited by children who have no memories of the past. She is sexually abused by the children, and when she tries to escape, she drowns.

Voltaire

Voltaire is the name Kundera gives to a famous university lecturer in Prague. In reality, Voltaire was a famous French writer known for his satire.

The Young Student

The student is a young man who meets Kristyna while vacationing in her small country town. He invites her to Prague, imagining that they will have an affair. When she arrives, he discovers that she is more unsophisticated and less lovely than he remembered, and he is embarrassed to be seen with her. He also wants to attend a meeting of writers on the same evening that Kristyna is in town, so he leaves her at his apartment while he goes to the meeting. When he returns, he discovers that she will not have sex with him, and he is very disappointed. He discovers the next day that it is not because she wants to preserve some romantic notion of their night together, devoid of sex, but rather that she is fearful of becoming pregnant. According to Kundera, the student is the embodiment of *litost*.

Zdena

Zdena is a woman with a large nose with whom Mirek had an affair some twenty-five years before the story opens. She possesses Mirek's love letters and refuses to part with them. Although Mirek suspects that she is in collusion with the secret police, she actually loves Mirek and wants to protect him.

THEMES

Memory and Forgetting

Clearly, in a book titled *The Book of Laughter and Forgetting*, memory and forgetting are likely to be dominant themes. Kundera is particularly interested in exploring how memories are created, then changed over time. In extreme circumstances, such as in the opening segment where a Communist leader is ultimately airbrushed out of Czechoslovakian history, memories can be totally erased. In his preoccupation with the state's intrusion into private memories, Kundera's work recalls George Orwell's *1984*. In Orwell's vision of the totalitarian state, public memory is controlled through bureaucrats such as Winston Smith, whose job it is to comb public records and change them according to the most recent edict from the rulers. Thus, someone who has fallen out of favor with the ruling party also falls out of institutional, political, and ultimately, private memory. Like Orwell, Kundera finds state censorship abhorrent, akin to a form of mind control.

Kundera's character Tamina demonstrates yet another facet of memory. In exile in Western Europe, the widowed Tamina finds herself unable to recall all of the details of her life with her late husband. Earlier in her marriage, she wrote down day-to-day events in a series of notebooks she left behind when the couple left Czechoslovakia. Now, with her memories fading, and a part of her own self fading with them, she desperately wants to recover the lost notebooks. Tamina has sacrificed the memory of her sexual life with her husband by having sex with a man who has offered to recover her notebooks for her. Ironically, it is her attempt to recover her memories that ultimately destroys them. Later, she enters a strange dream-like section where a young man promises to take her to a place where she will even forget forgetting.

The Idyll

An idyll is an extremely happy, peaceful, or picturesque episode or scene, typically an idealized or unsustainable one. For example, many people recall their childhoods as idylls. Often, people believe that the world was a kinder place when they were young. However, this idealization usually covers over some real unhappiness. Kundera uses the notion of idyll throughout *The Book of Laughter and Forgetting*. Many of the passages and many of the characters long for an Edenic past, a time such as that in which Adam and Eve enjoyed paradise in the Garden of Eden. Critic François Ricard asserts, however, that the "idyllic conscience" differs from person to person. That is, what one person might define as idyllic is not necessarily what another person would find idyllic. In Kundera's book, each of the characters define the idyll according to their own histories and their own circumstances. In the case of Jan and Edwige, as Ricard points out, their idylls are diametrically opposed to each other, leading to their mutual incomprehension of one another. Kundera uses these two characters to illustrate that individual conceptions of Paradise serve to undermine mutual understanding between people.

For Kundera, one idyll is that of innocence. This idyllic state is represented by the children's island. The children have no memory and exist fully in the present moment. Theirs is a life of unity, conformity, and innocence derived from their lack of memory. For Kundera, it is this lack and this conformity that allows them to commit torture and abuse without guilt. In the novel, Kundera also recalls the early days of the Communist movement as idyllic, a time when he, too, danced in the circle with other Party members before the idyll shattered into totalitarianism.

Opposed to the idyll of innocence is the idyll of experience. Kundera longs for the days when he was part of an innocent idyll as a young member of the Communist party. He is no longer able to be a part of this circle, however. His experience has destroyed his innocence. Although he has found some measure of peace, it is as a critic and a loner, not as a supportive member of a group. Like most of Kundera's ideas and themes, the oppositions between innocence and experience clash against one another.

STYLE

Intrusive Narrator

In *The Book of Laughter and Forgetting*, Kundera's most noticeable stylistic device is his use of the intrusive narrator. Narration in a novel is simply the manner in which the story is told. The narrator is, likewise, simply the voice that tells the story. An author can choose how noticeable or invisible he or she wishes the narrator to be. Sometimes a writer will choose to make a first person narrator a part of the story itself. F. Scott Fitzgerald's *The Great Gatsby* is an example of this; the narrator Nick Carraway both tells the story and participates in it. There is no separation between the narrator and the fiction itself.

In *The Book of Laughter and Forgetting*, however, Kundera plays a game with the notion of narration by creating a narrator who is named Milan Kundera. As critic John O'Brien writes in *Critique*: "Kundera weaves an author-figure into his texts with stark autobiographical intrusions." Likewise, Ellen Pifer notes in the *Journal of Narrative Technique* that "the author's narrating persona exposes both the characters and their author to skeptical scrutiny."

It is tempting to read this narrative "author-figure" as Kundera himself; after all, many of the details that the narrator provides are verifiable details from the author's life. But can the reader make the assumption that the narrative voice in *The Book of Laughter and Forgetting* is actually Kundera the author (and not Kundera the character)? The answer is probably not. A narrative voice is a deliberate creation, crafted to fulfill a specific function in the text, and in that a narrator exists only in words on paper, the narrator/character Milan Kundera cannot be identified as Milan Kundera the writer/person. Because the narrator speaks as if he is the author of the text, and because he speaks of the other characters in the book as characters, the narrator somehow seems more *real*. This is, however, an illusion, a deliberate blurring by Kundera the writer of the boundaries between fact and fiction. Indeed, when one considers this book carefully, it becomes evident that the narrator is the most important character in the book. He intrudes regularly in the storyline; he calls attention to parts of the story as fiction, and to other parts as history. He offers up bits of autobiography and quotes other writers. It is the narrator who appears to organize the order of events, the construction of the chapters, and the major themes and ideas. Nevertheless, that narrator is a creation, as much as Tamina is a creation.

Setting

The setting of *The Book of Laughter and Forgetting* is so important to the novel that it might as well be another character in the story. Indeed, after the narrator, the setting is the most important stylistic device in the book. The novel is largely about the country of Czechoslovakia; even those segments of the book that take place elsewhere always concern someone who is exiled from Czechoslovakia, someone who wants to return to Czechoslovakia, or someone who cannot leave Czechoslovakia. Oddly, Kundera generally does not refer to the setting as Czechoslovakia, but prefers to call his homeland Bohemia (an older, and more mythical, name that was once used to refer to the region). Nevertheless, the historical events that Kundera recounts belong to the actual history of Czechoslovakia. In several sections of the book, the characters are fearful because they live (or have lived) in a police state that monitors even private thoughts and conversations, and Communist Czechoslovakia was such a place. The result of this fear is a sense of claustrophobia in the sections set in Czechoslovakia. Even the characters who have chosen (or have been forced) to leave Czechoslovakia are controlled by their memories of their homeland, even in their forgetting. For Tamina, for example, it is just as painful to realize that she has forgotten parts of her life as it is to recall them. Kundera the narrator also speaks of his homeland with nostalgia and longing.

In addition to the geographic setting of the book, the temporal setting is equally important. The book was written between the Prague Spring of 1968 and the Velvet Revolution of 1989. In 1968, artists and writers were briefly able to speak their minds more freely than at any time during the previous two decades. However, many of these artists and writers were severely punished when the country returned to Communist rule by August of 1968. Oppression is all the more bitter when it follows a respite, and the satiric elements of the text reflect that bitterness. Furthermore, the images of the border that Kundera constructs only operate when the border is strictly enforced, as it was before the fall of the Soviet Union. Indeed, it is this impermeable border that creates the entire sense of exile. Emigrés who can return at will to the homeland do not have the same sense of exclusion as exiles who have had their citizenship revoked and for whom the homeland can exist only in memory. Tamina's story, for example, is only possible because she is in exile and cannot return to her home to recover her letters (which represent her memories). Across the border, she loses all sense of herself and of her identity. Consequently, *The Book of Laughter and Forgetting* requires both the geographic and the temporal setting to give the different strands of the novel an overall sense of connection.

HISTORICAL CONTEXT

Czechoslovakia in the Twentieth Century

Until the end of World War I, Czechoslovakia was not one nation but rather several separate regions ruled by the Habsburg Monarchy, then the Austrian Empire, and finally the Austro-Hungarian Empire. The people living in these regions were largely Czechs, living in Bohemia and Moravia; and Slovaks, living in Slovakia. In 1918, with the collapse of the Austro-Hungarian Empire brought about by the Allied victory in World War I, the Czechs and the Slovaks combined their joint territories as the independent Republic of Czechoslovakia. The country

COMPARE
&
CONTRAST

- **1960s:** As part of the Warsaw Pact, Czechoslovakia is firmly under the control of the Soviet Union. In Czechoslovakia itself, a totalitarian Communist government is installed.

  Today: The Czech Republic is a member of the North Alliance Treaty Organization (NATO), a military alliance that includes most western European nations as well as the United States. The government is a parliamentary republic.

- **1960s:** Under the leadership of Alexander Dubcek and other intellectuals, restrictions are gradually lifted on Czechoslovakian citizens. This triggers a military response from the Soviet Union. Their troops enter the country with tanks and restore control to hard-line Communists. Travel to and from Czechoslovakia is restricted by the government.

Today: The Czech Republic and Slovakia are full members of the European Union, having received membership on May 1, 2004, after a decade of economic reforms. Tourism is a major industry for both countries.

- **1960s:** Many writers and artists go into exile after suffering punishment and repression in Czechoslovakia. Those that remain must submit their work to the government for approval or censorship. Many writers, such as Milan Kundera, continue to write without publishing or write under assumed names.

  Today: Works by writers such as Milan Kundera and other dissidents circulate freely in the Czech language. Many exiled artists and writers are able to return home for visits or have returned to live there permanently.

---

enjoyed roughly twenty years of democracy after World War I.

In 1938, however, under the guise of protecting the German-speaking people of the Sudetenland (a small region of Czechoslovakia), Nazi troops marched into the country. England and France attempted to appease the Nazi leader Adolf Hitler and prevent another war by entering into the Munich Agreement, an act that disillusioned and disheartened the Czech and Slovak people. Hitler flouted the terms of the Agreement and ultimately overran the whole of Czechoslovakia. His troops occupied Prague, and many Czechs and Slovaks were sent to concentration camps. World War II ensued, and the exiled Czechoslovakian government, as well as the Czechoslovakian army, fought on the side of the Allied nations (against Nazi Germany).

At the close of World War II, following Hitler's defeat, the Communist Party grew dramatically, largely due to the warmth that Czechs felt toward the Soviet Union, whose troops were responsible for liberating Czechoslovakia from the Germans. In addition, many Czechs and Slovaks were disenchanted with what they viewed as abandonment by the West during Hitler's rampage. In 1948, the Communist People's Militia was successful in taking over Prague, forming an all-Communist government. The government bore a striking resemblance to Joseph Stalin's dictatorship of the Soviet Union, and the Soviets largely controlled the Czechoslovakian government. During the next twenty years, the Communist Party ruled all facets of life in Czechoslovakia; their reach extended not only to the government, but to the private lives of citizens. All art, culture, and education were under Communist control.

The Prague Spring of 1968 and the Soviet Invasion

In the 1960s, intellectuals (including Milan Kundera) under the leadership of Alexander Dubcek, attempted to reform their government. Life became briefly less repressive, and artists and writers flourished. In 1967, Kundera gave a famous speech to the Fourth Czechoslovak Writers

Soviet tanks drive on the streets of Prague, during the invasion of Czechoslovakia (now Czech Republic) by Warsaw Pact forces in 1968 (Hulton Archive / Getty Images)

Congress in which he called for an end to censorship. The gesture was not without consequence, however; many who spoke up against the state were later punished. Nevertheless, Dubcek, rising to the position of Secretary of the Czechoslovakian Communist Party in January, 1968, introduced a series of reforms aimed at improving life in Czechoslovakia. Dubcek, raised in the Soviet Union, was undoubtedly a committed Communist, convinced that the ideals of the Party were worth keeping. Nevertheless, he also believed that the Party was badly in need of reform. Thus, artists, musicians, writers, and the general population of Czechoslovakia experienced a few months of relative freedom after Dubcek came to power. This period became known as the Prague Spring.

The permissive activities in Czechoslovakia were viewed as threat to the Soviet Union. The Soviets feared that the so-called rebellion in Czechoslovakia might spill over into other nations such as Poland. Consequently, in August of 1968, Soviet troops invaded Czechoslovakia. Where there had been dancing in the streets of Prague just weeks earlier, now tanks rolled through the city.

Dubcek was quickly removed from power, and all the reforms that he had instituted were rescinded. The Soviets placed a new leader as head of government, and instituted an even more repressive state than the one that had preceded the Prague Spring. Kundera and other writers who had been a part of the Prague Spring movement lost their jobs, and were prohibited from publishing and even from speaking publicly. They were also not allowed to travel outside of Czechoslovakia, though Kundera finally received permission to leave in 1975.

For the next two decades, Czechoslovakia was a closed society, even as the Soviet Union became more liberal under the leadership of Mikhail Gorbachev. The fall of the Berlin Wall, however, opened the door for political change. In November and December of 1989, in what became known as the "Velvet Revolution," the Communist government was peacefully removed from power and a new democracy was established.

The growth of Slovakian nationalism led to another change in Czechoslovakia, however. In

1992, against the wishes of President Václav Havel, the nation voted to split into two nations, the Czech Republic and Slovakia.

CRITICAL OVERVIEW

Written in Czechoslovakian, but first published in French in 1979, *The Book of Laughter and Forgetting* became a literary sensation that was promptly released in English in 1980. Since that time, and with the subsequent publication of important works such as *The Unbearable Lightness of Being*, Kundera has been the subject of intense critical scrutiny.

In an early review of *The Book of Laughter and Forgetting*, Ted Solotaroff writes in the *New Republic* that Kundera "identifies the demonic with the burdens of history, adulthood, memory, remorse, and love; the angelic with the innocence, indifference, present-mindedness, sensuality, and conformity of childhood."

Later critics attempted to identify the main themes of the book. For example, R. B. Gill argues in *Critique* that laughter is the essential theme of the book: "Breaking through artificial limits of all kinds, [Kundera's] liberating laughter arises from humane individualism in a sad world of constrictions." Other critics see the novel as a treatise on the history of Czechoslovakia and on the nature of history itself. Nina Pelikan Straus, also writing in *Critique*, argues that *The Book of Laughter and Forgetting* "reveals the endangered positions of words, images, and theories in a historical context that subjects them to revision and deconstruction through the discourse of political orthodoxy." Vicki Adams, writing in *Imagination, Emblems and Expressions: Essays on Latin American, Caribbean, and Continental Culture and Identity*, also focuses on history, and Kundera's understanding of its malleable nature. She writes:

> Kundera's view of history has more to do with disorder than triumph of meaning. While his sentimental side years for a safe, unchanging, constantly returning, idyllic past, his skepticism tells us that ... alternative accounts are possible when authorities in Czechoslovakia tear down the old heroic monuments, give the streets new Russian names, and fabricate in schools a tidy and sentimental account of Czech history.

Likewise, Sheena Patchay, writing in *JLS/TLW*, persuasively argues that Kundera uses "fiction to comment on the way in which history has deliberately papered over the cracks of Czechoslovakian history, specifically the Russian Invasion of Czechoslovakia in 1968."

While the international audience has found Kundera's account of Czechoslovakian culture and history compelling, Czech critics have given the author's work a cooler reception. In a 2003 article in *Kosmas*, Petr Hruby concludes that while "it can be said that Kundera is an extremely capable, innovative and internationally successful writer," he is "also a man who has been severely criticized by his Czech colleagues, mainly for the dissimulation of his Communist past."

Nevertheless, other critics comment on the way that *The Book of Laughter and Forgetting* changes expectations. Jonathan Wilson asserts in the *Literary Review* that "Kundera has embarked upon an attempt to broaden the novel genre to consume all other genres of writing." Likewise, Fred Misurella in his book *Understanding Milan Kundera: Public Events, Private Affairs* goes so far as to argue that in *The Book of Laughter and Forgetting*, "Kundera created a historic shift in the way the contemporary audience regards the novel." No longer is the novel a plot-driven story with beginning, middle, and end. Instead, it may be a combination of many genres, including story, fable, allegory, history, philosophy, essay, and memoir. As British literary theorist Terry Eagleton writes in *Salmagundi*, Kundera "treats the novel as a place where you can write anything you like, anything, as it were, that has just come into your head, as a *genre* released from constraint rather in the manner of a diary."

That so many critics find so many ways of reading Kundera's work in general, and *The Book of Laughter and Forgetting* in particular, demonstrates the richness of the author's writing. It is likely that his work will continue to elicit intense critical debate throughout the twenty-first century.

CRITICISM

Diane Andrews Henningfeld
Henningfeld is a professor of English who writes widely on literature and theory. In the following

WHAT DO I READ NEXT?

- *The Unbearable Lightness of Being* is perhaps Kundera's best known work to English-speaking audiences. Published in 1984 in both Paris and New York, and made into a movie in 1989, the book is about the ambiguities and paradoxes of human existence.

- Laurence Sterne's classic 1759 novel, *The Life and Opinions of Tristam Shandy, Gentleman* is available in a 2004 Modern Library edition with an introduction by Robert Folkenflik. This novel, perhaps more than any other in English, utilizes the device of the intrusive narrator with hilarious results. Kundera names Sterne as one of his literary influences.

- Franz Kafka, born in Prague in 1883, wrote a number of books that were influential on Kundera's writing. *The Trial*, written in 1920 and published in 1925, prefigures many of the events that came to pass in Czechoslovakia as a result of Communist totalitarianism.

- Mark Kurlansky's *1968: The Year That Rocked the World* (2004) provides an overview of events that occurred throughout the world in 1968, putting the Prague Spring in a global perspective.

- *Milan Kundera* (2003), edited by Harold Bloom, provides fourteen critiques of Kundera's work by noted scholars, including a chapter on *The Book of Laughter and Forgetting*.

essay, she examines The Book of Laughter and Forgetting *as an example of magical realism.*

During the second half of the twentieth century, the term "magical realism" was coined for an artistic genre that included magical elements in an otherwise realistic setting. Often, in such artistic creations, the magical is treated as ordinary, and the ordinary treated as strange and marvelous. Originally, the term applied strictly to visual art; however, by the 1960s, the term

> INDEED, SUCH SCENES WOULD BE IMPOSSIBLE IN A REALISTIC TEXT; THE USE OF MAGICAL REALISM, ON THE OTHER HAND, ALLOWS KUNDERA TO CREATE ALTERNATE VERSIONS OF REALITY THAT BETTER DESCRIBE HIS FUNDAMENTAL THEMES OF LAUGHTER AND FORGETTING."

also came to be applied to literature. Magical realism became closely associated during the 1960s and the 1970s with South American writers such as Gabriel García Márquez, Carlos Fuentes, and Jorge Luis Borges. However, the use of magical realism was not limited to Latin America, but rather became a world-wide phenomenon. *The Book of Laughter and Forgetting*, for example, provides a European articulation of magical realism. An examination of this text through the lens of magical realism provides insight into the genre as well as into the book itself.

Wendy B. Faris, in her book *Magical Realism*, lists a number of characteristics of this literary style. Using her framework, it is possible to definitively place *The Book of Laughter and Forgetting* as a work of magical realism. Faris first notes that the magical realist "text contains an 'irreducible element' of magic, something we cannot explain according to the laws of the universe as we know them." Magic does not present itself in *The Book of Laughter and Forgetting* until the third section of the text. In this section, a completely realistic scenario of two American girls studying in Europe for the summer takes on a strange, magical cast. Kundera takes ordinary, realistic events, and renders them opaque and mysterious. For example, he describes the simple fact of the girls' laughter as follows: "They emitted short, shrill, spasmodic sounds very difficult to describe in words." This terminology makes the laughter seem somewhat strange, yet the fact that the girls laugh is not at all out of the ordinary. Later in the chapter, on the other hand, Kundera matter-of-factly describes an event without additional comment that is most definitely magical. In this scene, the two young girls and their teacher begin to dance and laugh, with the following result: "Suddenly Madame Raphael stamped her foot harder and rose a few centimeters above the floor, and then, with the next step, was no longer touching the ground." A few moments later, all three of the dancers begin to rise toward the ceiling: "When their hair touched the ceiling, it started little by little to open. They rose higher and higher through that opening ... and now there were only three pairs of shoes passing through the gaping hole." While the other students look on dumbfounded, Kundera ends the scene without interpretation or explanation, allowing his readers to make of it what they will.

Faris also argues that "metafictional dimensions are common in contemporary magical realism." Metafiction is a literary device in which a work of fiction comments on its own fictional nature. Certainly, *The Book of Laughter and Forgetting* amply illustrates Kundera's use of metafiction. Kundera begins Part Four of *The Book of Laughter and Forgetting* by stating: "I calculate that two or three new fictional characters are baptized here on earth every second. ... This time, to make clear that my heroine is mine and only mine (I am more attached to her than to any other), I am giving her a name no woman has ever before borne: Tamina." By intruding on the narrative to remind the reader that Tamina is a fictional character, Kundera undercuts the illusion of reality that traditional fiction attempts to maintain. Likewise, a little later in the chapter, Kundera directly tells readers that what they are reading is fiction, not real life: "This book is a novel in the form of variations. The various parts follow each other like the various stages of a voyage leading into the interior of a theme." Kundera thus not only reminds readers that they are reading fiction, he also tells them how he has structured the fiction. By constantly commenting on his work as fiction, he demonstrates that language can be shaped, changed, revised, and erased. Consequently, Tamina's story can be anything that the writer wishes. When Tamina, therefore, finds herself on the children's island, it is no more nor less "real" than when Tamina finds herself waiting tables in the restaurant. Both situations are equally created by the writer. In many ways, Kundera's use of metafiction allows for the seamless intrusion of magical situations and scenes.

Faris also argues that in magical realist texts, "descriptions detail a strong presence of the phenomenal world—this is the realism in magical realism, distinguishing it from much fantasy and allegory." In other words, texts of this genre include concrete details about the world as it is experienced through the senses. For the most part, the world that the writer presents closely mirrors the real world. Indeed, the details of the fictional world correspond to the real world, but the insertion of magical elements serves again to undercut the relationship between the text and the real world.

For Kundera, such a strategy serves an important purpose: he is able to demonstrate the way that all texts, including historical texts, can be altered, changed, or erased to fit the needs of its authors. Consequently, while Kundera includes realistic details about Czechoslovakian history in *The Book of Laughter and Forgetting*, his inclusion of magical scenes reminds readers that historical texts are no more true than fictional texts.

Finally, Faris writes that magical realist texts are antibureaucratic and often share "a carnivalesque spirit." That *The Book of Laughter and Forgetting* is antibureaucratic nearly goes without saying. Throughout the novel, Kundera satirizes and parodies the Communist bureaucracy of the Czechoslovakian government, so much so that the book cost him his Czechoslovakian citizenship. He is sharply critical of the government's intrusion in the private lives of its citizens.

The book's "carnivalesque spirit" is evident in its laughter. Kundera's laughter is that of the subversive; it is individualistic, and iconoclastic. It is, as Kundera himself defines it, demonic. Furthermore, Carnival, the period immediately preceding Lent, is traditionally a time of pointed celebration, emphasizing the lewd and the irrational. Also during Carnival, traditions are subverted, and the Church and governments are subjected to parody and satire. Likewise, *The Book of Laughter and Forgetting* contains many such elements. When Tamina is on the children's island, she is in a world where traditions are subverted. Tamina is subject to the childrens' customs and rules just as children are typically subject to adults' rules. Even more disturbing is the children's lewd fascination with Tamina's body. Her virtual rape causes her to lose all sense of herself. The scenes in which she is abused seem almost dreamlike or hallucinatory, yet they are nonetheless horrifying. Indeed, such scenes would be impossible in a realistic text; the use of magical realism, on the other hand, allows Kundera to create alternate versions of reality that better describe his fundamental themes of laughter and forgetting.

In *The Book of Laughter and Forgetting*, Kundera violates the basic laws of nature. Yet, through these violations, Kundera strives to achieve a certain truth. This essential paradox mirrors the ambiguity of human existence as Kundera sees it: that life is only and always experienced at the individual, lonely level (as is death). After death, the memories that create the individual persona vanish, and ultimately, all people are forgotten. In the face of this terrible truth, Kundera inserts the magical, and laughs.

Source: Diane Andrews Henningfeld, Critical Essay on *The Book of Laughter and Forgetting*, in *Novels for Students*, Gale, Cengage Learning, 2008.

Hana Píchová

In the following excerpt, Píchová argues that Tamina is the central character of The Book of Laughter and Forgetting. *Píchová also claims that personal memories are necessary for existence, and that Tamina's failure to sustain her memories leads ultimately to her death.*

Tamina—about whom the narrator of *The Book of Laughter and Forgetting* (1979) says, "It is a novel about Tamina, and whenever Tamina is absent, it is a novel for Tamina"—is one of the most heart-wrenching heroines in all of Kundera's fiction. Struggling to connect a bleak present with the recuperative fragments of the past, Tamina first tries to reconstruct her past life by writing down dates and places of its events. Later, her fear of continual forgetting leads to desperate attempts to retrieve eleven notebooks, left behind in Prague, that document her life before exile. When she fails and the diaries remain locked in a desk drawer behind the iron curtain, death soon follows for Tamina; she winds up trapped on a strange island inhabited solely by children, where no past or memories exist. Her story, although it appears deceptively simple, is integral to the entire narrative of *The Book of Laughter and Forgetting*. The story of Tamina, especially because of her failure, dramatizes the importance of sustaining personal memory through imaginative links to the past.

Tamina's ultimate failure to sustain imaginative connections is most clearly represented through her inability to re-create or retrieve her lost notebooks. At first, when Tamina is still in

> THE STORY OF TAMINA, ESPECIALLY BECAUSE OF HER FAILURE, DRAMATIZES THE IMPORTANCE OF SUSTAINING PERSONAL MEMORY THROUGH IMAGINATIVE LINKS TO THE PAST."

Czechoslovakia, her husband, who is ten years older than she and thus has "some idea of how poor the human memory can be," encourages her to keep a diary of their shared life. She complies, despite regarding this writing exercise as a mundane chore. The many empty pages and the overall fragmentary nature of her entries reveal Tamina's lack of interest and creativity. She is capable of only a literal transcription of the "days of dissatisfaction, quarrels, even boredom."

However, Tamina's husband dies shortly after their emigration, and once she is alone in exile, the diaries left behind in a desk drawer at her mother-in-law's house become increasingly important. They become her only means of recovering the past, the life she shared with her husband in Czechoslovakia. Since Tamina, as a political émigré, is unable to retrieve the diaries herself, she first tries to rewrite them: "Her project, like Don Quixote's, is predicated on an ingenuous belief that words and images in the mind possess the power to resurrect the past." Driven by the prospect of mimetically re-creating the past, she buys a new notebook and divides it into eleven parts, one part for each of the lost years of her life. But because in exile Tamina shares her past with no one with whom to double-check a forgotten event or date, and because she is unable to revisit the specific physical places that might help her recall events, she has a difficult time re-creating the precise details of her life. Devastated because she has "lost all sense of chronology," as well as any sense of location, and is thus unable to transcribe the exact dates and vacation spots of all eleven years, Tamina gives up on the project. It is this obsession with specific details that prevents her from re-creating the past more spontaneously, imaginatively, and freely, which ultimately prevents her from recreating it at all.

Finally, Tamina decides that the only other means of regaining her personal past is by reclaiming the original notebooks. She asks her

Western acquaintances to go to Prague and pick up the diaries at her mother-in-law's house. Thus, through these acquaintances, Tamina is trying to build an artificial bridge between the two countries, a bridge that would allow her past to be carried over onto the new shore. Significantly, she never tells these acquaintances the true contents of the diaries. Tamina's silence on this issue is tied to the protection of her identity, for she feels that, if her private life were to be made public, she would be stripped of her identity.

> She realized that what gave her written memories value, meaning, was that they were meant for *her alone*. As soon as they lost that quality, the intimate chain binding her to them would be broken, and instead of reading them with her own eyes, she would be forced to read them from the point of view of an audience perusing an impersonal document. Then the woman who wrote them would lose her identity, and the striking similarity that would nonetheless remain between her and the author of the notes would be nothing but a parody, a mockery.

It is not only the alteration of Tamina's eyes—reading her life from an outsider's perspective—that is at stake here. Tamina is also worried about the eyes of others; she compares them to "rain washing away inscriptions on a stone wall. Or light ruining a print by hitting photographic paper before it goes into the developer." In essence, she believes that these eyes have the power to destroy or erase the contents of her diaries, which now represent not just her identity but her entire life. Tamina knows that there is no need to worry about the prying curiosity of her acquaintances because they are too self-absorbed to ask any questions. She is, however, justifiably concerned with the interrogative gaze of the Czech secret police, who read all correspondence with foreign countries, and that is why she never has her mother-in-law mail the diaries. At the end, ironically, it is the very mother-in-law entrusted with these documents whose curiosity desecrates Tamina's private world.

The other motivation for Tamina's silence about what it is that she so desperately wants to retrieve is a cultural difference she encounters in the West. She feels that here privacy is not as sacred as it was behind the iron curtain, where people had nothing left but their few private moments, and even private moments were constantly jeopardized by the ever-present secret police. Explaining to her acquaintances why

she needs to keep her personal life private would prove difficult, if not impossible, because here people, as if to mock privacy, voluntarily give up their most intimate moments. This cultural difference becomes especially evident when Tamina and her acquaintances watch television together.

> "The first time I had sex I was fifteen"—the round old head looked proudly from one panel member to the next—"that's right, fifteen. I am now sixty-five. That means a sex life of fifty years' duration. Assuming I have made love on the average of twice a week—a very modest estimate—that means a hundred times a year or five thousand times so far. Let's go on. If an orgasm lasts five seconds, I have twenty-five thousand seconds of orgasm to my credit. Which comes to a total of six hours and fifty-six minutes. Not bad, eh?"

Unlike her acquaintances, who take the old man's bragging seriously, Tamina bursts out laughing, envisioning a continuous orgasm that makes the old man first lose his false teeth and then suffer a heart attack. His imagined death is grotesque, as well as revealing. To Tamina, the reduction of a life to a single act repeated without pause—an act that has been stripped of privacy, past, meaning, and context—is not glorious but deadly.

However, it is not only the cultural difference based on the importance of privacy that prevents Tamina from ever discussing her personal past. It is also her overall unwillingness to bridge the two cultures herself, for she realizes that it would be impossible to explain her previous life to nonémigrés in a way that would preserve and honor its richness and complexity: "Tamina had long since realized that if she wanted to make her life comprehensible to people here she had to simplify it. It would have been impossibly complicated to explain why private letters and diaries might be confiscated and why she set such great store by them." So Tamina allows these go-betweens to believe that the diaries are political documents, for as such their importance would seemingly be obvious and understandable. The narrator reflects Tamina's inability ever to explain fully her native country's historical reality by creating a textual gap precisely at the one moment she is "making a long and impassioned speech" about the situation in Czechoslovakia to Hugo, one of the potential retrievers of her diaries. The content of this long, impassioned speech, especially significant because it is the only speech that Tamina makes about her country, is not only missing, unnarrated, but the omission is emphasized by the narrator's following comment on the veracity of Tamina's words: "She knew the country inside out, and I can tell you—everything she said was true." The narrator's emphasis on the truth of Tamina's speech ironically calls attention to its inaccessibility to the reader. The narrator is reflecting Tamina's cultural difficulty on the structural level of the text here, but perhaps he is also suggesting that to bridge a cultural gap that separates an émigré from a nonémigré is nearly impossible.

When Tamina realizes that her diaries will never be retrieved (her last prospect ends with Hugo, who out of sexual and emotional frustration is unwilling to undertake the trip to Czechoslovakia), she collapses into a blurred and faded existence, into an abyss. No longer responsive to her customers, no longer lending them her ear, and no longer participating in their conversations, she alienates herself from the lives of those around her through silence. In essence, Tamina voluntarily chooses to exacerbate her outer, physical exile with an inner one. The double exile naturally results in a reductive existence. From now on, Tamina only silently and mechanically serves coffee, nevermore inquiring about her surroundings, nevermore phoning back home to ask about the diaries. The first section to deal with Tamina's story comes to a cold and simple narrative end: "She went on serving coffee and never made another call to Czechoslovakia."

Tamina's silenced present existence is reflected in the structural layout of the narrative, for her story is interrupted immediately following the line about her mechanically serving coffee. The narrator abruptly abandons the narrative thread of Tamina's story and begins a new part, which introduces other characters and issues. Part 2 presents the story of unfulfilled love between a butcher's wife, Kristýna, and a poet-student who spends an evening of debauchery with many famous Czech poets, a story that includes a discussion of the Czech word *litost*, which according to the narrator does not translate exactly into any other language. The narrator, in fact, takes the time to explain that *litost* is an open word denoting many different meanings all fused together: "It designates a feeling as infinite as an open accordion, a feeling that is the synthesis of many others: grief, sympathy, remorse, and an indefinable longing. The first syllable, which is long and stressed, sounds like the wail of an abandoned dog." The untranslatability of this word creates an epistemological gap within the text. In essence, translators are warned that they cannot do justice in translating this word and that the Czech original will always denote more than the translation. This linguistic gap mirrors the inherent cultural gap implied in Tamina's section.

Not until part 6, some forty pages later, does the narrator finally return to Tamina. This gap in the story line represents the narrator's own temporary exile of Tamina, as if to reflect her self-imposed exile, as if to honor her desire for silence. The double treatment of her story, in two distinct sections of the narrative (parts 4 and 6), also structurally mirrors the heroine's own doubly exiled existence (inner and outer).

The narrator's return to Tamina begins with the pronouncement that she simply disappeared one day (as she had from the text), explaining that the local police placed her name in the file of "Permanently Missing," "a bureaucratic category easily applied to the dead or exiled." Only then are we given a more detailed account of her disappearance. One day a young man in jeans walks into the café where Tamina works, and he strikes up a conversation. The reason Tamina breaks her silence and responds to this man is that he differs from all the others; he does not speak about himself but instead directs his fast-paced sentences at her. He encourages her, "Forget your forgetting," as he reveals to Tamina, "what she calls remembering is in fact something different, that in fact she is under a spell and watching herself forget." In the original, as pointed out by Maria Němcová Banerjee, the conversion of remembering to forgetting is underscored by a common verbal root that the words share—*vzpomínání* (the act of remembering) and *zapomínání* (the act of forgetting)—thus "remembrance turns into forgetting with a simple flip of a prefix (*za-* instead of *vz-*)" (*TP* 175–76). Furthermore, the man offers Tamina the classic vacation line—"Haven't you ever felt like getting away from it all?"—describing the place to which he can take her as a place "where things are as light as the breeze, where things have no weight." Tamina agrees to ride off in a red sports car with this young man, whose name, Raphael, is "not the least bit accidental."

The critic Fred Misurella takes up the narrator's hint and explores just how Raphael's name is more than accidental by reflecting on the angel Raphael in the Book of Tobit, a story found in the Apocrypha. The biblical story is indeed of interest here, for it contains parallels to Tamina's story in its concern with exiles and a journey guided by an angel, Raphael, to retrieve something from the past. The story is as follows:

> The ostensible setting of the story is the Assyrian capital, Nineveh, where the people of Northern Israel had been taken captive in the latter part of the eighth century B.C. (2 Kg. 17.1–6). There, it is said, dwelt the pious Tobit, who, despite his many charitable deeds, became blind and poor (chs. 1–2). But God heard his prayer, as well as the prayer of demon-haunted Sarah in faraway Media, and sent the angel Raphael to save them both (ch. 3). When Tobit commissioned his son Tobias to collect a deposit of money he had made long before in Media, the angel accompanied him and revealed magic formulas which would heal his father's blindness and exorcise Sarah's demon-lover, Asmodeus (chs. 4–6). Tobias successfully completed his mission and married Sarah (chs. 7–14).

In the biblical story, Raphael is an invaluable angelic intercessor who, with his magical powers, fulfills prayers and protects against evil. Tamina's Raphael, on the other hand, although he does act as a guide who helps to retrieve a moment from her past, ultimately proves to be far different from the helpful biblical guide. As elsewhere in *The Book of Laughter and Forgetting*, this angel is instead a frightening representative of a lifestyle that promotes the dangerous laughter of forgetting, which ends in death.

Tamina understands the danger of what Raphael represents and offers only after it is too late to resist the seductive lure of forgetting. When Raphael stops the car and they stand at the top of a clay slope with an abandoned bulldozer nearby, she suddenly experiences a strong sense of déjà vu, a feeling that the landscape looks "exactly like the terrain around where her husband worked in Czechoslovakia." She remembers the anguished love of their long-ago Sunday walks together, made more poignant because her husband had been fired from his original job and had become a bulldozer operator, and she could get from Prague to see him only once a week. She is overwhelmed by a sense of despair similar to what she felt then and is "glad for the lost fragment of the past [that the

landscape] had unexpectedly returned to her." For a brief moment, the two worlds have metaphorically merged for Tamina; she has created a bridge between the two shores. Therefore, feeling that her husband remains alive in her grief, just as all memories remain alive in the emotions of those still living, she begins to regret her decision to accompany Raphael. The narrative moves into exclamatory, free, indirect discourse to emphasize the importance of Tamina's epiphany: "No, no, her husband was still alive in her grief, just lost that's all, and it was her job to look for him! Search the whole world over! Yes, yes! Now she understood. Finally! We will never remember anything by sitting in one place waiting for the memories to come back to us of their own accord! Memories are scattered all over the world. We must travel if we want to find them and flush them from their hiding places!" Although Tamina's thoughts are powerful and passionate, they are never expressed aloud. On the outside, she remains passive; as if to confirm this passivity, she obediently joins Raphael's infectious laughter, a laughter that promises to erase her misery, a laughter that signals forgetting. And now Raphael truly becomes the messenger of forgetting when he grabs Tamina by the arm and both slide down the slippery slope of the clay bank, a "concrete" portrayal of the slide down the figurative slippery slope of no return. At the edge of the water is a rowboat ready with a boy who will become Tamina's new guide. Tamina's journey is increasingly turning into an allegorical one, and as noted by Misurella, "It's hard not to see this water as mythical—as the Lethe, for instance, the river of forgetfulness in Greek mythology, or the Acheron, the river Dante has dividing the borderland of Hell from Limbo" (39–40). From here Tamina is taken to the hauntingly perverse island of children, an island without past, without memory, without individual distinctions.

Just as the salesman Gregor Samsa of Kafka's *Metamorphosis,* whose transformation into a large insect during a night of bad dreams, has been interpreted as a literalization of his passive acceptance of humiliation and drudgery in his day-to-day life, Tamina too, we might say, is being punished by getting what she wants. If she wants to forget, she will be escorted away "to the place she had always longed to be; she had slipped back in time to a point where her husband did not exist in either memory or desire and where consequently she felt neither pressure nor remorse." In fact, an allusion to Kafka's Gregor Samsa is evident as Tamina departs with Raphael at the beginning of this section of the narration. When Tamina agrees (to Raphael's guidance) "in a dreamy voice" to go to this place "where things weigh nothing at all," the narrator steps in to tell us, "And as in a fairy-tale, as in a dream (no, it *is* a fairy-tale, it *is* a dream!), Tamina walks out from behind the corner." Recalling the famous opening paragraph of Kafka's story, in which the narrator bluntly emphasizes, "It was no dream," the denial of simile or metaphor in these lines from Kundera's text ironically suggests the opposite of what they say, for fairy tales or dreams are, of course, highly metaphorical. These lines are also ironic because Tamina's departure with Raphael quickly changes from a meeting narrated in plausibly realistic fashion to a journey marked by signs of the mythic or the fantastic: she is guided across a body of water by a strange, sexually precocious boy and then resides on an island inhabited solely by children, where the narrative slips into an allegorical or fairy-tale-like unreality. Tamina's ultimately fatal immersion in this world of literalized metaphor, or fairy tales come too frighteningly true, also serves to emphasize her inability to use metaphor or her imagination successfully to bridge the gap separating her from her past. Instead, she has repeatedly tried to re-create the past literally (by attempting to write a mirror copy of the lost notebooks and by planning to send people to retrieve the notebooks). Her failure suggests that such a literal return or recuperation is impossible and that, without an imaginative bridge, all access to the past is lost. Tamina fails to cross imaginatively over the geographic and temporal borders separating her from her past, and so she is led passively away into a metaphorical version of the kind of existence she has chosen for herself through this failure, an isolated island with no bridges of any kind, where she is condemned to a timeless, meaningless exile.

The island represents a frightful parody of the Pioneer camps found "everywhere east of the Elbe" and of utopian worlds built on innocence, inexperience, and the present tense. It is depicted as "enormously" different from the landscape she has left behind. All is green here as if it were a giant playground. What Tamina notices is the diminutiveness of the entire place as symbolized by the volleyball nets that are too close to the ground. Children are the only occupants of this island, and thus all is catered to their needs. The dormitories contain big open rooms full of little beds. The lack of privacy is most notable at evening's washing. The children, divided by groups, labeled with animal names, partake in an organized bathroom ritual. Since Tamina stands out as the only mature person among these children, she soon becomes an object of sexual discovery. The children touch her body, exploring, probing, as if she were "an open watch or a fly whose wings had been torn off." The wingless-fly simile foreshadows the switch that occurs in the minds of the children: the innocent touching suddenly leads to the desire to cause pain. The narrator explains this sudden shift: "Their only motive for causing pain to someone not of their world is to glorify that world and its law." Of course, Tamina realizes that she can no longer function in this world of dwarfs playing hopscotch and provocatively dancing as if "imitating intercourse" to the idiocy of guitars. She decides to escape the children's island, a place that offers only the opposite of her previous existence, a buoyant meaningless present. Tamina swims away. But no shores appear and so she drowns. Despite Tamina's death, however, the ending provides some sense of optimism. After all, she does escape this meaningless world, unwilling to conform to the rules laid out by the children, unwilling to lose her memory fully and thus her identity.

Yet another interpretive possibility comes to mind in regard to the children's island. The narrator's statement introducing the second part of Tamina's story, "as in a fairy-tale, as in a dream (no, it *is* a fairy-tale, it *is* a dream!)," hints that all this indeed may be a dream. Given Tamina's situation, it would be atypical if she did not suffer from what may be termed émigré nightmares. These nightmares appear to most people who find themselves in exile, especially in the first few years. The basic situation presented in these dreams—all are quite similar and repetitive in nature—is that an émigré finds a way back to the home country. The realization that being here is dangerous comes very quickly to the émigré. A desperate journey back to the country of exile follows but generally fails. The émigré wakes up with a feeling of desperate homelessness and utter alienation.

The second part of Tamina's story follows the general pattern of such a dream. At first,

Tamina finds a way to go back; the children's island represents the homeland, even if not fully recognizable. Of course, Tamina does not fit in; her situation even becomes dangerous when the children begin to hate her, and her need to leave this world grows stronger and stronger with each new day. Her attempt to swim back to the other shore, the country of exile, of freedom, fails. Tamina is left in between the two countries, helpless, alone, uncomprehended, and purposeless . . .

Source: Hana Píchová, "Variations on Letters and Bowler Hats," in *The Art of Memory in Exile: Vladimir Nabokov and Milan Kundera*, Southern Illinois University Press, 2002, pp. 46–66.

Norman Podhoretz

In the following excerpt, Norman Podhoretz addresses an open letter to Milan Kundera telling of his experience reading The Book of Laughter and Forgetting. *Podhoretz cites the "intellectual force" of the novel as its most important feature. He then goes on to assert that the novel is about how Communism affects society, and that the theme of the novel centers on totalitarianism.*

Dear Milan Kundera:

About four years ago, a copy of the bound galleys of your novel, *The Book of Laughter and Forgetting*, came into my office for review. As a magazine editor I get so many books every week in that form that unless I have a special reason I rarely do more than glance at their titles. In the case of *The Book of Laughter and Forgetting* I had no such special reason. By 1980 your name should have been more familiar to me, but in fact I had only a vague impression of you as an East European dissident—so vague that, I am now ashamed to confess, I could not have said for certain which country you came from: Hungary? Yugoslavia? Czechoslovakia? Perhaps even Poland?

Nor was I particularly curious about you either as an individual or as a member of the class of "East" European dissident writers. This was not because I was or am unsympathetic to dissidents in Communist regimes or those living in exile in the West. On the contrary, as a passionate anti-Communist, I am all too sympathetic—at least for their own good as writers.

"How many books about the horrors of life under Communism am I supposed to read? How many ought I to read?" asks William F. Buckley,

> BUT WHAT 'HITHERTO UNKNOWN SEGMENT OF EXISTENCE' DID YOU DISCOVER IN *THE BOOK OF LAUGHTER AND FORGETTING*? IN MY OPINION, THE ANSWER HAS TO BE: THE DISTINCTIVE THINGS COMMUNISM DOES TO THE LIFE—MOST NOTABLY THE SPIRITUAL OR CULTURAL LIFE—OF A SOCIETY."

Jr., another member of the radically diminished fraternity of unregenerate anti-Communists in the American intellectual world. Like Buckley, I felt that there were a good many people who still needed to learn about "the horrors of life under Communism," but that I was not one of them. Pleased though I was to see books by dissidents from behind the Iron Curtain published and disseminated, I resisted reading any more of them myself.

What then induced me to begin reading *The Book of Laughter and Forgetting*? I have no idea. Knowing your work as well as I do now, I can almost visualize myself as a character in a Kundera novel, standing in front of the cabinet in my office where review copies of new books are kept, suddenly being seized by one of them while you, the author, break into the picture to search speculatively for the cause. But whatever answer you might come up with, I have none. I simply do not know why I should have been drawn against so much resistance to *The Book of Laughter and Forgetting*. What I do know is that once I had begun reading it, I was transfixed.

Twenty-five years ago, as a young literary critic, I was sent an advance copy of a book of poems called *Life Studies*. It was by Robert Lowell, a poet already famous and much honored in America, but whose earlier work had generally left me cold. I therefore opened *Life Studies* with no great expectation of pleasure, but what I found there was more than pleasure. Reading it, I told Lowell in a note thanking him for the book, made me remember, as no other new volume of verse had for a long time, why I had become interested in poetry in the first place. That is exactly what *The Book of Laughter and Forgetting* did for my old love of the novel—a love grown cold and stale and dutiful.

During my years as a literary critic, I specialized in contemporary fiction, and one of the reasons I eventually gave up on criticism was that the novels I was reading seemed to me less and less worth writing about. They might be more or less interesting, more or less amusing, but mostly they told me more about their authors, and less about life or the world, than I wanted or needed to know. Once upon a time the novel (as its English name suggests) had been a bringer of news; or (to put it in the terms you yourself use in a recent essay entitled "The Novel and Europe") its mission had been to "uncover a hitherto unknown segment of existence." But novel after novel was now "only confirming what had already been said."

That is how you characterize the "hundreds and thousands of novels published in huge editions and widely read in Communist Russia." But "confirming what had already been said" was precisely what most of the novels written and published in the democratic West, including many honored for boldness and originality, were also doing. This was the situation twenty years ago, and it is perhaps even worse today. I do not, of course, mean that our novelists follow an official "party line," either directly or in some broader sense. What I do mean is that the most esteemed novels of our age in the West often seem to have as their main purpose the reinforcement of the by now endlessly reiterated idea that literary people are superior in every way to the businessmen, the politicians, the workers among whom they live—that they are more intelligent, more sensitive, and morally finer than everyone else.

You write, in the same essay from which I have just quoted, that "Every novel says to the reader: 'Things are not as simple as you think.'" This may be true of the best, the greatest, of novels. But it is not true of most contemporary American novels. Most contemporary American novels invite the reader to join with the author in a luxuriously complacent celebration of themselves and of the stock prejudices and bigotries of the "advanced" literary culture against the middle-class world around them. Flaubert could declare that *he* was Madame Bovary; the contemporary American novelist, faced with a modern-day equivalent of such a character, announces: How wonderful it is to have nothing whatever in common with this dull and inferior person.

In your essay on the novel you too bring up Flaubert and you credit him with discovering "the *terra* previously *incognita* of the everyday." But what "hitherto unknown segment of existence" did you discover in *The Book of Laughter and Forgetting*? In my opinion, the answer has to be: the distinctive things Communism does to the life—most notably the spiritual or cultural life—of a society. Before reading *The Book of Laughter and Forgetting*, I thought that a novel set in Communist Czechoslovakia could "only confirm what had already been said" and what I, as a convinced anti-Communist, had already taken in. William Buckley quite reasonably asks: "How is it possible for the thousandth exposé of life under Communism to be original?" But what you proved in *The Book of Laughter and Forgetting* (and, I have since discovered, in some of your earlier novels like *The Joke* as well) is that it *is* possible to be original even in going over the most frequently trodden ground. You cite with approval "Hermann Broch's obstinately repeated point that the only *raison d'être* of a novel is to discover what can only be discovered by a novel," and your own novels are a splendid demonstration of that point.

If I were still a practicing literary critic, I would be obligated at this juncture to show how *The Book of Laughter and Forgetting* achieves this marvelous result. To tell you the truth, though, even if I were not so rusty, I would have a hard time doing so. This is not an easy book to describe, let alone to analyze. Indeed, if I had not read it before the reviews came out, I would have been put off, and misled, by the terms in which they praised it.

Not that these terms were all inaccurate. *The Book of Laughter and Forgetting* assuredly is, in the words of one reviewer, "part fairy tale, part literary criticism, part political tract, part musicology, and part autobiography"; and I also agree with the same reviewer when he adds that "the whole is genius." Yet what compelled me most when I first opened *The Book of Laughter and Forgetting* was not its form or its aesthetic character but its *intellectual* force, the astonishing intelligence controlling and suffusing every line.

The only other contemporary novelist I could think of with that kind of intellectual force, that degree of intelligence, was Saul Bellow. Like Bellow, you moved with easy freedom and complete authority through the world of ideas, and like him too you were often playful in the way you handled them. But in the end Bellow seemed always to be writing only about himself, composing endless and finally claustrophobic variations on the theme of Saul Bellow's sensibility. You too were a composer of variations; in fact, in *The Book of Laughter and Forgetting* itself you made so bold as to inform us that "This entire book is a novel in the form of variations." Yet even though you yourself, as Milan Kundera, kept making personal appearances in the course of which you talked about your own life or, again speaking frankly in your own name, delivered yourself of brilliant little essays about the history of Czechoslovakia, or of music, or of literature, *you*, Milan Kundera, were not the subject of this novel, or the "theme" of these variations. The theme was totalitarianism: what it is, what it does, where it comes from. But this was a novel, however free and easy in its formal syncretism, whose mission was "to discover what can only be discovered by a novel," and consequently all its terms were specified. Totalitarianism thus meant Communism, and more specifically Soviet Communism, and still more specifically Communism as imposed on Czechoslovakia, first in 1948 by a coup and then, twenty years later in 1968, by the power of Soviet tanks ...

Source: Norman Podhoretz, "An Open Letter to Milan Kundera," in *Commentary*, Vol. 78, No. 4, October 1984, pp. 34–39.

Ted Solotaroff

In the following excerpt from a review of The Book of Laughter and Forgetting, *Solotaroff summarizes Kundera's political problems before his exile from Czechoslovakia and argues that in this book Kundera attempts to connect his past and his present.*

How does one stay in touch with the real in a brutally absurd world? This is the question that lies between the lines of this saturnine, grief-ridden, magical book, written by a Czech dissident in exile, a satirist with a tear in his eye whose telescopic property enables him to see all the way to Prague.

The Book of Laughter and Forgetting begins with a joke about repression and its double meaning. Back in 1948, party leader Gottwald made a speech to the people of Prague. It was a snowy day, he was speaking from a balcony, and one of his comrades, Clementis, gave him his fur cap. The speech proved to be historic, and a photo-

> THE BOOK OF LAUGHTER AND FORGETTING IS HIS FIRST WRITING FROM EXILE. IT IS MADE UP OF SEVEN NARRATIVES SUSPENDED LIKE BRIDGES FROM THE TWO THEMES OF ITS TITLE, AS THOUGH KUNDERA WERE TRYING TO WRITE HIS WAY ACROSS THE GAP BETWEEN EAST AND WEST, PAST AND PRESENT, REJOINING WHAT THE CONDITIONS OF THE COLD WAR AND OF HIS OWN LIFE HAVE SUNDERED."

graph featuring the two men became famous. Four years later Clementis, now foreign secretary, was hanged as a traitor and his figure was airbrushed from the photograph. Where he had stood was now a blank wall. All that remained of him was the cap on Gottwald's head.

Deep East European humor: a message flashing from Gogol to contemporary Prague—the void under the fact, the commonplace detail with a surrealist twist and a manifold meaning; a hatful of terror, oblivion, and an unruly, irrational element and its laughter that resist them. The joke is also typical Kundera—a Czech with iron in his irony who has never had to go out of his way to find his material.

A cocky, derisive, antinomian spirit from the start, Kundera was kicked out of the party in 1950, probably by a tribunal of his peers—the fate of Ludvik Jahn, the anti-hero of his first novel. Kundera describes watching his erstwhile comrades dancing in the streets of Prague, "its cafés full of poets, its jails full of traitors," on the day that Zavis Kalandra, a famous Surrealist, was executed, the smoke from the crematorium rising to "the heavens like a good omen." Excluded from "the magic circle" of the orthodox, Kundera realized that he belonged now to Kalandra, among the outsiders and the fallen. These early years of the "idyll for all," as he puts it—"timid lovers held hands on movie screens, marital infidelity received harsh penalties at citizens' courts of honor, nightingales sang, and the body of Clementis swung back and forth like a bell ringing in the new dawn of mankind"— appear to have confirmed him in his sensibility of extremes as well as in his skepticism and icon-oclasm. Amid the relentless positivism and dog-matism, he held to his view of the vanity of human desires, the crossing of purposes within and between people, the child that continues to father the man. Like the cap on Gottwald's head, Kundera placed what faith he had left in the irrational, the accidental, even the perverse, which provides now and then a little space in the interstices of an authoritarian society for life and truth to break through. He wrote a lot about gratuitous acts—particularly of people jumping out of windows, morally speaking, to spite and shame their persecutors—exploring through the private life the defenestration tendencies of his so frequently conquered country, placing the compelling fantasies of his sexual marksmen alongside those of the state and its henchmen. Having ruined his life by his political "joke," Ludvik Jahn then completes his humiliation by trying to seduce the wife of his chief betrayer. In *Life is Elsewhere*, a Nabokovian account of the short life of a precocious literary and political opportunist that parodies the tradition of romantic poetry and politics, Jaromil Volker simultaneously achieves the zenith and nadir of his life when he informs on his girl friend and her brother. The main interest of Kundera's last novel, *The Farewell Party*, surrounds the impulse that prompts a dissident intellectual to allow a young nurse to poison herself accidentally.

Since neither the political nor the sexual areas of Czech life were open to this kind of inspection, Kundera went unpublished, except for the period of the Prague Spring when *The Joke* appeared. It made him immediately famous and two years later, his country having returned to "the warm loving embrace of the Soviet Union," it made him again a non-person. The only work he could get was writing horoscopes for a socialist youth magazine under the pseudonym of a non-existent mathematician (satire never has had to go out of its way to find Kundera); when his identity was uncovered and a young editor fell with him, he decided he was bad news for everyone and managed to leave.

The Book of Laughter and Forgetting is his first writing from exile. It is made up of seven narratives suspended like bridges from the two themes of its title, as though Kundera were trying to write his way across the gap between East and West, past and present, rejoining what the conditions of the cold war and of his own life

have sundered. Thus the cap from Clementis's head finds a lovely parallel in a section of the final story, which describes the funeral of Victor Passer, a fellow refugee who goes on believing in his life even in its agonizing terminal stage, much as he had stubbornly clung to his vision of a new and humane politics. The funeral soon turns comic when the grave attendants miss their cue and lower the coffin into the grave, even as the speaker goes on addressing his remarks directly to the deceased. Then a gust of wind blows the hat from the head of Clevis, one of the mourners. A self-conscious, indecisive man, Clevis finally brings himself to chase down the hat, which has become the center of everyone's attention, but it continues to elude his furtive gestures and finally blows into the grave. The mourners are all racked by barely repressed laughter, particularly so when each of them must drop his shovelful of earth onto the coffin, on which sits the hat, "as though the indomitably vital and optimistic Passer were sticking his head out."

Another Czech who insists on being remembered and who illustrates the cruel, homely, perverse, and zany way things happen—the human comedy Czech style—is a dissenter named Mirek. Mirek still smarts from the realization that many years ago he took as his first mistress an ardent Stalinist who, worse yet, was ugly. It is 1971, the authorities are closing in, he has carefully kept many incriminating documents of his and his friends' activities, believing that "the struggle of man against power is the struggle of memory against oblivion." Instead of hiding his papers, however, he races off in his car to see his Zdena and ask her to return his love letters. Mirek has some revisionism of his own in mind, and though his trip is full of Proustian slips—the memory of his willingness to bark like a dog so that she wouldn't say he made love like an intellectual, even the memory of a begonia-decked summer house that delivers the astonishing message that he once loved her, big nose and all—none of this prevents Mirek from airbrushing her out of his life, for "Mirek is as much a rewriter of history as the Communist Party, all political parties, all nations, all men... The only reason people want to be masters of the future is to change the past."

Meanwhile, Mirek's other purpose—to pursue his fate as a soldier of memory—is going forward on its own: that is, when he arrives home the police are already going through his papers. "You don't seem to care much about your friends," one of them says. But though his son and 10 of his comrades will go to prison with him, Mirek is fulfilled.

> They wanted to erase hundreds of thousands of lives from human memory and leave nothing but a single unblemished idyll. But Mirek is going to stretch out full length over their idyll, like a blemish, like the cap on Gottwald's head.

Mirek's story is clear in its meaning but enigmatic in its tone, somewhere between bemusement and derision. Though he is deeply concerned about the "struggle of memory," Kundera is generally sardonic about the dissidents who carry it on. Politics seems to have set his teeth permanently on edge. Elsewhere he distinguishes between the "demons" and the "angels"—and their respective modes of laughter, the former being generated by the irrational, incongruous, disorderly principle, the latter by the rational, harmonious, dogmatic one. He tells us that both principles are needed but since the angels are in control everywhere he looks ("they [have] taken over the left and the right, Arab and Jew, Russian general and Russian dissident") he sides with the demons of heresy rather than the angels of dogma. Which is hardly a contest for him: a subversive conservative, he identifies the demonic with the burdens of history, adulthood, memory, remorse, and love; the angelic with the innocence, indifference, present-mindedness, sensuality, and conformity of childhood...

Source: Ted Solotaroff, "A Czech Artist of Memory," in *New Republic*, Vol. 183, December 20, 1980, pp. 28–31.

SOURCES

Adams, Vicki, "Milan Kundera: The Search for Self in a Post-Modern World," in *Imagination, Emblems and Expressions: Essays on Latin American, Caribbean, and Continental Culture and Identity*, edited by Helen Ryan-Ranson, Bowling Green State University Popular Press, 1993, pp. 233–46.

Eagleton, Terry, "Estrangement and Irony," in *Salmagundi*, No. 73, Winter 1987, pp. 25–32.

Faris, Wendy B., "Scheherazade's Children," in *Magical Realism*, edited by Lois Parkinson Zamora and Wendy B. Faris, Duke University Press, 1995, pp. 164–90.

Gill, R. B., "Bargaining in Good Faith: The Laughter of Vonnegut, Grass, and Kundera," in *Critique*, Vol. 25, No. 2, Winter 1984, pp. 77–91.

Hruby, Petr, "Milan Kundera's Czech Problems," in *Kosmas*, Vol. 17, No. 1, Fall 2003, pp. 28–49.

Kundera, Milan, *The Book of Laughter and Forgetting*, translated by Aaron Asher, Perennial Classics, 1996.

Misurella, Fred, "A Different World: *The Book of Laughter and Forgetting*," in *Understanding Milan Kundera: Public Events, Private Affairs*, University of South Carolina Press, 1993, pp. 19–45.

O'Brien, John, "Milan Kundera: Meaning, Play, and the Role of the Author," in *Critique*, Vol. 34, No. 1, Fall 1992, pp. 3–18.

Patchay, Sheena, "'Re-Telling Histories' in *The Unbearable Lightness of Being* and *The Book of Laughter and Forgetting*," in *JLS/TLW*, Vol. 14, No. 3–4, December 1998, pp. 245–52.

Pifer, Ellen, "*The Book of Laughter and Forgetting*: Kundera's Narration against Narration," in the *Journal of Narrative Technique*, Vol. 22, No. 2, Spring 1992, pp. 84–96.

Ricard, François, "The Fallen Idyll: A Rereading of Milan Kundera," in *Review of Contemporary Fiction*, Vol. 9, No. 2, Summer 1989, p. 17–26.

Solotaroff, Ted, "A Czech Artist of Memory," in the *New Republic*, December 20, 1980, pp. 28–30.

Straus, Nina Pelikan, "Erasing History and Deconstructing the Text: Milan Kundera's *The Book of Laughter and Forgetting*," in *Critique*, Vol. 28, No. 2, Winter 1987, p. 69–85.

Wilson, Jonathan, "Counterlives: On Autobiographical Fiction in the 1980s," in the *Literary Review*, Vol. 31, No. 4, Summer 1988, p. 393.

FURTHER READING

Banerjee, Maria Němcová, *Terminal Paradox: The Novels of Milan Kundera*, Grove Press, 1990.
> Banerjee devotes a chapter of this book to *The Book of Laughter and Forgetting*. Of particular interest in this book is Banerjee's discussion of using music to interpret Kundera's writing.

Kundera, Milan, *The Art of the Novel*, translated by Linda Asher, Grove Press, 1988.
> This collection of essays by Kundera concerns the nature of fiction. The last section includes a fascinating dictionary Kundera created for the benefit of his translators.

———, *The Curtain: An Essay in Seven Parts*, HarperCollins, 2007.
> In this book-length essay, Kundera traces the history of the novel, demonstrating that the purpose of the novel is to show readers their own lives. Students will find excellent authorial commentary on *The Book of Laughter and Forgetting* in this volume.

Petro, Peter, ed., *Critical Essays on Milan Kundera*, G. K. Hall, 1999.

This is an excellent collection of scholarly articles and interviews with Kundera that will help students develop a better understanding of his works.

Woods, Michelle, *Translating Milan Kundera (Topics in Translation)*, Multilingual Matters, 2006.

Woods provides a fascinating look at the decision making process that goes into translating an author's work, discussing the multiple translations of Kundera's novels, and the pressure of translation on the writer.

The Golden Notebook

DORIS LESSING

1962

Doris Lessing's novel *The Golden Notebook*, with its themes and setting reflecting the attitudes of the 1950s, was published in 1962. It is considered the author's most significant work. The form of the novel, and its topics, were praised by some and scorned by others when the book was first released. Over time, however, scholars have recognized that *The Golden Notebook* was published ahead of its time. Indeed, the novel experiments with chronological sequence and narrative voice, and it deconstructs language as an endeavor to search for meaning and truth. All of these experimental aspects became the principle elements of the postmodernist movement that followed the book's publication. *The Golden Notebook* also touches on feminist issues that were only just beginning to be debated at the time it was published. Additionally, the book openly discusses the protagonist, Anna, as being attracted to communism (a social theory that stresses that the economic goods of a society should be managed by the laborers who produce those goods and that a society's wealth should be distributed equally among its citizens). At the same time, however, Anna is dissatisfied with communism as a practice.

Lessing's novel is experimental and sometimes difficult to read. What holds it together is the author's skillful treatment of language and her sensitivity to her characters. *The Golden*

Notebook, some fifty years after it was first written, still strikes powerful chords. It probes women's identities, the value of male and female relationships, the ability of language to accurately communicate experience, the definition of sanity, the power that one person has to affect his or her world, and the value and purpose of literature. These are universal themes that may never be fully exhausted.

A recent edition of *The Golden Notebook* was printed by HarperCollins in 1999.

AUTHOR BIOGRAPHY

Lessing was born on October 22, 1919, in Kermanshah, Persia (now Iran) to British parents, Emily Maude McVeagh and Alfred Cook Taylor. According to Lessing's biographer, Carole Klein, Lessing's mother had been expecting a boy and was so disappointed her baby was a girl, she could not think of a name for the child. The physician attending the birth suggested the name Doris.

In 1925, when Lessing was six years old, her family moved to a farm in Rhodesia (now called Zimbabwe). Lessing attended a convent school until she was thirteen, when her formal education ended. When Lessing was nineteen, she married Frank Wisdom and gave birth to two children in quick succession (a son and a daughter). She divorced Wisdom in 1943, leaving him to care for their children. Two years later, she married Gottfried Lessing, a central figure in the local Communist Party and a refugee from Nazi Germany. They had a son, Peter.

In 1947, Lessing completed her first novel but had trouble finding a publisher. She also wrote many short stories about her experiences in Africa. In 1949, after divorcing her second husband, Lessing moved to London with Peter. A year later, her first novel, *The Grass is Singing*, was finally published. From then on, Lessing was able to live on the money she made as a writer. Upon the success of *The Golden Notebook* (1962), Lessing's role as a major British author was confirmed.

Regular topics in Lessing's writing include cultural conflicts, political conflicts, and psychological conflicts; in particular, her work often focuses on the conflicts between men and women. Lessing

Doris Lessing *(David Levenson / Getty Images)*

also reflects on the social pressures of conformity and mental breakdown in her novels *Briefing for a Descent into Hell* (1971) and *The Summer before the Dark* (1973). After reading about the spiritual principles set forth by Sufism, and those set forth in the Bible and the Koran, she began writing science fiction to reflect upon what she had learned, such as in her novel *The Marriages between Zones Three, Four, and Five* (1980).

During her career as a writer, Lessing has won many awards, including the Somerset Maugham Award in 1954 for her book *Five: Short Novels*; and the James Tait Black Prize in 1995 for *Under My Skin*, the first volume of her autobiography (the second volume is *Walking in the Shade* (1997)). In 2001, Lessing was awarded the David Cohen Memorial Prize for British Literature. The following year, she received the S. T. Dupont Golden PEN Award for a Lifetime's Distinguished Service to Literature. In 2007, Lessing was awarded the Nobel Prize for Literature.

PLOT SUMMARY

Free Women: 1

ANNA MEETS HER FRIEND MOLLY IN THE SUMMER OF 1957 AFTER A SEPARATION

The Golden Notebook is divided into six sections. Five sections are further subdivided into a storyline and into entries from the notebooks of the protagonist, Anna Wulf.

Anna is visiting with Molly Jacobs as the story opens. The two friends live in London. Anna and Molly refer to themselves as free women because they are not tied down by social conventions. Molly is an actress and Anna is a writer.

Richard Portmain, Molly's ex-husband, arrives to talk about Tommy, Molly and Richard's son. Molly and Richard were divorced after a year of marriage, and Tommy has been living with his mother. There is mention of Richard's second wife, Marion, who is very unhappy with Richard's blatant extramarital affairs.

Molly, Richard, and Anna are concerned about Tommy. He is almost twenty years old, and sits on his bed all day thinking. Richard, a very successful businessman, has offered Tommy a job in one of his international corporations.

Molly, Anna, and Richard point out the differences between Richard and the women but also the subtle differences between Molly, who is outgoing and a dilettante (or poser) in the arts, and Anna, who is subdued, introspective, and a true artist.

Tommy appears and turns down his father's job offer, explaining that he is trying to determine who he is. Tommy has been influenced by his mother and Anna but he is not like them, and he does not want to be like his father because Richard is completely defined by his job.

Richard and Tommy leave without anything being resolved. Molly and Anna discuss Anna's writer's block. Anna has published one bestselling novel, *Frontiers of War*. Now Anna writes only in notebooks that she does not want anyone to see. She has become frustrated by the form of the traditional novel and wants to experiment with writing that is somehow more truthful. She hopes her journal writing will show her how to do this.

Anna returns home and begins to describe her notebooks.

MEDIA ADAPTATIONS

- A video of Lessing reading excerpts from *The Golden Notebook* is called *Doris Lessing Reads: The Golden Notebook*. It was recorded in 1986 and was released by Caedmon (a division of HarperCollins).

THE NOTEBOOKS

Anna has four different notebooks: black, red, yellow, and blue. The black notebook contains Anna's reflections about her novel and her experiences living in southern Rhodesia—the experiences that inspired her novel. In this notebook, she has recorded her thoughts about communism and the different relationships she had while in Africa, where she lived during World War II. Anna's friends Paul Blackenhurst and Jimmy McGrath are both in the military. Anna is also friends with Maryrose, a young, white African woman, and Willi Rodde, a refugee from Germany. Although Anna and Willi begin living together, Anna states neither she nor Willi really like one another.

Most of the action in these first passages occurs at the Mashopi Hotel, a place in the Rhodesian countryside. On weekends, the group of friends drives out to the Mashopi, where they get very drunk and discuss sex and politics. Parts of their discussions involve the racial situation in colonized Africa.

One particular weekend at the Mashopi Hotel, Paul tells Jackson, the black cook at the hotel, indicates that the racial oppression is not as bad in other countries as it is in Africa. Mrs. Boothby, the wife of the hotel owner, is threatened by this and bans Paul from the kitchen. When she catches Jackson and Paul together again, Mrs. Boothby fires Jackson, who had worked for her for fifteen years. The group of friends leaves and never returns to the hotel.

The red notebook begins with Anna's involvement with the Communist Party in

England. Most of the entries in this notebook are about Anna's reflections on Communist philosophy or her frustrations with the way that philosophy is put to work.

The yellow notebook begins as if it were a novel, the main characters of which are Julia (who represents Molly) and Ella (who represents Anna). Ella works at a women's magazine. Ella's boss is Patricia Brent, who is editor of the magazine. At a party, Ella meets Paul Tanner, a psychiatrist. Paul is married, and he and Ella begin an affair that will last five years. Ella feels that Paul is the first man she has ever loved. As the story in the yellow notebook continues, Ella's affair with Paul disintegrates. Paul goes to Nigeria, and Ella expects Paul to ask her to join him. He does not.

While pondering her story in the yellow notebook, Anna mentions Michael, a man with whom she is having an affair. It seems that Paul represents Michael.

The blue notebook's entries recount Anna's relationship with Max (called Willi in the black notebook) who is Anna's ex-husband and the father of Anna's daughter, Janet. Anna also writes about Mrs. Marks, the therapist who Anna began to see when she could no longer write. The blue notebook then switches back and forth between Mrs. Marks and Michael, and then to news accounts of the day—war, peace talks, and the Cold War between the United States and Russia.

The first section of Lessing's novel ends with the suggestion that Anna's therapy sessions with Mrs. Marks are over and that Anna will be able to write again.

Free Women: 2
TWO VISITS, SOME TELEPHONE CALLS AND A TRAGEDY

Molly telephones Anna because she is concerned about Tommy. When Anna hangs up the phone, she hears footsteps and sees Tommy, who wants to talk. While she listens, Anna feels that Tommy is accusing her and Molly for the way they have influenced his life. Tommy reads parts of Anna's notebooks without asking permission, then leaves without achieving any resolution. Later, Molly calls Anna and tells her that Tommy has shot himself in the head. He is in the hospital and is not expected to live.

THE NOTEBOOKS
In the black notebook, Anna records attempts by movie and television producers to buy the film rights to her novel. However, the directors want to make changes to the story, and suggest that it could become a romance. Another producer wants to set the story in England rather than in Africa and change the racial components to differences in class and wealth. Someone else wants to turn the novel into a musical. Anna turns down all of these offers. Although she could use the money, she believes she must stay true to her story.

The red notebook entries begin as Anna meets with a group of writers who are members of the Communist Party. She is disturbed by what is happening in the Party. Many members disregard reports that Stalin is a murderer because they do not want to face the failures of the Communist system. As a result, no one is willing to criticize Stalin, though many members realize that what they are writing and publishing is not based on the truth. Their inability to openly admit this makes Anna angry with them and with herself.

The yellow notebook returns to Ella, who is depressed because Paul has left her. Ella's boss, Patricia, suggests that Ella go to Paris to interview the editor of a French magazine. In Paris, Ella realizes how much Paul has hindered her life. She had, without being aware of it, become dependent on Paul. While she considers herself a free woman, Ella realizes she is not much better off than any of the sad married women whom she meets, women who have lost themselves in meaningless and unfulfilling marriages, women who are not free.

On her flight home, Ella meets an American doctor, Cy Maitland, and the next evening she meets him for dinner. Cy is married with five children. After dinner, they end up in bed. Ella is surprised by her objective stance with Cy. She is not emotionally involved and therefore is able to sexually satisfy him without the need to love him or even be sexually satisfied by him. Her satisfaction only stems from his. She feels more in control this way.

In the blue notebook, Anna records that she feels tension between her role as a mother to her daughter and her role as Michael's lover. Michael is jealous of Anna's attention to her daughter, so Anna tries to schedule his visits at times when her daughter will not need her. Also, Anna senses that Michael is about to end their affair.

Nevertheless, on an evening when Michael is supposed to come see her, she dresses herself in an outfit that he likes and prepares dinner for him. Michael does not show up and shortly afterward ends the relationship.

Anna attempts to record all the details of her life in this journal as simply and as honestly as she can. She focuses on writing about one day to see if she is capable of capturing the reality of her actions through words. By the end of the day, when she rereads her entry, she draws lines through it, canceling it out. The experiment, for Anna, was a failure. After scoring through her words, Anna writes one paragraph, a synopsis of the day, listing only the barest details without any reflection. Neither version satisfies her.

Free Women: 3

TOMMY ADJUSTS HIMSELF TO BEING BLIND WHILE THE OLDER PEOPLE TRY TO HELP HIM

Tommy does not die, but his gunshot wound leaves him blind. Although he seems to be adjusting well, Molly and Anna sense that this is not truly the case. It seems as if Tommy is happy with his new situation and is using it to punish Molly and Anna. He has also developed a strong intuitive sense that allows him to read Molly's and Anna's minds. The women become uncomfortable around him, unable to speak confidentially with one another. Molly feels trapped by him. Anna feels guilty. She worries that Tommy shot himself because of something he read in her notebooks.

Meanwhile, Richard's second wife, Marion, stops drinking and spends every day with Tommy. Tommy, in turn, encourages Marion to become stronger and to make decisions for herself. Richard does not like the effect Tommy has on Marion and calls Anna for help, telling her that Marion has all but abandoned her children and him. Richard feels hurt, but he is also somewhat relieved. Since Marion has left him, Richard decides to divorce Marion and marry his secretary, Jean.

THE NOTEBOOKS

In the black notebook Anna recounts a memory. While at the Mashopi Hotel, Paul has gone hunting, at Mrs. Boothby's request, for pigeons so she can make a meat pie. The group of friends goes with him but are later sickened by the smell of blood and death.

In another section, Anna has pasted published reviews of her novel up in her house. All the reviews are from Communist publications. They all find fault with her work but encourage her to continue writing so she can improve.

The red notebook tells of new hope in the Communist Party following the Stalin's death. Members are energized with thoughts of refurbishing the Party. Anna becomes enlivened at first and then becomes disillusioned as nothing really changes.

The story of Ella continues in the yellow notebook. Ella promises herself that she will not go to bed with a man unless she can potentially have romantic feelings for him. Nevertheless, she continues to sleep with men she does not care for. Ella and Julia discuss the cost of being free women. Men are aroused by them because they are not their wives, but neither Julia nor Ella get any deep sexual satisfaction from their affairs because they are loveless encounters.

There is a change in the style of writing in the blue notebook. Anna records only very dry details, such as the date of her birth, her maiden name (which is Anna Freeman), and other details of her life. In another entry, Anna states that she is a new type of woman, one that has never before existed. She feels cracks developing inside of her. This means her new personality is ready to emerge, she tells Mrs. Marks.

It is at this point that Anna defines how she has divided her writing in the notebooks. The black one is meant to focus on Anna Wulf, the writer. The red one is devoted to politics. The yellow is an exercise in making up stories that reflect real experiences. The black one is like a diary.

Anna writes that she is losing her hold on who she is. Words are no longer making sense to her. If words have lost their meaning, than she, as a writer, is also losing meaning. She starts to feel that she is nothing, and this frightens her.

Free Women: 4

ANNA AND MOLLY INFLUENCE TOMMY FOR THE BETTER, MARION LEAVES RICHARD, AND ANNA DOES NOT FEEL HERSELF

Marion moves into Molly's house. Marion takes Tommy to a political rally, during which they are arrested. Richard and Molly want Anna to talk to Marion and Tommy because Richard is embarrassed by the news coverage of the story and Molly is concerned for Tommy's safety during the protests. Anna agrees, though she has no idea what to say. When she gets to the house, she first meets with Marion before meeting with Tommy. Anna says things and reacts as if she were watching herself from a distance. Anna does not know why, but Tommy miraculously drops his hostile stance against both herself and Molly. Richard and Molly visit Anna later, asking how she persuaded Tommy to change his attitude.

THE NOTEBOOKS

The black notebook contains a recurring theme, Anna's novel being turned into a disastrous movie. The entry ends with the statement that Anna is closing this notebook, and will not write in it any longer.

The red notebook contains information about Jimmy, one of Anna's friends from her earlier years in Africa. Jimmy tells Anna a story about Harry Mathews, a British teacher and Communist who becomes obsessed with Russia. Mathews learns to speak Russian and compiles a detailed history of Russian Communism. He believes the post-Stalin Communist Party officials will ask him to help guide them in their search for a new identity for the Party, though this never comes to pass.

Then Anna records several ideas for future short stories and novels that she hopes to write, all dealing with relationships between various types of men and women. This is a departure from other entries in the red notebook, which formerly focused exclusively on politics.

The blue notebook records a very long entry about a new man in Anna's life, Saul Green. Saul is a disturbed man, and he uses women and then hurts them when they become emotionally affected by him. Saul and Anna enter into an affair, which drags Anna further into a mental breakdown. With Saul, Anna loses her connection with reality. She moves in and out of different personalities, much like Saul does. Her emotions swing from depression to euphoria. She suffers from recurrent nightmares. At the end of the blue notebook, Anna states that she has bought a new golden notebook and will lock away her other four notebooks. When Saul sees the new golden notebook, he asks for it. Anna refuses to give it to him.

The Golden Notebook

Anna becomes further detached from herself and her surroundings and states that sanity is based on enjoying the simple pleasures of the senses,

which she is no longer able to do. She tells Saul that they are not good for one another and that she is not strong enough to make him leave. Saul says she must write and forces her to try. He provides the first sentence of a new novel that she will write. This sentence is the first sentence in Lessing's *The Golden Notebook*. Anna decides to give the golden notebook to Saul and recites the first sentence that he will need to use to begin his own novel.

Free Women: 5

MOLLY GETS MARRIED AND ANNA HAS AN AFFAIR

Anna, in an attempt to reconnect with the world around her, develops a voracious appetite for newspapers. She cuts out articles and pins them to the walls. Soon, the main room of her flat is covered in newspaper clippings. She is surrounded by words, but language cannot capture the world, and it can no longer express her feelings. She continues to sense that she is going mad but knows that when her daughter comes home, Anna's role as a mother will bring her back to sanity. In the meantime, she allows herself the freedom to flounder. Molly calls one day and sends an American named Milt over to rent one of Anna's rooms. Milt is stronger and more confident than Saul, but in many ways he is a reflection of Saul (or maybe he is Saul and Anna is using a different name to refer to him). Milt stays with Anna for a short time. At first, he tears down all the newspaper clippings so Anna will not go mad, then he tells her that he cannot make love to her. He leaves shortly afterward, when Anna suggests that he should go.

The novel ends with Molly and Anna discussing Molly's upcoming wedding to a businessman who has a lot of money. Molly's fiancé is only mentioned in passing, and he is never named. Molly states that Tommy, her son, has taken over his father's business. Anna will no longer write, she says, and she has accepted a job counseling married women. The two women part with a kiss.

CHARACTERS

Paul Blackenhurst

Paul is one of the airmen who is stationed in Africa. He flies missions to Germany during World War II. When he is not flying, he spends his time with Anna and her group of friends.

Paul is very outspoken and taunts Mrs. Boothby, who manages the Mashopi Hotel. Paul also befriends Jackson, the African cook at the hotel. Paul tries to tell Jackson that he could declare his rights as a human being if he did not live in colonial Africa. Paul dies before the end of the war. He gets drunk one day and walks into the propellers of a plane.

June Boothby

June is the Boothby's teenaged daughter. When a young man appears one day, June becomes very enthralled by him. She disappears during the night and when she returns she announces that she is engaged. Anna and Maryrose remember their own adolescence and announce that they are glad they never have to revisit that period of their lives again.

Mr. Boothby

Mr. Boothby is the owner of the Mashopi Hotel and, despite his gruffness, he welcomes Anna and her group, fixing them late night dinners even after the kitchen has been closed. He is hard on his wife, which, Paul points out, is the way some women like to be treated.

Mrs. Boothby

Mrs. Boothby, along with her husband, runs the Mashopi Hotel in Africa. She is a bigoted woman who believes white people are more evolved than black people. Mrs. Boothby accommodates Anna and her friends, cooking them the British food that they miss, but she does not appreciate it when they try to liberate black Africans, particularly her own employee. Mrs. Boothby represents England, not only with the food she prepares, but with the attitudes that many British colonizers held towards black Africans.

Patricia Brent

Patricia is a fictional character from Anna's yellow notebook. She is an editor at the magazine where Ella works. Patricia is not married and has affairs with married men, like Ella (and Anna).

Ella

A character in Anna's yellow notebook, Ella is Anna's alter ego. Although she changes the names of the characters in Ella's life, it is clear that Ella, a single mother who has an affair with a doctor, as well as several other men, is meant to represent Anna. Indeed, Anna uses Ella to reflect on and interpret her own life experiences.

Maryrose Fowler

Maryrose is mostly described in terms relating to her feminine charms. She is beautiful, demure, and sexually attractive. She is the only other female in Anna's group of friends in Africa. Maryrose often does not make comments when the others discuss Communism, but when she does, she helps to sort out the confused communications between the rest of the group. Most of the men want to go to bed with her. However, Maryrose is still consumed by a love affair she had with her brother, who later died.

Saul Green

By the time Saul Green enters the story, Anna has lost most of her connection to the real world, so it is not clear if Saul is real or if he is an imaginary reflection of Anna's thoughts. Saul meets Anna when he comes to her home to rent a room. He is a very confused and sick young man. Despite this, Anna goes to bed with him. They have a very troubling relationship, and they always communicate through anger. Saul only likes women who do not like or need him. Saul is the worst example of every man that Anna has ever had an affair with, and he encourages Anna's slide into madness. Anna finally tells Saul she is not strong enough to tell him to leave, but that he must do so. Anna feels it is the only way that each can begin to recover any semblance of mental health. Ironically, it is Saul who helps Anna start writing another novel.

George Hounslow

George meets with Anna and her friends at the Mashopi Hotel in Africa. One night he confesses he has been having an affair with Marie, Jackson's wife. He suspects that Marie has given birth to his son. He worries about the boy and what his own responsibilities are to his illegitimate son. The relationship between George and Marie (George is white and Marie is black) inspires Anna's bestselling novel.

Jackson

Jackson, who is married to Marie, is the African cook at the Mashopi Hotel. He has worked at the hotel for over fifteen years. Jackson listens to Paul's stories about life in England (where blacks are not as oppressed as they are in Africa). When Mrs. Boothby fires Jackson for his association with Paul, Jackson asks for his job back. Later he is seen walking away from the hotel with his family.

Molly Jacobs

Molly Jacobs is Anna's best friend. She is similar to Anna in that she is a single mother who considers herself a free woman. Molly believes that Anna is a true artist and scolds Anna for wasting her talents. Molly is an actress, but not a very successful or talented one.

Molly has a son, Tommy, from her marriage to Richard. At one time, Molly and Richard had common interests; now, Molly abhors most of what Richard stands for. He has a conservative political outlook, and he is only concerned with maintaining his high social status and extreme wealth. Molly has many love affairs, though the novel does not provide details. Although she shares many characteristics with Anna, the two women are also quite different. Molly is described as a woman who appears "boyish." She is a woman who "took pleasure in the various guises she could use." Anna, on the other hand, is soft and more feminine and prides herself on always looking the same.

Molly is more committed to the cause of socialism (a social theory proposing that land and businesses should not be privately owned but instead managed by a central public government) and women's rights than Anna, and she sticks with the Communist Party longer than Anna does. By the end of the novel, however, Molly announces she is going to marry a successful businessman. Anna shows surprise at this, but the story ends with Molly and Anna still friends.

Jean

Jean is Richard's secretary, with whom Richard has a long affair while married to Marion, his second wife. At the end of the novel, Richard marries Jean.

Julia

Julia is a fictional character in Anna's yellow notebook. Although the similarity is never noted explicitly, Julia is very much like Molly. Julia is Jewish, an actress, and is Ella's roommate. Molly is also an actress.

Cy Maitland

Cy is a character from Anna's yellow notebook. He is an American doctor whom Ella meets on her trip back to London from Paris. Ella has dinner with Cy and then sleeps with him. Cy is a married man whose wife no longer wants to have sex with him. He loves the way Ella makes love to him. With Cy, Ella feels in control because she has no romantic feelings for him. The affair is a one-time encounter.

Marie

Marie, Jackson's wife, has a long affair with George Hounslow and gives birth to a son, whom George believes is his. Marie appears only briefly in *The Golden Notebook*, but it is her story, that of a black African woman having an affair with a white English man, that inspires Anna's novel.

Mrs. Marks

Mrs. Marks, occasionally referred to by Anna as Mother Sugar, is a psychologist who treats Anna. Mrs. Marks has also been Molly's psychologist at times. Mrs. Marks helps Anna work through her inability to write. Even after her therapy sessions with Mrs. Marks end, Anna often thinks about what Mrs. Marks might say to her, depending on the circumstances that Anna finds herself in. Mrs. Marks helps Anna by pointing out the various types of mythological archetypes, such as those examined by the famed psychiatrist Carl Jung, particularly Jung's archetype of motherhood, which might make Anna feel like she has to mother not only her child but also the men in her life.

Tom Mathlong

Tom is an African rebel fighting for his country's freedom from Colonial powers. Tom's country is unnamed in the book, but much of Africa was colonized and ruled by Britain at the time. Once, when he visits Anna, he is amazed at how progressive and settled London is, and he realizes that it will take his country a long time to achieve this status.

Max

See Willi Rodde

Jimmy McGrath

Jimmy is a member of Anna's group of friends in Africa. He is in the British air corps and flies bomber missions to Germany during the war. He is terribly afraid of many things, but his colleagues say that as soon as Jimmy gets into the airplane, he is a great pilot. Jimmy shows up later in the novel to tell Anna a story about a British teacher, Harry Mathews, a man obsessed with the Russian Communist Party.

Michael

Michael is Anna's long-time lover. Michael is a psychiatrist, and is referred to in the novel as a doctor who works in mental health. Their affair lasts five years, and Anna claims that Michael is the only man she has ever loved. Michael is jealous of Anna's daughter, her writing, and other men (basically anything outside of himself that commands Anna's attention). Michael subsequently ends the affair. Michael becomes a sort of archetypal male for Anna, as she compares her feelings toward all men to the feelings she once had for Michael.

Milt

Milt is the last man in the novel to begin a relationship with Anna. He appears much as Saul had, and it is hard to figure out if Milt and Saul are actually the same person. Both men come to Anna to rent a room after Molly has referred them to her. Milt even says things that Saul has said to Anna. However, where Saul was weak, dragging Anna deeper into her madness, Milt is strong. Milt helps Anna get back to being normal. He tears down all of the newspaper clippings on Anna's walls and gets her to write again.

Mother Sugar
See Mrs. Marks

Nelson

Nelson is an American who moves to England because he is a Communist who has been blacklisted and cannot find work in the States. Nelson has a brief affair with Anna, and he tells her that he is afraid of being sexually or emotionally intimate with women. Nelson invites Anna to a party that he and his wife are giving, where he announces in the heat of an argument with his wife that he wants to go to bed with Anna. For a while afterward, Anna states that she does not want any men in her life because she no longer wants to be hurt by them.

Marion Portmain

Marion is Richard's second wife. She is bored, unfulfilled, unloved, and an alcoholic. She lives virtually without her husband, who works all day and carries on extra-marital affairs most nights.

Marion stops drinking after Tommy has blinded himself. Marion starts to better comprehend her husband's lack of love for her or for any woman. This makes Marion stronger. In the end, Marion becomes more independent, opening up a small dress shop.

Richard Portmain

Richard is Molly's ex-husband, and he is from a well-to-do family. Richard and Molly married young, at a time when Richard was rebelling against his background and leaning toward supporting the socialist movement. However, when Richard's family threatens to cut him off from any further funds, Richard renounces his political beliefs and goes on to develop a multinational corporation, becoming one of the most powerful men in England.

Richard is married to Marion, an alcoholic. He is a womanizer, seeking sexual satisfaction from women, but unable (or unwilling) to express affection. He represents most of the men with whom Anna and Molly have affairs. Richard also represents British society, particularly the British upper class. He mocks Molly and Anna for their artistic and bohemian lives, that of women who neither care about wealth nor status. Because of his entrenched views of Anna and Molly, Richard often does not hear what either tells him; or, he simply does not believe what they say. He also has trouble talking to his son, Tommy. By the end of the story, Richard has barely changed. His wife has divorced him, and Richard has remarried, but it is suggested that he is now cheating on his new wife.

Tommy Portmain

Tommy is the son of Molly and Richard. He is about twenty years old. He seems unable to reconcile himself with the adult role models with which he has been provided. His mother and father are drastically different, and Tommy does not fully identify with either of them.

Tommy shoots himself, and though he does not die, the wound causes him to go blind. In his blinded state, Tommy finally sees who he is. He takes a greater interest in the people around him, especially in his father's second wife, Marion. Molly and Anna believe Tommy is using his blindness to manipulate the people around him. Finally, Anna is able to reason with Tommy, and he becomes more sensitive to the needs of the people in his life. By the end of the story, Tommy accepts a position in his father's corporation, hoping that he can use his new power to help create a better world. Tommy, despite his attempted suicide, is one of the few characters who actually progresses emotionally in this story.

Willi Rodde

Willi (also referred to as Max) is the intellectual and leader of Anna's group of friends in Africa. He and Anna end up sharing a room together, though their friendship is almost completely platonic. He and Anna live together for three years. They get married only so their daughter will be considered legitimate. After Janet is born, Willi and Anna separate. Anna states that she and Willi never really liked one another.

Paul Tanner

Paul is a fictitious character in Anna's yellow notebook. He is a psychiatrist and one of Ella's main lovers. Paul represents Anna's real-life lover, Michael. Ella's love affair with Paul is a long and warm one, lasting five years. However, in the end, Paul, a married man, leaves for Nigeria and does not ask Ella to come along.

Anna Wulf

Anna is the protagonist of Lessing's novel. She is a writer and her close friend is Molly. Anna is a single mother, who was married to Willi. Now she lives with her daughter, Janet. Throughout the novel, Anna explores what it means to be a free woman—to think for herself, and to be sexually liberated from social norms. As the story develops, however, Anna begins to question her freedom. Just how free is she if she is almost constantly saddened by the many roles that she plays as a mother and as a mistress.

Anna questions many things in her life, including her belief in the Communist Party. She also questions her ability as a writer. The last portion of the novel follows Anna as these questions become so powerful that she can no longer define her world or reality. She loses contact with the people around her as well as with language, the tool she has used all her life to frame her reality. Toward the end of the novel, Anna believes she is going mad. She places herself in situations that hurt her, unable to avoid them because she does not have the mental strength to turn away from them. She is tormented by men who do not love her, by guilt that she is not a good role model for her daughter or for Molly's

son, and by menacing and terrifying nightmares. At the depth of her madness, Anna becomes alienated from everything around her, including her own body and all its physical senses. By the end, however, it is her writing and her role as a mother that bring her back to sanity.

Throughout the story, Anna stays true to her definition of the Free Woman; she does not need to be married or supported by a man. Anna is a woman who has come to understand who she is, and she is willing to face the challenges that confront her as a single mother and as a free thinker. Most importantly, Anna does not derive her identity from social conventions.

Janet Wulf

Janet is Anna's daughter. She lives with Anna but later asks to go to boarding school. Anna describes her daughter as intelligent but ordinary. Anna concludes that Janet does not want anything to do with her mother or her mother's lifestyle. On the other hand, Janet, and Anna's perception of herself as a mother, help to keep Anna sane.

THEMES

Cracks, or Mental and Emotional Breakdown

Lessing indicates in her 1971 introduction to her novel that the major theme of *The Golden Notebook* is that of cracks or mental breakdown. To emphasize the significance of this theme, in the opening page of the novel, one of the first statements made by Anna is: "everything's cracking up."

In the first section of the novel, the most obvious examples of breakdown begin with Tommy, Molly's son, a young adult who is struggling to define himself. He has been heavily influenced by his mother's and Anna's socialist beliefs, but he does not want to be like them. Neither does he want to be like his father, Richard, a business tycoon whose philosophies of capitalism are directly opposed to Molly's. Tommy becomes more and more disturbed as he attempts to pull away from his mother's and his father's influences. Later, Tommy shoots himself in the head.

Anna, the protagonist, has a more fully explored mental breakdown in this story. She specifically mentions to her psychiatrist, Mrs. Marks,

TOPICS FOR FURTHER STUDY

- One of the major driving forces in Anna's life is her creativity. She lives for it and is challenged by it. But what, exactly, is creativity? How do leading psychologists and philosophers define creativity? How are these theories the same? How are they different? How have they changed over time? Write an essay on your findings.

- How do men and women differ in their definitions of a good relationship? Interview at least twenty-five male students and twenty-five female students. Have a list of questions ready and record their answers. Examples of questions might include how important is monogamy in an intimate relationship? How important is sex? How significant are good looks? Create more questions that require value rated answers (rating the importance from a scale of one to ten), then create a chart of the results and share your findings with your class.

- Create a display that attempts to portray a typical woman during the 1950s. What did women wear then? How educated were they? How many children did they have on average, and how old were they when they had their first child? Find at least twenty different characteristics or statistics and accompany them with illustrations, if possible.

- Define socialism, and then compare a country currently governed by the socialist system to the capitalist democracy of the United States. What are the benefits of each system? What, if any, are the negative effects of each? Write an essay discussing which system you prefer and why.

the cracks she feels developing inside of her. When Anna tells Mrs. Marks about these cracks, she speaks of them in a positive light. Indeed, she tells the doctor that she feels she is about to become a new type of woman, one who is emerging through the cracks. However, in her notebooks, Anna does not view the process of cracking, or breaking down, with such a positive attitude. Anna says she is afraid that she is slipping deeper and deeper into madness. The process of breaking down is filled with terror and disgust as Anna loses not only a sense of self (as Tommy did) but also her connection with reality. Although Anna goes mad, Lessing indicates that this is part of Anna's attempts to bring her writing closer to the truth. The novel's emphasis is on Anna's writer's block and on the 'cracks' that she must undergo in order to recover her creativity.

Cracks are also exposed though politics. For instance, members of the Communist Party become disillusioned by the movement's failings and its use of violence. In the United States, people who are accused of being Communists lose their jobs and their reputations are irrevocably damaged. The Cold War between the United States and Russia also represents a breakdown, though one of trust and communication.

The breakdown of marriage and of the general relationship between men and women is also discussed in this story. Men, Lessing implies, need mothering and physical satisfaction, whereas women need emotional fulfillment. When a woman becomes too dependent on a man to fulfill her emotional needs, the man loses interest. There are many male characters in this novel who are incapable of being intimate with women, and there are many more who are incapable of being faithful. In these cases, the cracks in the relationships between men and women become more like chasms.

Anna also mentions the cracks that she feels developing among the various roles that women must play, such as the gaps between the role of mother and the role of lover, or the role of wife and the role of mistress. There are also cracks between free women and wives. Free women are supposedly not tied down by the norms with which society attempts to define women. Free women can have sex and as many relationships with men as they please. However, Anna realizes that she is often jealous of married women, who have more security than she does. At one point, Anna also confesses that she, in many ways, is no different than a married woman, as she is just as emotionally dependent on her lovers as wives are on their husbands. Thus, there are also cracks in what Anna and Molly believe to be their definition of freedom.

Writer's Block

Anna suffers from writer's block throughout the novel—she is unable to either begin or to continue writing a story. Anna's struggle to overcome her writer's block is, in many ways, the theme that ties *The Golden Notebook* together. One of the causes of Anna's inability to write is her desire to write only what is objectively true. She tries several different ways to capture the truth, stripped of sentimentality, as she states. But the closer she gets to the truth, the more she realizes that words can never fully express what someone feels or what someone has experienced. This realization is what pushes her deeper and deeper into madness.

Emotional Intimacy

The need to achieve emotional intimacy is another theme that is incorporated in this story. Anna struggles with her need to be loved by a man even as she continues to consider herself a free woman. She can have sex with a man, she discovers, but is not fulfilled in any way if there is no emotional intimacy between herself and her partner (the same is true for Molly). Anna also discovers that most men in her life, many of whom are married, leave her when she begins to depend on them to fulfill her emotional needs. Married women, according to this story, fare no better, as their husbands have affairs and leave them at home to take care of the household and the children. Furthermore, several of the men in this story state that they have a fear of being emotionally intimate. Very few characters in the novel are able to fulfill their emotional needs. Tommy might come closest, as he finds a way to work for the betterment of mankind. Molly, who decides to marry at the end of the story, sounds as if she may have found a path to security, but not necessarily a means towards achieving love. At the end of the book, Anna continues along the same path that she has followed throughout the story. She remains a free woman, detached from the men who do little more than use her.

STYLE

Journal Writing

Most of Lessing's novel is written as Anna Wulf's journals. This technique helps to draw readers into the story because Anna's character is much more exposed than it would be if the novel were written in the third person. Readers might also feel like they have come across something very private and secretive and that they are being privileged with Anna's innermost thoughts. By presenting the novel as a series of journals, Lessing is able to forego the traditional form of the novel in terms of plot development and chronology, concentrating instead on the internal changes in Anna's character. Although the fictitious journals provide more depth of character, they do cause some problems or challenges. There are portions of the writing that are repetitive or out of synch with previous entries. However, Lessing uses the journals as an opportunity to categorize Anna's thoughts, as the four differently-colored notebooks focus on specific topics or areas of Anna's life. The notebooks remain neatly separated, and readers become familiar with the repeated pattern in which they appear. Lessing also uses the different notebooks to emphasize the divisions in Anna's life. Then, as Anna's personality begins to break down, the boundaries between the notebooks begin to fade. In this way, the journals are used to further symbolize and reinforce Anna's descent into madness.

Unreliable Narrator

An unreliable narrator is just that—a narrator that cannot be trusted. In Lessing's novel, it is not clear if the narrator is telling the truth. First of all, Anna warns her readers that she is in search of the truth through her writing. Then she begins to explain the problems of finding that truth. When she attempts to record memories, she admits that her memories may have faded and she is making up details that are not necessarily correct or true. She also confesses that her memories are colored by her emotions, both the emotions she had during the actual experience as well as the emotions that have developed over time as she looks back at the experience.

In addition to this, Anna develops fictitious characters within her journals. This is a bit confusing because journals normally record what has actually happened or thoughts about what has actually happened. The characters Anna creates are supposed to represent Anna and her relationships with other people, so why doesn't Anna simply record these things as they are? Essentially, Anna has more liberty to recreate the truth by presenting it as fiction, and this adds to the feeling that Anna is not a reliable narrator.

COMPARE
&
CONTRAST

- **1950s:** The media in both the United States and Europe encourage women to stay home and have children. Television shows such as *Father Knows Best* and *The Adventures of Ozzie and Harriet* portray happy homes with a wife/mother figure who stays home to cook, clean, and care for the children.

  Today: Many women juggle a full-time career while simultaneously acting as the primary caregiver for their children. Being a full-time homemaker has become a luxury because families can no longer support a middle-class lifestyle on one income. In some families, the father may take on the role of homemaker while the mother supports the family with her career and income. This is still relatively rare, however.

- **1950s:** The communist Soviet Union under Stalin's brutal regime becomes an emerging world power.

Today: After the Soviet Union breaks apart (becoming Russia and fourteen other countries), Communist rule deteriorates as a free market economy and democratic government are attempted. Russia's world influence has also lessened considerably.

- **1950s:** The United Kingdom ruled the world's largest empire at one time, but suffered heavy economic losses stemming from World War II. As a result, many colonized countries are successful in their bids toward independence during the period just after the War.

Today: The United States (a former British colony) acquires Britain's political and military support for the war in Iraq. People in Britain criticize their government for acting as a puppet government to the U.S. administration, further emphasizing the loss of political power that Britain has sustained over time.

Once Anna begins to lose her sanity, her reliability can be questioned even further. If she is not experiencing reality as most people would, how can she record incidents that can be accepted as truthful? Adding to this confusion are the hazy outlines of the different people Anna writes about. Anna uses different names for Willi, her ex-husband. It is also unclear how closely the fictional Paul Tanner resembles Michael, Anna's lover. Details in the story also appear out of focus at times. Did Tommy run away with Marion, or did he marry a different woman that he had been dating (a girl that Tommy's mother has briefly mentioned in a conversation with Anna)? Milt and Saul, Anna's lovers, are interchangeable. Sometimes, Anna even records events in her journal before they actually happen.

It is possible that the journals are meant to create a sense of truthfulness or reliability, but

the novel's vague details offset this effect. Perhaps this too is purposeful: Lessing proves the point that, though an author might attempt to reach the truth, the feat itself is impossible.

HISTORICAL CONTEXT

Communism in Russia
According to Karl Marx (1818–1883) and Friedrich Engels (1820–1895), creators of the *Communist Manifesto of 1848*, capitalism would, with time, give way to communism. These two German intellectuals proclaimed that through their study of history they could predict a new social order in which the proletarians (labor force) would overtake the bourgeois (the moneyed classes). The organization of the proletarians would give them the power to do this and would lead to socialism—a system of social organization

in which producing and distributing goods would be controlled collectively or by a centralized government. Communism, then, would be a more evolved form of socialism in which a single party holds power and distributes goods to be shared equally by all citizens.

Vladimir Lenin (1870–1924), the first leader of the Communist government in Russia, was greatly influenced by the writings of Karl Marx and spent most of his early adult years working toward the unionization of Russia's working class. Lenin then worked to overthrow the Russian Tsar. In 1903, Lenin formed the political group known as the Bolsheviks and spent many years in exile, writing powerful pamphlets, urging the workers of Russia to revolt and urging peasants to claim the land. Lenin proclaimed that Russia should be ruled by soviets, a government controlled by small groups of workers. In 1917, after a successful revolt, Lenin was elected chairman of the Council of People's Commissars. According to the Communist theories, only one party could be in power at a time. To achieve and maintain this, a special group of secret police was formed. Their job was to find any political dissenters, who were then imprisoned and/or tortured. Many dissenters were also killed. This was necessary, according to Lenin, to ensure that Communism would be successful.

The fight to control Russia was a bloody one, both before and after Lenin came to power. There were wars as well as economic failures. There was also a famine in which millions of people died. Nevertheless, Lenin created the first communist government, and in 1922, the Union of Soviet Socialist Republics (USSR) was formed. Two years later, Lenin suffered several strokes and died. It is likely that the strokes that killed him stemmed from an attempted assassination in 1918 that left a bullet lodged in Lenin's neck.

Although Lenin had been very critical of him, Joseph Stalin maneuvered his way into power, succeeding Lenin as the authoritarian leader of the Soviet Union. Stalin successfully industrialized the country and made it a world power, but he did so at the cost of millions of lives. He ordered the deaths of any person suspected of disagreeing with him. Under Stalin, the basic tenets of Marxism were ignored. Instead, Stalin used terror to control the citizenry. Stalin died in 1953. Three years later, Nikita Krushchev, who succeeded Stalin, denounced his predecessor for having reigned through terror, lies, and self-glorification.

Throughout most of Lessing's novel, the main characters, Anna and Molly, struggle with their belief in communism. At its center, communism was a good idea. Unfortunately, much violence was enacted in the name of communism. This is the conundrum that Anna and Molly struggle with.

British Colonialism in Africa

At one time, the British government was one of the strongest nations in the world, controlling an empire that covered almost one fourth of the earth's land area and population. British Colonialism in Africa reached its peak in the nineteenth and early twentieth centuries. During this time, Britain controlled the Suez Canal, Nigeria, and what was called British East Africa (now Kenya, Uganda, Tanganyika, and Zanzibar). Britain also controlled South Africa, parts of Togo, and what was called German Southwest Africa (now Namibia).

As the twentieth century dawned, the fight for independence in Africa began with South Africa, which achieved self-rule in 1910. Other African nations in the east, central, and southern parts of the country were slower to gain their independence, but by the 1950s and 1960s, Britain's control over Africa was greatly diminished. Kenya gained independence in 1963. Somalia, Uganda, Tanzania, Malawi, Zambia, Botswana, Lesotho, and Swaziland had all gained independence by 1968. In West Africa, Ghana, Nigeria, Sierra Leone, and Gambia all gained independence in the late 1950s and into the 1960s.

Carl Jung (1875–1961)

Carl Jung, famed Swiss psychiatrist, based much of his psychological analysis on his concept of archetypes, idealized models that people hold in their psyche and that are often experienced in dreams. Jung believed that people's situations in life were mirrored in their dreams. He studied world mythologies and noted similar symbols in every culture, and this led him to believe that while people have a personal unconscious, all of humanity also shares what Jung called a collective unconscious. One of his better known books is *Man and His Symbols*, published posthumously in 1964. Jung's teachings influence Lessing's characters, as both Anna and Molly

9 2

Novels for Students, Volume 27

attend sessions with Mrs. Marks, a doctor who applies Jung's theory of archetypes to help the women better understand themselves.

Feminism in the 1950s

Feminism in the 1950s was stimulated in part by the end of World War II and the return of soldiers to the labor market. As veterans returned from the war, women were forced out of the jobs they had held while the soldiers were at war. Many women had grown used to the independence that their jobs had provided, and they began to demand equality in the workforce.

Even as the economy improved in Britain and in the United States after the war, women were largely unable to find jobs due to a lack of childcare programs and widespread discrimination. When women did hold jobs, they were paid far less than their male counterparts. The media (i.e., newspapers, women's magazines, and television) promoted the virtues of women as housewives. One popular book, published in 1947, titled *Modern Women: The Lost Sex*, written by Marynia Farnham and Ferdinand Lundberg, claimed that in order to stay in good health, women must raise children and take care of the household.

However, as divorce and better birth control became more accessible, women began claiming their rights to end poor marriages and to have fewer children, or even to not marry at all. Adding inspiration to the feminist movement was another book, this one encouraging women to claim their rights as equals to men. Indeed, Simone de Beauvoir's *The Second Sex* (1949) emphasized just how much women were oppressed. Lessing's *The Golden Notebook* was also very influential at this time, and it is often studied as a Feminist text because the main characters are women who rebel against social norms. Women in the 1950s were supposed to stay home and raise their children. Working women, single mothers, or sexually free women were often ostracized because they did not fit into socially accepted roles.

CRITICAL OVERVIEW

The Golden Notebook has often been cited as the Lessing's best work. It has been praised for its fascinating and experimental form and for its subject matter. Indeed, Lessing wrote on topics that were very controversial for her time, and her style of writing was well ahead of that of most of her peers.

Lessing's novel was initially praised by reviewers, and positive critical opinions of the book have actually grown over the years. In a 1962 review for the *New York Times*, Ernest Buckler writes, "one can only salute and marvel at the staggering fecundity of ideas and insight that turns almost every remaining paragraph into a hive of constellated meaning." Although Buckler comments that some of Lessing's discussions about politics are not fully developed, and that her exposition of her characters' emotions are, at times, overdrawn, he concludes that in comparison with other highly praised novels of the time, *The Golden Notebook* stands out significantly because of Lessing's powerful writing.

In another *New York Times* article, written ten years later, Richard Locke states "that of all the postwar English novelists Doris Lessing is the foremost creative descendant of the 'great tradition' which includes George Eliot, Conrad, and D. H. Lawrence." Although he praises Lessing, Locke admits that *The Golden Notebook* has some faults. Lessing can "write too casually," at times; can produce writing that sounds like it is inspired by a "preacher's fervor"; and she is sometimes repetitive. However, Locke also finds the novel to be intelligent but unpretentious, and Lessing shows great "courage to stick to her perceptions and tell home truths." Locke notes that Lessing's writing is "dense with intelligence," and that her stories provide "new information about our inner lives and social evasions."

Sandra Brown, writing in *Approaches to Teaching Lessing's The Golden Notebook*, states that "the novel can vex readers" who are looking for a traditional story, but that the form of the novel "is far from a 'jumble.'" This is due to Lessing's "individualizing each of Anna's voices," through which the author "defines the whole: the woman and the modern world." In *Doris Lessing: Critical Studies*, John L. Carey also addresses the form of Lessing's novel. Carey writes: "Without its structural plan *The Golden Notebook* could not make the comment on life Lessing desires; without the content the structure would be grandiose and bare, complicated rather than complex."

WHAT DO I READ NEXT?

- In Lessing's *The Golden Notebook* there are long sections devoted to a fictional novel that the protagonist wrote, and the plot described there is actually the plot in Lessing's first novel, *The Grass is Singing* (1950). The novel takes place in Rhodesia (now Zimbabwe) and particularly focuses on the racial tensions between white colonizers and local Africans.

- Lessing has written a two-volume autobiography. The first volume, called *Under My Skin*, was published in 1994 and chronicles the author's life up until the 1950s. The second volume, *Walking in the Shade*, was published in 1997 and deals with a period of time stretching from the 1950s until 1962, the year *The Golden Notebook* was first published.

- Just as Lessing's novel explores women's relationships with men, Lynn Freed does the same in her 2004 collection of stories *Curse of the Appropriate Man*. From widows to young teens experimenting with sex, Freed's stories explore women's emotions and experiences as they search for love.

- Paul Theroux provides another take on the inner life of a writer in his 2005 novel *Blinding Light*. Theroux's protagonist, Slade Steadman, is a blocked writer who travels to the Ecuadorian jungles in search of a drug that reportedly frees the mind. Steadman finds the drug, which proves to be quite effective in unlocking his creativity, but it also causes him to go blind.

CRITICISM

Joyce Hart

Hart has degrees in English and creative writing and is a freelance writer and published author. In the following essay, she examines the male characters in The Golden Notebook.

> RICHARD, MARION, ANNA, AND MOLLY ARE ALL DEEPLY AFFECTED BY TOMMY, WHO IS THE ONLY MALE CHARACTER THAT TRULY EVOLVES OVER THE COURSE OF THE NOVEL."

In *The Golden Notebook* Lessing examines the role of the 1950s woman and, in doing so, stimulates feminist thoughts and ideas. Lessing does this partially by presenting her characters, her so-called *Free Women*—Anna and Molly—in an endless series of unfulfilling relationships with men. Lessing defines these women and their needs by demonstrating their interactions with men. But what of the men portrayed in the novel?

Richard, Molly's ex-husband, is the first significant male character to appear in the story. Richard is a flat character in that little can be said about him aside from his being a multi-millionaire and the head of an international corporation. Indeed, Richard is one of the more financially powerful men in England. Richard represents everything that Molly and Anna disagree with. He is a stock character, the stereotype of a capitalist patriarch and womanizer. Richard may be rich and powerful in the world of economics, but he does not know how to communicate with people, especially his second wife, Marion, and his son Tommy. In the novel, Marion does a good job of summing up Richard's personal faults. She realizes that Richard sees people as types, not as individual human beings, and that he defines those around him based on their sex, financial status, and other similarly shallow categories. Marion recognizes this when she first sees Jean, Richard's most recent lover. Jean, Marion notices, looks just like her, only twenty years younger. In effect, Richard has traded in Marion for a newer version, just as one might do with a car. Richard's relationship with Tommy fares a little better, but not without the help of Anna and Molly. It is not clear if Richard offers his son a job to help Tommy, or, more likely, to help himself. Furthermore, Richard views Tommy's arrest for political protest as a deliberate attempt on Tommy's part to embarrass his father. Thus, readers might wonder if Richard has offered Tommy a job in order to avert further embarrassment brought on by Tommy's depression and lack of ambition. Tommy's judgment of his father fairly sums up Richard when he declares that his father is completely defined by his job. In these ways Richard represents a conventional class- and money-conscious man who uses women as little more than stylish accessories.

Michael, whom Anna fictionalizes as Paul in her yellow notebook, is somewhat more evolved than Richard. He makes love to Anna rather than just having sex with her. He is tender and listens to what she has to say. However, Michael is married. As a result, his relationship with Anna will never develop into more than it already is: an illicit affair. Still, the affair is, according to Anna, the most loving affair she has ever had. On the other hand, Michael is also a jealous man (and perhaps this jealousy stems from his aforementioned affection). He is particularly jealous of Anna's writing career and of her child. These two areas encompass two of Anna's main roles (writer and mother). Basically, Michael is uncomfortable with the fact that Anna's sense of self is not wholly derived from her role as his lover. Michael needs to dominate Anna; her independence makes him feel insecure. Indeed, Michael has placed a price tag on the affection he shows her, demanding that she focus mainly on him. Meanwhile, Michael actively pursues his profession, has a wife and children, and he comes into and goes from Anna's life whenever he wants, all regardless of what Anna or his wife may need. Michael also takes this fundamental imbalance in his relationships as a given. Therefore, although Michael is not quite as conventional as Richard, his views of women are still dominated by the widely held societal belief that women are second-class citizens. Michael unquestioningly believes that men and women have different rights, as readers can surmise through his actions.

Cy Maitland, the American doctor with whom Anna has a one-night stand, chose his wife only for her good looks. Anna, in turn, only sees Cy as a sexual object. If she were a man, she comments, she probably would be a lot like Cy. There is a physical attraction between Cy and Anna, but they do not share any emotional intimacy. Cy tells Anna that she is easy, which, believe it or not, is his way of complementing her. In other words, Cy indicates that Anna does not have any emotional baggage. This is not really

an accurate perception of Anna. However, Cy reacts this way because Anna can remain detached from him and thus remains in control of her emotions when she is with him. Notably, Cy is gentle and appears understanding when he is with Anna or with his wife. His wife does not want sex, and Cy seems to accept this without pressuring her. Still, Cy is not an emotionally developed character. His real passion, if he has any at all, is his profession. He is not a misogynist (a person who hates women) or a womanizer. But his relationships with women are exceedingly shallow.

Anna's relationships with men begin to take a downward turn towards the end of the novel. Nelson, one of Anna's many lovers, shows real interest in Anna's writing and in her life. He even demonstrates real tenderness for Anna's daughter. Anna describes Nelson as a mature man until she goes to bed with him. Nelson is afraid of sexual intimacy. He rushes through the sex act and quickly dresses. Later, at a party, Nelson lashes out at his wife and purposefully hurts her by telling everyone that he wants to go to bed with Anna. Nelson is a torn man. He is attracted to women but is afraid that they will hurt him. So he hurts them first. Initially, he is gentle and even humorous, a great companion, but this changes as soon as he has had sex with his lovers. Nelson is clearly psychologically ill, and he is not the only man whom Anna encounters with these neuroses.

Saul is also afraid of intimacy with a woman. But he is even worse than Nelson. Saul's anger at the world is all encompassing and eventually affects Anna. The only way Saul and Anna can communicate with one another is through anger. Anna's unstable state of mind at the time further compounds the negative effects of her unhealthy relationship with Saul. When Anna can no longer define herself, she takes on Saul's identity. Saul has only two redeemable traits. He listens to Anna when she tells him that he must leave (and he leaves), and he has enough insight to understand that the only thing that will save Anna is her writing, which he encourages her to do. Regardless, Saul is everything that Anna does not want in a man.

Tommy is yet another important male figure in the novel. Tommy is almost always a background character. He appears throughout the story, yet he is rarely an active participant in the storyline. Much that he does or says is often related through other characters. Tommy's actions, however, affect several people. Richard, Marion, Anna, and Molly are all deeply affected by Tommy, who is the only male character that truly evolves over the course of the novel. At first, Tommy is depressed because he has no role models he can relate to. Given the candidates he has to choose from, this is not surprising. His father is not an ideal role model, and neither are the other male characters in the novel. Even Anna and Molly are found to be lacking. Tommy's depression leads him to attempt suicide, and though he survives, he goes blind in the aftermath. On both a symbolic and practical level, Tommy's botched suicide is also a sort of rebirth. With the loss of his sight, Tommy develops a keen intuition. His intuition helps him to understand his mother and Anna, something he had struggled with previously. He also sees his father in a more positive light. In this new mode of seeing, Tommy learns from his parents what he wants to become, and he decides to use the power that he has inherited from his father (in the form of Richard's business) to change the world for the better. Significantly, the improvements that Tommy wishes to achieve are informed by the moral principles he has inherited from his mother. Tommy takes the only two good things that his parents have passed on to him and combines them in way that will cause growth and positive change. Thus, by the end of the novel, Tommy evolves more than his father, who remarries yet again and continues to chase after other women. Tommy also evolves more than his mother, who abandons her principles and marries a businessman. Of all the men in *The Golden Notebook*, Tommy is the only one who is able to emerge as a new man.

Source: Joyce Hart, Critical Essay on *The Golden Notebook*, in *Novels for Students*, Gale, Cengage Learning, 2008.

Lorelei Cederstrom

In the following excerpt, Cederstrom examines the material in the notebooks through which Anna enacts the psychological breakdown and subsequent recreation of a new self. This process is also viewed through the teachings of psychologist Carl Jung.

... Anna rigidly rejects all hints that she is not unique. Mrs. Marks is aware of what she is doing and tells her, "My dear Anna, you are

> AS THE COLLECTIVE UNCONSCIOUS BREAKS LOOSE, ANNA ENCOUNTERS SEVERAL ARCHETYPAL FIGURES WHICH REPRESENT ASPECTS OF HER PERSONALITY THAT SHE MUST RECONSIDER AND REINTEGRATE ON HER ROAD TO WHOLENESS."

using our experience together to re-enforce your own rationalizations for not writing."

Immediately after this abortive encounter, the old Anna begins to disintegrate. She attempts to re-solidify the divisions of the notebooks, but is forced to recognize the tenuous hold of her ego: "I remain Anna because of a certain kind of intelligence. This intelligence is dissolving and I am very frightened." Anna moves now into an encounter with the collective unconscious. All the chaotic elements kept firmly repressed by her compartmentalizing intelligence break loose, and she undergoes the flooding of unconscious contents into her conscious mind. Her ego, the controlling persona, is destroyed, and she is forced to create a new Anna, related to those women within about whom Mrs. Marks told her, an Anna who has achieved wholeness through individuation.

As the collective unconscious breaks loose, Anna encounters several archetypal figures which represent aspects of her personality that she must reconsider and reintegrate on her road to wholeness. The first of these appears in a recurring dream Anna has. The dream is of a threatening figure whom she sees as "pure spite, malice, joy in malice, joy in a destructive impulse." The image goes through several transformations in the course of the novel. It begins as an inhuman figure, a vase, then becomes a dwarf, then turns into Saul Green, and finally Anna sees her own face on this creature that mocks, jibes, hurts, wishes murder and death. Anna describes to Mrs. Marks the common denominators of this dream figure: "The element took a variety of shapes, usually that of a very old man or woman (yet there was a suggestion of double sex, or even sexlessness) and the figure was always very lively, in spite of having a wooden leg, or a crutch, or a hump, or being deformed in some way." Anna is terrified by this figure, but Mrs. Marks warns Anna that she must learn to dream this figure positively, for as a Jungian she would see him as a spirit goblin, a *kabeiros*, "an archetypal figure [like Rumpelstilt-skin] whose alluring 'help' brings ruin to woman, and threatens what is most precious to her but, precisely because she has recognized and named it, releases her from its power and leads her toward salvation" (Jacobi, 101). Jung frequently encountered spirit goblins like Anna's in the dreams of patients during individuation. He terms the positive aspect of this figure the Wise Old Man or Wise Old Woman, for it directs the dreamer, ultimately, toward the path he/she must follow. He notes, also, that the negative side of this figure is associated with malice and evil. Thus, before Anna can be saved from this monster of her unconscious, she has to recognize it as an element of her own personality and counter its negative aspects with a positive figure from within.

The internal archetype which Anna can summon to her aid in this cause is that of the Wise Old Woman, the Witch, an image of the strength of Mrs. Marks that she finds in herself. Anna's unconscious provides this knowledge in a dream in which both figures appear:

> I had the dream again—I was menaced by the anarchic principle, this time in the shape of an inhuman sort of dwarf. In the dream was Mrs. Marks, very large and powerful; like a kind of amiable witch. She heard the dream out, and said: "When you are on your own, and you are threatened, you must summon the good witch to your aid.' 'You,' I said, 'No, you, embodied in what you have made of me.' So the thing is over, then. It was as if she had said: Now you are on your own. For she spoke casually, indifferently almost, like someone turning away. I admired the skill of this; it was as if, on leave-taking, she were handing me something—a flowering branch, perhaps, or a talisman against evil."

A part of Anna's problem with the dwarf is that she has projected this frightening breakthrough of energies from the self onto the world at large. The clippings about war and violence that Anna has affixed to her Blue Notebook are another indication that she has externalized her own destructive qualities. "Projections," Jung has said, "change the world into the replica of one's own unknown face." It is only when Anna dreams of the dwarf wearing

her own face that she begins to dream positively. She is released from its power when she sees that that which she has feared is within and can be controlled by the strong "amiable witch" she also has within.

The second problem Anna confronts in her process of individuation, as outlined in this notebook, is the conflict between her need for freedom and the restrictions of motherhood. The situation between Anna and her daughter, Janet, is essentially a Uroboric—primordial, instinctual—one in which there is a strong identity of mother and daughter, ego and self. There is a great tendency for every woman to fall back into the archetypal instinctual role in which the demands of consciousness are secondary to the unconscious demands of the Great Mother.

... The conflict between motherhood and her own needs is vividly embodied in a few scenes in Anna's diary where she forces herself out of bed with her lover in order to get her daughter off to school. She resents having to leave her lover, yet she resents him for making her feel guilty about leaving his bed. This is so much a part of Anna that even when her daughter leaves her home for boarding school, Anna plays the Great Mother to several men in her life, most notably Saul Green. The combination of Saul's need for a mother and Janet's leaving home forces Anna to realize that she has put off her own development for too long: "I haven't moved, at ease, in time, since Janet was born. Having a child means being conscious of the clock, never being free of something that has to be done at a certain moment ahead. An Anna is coming to life that died when Janet was born."

In the individuation of the feminine psyche, the stage beyond the assimilation of the primordial Great Mother is the one already touched upon in the Red Notebook sections. The dominance of the Great Mother gives way to the Great Father, as the developing consciousness moves from the instinctual roles of motherhood to the roles of the dominant collective consciousness, in this case typified by the patriarchal attitudes Anna encounters working for the Communist Party. It is symbolic that Anna's last day at work for the Party is characterized by frequent trips to the bathroom to be sure that her co-workers remain unaware of her menstrual flow. Anna's instinctual feminine unconscious has no place here; however, the way to move beyond the instinctual feminine is not by moving into a purely masculine sphere where it is afforded no existence, but rather by establishing contact with the feminine self of which the instinct is only a part.

There is still one important element of the psyche with which Anna must come to terms. While she has rejected the masculine biases of the collective consciousness, she must come to terms with the man within, her animus, through Saul Green. Neumann notes that beyond the sphere of the Great Mother and Great Father, the individuating woman enters a stage of encounter in which the masculine and feminine confront each other individually. In Anna this phase has already moved beyond the individual encounter and entered the arena where the masculine spirit within her, her animus, battles for existence with her ego. Anna's animus, Saul Green, is so strong that he breaks down the hold of her ego completely: "I longed to be free of my own ordering, commenting memory," Anna writes. "I felt my sense of identity fade." Previously, Anna had rejected any implication that her sense of uniqueness was unhealthy. She refuted Mrs. Marks' statement that there were long lines of women stretching out behind her who shared her experiences. Where she once clung to her unique, ordering, frozen ego, she now pays the price for the repressions demanded by that ego. The flooding of her conscious mind with unconscious contents through the animus occasions an excursion into madness.

Anna learns, eventually, that breakdown can be positive, and she begins the painful process of reconstruction. Anna admits to Saul Green, for the first time, that she is suffering from a writer's block. While Saul, as animus, has aided in the destruction of Anna's ego, he has provided, at the same time, a constructive link with her creativity. Through Saul, Anna achieves an awareness of the integrated self. By forcing her to face her own destructive maternal qualities, he sets her free. In an act which symbolizes the creativity of the positive animus, Saul gives Anna the first line for her novel, a novel she writes as the "Free Women" sections of *The Golden Notebook*. As a symbol of her integration, Anna replaces the four notebooks with the single Golden Notebook which contains all the elements of her personality. The Anna of the Golden Notebook is feeling intensely and is no longer rigid. Her self is not yet stabilized, for she moves back and forth

between disintegration and assimilation several times. Eventually, though, the self emergies in the form of a "new, disinterested person" who is capable of controlling her dreams and ordering her unconscious into form. Her new self is based on the awareness of a small endurance, an inner strength equal to the greatest tasks. Anna begins to see her fictional Ella again and sees how valuable the creative imagination can be in the face of death, fear, and a sense of dissolution: "I was thinking that quite possibly these marvellous, generous things we walk side by side with in our imaginations could come in existence, simply because we need them, because we imagine them."

The novel ends with Anna's completed individuation. With the help of Mrs. Marks and rigorous exploration of her inner being, Anna has achieved integration. She has learned the lessons of her unconscious, has found strengths in the depths of her personality, and, most importantly, has learned to utilize her demons creatively. Lessing, like Jung, believes that cures for world-wide disintegration will come only from integrated individuals. With this novel, Lessing has shown the way the writer can do more than reflect the chaotic consciousness of his age. Disintegration can be turned against itself; it can be used to probe the depths of the unconscious to the point where a truer sense of wholeness can be discovered. "Individual consciousness," Jung wrote, "is only the flower and the fruit of a season, sprung from the perennial rhizome beneath the earth." With this novel, Lessing has begun to explore these roots in earnest.

Source: Lorelei Cederstrom, "The Process of Individuation: Disintegration and Reintegration in *The Golden Notebook*," in *Fine-Tuning the Feminine Psyche: Jungian Patterns in the Novels of Doris Lessing*, Peter Lang Publishing, 1990, pp. 117–34.

Betsy Draine

In the following excerpt, Draine defines postmodernist fiction and classifies The Golden Notebook *as a postmodern novel. Draine next explains this classification by reviewing the patterns and themes that appear in each section of the story.*

... In postmodern fiction, form is forced to acknowledge and accommodate the force of chaos, the source and destroyer of all form. Thus it is a kind of fiction ideally suited to express the simultaneous destruction and reconstruction that occurs within the psyche in times

> THE POSTMODERN WRITER REALIZES THAT IN ALL REALMS OF LIFE CHAOS AND ORDER ARE CONSTANTLY IMPINGING ON ONE ANOTHER IN A PROCESS OF CONTINUAL TRANSFORMATION."

of personal and social metamorphosis. The postmodern writer realizes that in all realms of life chaos and order are constantly impinging on one another in a process of continual transformation. It becomes the novelist's task to provide a fictional form that can give ample scope to this dynamic interplay of order and chaos.

In *The Golden Notebook*, Lessing succeeds in creating such a form. In her new identity as a postmodern writer, she refuses to put a lid on chaos; neither does she let chaos freely reign. Instead she shapes the novel so that its structure and story express the powerful tension between chaos and order—a tension that characterizes the postmodern consciousness.

The reader's first impression is one of dissonance. The complicated, highly ordered superstructure of the novel is clearly at odds with the apparent disorder of the content within that structure. This form-content split in the novel in turn mirrors the heroine's awareness of the split between the forms (social, artistic, emotional, intellectual) of her own consciousness and the experiential chaos that these forms attempt to control. It is important to realize, however, that this pair of parallel contrasts, so immediately apparent to the reader, is actually an over-simplification. There is more to the content of Anna's notebooks than mere chaos, if what we mean by chaos is utter formlessness. Rather, the various notebooks contain material that has been liberated from outworn forms and that holds its state of formlessness only as potentiality, beginning quickly to move toward new and provisional form, toward the constitution of a new cosmos. Thus there is no final *opposition* in the novel between chaos and form. Rather, chaos itself is seen to be continually destroying forms while moving itself to create new ones. Chaos and form are inextricably bound to one another in a dialectical process. Toward the end

of the novel, Anna herself imagines two people in the process of falling out of form into chaos: "Both cracking up because of a deliberate attempt to transcend their own limits. And out of the chaos, a new kind of strength." Outmoded form is broken by the force of chaos, primordial being, but the matter of chaos regroups itself into a new form, based on new values or strengths.

In Anna's first line of dialogue, she declares, "As far as I can see, everything's cracking up." The structure of the novel is designed to emphasize this fragmentation. The four colored notebooks reflect the four aspects of life that Anna can no longer reconcile with one another; her success as a published novelist (Black), her failure in political work (Red), her efforts of imagination (Yellow), her struggle to revise her own self-concept (Blue). In addition to these notebooks, written in the first person by Anna, there is a framing novel, called "Free Women," about the Anna who writes the notebooks. The four notebooks and the novel are additionally split each into sections and arranged in a neat pattern: "Free Women" 1, Black 1, Red 1, Yellow 1, Blue 1; "Free Women" 2, Black 2, Red 2, Yellow 2, Blue 2, etc. Lessing accomplishes several purposes by this dizzying arrangement of the novel's parts. First, she reflects the fact that, for Anna, existence has fragmented and threatens to return to an undifferentiated state of chaos. However, the mathematically neat arrangement of the splintered parts of Anna's experience suggests that in the face of threatened chaos, she is overreacting by imposing an order in her novel that does not properly belong to the material. Finally, Lessing suggests to the reader that while the many parts of the book treat separate subjects, they are actually unified by an underlying pattern, which their odd juxtaposition is designed to highlight.

The first striking element of that pattern is that each notebook (as well as "Free Women") starts just as "the stage sets collapse" in one theater of Anna's life, leaving her without a context within which to play her part. That is, each notebook begins as one form of her life begins to yield to chaos. The drama of each notebook is her battle not to be seduced by "a lying nostalgia"—a yearning for the recovery of the sense of form, the stage illusion of moral certainty, innocence, unity, and peace. In effect, this yearning is a desire for unreality and nonexistence. Since the yearning can never be fulfilled, it always leads to painful frustration and often to nihilism and despair.

Although Anna's nostalgia for moral sleep is acute, it is countered by an aspiration toward full, waking consciousness. In the battleground of each notebook, moreover, consciousness conquers, and Anna takes a victory, in existentialist terms. For her, as for Camus, "everything begins with consciousness and nothing is worth anything except through it." In Anna's case, full consciousness means facing up to the power of chaos and accepting its effect on her life. Yet Lessing does not let the case rest there. More acutely than her precursors Camus and Sartre, Lessing senses that every bit of ground gained for consciousness is saturated with irony—and that an excess of irony easily leads to bitterness, cynicism, and despair.

If the plot of each notebook concerns Anna's struggle to subdue her nostalgia for form and attain consciousness of chaos, the hidden and opposing plot of the novel as a whole concerns her struggle against the poisoning cynicism that accompanies her new knowledge. In the first three notebooks—Black, Red, and Yellow—Anna as a lone character moves from naïveté, through awareness, to cynicism, withdrawal, and loss of faith. Moreover, in the process of writing each of these three notebooks she loses confidence, becomes disoriented, doubts her own veracity, and finally despairs of communicating at all. In the Blue Notebook, on the other hand, there is a slow movement away from detachment, ennui, and self-consciousness toward commitment, passion, and unself-consciousness. This positive movement flows into the Golden Notebook, where Anna, by opening herself to chaos and emotion, achieves a mature vision that is simultaneously ironic and committed, detached and involved. In the overall dynamic of the novel, the detachment and irony that accompany awareness of chaos finally come to balance with the attachment and warmth that accompany commitment to the forms we impose on chaos.

Within each notebook, then, there is a pattern of opposition between nostalgia and awareness, as between their concomitants, pain and irony. In an analogous but larger pattern, the first three notebooks, where awareness is bought at the cost of irony, are opposed by the Blue Notebook, where moral and emotional passions reawaken. The Golden Notebook is the vehicle through which these antitheses are channeled into dialectic. Failure to take account of this dialectical structure is bound to result in a distorted reading of the major themes of the novel. "Living inside the subjective highly-coloured mist" of any one notebook, the reader is apt to be so intensely struck by a theme or attitude that he will fail to appreciate the countertheme or countertone developed elsewhere in this long and sometimes perplexing novel.

I propose an unorthodox method of examining the workings of this dynamic in the novel—that is, to unshuffle Lessing's deck and take a look separately at each colored notebook and the novel "Free Women." This is to play Anna's game—to "name" the pattern of each notebook, rescuing it from chaos, as she would say. So long as we take care to return the pieces to their splintered condition, we should do justice to both impulses in the novel—the one toward form and the one toward chaos...

Source: Betsy Draine, "*The Golden Notebook*: The Construction of a Postmodern Order," in *Substance under Pressure: Artistic Coherence and Evolving Form in the Novels of Doris Lessing*, University of Wisconsin Press, 1983, pp. 69–88.

Ellen Morgan

In the following essay, Morgan explores Ella's relationships and Anna's relationships to show how their interactions are or are not authentic. Morgan notes that the charcters are themselves aware of this dichotomy, and she concludes her critique by observing that Lessing's writing style further reflects the conflict between embracing feminism and turning away from it.

In her interview at Stony Brook (1969), Doris Lessing said, "I'm impatient with people who emphasize sexual revolution. I say we should all go to bed, shut up about sexual liberation, and go on with the important matters." But looking at the text of *The Golden Notebook*, which is, after all, about the female-male relationship in the middle of the twentieth century and about the meaning of femaleness in contemporary Western culture, one cannot help being [...] aware of the tension that exists between Lessing's sensitive observations of the malaise between the sexes and such denials of the importance of discomfort with the sexual status quo.

THE OVERRIDING WEAKNESS OF *THE GOLDEN NOTEBOOK* IS ALIENATION FROM THE AUTHENTIC FEMALE PERSPECTIVE, A PERSPECTIVE WHICH REPEATEDLY IS CLEARLY SKETCHED IN AND THEN SMEARED BY THE CENSOR IN LESSING."

In the course of *The Golden Notebook*, Lessing writes in the persona of Anna: "the quality a novel should have to make it a novel [is] the quality of philosophy... Yet I am incapable of writing the only kind of novel which interests me: a book powered with an intellectual or moral passion strong enough to create order, to create a new way of looking at life." This statement is a good entrance into *The Golden Notebook*, for the novel contains all the perceptions necessary to create a radical transforming and ordering vision of the relationship between women and men. These perceptions, however, are not gathered into the philosophical form proper to and inherent in them. Reading *The Golden Notebook* carefully forces one to realize how women writers can be, and have been, alienated from their own authentic, sensitive, and accurate perceptions of sexual politics because nowhere in their culture, in eras in which feminism is kept quiescent and latent, do they see such perceptions corroborated rather than made targets of antifeminist criticism, ridicule, and disparagement.

The world of *The Golden Notebook* consists, in addition to its artistic, racial, and other political dimensions, of Anna Wulf's closely rendered experiences with a number of acquaintances and lovers, sometimes told through Ella, her alter-ego and literary creation. But more significantly, the book consists of Anna-Ella's interpretations of these experiences, her judgments and evaluations of them and of herself. Repeatedly, as I shall attempt to show, her judgments belittle, deny, or distort her experiences and censor her spontaneous responses to them. The difference between Ella's actual attitudes and responses and those she does not permit herself is the measure of her alienation from her own perceptions

and, I believe, the extent of Lessing's failure to come to terms with female authenticity.

Ella and her friend Julia quite obviously feel, on the one hand, an instinctive human need to respect themselves as people, and, on the other, a conditioned contempt for themselves as women. Spontaneously they trust one another and are very close, but they *judge* this trust to be less valuable than they *feel* it to be, less valuable than their far less trusting relationships with men. As Anna says of herself and Molly, no matter how close they are on the basis of shared understanding, experience, and life style, their "real loyalties are always to men, and not to women." Anna-Ella feels strongly inclined to discuss with Molly-Julia her problems with men, but she judges that all the "complaints and the reproaches and the betrayals" ought not to be voiced. These judgments, which undermine the solidarity between the two women, are the result of their conviction that men are superior to women and that their own self-interest lies not in relationships with women but in those with men, however damaging individual female-male relationships may be. The two women share a minority-group psychological orientation which compels them to depreciate their femaleness and their friendship and seek approval from and identification with men. This fact becomes clear when Ella describes the contempt she feels for the magazine for which she works and even for the stories she writes because they are "feminine." The two women also reveal this self-deprecatory orientation by blaming only themselves for troubles to which men have contributed, as Julia wryly recognizes.

Ella judges that the future without a man is unimaginable. But she hates the parties she has to go to in order to meet men because the parties make her aware of the fact that she is "on the market again." Neither Ella nor Julia, however, thinks that there is any use indulging in complaint over this fact. Julia says, "It's no good taking that attitude—that's how everything is run, isn't it?" The two women thus dismiss their feelings, convinced that they have no legitimate grounds for complaint and that complaining would only be self-pity.

The pattern of opposition between feelings and judgment is shown in particularly high relief when Dr. West, Ella's employer, tries to start an affair with her while his wife is away. When she refuses, he turns to the other women in his office and finally to the eldest, who is grateful and flattered. Ella's spontaneous reaction is to become "angry on behalf of her sex," but she quickly turns away this feeling, telling herself that the emotion really is "rooted in a resentment that has nothing to do with Dr. West," a resentment which she sees as shameful. Ella retreats from sympathizing with the older woman for fear of "cutting off some possibility for herself." She feels a natural bond with other women but judges solidarity with them dangerous because it is to men that women, she believes, must turn for any advantages which they may gain.

"Sometimes," says Julia, "I think we're all in a sort of sexual mad house." But Ella tries to quash this rebellious reaction in her friend and in herself: "My dear Julia, we've chosen to be free women, and this is the price we pay, that's all." Neither woman considers actually fighting back; there is no visible solidarity among women which would sanction and support such rebellion. Moreover, their analysis of the situation is fundamentally apolitical. For example, Ella says that unlike men, women cannot obtain sexual satisfaction without love, and that therefore the inequality in sexual relations is inherent. Neither woman sees that the vulnerability she feels may be caused not by some kind of fixed biological or psychological difference between the sexes, but by the fact that in a culture in which sex is still apt to be viewed as a kind of conquest for the man, the psychologically healthy woman cannot afford to experience sexual relations without asking love in return to even the bargain. Ella and Julia know that the kind of sex offered them is a threat to their dignity and self-respect. They cannot act directly while holding the apolitical view they do of female-male relations, but neither is willing simply to capitulate—hence their bickering and criticism of men and Ella's inability to function sexually unless she is in love.

Most of Ella's keenest observations are followed by turnings away, efforts to escape the essentially political consequences of their logic. She is very much afraid that her perceptions, because feminist, are illegitimate and inconsistent with the broader humanism to which she is committed. But the woman who has permitted herself to consider the real extent of her oppression as a woman, and has stopped being ashamed of her anger and bitterness before asking of herself the humanism to view men as co-victims of the cultural web of power patterns, is one phenomenon.

Quite another is the Lessing woman, who consistently tells herself that her oppression is her own fault or an unchangeable condition to which one must gracefully resign oneself. She refuses to face and deal with the anger always just under the surface and forces herself not only to regard men as co-victims, but to sympathize with them against the healthy interests of her own sex.

It is only in the vignettes Ella writes that she shows the willingness to describe, albeit indirectly, the reality of female-male relations as she has experienced them. The vignettes are about Ella's openness to men as persons, her desire to communicate with them as people both sexually and emotionally, and their refusal to relate on this personal basis to her and to love. Ella grasps the fact that this refusal in the men to connect sex and love (and thus integrate the emotional and sexual components of personality) is a sickness. But she fails to make the connection between the fact that society teaches men not to allow themselves to be fully trusting, open, and involved emotionally with women and her observation that men ask women for refuge, strength, commitment, and loyal support while withholding these things from them. Neither of the women in *The Golden Notebook* connects this male fear of reciprocity to prevailing concepts of masculinity. Neither does either woman see that healthy men may retreat from women rather than try to fill the emptiness and assuage the self-contempt women often feel because, having internalized the prevailing social estimate of femaleness, they feel incomplete and inferior as persons.

Ella's relationship with Paul gives the reader even more convincing proof that the pattern of her psychic life is withdrawal from and censorship of her perceptions, of failure to live an authentic existence. Believing that female-male relationships are inherently unequal and therefore not susceptible to transformation, she seeks to justify the inequalities so that she may convince herself to accept them without the resentment and rebellion she constantly feels.

She senses and resents, for instance, Paul's will to dominate her. But Ella, like the other women in this book who are confronted with the choice of taking a man on terms which are less than egalitarian or of turning away from him to uphold her own terms, chooses the man on his own terms. When a sexual relationship is offered, she is unable to refuse because the terms available are the only ones imaginable to her. She does not make any attempt to change the basis of relating from exploitation to genuine egalitarian friendship and love. The idea that she could refuse to deal with men in the style suggested by their behavior does not occur to her. Rebellion and self-assertion are present in her propensities for condemning men with Julia and for feeling mistreated and hurt, but she tries to hide from herself the kinds of thoughts which encourage these propensities. Thus Ella perceives that part of Paul's personality is rakish, corrupting, and detrimental to her dignity, but she refuses to connect this part of him with the rest, which she calls his true self. His rakishness, she tells herself, "was on a level that not only had nothing to do with the simplicity and ease of their being together; but betrayed it so completely that she had no alternative but to ignore it. Otherwise she would have had to break with him." She is happy only when she does not think about the ugly aspects of their relationship. Anna writes of her, "she drifted along on a soft tide of not-thinking." At one point Paul's behavior makes her envision his paying her money as if she were a prostitute: "It was somewhere implicit in his attitude." But Ella pushes the thought away: "What's that got to do with all these hours we've been together, when every look and move he's made told me he loved me?"

After five years as Paul's mistress, Ella begins to be disturbed by thoughts about his wife and not only stops feeling triumph over her for having captured her husband, but envies her. Ella builds up a picture of the other woman as a "serene, calm, unjealous, unenvious, undemanding woman, full of resources of happiness inside herself, self-sufficient, yet always ready to give happiness when it is asked for." She realizes that this picture is not derived from what Paul says about his wife, but that this is the kind of woman she herself would like to be, especially since she has grown aware and afraid of the extent of her dependence upon Paul. It is interesting to note that Ella's idea of a defense against her own dependency is selflessness, the old ideal of the woman as giver who does not require gifts for herself. She is incapable of thinking of less self-damaging ways than self-abnegation to reduce her vulnerability. Significantly it is not because Ella wishes to respect herself more for being a complete, self-sufficient, self-motivated person that she admires and envies this figure; it is because she envisions such a woman as relatively invulnerable

to being hurt by people like Paul. The attraction to the figure has a negative motive, as all of Ella's emotional life is negative, because she does not allow her spontaneous reactions to her experience to govern her behavior and shape her values.

When Paul finally leaves Ella, she is devastated. She feels "as if a skin had been peeled off her" and realizes that the relationship was not free for her, as she had thought, simply because she had remained unmarried; nor was it really a love relationship, since it pulled her out of herself, unbalanced and diminished her, and proved altogether a destructive experience with regard to her self-respect and firmness of identity. Openly she admits, "I am unhappy because I have lost some kind of independence, some freedom," and she acknowledges that her attitude toward Paul has been "dishonest." But then Ella turns away from this realization. She concludes that it is not Paul, or society's sexual mores and views, but she herself who is to blame for the failure she feels.

Ella's life is a long series of encounters with the unhappy dislocation between the sexes, the implications of which neither Ella nor her creator Anna can face. The extraordinary amount of energy Ella expends in interpreting her relationships with men and compartmentalizing, disapproving of, and suppressing her feelings is a good indication of the seriousness of the discrepancy between what Ella is capable of perceiving and what she can afford to admit to herself, and therefore of her alienation from her perceptions and distance from personal authenticity.

The pattern of alienation, of withdrawal from authenticity, is also apparent in the Anna-Molly spectrum of *The Golden Notebook*. The two women allow Molly's ex-husband and son to bully them despite the fact that they are aware that the two men are hurting them. They extend friendship to other men who also mistreat them, such as Nelson, de Silva, Willi, George, and Paul, who are sadists and misogynists. In connection with one of these relationships Anna comments, "Sometimes I dislike women, I dislike us all, because of our capacity for not-thinking when it suits us; we choose not to think when we are reaching out for happiness." Again one sees Anna turning the anger she feels at being ill-used against herself and other women and refusing to curtail relationships with men which damage her. One could interpret her responses to these men as humanistic in the profoundest sense—as evidence of a mature ability to see that no human being is all good or bad, that most have something to offer which redeems at least in part that which is ugly in them. But such a view misses the crucial point here, which is that Anna and Molly have legitimate cause for anger, and that they feel the anger but believe it to be an illegitimate reaction to their experiences. Their behavior is inconsistent with their real self-interest and shows them once again to be alienated from themselves.

With her two rabidly antiwoman homosexual tenants, Anna permits some of her anger to surface and links their attitudes toward women with those of men in general. "The mockery," she says, "the defence of the homosexual, was nothing more than the polite over-gallantry of a 'real' man, the 'normal' man who intends to set bounds to his relationship with a woman, consciously or not." She continues, "It was the same cold, evasive emotion, taken a step further; there was a difference in degree but not in kind." But Anna, true to form, then criticizes herself for her anger and feels unfree to oust the tenants simply because they are so disagreeable to her. Finally she also rejects her perception of the connection between the tenants' attitudes toward women and those of men in general. Deciding to throw one tenant out so her daughter will not be damaged by his misogyny, she declares that her daughter is someday to have a "real" man, implying that the attitudes toward women of "real" men are not, after all, classifiable as damaging as she had spontaneously remarked.

The discrepancy between Anna's spontaneous perceptions and superimposed judgments is even clearer with regard to two men at a further remove from her: one who follows her out of the subway and another who exposes himself to her. Her immediate reaction to both is, naturally, fright. On second thought she tells herself that something is abnormal about her. "This happens every day, this is living in the city," she says, refusing to indict a society in which such treatment of women is to be expected.

The discrepancy is most obvious, however, in Anna's major relationships with men. With Michael, she is periodically happy and resentful. She resents his inability to accept her as a writer and a responsible mother and his refusal to give her the kind of unmeasured love and support he

asks of her. She also resents the fact that because he is a man, the petty details of his life are taken care of for him by women, whereas because she is a woman, her life is composed largely of seeing to the details of others' needs. Anna calls this resentment the "housewife's disease." But instead of facing squarely the fact that she resents Michael because he is a holder of the privileges which accrue to males in a patriarchal society and is taking advantage of this fact and of her, she turns her anger away, depersonalizing and depoliticizing it. She tells herself the anger has nothing to do with Michael. It is "impersonal," the disease "of women in our time" which is evident in their faces and voices, a protest against injustice, but nevertheless a protest which should be fought down and not on any account turned against men. The idea is that one must adjust rather than act in one's own self-interest to change the system.

With Saul the relationship is more complex because he alternates communicating with Anna on a very high level with misogynistic, hostile withdrawal from her. But the pattern still holds. For example, at one point she gets angry enough to explode at him for referring to women and sex in demeaning terms. But predictably there follows the retraction, the denial of legitimacy of her own spontaneous emotion. She feels "ridiculous" and softens toward Saul. As with Michael, Anna is ambivalent, but she only accepts her positive feelings for him.

Anna sees that any relationship structured along the lines of the heterosexual model of our culture, as are the female-male relationships in *The Golden Notebook*, pits the interests of women and men against each other, women being driven to need and grasp for security and protection and men resisting being drawn into the restrictive role of provider: "I am the position of women in our time." But although she is aware of this separation of interests, and also of the rhythm of alternating love and hate in her relationships with men, she never connects these two phenomena. And because she does not make this connection, the sexual pain which she experiences never is recognized as a problem susceptible of solution, a problem calling for remedial action. Thus when Saul vents hatred upon her, Anna does not *act* to alter the situation. Instead she follows her preestablished pattern, turning her anger and frustration in upon herself. Instead of defending herself from his attacks, she disparages herself for the very strength with which she meets them. "I longed," she writes, "to be free of my own ordering, commenting memory." Her stomach clenches and her back hurts, but she does not connect these details with the fact that her refusal to act in her own self-interest hurts her and is making her lose her sense of personal worth and identity. She relates the physical ills rather to Saul's hostility. The solution to the pain is thus made to lie with him and not with herself; she adopts the posture of a helpless victim instead of acting to bring herself relief.

Anna is aware that what is wrong between her and Saul is a problem common to women. She wonders to herself what it is that women need and are not getting from men and senses that perhaps this unfulfilled need is the cause of the note of betrayal that women strike in this era. But predictably, instead of permitting herself to conclude that this "note" is legitimate, she disparages women by describing it as self-pity, a "hateful emotion" which is "solemn" and "wet." She never really stands up for herself as a woman and never opts out of the self-damaging collusion of tolerating and playing a role in the submission-dominance syndrome which is the leitmotiv of female-male relations in patriarchal societies. The only approach to the problem which she feels legitimate is described in her dream about Saul as a tiger. The tiger claws her and she sympathizes with it instead of with herself; she then concretizes this approach in the image of flying above the tiger's cage: it is legitimate to try to "rise above" the situation, but not to change it.

As she views the imaginary movie composed of scenes from her past life, Anna realizes that the meaning with which she has endowed each scene has been "all false." She finds that the judgments she has been making have ordered the material "to fit what I knew" rather than emerging in a direct response to her experience. But she never escapes her pattern of self-punishment and alienation. The novel ends with Molly getting married although she knows "the exact dimensions of the bed" and with Anna entering marriage counseling work and the teaching of delinquent children. There is a "small silence" as the two women together contemplate their capitulation, their integration "with British life at its roots."

The Golden Notebook, therefore, reveals the peculiar problem of the woman writer working in a climate of assumptions and sympathies about women and sex roles which do not support female authenticity. The woman writer in this situation is unlikely to conceive of the relative status of women and men in political terms; prevailing opinion convinces her that the condition of women in society is rooted in biological and psychological immutables. She may, nevertheless, be acutely sensitive to and resentful of the power dynamics which characterize female-male relations, aware to a large extent of what we have come to call sexual politics. If so, she finds herself on the horns of a dilemma: she cannot completely deny her awareness, but, unencouraged by any cultural sanction for those of her perceptions which are, at the deepest level, feminist and potentially political, she doubts these perceptions and feels they are indicative of some aberration or defect in herself. It is not necessary to assume that this book is autobiographical to arrive at the idea that Lessing, and not simply her characters Anna and Ella, is confronting this dilemma. Lessing has so conceived the book that nowhere within it are Anna's and Ella's judgments of their experiences implied to be anything but unavoidable.

The overriding weakness of *The Golden Notebook* is alienation from the authentic female perspective, a perspective which repeatedly is clearly sketched in and then smeared by the censor in Lessing. The discrepancy between the perceptions and the alien standards which are imposed upon them seriously flaws the novel. But at the same time, the tension produced by this discrepancy makes the book a superb rendering of that state of alienation from themselves, from authentic selfhood, to which women, like blacks and members of other minority groups, are subjected until they find solidarity and begin to confirm and legitimize their experience. In addition, Lessing's study of the malaise and dislocation between the sexes in Western society does set a very important precedent in literature because it examines the relationship between women and men so humanistically and analytically, in such great detail and variety, and with a good faith which never permits a descent into vituperation or abuse.

Source: Ellen Morgan, "Alienation of the Woman Writer in *The Golden Notebook*," in *Doris Lessing: Critical Studies*, edited by Annis Pratt and L. S. Dembo, University of Wisconsin Press, 1974, pp. 54–63.

SOURCES

Brown, Sandra, "'Where Words, Patterns, Order, Dissolve': *The Golden Notebook* as Fugue," in *Approaches to Teaching Lessing's The Golden Notebook*, edited by Carey Kaplan and Ellen Cronan Rose, Modern Language Association of America, 1989, pp. 121–26.

Buckler, Ernest, "Against the Terror, the Spirit of Sisyphus," in the *New York Times*, July 1, 1962, p. 158.

Carey, John L., "Art and Reality in *The Golden Notebook*," in *Doris Lessing: Critical Studies*, University of Wisconsin Press, 1974, pp. 20–39.

Klein, Carole, *Doris Lessing: A Biography*, Carroll & Graf Publishers, 2000.

Leonard, John, "More on Lessing," in the *New York Times*, May 13, 1973, p. 385.

Lessing, Doris, *The Golden Notebook*, Perennial Classics, HarperCollins, 1999.

Locke, Richard, "In Praise of Doris Lessing," in the *New York Times*, October 21, 1972, p. 31.

FURTHER READING

Fishburn, Katherine, *The Unexpected Universe of Doris Lessing: A Study in Narrative Technique*, Greenwood Press, 1985.

> Fishburn examines Lessing's science fiction in order to identify the author's underlying philosophies. Significant influences on Lessing, Fishburn finds, are Marxism and Sufism. Fishburn then demonstrates how these philosophies shaped the various narrators and imaginary worlds in Lessing's work.

Galin, Muge, *Between East and West: Sufism in the Novels of Doris Lessing*, State University of New York Press, 1997.

> The spiritual beliefs of Sufism greatly inspired much of Lessing's writing. In this study by Galin, readers come to understand the basic principles of Sufism and are then shown how these beliefs influenced Lessing's novels.

Hague, Angela, *Fiction, Intuition, and Creativity: Studies in Brontë, James, Woolf, and Lessing*, Catholic University of America Press, 2003.

> Hague examines the writing of four major authors in her exploration of literary creativity. Included are notes on Hague's research into philosophy and psychology, in particular the studies of Jung and psychologist William James.

Newman, Michael, *Socialism: A Very Short Introduction*, Oxford University Press, 2005.

> Newman presents a very enlightening view of socialism, how it has been manifested in the past, and what it might hold for the future. This is a very readable text that provides insightful information as well as Newman's thoughts on what socialism would look like in the United States.

Smith, Sharon, *Women and Socialism: Essays on Women's Liberation*, Haymarket Books, 2005.

> Smith is the author of many studies on women and socialism. In this book she looks at what she defines as a lack of progress in the women's movement since the 1960s. Smith also explores how socialism can aid the feminist movement.

Ida

GERTRUDE STEIN
1941

A good way to read Gertrude Stein's 1941 novel *Ida* is aloud. The prose is musical, its rhythm is sing-song and comparable to children's stories. Its lilt carries the reader along even though there is no conventional plot development, conflicts, or resolutions, and little actually seems to happen.

Usually a novel tells a story, developing a narrative of events connected to each other by cause and effect. One thing leads to another; tensions are created; tensions are resolved. As characters act and react to events and to each other, their human characteristics and concerns are revealed. These characters and their concerns, if the author is skillful, become important to the reader. The most common responses to a story are: What is going to happen next? and Why? Indeed, a story usually shows how the past has led to the present, how the present becomes the future, how the characters direct events, and how events direct them.

In *Ida* Stein sabotages the novel, destroying the tensions that make a reader keep reading to find out what happens next. She eliminates cause and effect from the narrative. What happens in *Ida* is not, fundamentally, a story with a plot (a sequence of events moved forward by cause and effect), but is instead a musical flow of words tracing perception and consciousness.

Ida uses, in distorted form, many incidents from Stein's life, her quests for love, her

Gertrude Stein (AP Images)

achievement of fame, her artistic focus on the consciousness of her own perception. *Ida* is the story of a lonely woman whose parents die soon after her birth. The title character, Ida, becomes well known for her beauty, but she is not genuinely known by anyone. Thus, the novel traces Ida's attempts to find a true companion.

In *Ida* Stein does not attempt to present the psychology of her protagonist's actions, reactions, and interactions, as most novelists would. Instead, thoughts, observations, feelings, dreams, and apparently actual occurrences are treated with the same tone, as if they are not distinguishable from each other. Perception, as it occurs spontaneously, independent of knowledge of what is actually happening, guides Stein's narration. Reading *Ida* is like sitting on a bus overhearing a conversation between two strangers. They talk about things with which one is unfamiliar, as one looks around, taking in the surroundings, and being aware, at the same time, of one's own thoughts reveries, and associations.

A somewhat more recent printing of *Ida* is available in *Gertrude Stein: Writings, 1932–1946*, edited by Catherine R. Stimpson and Harriet Chessman, and published by the Library of America in 1998.

AUTHOR BIOGRAPHY

The youngest of five children, Gertrude Stein was born on February 3, 1874, in Allegheny, Pennsylvania. Her parents, Daniel and Amelia Stein, of German-Jewish descent, were financially successful and determined to raise their children to be educated, cultured adults. When Stein was less than a year old, Daniel took the family to Vienna in order to establish a branch of the family banking business there. When Daniel returned to the United States on business, Amelia moved the children to Paris.

In 1878, Daniel brought the family to Baltimore. The next year, they settled in Oakland, California. Daniel was stern; the children lived in fear of him. In 1888, Amelia died, and Daniel died in 1891. The eldest son, Mike, who worked for a cable car company in San Francisco, saved the family from poverty after discovering the debts their father had left. Mike sold a plan for consolidating all the cable lines to one of the chief cable car operators. Then he sent Stein and her sister Bertha to live with relatives in Baltimore.

In the fall of 1893, Stein was admitted to Harvard's women's college, Radcliffe. She received her degree in 1898 and published a paper on "Character in its Relation to Attention" that May in *The Psychological Review*. In 1897, before receiving her degree from Radcliffe, Stein entered Johns Hopkins to study medicine. After four years she left, bored, and disgusted by the condescension with which women in the program were treated. While in medical school, Stein traveled during the summers, to San Francisco, where she fell in love with May Bookstaver, a recent graduate of Bryn Mawr, who later jilted Stein for another woman. She also traveled throughout Europe with her brother Leo. In 1904, Stein became a permanent resident of Paris, where her brothers Michael and Leo already lived.

Before the First World War, she and Leo used some of the fortune Michael accumulated to buy some of the great paintings of the late nineteenth and early twentieth centuries. The paintings were still affordable at the time. Stein became friendly with Pablo Picasso, who painted her portrait in 1906, and also with Henri Matisse. She established a salon where writers and painters gathered. In 1907, Stein met Alice B. Toklas, an American expatriate from San Francisco. They began what became a marriage that lasted until Stein's death in 1946. To the outer world, as protection against the penalties for being openly lesbian, Toklas was usually cast as Stein's housekeeper and secretary, which, in fact, she also was. During the First World War, Stein and Toklas served the American, French, and British forces as ambulance drivers. After the war, their salon attracted such writers as Ezra Pound, Thornton Wilder, T. S. Eliot, and Ernest Hemingway, and Stein coined the term "the lost generation" to describe the war-wizened writers who gathered round her and were mostly American expatriates.

Stein had begun writing a novel about her family, *The Making of Americans* in 1903. That year, too, she wrote *Q.E.D.*, a novel about her relationship with Bookstaver. In 1905, Stein began writing *Three Lives*, which was published in 1909. Stein was paid 600 dollars by her publisher, and the book garnered mostly favorable reviews despite its radical departure from conventional style and narrative. By 1913, Gertrude and Leo, who had been nearly inseparable at one time, had become so alienated from each other (partly because of her lesbianism and his insecurity about his talents as a painter) that they divided their possessions and he moved to Italy. From then on, they never again saw each other or spoke with each other. In 1914, Stein published *Tender Buttons*, a long prose poem with a buried lesbian subtext.

In 1932, pressed for money, Stein wrote *The Autobiography of Alice B. Toklas*, a book about herself masquerading as Toklas's autobiography. Far easier to read than her previous writings, it became a bestseller and Random House became her publisher, bringing her work into the literary and commercial mainstream. Following this, Stein was invited in 1934 to tour the United States. She lectured and gave newspaper and radio interviews across the country. *Ida*, was published by Random House in 1941 following her tour.

Stein and Toklas return to Paris in early 1936. Threats of a looming German attack were apparent, and many of Stein's friends and family advised her to return to the United States. Stein remained dubious about the threat, though the Nazis did indeed invade France during World War II. Nevertheless, despite being a Jew and a lesbian, Stein survived the Nazi occupation of France, in large measure because she enjoyed the protection of Bernard Fay, a scholar of American history with whom she became close in 1926. Fay was an official in the pro-Nazi Vichy government and was incarcerated by the Allies after the war for working with the Nazis. Stein and Toklas worked to have him released, but Stein's major efforts once World War II had ended involved playing host to American servicemen in her salon in Paris and giving lectures to gatherings of American soldiers. Stein died on July 27, 1946 of stomach cancer in a hospital in the Paris suburb of Neuilly-sur-Seine and was interred that October in Père-Lachaise Cemetery in Paris.

PLOT SUMMARY

First Half: Part 1

Ida is the story of a woman variously called Ida, Ida-Ida, Winnie, and, once, Virginia. Although the novel seems to reflect Ida's inner consciousness, it is told not in the first person but by a narrator outside of the story. Ida is presented as a piece of data being examined, first as a child, then as a girl growing up, then as a woman and as a celebrity. The story begins with her birth and continues in a mostly linear fashion, stopping occasionally to loop back in time.

Ida is born despite her mother's effort to prevent her from being born. Soon after Ida's birth, her parents die (they "went off on a trip and never came back") and Ida goes to live with her great aunt. About Ida's parents, all the narrator says is that they were "sweet and gentle." Her aunt is not. Ida's life is a story of perceptions more than of actions: "She saw the moon and she saw the sun and she saw the grass and she saw the streets."

Even an event that might have some dramatic possibility is described only as a phenomenon of Ida's consciousness: "The first time she saw anything it frightened her." Juxtaposed with these accounts is an inventory of details about Ida, things that define her as a person. For instance, Tuesday is special to her, and although there is plenty to eat, she "always hesitated before eating." While actions and reactions are reported, the characters and the plot are not developed through the action.

When Ida is sixteen, her aunt apparently dies ("went away so she lost her great aunt"). Ida then gets a dog that has been blind since birth. Ida calls the dog Love and speaks to Love about her desire to have a twin and live in a big house. Next Ida meets a family of "little aunts," goes to church with them, where she cannot see them, but where she enjoys the warmth of the crowd. Outside the church, she sees the aunts again. She also sees a man and then another jump out from behind some trees. Ida tells the aunts to walk ahead so that she can protect them. Nothing further happens and she never sees either the men or the aunts again. The aunts are "the first and last friends she ever had," but no drama of friendship is described and Ida later seems to know many people.

Ida "gradually" gets older. She thinks about her parents, talks to her dog, moves from house to house, and is cared for by a number of undifferentiated people. After she wishes for a miracle, she sees a black dog and a white dog run away together during a summer snowstorm and she regards this as the miracle. Ida lives with her grandfather and has a new dog, Iris, though there is no mention of what happened to Love. When Ida looks through the gates of a public park, she sees a policeman looking at her, or perhaps he is looking at an old woman beside her, but perhaps the woman is not a woman. Ida cannot tell because the woman has so many clothes on. Ida also considers marriage, but is reluctant to change her name because she has endured so many other changes. Ida then sees a man carrying a sandwich board on his back advertising something and talking to a rich man. While walking in the park she sees a prostrate Arab man. Her dog approaches the man but does not bark or bother him. The man rises and, by signs, asks Ida for something to drink. She indicates she has nothing; the man goes away. Ida might have been frightened, the narrator says, implying she was not, had it been evening and had she been alone. Then the narrator notes that it is evening and Ida is alone. When the Arab walks away, Ida does not continue her walk but goes back in the direction from which she came. Perhaps this short section demonstrates one of Stein's techniques. She presents an image or series of images rather than an exploration or analysis of Ida's thoughts and feelings in regards to them.

Ida is not religious, and when she encounters people performing a religious ceremony she observes it, but leaves. Then she comes upon a group of people walking. She walks with them. "She kept on moving, sleeping or walking," suggesting that the narrative encompasses waking events, memories, dreams, day dreams, fantasies, desires, and reveries all presented without differentiation. The section concludes as Ida, at age eighteen, decides to have a twin, writes a letter to her twin telling her she is beautiful and that she must enter a beauty contest. Ida not only enters but also votes in the beauty contest and wins.

First Half: Part 2

After becoming a famous beauty queen, Ida is surprised to encounter a washerwoman who has a picture of Ida's dog Love. Ida snatches the picture from her and jumps into a car that has stopped and from which two women have emerged to see "what was happening." Ida tries to drive away but the women reenter the car, throw her out, and leave. Ida finds a package she thinks one of the women must have dropped. Later, on another day, Ida sees the washerwoman again. She also sees two women in a car, and in the car is Ida's dog Love. There is a farmer with several small women, and a young man. All these people look at each other and say nothing.

Ida writes a letter to her twin congratulating her on winning the beauty contest and gives her the name Winnie because she is a winner. Winnie becomes widely know to everyone, a celebrity just for being who she is. People go to see her and recognize her in public places. They do not notice Ida, even though Ida and Winnie are the same person. The celebrity Winnie is the public version of Ida. A man from Omaha follows her, and when he rings her bell, he only meets Ida. Though the narrative is unclear, he and Ida most likely make love, but afterwards, they part, and the man never returns, having seen Ida as Ida and not as Winnie. It appears soon after their encounter that Ida has had a miscarriage.

The narrative recounts encounters and flirtations Ida has with several men, most of them soldiers. Ida begins to think about marriage. She moves to Connecticut. As she is leaving Connecticut, Ida meets Sam Hamlin. She then goes to California. She stays with a woman named Eleanor Angel. Ida then meets and marries Frank Arthur. Frank and Ida part and she never sees him again. She becomes aware of the economic depression of the 1930s, seeing rallies for the unemployed, but she is not interested because she is not unemployed and "always had enough."

After her marriage to Frank ends (although there is no account of its ending, or of any other aspect of it) Ida lives with a cousin of her uncle, an old man who gilds picture frames. He has a son who runs a garage, quarrels with his partner over money, shoots his partner, and is sent to jail. Ida leaves her uncle, gets a dog named Claudine, and gives her away. People recognize Ida in the street, but she is lonely and again wishes for a sister or for sisters. Ida again thinks about marriage, but she decides not to marry or have children and to concentrate on her relationship to herself instead. She becomes a photographer in order to earn a living, but gives that up and decides to earn a living by talking. At one point, Ida sits on a hillside between two brothers, a painter and an engineer. They both leave her and Ida is overcome by the sense that she is entitled to anything she wants and is strong enough to help herself to anything she desires. Ida travels, meets people, parts from people, and moves to New Hampshire, where she marries.

First Half: Part 3
Ida's marriage does not last long. Her husband sighs a great deal and repeats her name. They travel throughout the United States, settling in Virginia and then in Ohio. Ida sees herself as resembling water. She travels more and looks at trees, particularly at what falls from trees. After traveling, she settles in Washington. Stein does not indicated whether they are in Washington state or Washington, D.C. Frederick, an army officer, meets her there.

First Half: Part 4
In Washington, Ida becomes the center of a circle of visitors. Frederick falls in love with her. They marry. Frederick is in the army and they move from Washington to Ohio, then to Texas. After a while she leaves him and Texas. Ida settles again in Washington. She meets many people, including a man from Minnesota. When she is leaning against a wall, Ida sees Andrew Hamilton. They begin to walk together. They get married and remain in Washington.

First Half: Part 5: Politics
While still in Washington, men visit Ida and leave her, often buying something unspecified from her, but there is a suggestion of sexual relations. In Washington, Ida is a celebrity. Sometimes she is married and sometimes she is not. One of the men who sometimes calls on her, Eugene

Thomas, wants to marry her. But after he is nearly drowned in a flood in Connecticut, he does not return to Washington and does not marry her. Ida lives with Edith and William. Each of them has been previously married. They also have "a" mother, who is not living with them. The "a" for the two suggests that they are as much brother and sister as they are husband and wife. During this time, Gerald Seaton is interested in marrying Ida. Ida and Gerald get married and they move away from Washington.

First Half: Part 6
Ida lives contentedly with Gerald in a small apartment in Boston. Domesticity makes her unlike the person she was. They leave Boston and move away from the metropolitan bustle. Though Ida's marriage to Gerald is the most successful of her marriages thus far, by the end of the section Gerald has disappeared and Ida has met Andrew and married him. When Ida becomes "Andrew's Ida," she changes and becomes "more Ida."

Second Half: Part 1
The First Half of *Ida* portrays the protagonist as she seeks a sense of her own completeness, mostly through her relationships with men. The Second Half of the novel is concerned with Ida in her maturity, depicting her as having achieved the completeness she once sought. Ida first appears walking along a wide road in bright moonlight. In the moonlight, a white dog that is with her seems gray. By thinking about the changed color of the dog, Ida realizes that context affects perception. Nothing is absolute in itself; instead, things attain their meaning in relation to the attributes of the things that surround them. This provides a key to understanding *Ida*. The book recasts how stories are told, and thus it challenges the conventions of perception.

In the moonlight Ida not only turns over these thoughts about context, she becomes frightened by the brightness of the moonlight itself. In the first half of the book, Ida has mostly been frightened by men. Now she is frightened by another kind of power, by the reflected light of the sun as it is transmitted through the moon. The moonlight is an emblem of the writer's power to receive experience from the world and to reflect it back as fiction. Here, Stein is commenting about the power of art and the consciousness of the artist.

Following this episode, the narrative begins to resemble a fairy tale, offering a symbolic account of Ida's encounter with her talent and how she takes command of it. Stein seems to be alluding to her own assumption of authorship through Ida: When Ida goes home, it is cold and the fire is out in her room. There is a fire burning in the servant's room, but the servant is not present. Ida is angry and takes "every bit of lighted wood" and brings it "into her room." Obviously impossible, the fact that Ida can carry burning wood into her room signals that this is a symbolic narrative (like the heroic Greek demi-god Prometheus, she is stealing fire) and as it proceeds, readers are also shown that symbolic expression is unstable, like consciousness and perception, and can change. Ida stays at home and "Andrew's name changed to Ida and eight changed to four and sixteen changed to twenty-five." Andrew is unaccountably present or absent. Ida fills her days with walking and talking and particularly with listening. She listens to herself talk and she listens to Andrew. It is part of a writer's work to listen. Ida develops on her own without Andrew, forging a relation with Susan Little, which is described only symbolically: "she walked with Susan Little." This suggests a homosexual relationship, one that was taboo and could not be explicitly mentioned at the time when Stein was writing *Ida*.

The fullness of Ida's life is followed by a period when everybody goes away. Ida's response, alone, is to think "about her life with dogs." Nearly the rest of Part One narrates the stories about dogs that Ida tells herself. With lively precision Stein describes dogs playing tag and tells stories about dogs with unusual attention to detail and chronological sequence. Ida is diverting herself, and Stein is telling stories inside a novel that resists telling stories.

As the section began with moonlight, so Ida's reverie about dogs ends with a fantasy about Ida's connection to the moon. The moon is Ida's because the moon symbolizes the way an artist works. Part One of the Second Half then ends with a coda (or afterthought) on the death, caused by meningitis, of a young man at the age of twenty-six.

Second Half: Part 2

Almost married to Andrew, Ida dreams that he is a soldier. She is notified that he is dying. The food and the car intended for the wedding, Ida thinks, will do just as well for the funeral, but the clothes will not do. The dream ends. Ida is alive and so is Andrew. Buried in the dream is Ida's own ambivalence; she imagines Andrew dying but avoids a confrontation with the fantasy of his death by focusing instead on practical matters.

Second Half: Part 3

Ida is a girl. Frank—it is not clear if this is Frank Arthur or a different person named Frank—is teaching her to swim. Accidentally, Ida kicks his testicles. Frank goes under on account of the ensuing pain and, letting go of Ida, she goes under. The narrator comments that they did not drown but might have. The section ends by noting that Ida has never been much younger that she is now, signifying, perhaps, the unity or completeness of her persona despite the movement of time.

Second Half: Part 4

This section celebrates Ida's fulfillment and her power to live in the present. Ida's condition is narrated by two short anecdotes. In the first anecdote a soldier takes home cuttings from an apple tree, plants them and subsequently always has apples. In the same story another soldier brings back a shepherd dog from the war. It sires a line of shepherd dogs. Similarly, Ida experiences a continuing abundance established by something she has brought forth from her own struggles (her complete sense of self). The second anecdote tells of Ida's dislike for riding in trains. It ends with an explanation. Ida never got on the train after her first time because "she was always there." Being always there seems to imply feeling that wherever she is at a given moment is where she belongs.

Second Half: Part 5

A digression ensues concerning the conflict between the actual and the symbolic and about the role perception plays in determining the existence of anything. This conflict is represented by a fable Ida tells Andrew, which is ostensibly about luck, concerning a spider, a cuckoo, a goldfish, and dwarfs. When Ida finishes telling her story, in which each symbolic entity, goldfish, spider, dwarfs, and cuckoo, argues for its real existence, "Everybody in the room was quiet and Andrew was really excited and he looked at Ida and that was that." Ida is acclaimed as a storyteller and Andrew is excited by her success.

This reaction is not typical of conventional gender roles at the time.

Second Half: Part 6

Ida, the narrator asserts, has luck on her side: she is settled with Andrew. She likes being with him. Together he and Ida form a sociable couple, and everyday becomes a Saturday. When Ida thinks about her good fortune, it seems to her to be the result of her ability to say "yes," to experience. This might indicate that Ida could not have become happy or whole if she had not lived through all that came before.

Second Half: Part 7

Experience, for Ida, however, is the experience of an uninterrupted present. Her difference from Andrew is symbolically represented by the metaphor of doors. Ida does not like doors. She likes rooms and being in rooms. She does not like going in and out of doors herself or when others do. Doors seem to be obstacles to Ida who likes, cultivates, and lives in an uninterrupted present. Although Andrew is steady and not moody, a husband who is always pleasant, he enters and exits through doors. Experience then, it seems, is more fragmented for him than for Ida. Certainly, Andrew is a more fragmented character than Ida. Ida, on the other hand "always did the same thing in the same way." In addition, all circumstances seem equal to her: "they said do you like the sunshine or the rain and Ida said she liked it best."

Second Half: Part 8

Ida concludes by celebrating the way Ida has become herself and her relationship with Andrew. Their union exists within the context of "yes." The section swells in the center: "something did happen and it excited everyone that it was something and it did happen." What that is, is not revealed, and this detail is not important. That it happened, however, is important. The events of the story suggest that what happened may have had something to do with Ida's fame. Stein, like Ida, had become an international celebrity after writing *The Autobiography of Alice B. Toklas*. There are also indications that the excitement is a result of Stein's acknowledging, even if only cryptically through the medium of her camouflaged prose, the possibility of a complete bond with women. Stein felt that the contempt shown to women as persons by men subverts women's perceptions of themselves and

each other, limiting their ability to fully bond with others. However, Stein believed that sexual or romantic relationships were a means to subvert this constraint and achieve a complete bond. As the excitement tapers off, Ida becomes calm. She eats fine foods, rests, lives with Andrew contentedly. "They are there," the narrator says conclusively. "There" seems to indicate a condition of fulfillment rather than a place. Then the narrator thanks her characters, Ida and Andrew, and asks the reader to: "Thank them." *Ida* ends with the single word, "Yes." This signifies an expansive acceptance of perception, character, experience—the world, or life in general.

CHARACTERS

Eleanor Angel
Ida lives with Eleanor in California. Eleanor has found gold and other precious minerals on her property.

Frank Arthur
Frank Arthur is Ida's first husband. They are not married long. He is described as a man who is not surprised by experience.

Aunt
After the death of her parents, Ida lives with her great aunt, whom the narrator categorizes as not gentle, unlike the rest of Ida's family. There is a rumor indicating that she buried an aborted fetus under a pear tree after an affair with a soldier.

Blanchette
Blanchette is Ida's dog and Mary Rose's pup.

Chocolate
Chocolate is Ida's dog and Mary Rose's pup.

Claudine
Claudine is one of Ida's dogs.

Edith
For a time, Ida lives with Edith and her husband William in Washington. Edith has a son from a previous marriage and she speaks brusquely to William. She is also said to share a mother with William.

Frank

Ida kicks him, apparently accidentally, in the testicles as he is teaching her to swim. It is not clear whether he is the same Frank as Frank Arthur.

Frederick

Frederick meets Ida in Washington. He is a soldier. He falls in love with Ida and marries her. They move from Washington to Ohio, then to Texas. Ida leaves him in Texas.

Andrew Hamilton

Andrew is Ida's enduring husband. With him she becomes "more Ida." He embodies her ideal of what a husband ought to be (the means for her to realize herself). Andrew is also said to be like violets, flowers "that last the longest if you do not pick them." He is different from the other men in Ida's life. They did not last.

Andrew, although not active, is not quiet, either, or alone, and he is not sad. Occasionally, Andrew seems to become other people. Sometimes he is called William, not to be confused with Edith's husband William. Sometimes he seems to be sitting across from himself. Stein presents character, through Andrew, as the changing aspect of a person.

Sam Hamlin

Sam meets Ida when she is leaving Connecticut and tells her he would divorce his wife for her if he had a wife. He also tells her that he will not leave Connecticut.

Henry Henry

Henry is a man who visits Ida when she lives in Washington.

Ida

Ida is the protagonist. The novel traces the course of her life and depicts her character and development from someone who seeks her sense of self through others to someone who finds her sense of self from within. Early in her life, her parents die. She often wishes she had a twin and sometimes even thinks of herself as twins, giving herself several names. She becomes a beauty queen and a celebrity, and she has a number of friends and lovers. She marries several times, but it is only in her marriage to Andrew that she can become her full self rather than be consumed and diminished.

Ida-Ida

The name for Ida when she appears as a composite with her imaginary "twin."

Iris

Iris is another of Ida's dogs. Iris is sometimes blind and sometimes not blind.

Susan Little

Ida becomes close with Susan Little while she is married to Andrew. It is likely that they shared a homosexual relationship.

Love

Love is the name of one of Ida's dogs. He was born blind. The dog's name and handicap are a pun on the saying: Love is blind.

Man from Omaha

The man from Omaha follows Ida because she is famous. The man never returns, however, because he does not meet Winnie, he only meets the real Ida.

Mary Rose

She is a dog that Ida tells a story about. Chocolate, who is run over, and Blanchette are her pups.

Gerald Seaton

Ida marries Gerald before she marries Andrew. Ida likes Gerald and likes hearing him talk. Gerald sees Ida for who she is rather than as the person others have made of her. Nevertheless, their contact is shallow and Ida has "met." him once only. After that "they never met again." By "met," Stein might mean sexual intimacy, but more than likely, she means to indicate emotional intimacy; i.e., Ida and Gerald have only once connected deeply as people who reach into and know each other. Gerald and Ida live in domestic familiarity, but not with human intimacy.

Eugene Thomas

Although he wanted to marry Ida, Eugene nearly drowns in Connecticut while Ida is in Washington. He does not return for her.

Virginia

Virginia is the least referenced of Ida's many personalities.

William

Stein reports that he speaks in poetry, although none is included in the text. Ida lives with him and his wife Edith in Washington. William has a daughter from a previous marriage, likes gardening, and supposedly shares a mother with Edith.

Winnie

Winnie is the name Ida gives her twin after she wins a beauty contest. Winnie represents Ida as she sometimes appears to others.

THEMES

Celebrity

Towards the end of the first chapter, Ida advises her twin—the hidden part of herself that she is trying to liberate—to enter a beauty contest. Her twin, Ida-Ida, or Winnie, wins. Ida becomes a celebrity. This mirrors Stein herself, who attained celebrity status some six years before the publication of *Ida* with her book *The Autobiography of Alice B. Toklas*. In *Ida* Stein explores the effect of celebrity. She is particularly intent to show that the person-as-celebrity is not an actual person. When a man introduces himself to Winnie, for example, he soon discovers that he is speaking with Ida. The real Ida is not the same person as the celebrity, Winnie, even if they are actually the same person. The man seems to be disappointed at his discovery.

Democracy

It may seem odd to assign to prose a term usually confined to politics and government. Nevertheless, the theme of democracy is implicit in *Ida* because of Stein's philosophy of perception and identity. Each perception, each observation, each event in *Ida* is narrated with the same emphasis, even when something is explored at a greater length than something else. Nothing takes priority over anything else. Stein gives equal importance to everything, and this reflects the egalitarian philosophy of democracy.

Feminism

Feminism as an idea or a social movement is not an explicit theme of Ida, but *Ida* is the work of a woman with a strong feminist consciousness. Indeed, Stein lived outside of conventional gender expectations her entire life. *Ida* bears the marks of a feminist sensibility and in certain

TOPICS FOR FURTHER STUDY

- Stein's fame rests not only on her own work but on her role as the hostess of a Parisian salon in which many of the great painters, writers, and musicians of the early twentieth century gathered. Among them was Pablo Picasso, one of the most important painters of the twentieth century. His 1906 cubist portrait of Stein now hangs in the Metropolitan Museum of Art in New York City. Explore Picasso's cubist period (reproductions of his work are available in books and on the Web), paying attention to the way Picasso decomposed the images he painted. Using some of these reproductions, prepare a twenty-minute presentation for your class, citing examples from Stein and Picasso, exploring the similarities between Picasso's cubism and Stein's prose in *Ida*.

- Using Janet Flanner's *Paris Was Yesterday*, or other books you may find in the library or on the Internet, write an essay about the artistic, intellectual, and political life of Paris from the turn of the century up until the start of World War II.

- Write a short story following the narrative conventions of sequence, coherence, and clarity. Then take your story and rewrite it in the manner of *Ida*. Read the second version of your story to your class and lead a discussion about it. Following this discussion, read your original version to the class.

- Using the library and the Internet, research the *nouveau roman* or New Novel, as it came to be called. Introduce this literary style to your class in a short presentation, explaining what it is, why it came into being, what its debt might be to Stein's writing, and how it has influenced subsequent literary trends.

instances, the narrative shifts personal pronouns, using she and he indiscriminately. Furthermore, *Ida* may be viewed as Stein's attempt to break

Monica Salisbury and Leonard Rupert Norris illustrate a society wedding in 1930 (Sasha / Getty Images)

the accepted structure of novels (established mostly by men) by sabotaging the conventions that guide the way novels are written and read. In traditional novels, readers can rely on a center of meaning and reference, and this is not the case in *Ida*. Stein's narrative is designed to exist outside of ideas or world views and the authority they seem to confer. It is designed simply to record what its subject perceives, thinks, feels, remembers, or imagines. This occurs not through a centered first person narrative but through a third person narrator whose power is to perceive and observe but not to orient. *Ida* is a collection of data, and Ida is the hero of an "educational romance," a type of novel that shows the growth of its major character. Novels centered upon character growth are also refereed to as bildungsroman (though the term is conventionally used when discussing the growth of a young male character on his path to achieving manhood). Further contradicting conventional scripts, Ida achieves fame, and her husband Andrew exists in order to facilitate her accomplishments rather than vice versa.

Identity

It is tempting to talk about the "problem" of identity in *Ida*, especially considering how Ida and Winnie are and are not the same person. One should also consider that Ida's identity in great measure depends on perception. Ida exists according to her own perception of herself and according to other people's perceptions of her. Consequently she is both one person and also several people. But identity, even as fragmented as it is in *Ida*, is not treated in the novel as a problem. The variety of identities within one person is treated as a commonplace, as is the existence of varying perceptions. Every phenomenon is reported without being positioned, valued, or judged as "real" or as "imaginary." If one thinks of Ida as a canvas, one can imagine Stein simply including every detail on a flat surface without any perspective. Thus, the viewer's gaze (or the reader's attention) is not directed in any particular way.

STYLE

Incoherence

Incoherence in writing or in speaking is usually regarded as a fault rather than a device. It usually signifies, in literature or in life, a state of disease or derangement. Schizophrenics, drunkards, and people under great stress may be or seem to be incoherent. In *Ida*, Stein turns incoherence into a literary device; it becomes the way she tells the story. Stein typically strings together sentences in the book like so:

> She liked apples. She was disappointed but she did not sigh. She got sunburned and she had a smile on her face. They asked her did she like it.

Taken as a unit, this adds up to incoherence. A reader might guess that these are sentences taken out of context and printed one after the other. Each sentence, sometimes even each word, seems to be a free floating unit. The essential fact about incoherence is that nothing has anything to do with anything else. Through incoherence, Stein conveys the fragmented nature of experience and highlights the present by conveying thoughts and experiences as they happen. Each moment is its own.

Additionally, incoherence may suggest that the words are actually codes, words substituted for other words that must be kept hidden. Posing as one unacknowledged part of herself, Virginia, Ida wonders what water is and then realizes that she herself is like water, perhaps because of the fluidity of her experience, perception, and identity. Married, Ida does not love "anybody in Ohio," not even her husband (he is, after all, "somebody" in Ohio). Perhaps, then, the word "apples" signifies women, not fruit.

Repetition

Throughout *Ida* Stein uses the incantatory device of repetition, repeating nouns, verbs, prepositions, phrases and language patterns. This device may be meant to provide a sense of unity and coherence to a world narrated in a way that simultaneously challenges coherence.

Selection: What Is Left Out and What Is Left In

Selection, although seldom evident, is one of the principle devices novelists use to compose stories, reveal characters, and move plots forward. Indeed, if selection is noticed, the very effect it is designed to achieve is essentially ruined. Novelists attempt to select material in order to create the illusion that the novel is an authentic, complete rendition of a particular segment of reality. But the apparent completeness the reader experiences is an illusion based as much upon the details that are left out of the story as the details that are included in the story. *Ida*'s radical peculiarity is as much a consequence of what Stein has chosen to omit as what she has chosen to include. Connectives, sequence, cause and effect relations, and motivation are not part of the story. The story is built on the perception of a random flow of data. If anything, one could say that the selection exercised by Stein is directly opposed to conventional selection. Where most novelists would focus on sequence, cause and effect relations, and motivation, choosing to leave out most random data, Stein does just the opposite.

Stream of Consciousness

Most frequently associated with the novels *Ulysses* and *Finnegan's Wake*, both by James Joyce, stream of consciousness is a narrative technique that short circuits the usual narrative categories of past, present, waking, dreaming, thinking, feeling, or imagining, among others. Stream of consciousness indiscriminately relies on all of these modes without regard to the boundaries between them. This narrative form is prominent in *Ida*, and Stein seems to be telling Ida's story through Ida, but Ida is not the first person narrator.

HISTORICAL CONTEXT

Celebrity

The growth of mass media through radio and movies during the 1920s and 1930s brought about an increased awareness of celebrities. The massive enthusiasm for Charles Lindbergh when he flew nonstop across the Atlantic Ocean in 1927 was unlike anything that had come before. Similarly, the interest aroused by Wallis Simpson, who became the Duchess of Windsor when King Edward VIII of England gave up his throne to marry her, was immense. Sales of undershirts were reported to plummet when the actor Clark Gable undressed for bed in the 1934 movie *It Happened One Night*—he was not wearing an undershirt in the scene. Political leaders, too, were not only political leaders but celebrities in their own right. Stein herself became a celebrity after the publication of *The Autobiography of Alice B. Toklas*. Her subsequent reading and speaking tour of the United States was covered extensively by the press.

Freudianism

In 1900, Sigmund Freud published his revolutionary book, *The Interpretation of Dreams*. Beside the fundamental assertion that dreams are expressions of frustrated wishes, Freud's book introduced the idea that each person possesses an active unconscious that is mostly responsible for their emotions, desires, and behavior. Freud posited that this unconscious was subjugated (repressed) by the conscious because not all human emotions, desires, and behaviors are acceptable in human society. Following the book's publication, many writers attempted to write from this unconscious, using techniques like automatic writing (holding a pen in one hand and moving it across the page— writing without thinking), writing when in a trance, and generally trying to keep the censorious consciousness from blocking the emergence of deeper, repressed material. *Ida* clearly shows the influence of this school of writing and of this technique.

The Rise and Consolidation of Totalitarian States and Charismatic Leaders

Between the two world wars, Russia, Germany, Italy, and Japan arose as powerful, totalitarian states. It seems obvious to point out that the heads of state for each country were males, but

COMPARE
&
CONTRAST

- **1930s:** The advent and popularity of radio and the movies creates cultural awareness of national and international celebrities.

  Today: Media (now mostly in the form of television and the Internet) is even more ubiquitous, as is the corresponding focus on celebrities. Through the power, reach, and diversification of media, many people become famous not for their talents, beauty, or political power, but simply because they are objects of national and international gossip.

- **1930s:** Powerful nations and their governments are arming in preparation for major war while simultaneously attempting last ditch negotiations to prevent war. Contained, although savage, violence is also occurring in Ethiopia, Spain, and Czechoslovakia.

  Today: Conflicts between governments and rebel groups have resulted in wars in Iraq, Afghanistan, Palestine, Somalia, and Lebanon. These conflicts threaten to expand into global war.

- **1930s:** Workers in industrialized nations struggle to establish unions and to secure a livable wage, humane working conditions, and a forty-hour work week.

  Today: Globalization, outsourcing, and technology create an underclass of cheap laborers without basic rights.

- **1930s:** Through Franklin D. Roosevelt's New Deal, the U.S. government creates a number of programs and projects to establish social services and financial security for most Americans.

  Today: The U.S. government is attempting to reverse many of the social benefits of the New Deal, engineering the privatization of what were formally government responsibilities, including health care, education, retirement, and most recently, imprisonment.

---

it is worth noting when considering that Stein wrote *Ida* within an international context formed by male brutality. In *Ida*, Stein seems to be withdrawing from that world of masculine brutality, focusing instead on the inner world of a woman.

The Years between World War I and World War II

The twenty years between the end of World War I, in 1919, and the start of World War II, in 1939, were years marked by tremendous upheavals in politics, economics, sexuality, and art. Change was ubiquitous. The way people lived together, the way they described their experience, the way they saw the world, all were challenged and altered. During this period there was the success of the Russian Revolution, economic depressions in Europe, and the 1920s economic boom in the United States preceding the Depression of the 1930s. After the fall of the German monarchy, and after a brief period of faltering attempts at democracy, Germany reemerged as a fascist state more powerful, disciplined, and dangerous than its predecessor and its initial ally, Italy.

In music, the dissonance of Igor Stravinsky and the atonal concision of Anton Von Webern replaced the emotionalism and melody of the nineteenth century. In painting, Juan Gris, Pablo Picasso, Georges Braque, and Henri Matisse changed the way artists saw the world, how they used the canvas, and even what painters were supposed to paint. Authors like James Joyce, Marcel Proust, Virginia Woolf, T. S. Eliot, and Stein set about breaking down the way experience is recorded in literature, sabotaging the convention of orderly narrative sequence.

Miss America 1927, Lois Delander of Joliet, Illinois, holds up her title sash (Hulton Archive / Getty Images)

CRITICAL OVERVIEW

Clifton Fadiman admits in *A Subtreasury of American Humor* that upon reading *Ida* he had no idea what the book was about. He adds impishly, "I have a theory ... that Miss Stein has set herself to solve, and has succeeded in solving, the most difficult problem in prose composition—to write something that will not arrest the attention in any way." Fadiman's response, although designed to be humorous, well represents the response of most readers approaching *Ida* and the work of Gertrude Stein in general.

What is at first baffling, often over the course of time and through the intervention of scholars and critics, can become less so. Writing more than thirty years later in *Twentieth-Century Literary Criticism*, Michael J. Hoffman explains that "Like Matisse who wished to paint with the eyes of a child, Stein combines primitivistically simple diction with interlocking repetitions, as well as a humorous tone that mixes the pretense of seriousness with the fun of writing." Where Fadiman finds tedium, Bettina L. Knapp, writing in *Gertrude Stein*, finds "humor, banter, frolic, satire, as well as recognizable action ... implicit in what might be identified as a heroine in *Ida*." Unlike Fadiman, Knapp characterizes Stein's prose, generally, as "discursive, meandering, and childlike." She calls *Ida* "a collective figure" incorporating "such fascinating ancient and modern women as Helen of Troy" (among others), and Stein as well.

Donald Sutherland, in *Gertrude Stein: A Biography of her Work*, asserts that "*Ida* is strictly speaking no novel at all but belongs to the tradition of the philosophical farce or romance which is probably at its purest in Voltaire's *Candide*." According to Sutherland, *Ida* is "the story of ... a person who neither does anything nor is connected with anything but who by sheer force of existence in being there holds the public attention and becomes a legend." Sutherland sees *Ida* as a book of external inaccuracies that are "internally true." Ida herself, Sutherland maintains, "is a human mind. She has no personality ... she exists and is in the present, like a legend or a masterpiece or the human mind, and that existence is all there is to her, though she is surrounded by everything else in perpetual happening."

In his 1959 book, *The Third Rose: Gertrude Stein and Her World*, John Malcolm Brinnin, attempts to explicate Stein's writing style. Stein, he argues, wrote as she did in order to "bring space into the vocabulary of an art whose aesthetic was concentrated in its manipulations of time." To do so, he continues, Stein "would follow the pictorial cubists, moving around an object to seize several subjective appearances, which, fused in a single image, reconstitute it in time." Brinnin warns that "works attempting to bring this new dimension to writing are, for all but those readers who no longer demand what literature has always offered, impossible to read."

Nevertheless, writing in *Axel's Castle: A Study in the Imaginative Literature of 1870–1930*, Edmund Wilson (writing ten years before *Ida* was published) pinpoints Stein's importance as an author. Indeed, his comments are often echoed today by contemporary critics. He observes:

> Widely ridiculed and seldom enjoyed, [Stein] has yet played an important role ... Most of us balk at her ... half-witted-sounding catalogues of numbers; most of us read her less and less. Yet ... we are still aware of her presence in the background of contemporary literature ... eternally and placidly ruminating the gradual developments of the processes of being.

CRITICISM

Neil Heims

Heims is a writer and teacher living in Paris. In the following essay, he argues that Stein shifts the narrative focus in Ida *away from telling a story to challenge the reader's basic expectations of, and approach to, reading a novel.*

The story in *Ida* is shaped by the responses the mind makes to the data it perceives in its environment. Gertrude Stein is less interested in narrating a recognizable story in *Ida* than in portraying reality as it is experienced through stream of consciousness. But Stein also plays with language. In *Ida* the meaning or sense of

> *IDA REQUIRES THE READER TO RENOUNCE LONG-HELD READING HABITS, MOST NOTABLY THE EXPECTATION AND THE DESIRE FOR A NARRATIVE TO PROVIDE VICARIOUS EXPERIENCE AND SUSPENSE."*

language is often secondary to its sound. Consequently, words stripped of their meaning and context raise the reader's awareness of their interaction with words (either as conveyors of meaning or sound, or both). In *Ida* Stein represents the activity of consciousness and the phenomenon of perception. Through *Ida* Stein enables the reader to experience, in the act of reading, acts of pure perception and of consciousness freed from meaning.

Ida does not offer readers the opportunity or the pleasure, as most novels conventionally do, of meeting recognizable or intriguing characters, or of experiencing the details and the drama of the typical situations that drive a story, like growing up, or being in love, or following a profession, or fighting in a war, or raising children, or facing death. Nor does Stein, in *Ida*, organize a series of interconnecting events that form a sequentially unfolding and suspenseful narrative fueled by conflict. It may be unusual to describe a work in terms of what it is not. But the experience most readers will first have of *Ida* is a sense of everything that seems to be missing: story, plot, sequence, coherence, excitement, character development, suspense. Reading *Ida* can be something like the experience of repeatedly falling asleep during a movie and, during periods of being awake, seeing scenes that, consequently, make little sense; or, it is very much like quickly flipping through the channels on a television set, catching little more than brief phrases and images from each program.

The words in *Ida*, even as they seem to be signifying actual characters, events, things, and actions, are more particularly being assembled to represent themselves as linguistic elements with a shape, dimension, and contour that is independent of their meaning. Stein uses words in the

WHAT DO I READ NEXT?

- *Nadja* (1928), by the French surrealist André Breton, traces the career of a woman in Paris making her way through the city's bohemian underworld. Following the surrealist desire to confound the senses and upset the common order by using prose that does not follow the conventions of narrative and dramatic coherence, *Nadja* resembles *Ida* while providing a more concrete sense of person and place.

- *The Autobiography of Alice B. Toklas* (1933), despite the title, is a book written by Gertrude Stein about herself, told as if she were her companion, Alice B. Toklas, rather than herself. Notably, Stein wrote the book when she needed to make money, and this may explain why it is one of her most accessible works.

- In a schematic or abstract way that retains sensations but purges those sensations of the events that caused them, Conrad Aiken's poem "The Room," published in 1930, is the poet's meditation, without specifically naming it, on his father's murder of his mother followed by his father's suicide.

- Raymond Queneau's *Zazie dans le métro* (Zazie in the Subway; 1959) is a comic novel written in a disconnected, slapstick style. It was made into an absurdist movie by Louis Malle in 1960.

- *The Time of Our Singing* (2003), by Richard Powers, uses many techniques pioneered by Stein, yet it also provides a strong narrative presence and a complex plot that spans several generations and integrates a number of social and racial cultures. This gives the book more of a conventional aspect than that of an experimental novel.

- *The Divided Self*, published in 1960, by R. D. Laing, is a study of schizophrenia, treating the disease, in large part, as stemming from a skewed language system. The words of the schizophrenic speaker, Laing argues, are taken to be mystifying or "crazy" because the background they refer to, the situations from which their speech emerges, are hidden from their interlocutors.

---

same way painters use pigments, composers use notes, or sculptors use three-dimensional shapes. The art lies in the process of combining the building blocks (words, pigments, notes, shapes), and these can be combined to create a story, a recognizable image, a melody, or a recognizable object. However, they can also be combined to create a string of words, blotches of color, dissonance, or a shape without any recognizable form. Such art is usually referred to as abstract, and Stein was one of the first writers to experiment with abstraction in favor of creating a story that is a recognizable representation or imitation of something else. Stein, then, like the abstract painter or sculptor, seeks to create an aesthetic object that is not attached to meanings or morals.

The text of *Ida* is not a reliable indication of what reality conventionally is like or of how things ought to be. Where a story can be said to be two dimensional, the reader can be said to provide the third dimension. *Ida* (or any book, really) is only a collection of printed paper sitting on a shelf until it is being read. Then, it becomes something that provides meaning, sound, or images as it interacts with the consciousness of the reader, setting off associations in the reader's mind. These associations are, in a sense, what makes a book a story. In a conventional novel, most of the meaning is easily extracted; whereas in *Ida*, meaning is not so easily derived. For instance, if ten people were to look at a conventional painting portraying a horse, each of these

ten people would likely report that they saw a horse in the painting. If ten people were to look at an abstract painting, each would likely report that they saw vastly different items in the painting.

In *Ida* Stein still references novelistic conventions to some degree. Indeed, the novel still revolves around a character and her experiences. Stein uses this conventional skeleton in order to outline the landscape of Ida's consciousness (or perhaps consciousness in general) and to provide a schematic diagram of the dynamics of perception:

> She liked to talk and to sing songs and she liked to change places. Wherever she was she always liked to change places. Otherwise there was nothing to do all day. Of course she went to bed early but even so she always could say, what shall I do now, now what shall I do.

Read out loud, this passage is striking for its narrative rhythm. It sounds like a children's story: "She liked to talk and to sing songs and she liked to change places." The sentence is a sing-song compound of three simple sentences, simultaneously joined together and kept separate by the word "and." It has the fairy tale quality of the following example: "The prince was rich and the prince was handsome and the prince was lonely." In this sentence, although there is no stated connection between its three parts, there is an implicit connection. "Although," or "nevertheless" seems to be hinted at. "Although the prince was rich and handsome, still he was lonely." But in Stein's sentence, there is no such relationship. Stein is not saying "Because she liked to play and sing, she liked to change places," or "Although she liked to play and sing, etc." There is no reasonable connection between talking, singing, and changing places. These elements are related only by the rhetorical device of polysyndeton, the repetition of the word "and."

The sentences that follow, "Wherever she was she liked to change places. Otherwise there was nothing to do all day," in their apparent simplicity, actually reveal an important fact: experience is a function of alteration, of going from one place or thing to another. Even the most mundane day consists of a great deal of movement, beginning with getting out of bed.

The final sentence of the paragraph, "Of course she went to bed early but even so she always could say, what shall I do now, now what shall I do," abandons the compound simplicity of the preceding sentences. Now there is some relation between the parts of the sentences described! "Even so" going to sleep did not free her from the problem of "doing," of changing from place to place. But just as the reader may be trying to puzzle out a meaning, Stein changes the context (something Ida, she has just reported, likes to do). The sentence exists less as a narrative fact about Ida than as literary allusion (or a reference to something else). Stein first references Marcel Proust's, great work of exploration of consciousness, *In Search of Lost Time.* Its first volume, *Swann's Way* (published in French in 1912) begins with the words, in Scott Montcrieff's 1922 translation: "For a long time, I used to go to bed early." Then the last half of Stein's sentence echoes the desperate cry from T. S. Eliot's poem *The Waste Land:* "What shall I do now? What shall I do?" The cry is meant to express the barrenness of experience.

Stein's narrative technique in *Ida* is a formal assault upon the conventions of the novel and, by extension, upon the reader. *Ida* requires the reader to renounce long-held reading habits, most notably the expectation and the desire for a narrative to provide vicarious experience and suspense. The risk Stein takes as a writer, or, perhaps, the challenge she presents to the reader, is that Stein repeatedly takes the reader to the edge of boredom and confusion. Vicarious experience is nullified. Stein's writing is hypnotic, but not hypnotic in the sense of fascinating. It is hypnotic because meaning is replaced by resonance. Think of a musical experience where the drama of melody is replaced by the mesmerism of drone. Indeed, the emotions, the associations, the techniques that cause a novel to be exciting and compelling are cancelled out and are replaced by a steady sing-song rhythm. The novel's narrator, although not a character in the novel and nondescript, is nevertheless a strong unwavering presence. Despite the fact that the novel is narrated using the past tense, the lack of sequential chronology makes even past events seem as if they are removed from the continuum of time and the rule of cause and effect.

A novel like *Ida*, because of its obscurity and because of its unconventionality and experimental quality, may seem richer and more interesting when it is talked about than it does when it is read. Analysis may clarify some of its aspects.

When a reader returns to it, however, even after getting a sense of its aesthetic resemblance to cubism or to the modernist narratives of authors like James Joyce and Virginia Woolf, *Ida* still may seem opaque, confusing, and, consequently, not engaging. And "not engaging" may be the worst thing that can be said about a book. A narrative that does not engage the reader also does not captivate or dominate. However, it can liberate the reader from being a passive respondent seduced by vicarious excitement. It can give the reader an opportunity to engage the novel as all works of art must be engaged, in the imaginary space forged midway between the work of art and the person who beholds it; i.e., in an engaged experience of the text, actually reading without regard to the content of what is being read.

Source: Neil Heims, Critical Essay on *Ida*, in *Novels for Students*, Gale, Cengage Learning, 2008.

Cynthia Secor

In the following excerpt, Secor suggests that Ida *is a great American novel whose heroine can be classified among the great heroines of literature.*

... *Ida* is a novel about a woman, a woman whose presence excited comment. Critical allusions to the novel have for the most part limited themselves to Ida as a study of identity and entity, as a portrait of a publicity saint, as a study of the Duchess of Windsor, as a comment on the dilemma of Stein as a publicly celebrated author, and as the chronicling of her first real whore since Melanctha. All of these conceptions have merit, and they are compatible. Ida is not Gertrude Stein, and it is important to sense the variety of interests at play in the novel. As Stein says, "I like a thing simple but it must be simple through complication. Everything must come into your scheme, otherwise you cannot achieve real simplicity."

Closely related to Stein's intention to bring everything into her scheme is her gift for rendering significant that which is deemed ordinary. Ida is in most respects a very ordinary woman of her period. She is not really a whore, though she gets married rather more often than usual; she is not really a publicity saint, whatever Stein meant by that charming phrase, but she is one of those persons people do talk about. Ida is fundamentally a woman in search of marriage, a marriage in which she can become more herself. Ida moves from marriage to marriage, state to state, city to city, until she comes to rest in a

> STEIN'S INTENSE CONCENTRATION ON THE PRESENT MOMENT, HER FOCUS ON THE HUMAN MIND COMPOSING AN IMAGE OF HUMAN NATURE, ALLOWS HER TO TREAT WOMEN AS SERIOUSLY AS MEN HAVE BEEN TREATED IN TRADITIONAL LITERATURE."

relation that allows her to be herself more fully than has any previous relation or occupation. The relation is not enough, her resting is not enough, but then what ever is? Life continues. One is maturing, aging, slowing down. Ida and Andrew are together. For this their life we can thank them. It is of interest to us...

Ida is a woman, every woman, an American woman, a woman not defined by her relation to woman or man, but to herself. Ida is herself. She is in quest of herself, though quest is much too self-conscious a term for her travels. In her youth she says to a friend, "... I am never tired and I am never very fresh. I change all the time. I say to myself, Ida, and that startles me and then I sit still." Later she dreams:

> ... that now she was married, she was not Ida she was Virginia ... She dreamed that she often longed for water. She dreamed that she said. When I close my eyes I see water and when I close my eyes I do see water.

> What is water, said Virginia.
> And then suddenly she said. Ida.

At both the conscious and the unconscious levels, Ida already experiences herself as complete. There is in this *Bildungsroman* no conventional maturation and no crises of identity. On the eve of her final marriage, to Andrew the first, there is the perception that she is "Andrew's Ida," "more that Ida she was Ida itself." But even this moment of "identity" is short-lived. Only briefly is her essential self, her "entity," heightened and augmented by a relational role, by being the focus of Andrew's romantic interest. Almost immediately Stein tells us that "Andrew had changed Ida to be more Ida." She is herself, now, more complete than ever for the experience of having seen and been seen. It is here that the first half of the novel culminates—with themes of entity and marriage firmly entwined.

The idea of marriage, so frequent a theme in the first half of the novel, is scarcely mentioned again, as in slow motion Stein proceeds in the second half to portray the gradual coming together of Ida and Andrew. Their coming together might be called marriage, but it is not Stein's purpose to explore the patriarchal institution of marriage. It is her purpose to explore the process through time of two persons bringing into step their characteristic rhythms... In traditional narratives and dramas focused on the female person, whether they be popular or serious literature, marriage is the proper culmination. Events and interactions may follow upon the marriage of the female person; but ritually and metaphorically the moment of completion for the female person, within patriarchal literature, whether written by women or men, is the moment of union with the male person, the taking of the hymen. We may decorate and elaborate the event with issues of dowry, morality, and whatnot, but the moment is relational. Her role, her identity, her entity, are one: she is the helpmate of her lord, the bearer of his progeny. Or worse, she is fallen, too many men making use of her. All of this is precisely what Stein is not saying. Stein is the harbinger of the articulate feminist literary community that is currently emerging, challenging all of the generic conventions that have sought to portray women as the other, the anonymous, the helpful. What can a heroine do? She can be herself, that's what she can do...

Stein's own experience as a lesbian gives her a critical distance that shapes her understanding of the struggle to be one's self. Her own identity is not shaped as she moves into relation with a man...

Her women thus come into the world complete, static, centered in their own space. They are not androgynous. There is in their lives no strenuous dialectic of gender. No man comes to provide for them the masculine qualities lacking in their own feminine natures. Their individual rhythms are distinct and complete from childhood...

It can be argued that Stein's entire effort to create the continuous present, intensely experienced for itself without reference to ideas, traditional syntax, and familiar metaphors, is her solution to the problem of having been born a female artist whose only tradition is a patriarchal one. Her method forces one to look slowly and carefully at what is in front of one, without explaining it in terms of ritual, myth, or other cultural artifacts. James Joyce is an archetypal patriarchal artist...

Within Joyce's tradition women do not exist as active figures, as embodiments of the Godhead, as definers of reality; they are vessels, handmaidens, and at their most exciting temptresses of gods and men. Stein, predictably, has no interest in excitement, except as an expression of the self.

Saturday, Ida.

> Ida never said once upon a time. These words did not mean anything to Ida. This is what Ida said. Ida said yes, and then Ida said oh yes, and then Ida said, I said yes, and then Ida said, Yes.

> Once when Ida was excited she said I know what it is I do, I do know that it is, yes.

That is what she said when she was excited.

Stein repeatedly rejects liveliness that she might embody life. Ida has life. Stein puts it succinctly:

> But a continent can always be changed and so that is not why Ida and Woodward did not always meet.

> Very likely Ida is not anxious nor is Woodward. Well said Ida, I have to have my life and Ida had her life and she has her life and she is having her life.

Stein's intense concentration on the present moment, her focus on the human mind composing an image of human nature, allows her to treat women as seriously as men have been treated in traditional literature. Hers is not a vision preempted by kings and ministers of state. Ida in her less literary way says all there is to be said on the subject of patriarchy in response to her first husband.

> He met her on the road one day and he began to walk next to her and they managed to make their feet keep step. It was just like a walking marathon.

> He began to talk. He said, All the world is crying about it all. They all want a king.

> She looked at him and then she did not. Everybody might want a king but anybody did not want a queen.

Stein is clear enough. Yet even the best and most sympathetic of her critics have been loath to see her subject matter—when that subject matter is women—and to understand what it means that hers is a lesbian perspective. So good a critic as Donald Sutherland seems almost unaware of the metaphysical, erotic, even political content of *Tender Buttons*, and so fine a collaborator as Virgil Thomson finds "Patriarchal Poetry" hermetic. The first is a celebration of the domestic and sensual aspects of her relation with Toklas, and the latter is a brilliant and witty comment on the political nature of the traditional masculine literary establishment. Neither work is without meaning if one is interested in sharing with Stein her understanding of love, identity, and power. Both are good preparation for *Ida*, which asks her reader to look at a contemporary American woman moving from birth into her golden years, realizing as she goes the opportunities open to her. What do identity and entity mean for an American woman living in America in the twentieth century? The Stein of *Everybody's Autobiography*, *Paris France*, *Wars I Have Seen*, and *Brewsie and Willie* is a social commentator. No less the Stein of *Ida*.

It is impossible to read *Ida* with anything approaching a complete understanding of Stein's accomplishment without sensing her own acceptance of herself as a complete physical and intellectual human being and her understanding of just how pervasive and disfunctional is the patriarchal understanding of the human mind and human nature. She understands that marriage, romance, and the roles of husband and wife are patriarchal institutions. It is out of this understanding that she creates the marriage of Ida and Andrew. Their union, while not denying their individual natures, has them meet on a plane that is truly the function of the human mind and not human nature.

> Slowly Ida knew everything about that. It was the first thing Ida had ever known really the first thing.
>
> Andrew was there, and it was not very long, it was long but not very long before Ida often saw Andrew and Andrew saw her. He even came to see her.

It is Stein's genius to couch in the traditional setting of their courtship Ida's emergence as a more and more present person. Marriage is not the beginning of her real life as traditionalists would have it, nor the end of her real life as some would have it. This marriage is a deepening of her actual life. The same is true for Andrew...

Entitling her work *Ida, A Novel*, Stein signals that it is meant to be read as an example of the form. Novels in Stein's understanding focus on character, a subject of concern for her from her youth...

In writing *Ida*, Stein rises to the challenge of creating a character with sufficient life to count in the life of the reader. That is why she so prominently labels it a novel. It was her own endless ruminations about publicity, reputations, identity, and entity that led her to the form of narration that gives to Ida the life that in the twentieth century is commonly reserved for movie stars, famous artists, war generals, and psychotic killers. Ida is food for the imagination...

What the human mind of the writer must grasp completely and uniformly is that which is the essential rhythm of the character being seen, the rhythm that through all variations remains constant. Ida is seen as striving to cease to be alone. The activity is not conscious, it is constant.

Stein, so little interested in or influenced by her contemporaries Freud and Jung, comes, nonetheless, to define the novel as a dream. Her definition grows out of her own understanding of the time sense that is necessary for a serious writer: "You can have a historical time but for you the time does not exist and if you are writing about the present the time element must cease to exist... There should not be a sense of time but an existence suspended in time." The character at the center of the novel then must be both food for the imagination and an existence suspended in time. *Ida* accomplishes this end by using a mode of narration so concrete and spare that the reader comes to feel that she is dreaming through Ida's mind the dream that is Ida. The intention of the novel is surely to provide an extended portrait of a woman, a woman whose human mind is the subject. The prose must embody her perception of successive moments in time—each frame as complete and accurate as the successive frames of a strip of celluloid movie film. Each paragraph is a frame; viewed successively they provide a portrait over time of reality as Ida sees it. Stein is not meant to be present; she is the camera.

This mode of narration is a solution to the problem of identity and entity as literary subject matter. The totality of the novel is the entity of Ida, whereas the successive frames—sometimes vignettes or anecdotes as well as straightforward accounts of activity—record successive identities. Ida's memory of Frank, the Lurline Baths, and the wild onions is typical. The episode is neither gratuitous nor randomly placed. *Ida* is a distillation of all that is Ida, not a loosely ordered chronicle of her travels and loves. In each successive frame she repeats her essential self. The dreams, memories, and impressions recorded are the ones that impinge deeply on Ida, that sink deeply into her, as Wordsworth's stone into the lake. They are the scenes her perception sees and retains. The Lurline Baths episode confirms that the girl and the woman are the same person. Their anxiety is the same anxiety. When "Ida was also married to Andrew," she recalls the Lurline Baths in San Francisco and a youth named Frank teaching her to swim:

> ... he leaned over and he said kick he was holding her under the chin and he was standing beside her, it was not deep water, and he said kick and she did and he walked along beside her holding her chin, and he said kick and she kicked again and he was standing very close to her and she kicked hard and she kicked him. He let go her he called out Jesus Christ my balls and he went under and she went under they were neither of them drowned but they might have been.

The moment is recalled forcefully. She continues thinking: "Strangely enough she never thought about Frank, that was his name, Frank, she could not remember his other name, but once when she smelled wild onion she remembered going under and that neither were drowned." The incident is recalled because: "Any ball has to look like the moon. Ida just had to know what was going to be happening soon." Immediately after the incident is recalled, the narrative continues: "And now it was suddenly happening, well not suddenly but it was happening, Andrew was almost Andrew the first. It was not sudden." Her anxiety during the process of their coming together is the anxiety of her youth when during the process of being supported in the water she kicked her mentor unexpectedly and accidentally. It is just this anxiety that causes her so often throughout her life unexpectedly and seemingly without cause to pick up and leave. It is just this anxiety that the girl child experienced in her "nice family" that "did easily lose each other." It is the anxiety of the child who "the first time she saw anything it frightened her." It is the anxiety associated with romance as she becomes at once both more herself and less herself; it is the anxiety connected with sex and love. The presence of the episode does not argue for causation. The adult anxiety does not stem from the

youthful event. It simply demonstrates that the adult woman coming together with the adult man is the same person who came into the world as Ida-Ida, held back by her mother, and who one more time "will get up suddenly once and leave but not just now."

A novel, then, is just like a dream. "And some dreams are just what any one would do only a little different always just a little different and that is what a novel is." Like a dream, a novel ends when there is no more interest in it. Ida's story ends with marriage. What more can happen? Ida's quest for entity within marriage is achieved. What can happen to Ida by virtue of marriage has happened, and any further exploration of entity would turn out to be another novel, a novel about aging: "If Ida goes on, does she go on even when she does not go on any more." Ida rests in her marriage ...

In a ... domestic, familiar fashion Andrew and Ida live ordinary lives "and Andrew is in, and they go in and that is where they are." They are as commonplace a couple as Mr. and Mrs. Reynolds. There is no more story to tell. The novel is over.

Clearly much of the force of this novel, that "complex force of femininity" which Woolf celebrates, comes from the fact that in creating the life of Ida, Stein does draw on her own past for emotional content. During the years preceding her writing the novel, she seems preoccupied with the relation of the child to the adult, ruminating on this theme in *The Geographical History of America*, *Everybody's Autobiography*, and *What Are Masterpieces*? In a wonderful turn on Wordsworth's idea that the boy is father to the man, Stein inquires: "What is the use of being a little boy if you are growing up to be a man." And she continues, in a sentence, wryly universalizing the discussion: "And yet everybody does so unless it is a little girl going to grow up to be a woman." What is the use of having been the youthful Gertrude involved with May Bookstaver and Leo Stein if she was to become the companion of Alice Toklas, to have lived so many places if she was to settle in Paris for most of her adult life?

Ida, then, which at the first reading seems so technically curious in the apparent break in tempo and focus between the first and second halves, reenacts the watershed in Stein's own life when after *Three Lives* and during *The Making of Americans* Alice arrived in her life. Her marriage to Alice was clearly the central emotional event in her own life. It both limited her options and freedom (Alice manipulated both her personal and her literary friendships, as Linda Simon notes), and it created the domestic and critical support that sustained her over the decades that marked the gradual recognition of her stature. This novel is not meant as fictionalized autobiography, but it does bring into conjunction the two themes which would surely have been prominent had Stein written the autobiography of Gertrude Stein—entity and marriage. Such careful critics as Richard Bridgman and Michael J. Hoffman have found the novel tedious with the departure of Winnie, but surely this is because they are focused on the theme of publicity rather than of marriage among Americans.

The rapid movement of Ida from place to place and from marriage to marriage is crucial to the portrait of her as a twentieth-century American woman. This restlessness and rootlessness, her lack of enduring connection with place or family, for Stein characterizes her as American . . .

It is this mobility, this gift for abstraction, which Ida embodies, that makes it possible for any American to know anything about men and women, and so to understand the coming together of Ida and Andrew as that of two persons, to be experienced directly, unmediated by traditional conceptions of husband and wife, identities that the traditional culture of an earlier century would have taken as reality.

As Stein's geographical history of Ida concludes, the curious two-part structure of the novel takes on meaning. It is a curious blending of picaresque and epithalamium. Ida has traveled and now she rests much as Leopold Bloom [from *Ulysses* by James Joyce] does, but with the difference that her geography is meant to be literal geography, states crossed and recrossed, not mythical regions. In turn Ida and Andrew's motion is meant to be the stately and joyous rhythm of the epithalamium, not to recall it.

> Poetry and prose is not interesting.
> What is necessary now is not form but content.
> That is why in this epoch a woman does the literary thinking.
> Kindly learn everything please.

The novel as Stein writes it understands these forms and their origins in patriarchal culture. And it is her genius as a critic and a writer that she creates for Ida a contemporaneous

vehicle suited to her reality. "Ida did not get married so that never again would she be alone." At first Ida experiences reality by herself, then upon maturity in the company of another person. Stein's own marriage with Toklas was by the writing of *Ida* in its fourth decade, and it had given her to understand well the nature of marriage, the spaces within it, its mythology, rituals, and processes. Gertrude in relation to Alice became over the years both more Gertrude and less Gertrude. In the beginning before she met Alice she was Gertrude. In the end she was Gertrude.

The thrice rewritten novel rewards the labor Stein put into it. The Ida-Ida of the first page is a cypher, an abstraction, whereas the Ida of the final page is a fully seen person. Through the successive relations—Love, Winnie, the three men she loved, and Andrew—that mark her passage from place to place, Ida gains intensity, density, and finally luminosity. At the novel's end the abandoned child of nineteenth-century fiction has emerged as a woman of common substance, at once fragile and majestic, complete in herself, and in enduring balance with another of her kind. When all is said and done, she rests before us an aging woman. "Not too much not too much Ida . . . And not enough Ida." Stein intends Ida to join the invisible choir of those who have gone before—Moll Flanders, Dorothea Brooke, Madame Bovary, and Isabel Archer.

Source: Cynthia Secor, "*Ida*, A Great American Novel," in *Twentieth Century Literature*, Vol. 24, No. 1, Spring 1978, pp. 96–107.

SOURCES

Brinnin, John Malcolm, *The Third Rose: Gertrude Stein and Her World*, Weidenfeld & Nicolson, 1959, pp. 140–41.

Eliot, T. S., "The Waste Land," in *T. S. Eliot: The Complete Poems and Plays*, Harcourt Brace, 1958, p. 41.

Fadiman, Clifton, "Getting Gertie's Ida," in *A Subtreasury of American Humor*, edited by E. B. and Katherine S. White, Modern Library, 1941, pp. 544–45.

Hoffman, Michael J., "Gertrude Stein," in *Twentieth-Century Literary Criticism*, Vol. 28, edited by Dennis Poupard, Gale Research, 1988, p. 334, reprinted from Twayne Publishers, 1976.

Knapp, Bettina L., *Gertrude Stein*, Frederick Ungar/Continuum, 1990, p. 166.

Proust, Marcel, "Swann's Way," in *Remembrance of Things Past*, Vol. 1, translated by C. K. Scott Moncrieff, Henry Holt, 1922.

Stein, Gertrude, *Ida*, in *Gertrude Stein: Writings 1932–1946*, Library of America, 1998, pp. 611–705.

Sutherland, Donald, *Gertrude Stein: A Biography of Her Work*, Greenwood Press, 1951, pp. 154–55, 159.

Wagner-Martin, Linda, *"Favored Strangers": Gertrude Stein and Her Family*, Rutgers University Press, 1995.

Wilson, Edmund, "Gertrude Stein," in *Twentieth-Century Literary Criticism*, Vol. 28, edited by Dedria Bryfonski and Phyllis Carmel Mendelson, Gale Research, 1978, p. 252, reprinted from *Axel's Castle: A Study in the Imaginative Literature of 1870–1930*, Charles Scribner's Sons, 1931.

FURTHER READING

Flanner, Janet, *Paris Was Yesterday, 1925–1939*, Viking Press, 1972.

> This is a collection of essays, published in 1972, though most of them were first written for the *New Yorker* under the name "Genet" between 1925 and 1939. The articles document the life and culture of the city and especially its bohemian population, and they also describe the milieu that Stein inhabited.

Forster, E. M., *Aspects of the Novel*, Harcourt Brace, 1927.

> Forster is one of the major early twentieth-century English novelists. In this book, drawn from lectures delivered in 1927 at Cambridge University, Forster explores the nature of the novel as a form.

Gallup, Donald C., ed., *The Flowers of Friendship: Letters Written to Gertrude Stein*, Alfred A. Knopf, 1953.

> This collection of letters written to Stein by friends provides an insightful view of her life.

Mellow, James R., *Charmed Circle: Gertrude Stein & Company*, Phaidon Press, 1974.

> Mellow correlates the events of Stein's daily life with her writings.

Wineapple, Brenda, *Sister Brother: Gertrude and Leo Stein*, G. P. Putnam's Sons, 1996.

> This study of Stein and Leo Stein explores not only their relationship but the bohemian world of Paris in the first decades of the twentieth century.

Life of Pi

YANN MARTEL
2001

Considered most simply, Yann Martel's acclaimed novel, *Life of Pi* (2001), can be described as a postcolonial novel, focusing on the culture and stories of a former British colony (in this case, India.) But to see this novel only as a postcolonial story is to limit its possibilities. Set against the backdrop of a period of Indian history known as the Emergency, the novel opens in the southern Indian city of Pondicherry, which was once the capital of French India, and the story explores the tensions facing this tiny city during a time of deep political turmoil. In the midst of this, the protagonist, Piscine Patel (known as Pi) emigrates from India to Canada with his family. They leave India by boat, but the ship sinks on the way. Pi and a Bengal tiger are the only survivors. As Pi struggles to coexist on a lifeboat with a tiger, he comes to understand the human condition. Indeed, Martel's novel quickly changes from a postcolonial novel to a deep meditation on the complex nature of faith, morality, and, ultimately, identity. The story also stands as an argument for the existence of God, or at least for sustaining belief in that existence.

A recent edition of the novel was published by Vintage Canada in 2002.

AUTHOR BIOGRAPHY

Yann Martel was born in Salamanca, Spain, on June 25, 1963, to Canadian parents. Soon after the birth of their son, Martel's parents joined the

Yann Martel (*AP Images*)

Canadian Foreign Service, and the family traveled often, living in Alaska, Costa Rica, France, Mexico, and a number of Canadian provinces. Martel continued to travel well into his adulthood, spending time in Iran, Turkey, and India before returning to Canada to study philosophy at Trent University in Ontario. After graduating from Trent in 1986, he worked variously as a tree planter, dishwasher, and security guard while developing his writing.

With years of travel and writing behind him, Martel published his first book in 1993, a collection of short fiction titled *The Facts Behind the Helsinki Roccamatios*. The stories focus on such themes as illness, the anguish of youth, grief, and death. The collection was awarded the 1993 Journey Prize in Canada, and was followed in 1996 by his first novel, *Self*, a story of shifting identities. Martel's first novel was on the short list for the Chapters/Books in Canada First Novel Award.

In 2002, Martel was recognized internationally when his second novel, *Life of Pi* (2001), was awarded the Man Booker Prize for Fiction, the Boeke Prize (South Africa), and the Hugh MacLennan Prize for Fiction (Canada). The novel was also short listed for the prestigious Governor General's Literary Award for Fiction (Canada) and the Commonwealth Writers Prize (Eurasia Region, Best Book). The accolades continued into 2003, with *Life of Pi* being selected as the recipient of the Quality Paperback Book Club's annual New Voices Award. The novel has been translated into more than thirty languages, has found readers in more than forty countries, and has been optioned for film adaptation. Notably, the French-Canadian edition of the novel was translated by Martel's own parents, Nicole and Emile.

Martel followed this remarkable success with a collection of short stories, *We Ate the Children Last*, in 2004. In April, 2007, Martel returned to prominence when he began a very public and much publicized project to mail the Prime Minister of Canada, Stephen Harper, a new book every two weeks. Martel noted that he hoped to help the political leader expand upon a sense of what the author called "stillness." The three initial mailings, for instance, were Leo Tolstoy's *The Death of Ivan*

Ilych, George Orwell's *Animal Farm*, and Agatha Christie's *The Murder of Roger Ackroyd*. Martel spends his time between creative projects in Montreal, Quebec, and he also serves as writer-in-residence with the English department at the University of Saskatchewan.

PLOT SUMMARY

Author's Note

A brief, italicized section establishes some background on the author of the novel, who is also a character in the text of the novel itself. (Each of the author's sections are similarly italicized, setting them off visually as well as thematically from the rest of the novel.) Confiding that he flew to Bombay in order to rejuvenate his mind and his writing following the lukewarm response to his first two books, the author is forced to admit, too, that he is suffering from writer's block. Leaving Bombay for a period of intellectual and spiritual wandering, he ends up in the small southern Indian city of Pondicherry, which had for many years been the centerpiece of "that most modest of colonial empires, *French* India."

Visiting a local coffee shop, the author has a chance encounter with a small elderly man, Francis Adirubasamy, who promises to tell him "a story that will make you believe in God." Taking notes of the fragmented tale that unfolds during their conversation, the author finds the story magnetic and it continues to fascinate him after he returns to Toronto. Searching for the protagonist of Adirubasamy's story, the author tracks down and speaks at length with Mr. Piscine Patel, whose story is told in the bulk of the novel. The author's conclusion, and his aim in writing the novel, is made very clear: "It seemed natural," he concludes, "that Mr. Patel's story should be told mostly in the first person, in his voice and through his eyes." At the same time, the author is quick to point out, "any inaccuracies or mistakes" that might find their way into the story are the responsibility of the author.

Part One: Toronto and Pondicherry

CHAPTER 1

The main narrative begins with Piscine (Pi) Patel's declaration that his early life had been one of great suffering, the cause of which is never made clear. Nonetheless, this suffering leaves the youthful Pi oscillating in emotion between sadness and

MEDIA ADAPTATIONS

- HarperCollins released an audio version of the novel (read by Kerry Shale) in 2003.

despondency. His mood lifts, and his life takes a turn for the better, when he decides to commit his energies to the study of two different topics: religious studies and zoology. Speaking at length about his research into sloths, Pi uses the discussion to hint at a number of facts that will appear in subsequent chapters: that he misses India; that he misses someone named Richard Parker; and that he has spent an extended period of time in a Mexican hospital suffering variously from anemia and dehydration.

CHAPTER 2

In a very brief chapter, the author reenters the narrative with details about where Pi currently lives in Toronto, what he looks like, and the way he speaks.

CHAPTER 3

The chapter discusses the history of Pi's full name, Piscine, which came from the name of the pool where a family friend, Francis Adirubasamy (whom Pi calls Mamaji), taught Pi to swim. Pi is the only member in his family who is not afraid of the water, and he has an almost obsessive love for the ritualistic nature of swimming. Readers learn details, too, about Adirubasamy's own life as a champion swimmer and later as a student in Paris.

CHAPTER 4

Pi shares a series of reflections upon his childhood in India. Most tellingly, he speaks about growing up as the son of a zookeeper, Santosh Patel. Pi's father ran the famous zoo at Pondicherry. As a child, Pi considered the zoo to be a kind of paradise in which various rituals and an almost clock-like precision combine to create a logical world of balance and coexistence. Pi also offers a lengthy and detailed defense of the practice and philosophy of zoo keeping, which is grounded in a complex balancing of respectful stewardship, authoritative control of territory, and applied theory. Sadly, Pi concludes, zoos have fallen into disrepute in the contemporary world.

CHAPTER 5

Teased at school because of his name (Piscine became Pissing), Pi gets the teachers and his fellow students to call him by the shortened (and geometrically significant) name of Pi. In his renaming, Pi finds a new beginning: "And so, in that Greek letter that looks like a shack with a corrugated tin roof, in that elusive, irrational number with which scientists try to understand the universe, I found refuge," he declares.

CHAPTER 6

In another brief chapter, the author interjects once again to talk about Pi's love of food, his excellent cooking, and his exotic and well-stocked kitchen.

CHAPTER 7

Returning to Pi's recollections of life in Pondicherry, this chapter opens a series of chapters that catalogue a number of important people, moments, and ideas that shape Pi as he matures. This chapter focuses on the influence of Mr. Satish Kumar, Pi's biology teacher, an avowed atheist, and an active Communist. He visits the zoo often, seeing it as a reassuring embodiment of the powers of reason and logic over the chaos of the natural world.

CHAPTER 8

After commenting at length on the cruelty that defines the relationships between animals in the natural order of things, Pi notes that the most dangerous animal is the human animal. In one of the more shocking scenes of the novel, Pi is also taught a powerful lesson when his father feeds a live goat to a caged tiger in order to demonstrate the dangers posed by wild animals, and the need for man to position himself as the dominant animal in any inter-species relationship. The keys to securing this balance of power are laid out clearly for Pi: understand how each animal responds to a potential threat or enemy; create a safe distance between yourself and that animal; be sure that each animal has sufficient food and water; and, most importantly, watch and learn the tendencies of each animal.

CHAPTER 9

Following a chapter on the dangers inherent in the relationship between humans and animals, Pi reflects on what he considers to be the strategy at the heart of zookeeping: nurturing animals so they get used to the presence of humans.

CHAPTER 10

In this brief chapter, Pi explains that even in the best of zoos there are animals that will try to escape. His point is clear: "animals don't escape *to somewhere* but *from something*."

CHAPTER 11

Continuing from chapter 10, Pi discusses a number of anecdotes about escaped zoo animals.

CHAPTER 12

Continuing his reflections from chapter 2, the author again speaks of Pi's cooking, with particular attention to the effects that the Indian man's spices have had on his untrained digestive tract. As an aside, the author notes that the mysterious Richard Parker is still often on Pi's mind, even so many years after their adventure together.

CHAPTER 13

Refocusing to the dynamics of animals and their territory, Pi talks about the example of a circus trainer and how he establishes the circus ring as his territory. By doing so, Pi argues, the trainer establishes himself at the top of the animal hierarchy.

CHAPTER 14

This chapter continues the discussion of circus trainers and their control of the animals in their ring.

CHAPTER 15

The author steps forward once again to describe Pi's house in Toronto, which is described in detail as containing a blend of religious icons and art from Hindu, Islamic, and Christian traditions.

CHAPTER 16

Pi explains his youthful relationship with the three major religions that shaped his ideas about the world. Born into a Hindu family, he describes his almost insatiable hunger for Prasad (an offering to God) and the ways that his hands almost automatically would fall into the prayer position. More importantly, he points out, is the Hindu philosophy of life, which he will always hold, he claims, as the centerpiece of his religious beliefs: "That which sustains the universe beyond thought and language, and that which is at the core of us and struggles for expression, is the same thing."

CHAPTER 17

Pi then goes on to recount the story of his almost casual introduction to Christianity. Stepping into a local church one day, the fourteen-year-old Pi enters into a discussion with Father Martin, who tells the young Hindu the story of the crucifixion of Christ. When pushed to explicate the deepest meaning of the story, Father Martin explains to Pi that the main idea shaping the stories of Christianity is always the same: love. Following some days of reflection, Pi decides that he will become a Christian. To Pi, this does not mean that he will no longer be a Hindu. In fact, he intends to be both.

CHAPTER 18

As Pi states almost casually, "Islam followed right behind" his decision to accept Christianity. Pi meets a Muslim mystic and baker who also becomes the second person named Satish Kumar to enter Pi's life.

CHAPTER 19

Through the second Mr. Kumar, the young Hindu/Christian comes to be intrigued by the daily rituals of Islam and by the stories of Mohammed that the baker shares with him.

CHAPTER 20

In this chapter, Pi comes to understand religious belief as a series of stories developed by humans in order to make their lives more understandable, more readily explainable, and generally more meaningful.

CHAPTER 21

This chapter opens with the author sitting in a café, reflecting on the story he is being told and, less comfortably, the "glum contentment" that has come to characterize his own life. Significantly, he remembers two phrases that had particularly intrigued him from his most recent conversation with Pi: "dry, yeastless factuality" and "the better story." Both of these phrases echo again and again as the novel unfolds.

CHAPTER 22

Referring to the previous phrases, Pi imagines the final words of an atheist versus those of an agnostic. Pi indicates that while an atheist would likely undergo a last-minute conversion as he experiences death, the agnostic would likely try to explain the experience in scientific terms.

CHAPTER 23

Pi recounts an episode where a representative from each of Pi's religions approach his parents. They state that a combination of faiths is not possible and that Pi must choose a single religion and a single mode of worship. His parents are shocked, for this is the first time they have even heard of their son's fascination with religion. Arguing that people who use the name of God to support violence or factionalism do not understand the word of God, Pi answers his challengers with a simple yet profound idea: he just wants to love God.

CHAPTER 24

In this brief chapter, Pi's brother, Ravi, teases Pi mercilessly upon discovering Pi's religious views.

CHAPTER 25

In this chapter, Pi recounts how people from the various religious groups react negatively to his complex spiritual quest.

CHAPTER 26

Now that his parents know about his religious beliefs, Pi asks them to allow him to be baptized and to have a prayer rug of his own. After some attempts to dissuade their son, his parents give in to both requests, marking the end of this early stage of Pi's spiritual journey.

CHAPTER 27

Pi's parents discuss, with some humor, the spiritual route chosen by their youngest son.

CHAPTER 28

Upon getting a prayer rug and a baptism, Pi feels that both events combine to give him a rejuvenating cleansing that he compares to a monsoon rain.

CHAPTER 29

The focal point of the novel shifts dramatically from religion to politics when Pi's father announces that the political situation in India during the time of the Emergency has effectively ruined the business of the Pondicherry zoo. Thus, Pi's father has decided that the zoo animals will be sold and that the family will emigrate to Canada.

CHAPTER 30

The author begins this chapter with a declarative statement: "He's married." Upon being introduced to Pi's wife, Meena, the author begins to see the house in a new light, paying attention to items and details that had gone unnoticed during his previous visits. His view has been limited, the author is forced to acknowledge, because he was not looking closely enough for details that might illuminate more clearly the corners and edges of the story he is being told.

It seems that even the author must admit to himself that a story (in this case, the story about Pi) can change drastically depending on the details that one chooses to pay attention to. This is an important revelation in that it anticipates the final section, when two versions of the same story are presented. Each story shares the same basic details (a boat sank, there are a certain number of survivors, the survivors die off in a certain order, etc.). However, each story presents those details through a distinct and often contradictory lens.

CHAPTER 31

Pi recounts the one-time meeting of the two Misters Kumar (one an atheist, the other a Muslim mystic). Joining Pi for a tour of the zoo, the two men see a zebra for the first time. Both are in awe of the exotic creature, and try to explain its marvelous markings.

CHAPTER 32

Pi takes this discussion as an opportunity to discuss zoomorphism, which is what happens when an animal takes a human being or any other animal outside of its species to be one of its own. Pi also speculates as to the psychological and emotional causes of this phenomenon.

CHAPTER 33

The author recalls the time he has spent with Pi exploring Pi's very minimal family memorabilia, including photos of weddings, the Pondicherry zoo, and the (still) mysterious Richard Parker. The chapter closes with Pi lamenting that he has lost so many of his memories, most sadly those of his mother, Gita, of whom he does not even have a picture. "It's very sad not to remember what your mother looks like," Pi says sadly, closing the book that contains images of his past.

CHAPTER 34

In preparation for the move across the Pacific, Pi's father sells off many of the zoo animals, agreeing to oversee the transport of the remainder in the same cargo ship that will carry his family to their new life in Canada. Pi reflects upon the fact that some animals are in high demand, while others are more or less ignored. He compares the inspections of the animals prior to receiving transport papers to the preparations of his own family to leave Pondicherry.

CHAPTER 35

Pi describes the mixed emotions with which the family leaves India aboard the Japanese ship *Tsimtsum* on June 21, 1977. He talks about packing the animals into cargo as well as his philosophy of how a person deals with life when things do not turn out as planned.

CHAPTER 36

The first part of the book ends as the author remembers his first meeting with Pi's two children, Usha and Nikhil. Now that the author has met Pi's family, but with much of Pi's story yet to be told, the author closes the chapter by stating: "This story has a happy ending."

Part Two: The Pacific Ocean
CHAPTER 37

Part Two opens with the sinking of the *Tsimtsum*, which leaves Pi suddenly separated from his family, floating in a lifeboat with an injured zebra. He sees Richard Parker, a 450-pound Bengal tiger, swimming toward the lifeboat. Rather than share the boat with a huge Bengal tiger, Pi leaps overboard.

CHAPTER 38

In a flashback to the moments preceding the sinking of the ship, Pi remembers his excitement at the possibilities that await him and his brother in Canada. His optimism turns to confusion when he feels the ship shudder with an explosion, and then to fear as he witnesses the chaos unfolding around him.

CHAPTER 39

Tossed into a lifeboat, Pi finds himself joined suddenly by an injured zebra.

CHAPTER 40

Picking up where he left off in chapter 37, Pi recognizes his dilemma: stay in the water with the sharks that are beginning to gather, or climb back aboard the lifeboat, where Richard Parker has taken refuge under a tarpaulin.

CHAPTER 41

Having climbed back aboard the lifeboat, Pi watches as the ship sinks. He also realizes that he is sharing his new home with not only a tiger and an injured zebra, but also with a mean-spirited hyena.

CHAPTER 42

A Borneo orangutan named Orange Juice floats by the boat on a raft of bananas. Pi rescues Orange Juice from the disintegrating raft of fruit, but forgets to bring any of the bananas aboard.

CHAPTER 43

Pi begins to establish the power structure within the group of animals aboard the lifeboat. His most immediate threat is the hyena, which is racing in circles around the boat.

CHAPTER 44

During his first night aboard the lifeboat, the hyena kills the injured zebra, as a terrified Pi listens helplessly from his end of the boat.

CHAPTER 45

The following morning, Pi contemplates the meaning of life and death as it is now presented to him. He also watches Orange Juice's reaction to recent events.

CHAPTER 46

What Pi sees at first fascinates him, as Orange Juice raises herself to her full height to intimidate the hyena into submission. Violence is averted this time, but Pi is aware that the peace aboard the lifeboat is temporary.

CHAPTER 47

As sharks circle the lifeboat, Pi watches once again as violence breaks out, this time between the still ravenous hyena and Orange Juice. He is surprised and somewhat appalled as the orangutan attempts to club the hyena to death. In the end, Orange Juice dies, and Pi is left in an almost delirious state of fear that he will be the next victim.

CHAPTER 48

Pi recalls the clerical error that led to the tiger being named Richard Parker instead of Thirsty, which was the animal's intended name.

CHAPTER 49

The story resumes with Pi tentatively exploring the boat in search of water and supplies. He

must remain aware at all times, he knows, of the location of both the murderous hyena and the quiet, but always dangerous, Richard Parker.

CHAPTER 50

This relatively brief chapter is dedicated to a detailed description of the physical dimensions of the lifeboat and the equipment discovered in it.

CHAPTER 51

Discovering the rations in the boat, Pi finds his spirits uplifted. He calculates that he has enough food and water to last for 124 days.

CHAPTER 52

This chapter is dedicated almost totally to recounting the list of items that Pi discovers aboard the lifeboat.

CHAPTER 53

Awakening to what he calls "the reality of Richard Parker," Pi prepares himself to battle the animals that share his limited space. When Richard Parker raises his powerful body to attack, Pi is certain that he is the intended victim. He is surprised, relieved, and somewhat horrified when the tiger instead kills the hyena.

Certain that he will be next to die, Pi is saved when a rat scrambles over the tarpaulin and climbs onto Pi's head. Grabbing the rat, Pi throws it to the tiger, who accepts the offering. Pi senses that a balance has been reached between them, for the moment at least.

CHAPTER 54

Pi contemplates the pros and cons of each of six plans for dealing with Richard Parker, ranging from pushing him off the lifeboat to waging a war of attrition that will end with one of them dying from starvation or dehydration.

CHAPTER 55

Thinking and thinking again about each of his six plans, Pi settles momentarily on the plan to outwait Richard Parker and hope that he starves to death. Pi immediately recognizes the faulty logic and inevitable failure of this plan.

CHAPTER 56

In this brief but important chapter, Pi reflects upon the nature of fear, which he classifies as "life's only true opponent."

CHAPTER 57

Ironically, the presence of Richard Parker calms Pi during their initial days aboard the lifeboat. Watching the tiger rest under his tarpaulin, Pi thinks back on what he has learned about circus trainers and decides to train the tiger rather than compete with him.

CHAPTER 58

Pi details the wealth of practical information that he discovers in a survival manual he finds in the lifeboat.

CHAPTER 59

Learning a variety of strategies for marking his territory aboard the lifeboat, Pi begins training Richard Parker. More importantly, he discovers and learns to operate a solar still that can convert salt water into the drinkable water that he will need to survive. He also knows that the ocean around him is literally teeming with fish and turtles, both of which might prove a regular form of sustenance if he can figure out a method of catching them.

CHAPTER 60

Pi reflects upon the various life lessons learned during his spiritual development.

CHAPTER 61

Learning to catch fish, Pi also learns that food can be used as a training tool when dealing with Richard Parker. Pi further learns that he can adjust quite readily to killing another living creature in order to keep himself alive (Pi was previously a vegetarian). Upon this discovery Pi begins to deeply question his faith. The longer Pi is left to float upon the Pacific, the more his questioning will continue to deepen.

CHAPTER 62

The routine of catching food and making fresh water in the solar still occupies Pi's days at sea.

CHAPTER 63

Comparing himself to other famous survivors of lengthy sea journeys, Pi recounts an average day on the lifeboat. He juxtaposes this new routine with the increasingly fragile condition of his memories of life in India.

CHAPTER 64

This brief chapter details the physical ailments that begin to affect Pi as the days wear on.

CHAPTER 65

Believing firmly that knowledge will be crucial to his survival, Pi spends hours trying to decipher the navigational instructions in the survival manual. In the end, he is not successful.

CHAPTER 66

In this chapter, Pi recounts in detail how he came to master the techniques of hunting and killing fish and turtles. They are the basis of his entire diet, and Richard Parker's, as Pi shares all of his food with the tiger.

CHAPTER 67

Pi watches the small sea creatures that attach themselves to the lifeboat, recognizing that as he struggles to survive in inhospitable circumstances, he does so just above a complete, self-supporting ecosystem.

CHAPTER 68

Pi describes his sleeping patterns and Richard Parker's sleeping patterns.

CHAPTER 69

Pi spends his nights watching for a distant light, shooting flares in the hopes of attracting the attention of what he imagines to be ships passing nearby. As both he and Richard Parker watch the flares sink into the horizon, Pi realizes the futility of his efforts and the overwhelming barrenness of the ocean that surrounds him.

CHAPTER 70

Pi relates details of butchering a turtle. The chapter closes with Pi's determination to carve out his territory from Richard Parker once and for all.

CHAPTER 71

Pi makes a list of essentials for survival, which he offers as advice for anyone who might find themselves in a similar situation. The list has nine points.

CHAPTER 72

Richard Parker's training begins with Pi experimenting with various styles of shields, a piece of equipment that he feels will be necessary for the exercise he is about to undertake.

CHAPTER 73

Pi wishes for a book other than the survival manual. He also begins keeping a diary, written in tiny letters and detailing his feelings as well as the practical considerations of each day.

CHAPTER 74

Pi recounts how he maintains his religious rituals during the early days of his journey.

CHAPTER 75

In this one-sentence long chapter, Pi believes it is around the time of his mother's birthday, so he sings to celebrate it.

CHAPTER 76

Pi recalls how he got in the habit of cleaning up the feces left by the tiger, and how his own constipation was a source of great pain.

CHAPTER 77

As the rations aboard the lifeboat dwindle, Pi begins to deteriorate physically and mentally. He finds himself increasingly obsessed with food and water.

CHAPTER 78

Pi reflects upon the nature of the sky when seen from the point of view of a castaway. He also reflects on the loneliness of his position.

CHAPTER 79

This chapter is dedicated to sharks: how to capture them, how to butcher them, how they fight each other, and Pi's general observations of the various species.

CHAPTER 80

Opening with a discussion of the dorado (the most common fish that Pi catches), this chapter shifts gradually towards a meditation on Pi's interactions with Richard Parker and on the strength of the human mind to endure the most grueling of challenges.

CHAPTER 81

Pi acknowledges that the story of his survival might appear unbelievable to many people. He counters this disbelief by detailing a number of the key reasons why people should believe him.

CHAPTER 82

Pi again recounts the routine of gathering rainwater and food. He also shares more on the patterns that sustain both man and tiger in a variety of ways.

CHAPTER 83

A tremendous storm hits, and the lifeboat is tossed from wave to wave. Both Pi and Richard Parker struggle to remain upright in the boat, which begins to disintegrate in the ferocity of the storm. Terrified, the two passengers survive the storm.

CHAPTER 84

Following the storm, Pi again takes to recounting the setting in which he finds himself. He remarks on whales and dolphins, as well as how he ingeniously captures and kills a large sea bird for food.

CHAPTER 85

This brief chapter is dedicated to exploring the different responses of man and tiger to the occasional lightning storms that sweep over the small boat.

CHAPTER 86

In a brief but futile moment of hope, Pi spots a ship moving towards them. Planning the details of their rescue, Pi is aware suddenly that the huge ship is bearing down on them with no sign of slowing down or stopping. Almost overturned when the ship passes them by, the lifeboat continues to drift. Pi and Richard Parker both seem to give up hope.

CHAPTER 87

Pi recalls one of his favorite means of mental escape during his time on the lifeboat—choking himself almost to the point of unconsciousness.

CHAPTER 88

The lifeboat drifts through some trash. Pi snags a bottle, into which he places a note before launching it back into the sea.

CHAPTER 89

Pi reaches the lowest point of his journey. Without sufficient food or water, he begins to sleep more and more. When he does awaken, he has no energy, and he gives himself over to thoughts of death. He quits writing in his diary.

CHAPTER 90

Physically broken down to the point of blindness, Pi declines into a state of delirium. Hearing a voice with a French accent that he believes at first to be that of Parker, Pi encounters, or so he believes, another castaway adrift at sea. Indeed, it is not clear if the incident is real or imagined. The castaway is alone, and he is blind like Pi. The two men talk about food, which gradually leads the Frenchman to confess that he killed and cannibalized his shipmates (a man and a woman). When the Frenchman boards Pi's lifeboat with the intention of making Pi his next victim, he is immediately killed and eaten by the starving tiger.

CHAPTER 91

After rinsing his eyes with seawater, Pi regains his vision, sees the butchered body and, in a moment of extreme desperation, dries small strips of its flesh for his own consumption.

CHAPTER 92

Making "an exceptional botanical discovery," Pi and Parker come across a low-lying island made of algae that is drifting freely upon the sea. Beaching the lifeboat, Pi finds that the island has plentiful fresh water, fruit, and fish. It is also populated, he discovers, by a massive colony of meerkats who, Pi realizes, have come to understand the intricacies of the strange island's ecosystem.

And it is this ecosystem that is problematic, as Pi soon discovers. Upon realizing that the algae comprising the island floor turns toxic at night, Pi takes to sleeping in the trees with the meerkats. One day, discovering a tree that bears fruit-like objects containing human teeth, Pi concludes that his island paradise is carnivorous, and that eventually he, too, will be absorbed by the toxic algae as food for the island itself.

CHAPTER 93

Stocking the lifeboat with water and food, Pi and Parker set off once again in the lifeboat. Seeing all of his efforts as pointless and futile, Pi gives himself over to God's will by way of easing his suffering and desperation.

CHAPTER 94

Drifting for days, the two are finally washed ashore in Mexico. As Pi clambers onto the beach and collapses onto the sand, Parker disappears into the jungle. Pi is haunted by the suddenness of Parker's departure, and the fact that the two voyagers never had a proper farewell.

Discovered by local villagers, Pi is taken to an infirmary where he is nursed back to health.

Part Three: Benito Juárez Infirmary, Tomatlán, Mexico

CHAPTER 95

After returning to the voice of the author, he recounts the appearance of two officials from the Maritime Department in the Japanese Ministry of Transport, Tomohiro Okamoto and Atsuro Chiba. Traveling in California on unrelated business, they are redirected to Mexico to interview the sole survivor of the sinking of the *Tsimtsum*. After a confused journey to the small village, the men begin to interview Pi as he recuperates. Much of the conversation is presented in the form of interview transcripts.

CHAPTER 96

Introducing themselves to Pi, the two investigators give him a cookie and invite him to recount the details of the ship's explosion and his journey. Pi is happy to oblige their request.

CHAPTER 97

This two-word chapter simply says "The story," as Pi presumably recounts what the reader has already been told.

CHAPTER 98

The investigators take a break to consider the implications of the story.

CHAPTER 99

Pi is told by the Japanese investigators that his story is entertaining but wholly unbelievable. They push him to tell them what really happened during his 227 days at sea. At first, Pi challenges the men for their doubts, but gradually comes to recognize what they really desire to hear: "I know what you want," he says one day. "You want a story that won't surprise you. That will confirm what you already know. That won't make you see higher or further or differently. You want a flat story," he challenges them. "An immobile story. You want dry, yeastless factuality."

With this understanding, Pi tells the Japanese men another story. In this version, there are three other occupants in the lifeboat with Pi: his mother, a foul-mannered French cook, and a beautiful, young Chinese sailor. When the sailor dies from injuries that are exacerbated by the cook's attacks upon him, he is used for food by the Frenchman, much to the disgust of Pi and his mother, who attempt to intervene. The Frenchman then kills Pi's mother before being killed by Pi himself. Pi survives his journey, he tells the investigators, by eating the flesh and organs of the murdered Frenchman. If one considers the order and manner in which these deaths occur, they largely mirror the deaths of the animals as Pi had earlier described. Looked at this way, the Frenchman is the hyena who kills the sailor (the zebra), and then Pi's mother (the orangutan), before being killed by Pi (the tiger).

Appalled at the savagery of the second story, but also aware of the parallels connecting the two versions of the tale, Okamoto and Chiba continue to question Pi and to debate over which story they will file in their official report.

CHAPTER 100

The senior investigator, Okamoto, is charged with filing the report, which comprises the final chapter of the novel. Okamoto settles on the story that includes Richard Parker. He does so because Pi asks the investigators which story is "better," and they respond that the "better story" is the one with the animals. Pi replies: "And so it goes with God." Here, Pi slyly indicates that the story of a world where God exists is better than the story of a world where God does not exist. Like Pi's stories of survival, one version is less believable than the other, but the less believable version is more thrilling than its counterpart. Thus, as Francis Adirubasamy promises the author at the beginning of the book, Pi's story is "a story that will make you believe in God."

Okamota therefore chooses the version of Pi's story that reaffirms belief in the existence of God. He notes, too, that Pi's tale "is an astounding story of courage and endurance" and that it "is unparalleled in the history of shipwrecks."

CHARACTERS

Francis Adirubasamy

Sitting in a Pondicherry coffee shop, Francis Adirubasamy is the elderly man who promises to tell the author a story that "will make [him] believe in God." He is, in other words, the catalyst for the novel that is about to unfold. At the same time, he is a character involved in Pi's childhood, the man who teaches Pi to swim and who is influential in naming the young protagonist. There is a closeness and a respect connecting Pi with Francis Adirubasamy; throughout the novel Pi refers to him as "Mamaji," which means "respected uncle."

The Author

The voice of the author surfaces at various points throughout the novel, commenting on Pi as he lives in the present-day city of Toronto while serving as the conduit for the story of Pi's journey with Richard Parker. A frustrated writer, the author is himself a student of storytelling who reflects on the tales laid out before him by Pi Patel.

The Blind Frenchman

The blind Frenchman is the castaway that Pi Patel meets in the midst of his most intense delusions at sea. Whether the blind Frenchman actually exists or is a figment of Pi's imagination is not clear. The blind Frenchman is, like Pi, delirious and hungry. He is also a storyteller, who recounts his own tale of murder and cannibalism. After boarding Pi's lifeboat with the intention of killing and eating Pi, he is instead eaten by the now ravenous Richard Parker.

Atsuro Chiba

One of the Japanese investigators from the Maritime Department in the Japanese Ministry of Transport sent to gather information about Pi's ordeal and the sinking of the *Tsimtsum*, Chiba is the junior colleague of Tomohiro Okamoto. He is the not as skeptical of Pi's tale as Okamoto. In the end, though, it is Okamoto who makes the final decision about which of the two stories appears in their official report.

The French Cook

The French cook becomes the human equivalent of the hyena when Pi remodels his version of the tale to suit the Japanese investigators, who do not believe Pi's initial tale. A violent and uncouth cannibal of a man, the cook kills the beautiful young sailor and then Pi's mother before he is killed by Pi in retaliation. As with most characters in the revised version of the story, there is much debate as to whether the cook is real or not.

The Hyena

One of the castaways aboard the lifeboat in Pi's first version of events, the hyena kills the zebra and then the orangutan before being killed in turn by the Royal Bengal tiger, Richard Parker. In the revised version of the story (the version without animals) the characteristics of the hyena are represented in the character of the French cook.

Satish Kumar

Sharing a name with Pi's high-school biology teacher, Satish Kumar is a Sufi, a Muslim mystic who works in a local bakery. An influential figure in Pi's development, Kumar is instrumental in leading Pi towards his lifelong interest in religion. When Satish Kumar visits the Patel family zoo, he sees the zoo animals as proof of the existence of a glorious god. He is a counterpoint to the almost identically named character of Mr. Satish Kumar, who is an atheist.

Mr. Satish Kumar

Pi's high-school biology teacher, Mr. Satish Kumar is an atheist and an active Communist, who was also afflicted with polio in his childhood. He inspires a love for empirical explanations of the world in Pi, and is a key figure in developing Pi's interest in zoology. When Mr. Kumar visits the Patel family zoo, he sees the way in which the animals have been arranged as proof of a scientific and rational logic. His character is a counterpoint to the other Satish Kumar, a devout Muslim.

Father Martin

Father Martin is the central figure in Pi's Christian education during the first part of the novel. His role is to offer comfort and guidance to Pi. His message is clear and well received by Pi; Martin states that the story of the Christian God is love and acceptance.

Tomohiro Okamoto

Tomohiro Okamoto is the lead investigator from the Maritime Department of the Japanese Ministry of Transport. He is in charge of the enquiry into the sinking of the *Tsimtsum*. Working with his assistant, Atsuro Chiba, he is the more suspicious of the two, as he is highly skeptical of the truthfulness of Pi's original story. He is also the final arbiter as to which version of events is included in his final report, the one with animals or the one without. The decision, Okamoto recalls when talking with the author, was both memorable and difficult. In the end, Okamoto chooses the story with animals, which, as indicated in the Author's Note, is the story that reinforces belief in the existence of God. To base his report on the story without animals would mean, also, that Okamoto readily accepts that the thin veneer of humanity crumbles into animalistic behavior almost immediately when placed outside of society (leading in this case to murder and cannibalism). Okamoto, like the author, prefers the story with animals to the dehumanizing and spiritually void alternative.

Orange Juice

Another of the castaways aboard the lifeboat in Pi's first version of events, Orange Juice is the prized Borneo orangutan whom Pi pulls into the lifeboat as she floats by on a raft of netted bananas. She is the second victim of the hyena, who turns on her after killing the zebra. Pi is particularly attached to Orange Juice, seeing her as a symbol of maternal affection and matriarchal protection (she attempts to protect the injured zebra, reminding him of his own mother who often acted as his protector). At the same time, Pi is taken aback when she lashes out violently at the hyena in the moments leading up to her death. In Pi's second version of events, Orange Juice is transformed to fill the role of Pi's mother.

Richard Parker

Richard Parker is the Royal Bengal tiger who shares the lifeboat with Pi following the sinking of the *Tsimtsum*. Originally named Thirsty, his name was changed through a clerical error that accidentally listed his captor's name as his own. A symbol of the ferocity of the natural world and of Pi's own unconscious, Parker is both a threat and a companion to Pi during their 227-day journey across the Pacific Ocean. Having already killed the hyena, Parker is an intelligent and brutal force that Pi must learn to control if the two are to coexist in the lifeboat. Whereas Pi is a man of faith and intellect, Parker sees the world as an animal does, guided by instinct and concerned mainly with hunger and thirst. It is he, for instance, who first recognizes the dangers of the algae island, returning to the boat every night to sleep safely away from the carnivorous algae. When the two companions finally arrive safely on a beach in Mexico, Parker disappears into the coastline jungle, leaving a void in Pi's emotional world. In Pi's second version of events, Richard Parker is transformed to represent Pi himself.

Gita Patel

Gita Patel is Pi's protective and loving mother. Raised a Hindu, but educated as a Baptist, she is, in many ways, a woman without formal religion, serving as a kind of counterpoint to Pi's seemingly perpetual quest for one. Through Gita, Pi learns to love reading. In the first version of Pi's story, she dies in the sinking of the *Tsimtsum*. In the second version, she is killed on the lifeboat by the French cook.

Meena Patel

Meena Patel is Pi's wife, whom the author meets very briefly while speaking with Pi in Toronto.

Nikhil Patel

Nikhil Patel, also known as Nick, is Pi's son. Defined primarily by his love of baseball, he is introduced to the author in a very brief meeting.

Pi Patel

Pi, born Piscine Molitor Patel, is the protagonist and first-person narrator of much of the novel. His name is derived from the French word for swimming pool (*piscine*) which rhymes uncomfortably with "pissing," prompting him to shorten it to the mathematical constant Pi.

In the chapters that constitute the first and third parts of the novel, Pi recounts both his upbringing at the Pondicherry zoo, his introduction to the religions of the world, and his later life in Toronto. Part Three also reveals his very open interpretation of reality and truth, as he willingly modifies his tale to appease the Japanese inspectors. But, as Pi reveals to them, the decision between the two stories is a relatively straightforward one: to believe in the story with animals is to believe in a world in which God can exist; but to believe in the story without animals is to be forced to acknowledge that human existence is nasty, brutish, and devoid of morality or spirituality.

In the substantive second part of the novel, Pi recounts his fabulous and often grisly story of survival. Sharing a lifeboat with a Royal Bengal tiger for 227 days, he finds that he is tested physically, intellectually, emotionally, and spiritually. Pi learns to fend off the natural impulses of fear and anger, as well as to allow those impulses to guide him (as in his hunting for food). He also learns that, in order to retain his sanity, he must achieve a deep personal honesty that allows him to acknowledge the animal within himself while still remaining human.

Piscine Molitor Patel

See Pi Patel

Ravi Patel

Ravi Patel is Pi's older brother. Where Pi is spiritual and intellectual, Ravi is athletic and social. He functions in the novel as a kind of foil to his younger brother. Through his relentless teasing, Ravi also tests Pi's developing religious beliefs.

Santosh Patel

Santosh Patel is Pi's father, who once owned a hotel in Madras before taking over the management of the Pondicherry zoo. Intrigued by animal culture and behavior, he passes his keen interest down to Pi. Due to the political climate in India during the years of the Emergency, Santosh decides to move his family to Canada. He dies when the cargo ship they are traveling on sinks into the Pacific.

Usha Patel

Usha Patel is Pi's shy but adoring daughter. The author meets her briefly.

The Sailor

In Pi's second version of events on the lifeboat, the sailor is the human equivalent of the zebra. The sailor is the French cook's first victim.

The Zebra

The zebra is one of the first animals on the lifeboat, and he is also the first animal that is killed by the hyena. In the revised version of Pi's tale, the zebra is represented by the sailor.

THEMES

The Possibility of the Existence of God

When the author first meets Francis Adirubasamy in the opening chapter of *Life of Pi*, the elderly Indian man promises the somewhat skeptical writer that he has "a story that will make you believe in God." When the author later meets the central character in this story, an older Pi Patel now living in Toronto, he comes to understand that this assertion is very much at the crux of Pi's story.

Life of Pi offers readers two versions of the same story. One of these stories, which constitutes the bulk of the novel, includes a collection of wild animals and a floating carnivorous island. In this version, Pi is a man whose belief in God is put to the most profound tests as he is forced each day to try to remain civilized in a world bereft of human contact and in which basic survival is a challenge. In the end, it is his belief that sustains Pi, guiding him to forge an unlikely relationship with a Bengal tiger, to discover a discipline and strength within himself that allows him to survive each day at sea, and to recognize the dangers of an apparently idyllic island despite his deep desire to see it as a refuge.

The other story, considerably shorter than the version with animals, recounts a tale of murder and cannibalism. This story indicates that

TOPICS FOR FURTHER STUDY

- Given that the Patel family leaves Pondicherry during the period of Indian history known as the Emergency, research the history of this period in India. Write an essay in which you comment on the relevance of this period to the journey that Pi is later forced to take following the sinking of the *Tsimtsum*. In your essay, consider the question: Do you think that *Life of Pi* can be read, in part, as a political commentary on such issues as political territoriality or the animal nature of human politics? Why? Why not?

- *Life of Pi* is a novel that is full of colors: the yellow of bananas; the orange of the orangutan and the Royal Bengal tiger; the blue of the sea and sky. Write an essay in which you discuss the meanings of each of the various colors mentioned in the book, and the importance of what or whom they are attached to.

- In chapter 58, Pi spends some time reading a survival manual that he discovers on the lifeboat. Written by a British Royal Navy commander, it is an eclectic collection of obvious and not-so-obvious hints for survival. Write a similar manual for surviving life as a student. Include at least twelve items, making some of the points practical and others more abstract. Feel free to include diagrams, calculations, or images if the mood strikes you.

- In chapter 5, Pi goes to great lengths to have his name translated from the embarrassing Piscine to the more liberating Pi, which is both a Greek letter and almost mythical mathematical constant. Research the visual art and music that has accumulated around this number, and create a timeline of paintings, cartoons, and musical scores (as examples) that have been inspired by this number. What information can you find about the number that indicates its spiritual significance? Present your findings to the class.

- The novel is a sly argument promoting spiritual belief, specifically belief in God. What other philosophers have also attempted to argue that God exists? Compile a report on your findings and include a brief description of each philosopher's argument.

human goodness is a flimsy and easily removable construct.

Indeed, as both the author and the Japanese investigators conclude after hearing both of Pi's stories, the version with animals is the "better story," and it is also the most meaningful of the two. The "better story" is the story that represents a world where God might exist, but the other story represents a world that is spiritually void.

The Power of Storytelling

Constructed as a series of stories within a story, *Life of Pi* is a blend of various storytelling forms, from first-person accounts (both by Pi and by the author) that move forward and backward in time, to the emotionally intense internal monologues and the ostensibly factual interview transcripts. Each form of storytelling is revealed within the novel to contain its own version of truth and accuracy, with none of the many stories able to explain exactly all that had happened aboard the lifeboat. With each new story, few answers are provided while more and more questions are raised.

Rather than collapsing the story into a debate about a solid and knowable set of facts or certainties regarding Pi's adventures (what might be called reality), *Life of Pi* opens outwards to explore other ways of seeing and knowing the world. When Pi meets his Japanese investigators, for instance, he offers them two very different but intimately related versions of the same tale, one with animals and the other without. Both versions are true in their own way.

In the end, the decision as to what version to believe is left to Okamoto and Chida, and, more importantly, to the reader of the novel itself.

Echoing such earlier stories as told in Samuel Taylor Coleridge's poem "The Rime of the Ancient Mariner" (1798), *Life of Pi* is also a novel that explores the human need to tell and believe in stories as a strategy for survival. As Pi explains often during the opening section of the novel, the various stories that shape world religions are necessary for human survival. Each of Pi's three religions has its own distinct set of stories (often shaped as parables) and narrative strategies. What Pi comes to understand about this plethora of stories is very profound: all of the stories, in the end, address a deeply rooted need to love and be loved, and in order to survive in the world every individual needs to put his faith in one or another story of this (divine) love. To remain an agnostic is to live without faith in the power of stories to shape one's very existence in meaningful ways.

The Conditions of Human Nature

The Pondicherry zoo serves as an important reminder of the distinctions separating human beings from wild animals. Yet the zoo also makes Pi aware of some similarities between the two. Just as animals find some solace in the rituals of zoo life, Pi believes that humans find solace in the rituals of daily life. The order and structure of the zoo comes to represent the human ability to bring order and harmony to a primitive world that is always on the cusp of reverting back to a natural, wild state. In its wild state, life is a constant struggle for survival, a perpetual race for food and safety in which death is a constant possibility.

As Pi's journey aboard the lifeboat begins, so, too, does his reeducation in the conditions of wildness and human nature. After witnessing the savagery of the hyena, Pi comes to realize that the world in which he now lives has been stripped of the false comforts and artificial harmonies of society. This new world is one in which his faith will be profoundly tested. As he learns to live peacefully with, rather than in fear of, Richard Parker, for instance, Pi also begins to recognize, much to his disappointment, that his own behaviors are becoming more animal-like. Pi learns to kill fish and turtles without any sort of guilt, for instance. He not only drinks their blood and eats their brains in order to survive, but he does so

with an almost bestial gusto. At first, Pi is appalled when he catches himself wolfing down a new catch of food, but he gradually comes to recognize how easy it is for him to slip away from the religion and vegetarianism that had defined his early life, and how easy it is to live a life that is discomfortingly similar to that of the zoo animals he had once tended.

Gradually, the distance separating Pi from Richard Parker is almost erased in the novel. Readers are left with the possibility that Parker and Pi are distinct but connected elements of the same character, with the tiger emerging as a symbol of Pi's primal nature and his instinctive drive for survival at all costs. If readers accept that the second version of Pi's story is true, then the invention of Richard Parker can be understood as a psychological mechanism that allows Pi to disassociate himself from the murder that he has committed. Read in either of these ways, the novel underscores what such writers as Joseph Conrad (*Heart of Darkness*, 1902) and William Golding (*Lord of the Flies*, 1954) had explored previously: that humans are not so different from animals as is traditionally believed. Deprived of the zoo-like structures (society) that sustain them in their daily lives, humans return quite naturally to lives guided by basic instincts and animalistic impulses.

STYLE

Magical Realism

The term was first used by the German art critic Franz Roh to describe paintings that present recognizable objects in an altered form or setting. More specifically, these works of art represented a kind of heightened reality in which elements of the marvelous or the unnatural appear alongside familiar elements of the everyday world.

In literature, including in *Life of Pi*, magical realism often blurs the familiar line between the internal/emotional world of the characters and the external/physical world through which these characters move. Serving as a literary counterpoint to traditional beliefs in a unified and knowable reality shared by all people and all cultures, magical realism acknowledges that everyday reality is a relative concept, and that what is seen as real or normal by one individual might at the same moment be seen as miraculous or magical by another. Promoting an openness to other ways of seeing the world and

Life of Pi

Symbols of three world religions (© Eyebyte / Alamy)

underscoring the need for tolerance of divergent opinions, magical realism has become increasingly important in a world fractured by territorial and cultural tensions.

The emergence of Richard Parker as an almost-human personality in the novel, for instance, and the floating, carnivorous island (which at first seems to be a paradise), mark *Life of Pi* as a novel written in the tradition of magical realism. Accordingly, *Life of Pi* can be read alongside works by such international writers as Isabel Allende (*The House of Spirits*, 1982) Italo Calvino (*Invisible Cities*, 1972) and Salman Rushdie (*Midnight's Children*, 1981) to name but a few.

Bildungsroman

The novel traces the intellectual, spiritual, and physical maturation of Pi Patel, and thus falls very neatly into the tradition of the Bildungsroman, a novel tracing the formation or education of its (typically male) protagonist. Known alternatively as the coming-of-age novel, the Bildungsroman in its more organized form usually includes a number of

elements, most of which appear in whole or in part in Martel's novel. The protagonist grows during the course of the novel from a boy into a man; Pi leaves India as a sixteen-year-old and recounts his story to the author many years later, as an older man living in Toronto with his family. The protagonist must also have an obvious motivation for undertaking his transformative journey, which for Pi can be seen as both the political implications of the Emergency and the more immediate motivation for survival following the sinking of the *Tsimtsum*.

In a Bildungsroman, once the journey is underway the protagonist must face a long and arduous trial (227 days in a lifeboat) that is punctuated with a conflict between his needs and those of others within his community (Pi versus Richard Parker). As the journey unfolds, the protagonist of the Bildungsroman traditionally grows away from a spirit of conformity towards a more individualized sense of the world and his place in it. Finally, as is apparent throughout *Life of Pi*, there is a thematic emphasis on the spiritual or the emotional and the practical problems associated with living outside of social norms. Mark Twain's *Huckleberry Finn* (1885) is a classic example of a Bildungsroman.

HISTORICAL CONTEXT

The Emergency Years in Indian History

When Santosh Patel decides to leave Pondicherry for a better life in Canada, he openly cites the political unrest that was sweeping India in the mid-1970s as his motivation to emigrate. The period known formally as the Emergency was a twenty-one-month period beginning on June 25, 1975, and ending around March 21, 1977. During this period, Indian President Fakhruddin Ali Ahmed, responding to the advice of Prime Minister Indira Gandhi, declared a state of emergency throughout India. Rooted in long-standing political disagreements and widespread disillusionment with policies of the day, the declaration effectively granted the Government the power to rule by decree and without pressure to recognize civil liberties or the due process of democratic elections.

Also during this time, the Government deployed its police forces to suppress protests and strikes, banned many parties that offered political opposition, and engaged in a sustained attempt to rewrite Indian laws with the sanction of Parliament.

The legacy of this period remains controversial. Although economic recovery was strengthened and the political climate of the country was stabilized through many of the decisions put into place, the Emergency years are also seen as a black mark against India's commitment to the principles of democratic rule.

The Rise of Post-Colonialism

Post-Colonialism refers to a collection of theories and critical approaches that look to explore the culture of countries that were once ruled by foreign governments (India is a former British colony). Although more a collection of ideas than a single, unified theory, post-colonialism does feature a number of common subjects that arise in *Life of Pi*: the heritage of European influences in local art, philosophy, and religion; racism; political territoriality; and the struggle for cultural identity. The beginnings of post-colonial thinking is mostly considered to have come from two writers: Frantz Fanon (*Black Skin, White Masks*, 1952) and Edward Said (*Orientalism*, 1978). Both men had a powerful influence on the intellectual climate of the 1970s.

One of the key strategies of post-colonial thinkers is to consider how the colonizer's culture has become hybridized in the culture of the colonized. The merging of old with new, colonizing with pre-colonial, is seen as creating something particularly unique to the post-colonial culture, and serves as a foundation for future growth. Pi Patel's bringing together of elements of Christianity, Hinduism, and Islam is an excellent example of what post-colonial thinkers would call a hybridized identity. Taking bits and pieces from old and new aspects of his culture, Pi positions himself as both a man of the past and a beacon of the emergence of that past into a new, hopefully progressive future. Indeed, Pi is a post-colonial figure. The fact that he resists traditional pressures to choose one path serves only to underscore both the limitations (territoriality) of the old ways and the necessity for an inclusive view of the world.

Significantly, *Life of Pi* resists the tendency of most post-colonial writing to settle too easily on a new, hybridized identity as the solution to all problems. What Pi discovers on his journey across the Pacific Ocean is that even his hybridized faith cannot answer all of the questions that confront him.

CRITICAL OVERVIEW

Somewhat surprisingly, given its meteoric rise as a novel of international standing, *Life of Pi* was greeted with what a contributor to the *Missouri Review* characterizes as "wildly disparate reactions." Writing in the *New York Review of Books*, for instance, Pankaj Mishra gives the novel only the mildest of praise. Mishra celebrates Martel's skill in "stretch[ing] our credulity through some hypnotic storytelling." The critic, however, is troubled by Martel's depictions of religious life generally and his "unpersuasive treatment of God" more specifically. The description of religious practices in India, for instance, "carry the whiff of an encyclopedia entry, or a tourist's scrupulously kept journal," while later in the novel "Martel is unable to reveal adequately ... the precise nature, or vacillations, of Pi's faith." In the end, Mishra concludes, Martel's "instincts as a storyteller prove to be keener than his ability to proselytize" in support of a new way of

Bengal tiger walking in surf *(Joseph Van Os | The Image Bank | Getty Images)*

making God relevant in an increasingly secular world. As Linda M. Morra concludes in *Canadian Literature*, *Life of Pi* is, for many readers, "inconsistently compelling and occasionally contrived."

Reviewing the novel for the *Christian Century*, Gordon Houser is far less hesitant in his praise of Martel's exploration of questions of a spiritual nature. Noting that the writing is "deceptively simple," Houser celebrates the "aplomb" with which "Martel lets the winsome narrative voice and the intriguing plot carry [readers], all the while winking as he tosses out thoughts on the kinds of metaphysical questions humans have pondered for centuries." Indeed, they are questions, notes Linda Shirato in *Library Journal* that tend to elicit "strong emotions" from most readers. This point is also made by Charlotte Innes, writing in the *Nation*. Martel "baits his readers with serious themes and trawls them through a sea of questions and confusion," she begins, "but he makes one laugh so much, and at times feel so awed and chilled, that even thrashing around in bewilderment or disagreement one can't help but be captured by his prose." Aligning the novel with such classic castaway tales as Defoe's *Robinson Crusoe* and Swift's *Gulliver's Travels*, Innes is ebullient in her praise: "above all," she

writes, this is "a book about life's absurdities that makes one laugh out loud on almost every page, with its quirky juxtapositions, comparisons, metaphors, Borgesian puzzles, postmodern games and a sense of fun that reflects the hero's sensual enjoyment of the world."

Comparisons alleging plagiarism have been drawn between *Life of Pi* and Brazilian author Moacyr Scliar's *Max and the Cats* (1981), an earlier book that shows remarkable similarities with Martel's novel. The various accounts about this are somewhat convoluted, but supposedly Martel mentioned that he had been intrigued by the premise of Scliar's novel after reading an unfavorable review of it by American novelist John Updike in the *New York Times Book Review*. Martel soon came under fire when it was shown that no such review existed and Updike publicly stated that he had no knowledge whatsoever of the Brazilian novel. Martel claims never to have read Scliar's book, despite the fact that the Author's Note in *Life of Pi* includes thanks to Mr. Moacyr Scliar "for the spark of life." The story has it that Scliar considered a lawsuit but changed his mind after personally speaking with Martel.

WHAT
DO I READ
NEXT?

- Yann Martel's *Self* (1996), like *Life of Pi*, raises questions about the nature of faith and whether it is possible to live a spiritual life in a world increasingly given over to secular ideas and sectarian politics.

- Discussions of magical realism as a literary style often cite Gabriel García Márquez's *One Hundred Years of Solitude* (1967) as one of the genre's outstanding examples. Considered a contemporary masterpiece, the novel chronicles a family's struggles, and the history of their fictional town, Macondo, for a period of one hundred years.

- No reading of the traditional Bildungsroman would be complete without Charles Dickens's *David Copperfield* (1850), a carefully structured novel that traces many of the events in Dickens's own life and is arguably the most intensely autobiographical of all his novels.

- Generally considered a balanced, accessible, and carefully detailed study, David Noss and Blake R. Grangaard's *History of the World's Religions* (2007) introduces readers to the origins of world religions, shows how they developed across generations, and how they continue to impact the world today.

CRITICISM

Klay Dyer

Dyer holds a Ph.D. in English literature and has published extensively on fiction, poetry, film, and television. He is also a freelance university teacher, writer, and educational consultant. In the following essay, he discusses the mystical algae island as the ultimate test of Pi's emerging and maturing faith.

Yann Martel's *Life of Pi* is a novel about belief and faith. More specifically, it is about survival, tracing a journey that takes Pi through both a profound trauma and the resulting

> THE EXPERIENCE OF THE ISLAND AND HIS OWN SELF-DELUSION LEAVES THE YOUNG CASTAWAY QUESTIONING HIMSELF AND WHAT HE BELIEVES IN. IRONICALLY, THIS SELF DOUBT BRINGS PI TO A GREATER UNDERSTANDING OF HIMSELF AND OF HIS GOD."

challenges to his developing religious faith. Marooned on a lifeboat with a 450-pound Bengal tiger, Pi finds his most intense struggle is not to stay alive but to remain hopeful about his prospects for survival (both physical and psychological). Before Pi ends his journey on a Mexican beach, however, he must endure his most profound spiritual test in the form of a mysterious island, which proves to be a symbol of the failure of blind faith as an uncritical framework for understanding the world. Indeed, during his stay on the island, Pi confronts the limits of his still immature philosophy. It is in this test of faith that Pi realizes he has participated in an act of self-deception by believing that the island will provide him with a stable haven for respite and nourishment. Pi's experiences on the island allow him to realize that believing wholeheartedly and unquestionably in anything will ultimately prove to be the path to his own demise. To question and to doubt, Pi learns during his stay on the island, is the key to survival.

In his opening notes to the novel, the author figure first emphasizes the word "bamboozle," leaving readers to expect, or at least to be aware of, some form of trickery that might appear as the story unfolds. This is a novel, the author warns, in which readers might come to expect "the selective transforming of reality." Indeed, Pi's time on the island is an episode in an already fantastic tale, he admits, that might stretch the cord of credulity to the breaking point. "There will be many who disbelieve the following episode," he admits.

Significantly, before he begins to recount his time on the island, Pi first reiterates his thoughts on the religions he has accumulated prior to his trials aboard the lifeboat. His uniquely synthetic blending of religious ideals and practices has provided him with a moral and philosophic framework that he uses to make sense of the world around him. Throughout his trials, Pi faithfully applies what he believes from Hinduism, which brings him "Truth, Unity, Absolute, Ultimate Reality"; from Christianity, which provides him with the belief in a saving grace that "exists only at one time: right now;" and from Islam, which Pi describes as "a beautiful religion of brotherhood and devotion." Together, these ideas help Pi negotiate the many trials of hunger, thirst, and spiritual survival that he faces during his time on the lifeboat with Richard Parker.

Having engaged this blended faith as his primary tool for mental and emotional survival, Pi's faith is tested most of all when he sees what appears to be an island on the horizon. Upon approaching the island, which he hopes will provide respite from the small lifeboat, Pi admits that what he sees in front of him leaves him with a "thrill to be deluded in such a high-quality way." Pi sees a "profusion of leaves" that are "brilliantly green," but even in this moment of thrilling delusion, readers see that critical questions begin to seep into Pi's mind. "Who had ever heard of land with no soil?" he asks himself, only to pass off the question as a "chimera, a play of the mind." At this point, Pi ties his religious faith to his belief in the island as a symbol of hope, noting that the island is "music to [his] eyes," and that the island's vibrant green color is "the colour of Islam."

Pi's first step toward what might be considered a leap of blind faith takes place as he steps onto the island, discovering that it is a somewhat disconcerting blend of stability and instability. It is, as he notes to himself, "flexible but solid." Turning away from his own questioning of the island, Pi experiences an almost religious experience as he becomes intoxicated by the first scent of "vegetable organic matter" that he has encountered since he first set sail from India. At this point, he comes to "believe" in the island, as he "babble[s] incoherent thanks to God and collapse[s]" on the forgiving surface. Exploring the island, Pi describes the trees as "a blessedly good thing to behold." Seeing the trees for the first time, Pi wishes "that [he] could be like" them, "rooted to the ground but with my every hand raised up to

God in praise!" Linking the existence of the trees to the threads of Islam that are woven through the fabric of his faith, Pi exults in "Allah's works." This declaration is a self-congratulatory confirmation that "the tree did indeed grow right out of the algae, as [Pi] had seen from the lifeboat."

Most tellingly, as Pi puts his faith in the island, Richard Parker remains guided by his animal instinct and is "afraid" to come ashore. The Bengal tiger "remain[s] tense" and at night in the lifeboat he is "unsettled and noisy." Parker returns to the lifeboat every night, deciding not to sleep on the island. When he awakens in the morning he "hesitate[s] for hours before jumping off the boat" to continue his hunting and his explorations of the island. From the moment the castaways discover the island, Parker's instinct is to approach it critically, to doubt it as a source of their salvation.

Whereas Parker's instinct is to approach the island as something that is not what it appears to be, Pi moves forward with a self-deluding confidence that the island is what he needs it to be. But after some weeks of retrospection and an extended exploration of the contours of this apparent paradise, Pi is forced to rethink his faith in the island. The forgiving ground is not as stable as he once thought it to be, and more specifically it "was Gandhian: it resisted by not resisting." What Pi thought was once a "small landmass rooted to the floor of the ocean," is, he realizes suddenly, a "free-floating organism" that must be perceived and judged from an entirely different perspective. Gradually, Pi begins to understand that what he once considered as truth and stability is exactly the opposite.

Not only does Pi come to acknowledge the unstableness of the island, he also discovers that it is not a complete ecosystem, meaning there are no "butterflies, no bees, no insects of any kind" as well as "no worms, no snakes, ... no shrubs, no grasses, ... no weeds." There is, he begins to recognize, no "foreign matter on the island, organic or inorganic," with the obvious exception of the omnipresent meerkats. The only other outstanding feature of the island is what attracted Pi to its surface in the first place, notably the "shining green algae and shining green trees." Pi's initial belief in the presence of a structural ecosystem based on a solid island is representative of his need to believe that he has finally found land.

As Pi starts to become skeptical of his belief in the island, he starts to put his trust in the pragmatism exhibited by Richard Parker. As Pi watches the meerkats gathering and "bending down at the same time" to nibble at the pond algae, they remind him "of prayer time in a mosque." While the meerkats appear to worship the island, they also recognize the island's dangers, which they have learned to respect and fear over time. As Pi begins to question what he sees, he also begins to question what he believes in. Pi first wonders about the "botanical strangeness" of the island after dark; the floor of the algae island turns toxic, burning him when he touches it. Discovering what he thinks is fruit on a tree, Pi realizes, after peeling off the "dense accumulation of leaves," that the object in his hand is "not a fruit." Pi then admits that if the so-called "fruit had a seed, it was the seed of my departure."

The peeling of the presumed fruit serves as a kind of stripping away of Pi's fervent, non-critical belief in the island as an ideal paradise. Shocked and disappointed by his discovery, and disappointed in himself for not recognizing his own self-delusion, he states: "Ah, how I wish that moment had never been! But for it I might have lived for years—why, for the rest of my life—on that island." Indeed, for the first time in months, all of Pi's "physical needs" are being met on the island. Because of this, "the thought of leaving the island had not crossed [his] mind"; that is, not until he discovered the secret of the island in the center of the so-called fruit.

Tucked in the center of the leaves that supposedly hid fruit, Pi finds human teeth, precisely "thirty-two teeth, a complete human set [with] not one tooth missing." At this moment "understanding dawned upon" Pi, who realizes, to his "horror," that the island is "carnivorous." Pi ponders the fate of the remains of the "poor lost soul" before him and wonders "how many dreams of a happy life [were] dashed" on the island, and "how much stored-up conversation died unsaid?" When Pi stops believing blindly in the island as a source of sustenance and begins to explore and question it, he sees the island for exactly what it is.

Ultimately, the island proves to be not only unstable but voraciously carnivorous, a self-

consuming reminder of the dangers of living in the world through blind faith. Taught early on in the novel that he must always assume that a Bengal tiger could devour him at any moment, Pi survives months aboard a lifeboat with this intense threat. Yet the island is another test, and Pi learns that he must approach the island (and thus the world) in much the same way that he approaches Richard Parker, by thinking critically and trusting his instincts.

Even if the island does not devour him, Pi knows that if he remains with the meerkats he will die a "spiritual death on [the] murderous island." He realizes, too, that he would rather "set off and perish in search of [his] own kind than to live a lonely half-life of physical comfort." Thus, Pi could choose to continue living by a false faith, but he would rather choose to seek out a truer faith. The experience of the island and his own self-delusion leaves the young castaway questioning himself and what he believes in. Ironically, this self doubt brings Pi to a greater understanding of himself and of his god. Indeed, left "bereft and desperate" by the ordeal of the island, he finds himself "in the throes of unremitting suffering" and more willing than ever to "turn to God." Pi discovers that maintaining a deep and critical faith means accepting that there is a negation to every assertion (a negative for every positive, and vice versa). Put simply, the world is filled with both good and bad things, Pi realizes, and to deny that there is any bad is, in a sense, to deny the world and, by extension, to deny God. This is the lesson of the island.

Source: Klay Dyer, Critical Essay on *Life of Pi*, in *Novels for Students*, Gale, Cengage Learning, 2008.

Stewart Cole

In the following excerpt, Cole claims the book's arguments regarding belief in God hinge upon the suspension of disbelief and the attribution or projection of human characteristics on anything that is not human.

. . . Despite its essential tenuousness, Martel's analogy does highlight an important similarity between fiction and religion: disbelief is anathema to both. I have already noted how *Life of Pi*, in claiming to be a story that "will make you believe in God," both presumes and to some extent depends upon the reader's initial disbelief in Him. This readerly disbelief is more explicitly analogized in the initial skepticism of the two Japanese interviewers when faced with the story

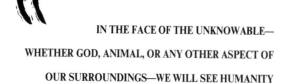

IN THE FACE OF THE UNKNOWABLE—
WHETHER GOD, ANIMAL, OR ANY OTHER ASPECT OF
OUR SURROUNDINGS—WE WILL SEE HUMANITY
WHEREVER POSSIBLE."

of Pi's survival for 227 days in a lifeboat with the tiger Richard Parker. In its treatment of the two central motifs of God and animal—Pi's apparently incongruous double majors of religious studies and zoology—the novel dramatizes disbelief in order to suspend it. Central to this tensile movement is the concept of anthropomorphism, often used in both theological and zoological contexts to indicate—as the *OED* has it—the "ascription of a human attribute or personality" to either God or animals.

Early in the novel, Pi directly addresses the problem of "Animalus Anthropomorphicus, the animal as seen through human eyes," noting that in attributing human characteristics to animals "we look at an animal and see a mirror," and going on to bemoan that "the obsession with putting ourselves at the centre of everything is the bane not only of theologians but also of zoologists." But religious scholar Stewart Elliott Guthrie, in his book-length examination of anthropomorphism entitled *Faces in the Clouds*, claims that rather than being a boon against the adoption of religious faith, anthropomorphism—or, "the obsession with putting ourselves at the centre of everything"—is the very foundation of religiosity. Guthrie's assertion that "religion may be best understood as systematic anthropomorphism" is bolstered by the fact, widely accepted by psychologists, that human modes of perception arise out of a fundamental perceptual uncertainty which forces us to always be interpreting, rather than simply seeing, the phenomenal world. Beginning from this premise that all perception is interpretive—all seeing is seeing as—Guthrie goes on to claim that the attribution of human characteristics to the non-human is an often unconscious strategy by which humans attempt to gain the benefit of whatever significance the world has to offer. He repeatedly returns to the example of the hiker who spots a large shape just off the trail and immediately jumps to the conclusion that it is a

bear, only to discover a few seconds later that it is in fact a boulder (45). Given ambiguity, humans will choose to perceive objects as animate until proven otherwise. This instinctual animism— "attributing life to the lifeless" (39)—finds us not only grasping after every opportunity to engage with our fellow sentient beings, but also performs a survival function: were the hiker to see as a boulder what is in fact a bear, her misperception could prove fatal, while on the other hand, little is lost in briefly hallucinating the bear. Guthrie notes how such a strategy is analogous to Pascal's wager—whether God exists or not, we should believe in Him, for we suffer nothing by our wrong belief if He does not exist, while we gain an infinitude for our faith if He does (Pascal 157)—and claims that anthropomorphism, and thus religion, arise from a similar perceptual bet:

> We do find apparent humans, and echoes and copies of humans, both in our immediate environments and in our ultimate conditions. Mailboxes appear as persons, plagues appear as messages, and order appears as design. Anthropomorphism by definition is mistaken, but it also is reasonable and inevitable. Choosing among interpretations of the world, we remain condemned to meaning, and the greatest meaning has a human face. (Guthrie 204)

The jubilation Pi feels upon emerging from the Muslim Mr. Kumar's bakery after an afternoon of prayer nicely exemplifies this link between anthropomorphism and meaning in a religious context. "I suddenly felt I was in heaven," he tells us, marvelling at the richness of his surroundings:

> Whereas before the road, the sea, the trees, the air, the sun all spoke differently to me, now they spoke one language of unity. Tree took account of road, which was aware of air, which was mindful of sea, which shared things with sun. Every element lived in harmonious relation with its neighbour, and all was kith and kin. I knelt a mortal; I rose an immortal. I felt like the centre of a small circle coinciding with the centre of a much larger one. Atman met Allah.

Pi here invokes "heaven" amidst earthly surroundings, attributes language and kinship to the various elements of those surroundings, and shows a willingness to place himself—prior protestations notwithstanding, and however coincidentally—"at the centre of everything," thus demonstrating that while he may oppose anthropomorphism as it applies to animals, he is willing to indulge in the fallacy as it applies to his surroundings while in the grip of religious exaltation.

That this rampantly anthropomorphic passage is one of the book's most convincing evocations of Pi's religious fervour is no accident. The affective power of anthropomorphism in works of literature—as personification or, more cautiously, the pathetic fallacy—has often been noted, from Coleridge's earnest hope to "transfer from our inward nature a human interest" (322) that would lend even the supernatural an emotive relevance and immediacy, to John Ruskin's initial coining and terse dismissal of "the pathetic fallacy" in poetry as "a falseness in our impressions of external things" (qtd. in Hecht 482), to Paul de Man's lukewarm endorsement of anthropomorphism as "the illusionary resuscitation of the natural breath of language (247). But the most important aspect of the anthropomorphic impulse, implicit in all the above accounts, is that it finds expression primarily in response to doubt or disbelief, the perceptual uncertainty into which we are all born and with which, consciously or not, our minds constantly grapple: Is that a ship on the horizon, or a trick of the sunlight? A fierce wind, or the angry breath of God? In the face of the unknowable—whether God, animal, or any other aspect of our surroundings—we will see humanity wherever possible.

Given the prevalence of anthropomorphism as a strategy for combating perceptual uncertainty, disbelief or doubt, Pi's tendency to humanize the animals that surround him—despite the zoological knowledge that affords him insight into the drawbacks of such a tendency—takes on a special significance, especially in light of his apparently incongruous and excessive engagement with religion. Although he attempts to excuse having humanized the pheasants, baboons and other animals of the zoo "till they spoke fluent English" by claiming that "the fancy was always conscious," Pi never entirely loses his youthful tendency to anthropomorphize. This is most obvious in his attitude to Richard Parker, the tiger with a human name, an anthropomorphic trope writ large. Though it might seem strange that a novel whose only direct comments on anthropomorphism are condemnatory should depend so heavily on it—to the extent of granting a tiger an honorary humanity to allow both narrator and reader a more convincing engagement with him—a careful reading reveals a much more fraught and ambiguous narrative relationship with the concept than Pi's vehement positioning suggests.

The first time we hear of Richard Parker, Pi laments: "I still cannot understand how he could abandon me so unceremoniously, without any sort of goodbye, without looking back even once," an anthropomorphic misunderstanding that jars quite strikingly with Pi's aforementioned oration on the dangers of "Animalus Anthropomorphicus," which occurs only a little further on in the novel. But although Pi presumably sees quite clearly the fallacy in daring to attribute fellow feeling to a tiger, the reader is not explicitly told that Richard Parker is a tiger until much later, ... and so would not recognize the contradiction on first reading. Besides, the rhetorical importance of the passage far outweighs the logical contradiction it embodies, as the narrative impact of Richard Parker's appearance in the lifeboat as "a wet, trembling, half-drowned, heaving and coughing three-year-old adult Bengal tiger" entirely depends on the reader having naturally assumed that Richard Parker is human. Or, put another way, given ambiguity, we assume Richard Parker is human because that is the most meaningful thing he could be; because, as Guthrie notes of our anthropomorphic impulse, "we look first for what matters most" (90). This is not to say that the revelation of Richard Parker's tiger-ness strips him of meaning. Not at all. Because by the time his biological status is clarified, he has already been sufficiently humanized for the reader to have placed him on a continuum with the novel's human characters. Although the believability of Pi's story depends on his detailed engagement with Richard Parker's tiger-ness—his account of how he kept him fed, watered, and obedient without getting killed—and although such passages convey a realism only meticulous zoological research can account for, much of Richard Parker's charm as a character subsists in his consistent humanization, a function his name subtly fulfils at every mention. And although Pi resists directly anthropomorphizing Richard Parker for most of the lifeboat journey, qualifying his statements with the verb to seem so as not to claim possession of an inaccessible knowledge—as in "'Where's my treat?' his face seemed to inquire"—he cannot avoid using human analogies to imbue Richard Parker with significance: in the space of a few pages, the tiger sports "formidable sideburns" and "a stylish goatee"; reveals his massive canine "coyly"; catches the rat in his maw "like a baseball into a catcher's mitt"; and settles in after feeding "the way you or I would look out from a restaurant table after a good meal, when the time has come for conversation and people-watching." Pi's avoidance of unqualified anthropomorphisms through most of the long lifeboat section might convince us that he has, as he claims, learned from the tiger "the lesson that an animal is an animal, essentially and practically removed from us." But at the end of the novel, while recounting their sad final parting, he takes up once again his anthropomorphic lament: "I was weeping because Richard Parker left me so unceremoniously. What a terrible thing it is to botch a farewell. I am a person who believes in form, in the harmony of order. Where we can, we must give things a meaningful shape." Further on, Pi admits that "that bungled goodbye hurts me to this day," an indication that though he may be intellectually resolved to the unbridgeable distance between himself and Richard Parker—a distance so vast that not even 227 days in a lifeboat together could bring them to anything more than spatial closeness—the fact still stings him emotionally. Also worth noting is Pi's shift to the present tense: he "believes in form," and that "we must give things a meaningful shape," thus evincing that however his experiences with Richard Parker may have disabused him of any faith in the truth of anthropomorphism, he still implicitly acknowledges its necessity. Anthropomorphism, as characterized by Guthrie and others, is a perceptual strategy by which we attempt to glean the greatest meaning from the world around us. Though by definition mistaken, it is reasonable and often unavoidable. So Pi's appeal to meaning in the above passage is not surprising; Richard Parker's presence during his lifeboat ordeal provides him with another proximate being to infuse with significance, a fellow mammal with whom to share the months of endless horizon. Like all humans, Pi remains "condemned to meaning," is a meaning generator, so Richard Parker's presence allows Pi to exercise a fundamental aspect of his humanity. Conversely, it is difficult to imagine the animal characters in *Life of Pi* conveying much of anything if stripped of their imposed humanness.

I have so far noted that while Pi generally avoids directly anthropomorphizing Richard Parker during their lifeboat ordeal, he tends to indulge in the fallacy more openly at places in the narrative set explicitly before or after their odyssey. This is in the interest of realism; the meticulously detailed lifeboat section would suffer in believability were the narrator's more wildly fallacious anthropomorphisms to emerge too often. Gone therefore are such elaborate comparisons as that of three-toed sloths to "upside-down yogis

deep in meditation or hermits deep in prayer"; or that of zoos to hotels with guests "either terribly repressed and subject to explosions of frenzied lasciviousness or openly depraved"; or that of the orangutan Orange Juice to the Virgin Mary, and the spiders that crawl around her to "malevolent worshippers." Except for the comment that Richard Parker's "mix of ease and concentration" while swatting and swallowing flying fish out of the air "would be the envy of the highest yogis," Pi's early proclivity for improbable comparisons is noticeably muted in the novel's long second part, with Richard Parker's name and a slew of indirectly humanizing analogies sufficing to carry the anthropomorphic conceit through to its re-emergence at the coda. That four of the five comparisons cited above have religious overtones also calls to notice how the religious content too is muted in the lifeboat section. Despite regular invocations of "Jesus, Mary, Mohammed and Vishnu," "God," or "Allah," and a single of the lifeboat's 57 chapters devoted to religious rituals on board (chapter 74), references to Pi's well-established religious fervour come mainly in passing. So remarkably slight is Pi's engagement with religion during this section that when he claims, just before striking land, that "it was natural that, bereft and desperate as I was, in the throes of unremitting suffering, I should turn to God," his piety rings a little false. At this point he has made no reference to God for thirty pages, none at all since first landing on the carnivorous island. James Wood points out that during the lifeboat section "we are not privy to any theological anguish or questioning," and notes that in the "bland closure" of the above-cited passage, "it is not Pi's theological conclusion—his religious fidelity—that puzzles so much as his oddly formulaic, empty method of reaching it." But given Pi's persistent conflation of aesthetic and religious belief, the absence of religious questioning during the lifeboat ordeal seems consistent. Neither Pi nor his author-narrator make any distinction between the temporary suspension of disbelief and firm religious faith, between the acceptance of a believable story and the embrasure of an omniscient God. From such a vantage point, the subjective aesthetic value of the lifeboat section—how it manages an intricate realism within an utterly implausible framework—effectively supplants objective religious truth. According to the worldview embodied in the novel, the religious aspects of the narrative do not simply fade to the background in part two, they are enacted: if we believe the story of Pi's ordeal, we believe in God, however temporarily . . .

Source: Stewart Cole, "Believing in Tigers: Anthropomorphism and Incredulity in Yann Martel's *Life of Pi*," in *Studies in Canadian Literature*, Vol. 29, No. 2, Summer 2004, pp. 22–37.

Randy Boyagoda

In the following review, Boyagoda simultaneously applauds the story in Life of Pi *while heavily critiquing its religious arguments as "piecemeal."*

Good news came from across the Atlantic late last year. England's most prestigious literary award—the Booker Prize—had been awarded to a work that made the following assertion on its inside cover: "This is a novel of such rare and wondrous storytelling that it may, as one character claims, make you believe in God. Can a reader reasonably ask for anything more?" That sophisticated English literary palettes thought this a reasonable claim—and that Canadian Yann Martel's *The Life of Pi* has since become a bestseller—may be an indication that growing numbers of people, thirsting for more substance in their lives, are beginning to seek more substance in their reading. Or, alternately, it may be a comment on the brand of popular piety Martel's novel proposes.

The protagonist of *The Life of Pi* is the precocious son of a pragmatic zookeeper, an Indian boy fascinated by his nation's many faiths but forced by its many political problems to emigrate to Canada along with his family and their animal charges. During the voyage, their ship suddenly sinks, leaving the boy on a lifeboat along with a few furry survivors; ultimately only Pi and a tiger remain. As the duo drift through the Pacific Ocean, struggling to survive the elements, Pi must also struggle to survive his shipmate; he

relies on his wits and his faith in, intermittently, Christianity, Hinduism, and Islam to do so. After a series of adventures—some wondrous, some gruesome—their boat washes up in Mexico and the two part ways. We never hear from the tiger again, but we do hear from Pi. In fact, he retells his story as an adult living in Toronto, in a house whose décor—a portrait of Our Lady of Guadalupe rests beside a photo of Kaaba; a brass statue of Shiva stands beneath paintings of Christ; a prayer rug lies near a bedside Bible—inadvertently displays our protagonist's eclectically tacky approach to religion.

The Life of Pi seems to have as many literary predecessors as India has religions. There are traces of Defoe's *Robinson Crusoe*, Hemingway's *The Old Man and the Sea*, Bunyan's *Pilgrim's Progress*, St. Exupéry's *Le Petit Prince*, and Aesop's *Fables*. But *The Life of Pi* also asks to be the latest in the long line of grand tales about India, novels that seek to capture what Martel himself calls "the rich, noisy, functioning madness" of the place, and a great deal of the novel's flaws rest in that ambition. The encounters of two more famous orphans with India's religions provide a sense of what Pi lacks. Kipling's Kim and Rushdie's Saleem Sinai dash from one end of India to another, experiencing the nation's religious panoply as it must be—as frenzied, vital, occasionally terrifying—rather than as a well-meaning Canadian might imagine it: as polite, passive, frequently meek.

For example, the adult Pi, an Indian orphan-cum-Canadian immigrant, recalls finding a Gideon Bible in a hotel room. He praises the Gideons, then advises: "They should leave not only Bibles, but other sacred writings as well. I cannot think of a better way to spread the faith. No thundering from a pulpit, no condemnation from bad churches, no peer pressure, just a book of scripture quietly waiting to say hello, as gentle and powerful as a girl's kiss on your cheek." The author's patent lack of appreciation for the intensity and particularity of religious devotion explains such myopic idealism and saccharine imagery. In telling us that the Bible (and "other sacred writings") is "just a book" to spread "the faith," Martel reveals his fundamental misunderstanding of the relationship between God and religious practices. Martel offers a confusing pastiche of devotions brought into unity by the sincerity of individual intention and action, rather than by virtue of the singular truth inherent in any of the religions Pi purports to follow.

Pi's repeated all-inclusive paeans to his private trinity of faiths detract from an otherwise enjoyable tale, which Martel achieves when he forgets about religion and concentrates on telling his young hero's adventures. Running through the chaos of a sinking ship; watching a tiger wrestle a shark; exploring a mysterious island; devising ways to catch turtles and gather fresh water—these are but some of the novel's small pleasures. In matters not religious, Martel chose the right narrator: Pi's innocent voice allows us to revel in the wide-eyed pleasures of this world as only a young boy on a fantastic voyage can experience them. Consider Pi's description of the fearful symmetry of raw elegance and sublime power occasioned by his tiger companion returning to their boat:

> He surged onto the stern, quantities of water pouring off him, making my end of the boat pitch up. He balanced on the gunnel and the stern bench for a moment, assessing me. My heart grew faint. I did not think I would be able to blow into the whistle again. I looked at him blankly. He flowed down to the floor of the lifeboat and disappeared under the tarpaulin. I could see parts of him from the edges of the locker lid. I threw myself upon the tarpaulin, out of his sight—but directly above him. I felt an overwhelming urge to sprout wings and fly off.

Like Pi, we are breathless, a tiger-training whistle dangling from our lips, as much from the beauty as from the terror of a wild animal in close proximity.

However grateful we may be to Martel for such moments, the third and final section of his novel limits our general appreciation by enlisting us in a clumsy postmodern game of narration and belief. The section is comprised of a transcript between two Japanese representatives of the shipping company and Pi, recuperating in a Mexican hospital room. The Japanese have no time for Pi's unbelievable musings and insist upon a factual account of the ship's sinking, so Pi retells his tale, turning his animal shipmates into humans. The new version is more comprehensible but less enjoyable: either way we can never know which version "actually" happened. We likely entered the novel as skeptical as are the Japanese, but having heard the story, we now face a test of faith: Which do we believe? Of course Martel wants us to believe in Pi's original version, with the floating banana island and the man-eating plants and the flying fish. In his view, to do so is a leap of faith, which in turn is a leap

towards God: the God brought into existence by the novel itself, a strange mishmash of religious notions and figures that together comprise the deity that Pi creates and celebrates. In short, a God of fiction.

Martel should have stuck to the metaphoric approach he takes to religion at the end of the novel's second section, when Pi finally reaches land. In his darkest moment, Pi perceives: "The lower you are, the higher your mind will want to soar. It was natural that, bereft and desperate as I was, in the throes of unremitting suffering, I should turn to God." The next chapter opens: "When we reached land," a phrase that with simple perfection conveys the foundation given to us when we rely on God's power, rather than on our own. In one of the novel's few instances of coherent religious meaning, Martel echoes St. Paul and Kempis' *Imitatio* in telling us that if we turn to God in our lowest moments, inevitably we will be raised up on high. A meaningful moment, sadly set adrift amongst so much faith-as-flotsam. If only we could agree with Pi's approach to religion, we could enjoy his *Life*. Were we to read in a compartmentalized way, taking bits and pieces from here and there that amuse or ennoble us, ignoring the deeper implications of such a piecemeal commitment to a unified whole, we could happily sail along with boy and tiger. But such a way of reading, of professing, indeed of living, while so symptomatic of our contemporary condition, ought not be our course.

T. S. Eliot made the following distinction: "We must believe that the greater part of our current reading matter is written for us by people who have no real belief in a supernatural order, though some of it may be written by people with individual notions of a supernatural order which are not ours." Martel falls into the latter camp: unfortunately, his invitation to believe in God through his novel is too individualized to be reasonable. We do not turn to fiction to find the true God, and we should not turn to it to find a recipe for making a God agreeable enough to our personal tastes to believe in. We turn to good novels in part to exercise our imaginations, and *The Life of Pi* allows for that in some places. Yet Martel goes much further, to imply that we can find God by using our imaginations freely. But we can only hope to find God by using our imaginations wisely. Fiction, on its own, cannot create truth. The finest books can at best sound the depths of the human condition and bring rumors of the highest truths. They help chart our course towards that undiscovered country where we all hope, someday, to land.

Source: Randy Boyagoda, "Faith, Fiction, Flotsam," in *First Things: A Journal of Religion and Public Life*, May 2003, pp. 69–72.

SOURCES

Houser, Gordon, Review of *Life of Pi*, in the *Christian Century*, February 8, 2003, pp. 34–35.

Innes, Charlotte, "Robinson Crusoe, Move Over," in the *Nation*, August 19–26, 2002, pp. 25–29.

Iyer, Pico, "The Last Refuge," in *Harper's* magazine, Vol. 304, No. 1825, 2002, pp. 77–80.

Martel, Yann, *Life of Pi*, Vintage Canada, 2002.

Mishra, Pankaj, "The Man or the Tiger?" in the *New York Review of Books*, Vol. 50, No. 5, March 27, 2003, pp. 43–54.

Morra, Linda M., Review of *Life of Pi*, in *Canadian Literature*, Vol. 177, Summer 2003, p. 163.

Review of *Life of Pi*, in the *Missouri Review*, Vol. 27, No. 1, 2004, pp. 179–80.

Shirato, Linda, Review of *Life of Pi*, in *Library Journal*, May 15, 2003, p. 164.

FURTHER READING

Ashcroft, Bill, Gareth Griffiths, and Helen Tiffin, *The Empire Writes Back: Theory and Practice in Post-Colonial Literatures*, Routledge, 2002.

This was the first major theoretical account of a wide range of post-colonial texts and their relation to the larger issues of post-colonial culture, and remains one of the most significant works published in this field.

Moretti, Franco, *The Way of the World: The Bildungsroman in European Culture*, Verso Books, 2000.

This seminal study positions the Bildungsroman as the great cultural mediator of nineteenth-century Europe, arguing that the form explores the many strange compromises between revolution and restoration; economic transition and aesthetic pleasure; and individual autonomy and social normality.

New, William H., ed., *Encyclopedia of Literature in Canada*, University of Toronto Press, 2002.

This book is an invaluable reference companion to the literatures of Canada, and it discusses Canadian authors and their work, related literary and social issues, and the major historical and cultural events that have shaped Canadian literature.

Said, Edward W., *Orientalism*, Vintage, 1979.

The Eastern world was first known to the West only through literature and texts that viewed it, for the most part, through a predominantly Western perspective. The crux of this study is a critique of how the academic world has regarded the East and how they have only helped to legitimize and feed this skewed perspective.

Lives of Girls and Women

ALICE MUNRO

1971

Alice Munro's only novel, *Lives of Girls and Women*, which was published in 1971, is a fictionalized coming-of-age work that is sometimes described as autobiographical. Munro is best known as a short story writer, whose work focuses on women's lives. *Lives of Girls and Women* consists of an episodic series of loosely linked short stories, all connected around the life of a young girl. Del Jordan, who is a child in the book's opening chapters, narrates a series of episodes from her life growing up in Jubilee, a small rural town in western Ontario. It is a reasonable possibility that Jubilee was modeled after Munro's own home town of Wingham, Ontario. Del's stories focus on her efforts to find her place in the small town in which she lives. She is not content with the kind of life that other young girls live and has no desire to be conventional. Instead, Del wants to find her own voice. Her efforts result in an interesting opposition between memory, truth, and imagination. As a narrator, Del relates events from different perspectives of time, recounting events from both the child narrator's perspective and from the viewpoint of the grown woman looking back on her life. This style of narration provides dimension and complexity to Munro's book. Munro's only novel also offers readers what seems to be an authentic glimpse into small town life. Her descriptions of locations and people create an image for the reader that seems very authentic. *Lives of Girls and Women* was

Alice Munro (*AP Images*)

awarded the Canadian Booksellers' Association Award. A recent edition of the novel was released by Vintage Books in 2001.

AUTHOR BIOGRAPHY

Alice Munro was born Alice Laidlaw on July 10, 1931 just outside Wingham, a small town in western Ontario, Canada. Her father, Robert, was an unsuccessful breeder of silver foxes, whose business failed completely during the depression. Her mother, Ann, had been a school teacher at one time and later helped her husband sell the pelts from their foxes. The Laidlaw family was poor, especially after her father's fox farm failed, and they lived in a poorer area just outside town. Alice began writing short stories when she was twelve and continued to write after she left Wingham to attend university. She won a

scholarship to attend the University of Western Ontario in 1949, but she was forced to leave after two years when the scholarship ended.

Rather than return to her home in 1951, she decided to marry a fellow student, James Munro. During the more than twenty years of their marriage, they had four daughters, one of whom died in infancy. The Munro family lived in Vancouver, British Columbia for many years, but eventually they moved to Victoria, where they opened a bookstore. During the time in Vancouver, Munro wrote infrequently, but after the move to Victoria, she once again began writing short stories. Her first collection of short stories was published as *Dance of the Happy Shades* in 1968. This first book, which included stories written in the 1950s and 1960s, won the Governor General's Literary Award, Canada's highest literary award. In 1971, Munro's only novel, *Lives of Girls and Women* was published and was awarded the Canadian Booksellers' Association

MEDIA ADAPTATIONS

- *Lives of Girls and Women* was filmed for television in 1994 by Paragon Entertainment.

- "Baptizing," a chapter from *Lives of Girls and Women*, was adapted and filmed for CBC's *Performance* series in 1975. The film stars Munro's daughter Jenny.

Award. The following year, Munro left her husband and moved back to Ontario, where she began teaching creative writing classes at the University of Western Ontario.

Another collection of short stories, *Something I've Been Meaning to Tell You*, was published in 1973. Munro and her husband were divorced in 1976, and she married Gerald Fremlin that same year. The publication of her third collection of short stories, *Who Do You Think You Are?*, earned Munro a second Governor General's Literary Award. She won this award for a third time in 1986 for *The Progress of Love*. Munro was awarded the inaugural Marian Engel Award in 1986 for her entire body of work.

In the years that followed, Munro continued to write short stories, some of which were published in the *New Yorker* and in *Atlantic Monthly*. Collections of her stories have also been published as *Moons of Jupiter* (1982), *Friend of My Youth* (1990), and *Open Secrets*, which won the W. H. Smith Award for the best book published in the United Kingdom in 1995. *Selected Stories* came out in 1996 and *The Love of a Good Woman* was published in 1998, with the second book winning the Giller Prize. *Hateship, Friendship, Courtship, Loveship, Marriage* (2001), *Runaway* (2004), which also won the Giller Prize, and *The View From Castle Rock* (2006) continue Munro's love of the short story as a way to explore women's lives and her own family's past life.

PLOT SUMMARY

The Flats Road

The narrator, Del, uses this first chapter of *Lives of Girls and Women* to briefly introduce her family and setting. Del lives at the end of Flats Road, which is just outside town but not quite in the country. Del lives with her mother, Addie, who hates living in the country and envisions herself more attuned to city living, and her father, who is comfortable with their semi-country existence. The narrator also shares her home with her younger brother, Owen, and a dog, Major. The area in which they live is described as "neglected, poor, and eccentric." Del is not explicit about her age, but she is probably about ten or eleven years old in this chapter. This opening chapter quickly establishes the narrator's position within the family and paints the world in which she lives. It is 1942 in rural Canada. The people are unsophisticated, poor, wary of strangers, and some are drunk much of the time. Readers are introduced to several strange and peculiar inhabitants of the countryside, including bootleggers Mitch Plim, and the Potter boys. The narrator labels Frankie Hall and Irene Pollox as the two idiots, who live on Flats Road, and readers learn about Sandy Stevenson, who marries a widow and is haunted by her unhappy deceased husband. All of these characters populate Flats Road and help to create an image of quirkiness in the first chapter of Munro's novel.

This opening chapter also recounts the story of Uncle Benny, who is not the narrator's uncle or anyone's uncle, as readers quickly learn. Benny Poole lives in his parent's home, which is filled with a variety of objects that the narrator describes as "a wealth of wreckage, a whole rich, dark, rotting mess of carpets, linoleum, parts of furniture, insides of machinery, nails, wire, tools, utensils." These are mostly the throwaways that Benny collects from the discards of other people's lives and what he can scavenge from the dump. Although the author provides some information about Uncle Benny's life, for instance that he subscribes to a tabloid newspaper filled with strange and unusual happenings, the larger focus of this chapter is on Benny's mail order bride and what happens to him after he brings her back to Flats Road. When Benny goes to meet this woman for the first time, he finds her family prepared for an immediate wedding, to which Benny agrees, without much thought. He brings his new bride back to Flats Road, Jubilee. Madeleine is not the bargain Benny hoped to find. She is only a girl, although she already has a small child. She is also dirty and ill kept and given to violence and the occasional outburst directed to anyone who displeases her. Readers also learn that she beats her daughter, Diane. When Madeleine disappears with some of his broken-down furniture, Benny goes to Toronto to search for her and to rescue Diane, but he is soon lost and discouraged and returns home without the child he had hoped to save. Years later, when he is reminded of Madeleine, Benny prefers to remember his brief foray into marriage "with a little contempt for being something, or somebody, so long discarded." The evidence that she beat her small daughter was easily forgotten as an inconvenient memory that was best ignored.

Heirs of the Living Body

In this chapter, Munro tells the story of Del's Uncle Craig, who is researching the family genealogy and accumulating a detailed history of the area. Although when the chapter opens, Uncle Craig is old and partially blind, Munro includes the description of Uncle Craig as he appeared in a youthful photograph, and so readers can see him as more than just the old man that Del sees. Uncle Craig's life work has been a ponderous written history of the area. He writes down the most exacting details, but his history is dry and uninteresting to Del. The two maiden aunts, Elspeth and Grace, are also purveyors of history. They relate the oral history of the people and land, infusing their stories with the kinds of details and personal antidotes that Del finds entertaining. The two sisters also find the telling of the stories entertaining, and Del notes that even without an audience, "they would have told them anyway, for their own pleasure." The sisters compliment one another, completing one another's sentences and filling in necessary details for each sister's stories. However, the sisters judge their own stories and work to be less important than the work of their brother, Craig. When he is busy recording his history, all noise, talking, or even slight movement must cease, so that he cannot be disturbed. In the sisters' world, men occupy a more important sphere than women. The sisters change when they visit Del's home and come into contact with her mother. They become "sulky, sly, elderly, eager to take offense." The aunts take offense easily and their conversation is often

laced with mockery, cold remarks, and pretension. The aunts also reveal an important family tradition. For example, Uncle Craig never ran for office, just as they never married. Del understands that they feared rejection so much that they never took a chance on doing anything that might result in being rejected, whether public office, marriage, or any other opportunity.

This chapter also tells the story of Del's cousin, Mary Agnes, who is described as "almost like other people." Del explains that Mary Agnes was deprived of oxygen at birth. Del knows that Mary Agnes must be shown the respect of an adult, since her age suggests that she is one, but her behavior is that of a child. She has been assaulted in the past, although Del does not know if Mary Agnes was sexually assaulted, but now she wears extra layers of clothing and is more closely watched. Her mother, Aunt Moira, is a victim of many physical maladies, which Del credits to Aunt Moria's having been married, since her two spinster sisters, Aunt Elspeth and Aunties Grace, are both in perfect health. Thus Del thinks that marriage is not as healthy for women as being single.

The climax of this chapter focuses on the death of Uncle Craig, whose passing leads to a discussion about dying and nature. The title for this chapter is taken from an article that tells about organ transplant, which Del's mother uses to try and dispel some of the mystery surrounding death. The prospect of seeing her uncle's body frightens Del and no amount of reassurance relieves her anxiety. When Mary Agnes tries to force Del to view the body, Del bites her. This chapter ends with Del outgrowing her two aunts and their stories. The two aunts seem to lose their vitality after Uncle Craig's death, which Del credits to "what became of them when they no longer had a man with them, to nourish and admire." The chapter concludes with the handing down of Uncle Craig's thousand page history to Del, who the aunts see as the one person most able to finish the work. Del stores Uncle Craig's life work in the cellar, where a spring flood eventually destroys it.

Princess Ida

In this chapter, readers learn about Del's mother. The title of the chapter refers to her mother's nom de plume, which she uses for a column that she writes, which is published in the local newspaper. Addie Jordan has become an encyclopedia salesman as the chapter begins. Del likes reading the encyclopedia, and initially she is pleased to recite what she knows, as part of her mother's sales pitch. Eventually, though, Del begins to understand that reciting a catalogue of facts is not especially attractive, and after a series of deliberate errors and embarrassing moments, the recitations end. Readers also learn that Del's mother, who has always hated country living, has rented a house in town. The family still goes back out to the house on Flats Road for the summer, but they no longer all live together as a family. Like her mother, Del enjoys the formality and order of living in town. Life is busier and far more interesting, as well. Del also describes a party that her mother threw for the other town ladies, whom she wished to impress. Del enjoys the party and admires her mother, until Aunt Elspeth and Auntie Grace's criticism make her see the party and her mother differently. She sees her mother's efforts to impress as embarrassing, and in some ways even pitiful, in her failed attempt to introduce new social customs to their small town.

Del tells her mother's personal story, as the chapter continues. Addie Morrison grew up very poor, with a father and two brothers, one whom she tolerated and another whom she hated. Del's maternal grandmother was a religious fanatic, who spent her time either weeping or praying. When she inherited money, it was spent on expensive bibles to give to nonbelievers, even though the family was in desperate need of money. Del is sometimes acutely embarrassed by her mother—by her stories, by her clothing, and by her mannerisms. When Del's Uncle Bill arrives for a visit with his new and much younger wife, Nile, readers learn more about Del's mother. Uncle Bill is the younger of the two brothers, who tormented her as a child. Both Addie and Bill remember their childhood differently. For Del's mother, their farm was bleak, sterile, incapable of growing any crops, an inhospitable place, from which she gratefully escaped. Her memories of their childhood farm color her choices as an adult and are the reason why she wants to live in town. For her brother Bill, the farm is a romantic memory of a simpler life that was closer to nature. After Uncle Bill and his wife leave, Addie tells Del that her Uncle Bill is dying. The chapter ends with the realization that the hatred and animosity and the terrible memories of that long-ago childhood are no longer as painful for her mother.

Age of Faith

In this chapter, Del relates her search for something tangible about God that she can believe. This is her search for the faith that she thinks is missing. Initially, Del explains that her belief in the burglars that her mother fears is more real than any belief in God. Del can picture the possible burglars quite clearly, but she soon comes to realize that while burglars do exist, they are not quite as clearly defined as she had imagined. Her belief in God is not clearly defined either, and so part of this chapter is devoted to her experiences with religion, especially the four churches that are present in the town of Jubilee. Her family belongs to the United Church, which is the largest and most successful of the Jubilee churches. Del is the only member of the family to attend church on a regular basis. Her mother is skeptical of organized religion and so Del cannot seek answers to her questions at home. She carefully assesses the different churches to determine their suitability and decides that the Catholic Church is mysterious, an "exotic dangerous faith." The Baptists are an austere group, but "their hymns were loud, rollicking, and optimistic." The Presbyterians are the "leftovers" who did not attend United and the elderly. The fourth choice is the Anglican Church, which had become unfashionable and was thus quite poor.

Del wants to know if God is real, and she looks for the answer at church. When she fails to find an answer at the United Church, she attends the Anglican Church. She likes the theatricality of the Anglican Church but still cannot determine if God is real. As a test, Del prays to God to help her in her Household Science class, where she is incapable of threading a needle and pleasing her teacher. Her prayers seem to be answered, but then Del begins to wonder if it was coincidence and not prayer that saved her from her teacher's anger. The real test comes when the family dog begins killing the neighbor's sheep. When Del's father decides that the dog, Major, must be killed, her younger brother Owen, begs her to pray that Major will not be killed. Del refuses; she understands on some level that God will not intervene in the death of a dog. Although Del thinks that she has her answer about whether God is real, she believes that God would not be interested in their objections to Major's execution, since their objections "were not His." As was the case in previous chapters, Del is very interested in death.

Her interest in religion stems, in part, from a concern about what happens after death.

Changes and Ceremonies

Much of this chapter focuses on the relationships between boys and girls, which change over time. Del begins her narration by recalling a scene in which a group of boys are harassing Del and her friend, Naomi. The name calling is common, and Del understands that with their slanders, the boys "stripped away freedom to be what you wanted, reduced you to what it was they saw." In this chapter, Del also reveals her first crush on a boy from her school, Frank Wales, who has the lead in the operetta, *The Pied Piper*, which is being staged in the Town Hall. Del is selected to be a dancer in the production. The rehearsals and costume design for the operetta consume the participants, but much of Del's energy goes into daydreaming about Frank, who is unaware of her passion for him. The teacher overseeing the operetta is Miss Farris, who, although she was born in Jubilee, always seems an outsider. She is often the subject of gossip, which focuses on her clothing and the possibility of a romance or scandal.

In the choosing of people to participate in the operetta, Del explains the hierarchy of classroom life. Some students are secure in the knowledge that they will be chosen. These are the boys and girls who radiate self-confidence. Their position is, in part, awarded to them by their classmates, who admire these students. There are also students who will never be chosen. These are the students who do not fit in somehow, either because of some physical identity that sets him or her apart or because of illness. Del and Naomi fit into a group of students who are sometimes chosen. Del's observations about her classmates and teachers are intermingled with the events surrounding the operetta, which culminates in a successful performance. The chapter ends, however, with a look ahead a few years and a report that Miss Farris drowned in the Wawanash River, a likely suicide, although no one knows for certain. As the chapter title suggests, Del does change as she evolves against the backdrop of so many different ceremonies.

Lives of Girls and Women

In this chapter, Del is in her first year of high school. She and Naomi are consumed with a growing awareness of their own sexuality and that of everyone with whom they have contact. Del and Naomi observe the differences in male and female peacocks and note that the males are far more beautiful and noticeable than the females. Even the sounds they hear in nature are linked to their growing sexual awareness. Virtually everything around them is connected in some way to this new interest in sex. They speculate about Addie's boarder, Fern, whose friend, Mr. Chamberlain, might even be her suitor. Mr. Chamberlain is a frequent guest in their home, and so it is easy for Del to appropriate Mr. Chamberlain as part of her sexual fantasies, as she tries to understand the changes that are occurring in her body. One evening, at a moment when they are unobserved, Mr. Chamberlain takes the opportunity to feel Del's breasts. After that stolen moment, Del continues to make it easy for Mr. Chamberlain to feel her breasts, which he does quite often. He also feels her buttocks and upper thighs. Although his touch is quite brutal, Del does not object, since she believes that sexual activity is violent. Del recounts two episodes with Mr. Chamberlain. In the first, he asks her to search Fern's room for some letters that he wrote, and in the second, he takes Del out into the woods and masturbates in front of her. After that episode, he leaves town but not before writing Fern a letter ending their relationship. In her new awareness of the world and of men and women, Del reads books by Somerset Maugham and Nancy Mitford. She learns about the social interactions of men and women in other places and fantasizes about a different life. The chapter ends with Del's mother prophesying that the world will change for women, who will no longer need to define themselves only by their relationships with men. Because Del automatically rejects anything that her mother tells her, Del believes that women should not be told to be careful; instead, women should be told to be more like men: "go out and take on all kinds of experiences and shuck off what they didn't want and come back proud."

Baptizing

When the chapter opens, Del is in her third year of high school. Her friend Naomi has quit school and gotten a secretarial job. Del struggles with her place in the world, since she does not see herself like the other girls she knows, nor is she like her mother. When she reads what a famous psychiatrist says about the differences between girls and boys, it seems that she is not like girls anywhere. After an episode in which she and Naomi meet two men that they know at a dance and have too much to drink, Del's friendship with Naomi is less important to her. Del is not interested in men, dancing, or drink and feels that she is different from other girls and young women, who are busy looking for potential husbands, planning for weddings, and preparing to be mothers. Del forms a relationship with Jerry Storey, her intellectual equal, given that the two of them are considered the smartest students in their high school. Their relationship seems to happen almost by accident and is not especially romantic or passionate. They are mostly friends, who play the role of girlfriend and boyfriend because it is convenient to do so.

At a revivalist meeting, Del meets Garnet French and suddenly she becomes someone different when she is with him. He is uneducated and does not admire education. He has been in jail and vows that religion has saved him. Del knows that she and Garnet share a physical attraction that is not intellectual at all. She understands that he reworks her, transforms her into someone she is not, but she also knows that she does the same for him. After Del and Garnet become sexually intimate, Del becomes obsessed with her discoveries about sexuality and intimacy and cannot focus on college plans. Naomi becomes pregnant and marries, but she also warns Del about taking precautions so that she does not get pregnant. Eventually, Garnet begins to speak of marriage and having a baby and he insists the Del must be baptized as a Baptist. It is only after she refuses that Garnet understands that Del is not the person he believed her to be. When Garnet tries to force her into being baptized by him, nearly drowning her in the process, their relationship changes; the violence of her rejection and their fight makes clear to both of them that the relationship is over. Del ends this chapter with the comment that now she can get on with her "real life."

Epilogue: The Photographer

In this final chapter, Del tells of her need to write a novel, since eventually, "all the books in the library in the Town Hall were not enough for me." She decides to base her book on the lives of a Jubilee family, who have suffered several tragic events. Del's imagination creates a tragic heroine and her pursuit of and affair with a strange photographer. The chapter and the book end with Del's impromptu visit with the son of this tragic family. It is then that she realizes that although she might leave Jubilee, she will always be a part of that town. The novel more correctly ends with the previous chapter, and if an epilogue is suppose to take place years later and offer some resolution for the reader, this chapter fails as an epilogue. However, it does succeed as a vehicle for Del to wrap up her ideas about being a writer and about the difference between fiction and reality. Del's attempts to write a novel capture her own attempts to rewrite her own past in the narration that she has told. Reality intrudes and can never be obscured completely.

CHARACTERS

Art Chamberlain

Mr. Chamberlain is the newscaster on Jubilee's radio broadcasts and a World War II veteran. He is also Fern's suitor and a frequent visitor at Del's house. He is aware of Del's growing sexual awareness and curiosity, and after taking several opportunities to feel her breasts and buttocks, he takes her out into the woods and masturbates in front of her. Mr. Chamberlain does not attempt to seduce Del and so he would not see himself as a sexual predator, but she is 14 years old and does not fully appreciate the risk that he poses. Del had earlier fantasized about Mr. Chamberlain, but she lacked the experience necessary to develop her fantasies fully. When Mr. Chamberlain masturbates in front of her, Del understands that he is performing for her and that he was also objectifying her as a sexual object. She never really grasps the danger she is in when she willingly obeys his request to follow him into the woods.

Uncle Craig

Uncle Craig is a life-long bachelor, whose life work is compiling a vastly detailed history of their town and the genealogy of the family. He is the brother of Del's paternal grandfather. Uncle Craig's death and funeral occupies a significant portion of Del's early narration, since grappling with death in any form is a curiosity that must be understood. Del inherits Uncle Craig's thousand page manuscript, and because she does not value that kind of writing, she allows its destruction.

Del

Del is the narrator. At points throughout the narration, she provides the reader with brief information about her age only through references about the grade she is attending in school at that moment. The stories that she tells are largely about her coming of age, as she learns about her mother, friendships, and men through a series of relationships and experiences. Del does not always tell her story in a chronological narration but through brief glimpses of time that shifts back and forth with ease. She is curious and intelligent but also intolerant of her mother's foibles once she becomes old enough to be embarrassed by her mother's actions. Throughout the novel, Del is transformed from a reader of stories to a writer of stories. In fact, she is writing her own story, in which she is a performer. Throughout the narration, Del sees herself as an observer, a performer who acts in her own composition and who is never fully involved as a participant in the story she is writing or in many cases, rewriting. After her sexual relationship with Garnet ends, the fantasies that she had nurtured about boys for so long are finally put to rest, and she plans, then, to get started on her "real life."

Fern Dogherty

Fern is Addie's boarder. She sings in the United Church choir and is also Addie's only friend. Fern works at the post office but at one time seemed to have a promising career future as a singer. She is rumored to have had an illegitimate child that ended her voice training. She is described in Rubenesque terms, more shapely, voluptuous, and more sensual than Del's mother. She has a sexual relationship with Art Chamberlain, and she reports that he had mentioned marriage in letters, but in the end, he leaves Jubilee and soon after, she also leaves town.

Aunt Elspeth

One of Del's aunts, Aunt Elspeth is virtually inseparable from her sister Auntie Grace. The two spinsters tell entertaining stories that are so well known and rehearsed that they can finish one another's sentences. Like her sister, Elspeth does not approve of Del's mother and tries subtly to undermine Addie whenever possible. Although on the surface she appears quite gentle, in reality she is judgmental and sometimes vicious in her pronouncements. She values her brother Craig and all that he does more than she

values herself, and yet her oral histories are far richer in real information than Craig's heavily researched text.

Elinor Farris

See Miss Farris

Miss Farris

Miss Farris is a third year teacher who serves as an example of unrequited love and dreams. Her artificial cheerfulness disguises an empty and unhappy existence. She comes alive during the rehearsals for the yearly operetta, when she is center stage in the planning of the performance. What Miss Farris wants is largely unknown. She dresses younger than her supposed age, which some observers suggest is an attempt to attract a man. Del, though, suggests that whatever it is that Miss Farris wants, "it could hardly even be men." Miss Farris drowns herself in what is generally understood by the townspeople to be a suicide.

Garnet French

Garnet becomes Del's first serious boyfriend and her first sexual experience. There is no intellectual connection, and in fact, they do not meet over words; they rarely speak of anything. Garnet is a physical attraction; he represents the passion that was missing in Del's crush on Frank and her relationship with Jerry. Garnet wants to marry Del and have babies with her, but first she must be baptized and become a Baptist. When she refuses, Garnet holds her head under the water of the Wawanash River, where only a few moments earlier they had been playing. With each of her refusals, Garnet becomes increasing violent in his attempts to force baptism on Del.

Auntie Grace

One of Del's two aunts, she is virtually inseparable from her sister Aunt Elspeth. The two spinsters tell entertaining stories that are so well known and rehearsed that they can finish one another's sentences. Like her sister, Grace does not approve of Del's mother and tries subtly to undermine Addie whenever possible. Although on the surface she appears quite gentle, in reality she is judgmental and sometimes vicious in her pronouncements. She values her brother Craig and all that he does more than herself, and yet her oral histories are far richer in real information than Craig's heavily researched text.

Princess Ida
See Addie Morrison Jordan

Addie Morrison Jordan
Del's mother is also known as Princess Ida, her pen name for the opinion pieces that she writes for the Jubilee newspaper. Addie's story is told in the chapter, "Princess Ida." She grew up very poor with a mother who was a religious zealot and a father and brothers who bonded together, excluding the daughter. Her memories are of a cruel childhood that denied her all that she wanted. Only after she runs away from home is Addie free of her home, although she is never free of the past. Addie yearns for knowledge and she covets respectability. She wants to be part of the Jubilee town scene and not a country wife. Addie is never really satisfied with her life as it exists and part of her personality is the constant striving to be something else and to achieve more.

Della Jordan
See Del

Father Jordan
Del's father, while present in the novel, has neither a name nor a personality. He shows up only occasionally and most often at meals. Because he utters only the occasional sentence, and Del never narrates his story, his role in the novel is minimal. Del's father represents the country life. He continues to live in the country, tending to his fox business, even though his wife and children live in town most of the year

Owen Jordan
Del's younger brother, Owen, plays a very peripheral role in the book. His biggest role is as a sounding board for Del in the chapter, "Age of Faith," in which he asks Del to show him how to pray for his dog, Major. Men's lives are not examined by Del except as they relate to her own growth, and so Owen is given little personality. As a young adult, he becomes like his father and Uncle Benny, just another man living at the house at the end of Flats Road.

Uncle Bill Morrison
Addie's younger brother brings his new wife and comes to Jubilee to visit his sister. He is dying and this visit is a last visit before he dies. His recollections of their childhood differ from Addie's. In his memory, their mother is not a cruel religious fanatic but a gentle loving mother. His role in the novel is really to help Del understand that memories are fluid and that her mother creates her own reality from the memories of her youth. Since Del wants to be a writer, it is important for her to understand that even reality is sometimes tinged with fiction.

Naomi
Naomi is Del's childhood friend and her best friend for many years. As children they share secret and experiences. As they grow older, Naomi is a source of information, much of it incorrect, that her mother supplies about other women and about sexual experience. Naomi changes, though, and emerges as a young woman, more focused on boys and marriage than Del. Naomi's maturation is more rapid than Del's. In addition, Naomi is also more of a young lady than Del, who still cannot keep her hair, clothing, or even perspiration under control. Naomi's change seems in many ways to be a betrayal to Del, who is still mired in adolescence when the change occurs.

Uncle Benny Poole
Benny is not really Del's uncle. He works for her father and he eats with the family. He possesses a subscription to a tabloid newspaper that fascinates Del, and he marries a woman he does not know but whom he met through the want-ads.

Madeleine Poole
Madeleine is the young mail-order bride who is forced by her family to marry Uncle Benny. She has an illegitimate child, and while she is violent and without any social skills, her story is important, since she teaches Del that not all women fit easily into the community definition of wife and mother.

Jerry Storey
Jerry is in large part a boyfriend of convenience. He and Del are linked together by their common intelligence, but Jerry has no tolerance for literature or history, which are passions of Del's existence. Jerry has no understanding of the non-literal world. He deals only in facts and not in figurative ideas. Jerry even tries to understand sexuality in a very literal way and as an experiment to gain knowledge. His request to view Del's body without clothing is not about sexual lust but about wanting to see and thus know about a woman's body. He lacks the passion that Del wants. Jerry is who he appears

TOPICS FOR FURTHER STUDY

- Research rural life in both Ontario, Canada, and the United States during World War II. Focus particularly on how people lived and worked during this period of time. Prepare a poster listing the similarities and the differences that you find.

- Munro uses events and people from her past to create characters and plots in her stories. Choose one of your own memories and use it as the basis for a short story. Like Munro, you should change the factual details to suit your plot and theme. Present your story to the class and note the details you've used that are based in fact.

- Del's mother, Addie, predicts that in the future, women will have more freedoms and choices than during her lifetime. Research women's lives in the 1940s and at the beginning of the twenty-first century. Write an essay in which you evaluate the changes that have occurred in women's lives and what changes you think are yet to come. Consider if these changes have improved women's lives, or if you think these changes have had mixed results.

- Much of Del's life centers around her time at school. Students in Del's high school could choose between studying academic subjects or vocational subjects, depending on whether or not they intended to attend college. Research the differences in elementary and secondary education in the 1940s and at the beginning of the twenty-first century. Prepare a speech in which you explain the different educational systems. Which do you like best and why?

- Del's father raises silver foxes and sells the pelts. In the past, furs were sold by trappers, who hunted and trapped wild animals, then processed the pelts. Although the slaughter of animals to make fur clothing is now controversial, the practice was once widely accepted. Research the history of the fur trade in Canada, including the differences between hunting and raising animals to provide consumers with fur. You might consider aspects of the fur trade such as the ethical treatment of animals, or the economics of raising animals versus trapping wild animals for their fur. Prepare an essay that discusses your findings.

---

to be, but Del wants him to be more of a mystery to be probed.

Frank Wales

Frank is Del's first childhood crush. Del's crush is a product of the operetta in which both have parts. Except that he is a terrible speller, she has no connection to him as a fellow student, but once they begin rehearsing for the performance Del begins to see Frank in a different way. Her love for him is because her imagination and the operetta are able to transform him into a different persona. Del's crush on Frank is in many ways a performance, a rehearsal for more complex fantasies about men.

THEMES

Fantasy

Del uses fantasy as a way to understand the relationship between girls and boys and later, men and women. In her first crush on a boy from her eighth-grade class, Del daydreams about Frank Wales and imagines him walking her home. In these daydreams, Frank wears his costume from the operetta and sings to Del. Later, when Del is a freshman in high school, she begins fantasizing about Art Chamberlain, trying to fill in the gaps of her knowledge about sexual experience between what she has read in books about the relationship between men and women and what she has experienced. Del imagines that Mr. Chamberlain sees her without her clothes, but her imagination can go no further because she has no experience or explicit knowledge about what comes next. Her dreams of seduction are halted because of her inexperience, but their purpose is to help her make that transition from innocence to experience. After Mr. Chamberlain masturbates in front of her, Del no longer needs fantasy to fill in the missing pieces of her sexual education.

Memory

Del understands early in life that memories are fluid entities. In the chapter "Princess Ida," Del tells the story of her mother's childhood, as her mother has told it to her. Addie's childhood is one of privation and isolation. Addie's mother is described as a religious zealot, so focused on her beliefs that her daughter lacks the basic necessities of food and love. But then Addie's brother, Bill, visits, and Del hears an entirely different story of parental love, gentleness and nurturing. Bill's memories of childhood offer an important lesson to Del, who understands that Bill's warm memories of home are of the same farm house that Addie wanted to escape, even if it meant suicide. Memory is an act of choosing what is to be remembered, and the choices reflect upon the individual. Uncle Bill chooses to remember a happy nurturing time when he felt safe because he is soon going to die from cancer. Addie's memories of deprivation serve as a way to motivate her to escape her childhood. Together, Bill's and Addie's memories suggest that memories of the past serve a purpose in protecting an individual in the future.

Religion

In the chapter, "Age of Faith," Del searches for answers about whether God is real. She describes each of the four town churches and then visits the Anglican Church, although it is not her family's church. Del is drawn to the theatricality of the Anglican service, which she attends at first without her mother's knowledge and later, with her mother's disapproval. Del's desire to discover God is linked to her experiences with death. In a previous chapter, she has described the death of Uncle Craig and her desire to touch a dead cow she had discovered. She is also aware of the pending death of her Uncle Bill. Del's test of God's existence is simple—can He save her from having to thread a needle in her Household Science class?

When her prayers seem to have been answered, Del begins to worry that she was saved through coincidence rather than divine intervention. Eventually, Del recognizes that God does not always respond to prayers, since the interests of men are not the interests of God.

Religion is also important in Del's relationship with Garnet. He has been saved from a life of crime by the intervention of a Baptist minister, who then baptizes Garnet. Religion is again the focus when Del and Garnet meet, since they meet at a revival meeting. Garnet wants to marry Del and have children, but he insists that she must be baptized first. When she refuses, he tries to forcibly baptize her, nearly drowning her in the process. For Del, Garnet's religious fervor illustrates what she has known all along—that she and Garnet have no intellectual connection. Their relationship is based solely on physical attraction.

Sex and Sexuality

In general, men are not well defined in *Lives of Girls and Women*. But as sexual beings, boys and men have a larger role in the novel. Del is very interested in the sexual connection between men and women. As adolescents, Naomi's mother provides clinical information about sexuality through books and prurient gossip about sexual behavior. But Naomi's mother cannot provide the kind of detail that most interests the two girls. Because they lack experience, their knowledge is limited. Consequently, both girls spend a great deal of time fantasizing about boys and imagining sexual experience. Del's relationship with boys undergoes a natural progression from the childhood crush over Frank Wales, to the experimental and largely clinical relationship with Jerry Story, to an intimate sexual relationship with Garnet French. There is also a voyeuristic relationship with Art Chamberlain. In each case, Del learned something more about how men and women relate sexually to one another. Sexuality and sexual experience provide a pattern of knowledge that helps to define Del's growth from adolescent to adult.

STYLE

Depth of Characterization

Characterization is the process by which the author creates a life-like person from his or her imagination. To accomplish this, the author provides the character with personality traits that help define who she will be and how she will behave in a given situation. Madeleine Poole is a complex character, whose role in the novel takes only a few paragraphs, but her influence is important in how Del sees the relationship between men and women. Characters can range from simple stereotypical figures to more complex multifaceted ones and they may also be defined by personality traits, such as the rogue or the damsel in distress. Munro portrays her characters with a great deal of depth, and this may be because they are loosely based on people that she has known in the past, as has been suggested about many of her stories. Munro writes about an area and types of people with whom she is most familiar, although her characters are based more on composites (combinations) of different people than on specific people whom she has met. By doing this, she makes her characters more interesting and complex.

Autobiographical Fiction

Fiction refers to any story that is created out of the author's imagination, rather than factual events. Sometimes the characters in a fictional piece are based on real people, but their ultimate form and the way they respond to events is solely the creation of the author. In *Lives of Girls and Women* the characters are fictional, but they are based on people or character types from Munro's life. Because Munro initially titled the novel "Real Lives," there has been speculation that her book is more autobiographical than fictional. In addition, since many of the details and locations in *Lives of Girls and Women* mirror Munro's own life, many critics analyze her novel by looking for autobiographical elements. However, Munro has stated in many interviews that *Lives of Girls and Women* is a fictional work, and for all intents and purposes, she is correct. The book is indeed a work of autobiographical fiction because it is a fictional story that contains elements of autobiographical fact.

Künstlerroman Novel

A Künstlerroman novel relates the story of a protagonist who labors from childhood to maturity in an effort to come to terms with his or her artistic talent. In Munro's novel, Del tries to understand and express her talent as a writer. This term is also used to refer to James Joyce's *A Portrait of the Artist as a Young Man*. This kind of novel is also sometimes called an "Apprenticeship Novel," which relates the story of a young person who is trying to find his or her place in the world. Furthermore, the apprenticeship novel is sometimes also called a coming-of-age novel or Bildungsroman. In this kind of novel, a young person, often an adolescent, matures into an adult. Indeed, Del matures from a child to an adult in *Lives of Girls and Women* as she undergoes a series of adventures and conflicts that ultimately help her grow into a mature adult.

Interlinked Stories

In this novel, there is no clearly defined beginning, middle, and end; this is why some critics refer to the book as a series of short stories, rather than a novel. A novel is an extended fictional narrative. The length allows for more complex character development than would be found in a short story and a more substantially developed plot, with a clear movement from beginning to end. In a conventional novel, each chapter is linked to the preceding chapter by the movement of the plot. In *Lives of Girls and Women* the plot consists of several loosely linked episodes (vignettes) in the protagonist's life. These vignettes are episodic and self-contained rather than continuing an overarching plot. Indeed, each chapter in Munro's book could stand alone as a short story, since it is not dependant on information that is contained elsewhere in the book. Yet, other elements aside from the plot hold these stories together, such as their overarching theme and the recurring characters. Books with these characteristics, like *Lives of Girls and Women*, are often referred to as interlinked stories. A well-known example is *Winesburg, Ohio* by Sherwood Anderson.

HISTORICAL CONTEXT

1940s Village Schools

In *Lives of Girls and Women*, many of the events that Del describes are part of her experience in school. School life in rural Ontario in the 1940s was very different than it is for students attending school in the twenty-first century. The latter part of the 1930s had been a time of school reform in Ontario, and Del would have experienced the new trend of progressivism in her elementary and secondary classes. Rather than prepare students for an academic education,

COMPARE
&
CONTRAST

- **1940s:** The Ontario Teachers' Federation approves the principle of equal pay for male and female teachers.

  1970s: In Canada, female university graduates earn 4,000 to 7,000 dollars less than men with equivalent jobs and skills.

  Today: In Canada, 74 percent of female university graduates are employed, while only 69 percent of male university graduates have jobs.

- **1940s:** Dating for high-school age boys and girls involves strict curfews that are designed to help protect young women from pregnancy. The rate of unmarried pregnancies is very low, less than 1 percent, but that is primarily because most couples get married as soon as a pregnancy occurs.

  1970s: The ready availability of the birth control pill does not decrease pregnancy rates among teenagers, as had been hoped. About 10 percent of all births in Canada are to unwed mothers.

  Today: The stigma that had been attached to unwed pregnancy has almost completely disappeared, and over one third of all births in Canada are to unwed mothers.

- **1940s:** The parents of the baby boomers get married for the first time at the average age of 28.5 (for men) and 25.9 (for women).

  1970s: The baby boomers marry at slightly younger ages than their parents. The age at first marriage drops to 25.2 years for men and 22.8 for women.

  Today: The age at first marriage has risen above that reported in the late 1940s. For men, the average age at marriage is 29.5 years and for women it is 27.4 years.

---

the emphasis in schools focused on preparing students for working. Many students did not continue on to secondary schools after completing their elementary education and even fewer attended university, and thus, the change in education was to provide practical knowledge, rather than academic knowledge. In *Lives of Girls and Women*, Del's friends Frank and Naomi drop out of school and find jobs. This was actually the more common scenario in rural villages, where in most cases children had only limited access to secondary schools. Del's village of Jubilee actually did have a secondary school, which Naomi attended for most of three years, but Frank dropped out before high school in order to work at the Jubilee Dry Cleaners. Because Jubilee has a secondary school, Del explains that almost everyone in her elementary class continued on to high school, although not all stayed long enough to graduate. In addition to providing the kind of vocational training that Naomi chose, which was typing and other secretarial skills, there was an increased emphasis on socialization skills, learning about good hygiene, and teaching self-confidence. In 1948, the year that Del became a senior in high school, 71 percent of all of Ontario's schools were still one room schools with only a single teacher. Nearly a third of all high schools only had five rooms and one teacher per room. By 1950, it was estimated that 54 percent of all students had dropped out of school by age sixteen. During Del's years in school, education was still very limited in rural areas, and thus her experience in completing high school was still unusual.

Women's Lives in the 1940s

Del's mother, Addie, often tells her daughter that women lives are changing and that in the future women will have more choices and greater freedoms. During World War II, Del was still just an adolescent, but her mother already knew that Canadian women were doing the work of men to help with the war effort. About 600,000 women held full-time jobs in 1939, the year that the war began. During the war years, though, that number doubled to 1.2 million women working, many of them doing men's jobs. Women worked in the aircraft industry making planes for the war, and many other women worked in drafting, electronics, and welding, traditionally men's work. Women also ran farms and helped to keep the economy flowing while men were in Europe fighting the war. However, in spite of their hard work, women were generally paid less than 60 percent of men's wages for the same jobs, and after the war ended, women were expected to quit their jobs, so that there would be sufficient employment for returning soldiers. When the men returned from the war, many women returned to their homes and their soldier husbands and became housewives once again. These women were not alone. When the war ended, there was an influx of war brides immigrating to Canada. At that time, Canada was still largely rural. Two-thirds of Canada's economy was farm based; 80 percent of farms still did not have electricity in 1945 and only 8 percent had indoor plumbing. Although Addie was optimistic that women's lives would be better in the future, life in rural Canada was still very difficult in 1945 for women. It was even more difficult for the estimated 48,000 war brides who left family and homes in Europe to follow their husbands to rural Canada.

CRITICAL OVERVIEW

Canadian women writers were still relatively rare when Munro began writing, and as Christopher Wordsworth observes in his *Guardian Weekly* review of *Lives of Girls and Women*, Canada is "not a great seed-bed of the arts," which makes Munro's achievement all the more notable. Wordsworth describes Munro's work as having "the core and growth of a good novel," and he acknowledges the influence of the short story genre on Munro's novel, which is "episodic in a way that shows its author's apprenticeship to the short story form." The book's protagonist, Del, is the "clever and receptive" connection that holds these series of stories together, but it is Munro's "sensitive and tensile writing [that] lends strength as well as charm" to the novel.

Indeed, reviews of *Lives of Girls and Women* echo one another in their appreciation of the writer's ability to take ordinary people and events and make them memorable. Because many writers use the ordinariness of small-town life as a subject in their novels, *Time* magazine critic Geoffrey Wolff writes that while "the threads of this yarn are common enough stuff," it is what "Alice Munro makes of it that is rare." She can take small-town life and everyday events and turn them into a "snapshot album of imperfect strangers" who readers want to know. According to Wolff, Munro's "achievement is small, but fine." She carefully chooses past events for her subject matter, and she brings the town to life with her words. "Call it fiction: praise it."

Similar admiration is also noted in Jane Rule's review in *Books in Canada*. Rule labels Munro "a writer of rare and clear gifts, who requires as much of herself as she does of her readers." After asserting that the publication of *Lives of Girls and Women* "should be announced on the front page of every paper in Canada," Rule suggests that this " is a book that will find its way into the libraries of everyone who cares about craft in writing and good reading." In her review of Munro's novel for the *Journal of Canadian Fiction*, Clara Thomas says of Munro that her "talent is both large and delicate." This is a writer, according to Thomas, who "succeeds in handling a vast number of details of places and persons and in weaving them into a strong and seamless fabric." For Thomas, Munro's characters "remain hauntingly real after the book is finished." Certainly, this accounts for the book's continued popularity.

CRITICISM

Sheri Metzger Karmiol
Karmiol has a doctorate in English Renaissance literature. She teaches literature and drama at the University of New Mexico, where she is a lecturer in the University Honors Program. She is also a professional writer and the author of several reference texts on poetry and drama. In the following essay, Karmiol discusses how Del is transformed by her interactions with other women, who provide her with different role models.

The female characters in *Lives of Girls and Women* are women in transition, women on the

WHAT DO I READ NEXT?

- *Dance of the Happy Shades*, published in 1968, is Munro's first collection of short stories. This award-winning collection explores life in western Ontario with the same attention to detail that makes her work so captivating to readers.

- Margaret Atwood's *Moral Disorder: and Other Stories*, published in 2006, is a collection of linked stories that explores 60 years of a Canadian family's history.

- *Women and Fiction: Stories By and About Women*, published in 2002 and edited by Susan Cahill, is a collection of short stories exploring women's lives. The stories cover a vast period of time and locations, and include works by some of the best short-story writers of the twentieth century.

- *Gender Conflicts: New Essays in Women's History*, published in 1992 and edited by Franca Lacovetta and Mariana Valverde, provides a close look at women's lives in Canada. Like Munro's novel, this nonfiction work explores such topics as marriage, sexuality, family, and religion.

- James Joyce's *A Portrait of the Artist as a Young Man* was first published in 1916. Del's journey in Munro's novel is often compared to the journey taken by Joyce's semi-autobiographical protagonist.

cusp of change, although it will be 30 plus years before real change happens. In 1940s rural Ontario, Canada, women are defined by their connections to men. They are sisters, wives, mothers, and daughters but not women in control of their own world. Del's aunts represent one end of the continuum, lives living in the past and with no possibility of change. They exist to give meaning to their brother's work and not to create meaning in their own lives. Addie Jordan and Madeleine Poole represent the other end of the continuum. They are

women who will forge their own way—one through intellectual pursuits and the other through violence. While many of the women in Munro's novel begin their adult lives defined by their connections to the men around them, several have begun to think that there are other ways to exist in a male dominated world.

One of the strongest women in *Lives of Girls and Women* is the child-bride of Uncle Benny. Madeleine is violent and hard, completely unwilling to play the role of dutiful wife. She throws tantrums, yells, and beats her child. While beating her child is not behavior to be emulated, as a model for strong feminine behavior, she teaches Del that women do not have to be docile and willing accomplices in their own subordination. In her book, *Dance of the Sexes: Art and Gender in the Fiction of Alice Munro*, Beverly J. Rasporich points to Madeleine as "a fascinating character of uncontrollable fury who, raging against her unchosen status of wife of Uncle Benny and mother of the illegitimate child Diane, refuses to conform to even the minimal social expectations of the Flats Road." As a mail-order bride, who has been forced into a shotgun wedding, Madeleine is brought back to live with Uncle Benny in a house filled with a "dark, rotting mess of carpets, linoleum, parts of furniture, insides of machinery, nails, wire, tools, utensils." This is a house crammed with what Benny could scavenge from the dump and his neighbor's discards. There is no reason to suppose that any woman would find living in Benny's house enjoyable, but Madeleine's options are limited. Her illegitimate child makes her family eager to marry her off to the first likely prospect to appear. When Benny arrives to meet Madeleine, he finds her family has a preacher waiting, a ring in hand, and a wedding celebration planned. Madeleine will not succumb to domestic life and within months, she has fled Flats Road and Benny's life forever.

Not all of the women in *Lives of Girls and Women* commit such radical acts to assert their strength. Aunt Elspeth and Auntie Grace live their lives in the shadow of their brother. They never marry and instead devote themselves to keeping their brother comfortable. Their meals and activities center around Craig's needs, and they govern their own lives to keep from disturbing his work. The aunts demonstrate that there is safety and comfort in daily routine. They embody a long family tradition in Del's father's family. Promotions are not sought, scholarships are declined, and spinsterhood is chosen because there is a perceived safety in not taking chances. For the aunts, "choosing not to do things showed, in the end, more wisdom and self-respect than choosing to do them." They teach Del an important lesson about taking chances. Being safe and not courting change, never allowing themselves the opportunity to either succeed or grow, is easier than the alternative (although not necessarily more rewarding). Del tells readers that her aunts "respected men's work beyond anything." The aunts "would never, never meddle with it; between men's work and women's work was the clearest line drawn." Although they may have respect for men's work, "they also laughed at it." The aunts' rebellion is slight and limited to laughter, but it is there nonetheless.

Sadly, Aunt Elspeth and Auntie Grace's limited lives become even more reduced after their brother's death. The two aunts seem less real, more artificial, their very lives "like something learned long ago, perfectly remembered." The aunts had no real life of their own while their brother was alive, and once he is dead, they even lack the ability to transform themselves as women who exist for more than their connection to a man. Del points out that the aunts have been so mired in their brother's life that they never had a real life of their own. The stories that they tell are rich in detail and history. Their oral history is as valuable and more interesting to Del than Uncle Craig's ponderously detailed and very dry history, but the aunts have denied the value of their own lives for so long that they can no longer see their own value as independent beings.

Where Aunt Elspeth and Auntie Grace cannot imagine change and Madeleine is only too eager for transformation, Del Jordan's character

falls somewhere between these two extremes. Life is not as clear for Del as it is for her role models. She wants knowledge and sees herself not as a wife but as a writer. She reads everything she can find and imagines what she cannot know. Yet Del has also been brought up to put men first, as her relationship with Jerry Story suggests. Although Del says that he is honest with her, she is not as honest. Del is willing to protect Jerry's feelings, but she is not willing to sublimate herself, as her relationship with Garnet French later proves. Rasporich argues that a very young Del is influenced not by her aunts' endless sacrifices for Uncle Craig but by the rarely seen and yet very visible Madeleine, whose exploits become mythic on Flats Road. Rasporich claims that Del's "concept of womanhood is influenced by one of Munro's most striking models of female savagery, Madeleine." Rather than provide a model of traditional subordinate womanhood, such as that presented by her aunts, Madeleine is, according to Rasporich, "victorious for Del Jordan, at least in comparison to the Calvinist women, her aunts, who practice proper domestic rituals, accept the division between women's work and important male enterprise, who center their lives about a man and deny the jurisdiction of the flesh." Madeleine's example suggests that women can have power over men. Indeed, Madeleine's power is more than the violence of her physical attacks, whether throwing a box of Kotex (a feminine hygiene product) at Charlie Buckle in the town grocery or throwing a kettle through a window or cutting up Benny's wedding suit. Her rebellion teaches Del that women can leave men, which Del does when she denies Garnet ownership over her body. Madeleine's lesson is that women can only be mastered when they agree to be mastered, regardless of social conventions that dictate otherwise.

The lives of most of the other women who inhabit Munro's novel reside in more conventionally defined roles, although not all of these women are happy. Del's friend, Naomi, is more conventional in her approach to life. She quits school for a clerical job at the creamery, a choice that other young women in Jubilee have also made. She conforms to the expectations of her cohorts, filling her hope chest on the layaway plan, focusing on her clothing and hair, and planning her life around meeting a prospective husband. She is betrayed by her own body when she becomes pregnant. Her mother, who for years has claimed knowledge about sexuality and women's bodies, cannot help her in any way except to push her towards marriage. Indeed, Naomi settles for marriage, home, and family in a way that Del could not. Years earlier she had told Del that girls are responsible if boys take advantage of them. Naomi was sure that "It's the girl who is responsible because our sex organs are on the inside and theirs are on the outside and we can control our urges better than they can." Naomi buys into the stereotypes that keep women in their place, but when she is pregnant and forced to wed, she warns Del to be careful and use protection, since "nothing works" to end the pregnancy. While she cannot, herself, rebel, Naomi can still urge Del not to be caught in the trap that binds other women.

Miss Farris, the tragic teacher, is also a conventional figure. In an examination of the lives of unmarried female teachers during the 1940s and 1950s, Sheila L. Cavanagh concludes in the History of Education Quarterly that female teachers were forced to meet a restrictive lifestyle that celebrated an "overriding commitment to education." Teachers were regulated by codes that governed their clothing, social interactions, friendships, and even where they lived. Teaching administrations during this time required that female teachers "adhere to social and professional directives to remain unmarried." Teachers in Ontario were obligated to be single, since a married teacher "was thought to be an occupational transient, underqualified, uninterested in professional development, and torn between divided loyalties to her family and the school." Women could not be both wife and teacher. Thus, Miss Farris is part of a profession that requires that she remain single if she wants to continue teaching, and yet her single status invites gossip and seemingly endless speculation. She dresses as if she is younger than her supposed age, which some observers suggest is an attempt to attract a man. Del, though, suggests that whatever it is that Miss Farris wants, "it could hardly even be men." Instead of a lover, all of Miss Farris's passion is directed toward staging the yearly school production of an operetta.

Miss Farris was born in Jubilee, educated there, and continued as an adult to live there. She is relegated to a traditional role not only through her sex but through her profession. If other women have the meager opportunity to change, Miss Farris's opportunity is even slimmer. She

can only permanently transform her world by committing suicide. Del suggests that Miss Farris exists in the past, "away back in time," and when she commits suicide, Del remembers Miss Farris as "imprisoned in that time," and Del is "amazed that she had broken out to commit this act." Miss Farris lacked the courage to recreate herself. Her choice as a single school teacher was spinsterhood, and a life that she ultimately found was not worth living.

Some of the girls and women in Jubilee are trapped in lives filled with dissatisfaction, lost dreams, and unrequited loves. The change that Addie predicts will not happen quickly enough to save them. But these are the women whose lives make Lives of Girls and Women so memorable. In Thomas E. Tausky's article, "Alice Munro: Biocritical Essay," the critic argues that Del is an exceptional female character, who acts "firmly, confidently, and constructively in order to shape her own future." Tausky suggests that "male figures are given roles of some prominence, but only as supporting actors in the drama of Del's life." The characters who linger in the memory as powerfully imagined creations are all women; Del herself, her mother, her mother's boarder Fern, her aunts." Throughout the novel, Del is on the cusp of change, and by the time she must choose to either break free of Garnet or be consumed by him, she is no longer as tender about men's feelings as she was when she dated Jerry. She has transformed herself. Addie warns her daughter that "all women have had up till now has been their connection with men." But by the end of the book, Del understands the possibilities of a real life, one that is removed from her many fantasies about men, and she is ready to get started with the next chapter in her life.

Source: Sheri Metzger Karmiol, Critical Essay on Lives of Girls and Women, in Novels for Students, Gale, Cengage Learning, 2008.

Rowena Fowler

In the following excerpt, Fowler explores the conflict between stories and reality in Alice Munro's Lives of Girls and Women. The stories told by men and women are different, but according to Fowler, as the novel progresses, Del learns that women's stories do not have to conform to romantic feminism or to the pragmatic realism of men's stories.

> DEL'S PERPLEXITY IN THE FACE OF SUCH
> NARRATIVE CHALLENGES UNDERLINES MUNRO'S OWN
> ACHIEVEMENT: HER ABILITY TO ACCOMMODATE BOTH
> THE ORDINARY AND THE BIZARRE IN HER FICTION, TO
> ENHANCE OBSERVATION AND EXPERIENCE WITHOUT
> WRENCHING THEM OUT OF TRUE."

As Del Jordan sets off from Jubilee, Ontario, in search of her "real life," she abandons the "black fable" she has concocted out of her small-town childhood and takes with her only the intuition of "Epilogue: The Photographer" that familiar things are both more ordinary and more amazing than she has given them credit for. They stubbornly resist being turned into fiction: "It is a shock, when you have dealt so cunningly, powerfully, with reality, to come back and find it still there." Like Catherine Morland in *Northanger Abbey*, Del sees the world in terms of her favorite novels, is disabused of her fanciful notions, and finally, we realize, undergoes experiences as exciting or disturbing in their way as anything she might read about.

What is false in her "black fable" is not plot but style. Extraordinary things do happen in Jubilee, but Del has distorted them, trapping people and events in topiary gardens, Regency romance poses, and mannered prose: the "bittersweet flesh" of her fictional heroine, Caroline, overlays her Jubilee prototype, "pudgy Marion, the tennis player." Del's stylized figures are set in a physical and psychological landscape that is recognizably Southern Gothic; given Alice Munro's acknowledged debt to Eudora Welty and Flannery O'Connor, it seems that she has her own "black fables" to exorcise: "Their speech was subtle and evasive and bizarrely stupid; their platitudes crackled with madness. The season was always the height of summer—white, brutal heat, dogs lying as if dead on the sidewalks, waves of air shuddering, jellylike, over the empty highway."

Del keeps her fragmentary novel folded inside a copy of *Wuthering Heights* and escapes from Jubilee into *The Life of Charlotte Brontë*: "The only world I was in touch with was the one I had made, with the aid of some books, to be peculiar and nourishing to myself." Emerging from the public library into the Ontario winter after reading [Sigrid] Undset's *Kristin Lavransdatter*, she sees a farmer on his sleigh as "a helmeted Norseman." From time to time, however, practical details, "niggling considerations of fact," impinge on her made-up world: if "Caroline" is to drown herself at the height of summer, how will there be enough water in the river?

Del's perplexity in the face of such narrative challenges underlines Munro's own achievement: her ability to accommodate both the ordinary and the bizarre in her fiction, to enhance observation and experience without wrenching them out of true. As a child, Del lurches from the world she reads about to the one she lives in and finds that one tends to obliterate the other. The stories in Uncle Benny's tabloid newspaper seem irresistible:

> I was bloated and giddy with revelations of evil, of its versatility and grand invention and horrific playfulness. But the nearer I got to our house the more this vision faded. Why was it that the plain back wall of home, the pale chipped brick, the cement platform outside the kitchen door, washtubs hanging on nails, the pump, the lilac bush with brown-spotted leaves, should make it seem doubtful that a woman would really send her husband's torso, wrapped in Christmas paper, by mail to his girl friend in South Carolina?

In the same way, Uncle Bill, when he turns up in the flesh, obliterates the monster of Del's mother's stories: "This was the thing, the indigestible fact. This Uncle Bill was my mother's brother, the terrible fat boy, so gifted in cruelty, so cunning, quick, fiendish, so much to be feared. I kept looking at him, trying to pull that boy out of the yellowish man. But I could not find him there. He was gone, smothered." Which is true?—her mother's picture of their childhood (miserable, narrow, blighted by religious fanaticism), or Uncle Bill's reminiscences of the simple country life and its "good spiritual example"? Not yet able to appreciate the different ways in which people recount their lives and shape the past to make sense of the present, Del is suddenly sarcastic about one of her mother's favorite stories. For a moment, in challenging her mother's version of the past she has cast doubt on everything she lives by: "there was something in the room like the downflash of a wing or knife, a sense of hurt so strong, but quick and isolated, vanishing."

The handing down of stories from mother to daughter, the re-interpretation of, even resistance to, these stories, the testing of them against experience, is an important structural principle of *Lives of Girls and Women*. Implicit in the narrative is the irony that Del, an aspiring writer, never realizes that the stories she is so used to hearing could provide the starting point of a book; she notices only the discontinuities and contradictions between what goes on around her and what she finds written down. Her attitude is natural in Jubilee, where "reading books was something like chewing gum, a habit to be abandoned when the seriousness and satisfactions of adult life took over." At school, "art" is the seductive artifice of the annual operetta, with its cardboard villages and peasant dances. At home, Del's father reads the same three books "over and over again, putting himself to sleep. He never talked about what he read." Her mother, the "Princess Ida" of a city newspaper column for "lady correspondents," coats in sentimental cliché the very countryside she has done her best to escape from: "This morning a marvelous silver frost enraptures the eye on every twig and telephone wire and makes the world a veritable fairyland." Writing under her own name to the Jubilee *Herald-Advance*, she expresses dispassionate reformist opinions that are at odds with Del's sense of glory and danger in the lives of girls and women.

As well as these unhelpful models, Del has two special handicaps to contend with in understanding the relationship between literature and life: being Canadian and being a woman. "Reality" is a special problem for a writer in rural Ontario, who cannot mention the nearest city without having to explain that her London is not the "real" London. It is also a problem for a girl who reads in a woman's magazine the opinion of "a famous New York psychiatrist, a disciple of Freud" that if a boy and a girl look at a full moon: "The boy thinks of the universe, its immensity and mystery; the girl thinks 'I must wash my hair.'" Del knows that that is not how she thinks, but instead of doubting the article she doubts herself—"surely a New York psychiatrist must *know*"—and feels trapped in a dilemma: "I wanted men to love me, *and* I wanted to think of the universe when I looked at the moon." It is left to Munro, at the end of the story, to redress the

balance by showing what men think about at important moments: "Sometimes when he had barely got his breath back [after love-making] I would ask him what he was thinking and he would say, 'I was just figuring out how I could fix that muffler—.'"

Del is surrounded by chroniclers and storytellers, by myths and memories and the "baroque concoctions of rumor." Dr. Comber's stories are paranoid, Uncle Benny's unlikely, Uncle Bill's formless and sentimental, but none of them seems as far from her conception of Jubilee as Uncle Craig's "public" version of events: a painstaking documentation of local history, "a great accumulation of the most ordinary facts which it was his business to get in order." Listening to the men of Jubilee talking about the war, Del notices a crucial difference of perspective and tone: it is only those not involved in the fighting who can see a pattern or wider significance in it. For Uncle Craig the war is "a huge eruption in ordinary political life"; he is "more interested in how it affected elections, in what the conscription issue would do to the Liberal Party, than in how it progressed by itself." Del's father, also a noncombatant, "saw it as an overall design, marked off in campaigns, which had a purpose, which failed or succeeded" whereas Mr. Chamberlain, who had fought in Italy, "saw it as a conglomeration of stories, leading nowhere in particular. He made his stories to be laughed at."

The art of Munro's fiction is to discover an "overall design" for a "conglomeration of stories." The resulting form is flexible without being artless. It is not a *Bildungsroman*, for women's lives are not comfortably accommodated in a genre which presupposes that characters are free to act, develop and make choices, to learn from, not succumb to, experience. Women's stories have their own tenor and direction. Del's aunts, Elspeth and Grace, keep up an endless, sharp dialogue of story-telling which runs along with the pace and mood of their work; stoning cherries, shelling peas, coring apples, "Their hands, their old, dark, wooden-handled paring knives, moved with marvelous, almost vindictive speed." These aunts are spinsters and their stories feel to Del "dried out, brittle." Aunt Moira, on the other hand, who is married, seems "one of those heavy, cautiously moving, wrecked survivors of the female life, with stories to tell."

The female version of the novel of education is about the conflicting claims of individual freedom and biological destiny; imagery of water, as women novelists know so well, is its natural expression. Will the heroine be swept away and drowned or left high and dry? Must her energies be damned up or diverted into narrow channels? Del Jordan's story begins on a river bank: "We spent days along the Wawanash River helping Uncle Benny fish." She hears from her mother and from their lodger, Fern, "stories about people in the town, about themselves; their talk was a river that never dried up. It was the drama, the ferment of life just beyond my reach." The movement of their narrative often takes the form of eddies and whirlpools: "Stories of the past could go like this, round and round and down to death; I expected it." As she grows up, Del protests against this inevitability—"Had all her stories, after all, to end up with just her, the way she was now, just my mother in Jubilee?"—just as she resists her first lover's attempt to "baptize" her, holding her against her will under the water. In the end it is the river itself, gathering force, flooding, receding within each story, which gives the novel its shape and form. In the end Del learns to keep her head above water; it is not she who is destroyed in the spring flood but her unwanted inheritance, Uncle Craig's dry archive of local history and genealogy...

Once the spell of her Gothic extravaganza is broken, Del is not tempted to opt instead for the utilitarian realism of documentary or journalistic reporting; even before she has finished her revelatory conversation with Bobby Sherriff, she sees the editor of the local newspaper "come out the back door of the Herald-Advance building, empty a wastebasket into an incinerator, and plod back in." "Voracious and misguided" as Uncle Craig writing his local history, she will begin her attempt to recapture Jubilee by compiling lists: "A list of all the stores and businesses going up and down the main street and who owned them, a list of family names, names on the tombstones in the cemetery and any inscriptions underneath." (The stratagem is reminiscent of much nineteenth-century American writing, where nothing can be taken for granted and everything must be painstakingly enumerated before it can be made over into art.) No list, though, can ever be accurate enough or exhaustive enough to contain the details of just one life, and only a story, not a list, can connect and make sense of the details so that they are "held together" as well as "held still": "no list could hold what I wanted, for what I

wanted was every last thing, every layer of speech and thought, stroke of light on bark or walls, every smell, pothole, pain, crack, delusion, held still and held together—radiant, everlasting." The paradoxical lesson of Lives of Girls and Women is that fiction can only transcend locality when it is firmly grounded in it...

Source: Rowena Fowler, "The Art of Alice Munro: The Beggar Maid and Lives of Girls and Women," in Critique, Vol. 25, No. 4, Summer 1984, pp. 189–98.

W. R. Martin

In the following excerpt, Martin suggests that Munro uses literary oppositions to create unfamiliar meanings from ordinary events.

Alice Munro has such a penetrating and sympathetic intelligence and is such an accomplished writer that there are more ways of seeing the paradoxes and ironies in the substance and style of her work than will occur to any one reader. The doubleness, or reciprocation, that I'd like to draw attention to in this essay might be expressed in this way: with vivid images and dramatic scenes that, as Sidney puts it in his Apologie, "strike, pierce, [and] possesses the sight of the soule," she presents, and makes real and convincing, concepts that we usually think of in cloudy, abstract terms and—Sidney again—"woordish description." Contrarily, she charges common and familiar incidents with surprising meanings and insights. In other words, like Coleridge, she makes the strange familiar, and, like Wordsworth, she makes the familiar wonderful; thus she illuminates and enriches both the strange and the familiar. Adapting the terms she herself used in the Weekend Magazine of 11 May 1974, one might say that Alice Munro makes the Mysterious Touchable, and the Touchable Mysterious...

A bold and conceptually brilliant exhibition ... on a grand scale, is presented in "The Flats Road," which opens *Lives of Girls and Women.* Uncle Benny occupies the stage at the very beginning of the first chapter, and this is an indication of his importance in the novel, which is about Del, and especially about the growth of her mind and imagination up to the point when she begins to practise as a conscious literary artist; so we must understand his significance for Del. He thinks and talks as if "the river and the bush and the whole of Grenoch Swamp more or less belonged to him, because he knew them, better than anyone else did. He claimed he was the only person who had been right through the swamp, not just made little trips in around the edges." Though the swamp belongs to him and he to the swamp, he nevertheless "ate at our table every day at noon, except Sunday"; "So lying alongside our world was Uncle Benny's world like a troubling distorted reflection." Others may merely accept him as an oddity, but for Del he is a knotty phenomenon that she must make sense of and place in some kind of relation to herself. Thus when she writes out his address for him—he can't write but seems to be able to read a little—she does it in full, thus: "*Mr. Benjamin Poole, The Flats Road, Jubilee, Wawanash County, Ontario, Canada, North America, The Western Hemisphere, The World, The Solar System, The Universe.*" She is trying to place him in a perspective in which she too appears, in order to make the strange familiar.

One can feel in the intentness with which Del observes him just how fascinating she finds Uncle Benny: "He stuck his gum on the end of his fork [as Henry Bailey does in '*Boys and Girls*' (Dance, p. 127)], and at the end of the meal took it off and showed us the pattern, so nicely engraved on the pewter-coloured gum it was a pity to chew it. He poured tea into his saucer and blew on it. With a piece of bread speared on a fork he wiped his plate as clean as a cat's. He brought into the kitchen a smell, which I did not dislike, of fish, furred animals, swamp." When we put all this together with the fact that he cultivates no crops or vegetables—in fact one of the reasons why he wants a wife is perhaps so that he can make the transition to agriculture: in the letter he dictates to his prospective wife he holds out the hope that she "could have a good vegetable garden if you could keep off the rabbits"—it is not I think too fanciful to suppose that to Del he represents something like the hunting or neolithic stage of man's development. There

is in him a hint of an even earlier phase of pre-history, and perhaps even of evolution itself—of the emergence of life from the swamps. His milieu is the swamp, and his surname is Poole!

It is a matter not only of Uncle Benny's habits but also of the quality of his mind and the patterns of his thoughts. He is naïve, believing in a literal "Heaven", he tells stories that in their simplicity and extravagant melodrama have the quality of myth, legend and folk-tale, stories "that my mother would insist could not have happened, as in the story of Sandy Stevenson's marriage." For all its extravagance, Uncle Benny's story about Sandy Stevenson is based on at least some literal truth—"I seen the bruises, I seen them myself"—and is also, ironically, true as prophecy, because it foreshadows Uncle Benny's own unfortunate matrimonial venture. His stories deserve to be pondered; they cannot be lightly dismissed as mythical, meaning untrue, as Del's rational mother supposes. In presenting the nature and quality of Uncle Benny's mind so completely, without making him a target for facile ridicule or diminishing him with undignified farce, but, on the contrary, by paying as it were oblique tribute to the validity of his experience, Alice Munro demonstrates how generous and yet illuminating she is in her art.

How alien Uncle Benny is in the modern world becomes very clear when, looking for his errant wife in Toronto, he "got lost among factories, dead-end roads, warehouses, junkyards, railway tracks." No wonder! His element is the primeval swamp, which to modern citified man is as strange as Toronto is to him. Despite his strangeness, Del's family makes him an honorary uncle and has him at its table. But Del goes further than mere social tolerance: she seems to accept him as a sort of spiritual forebear. Her imagination has been able to embrace his strangeness and make it truly familiar—an etymological pun is intended here!—because she has recognized in him herself, her part in mankind's history and pre-history. In this *Bildungsroman* Del passes through phases analogous to those of the foetus, which is said to reflect in the womb the stages of evolution; she also passes through the stages of pre-history that children are said to rehearse as they grow up. It is her intelligent imagination that allows her to do this so completely; it makes what is strange familiar by bringing her to the knowledge that she is a part of mankind and that nothing human is alien to her.

The second chapter of *Lives of Girls and Women* is "Heirs of the Living Body"; it deals with issues that are similar, more immediate, though in a sense more limited, in a much more specific form. Del's relation with her family is a matter that she can address herself to more consciously and deliberately. If the honorary uncle, Benny, represents pre-history, the real aunts and uncles of this chapter embody history, and with a very present and sometimes pressing force. They and Del are the heirs of the same living bodies, but we see the counter-weighted irony that Aunt Elspeth and Auntie Grace—their very names are long out of fashion—embody patterns and standards which, though they prevailed only a generation or two before, are strange, almost antediluvian—in some ways stranger even than Uncle Benny. But Del is nevertheless fascinated by her aunts' avocations, attitudes and codes; though they remain for her somewhat alien, she is able to admire and feel affection for them. Indeed she evokes their ethos lovingly and in detail.

But perhaps the deepest and most ironical truths of the chapter are reached through the portrayal of Uncle Craig, who is so very diligently and literally the transmitter of tradition that his life is now devoted to compiling a laborious and pedestrian history of Wawanash County: "During the spring, summer, and early fall of that year a large amount of building went forward in Fairmile, Morris, and Grantly townships . . ." When he dies the aunts piously and formally hand the unfinished opus over to Del to complete; because she has, as they put it, "the knack for writing compositions," they think she "could learn to copy his way"! Del is scornful of this pettifogging history and dedicated to Art with an ardour and confidence that seems to derive from Aristotle and Joyce's Stephen Dedalus; she believes that "the only duty of a writer is to produce a masterpiece," and allows the manuscript that has been accumulated with such care to lie in the cellar, where it becomes "just a big wad of soaking paper."

But Alice Munro, through her surrogate, Del, doesn't allow us easy laughs at Uncle Craig's expense any more than she does at Uncle Benny's. One of the most striking merits of Alice Munro's work is that in its final effect it is just, rising above all the snobberies of fashion,

class and the intellect. Uncle Craig's aim, which is to record "the whole solid intricate structure of lives supporting us from the past," is admirable and enlightened, and, by a telling irony, it later becomes Del's aim too; even Del's method is similar to his:

> It did not occur to me [at the time of the events described towards the end of *Lives*] that one day I would be so greedy for Jubilee. Voracious and misguided as Uncle Craig out at Jenkin's bend, writing his History, I would want to write things down.

> I would try to make lists. A list of all the stores and businesses going up and down the main street and who owned them, a list of family names, names on the tombstones in the Cemetery and any inscriptions underneath. A list of the titles of movies that played at the Lyceum Theatre from 1938 to 1950, roughly speaking. Names on the Cenotaph (more for the first World War than for the second). Names of the streets and the pattern they lay in.

> The hope of accuracy we bring to such tasks is crazy, heartbreaking.

> And no list could hold what I wanted, for what I wanted was every last thing, every layer of speech and thought, stroke of light on bark or walls, every smell, pothole, pain, crack, delusion, held still and held together—radiant, everlasting.

The mature artist that Del is yet to become knows that these methods will not achieve what she wants; only art can hold it all "still" and "together—radiant, everlasting," in the way that Hugo's story, in "Material," will lift Dotty "out of life" and hold her "in light, suspended in the marvelous clear jelly" that Hugo, the writer, "has spent all his life learning how to make."

But when she reaches that stage in her art, Del will not be as easily scornful of Uncle Craig's work as she was in her girlhood because, in the words of T. S. Eliot's *The Dry Salvages*, she will realize that Uncle Craig has nourished "the life of significant soil." She will know that in many senses, both literal and figurative, she is the heir of a living body that comprises many aunts and uncles, real and honorary, and that Uncle Craig deserves a high place among them . . .

But what about Miss Madeleine Howey, the almost unspeakable Mrs. Benjamin Poole, Uncle Benny's bride? Is she an indigestible bolus, beyond the reach of Del's, and our, sympathetic imagination, an unresolved complexity, too strange ever to become in any sense familiar or to be felt as kin? Del records her family's response at the end of "The Flats Road": "After a while we would all just laugh, remembering Madeleine going down the road in her red jacket, with her legs like scissors, flinging abuse over her shoulder at Uncle Benny trailing after, with her child … We remembered her like a story, and having nothing else to give we gave her our strange, belated, heartless applause. 'Madeleine! That madwoman!'"

It would be typical of Alice Munro's truthfulness, which often uses irony as its instrument, to present us in Madeleine with an exception, a member of the human race who is not part of the greater identity, the Living Body. But on the other hand, perhaps there is a suggestion of uneasiness and guilt in the family's laughter, and the very fact that Madeleine is having stories told about her, suggests that the folk imagination, and Del's too, is incorporating even her into the tradition. She provides the stiffest challenge of all, but she too in the end must be seen as a member of the human family.

There is more to be said about our theme in that second chapter of *Lives*: "Heirs of the Living Body." A fairly simple meaning declares itself in the scene at Uncle Craig's funeral in which Del bites Mary Agnes and is said to have blood on her mouth: she experiences a moment of great intensity, "the very opposite of the mystic's incommunicable vision of order and light." Del finds Mary Agnes inimical, even though she is her cousin—another case of Munrovian irony in family relationships—and is perhaps trying to force a sort of *Blutschwesterschaft* to correspond with what she knows she ought to feel for Mary Agnes. In spite of the intensity of her feelings of shame at her misbehaviour, Del knows that the family "would not put me outside," would not expel her from the Living Body. It's not surprising that Del "felt held close, stifled, as if it was not air that I had to move and talk through in this world but something thick as cotton wool." The community sense is by no means always an unmixed blessing; family feeling can amount to virtual suffocation.

But this scene is linked with another in the same chapter, where the meanings, though they are fully realized, are by no means simple, and in fact provide a sort of culmination of the movement towards an awareness of community that I have been largely concerned with thus far in this essay. It is the scene with the dead cow. Mary Agnes is unfeeling and even callous as "she laid her hand—she laid *the palm of her hand*—over it, over the eye" of the dead cow; Del is horrified at Mary Agnes's casualness. In contrast to Mary Agnes, Del feels an intense fascination with the cow, and this is conveyed in her description of it:

> The eye was wide open, dark, a smooth sightless bulge, with a sheen like silk and a reddish gleam in it, a reflection of light. An orange stuffed in a black silk stocking. Flies nestled in one corner, bunched together beautifully in an iridescent brooch. I had a great desire to poke the eye with my stick, to see if it would collapse, if it would quiver and break like a jelly, showing itself to be the same composition all the way through, or if the skin over the surface would break and let loose all sorts of putrid mess, to flow down the face. I traced the stick all the way round the eye. I drew it back— but I was not able, I could not poke it in.

> Mary Agnes did not come close. "Leave it alone," she warned. "That old dead cow. It's dirty. You get yourself dirty."

> "Day-ud cow," I said, expanding the word lusciously. "Day-ud cow, day-ud cow."

> "You come on," Mary Agnes bossed me, but was afraid, I thought, to come nearer.

> Being dead, it invited desecration, I wanted to poke it, trample it, pee on it, anything to punish it, to show what contempt I had for its being dead. Beat it up, break it up, spit on it, tear it, throw it away! But still it had power, lying with a gleaming strange map on its back, its straining neck, the smooth eye. I had never once looked at a cow alive and thought what I thought now: why should there be a cow? Why should the white spots be shaped just the way they were, and never again, not on any cow or creature, shaped in exactly the same way? Tracing the outline of a continent again, digging the stick in, trying to make a definite line, I paid attention to its shape as I would sometimes pay attention to the shape of real continents or island on real maps, as if the shape itself were a revelation beyond words, and I would be able to make sense of it, if I tried hard enough, and had time.

There are many meanings here. Faced with this death, Del feels herself close to the mysteries of life and death and longs to part the veil, but her spirit quails in awe. To her the dead cow is of the utmost importance. Even her impulse to desecrate it stems from her notion that it is in some sense sacred. The "day-ud cow" is for her the corpse of a fellow creature. Here she is on the edge of an awareness of being the heir not only of the Living Human Body, of human history and tradition, but of all life; she has gone even further, and with a fuller conscious awareness, than she went in her relation with Uncle Benny in the previous chapter. In contrast to Del, Mary Agnes, despite the meanings suggested by her names, or because—as well as being backward—she is as conventional as they are, has no such sense of respect or reverence. She is not mainly afraid, as Del thinks, but mainly indifferent, as she shows when, as we have seen, she puts the palm of her hand over the cow's eye.

All the scenes I have discussed thus far, involving a father with his daughter, and Del with Uncle Benny, her real aunts, Uncle Craig, Madeleine Howey, and a dead cow, show us a young girl—of exceptional intelligence and imagination, it is true—entering into a full human consciousness of her life in time and space. The word "tradition" is too feeble and abstract to suggest more than a thin shadow of the meanings entailed here. Have these meanings ever been rendered better, with fuller insight into the comic, ironic and pathetic complexities, with deeper sympathy, or a surer moral grasp of all the issues? . . .

What I have tried to illustrate is a single aspect of Alice Munro's art: like Blake's and James Joyce's, it deals with oppositions, contraries, tensions, inconsistencies, and then resolutions, implied or achieved; in literary terms the oppositions produce ironies and paradoxes, but also moments of vision in which the oppositions are reconciled, at least in the imagination. It is because Alice Munro's fiction is constantly addressing itself to and approaching these oppositions, and trembling on the edge of this sort of consummation, when the familiar and the strange, the touchable and the mysterious, the similar and the different, become one, when in Yeats's words "all the planets drop into the sun" ("There"), that her work is so readable, exciting and satisfying.

Source: W. R. Martin, "The Strange and the Familiar in Alice Munro," in *Studies in Canadian Literature*, Vol. 7, No. 2, 1982, pp. 214–26.

SOURCES

Cavanagh, Sheila L., "Female-Teacher Gender and Sexuality in Twentieth-Century Ontario, Canada," in *History of Education Quarterly*, Vol. 45, No. 2, 2005, pp. 247–73.

Coffey, Katelyn, "How Women's Role in Society has Changed throughout the 20th Century," http://www.youthlinks.org/article.do?articleID = 1376&sl; = e (accessed July 27, 2007).

Irvine, Lorna, "Changing Is the Word I Want," in *Probably Fictions: Alice Munro's Narrative Acts*, edited by Louis MacKendrick, ECW Press, 1983, pp. 99–111.

Long, John S., "Ontario's Educational Issues/Trending," http://www.nipissingu.ca/education/robfix/EDUC4202/Notes/Lecture_Week6_Dec12.doc (accessed July 27, 2007).

Munro, Alice, *Lives of Girls and Women*, Vintage Books, 2001.

Rasporich, Beverly J., *Dance of the Sexes: Art and Gender in the Fiction of Alice Munro*, University of Alberta Press, 1990, p 45.

Rule, Jane, "The Credible Woman," in *Books in Canada*, Vol. 1, No. 4, November 1971, pp. 4–5.

Tausky, Thomas E., "Alice Munro: Biocritical Essay," 1986, http://www.ucalgary.ca/lib-old/SpecColl/munrobioc.htm (accessed July 27, 2007).

Thomas, Clara, "Woman Invincible," in *Journal of Canadian Fiction*, Vol. 1, No. 4, 1972, pp. 95–96.

Vaidyanath, Sharda, "Exhibit Depicts Triumphs and Trials of 1940s Women," in the *Epoch Times*, May 18, 2007, http://en.epochtimes.com/news/7-5-18/55450.html (accessed July 27, 2007).

Wolff, Geoffrey, "Call It Fiction," in *Time*, Vol. 15, 1973, p. 79.

Wordsworth, Christopher, "Maple Leaf in Bud," in the *Guardian Weekly*, Vol. 3, November 3, 1973, p. 24.

FURTHER READING

"Appreciations of Alice Munro," in the *Virginia Quarterly Review*, Vol. 82, Issue 3, Summer 2006, pp. 91–107.
This article contains a series of brief examinations of Munro's work provided by several writers and many of Munro's friends.

Carter, Kathryn, ed., *The Small Details of Life: Twenty Diaries by Women in Canada, 1830–1996*, University of Toronto Press, 2002.
This book contains a series of excerpts from women's diaries. The texts include details about married life, including an account of domestic abuse, the experiences of new settlers and farming wives, and the experiences of single women teachers.

Munro, Sheila, *Lives of Mothers & Daughters: Growing Up with Alice Munro*, Douglas Gibson Books, 2001.
This biography of Munro is also a memoir written by her oldest daughter. The book is

filled with photos and personal information about Alice Munro's family and her work.

Thacker, Robert W., ed., *The Rest of the Story: Essays on Alice Munro*, ECW Press, 1999.
This book is a collection of eleven critical essays that focus on several of Munro's short stories.

Wine, Jeri Dawn, and Janice L. Ristock, eds., *Women and Social Change: Feminist Activism in Canada*, J. Lorimer, 1991.
This book is a collection of essays that explore women's lives. Topics include feminism in the academic field, in rural life, in agriculture, and in minority populations.

The Man Who Loved Children

Christina Stead's *The Man Who Loved Children* received little critical consideration when it was first published in 1940, and would probably have been forgotten by the literary world if not for the attention brought to it by the poet Randall Jarrell, who wrote a highly laudatory introduction for the twenty-five-year anniversary edition. Since then, the book has been considered a modern masterpiece.

The novel offers a harrowing look at a dysfunctional family, and is patterned on the household in which Stead grew up. Like the oldest daughter, Louisa, Stead was raised by her stepmother after her birth mother died when she was two; her parents went on to have six more children, even though they fought constantly. Stead's eye for detail makes these characters easily relatable to readers, and their hatred and self-destructive tendencies make them characters that are difficult to forget. Perhaps this is why the book has remained in print for so long, with a new edition published by Picador in 2001.

CHRISTINA STEAD

1940

AUTHOR BIOGRAPHY

Christina Stead was born in Australia, in the town of Rockdale in New South Wales, on July 17, 1902. Her father was a marine biologist and an active socialist. When she was two years old, her mother died. Three years later, her father

Christina Stead (AP Images)

remarried Ada Gibbons, with whom Stead did not get along. Her parents went on to have six more children, mirroring the family structure in *The Man Who Loved Children*.

Stead was educated in nearby Sydney, earning her degree from New South Wales Teachers' College in 1922. She found that teaching was not the right job for her, and in 1925 started working as a secretary. She moved to London in 1928, to follow a man with whom she had fallen in love, and when he rejected her, she took a job as an office clerk. At that job, she met Wilhelm Blech, who was to become her lifelong companion. With his influence, she became a Marxist. The two lived in Paris, then in Spain until the Civil War began in 1936. Then they moved to the United States.

Stead's first novel, *Seven Poor Men of Sydney*, was published in 1934, followed by *The Beauties and Furies* in 1936, and *House of All Nations* in 1938. The novels did not sell well, and were not even published in her native Australia. To support herself, Stead worked on a variety of writing jobs, including some scriptwriting for MGM. The publication of *The Man*

Who Loved Children in 1940 did little to raise her from literary obscurity; and the novel only started to gain widespread critical praise when it was reissued in 1965.

Stead and Blech, who had changed his name to William Blake, returned to Europe after World War II, finding it difficult to obtain writing jobs in the anti-Communist climate of the 1940s and 1950s. They were married in 1952. After the poet Randall Jarrell renewed interest in Stead's writing with his forward for the 1965 edition of *The Man Who Loved Children*, the couple found more financial stability. In 1968, though, Blake died of stomach cancer. In 1969, Stead returned to Australia as a visiting writer when she was given a Creative Arts Fellowship to the Australian National University. Stead, now recognized in Europe, America, and Australia as a major literary talent, kept writing, though she published few books in her later years. Also in 1969, Stead was passed over for the Britannica-Australia prize on the grounds that she had not lived in Australia for decades and was, thus, no longer Australian. She received the first Patrick White prize for fiction in 1974, and was nominated several times for a Nobel Prize in literature. Stead returned to live in Sydney in 1974 and lived there until her death on March 31, 1983.

PLOT SUMMARY

Chapter One
The first chapter of *The Man Who Loved Children* introduces readers to life at Tohoga House, the large Washington estate occupied by the Pollit family. Henrietta (Henny), the mother, comes home, and her children swarm around her, curious about where she has been and what she has brought. Instead of basking in their attention, though, she snaps at them in a manner that seems ferocious, but that they are obviously accustomed to, since they accept her anger with good nature. They fetch tea for her and kiss her as they watch her play solitaire.

Sam Pollit, the father, returns home from a party at work, with the happy news that he has just been appointed to the Anthropological Mission to the Pacific, a position that he has been seeking. He notices the neighbor's young daughter, Gillian Roebuck, and makes up a short poem about her that he recites to himself.

Once in Tahoga House, he talks with his eleven-year-old daughter Louisa, whose mother was his first wife (she died when Louisa was two). His other five children are not around.

On Sunday, Sam wakes up the children. His other daughter, Evie, is called into his bedroom to massage his head as soon as she wakes up. After breakfast, Sam and the boys—Ernie, the twins Sam Jr. and Saul, and Tommy, the toddler—go out to paint the house.

Chapter Two
The house painting progresses slowly, as Sam spends his time entertaining his sons and the children from the neighborhood with his plans, theories, and ideas. He talks to them in comic accents, and makes up funny, slanderous stories about people in the neighborhood.

Chapter Three
Louie goes to the house of an elderly couple in the neighborhood, the Kydds. Mrs. Kydd is kind to her and speaks lovingly of her husband, though the gossip around the neighborhood is that John Kydd abuses her. While Sam mocks Louie's sullenness to his boys, Mrs. Kydd invites the girl in and explains to her that they have a new cat, but that they cannot afford to feed it and she herself is too weak to kill it. Louisa drowns the cat for her.

Sam, sitting on the lawn with the boys, outlines his ideas for a utopian future society. When he assigns Ernest to be his lieutenant while he is away, his son Sam Jr. objects, and the other twin, Saul, stands up for little Sam. Sam encourages Saul and Ernest to settle their disagreement by fighting; he taunts Saul throughout. Meanwhile, Henny goes downtown and meets with Bert Anderson, a bachelor, at a restaurant, pleased because he lavishes attention and money on her.

Chapter Four
Sam's unmarried older sister, Jo, comes to him to tell him some scandalous gossip she has heard about their younger sister Bonnie, an aspiring actress. When Jo confronts Bonnie, she says that she has heard that the man Bonnie is involved with, Holloway, will not leave his wife, dashing Bonnie's hopes. After going to her room for a while, Bonnie eventually rejoins her siblings to sing and joke.

When Henny comes home after her assignation with Anderson, Jo tells her about Bonnie's

affair, but Henny is not interested. She waits until Sam's sisters leave, then argues with him about money. Sam takes a walk with Louisa, and on their return Henny is still quarrelsome. During their fight Sam hits her, but then as they calm down, he suggests that they should have another child together. Henny agrees, thinking as she does so that she will have her revenge on him.

Chapter Five
Louie goes to Harpers Ferry, Virginia, to spend the summer with her mother's family, the Bakens. The assorted people at her grandfather's house are poor, and they resent the fact that the Pollits, who they think are rich, do not send any money to care for Louie; still, they provide her with a happier family life than she finds at home. After her return, Henny and her daughters visit Monocacy, the opulent home of her wealthy father, David Collyer. Henny discusses methods of suicide with her mother, Ellen, a woman whom her brother Barry impregnated; they discuss the methods they would or would not try.

While Henny, her sister and her mother discuss the difficulties of their lives in the living room, the maid, Nellie, talks to Louie in the kitchen. She mocks Louie, calling her an orphan because her mother is dead and Henny is not her real mother. Louie later tells the adults about the way the maid treated her, and Nellie is fired.

Back home, Louie befriends a girl named Olive who is just a little older than her. Their friendship is short-lived, however—Olive, who is fourteen, announces that she is sick of her home and is running away to Baltimore.

Chapter Six
With Sam in Malaya, Tohoga House is unheated, because Henny spends all of the money he sends her to pay back loans. The children all write letters to Sam, and Louie puts them to bed at night with made-up stories about the interesting characters that their father has befriended in Asia.

In Malay, Sam walks through the streets of Singapore with his Indian secretary, Nadan, discussing religion and culture. Nadan sees Sam as naïve about the danger to a white man walking alone, and Sam thinks Nadan is too cynical. Nadan takes Sam to his home to meet his wife and child, expressing his honor at such a visit. Sam returns to his office and hears from Lai Wan Hoe, who runs the office for him, that his supervisor, Colonel Willets, is angry with him. Sam opens his letters, including one from Gillian Roebuck, a neighborhood child from home, with whom he has been corresponding. He writes back to Louisa and to Gillian.

When he finds out that Lai Wan Hoe has fled the city to escape creditors, Sam realizes that he knows too little about what he is supposed to be doing to continue with the expedition. He considers an offer to teach ichthyology at Hangkow University, but decides to return to Washington, to be with his family.

Chapter Seven

Sam's family—including his parents, brothers and sisters—gathers at Tohoga House (now called Tohoga Place, at Sam's will) to celebrate his arrival home from Asia. While his father, Charles, leads them in song and in his recitations of dramatic scenes, His brother Lenny mixes a punch with alcohol in it. Sam is infuriated because he does not allow alcohol in his house, and a fight breaks out between him and Henny, during which they insult each other viciously in front of all of the guests.

When Henny goes up to her room, a letter comes for her, saying that her father, David Collyer, has died. Sam decides to not tell her. Soon after, though, Henny goes into labor and the doctor is called. Sam stays up all night, and in the morning wakes all of the children to see the new baby, a boy whom they name Charles, because Sam's father asked that the baby be named after him.

When Old David Collyer's estate is settled, it is found that he has spent his family's fortune. There will be no inheritance, which Henny was waiting for to pay off her debts. Tohoga Place must be sold to pay off Collyer's own debts, and the family is forced to move.

Without the protection of his rich father-in-law, the people in his department who never liked Sam are able to start rumors about him: about his ineptitude and possible affairs. Colonel Willets testifies to the bad work he did in Singapore. Sam knows that there are rumors about him going around, but he refuses to answer them, feeling that he is above them.

Chapter Eight

The family moves to Spa House, in a poor section of Annapolis, Virginia. Sam is on unpaid leave from his job, and is not sure if he would go back to it if asked. He uses his time off to repair the decrepit house he could afford, claiming that he and his sons can do all necessary construction. When his official suspension comes, he welcomes the chance to spend more time with the children.

At school, Louisa finds she has a talent for writing poetry and plays. She makes friends with Clare Meredith, who is an artist like herself, and together she and Clare bond over their love for their teacher, Miss Aiden. One day, when walking with Louisa, Sam steers her over to Clare's house and has her ask Clare out with them for some ice cream. Though Louisa dreads how Clare will react when she hears the pet names Sam uses for her and his general air of superiority, Clare says nothing about it.

Later, when Sam is talking with the children, Ernie tells him that Louie has a diary hidden in his room. Sam brings it out to read to the whole family, but it is in code. Louie comes home and he makes her translate it to them, humiliating her. After that, when he tries to lecture her about what she can expect from the world, she can only laugh at his own ignorance and, like Henny, is openly spiteful toward Sam.

Chapter Nine

Henny spends time away from home, often visiting her sister, Hassie. Sam stays around his children, nominally supervising their work but more often distracting them with stories about the neighbors and his old work companions. When he discovers that Ernie, who has always been conscious about money, has been hoarding lumps of lead under his bed to sell later, Sam has the other children take it out, and he publicly makes fun of Ernie for his miserliness.

Ernie notices all of the luxury items that are missing from the house. He asks his mother where they all went: at first, she says that she stored them with relatives, but he eventually finds out that she has sold them. He also finds out that she has raided his money box, taken his life savings of five dollars, and replaced his money with worthless foreign money.

On Sam's birthday, Louisa has Ernie and Evie perform a play that she has written called "Tragedy: The Snake-Man." It is a one-act play about an overbearing, clueless father and his daughter, who has isolated herself from the world. When Sam is outraged by it, Louie is perplexed.

Louie's teacher Miss Aiden comes to dinner on Sam's fortieth birthday. She struggles to remain polite, but she is aghast to see the condition that the Pollits live in: they have only one glass for the whole family and the rough construction work that Sam has done with his sons looks shabby to her outsider's eyes.

After she leaves, Sam feels inspired to make a new bookcase in Louisa's room. Taking down the old bookcase, he finds a book of poetry that Louie has written to Miss Aiden, titled "The Aiden Cycle." He reads the poems aloud to the children, mocking Louie's deeply-held sentiments as he reads, until she shouts at him to give her her book back.

A letter that was delivered earlier but dropped on the lawn is given to Sam. It is an anonymous note telling him that his wife was having an affair while he was in Asia, and that his youngest son, Chappy, is another man's child. Louie distracts the other children with a story while Sam and Henny argue about the letter. Another letter that was dropped on the lawn is given to Louie: it is from her friend Clare, written that afternoon, commiserating with her sorrows and offering her support.

The following morning, Henny is distraught, screaming at Sam and the children, threatening to kill herself or kill all of them. She meets with Bert Anderson the following day. Bert has been avoiding her since the death of her politically powerful father, and he is shocked to see how haggard Henny has become. He has to get back to work, but agrees to meet her again later. Henny waits for him in a bar, but, when he doesn't come, she goes to her sister Hassie's home, where she stays a few days.

Chapter Ten

When Henny returns home, the family is in more disarray than usual. The children have been eating things like raw bacon and almonds for dinner, and the baby, left in the yard, is eating his own feces, which Sam thinks is normal and healthy.

Jo Pollit comes and tells Sam that their sister Bonnie has come to her home and given birth. Jo arranged for the baby to be taken away to an orphanage, but she wants Bonnie, who is too sick to move, out of her apartment before the neighbors start to talk.

Sam has been given a huge fish, a marlin, that his friend Saul caught. He has a scientific theory about the many uses of fish oil, and so he

decides to boil the fish and bottle the oil that comes out of it. The only thing big enough for it is Henny's large washtub. He starts it boiling at night, giving the children different shifts throughout the night to watch the fire under the tub. During his shift in the night, Sam wakes Louie to talk. He tells her about a young woman he has been seeing, who he would marry if not for Henny. She tells him of her desperate desire to get away, of her plan to leave with Clare and travel the country.

In the morning, when the fish oil is bottled, Sam has all of the children take the boiled-down shreds of the marlin out to the garbage heap. The smell of it is so bad that Little-Sam vomits. Sam mocks him for being weak, and, when he says he cannot carry these awful fish remains any more, he pours the stuff all over Little-Sam and gives him the job of cleaning out the washtub.

Louie cannot think of any way free of Sam and Henny and their constant arguing except to kill them both. She plans to put cyanide in their morning tea. In the morning, however, Henny comes in as she is preparing the tea, and suspects that something is up. When Sam comes in, Henny rages at him, tells him to not blame Louie, grabs the poisoned cup and drinks it down, falling dead almost immediately. They try to revive her, but are unsuccessful. Louie then finds that Ernie has hung a mannequin of himself in his bed with a rope around his neck, which she later deduces was a practice attempt at hanging himself.

After Henny's death, the family finds out that she was deeply in debt ever since Ernie was born, twelve years ago. People start treating Sam more sympathetically, though he insists on being responsible for what Henny owed. He secures a job that he thinks will be good for him—he will be the host of a radio program for children, telling them patriotic stories—and he runs across his estranged sister Bonnie, whom he convinces to move back into the house and help him with the children. After a talk in which she explains to Sam her plans to kill him and Henny, Louie leaves home with no definite plan for where she will go.

CHARACTERS

Miss Rosalind Aiden

Miss Aiden is the teacher that Louisa has a crush on. Sam, having read some of the poetry that

Louie has written in Miss Aiden's praise, tells her to invite her teacher to dinner on the night of his birthday. When Miss Aiden comes, she is shocked to find the poverty in which the Pollits live.

Bert Anderson

Bert is a government employee with whom Henny is having an affair. When her father dies and her family is forced to leave their house, he avoids her phone calls. When Henny is fed up with life with Sam, she goes to Bert; he arranges to meet her in the evening at a bar, but he never shows up.

Chappy

See Charles Franklin Pollit

David Collyer

"Old David," Henrietta's father, is a rich man who has raised her to expect a life of luxury. She goes to him to borrow money when she can, and the family rents Tohoga House from him for a nominal rent. After his death, it is discovered that he has spent his entire fortune taking care of his children. Henny does not receive the inheritance she had been counting on, and Tohoga House has to be sold, forcing the Pollits to move.

Ernie

See Ernest Pollit

Evie

See Evelyn Pollit

Aunt Hassie

See Aunt Eleanor Lessinum

Henny

See Henrietta Pollit

Aunt Jo

See Josephine Pollit

Aunt Eleanor Lessinum

Henrietta's sister and her confidante, Hassie, whose real name is Eleanor, is as sarcastic about her marriage as Henny is, but her husband Archie is weak-willed, which has allowed her to stay closer to her family than Henny can be.

Little-Sam

See Samuel Pollit

Little-Womey

See Evelyn Pollit

Louie

See Louisa Pollit

Megalops

See Charles Franklin Pollit

Clare Meredith

Clare is Louisa's friend when she transfers to school in Annapolis. They are both intellectuals and share an infatuation with Miss Aiden. Clare thinks of herself as a Socialist and reads intellectual works about class struggle. She understands Louie's home situation and sympathizes with her. When Sam insists on taking Clare out for ice cream, Louie is embarrassed by his attempts to be charming, but Clare says nothing about it to Louie. They make plans to run away together, to walk across the country, but, when Louisa comes to Clare as she is leaving town at the end of the book, Clare says that she has a responsibility to her little sister.

Hazel Moore

Hazel is the housekeeper from Henny's childhood. She was with the Pollits in the beginning of their marriage, but Sam fires her because she abused his reading materials, which offended her religious sensibilities. When Sam goes to Malay, Henny has Hazel move back into the house, but eventually they cannot afford her. In the end she marries her long-time beau, Mr. Gray, to whom she was engaged for more than fifteen years.

Nadan

Nadan is Sam's secretary in Malay, a Madrasi Kerani. He sees Sam as being a bit naïve, telling him to not roam the streets at night, that he might not be safe. Nadan takes Sam to see his wife and newborn child, feeling that his connection with this westerner makes him important.

Old David

See David Collyer

Saul Pilgrim

Sam's friend from the Conservation Bureau, Saul has published his own newspaper with an ongoing story. When Sam is the subject of a smear campaign, Saul stands by him.

Bonnie Pollit

Bonnie is Sam's younger sister, who lives in Tohoga House with them and does all of the work of a maid, without pay. Henny does not approve of her, and, when Sam goes to Asia, Henny has Bonnie moved out of the house, to bring in her old maid, whom Sam cannot stand.

For a while, the family loses track of Bonnie. She shows up at her sister Jo's place about to have a baby, and, while she is sick from childbirth, the baby is given away. Bonnie disappears again, but later, after Henny's death, Sam runs into her on a Washington street with a child that she is fairly sure is the one that Hassie forced her to give away, and Sam asks her to move in with him and his children again.

Charles Franklin Pollit

Charles is the baby of the family, born on the night of Sam's return from Malay. Rumors circulate that Henny became pregnant with this son while her husband was away. These rumors are unlikely, as Henny later thinks of him as being, just like the rest of the children, a Pollit. He is sometimes called by the nickname "Megalops," and, more often, "Chappy."

Ernest Pollit

The first born child of Henrietta and Sam, Ernest (Ernie) is ten years old at the start of the book. He is Henrietta's favorite. Ernie is obsessed with money: he hoards the coins relatives give him for birthdays and special occasions and frantically calculates what money is coming into the house and what is going out. He lends Henny money out of his cash box, at interest.

When Sam loses his job and the family, impoverished, has to move to the poor section of Annapolis, Ernie hoards lumps of lead. He refuses to sell them, or to even let others touch them. His insecurity about finances is magnified when he notices that his mother has sold all of the family's valuable possessions. Even worse, however, is when he finds out that Henny has found his cash box, hidden under a loose board in the floor, and stolen all of his money, replacing it with useless foreign money. As desperate as that act was for Henny, it is a catastrophe for Ernie to lose his life's savings, five dollars and eighty-nine cents. On the morning that Henny dies, Ernie has attached a dummy with a rope around its neck to his bed, and Louie speculates that Ernie is planning to hang himself.

Evelyn Pollit

Evelyn (Evie) is eight years old at the start of the book, and is her father's favorite. His nickname for her is "Little-Womey," for "little woman." His relationship with her is physically close: every morning he calls her, against her objections, to come to him in his bed and massage his head.

Unlike her older sister Louisa, Evie is a pretty girl. Because Louie is an intellectual, and is increasingly wandering off to think and to write, the household chores that their father determines should be handled by girls often fall to Evie. The boys go outside to paint or to build things, but Evie is left to wash dishes and change beds. She never objects to the tasks assigned to her, making her the model of the young compliant "woman" that her father admires.

Henrietta Pollit

Henrietta (Henny) Pollit is the mother of the family portrayed in the novel. Having grown up in a wealthy family, she finds her current situation, as the wife of a man with limited means and a mother to a large family, to be woefully disappointing. Henny has never learned to budget, and so lives beyond her means, spending money too freely while constantly worrying about paying back the money she has borrowed. After her death, it is discovered that Henny's debts went back years, to the birth of her first child, Ernest, ten years before the novel's beginning.

Although Henny is verbally abusive toward her children, she is also loved by them. They dote on her and ask her to sing favorite songs and recite poems, even when she asks them brusquely to go away and leave her alone. She forms a particular bond with Louisa, who is her husband's daughter by his previous marriage. Though Henny is vicious about Louisa's looks, her behavior, and even her hygiene, Henny still feels some empathy for the girl, and Louisa feels that she has more understanding for her stepmother than she does for her father.

To help accept the disappointments of her unhappy marriage, Henny sits in her room and plays solitaire, distancing herself from the rest of the family. She seldom goes out, though she does seek solace in an affair with Bert Anderson, who, like Sam Pollit, is a government bureaucrat. In the end of the book, Henny finally wins at solitaire without cheating and she finds herself abandoned by Bert, who promises to meet her at a bar but never shows up. Henny thus has little to look forward to in life, and this drives her to suicide.

Josephine Pollit

Josephine (Jo) Pollit is Sam Pollit's sister, older than him by about a decade. She is not married and rents out apartments in two buildings she owns for a living. Aunt Jo, as she is called, babies her younger brother by bringing him chocolate when she visits. She is a prude, complaining about their sister Bonnie's potentially scandalous behavior when she lives with Sam's family. Later, when Bonnie nearly dies at Jo's apartment during childbirth, Jo does what she can to have Bonnie moved to Sam's house before her neighbors can find out about the out-of-wedlock birth.

Louisa Pollit

Louisa (Louie) is eleven and a half years old at the beginning of the book. She is Sam's daughter by his first wife, Rachel. Because she is the oldest and not Henny's own child, Henny is particularly harsh toward Louie, picking at her every fault; still, there is a bond between Louie and her stepmother, so that she tends to sympathize with Henny when her parents argue. Often, when her parents are not talking, it falls to Louie to act as a parent to the younger children.

Louie is a big, lumbering child. She is not a pretty girl. She is, however, very intelligent, writing plays and verse in Latin. She is well-read, and fills her writings with literary allusions that her parents do not understand.

Because she can see Sam's hypocrisy, Louie has little use for men. She forms a few close friendships with girls her own age, but the greatest love of her life is her teacher, Miss Aiden, for whom she composes an entire volume of poems. Although Louie is generally embarrassed about her parents, she does not realize how pitiable Miss Aiden finds her home situation when she comes to visit.

Although Louie plans to end the family turmoil by killing Sam and Henny, she is saved the trouble when Henny, realizing the poison Louie has put in her tea, commits suicide by drinking it willingly. Still, Louie is honest enough to tell Sam of her intention, and just barely strong-willed enough to leave home on her own at age fourteen.

Rebecca Baken Pollit

Rebecca was Sam Pollit's first wife and is Louisa's mother. She died when Louie was a baby. Though she never appears in the story, Sam often refers to her in glowing terms.

Sam Pollit

Sam is thirty-eight when the novel begins. He comes from humble roots—his father was a bricklayer—but he has worked himself up in the Conservation Bureau in large part because of the political influence of his wealthy father-in-law, David Collyer. After Old David's death, rumors spread around the office, and Sam loses his job.

Throughout the novel, Sam forms relationships with women outside of his marriage. Whether these relationships ever blossom into sexual affairs is never made clear: he thinks about his desires for Madeline Vines, his secretary, and his correspondences with Gillian Roebuck, who he later thinks he could marry if Henny were not his wife. He is flirtatious with women while stationed in Malay, with Louie's teacher, and with her friend, Clare.

Despite his self-image as a kind and loving father, Sam is cruel whenever he senses that his children are thinking independently. He forces Saul and Ernest to fight, even though the younger boy is hopelessly outmatched; he reads Louie's poetry aloud to the family, mocking it; he pours fish offal all over Little-Sam's head when the smell of it has already made the boy sick. Sam pretends that his cruel behavior is in their best interest, to make them stronger.

Sam's ego blinds him to the results of his theories about child rearing and family. He looks at his marriage to Henny as a mistake, but one that he has been bound by honor to follow through, despite the misery that it inflicts on everyone around them. He refuses to see the suffering of his children, living in poverty and surrounded by hatred, and even blocks out the terrible truth when Louie tells him that she tried to poison both parents and that Ernie was probably planning suicide.

After Henny's death, things work out well for Sam. People look at him sympathetically, blaming her for the troubles of the Pollit household. He starts a new job with a radio program, where, presumably, he will be able to expand upon his own delusions and self-justification.

Samuel Pollit

The blonde seven-year-old twin son, Little-Sam, is one of the most sensitive of the Pollit children. When Sam forces the children to boil down a fish for the oil and help him dispose of the remains, the stench of the fish pieces that they are throwing out make Little-Sam vomit. Instead of showing sympathy, Sam pours the disgusting fish liquid all over Little-Sam's head and refuses to let him shower it off.

Saul Pollit

The technically older of the seven-year-old twins, Saul is considered the hothead of the family. He is ready to enter into a fight without thinking, a "manly" trait of which his father approves.

Tommy Pollit

At the beginning of the book Tommy is the four-year-old baby of the family. By the end he is old enough to have befriended a girl in the neighborhood. His mother and father look at him as a young womanizer.

Gillian Roebuck

Gillian is a child at the beginning of the novel, when Sam Pollit notices her on the street and makes up a poem about her. Later, when he is away from home, he writes letters to her. When life between Sam and Henny is at its worst, Sam implies that Gillian is in love with him and he with her, and that they would be married if he were single.

Lai Wan Hoe

A Chinese citizen born in Singapore, Wan Hoe is Sam's office secretary in Malay. Because Sam is almost crippled by the heat of southeast Asia, Wan Hoe does all of the work that his office generates. He has to borrow money to take care of his family, however, and he ends up running away, leaving Sam with no one to do his work for him.

Colonel Willard Willets

Colonel Willets is Sam's superior at his Malay job. He resents Sam, and feels he does not respect his authority. Later, when Sam's career at the Conservation Bureau is in jeopardy, Colonel Willets writes letters to do anything he can to get Sam fired, out of spite.

TOPICS FOR FURTHER STUDY

- Research the cost of household goods during the Depression and make out a budget for a family of eight living in an urban area. Include costs for utilities (telephone, electricity, heat, etc.).

- Near the end of the novel, young Charles Pollit develops *coprophagia*, eating his own excrement. Research the symptoms of this condition, and, using the descriptions of his family background, write a diagnosis for him just as a psychologist would write it.

- Some critics have categorized *The Man Who Loved Children* as a "feminist" novel, while others have said that it is not one. Make a list of eight to ten characteristics that you think a feminist novel should have, and then chart how each item is or is not found in the work. Write an essay discussing your findings.

- At the end of the novel, Sam Pollit is about to host a radio program that will allow him to broadcast his theories about children across the country. Write a script of a radio show that Sam Pollit would likely broadcast. Perform your script for the class.

- The short play that Louisa writes for her father's birthday gift horrifies and enrages him. Write a one-act play that mirrors the kind of relationship that you have with someone that you admire.

THEMES

Family

The central theme of *The Man Who Loved Children* is the way that the Pollit family sticks together despite the fierce animosity between the two parents who run the household. From the start, Stead establishes Henrietta Pollit's lack of respect for her husband, whom she usually communicates with through the children. Regarding Henny, Sam seems more frustrated than angry:

he showers the children with attention, telling them stories and keeping them occupied with chores around the house. Henny's inability to keep the house, cope with the children or remain within her budget causes him concern.

It is only as the novel progresses that it becomes clear that the problem with the Pollit family structure is not simply a matter of Henny's bad attitude, but is solidly established in the family's roots. Although she is sarcastic and sharp-tongued, Henny can actually be a caring person at heart: her stepdaughter, Louisa, senses this, and dotes on Henny in spite of the verbal abuse she receives from her. And Sam's culpability for the unhealthy family structure is revealed as readers become more able to see through his cheerfulness—which is often masked by his unique, exuberant way of talking—to see what a cold and demanding man he really is. The early episode in which he sets Saul and Ernest against each other in a fight, for instance, seems to be misguided but at least grounded in his moral principles, as Sam tells them that brothers should always clear the air with fighting and then make up. Later episodes, however, in which he leads the family in mocking Ernest for collecting lead or in mocking Louie's love poetry, show Sam to be nothing more than mean-spirited. Although Stead presents Henny's hostility from the start, it is when Sam's suppressed hostility gradually develops that readers can see that the Pollit family is not just a family where something has gone wrong, but that it is a family built around anger, and that the cheerful and well-behaved personalities of the children are a response to the insecurity and hostility they have known all their lives.

Narcissism

Narcissism is a psychological condition in which a person views the world only in terms of how much they see themselves reflected in it. Although this novel's title character, Sam Pollit, seems to sincerely enjoy the company of his own children and welcomes other children from around the neighborhood to join his family, Stead makes it clear that he is fooling himself as well as others about his apparent love. He says that his family is the most important thing in his life, that he would like to have children from all nations and races, and that he welcomes his suspension from work as an opportunity to spend more time with his children, but there are clear indicators that this talk is only there to hide

his real interest in drawing attention to himself. For one thing, the specific language that he uses with the children is not as whimsical as it might at first seem: though it might seem a fun way to amuse his children, Sam uses this way of talking all of the time, in effect alienating the family from the outside world with it and forcing the children to focus on him. When he works on projects with the children, he seems to mix fun with work (as indicated in the title "Sunday a Funday," used for two chapters at opposite ends of the book); in actuality, however, Sam does little work and more talking, designating himself as a project supervisor. Not being a role model, he still requires the attention of the children, doubling their burden as they are expected to work and listen to Sam weave his amusing tales.

Sam's narcissism becomes most apparent as his oldest daughter, Louie, begins to develop her own personality. When she makes a friend outside of the home, Clare Meredith, he tries to bring her into his circle of influence, taking Clare out for ice cream and trying to charm her. He does the same thing with Miss Aiden, Louie's teacher, although it is clear that Sam's wordplay and boyishness have minimal success with adults. One of the most telling aspects of his narcissism is the way that he proves to be so upset over Louie's love poetry for Miss Aiden: in mocking it, even though he clearly does not understand whether it is good poetry or not, Sam is showing his fear that his oldest daughter has reached an age at which she can become emotionally attached to someone other than himself.

Art

Throughout the novel, Louisa receives little encouragement from any members of her family. She is not pretty, as she is told often. She is not accommodating, as her younger sister Evie is. She is an outcast at Tahoga House, where her family lives; at Monocacy, where her stepmother Henny's family lives; or at Harpers Ferry, where she spends her summers with her real mother's family. As she matures, though, Louie realizes that she has a gift for art. Instead of channeling her frustrations with the world into anger, as Henny does, or into seeking the attention of children, as her father does, she learns to express herself through writing. She writes clever poems that her friend Clare appreciates. She channels her admiration for her teacher into an extended cycle of poetry, expanding her basic talent by linking it to increasingly complex forms. She reads extensively, quoting freely from Herman Melville, La Rochefoucauld, and the letters of the Russian ballet genius Njinsky. Perhaps the most sure sign that art has become Louie's identity as she has outgrown her family is the fact that she writes a play for her father's birthday, oblivious to the fact that he will not be able to appreciate it for its artistic merits and can only see the ways in which it makes him look bad. Understanding art but not her father, Louie seems sincerely surprised by the offense that Sam takes at her play.

STYLE

Stylized Language

Throughout *The Man Who Loved Children* the members of the Pollit family speak in a particularly stylized language invented by the father, Sam Pollit. This language is a mix of baby talk, ethnic dialect, and some sort of stylized version of the homey rural colloquialisms used by the 19th century American humorist Artemus Ward. At times, Stead's use of this strange Pollit language is so far removed from standard English that she needs to provide readers with a translation in parentheses, knowing that they will never be able to sound out the meaning of what Sam or the children are saying to each other from the words on the page. Their use of the specialized language with each other makes the Pollits initially seem to be a close-knit group, but Stead shows by the end of the book, when Miss Aiden comes to visit, that their closeness has made them unable to recognize how odd they are to outsiders.

Foreshadowing

Even from the start of this long novel, Stead foreshadows the events that are eventually going to take place in the final chapter. Foreshadowing is a device that authors use to prepare readers for what is to come. Usually, it is difficult to identify foreshadowing in advance, and it is only after reading to the end of a work that readers can look back and see how earlier events predicted later ones. In *The Man Who Loved Children* for instance, Henny seems to be on the verge of violence from the novel's opening pages. There are numerous times when Henny threatens to kill herself, as she actually does in the end. There are, however, also many times when she threatens to kill Sam, or the children, so readers would be in their rights to expect either of those events to occur as well. Even so, once they move to Spa House, a death by the end of the book is almost certain, not only because of Henny's spiraling depression, but also because of the presence of a coffin maker across the street.

HISTORICAL CONTEXT

The Great Depression

The Man Who Loved Children was written in the late 1930s, which is when the action takes place. Although it is not a fact that is dwelt upon in the book, this time frame marked the depth of the Great Depression in America. The poverty that seems to creep up on the characters in the book is, in fact, the natural result of years of economic stagnation throughout the country.

While economic shifts usually occur gradually, most historians identify the start of the Great Depression as October 24, 1929, when the U.S. stock market faced a massive sell-off. On that one day, U.S. stocks lost a total of 12.8 percent. The panic that ensued as people tried to take their money out of stocks created an even worse crisis, so that by November it was down 40 percent from where it had been in September. Personal fortunes and businesses were wiped out, and the lack of money caused a chain reaction, bankrupting other businesses and putting people out of jobs, which glutted the employment market with skilled workers. The Depression grew in the United States and spread to markets overseas, to become a worldwide phenomenon. It lingered on until the United States entered World War II in 1941.

Economic conditions declined over the first few years, hitting their low point in March of 1933. That month, President Franklin D. Roosevelt was inaugurated for his first term. Roosevelt came into office enacting economic changes to ease the Depression's effects. His New Deal program created new government agencies, such as the Civilian Conservation Corps, which gave unemployed men outdoor work on construction projects. Many other New Deal agencies focused government resources on the environment.

Because Sam Pollit draws his salary from the government, which was in no danger of going out of business, it makes sense that he would be able to hold onto his job throughout the 1930s.

COMPARE
&
CONTRAST

- **1930s:** Singapore is a colony under British control. Its economic output is the property of the United Kingdom.

  Today: Singapore is an independent country and one if the economic centers of Asia, with one of the continent's highest standards of living.

- **1930s:** An out-of-wedlock birth, like that experienced by Bonnie Pollit, can create such a scandal that family members, like her sister Jo, would feel compelled to throw the single mother out of their household to avoid shame being attached to them.

  Today: The social stigma surrounding unmarried parenting is almost entirely diminished, with nearly 40 percent of all births in the United States occurring out of wedlock.

- **1930s:** At the height of the Depression, families are evicted from their homes and broken up as each family member, including children and teens, set out to seek work. A fourteen-year-old girl traveling on her own (like Louie prepares to do at the end of the novel), would be viewed and treated almost as any other adult would.

  Today: Economic prosperity in America has resulted in extended childhoods, and minors are no longer required to support themselves or their family. Children rarely leave home before the age of eighteen, and a fourteen-year-old girl would not be able to travel far on her own before being victimized or reported to police as a runaway.

- **1930s:** Many Americans, like Henny Pollit, suffer for years as they try without hope to pay back debts that have accrued interest.

  Today: More Americans are in debt than ever before. However, agencies that provide services to restructure debts (so that they can be managed and eventually paid off) have proliferated.

Still, the glut of able workers would have made his job increasingly vulnerable, just as the shortage of investment money would have dried up a fortune like the one held by his father-in-law, David Collyer. The fact that the Pollits, and many of the Collyers, end up in poverty at the end of the novel, or that a child from a poor family like Louisa would have left home to aimlessly travel the world, would not have seemed that unusual during the Great Depression.

Malay

Sam travels to Malay (the term that was once used to describe the Malay Peninsula). Starting in the early 1920s, most of the peninsula was under the political influence of Great Britain. That changed, however, with World War II, when Japan spread its control over the entire region. After the war, there was a brief-lived Malayan Union under British control from 1946 to 1948, but the indigenous people of the area objected to the way that power in this federation had been ceded to Britain without their consent. In 1948, the Federation of Malaya replaced it, recognizing the sovereignty of the Malaysian people. In 1963, a new federation formed under the name Malaysia.

Today, the Malay Peninsula is comprised by the southwest portion of Burma, now called Myanmar; the southern reaches of Thailand; and part of the country of Malaysia (referred to as West Malaysia or Peninsular Malaysia). Singapore, where Sam Pollit served on his economic mission in the novel, is a series of islands off of the tip of the Malay Peninsula: it had been considered a part of Malaya at the time of the novel, but it is not currently joined to Malaysia.

CRITICAL OVERVIEW

The story of how *The Man Who Loved Children* emerged from obscurity twenty-five years after its initial publication is one of the great stories of the power of literary criticism. When the book was published in 1940, it received tepid reviews, its sales were poor, and it was soon forgotten. Stead went on to write four more novels in the 1940s and 1950s, but none gained widespread popularity. Then, in 1965, Rinehart & Winston re-released *The Man Who Loved Children* with an introduction by the poet Randall Jarrell. Suddenly, the literary world accepted the case that Jarrell made for the book's excellence. Indeed, a contributor to *Time* magazine explains in a 1965 review that the book's newfound attention: "a slowly enlarging circle of literati insisted that a magnum opus had been overlooked, and the publisher at last consented to a second edition that proves the literati right." The same article also reports: "*The Man Who Loved Children* is one of the most truthful and terrifying horror stories ever written about family life."

The book has been in print continuously since 1965, and, since that reissue, Christina Stead has been acknowledged as one of the great Australian novelists. In the ensuing years, as the book has become an accepted part of the literary canon, there has been a tendency to categorize it as one type of writing or another. Most often, it has been used as a text in Women's Studies curricula. As Susan Sheridan, a Lecturer in Women's Studies at the Flinders University of South Australia, points out in her 1988 study titled *Christina Stead*, "many of Stead's stories of women's lives seem at first to invite the attention of feminist critics seeking in women's writing testimony to the common feature of female experience which are not represented in patriarchal discourses." As recently as 2001, in discussing the book in a review for *Slate*, Katha Pollitt comments that Lillian Hellman, the famed playwright, once referred to Stead as "the best woman writer alive," but Pollitt dismissed that praise as a patronizing "kiss of death," noting that "nobody ever calls a man 'the best male writer alive.'" Pollitt settles the matter by stating: "Christina Stead is a great writer, period."

CRITICISM

David Kelly

Kelly is an instructor of creative writing and literature. In the following essay, he examines the

careful balance between the essential personalities of Sam and Henny Pollit, and how that balance crumbles over the course of the novel.

One of the finer achievements of Christina Stead's 1940 masterpiece *The Man Who Loved Children* is the presentation of a dysfunctional household as if it is suspended in a state of absolute balance. The parents, Sam and Henny Pollit, are so perfectly unlike one another in their worldviews that it is easy to accept that they have, up to the time of the novel, canceled each other out. Henny, who comes from an old, staid, moneyed family, has a sharp tongue with her children (when she interacts with them at all), though she is more often crippled by her inability to handle money to the point where it consumes her every thought. Sam, who was the baby of a boisterous family of singers, actors, and general attention seekers, makes up for Henny's absence in his children's lives by lavishing attention on them, talking to them in a silly, fanciful language. As the novel progresses, the psychoses of these two individuals become increasingly clear. What also becomes clearer is that their personalities represent natural forces: Henny provides permanence (in that she does not change), while Sam provides the opposite, moving forward with one eye to the future. Unfortunately for the Pollits, this culminates in disaster. Henny is a case study in inertia, and Sam is pitifully out of touch with the world he lives in.

Henrietta Pollit is not an easy character to like. Her first line in the novel is "I come home and find you tearing about the streets like mad things!" This sets the pace for the bitter, sarcastic tone that she takes toward her children throughout the entire book. Readers soon come to recognize that her way of speaking does not bother the children in the least: they still kiss her and dote on her as much as they would a mother who doled out constant praise to them. Toward the five children to whom she has given birth, and especially toward her favorite, Ernie, Henny can be gentle and sympathetic at times. Toward Louie, Sam's daughter from his previous marriage, though, Henny has nothing but vicious words: it is only in her thoughts or in Henny's conversations with her sister that readers learn that Henny pities the child.

Henny does not seek out occasions to persecute her family; in fact, she tries consistently to isolate herself from them. She locks herself in her room playing patience, a kind of solitaire, and takes off, in the middle of what Sam and the

WHAT DO I READ NEXT?

- Studs Turkel's book *Hard Times: An Oral History of the Great Depression* is a collection of interviews with people from all walks of life remembering what everyday living was like for them during those years. First published in 1970, it has stayed in print and is considered an invaluable tool for historians interested in the period. It is currently available from W. W. Norton, reprinted in 2000.

- After *The Man Who Loved Children*, critics consider Stead's novel *Letty Fox: Her Luck* to be her most successful work. Published in 1946, it is a vast, sprawling work about a young woman living in New York during World War II and dealing with her eccentric extended family.

- Sam Pollit acknowledges that the language that he uses with his children is based, at least in part, on the writings of American humorist Artemus Ward. Ward's essay "The Shakers," about a religious sect popular in his time, is included in *The Complete Works of Artemus Ward*, published in paperback in 2005 by Kessinger Publishing.

- The introduction that Randall Jarrell wrote for the twenty-fifth anniversary edition of *The Man Who Loved Children* was instrumental in reviving critical interest in the book, and it also revived Christina Stead's literary career. The introduction, titled "An Unread Book," is included in Jarrell's *No Other Book: Selected Essays* (2000).

- Marilynne Robinson's 1980 novel *Housekeeping* is about two sisters raised in Fingerbone, Idaho, by their grandmother and various aunts in circumstances that are as unconventional and dysfunctional as those in Stead's novel.

- The personal correspondence of Christina Stead and her husband can be found in *Dearest Munx: The Letters of Christina Stead and William J. Blake* (2005). Unlike the many good biographies written about Stead, this volume gives readers insight into her life in her own words.

---

children call "Sunday-Funday," to meet her lover Bert. She yearns for freedom from her husband and her children.

In her anger and isolation, Henny exhibits all the symptoms of chronic depression, but Stead offers an explanation for her behavior that does not require readers to go beyond the pages of the novel. In the end, after she has committed suicide, it is discovered that her financial troubles have been longer held and much deeper than anyone could have guessed, going back twelve years, and coinciding with the birth of her first child. Though readers have known throughout the book that Henny was concerned with money, this revelation at the end changes her behavior so that it is viewed as a constant, enduring state of panic. It defines her personality, reversing the psychology that has been intact up to that point: Henny is not just a depressed person who cannot cope with her debts any more than she can cope with the other aspects of her life, such as her marriage and her children. She is a woman mired in the past, frozen in place by twelve-year-old loans with accruing interest which increase her financial burden with every passing day. The future represents nothing to Henny but a worsening of her situation.

In contrast, her husband, Sam, spends every day looking to the future. In one early segment, he spins tales for his children about what he thinks the world could be like in the future, if he had control of it. His trip to Malay, during which he seems incapable of doing any of his assigned work, is, in Sam's mind, a chance to get to know his fellow man, to make the world a better place. Sam's noble sentiments, however, skip over the complexities of the present; he blithely ignores the details, as he does the financial quagmire that Henny has gotten herself into. While he dreams of the future, the world around him collapses: by the end, the home of this "man who loved children" is a place where there is only one water glass for nine people; where the baby is left to eat his own feces; where one child thinks of suicide while another plots the murder of her parents. Readers can easily see this situation developing. Sam doesn't see it for what it is.

Sam's love for children and his hopes for the future are tied together, only not in the way that he thinks. He is an idealist, but his ideals never really connect with actual people. He imagines himself having a hundred children, building a new society with them, yet he is woefully unaware of what is happening to the children he already has. When he goes to Singapore to study Asian culture, he ends up blocking out almost everything he experienced there, retaining only the fact that, during a discussion about different theological understandings, his secretary Naden told him: "Sah, you are as the gods."

Sam's interest in children is, in fact, no more deeply-held than his interest in the servants that he rules over within the colonial system. His is an imperial ego supported by feeble competence: children and servants are the only ones who are forced to look up to him. Stead's ironic fate for Sam at the end of the book is consigning him to the bliss of broadcasting his half-baked ideas over the radio to an audience of children, and to people with childish dispositions who would be willing to listen to someone like him.

There are occasionally circumstances that drive Sam Pollit to panic and to drop his veil of benevolence toward children. His true nature appears when his children show any sense of independence. This, of course, is most evident with his daughter Louie. Not only is Louie the oldest child, and therefore the first to mature and realize that Sam is not the wise and "bold" character he claims to be, she also is the only one of the children who has other relatives to learn from. Her summers at Harpers Ferry with her mother's family give Louie a different perspective on how the world operates outside of the insular walls of Tohoga House or Spa House.

Not only do Sam and Henny fear her physical maturity—both make constant remarks about her size, dreading the approaching day

> HENNY'S DEBT AND SAM'S NEGLECT FORCE THEM TO MOVE TO POORER CIRCUMSTANCES, WHILE HENNY'S ISOLATION AND SAM'S DESPERATION FOR THE REVERENCE OF HIS AND OTHERS' CHILDREN DRIVE THE FAMILY TOWARD INCREASINGLY ANTISOCIAL BEHAVIORS."

when she will be an adult—but they know that if she reaches emotional maturity, Louie will see their personality defects for what they are. Henny's only response is to criticize the child more and more, but Sam takes steps to impede her development. When she forms friendships outside of his sphere of influence, he tries to charm her new friends. When he is not successful, his cruelty comes out: his mocking of Louie's poetry is transparent jealousy for her reverence toward her new parent figure, Miss Aiden; when he reads her diary and finds that it is written in code, he demands that she have no secret thoughts from him. He is too egocentric and naïve to see that his battle against Louie's emerging adolescence is a battle he is bound to lose.

Stead offers other examples of his true nature, such as when he sets two sons fighting against each other or when he tortures Little-Sam, who is sickened by the smell of boiled-down fish, by pouring the very thing that makes the child vomit all over his head. In each case, Sam defends his actions with some weak justification based in ill-considered child-rearing techniques, but it does not take much to see that the real motive behind his actions is simple, childish bullying. Clearly, he has little love for children, but he does need them around. He simply wants to be a child. At age forty, the best that he can do is pose as a man who spends his time with children because he enjoys their company.

Sam Pollit's view of the world is that of a child; he feels that life has yet to arrive. Henny Pollit's view is that of a hopeless debtor, whose burden increases every day; she feels that life can only get worse. At the time of the novel's start, they are in an unpleasant situation, but they are also in stasis, a place of balance, of equilibrium. Throughout the course of *The Man Who Loved Children*, each parent's basic nature grinds the household down. Henny's debt and Sam's neglect force them to move to poorer circumstances, while Henny's isolation and Sam's desperation for the reverence of his and others' children drive the family toward increasingly antisocial behaviors. At the end of the novel, even with the good fortune befalling Sam Pollit at that point of his life, it is quite unlikely that he will be able to survive for long without his opposite, Henny, to provide a counterbalance to his personality.

Source: David Kelly, Critical Essay on *The Man Who Loved Children*, in *Novels for Students*, Gale, Cengage Learning, 2008.

Michael Ackland

In the following excerpt, Ackland compares The Man Who Loved Children *to the writings of William Blake. While doing so, Ackland also attempts to ascertain Stead's familiarity with Blake's philosophies by identifying the possible influences his writing may have had on Stead's novel.*

... Stead's knowledge of Blake has long been assumed but rarely pinned down. That she was thoroughly acquainted with at least his more accessible works can hardly be doubted. Blake's writing had begun to emerge from obscurity with the influential commentaries and editions of E.J. Ellis and W.B. Yeats in 1893 and 1907, and the foundation for future Blake scholarship had been laid with S. Foster Damon's *William Blake: His Philosophy and Symbols* (1924). Henceforth readers, undaunted by Blake's unorthodox art and poetry, could grasp in detail his radical critique of everyday life. Attacking the restrictive nature of empirical and scientific thinking, the Romantic posited the existence of an eternal realm, portions of which appear to our fallen senses as solid and real. These, according to Blake, are illusory perceptions, destined to be expunged when humanity rediscovers its full spiritual potential. Organized religion, government, social hierarchies and inherited beliefs need to be overthrown. These tenets could be readily assimilated by convinced Marxists like Stead and her life-companion Wilhelm Blech—although Stead, true to her own convictions, consistently located her visions of individual regeneration in the physical here-and-now, not

in Blake's otherworldly "Eternal Life" (146). One measure of the poet's new fame and notoriety as a revolutionary thinker was the decision of Blech, in 1936, to change his name to William Blake in a profound acknowledgment of intellectual kinship and respect, and two years later the narrator of Stead's *House of All Nations* confirmed the essential promise of Adam, a young socialist employed in a dubious financial institution, by likening him to "the frail earthly first man hearing the strains of sun music in one of William Blake's dawn pictures." Other "sporadic affinities" between Blake and Stead have been noted (Green 69), and Angela Carter has credibly asserted that the most fitting motto for Stead's entire oeuvre would be: "Without Contraries is no progression. Attraction and Repulsion, Reason and Energy, Love and Hate, are necessary to Human existence" (262). And like most of her works, *The Man Who Loved Children* abounds in contraries. Most obviously, the lifestyles of Sam and Henny afford a series of binary oppositions. Sam is identified with scientific treatment of the natural world, a drive to order, name and create pedagogically rewarding exhibitions, with rule and the tables of the law, and linked with either Darwin or despotic czarism. Henny is aligned with great, mysterious forces, an esoteric personal space that affords joyous refuge or "a cave of Aladdin," with primal instinct and natural law; she is diversely cast as anarchist, perennial adversary, and hyena. Their clash, Carter suggests, may be read as an illustration of Blake's adage.

But what was Stead's attitude to this doctrine of contraries, and is it, of all Blake's tenets, the most important to an understanding of *The Man Who Loved Children*? *The Marriage of Heaven and Hell* asserts unambiguously that contraries are necessary to life itself. On plate 16 this article of faith is reiterated in terms relevant to Stead's novel:

> Thus one portion of being, is the Prolific, the other, the Devouring: to the devourer it seems as if the producer was in his chains, but it is not so, he only takes portions of existence and fancies that the whole.

> But the Prolific would cease to be Prolific unless the Devourer as a sea recieved [sic] the excess of his delights.

> These two classes of men are always upon earth, & they should be enemies; whoever

> MOREOVER, GIVEN STEAD'S NEED TO
> PORTRAY THIS COUPLE'S FLUCTUATING STATE OF
> TURMOIL, SHE WOULD PRESUMABLY HAVE BEEN
> DRAWN TO BLAKE'S MANY DEPICTIONS OF THE
> 'VARIOUS ARTS OF LOVE & HATE' PLAYED OUT
> BETWEEN THE SEXES."

tries to reconcile them seeks to destroy existence. (Blake 40)

Translated into breathing human situations, the unceasing enmity projected by Blake had little appeal to Stead. In *For Love Alone*, for instance, the narrator utters a damning *cri de coeur* about "the naked domestic drama and hate of parent and child" and its bleak consequences (463), while the last line of the novel resonates with Teresa's despair at the possible recurrence of a pair of contraries in herself and Jonathan: "'It's dreadful to think that it will go on being repeated for ever, he—and me! What's there to stop it?'" (502). Similarly, neither Stead nor Louie locates much that is positive in the war of attrition waged between Sam and Henny. In fact, it degenerates into bloodshed, saps their moral stature, and seems destructive of worthwhile human existence. Moreover, given Stead's need to portray this couple's fluctuating state of turmoil, she would presumably have been drawn to Blake's many depictions of the "various arts of Love & Hate" played out between the sexes. But less expected, and as elusive as Louie's "hard-soft" nightmare, is her interest in the Romantic's notion of the dialectics of vision, or the ability of a strong ideology or mindset to alter radically the reality perceived by others.

The Man Who Loved Children contains a brief, well-disguised allusion to a key scene in Blake's writing that deals with this issue. Again it appears in the course of an enigmatic, longer dream:

> As they stood in front of the snake cage, he said anxiously, "Kids, last night I was dozing on Bonniferous's [his sister's] bed...and I had my snake dream. Great snakes alive were crawling around da kitch [the kitchen] and out of one of my boxes jumped two beautiful

young spotted cats, ocelots, *Felis pardalis*, which relieved me considduble, because they began to fight the naiks [snakes], and then an ocelot with a snake curled round him and hissing at me tried to break through the netted back door here at me and I pushed with all my strength against them, crying out, but they gradually opened it, when I saw the door opened right on the city of Washington! There it was, with all its marbles like bones gleaming under me, and I hung on the edge of a precipice—it was the snake, or the bone yard!"

Visually compelling and personalized by Sam's idiolect, the dream nonetheless has complex literary antecedents. The novel's debt to Twain has been demonstrated (Arac 175–89), and the initial comic register and mayhem of the dream reveal a distant kinship with a scene of slapstick comedy in *The Adventures of Huckleberry Finn*, where another Sam (Samuel Clemens) depicts snakes, so laboriously collected by Huck and Tom Sawyer, escaping to run amok in Aunt Sally's home, which inspires Huck's laconic remark: "No, there warn't no real scarcity of snakes about the house for a considerble spell" (338–39). Embedded still deeper, a Blakean reference reverberates in the one incongruous line in the passage: "And I hung on the edge of a precipice"—an allusion clinched by the dominance of serpents in the scene and by the alternating visions of Washington.

The allusion, together with Blake's hallmark statement of the doctrine of contraries, is drawn from the longest "Memorable Fancy" of *The Marriage of Heaven and Hell*. It consists of two scenes of hellish menace, linked by an authorially endorsed explanation. In the first a self-assured Angel offers to show the young male speaker the perdition, or "hot burning dungeon," awaiting him for all eternity. A long descent through a cavern brings them to "a void boundless as a nether sky"—Stead's "precipice"—at whose edge they rest "suspended in ... [oak roots and] fungus which hung with the head downward into the deep." Beneath them in "the infinite Abyss, fiery as the smoke of a burning city," unfolds a series of terrifying scenes: "vast spiders, crawling after their prey," "animals sprung from corruption," and "a cataract of blood mixed with fire." When asked where the narrator's "eternal lot" lies, the Angel responds: "between the black & white spiders." All these, however, are eclipsed by a climactic image of infernal threat and retribution as Leviathan appears "a monstrous serpent... advancing toward us with all the fury of a spiritual existence" (41). The Angel, his intuitions of everlasting damnation confirmed, flees, leaving the narrator to make sense of a sudden visual reversal:

> I remain'd alone, & then this appearance was no more, but I found myself sitting on a pleasant bank beside a river by moon light hearing a harper, who sung to the harp. & his theme was, The man who never alters his opinion is like standing water, & breeds reptiles of the mind.
>
> ...I found my Angel, who surprised asked me, how I escaped?
>
> I answerd. All that we saw was owing to your metaphysics: for when you ran away, I found myself on a bank by moonlight hearing a harper, But now we have seen my eternal lot, shall I shew you yours? (41–42)

Then follows a satiric scene of apes cannibalizing each other, rounded off by a final antagonistic exchange: "So the Angel said: thy phantasy has imposed upon me & thou oughtest to be ashamed. / I answered: we impose on one another" (42).

The effect of mental impositions is Blake's primary concern. The central encounter involves three participants: the speaker, the Angel, and what they see before them in "the infinite Abyss." Blake registers two changes to this configuration. First, the Angel leaves (he "climb'd up from his station into the mill" [of analytical reason]); next, whatever is in front of the speaker undergoes a radical change of form: from Leviathan to harper. Nowhere, however, is there any indication that the principal constituent of the abyss has moved away. What alters are the audience's perceptions of it. Remove the Angel and what had assumed the shape of Leviathan metamorphoses into something far less threatening and more productive: a harper who advocates the need to alter individual opinions or mindsets. Blake's message, in a work that celebrates the redemptive uses of energy, is clear. To orthodoxy, unchained energy is unambiguously dangerous and infernal. To a viewer not subjected to the "mind-forg'd manacles" of institutional belief (27), the same energy is creative; and the theme of the harper, a figure akin to Blake's beloved poets and prophets, suggests that the preceding vision of Leviathan was a "reptile of the mind." ...

Source: Michael Ackland, "Breeding 'Reptiles of the Mind': Blake's Dialectics of Vision and Stead's Critique of Pollitry in *The Man Who Loved Children*," in *Studies in the Novel*, Vol. 38, No. 2, Summer 2006, pp. 234–49.

Brooke Allen

In the following excerpt, Allen discusses aspects of Stead's life and how they correlate to events in The Man Who Loved Children.

... The Australian-born novelist Christina Stead is an author whose reputation perpetually hovers somewhere between apotheosis and oblivion. As a novelist, she was one of those unfortunates whom critics admire in the abstract but often find distasteful or harsh in reality. She never achieved a popular or even a real critical success; during her lifetime she complained, with justification, that each new novel was greeted with cries of disappointment by reviewers, who accused it of not measuring up to her earlier books—books that themselves had all too often met with indifference, incomprehension, or hostility.

One of her publishers said that "Christina Stead is a writer who makes absolutely no concessions to the reader." This is true, and the result was that at no time during her life or beyond it could Stead be even remotely considered a popular writer. But her talent, raw and undisciplined as it undoubtedly was, has proved impossible to dismiss. Beginning in 1955 with Randall Jarrell's famous essay on *The Man Who Loved Children* in *The New York Times*, a handful of influential writers have urged the public to take notice of this largely ignored artist. While most of her books are out of print at any given time, publishers, ever hopeful, continue to put out new editions of the better-known and less "difficult" ones: this year Henry Holt is republishing *The Man Who Loved Children*, *I'm Dying Laughing*, and *The Little Hotel*. Holt is also bringing out a comprehensive biography by Hazel Rowley, the first that has been written.

But the ranks of Stead fans are unlikely to swell greatly, however hard her admirers try to share their enthusiasm. As many have pointed out, her prose is inaccessible to the casual reader—repetitive, verbose, often precious. At the same time Stead is insufficiently pretentious to appeal to the intellectual snob. She rejected the more self-conscious tricks of the second-string modernist, and while she was plainly influenced by Lawrence, Joyce, and Stein, the nineteenth-century masters—Balzac, Stendhal, Dickens, Thackeray, Goethe, Nietzsche, Strindberg, and many others— were really more important to her aesthetic. Clifton Fadiman, Stead's onetime editor and a lifelong admirer, knew that most readers would never

> HER TECHNIQUE OF TURNING LIFE INTO FICTION WAS STARTLINGLY RUDIMENTARY. SHE WOULD REPRODUCE HER MODEL'S SPEECH PATTERNS, APPEARANCE, LIFE CIRCUMSTANCES EXACTLY; SHE EVEN TRANSCRIBED THEIR LETTERS VERBATIM. STEAD'S NOVELS CAN IN EFFECT BE READ AS A CHRONICLE OF HER LIFE."

swallow Stead whole. "Her humor is savage, her learning hard to cope with, her fancies too furious. Like Emily Brontë, she has none of the proper bearing, the reassuring domestic countenance of a 'lady author.'"

In the American literary climate dominated for so many decades by the stylistic dogma of Hemingwayesque simplicity, Stead's all-over-the-map excess was viewed with puzzlement if not active annoyance, and Stead herself, much as she desired at least a modicum of popular recognition and the financial rewards that accompany it, never even paid lip service to middle-highbrow tastes: "That brainless pamphlet of monosyllables!" she raged when her publishers suggested that she write more in the style of Steinbeck's latest best seller. When she edited her work she might throw things away, but by throwing away she emphatically did not mean "what is called 'paring to the bone.'" Her own style was distinctly unfashionable.

> The sensuality, delicacy of literature does not exist for me [she once wrote]; only the passion, energy and struggle, the night of which no one speaks, the creative act: some people like to see the creative act banished from the book—it should be put behind one and a neatly-groomed little boy in sailor-collar introduced . .. But for me it is not right: I like each book to have not only the little boy, not very neat, but also the preceding creative act ... Most of my friends deplore this: they are always telling me what I should leave out in order to have "success." But I know that nothing has more success in the end than an intelligent ferocity.

The execution of such a credo virtually demands an anti-naturalistic style, and while Stead's prose is not exactly what most people call "experimental," it was also not what mid-century readers,

saturated in Hemingway/Steinbeck minimalism, thought of as realistic. Stead saw herself as serving psychological rather than literal truth, hence her practice of making all her characters far more articulate than their real-life models could possibly be. Marpurgo, the cosmopolitan lace-merchant in *The Beauties and the Furies*, speaks in a fashion which we should find hideously affected in a real person—nevertheless, he remains sympathetic to the reader: "Humidity height is bad for the lesion: I was born for the nocturnes, the chiaroscuro, but a soggy lung makes indwelling constant, for relief, sustenance, it insists on the dry fresco of midday." One could criticize this kind of stylistic liberty at length, even mock it, but Stead's own words of justification ought first to be considered:

> My purpose, in making characters eloquent, is the expression of two psychological truths; first, that everyone has a wit superior to his everyday wit, when discussing his personal problems and the most depressed housewife, for example, can talk like Medea about her troubles; second, that everyone, to a greater or lesser extent, is a fountain of passion, which is turned by circumstances of birth or upbringing into conventional channels.

If Stead saw her characters as fountains of passion, it is because she knew herself to be one. As a plain, unloved Australian schoolgirl she saw herself as a Nietzschean heroine; as a lonely elderly woman she concocted a romantic "past" for herself and almost succeeded in making herself believe that she was an object of sexual desire to the most glamorous men of her acquaintance. Speaking of Louisa Pollit, Stead's alter-ego in *The Man Who Loved Children*, Randall Jarrell pointed out that "it is ugly ducklings, grown either into swans or into remarkably big, remarkably ugly ducks, who are responsible for most works of art." Christina Stead was fated to become one of those big, ugly ducks. To her credit, she had the courage to acknowledge her passionate nature rather than set it into "conventional channels," though she was often humiliated and made to look ridiculous for her sexual aggression.

It is not only in her two autobiographical novels, *The Man Who Loved Children* (1940) and *For Love Alone* (1944), that Christina Stead fictionalized herself and the people she knew. All of her novels were based on real people, the cruelest portraits of all, the real "monsters," on people who had had reason over the years to consider her a good friend. Her technique of turning life into fiction was startlingly rudimentary. She would reproduce her model's speech patterns, appearance, life circumstances exactly; she even transcribed their letters verbatim. Stead's novels can in effect be read as a chronicle of her life. Her lifelong tirade against the libel laws was hardly disinterested.

Though she spent her first twenty-six years in Australia (she was born in 1902), it is doubtful whether Stead in later life felt "Australian," and it is equally doubtful whether Australia liked to consider her a native daughter. Stead was too European and too intellectual. She made her home abroad, and with few exceptions she set her novels there, too. The Australian intelligentsia had always suffered from what one writer memorably termed "cultural cringe," an attitude both deferential and defensive toward European cultural products and institutions. The pull of London, Paris, and New York had stripped Australia of many of her best artists: during Stead's childhood, Miles Franklin moved to America, and Henry Handel Richardson, the most important Australian writer of the period, had been living in Europe for years. As an expatriate, Stead was resentfully branded "un-Australian," a label that was to color her reputation in her native country for the rest of her life.

Stead's childhood, described unforgettably and almost literally in *The Man Who Loved Children*, was a bitterly unhappy one. Her father, David Stead, was a self-educated naturalist who eventually became the General Manager of the State Trawling Industry and co-founder of the Wildlife Preservation Society of Australia. Stead characterized him as "Huxley-Darwin reasonable-rational nature-agnostic mother-of-all-things-fresh-air-panacea eclectic-socialist universal-peace-manhood suffrage-and-vegetarianism of the English breed, inheriting from the eighteenth century age of light and Jean-Jacques ..." David was a strange combination of atheist and Puritan, allowing no tobacco or alcohol, no kissing, dancing, or embracing in the home. Christina's mother, Ellen Butters, died when her daughter was two, and David then married Ada Gibbins, a delicate girl from a faded-genteel background, totally unsuited to the life of poverty and squalor the Stead family eventually descended to. Before her marriage, she had never learned anything but "water-color-painting, embroidery, and the playing of Chopin."

> My stepmother did not like me, very natural, as I was the kind of child only a mother could love

and then probably with doubts: her treatment of me was dubious. Sometimes servants thought I was my father's illegitimate child, at other times, they fancied I was an orphan on my stepmother's side: friends who came to the house took me aside and told me what I owed the kind people who had taken me in.

But while Stead obviously despises the furious, impotent Henny Pollit, Ada's representative in *The Man Who Loved Children*, she retains, too, a certain amount of sympathy for her, trapped as she is in a hated union. It is for the father, Sam, that Stead reserves the full force of her hatred. Of all Stead's monstrous characters, Sam is the greatest monster, because he is the most supreme egotist. Other people, especially his own children, have no independent life for Sam; he sees them only as the very palest reflections of himself. He loves little children because he can be their god, and he forces his way into the very center of their small lives, tirelessly organizing games and fantasies. He speaks to them in a playful dialect, a cross between Uncle Remus and Artemus Ward—a dialect that eventually enrages the reader as Sam uses it to deflect every challenge and confrontation.

Sam is less fond of older children, children who have reached the age of dissent, and *The Man Who Loved Children* is in large part an account of the conflict between Sam and the adolescent Louisa. Louisa is brilliant, angry, and powerless. Her every assertion of intellectual independence is annexed by Sam into his own story, her every experience is made somehow less authentic than his own.

> "You cannot appreciate what I mean and will not for years to come, perhaps never. My sorrows, while all the time I was struggling upward, were more than man should bear."
>
> "I had sorrows too," she piped up.
>
> "I know, Looloo, I know," he said hastily, squeezing her hand. "We are close to each other: you are nearly of an age to begin to understand me."

As Louie makes her strikes for independence, Sam becomes cruel, even sadistic, in his efforts to retain her as his satellite, prying among her things, forcing her to read her diaries aloud, ridiculing her appearance—"You'll find your place in the world, Looloo, but whatever we eventually find in that mountain of fat, it isn't going to be a Pavlova!" Louie, meanwhile, who sees herself as Beatrice in *The Cenci*, bides her time, plans her escape, and keeps in mind

Nietzsche's exhortation to throw not away the hero in her soul—for within the unlikely person of this tubby schoolgirl is a Nietzschean heroine, as she proves at the end of the book, when her achieved act of will brings the Pollits' untenable life to a sort of resolution.

Clifton Fadiman wrote about Sam that "you're ready to scream at him as if he were not a character in a book but a man in your living room"—somewhat in the manner of the characters in *Who's Afraid of Virginia Woolf*. This infuriating but powerful effect is achieved partly through force of repetition, a technique Stead always used to an unorthodox degree. In all of her novels she treads a very fine line between the power of controlled reiteration and the diffusion caused by an ill-disciplined unwillingness to edit.

What Stead achieved with Sam Pollit was a character who is at once unique and universal: however different he is from one's own parents, he still represents the abstract notion of Parent. This is because Stead penetrated the secret that egotism is an essential condition of parenthood, that all parents are wounded to the heart to think that their children have an emotional and intellectual life independent of them; some parents, like Sam, never accept the existence of that life at all. This universality is why *The Man Who Loved Children* has survived where another book, *I'm Dying Laughing*, equally interesting and well-written, is hardly known. The former is a critique of family life as memorable as *The Way of All Flesh*; the latter is very much of a particular historical moment, and fatally inscribed within it. ...

Source: Brooke Allen, "'A Real Inferno': The Life of Christina Stead," in *New Criterion*, Vol. 13, No. 2, October 1994, 16 pp.

SOURCES

Pollitt, Katha, "A Monster of Selfishness and Irresponsibility," in *Slate*, March 6, 2001, http://www.slate.com/id/2000238/entry/1007210/ (accessed July 27, 2007).

Sheridan, Susan, "A Challenge to Feminist Criticism," in *Christina Stead*, Indiana University Press, 1988, p. 9.

Stead, Christina, *The Man Who Loved Children*, Picador Press, 2001.

"There's No Place Like Home," in *Time*, April 2, 1965, http://www.time.com/time/magazine/article/0,9171,941052,00.html (accessed July 27, 2007).

FURTHER READING

Blake, Ann, *Christina Stead's Politics of Place*, University of Western Australia Press, 1999.
This book traces Stead's travels as an expatriate throughout her adult life and the development of her political sensibilities, and charts how her political development is reflected in her fiction.

Lidoff, Joan, "Family Fictions: *The Man Who Loved Children*," in *Christina Stead* Frederick Ungar Publishing, 1982, pp. 14–56.
This chapter of Lidoff's book on Stead analyzes the major characters from the novel one at a time, discussing them both independently of one another, and exploring how they work together as a family unit.

Peterson, Teresa, *The Enigmatic Christina Stead: A Provocative Re-Reading*, Melbourne University Press, 2001.
Rather than focusing on an analysis of *The Man Who Loved Children*, as so many critical studies of Stead do, Peterson works around the novel, examining Stead's other major works with a depth that they seldom receive elsewhere.

Stewart, Ken, "Heaven and Hell in *The Man Who Loved Children*," in *The Magic Phrase: Critical Essays on Christina Stead*, edited by Margaret Harris, University of Queensland Press, 2001, pp. 133–44.
As its title indicates, Stewart's essay contrasts the elements of the divine in the novel with the hellish imagery that appears throughout the story.

West, Diana, *The Death of the Grown-Up: How America's Arrested Development is Bringing Down Western Civilization*, St. Martin's Press, 2007.
This recent study traces the phenomenon that Stead attributes to Sam Pollit in the novel: a fixation with the toys and games of childhood and the worldview of the child. In West's analysis, this attitude is widespread today and dangerous to society as a whole.

My Name Is Red

ORHAN PAMUK

2001

My Name Is Red is a novel by Turkish writer Orhan Pamuk, who won the Nobel Prize for Literature in 2006. Set in Istanbul, the capital city of the powerful Ottoman Empire, in 1591, the novel functions at many different levels. Covering a period of about a week, it is at once a murder mystery, a love story, and an examination of the cultural tensions between East and West. These tensions center around different theories of art. The Ottoman Sultan has commissioned an illustrated book to celebrate the power of his empire, and he has ordered that the paintings employ the techniques of the Italian Renaissance, in which the use of perspective and shadow create realistic portraits that are quite different from the stylized representations of Islamic tradition. The use of the new style creates fear amongst the artists commissioned to produce the book, and two murders are the result. Black, an artist who has just returned to Istanbul and is courting the beautiful Shekure, is told by the Sultan that he must solve the case within three days or he and the other master artists will be tortured. With its theme of East-West conflict, and its examination of what happens when Western ideas creep into a restrictive Islamic society, *My Name Is Red*, although set four hundred years ago, has much relevance for the cultural conflicts of today.

A recent edition of the story, translated from the Turkish by Erdağ M. Göknar, was released by Vintage International in 2002.

Orhan Pamuk (*AP Images*)

AUTHOR BIOGRAPHY

Orhan Pamuk was born in Istanbul, Turkey, on June 7, 1952, and grew up in a large family in a wealthy area of the city. When he was a child he acquired an interest in painting and wanted to become an artist, a desire he entertained until he was in his early twenties.

Pamuk graduated from the American Robert College in Istanbul and studied architecture for three years at Istanbul Technical University. But he decided not to pursue his earlier goals of becoming an artist or architect and instead turned to journalism. He graduated from the Institute of Journalism at the University of Istanbul in 1976. However, he never pursued a career in journalism. Instead, at the age of twenty-three, he decided to become a novelist. For the next seven years, he lived with his parents, who supported his writing.

Pamuk's first novel, *Cevdet Bey ve ogullari: roman*, was published in 1982. It is the story of three generations of a wealthy family living in Istanbul. Pamuk then wrote *Sessiz ev: roman* (1983). His third novel, *Beyaz kale: roman*

(1985), was translated into English and published as *The White Castle: A Novel* (1990 in England, 1991 in the United States). About the interaction between East and West in Istanbul, the novel earned Pamuk an international reputation.

Pamuk was a visiting scholar at Columbia University, New York, from 1985 to 1988. During this time he wrote most of his next novel, *Kara Kitap*, which was published in Turkey in 1990 and in the United States in 1994 as *The Black Book*. *Yeni hayat* (1994) was translated as *The New Life* (1997).

Benim Adim Kirmizi (2000) was translated from Turkish and first published as *My Name Is Red* in the United States in 2001. The novel won the French Prix Du Meilleur Livre Étranger (2001), the Italian Grinzane Cavour (2002) and the prestigious International IMPAC Dublin literary award (2003).

Kar (2002) published in English as *Snow* (2002), which Pamuk described as the only political novel he has written, is about tensions between political Islamists, secularists, and Kurdish and Turkish nationalists.

Over the years, Pamuk has been critical of the Turkish government over human rights issues, and in 2005, he was subjected to criminal charges over remarks he made in an interview with a Swiss magazine. Pamuk commented that thirty thousand Kurds had been killed in the conflict between Kurdish nationalists and Turkish security forces, and that a million Armenians were killed in Turkey in 1915, but that no one spoke about it.

After an international outcry, the charges against Pamuk were dropped in January 2006. He has subsequently stated that his intent in making the controversial statements was to draw attention to freedom of expression issues in Turkey.

In 2006, Pamuk was awarded the 2006 Nobel Prize in literature. In the same year, he was appointed visiting professor at Columbia University. As of 2007, Pamuk is a Fellow with Columbia University's Committee on Global Thought.

PLOT SUMMARY

Chapters 1–10

Set in a winter in Istanbul in 1591, *My Name Is Red* is told in brief chapters by multiple narrators; the narrator is identified in the heading of each chapter. Chapter 1 is told by a murdered man whose as-yet-undiscovered-corpse lies at the bottom of a well. His name was Elegant and he was an artist working on illustrations for a secret book commissioned by the Sultan.

Chapter 2 is narrated by Black, who has just returned to Istanbul after a twelve-year absence. For all that time he has been in love with his cousin, Shekure. He is returning to Istanbul at the invitation of his uncle, Enishte, to whom he was formerly apprenticed. Enishte is also an artist, and it is he who is in charge of preparing the secret book for the Sultan. Enishte has asked Black for assistance, since Black has experience commissioning artists. Black walks the streets of Istanbul and enters a coffeehouse, in which a storyteller has hung a picture of a dog. He is giving voice to the dog and pointing at the drawing. The next chapter is narrated by the dog. He questions why some people dislike dogs.

Chapter 4 is narrated by the man who murdered Elegant, although he does not identify himself. He is also in the coffeehouse, and he reveals that, he, like Elegant, is a miniaturist. He discusses what it feels like to be a murderer and reveals that Elegant had believed the illustrations they were doing were heretical. The murderer feared that they would all be denounced to the fundamentalists.

Chapter 5 is narrated by Enishte, Black's uncle, who recalls the circumstances of Black's departure, twelve years ago. This happened because Black fell in love with Enishte's daughter, Shekure, but was not considered a suitable match, so he was asked to leave the house. Several years later, Shekure married a cavalryman and had two children. But her husband, after going off to war, has now been missing for four years. Enishte tells Black that the portrait of the Sultan that is to be included in the secret book will be painted in the Venetian style, as a genuine portrait of the man. This will be a departure from the impersonal style of the Islamic miniaturists.

Chapter 6 is told by Orhan, Shekure's six-year-old son. Orhan overhears his grandfather telling Black that he thinks Elegant was murdered because of the controversial nature of his work, even though Elegant worked in the old style. Orhan and his brother Shevket misbehave and their mother makes them wait in the kitchen until Black leaves.

Black takes up the story in chapter 7. He relates his feelings on visiting Enishte's house. He desperately wants to see Shekure again. Enishte tells him he must visit all the miniaturists working on the book, as well as Master Osman, the Head Illuminator. As he rides away, a clothes peddler named Esther hands him a letter from Shekure, and he also catches a glimpse of Shekure's face in the window.

In chapter 8, Esther, who delivers letters as she hawks her wares around the city, relates how she came to deliver the letter to Black. She knows that Shekure has told Black not to return. Esther guesses, however, that Shekure does not mean what she says.

Shekure tells her own story in chapter 9. She confirms Esther's intuition that she does not want to discourage Black, and also tells the story of how she fell in love with her husband. After he went missing, she had to move back in with her father. She knows that Hasan, her brother-in-law, wants to marry her, but she does not want to marry him.

Chapter 10 is told by a tree, which says it does not want to be depicted in the Western, Venetian style, like a real tree. Instead, it wants to reveal what the meaning of a tree is.

Chapters 11–20

Black is the narrator in chapter 11. He reads Shekure's letter and dreams of being married. In the morning he visits the royal artisans' workshop, and senses that Master Osman is suspicious of him. Osman reveals that the miniaturists Olive, Stork, and Butterfly work on the special book—not at the workshop but at home. Black is given a tour of the workshop, and on his way back he gives Esther a letter for Shekure.

The next three chapters are related by, respectively, Butterfly, Stork, and Olive. Each artist receives a visit from Black, who questions them about their philosophical approach to art and looks at some of their paintings. Each artist tells three stories that allude to the matter of artistic style (Butterfly), the nature of painting and time (Stork), and blindness and memory (Olive). Black observes everything in their homes, searching for any clue to Elegant's disappearance. News arrives that Elegant's body has been found.

Chapters 15 and 16, narrated by Esther and Shekure respectively, return to the love story of Black and Shekure. Esther visits Hasan and shows him the letter Black has written to Shekure, in which he says he wants to marry her. Hasan, who also wants Shekure, gives Esther a letter he has written to Shekure. He asks Esther what he can do to convince Shekure and her father that he would make a suitable husband. Shekure is confused by the situation.

In chapter 17, Enishte tells of his attendance at Elegant's funeral. Butterfly tells him that the miniaturists were jealous of one another over who would assume leadership of the workshop after Master Osman died. Butterfly admits that he had a bad relationship with Elegant, but believes Olive and Stork are exploiting this in order to blame him for the murder.

Chapter 18 is narrated by the murderer, who attended Elegant's funeral and wept more than anyone else at the graveside. Chapter 19 is told by a gold coin, which narrates its travels across Istanbul.

The story returns to Black's viewpoint. He listens to Enishte speak of the portraits he had seen in Venice, where portraiture is popular amongst the affluent. Enishte is both attracted to the portraits and appalled by them.

Chapters 21–30

In chapter 21 (told from Enishte's point of view), Enishte explains to Black how he had persuaded the Sultan to fund the secret book, and that the last picture was nearly finished. He shows Black a picture of Death, painted by Butterfly, and all the other illustrations to the book. Black goes home thinking of Shekure, believing that she was watching him while he visited her father. He contemplates the task Enishte has given him, which is to write a story to accompany each illustration in the book, and he knows he must do this if he is to win Shekure.

In chapter 23, which is narrated by the murderer, the culprit describes how tormented he is following the murder. He reveals that he is also in love with Shekure. In the next chapter, Death reveals that the miniaturist who was persuaded by Enishte to illustrate Death regrets his decision because in painting the picture, he was unwittingly imitating the Frankish (Western) method.

Esther narrates how, in a letter, Shekure tells Black that he must complete the manuscript if he is to win her love. Black asks her to meet him at an abandoned house.

In chapter 26, Shekure tells of reading Hasan's letter, in which he says that he is going to the judge in order to force her to live with him. Shekure ignores Hasan's letter but agrees to meet Black at the abandoned house. When they meet, they embrace and kiss. In chapter 27, Black agrees to testify that he has seen the corpse of her husband, so that she can be declared a widow and be free to marry him.

Chapter 28 is narrated by the murderer, who visits Enishte and tells him about the rumors that the book they are preparing is blasphemous. He is worried about the final illustration and fears it is painted in the Frankish style. Enishte replies that two styles can be brought together to create something new. But the two men grow suspicious of each other, and then the murderer confesses that he killed Elegant.

The narration is taken up by Enishte in chapter 29, who fears that the murderer will kill him, too. After a lengthy discussion about the nature of painting, the murderer hits him on the head with an ink pot, killing him.

Shekure narrates how, when she comes home, (Chapter 30) she discovers her father's body. She moves it into a back room and tells the children that their grandfather is sleeping. She informs Hayrire of the murder but tells her to behave as if nothing has happened.

Chapters 31–40

After chapter 31 is narrated by the color red, Shekure continues the story. She tells Black she wants to conceal Enishte's death because otherwise Hasan and his father will be appointed her guardians. She says that she will marry Black, but until the murderer is caught and the Sultan's book is finished, she will not share his bed. Chapter 32 is then narrated by Black, who bribes the authorities to grant Shekure a divorce. At the wedding ceremony, the dead Enishte is dressed in nightclothes, as if he were sick, so he can act as Shekure's guardian.

After the wedding, Shekure and Black agree, in chapter 34 (told by Shekure), to announce in the morning that Enishte has died in his sleep. Shekure awakes during the night, goes outside and finds Hasan and Black arguing. Hasan claims the marriage is invalid. He also claims that Shekure, in league with Black, killed her father. He says he will forgive her if she returns to live with him. Black responds by accusing Hasan of killing Enishte.

Chapter 35 is narrated by a horse, who argues in favor of the Frankish style of painting. In the morning, Shekure announces Enishte's death. Black gets an audience with the Head Treasurer and tells him that he suspects the secret book Enishte was working on was the cause of his murder because it fostered jealousy among the artists.

In chapter 37, the dead Enishte tells of his public funeral, which was attended by many dignitaries. He says his soul is at peace. Chapter 38 is narrated by Master Osman, who is summoned to a meeting with the Head Treasurer and the Commander of the Imperial Guard. The Head Treasurer says the Sultan is furious that Enishte has been murdered. He wants the book finished and the murderer caught. Black, Olive, Stork, and Butterfly are all suspects. The Commander says he is authorized to torture Black and the others if necessary during interrogation.

Chapter 39 is narrated by Esther. Esther visits the widow of Elegant, who informs her of some sketches of horses that were found with the body of her husband. Since Elegant did not draw horses, they might be the work of the murderer. In chapter 40, Black tells readers that he is summoned to the palace, where he is tortured. He denies knowing anything of Elegant's murder, and Master Osman informs him that the torture was only a test. But Osman also informs him that unless he finds the murderer within three days, as well as the missing final illustration, he will be the first to be tortured.

Chapters 41–50

Master Osman tells of how he and Black examine illustrations from the secret book to determine which miniaturist illustrated which one. Osman dislikes the pictures and has no desire to finish the book. With Black, Osman discusses the talents and temperaments of Olive, Butterfly, and Stork. He reveals that he favors Butterfly to succeed him as leader of the workshop because he is the only one who could resist the lure of Venetian artistry.

In chapter 42, narrated by Black, Shekure's letter enclosing the sketches of the horses is delivered to the palace, where Master Osman and Black receive it. They try to match the

sketches to an illustration of a horse in the secret book, concluding that they were drawn by the same hand. They notice that the horse's nostrils are drawn oddly. It is a clue as to which miniaturist might have drawn the picture. They examine hundreds of other horses painted by Butterfly, Stork, and Olive, but none of them bear this peculiarity. Master Osman suggests to the Sultan that they ask each miniaturist to draw a horse quickly and say it is for a contest.

In chapters 43–45, Olive, Butterfly, and Stork respectively narrate how they were asked to draw a horse to see who could draw the best horse in the shortest time. They describe their technique. In chapter 46, the murderer reveals that he knew it was not a competition, and that the authorities wanted to catch him. However, he believes he has no peculiarity of style that will betray him.

Chapter 47 is narrated by Satan, who has just been identified by the murderer as the being who first separated East and West by asserting his own individuality and thus, in artistic terms, adopting a particular style. But Satan refutes this argument, which is also put forward by the fundamentalists.

Chapter 48 returns to Shekure's point of view. She has doubts about her decision to marry Black. Black tries to reassure her by saying how much he loves her. Black (in chapter 49) goes to the palace, where Master Osman tells him that they are unable to determine from the three horse illustrations who drew the horse in the sketches found on Elegant. Osman persuades the Sultan to allow him to examine centuries-old books in the Treasury to find out whether the unusual depiction of the horse's nose is a mistake or whether it reflects other techniques from the past. They examine thousands of pictures.

Chapter 50 is related by two dervishes, characters in a painting over one hundred years old rendered in the Venetian style.

Chapters 51–59

In chapter 51, Master Osman relates how he spends the entire night in the Treasury with Black studying thousands of illustrations. He feels deep affection for all the masters of old, and he relives with delight all the years he has labored as a painter. He knows that the artistic world he knew is coming to an end. After studying the legendary *Book of Kings*, he finds the needle that the great master Bihzad had used to blind himself. Knowing that he cannot prevent the spread of the new method of painting, Osman presses the needle into his eyes, which means he will soon go blind.

Chapter 52 is narrated by Black, who discovers in an album a picture of a horse with peculiar nostrils and takes it to Osman. Osman identifies the nose as resembling the noses of Mongol horses, who had their nostrils cut open. It is painted in the Chinese style. Osman then says he thinks Olive is the one who drew the horses in Enishte's book, because he is the one who best knows the old styles. But he does not believe Olive is the murderer, because both Olive and Elegant were devoted to the old methods. Osman believes the murderer was Stork. Black is confused, and even suspects that Osman orchestrated the murders. As he leaves the Treasury he takes with him the needle that Bihzad and Osman used to blind themselves.

Chapter 53 is narrated by Esther, who receives a visit from Black. She informs him that Shekure's former husband is on his way back and that Shekure and her sons are now living at Hasan's home. Black and some armed men go to the house. Hasan is not at home so Black sends Shekure a note. Esther notes how confused she is, ready to love either Black or Hasan if either of them prove to be a good father to her boys. She finds out that the former husband is not really returning; that was Hasan's lie. Black and his men attack the house although they do not enter it. Eventually Shekure agrees to return to live with Black.

After a chapter narrated by a man who dresses as a woman, the story returns to Butterfly's point of view in chapter 55. Butterfly reports an attack by the followers of a fundamentalist preacher on a coffeehouse. On his way back, Butterfly is accosted by Black, who presses a dagger to his throat. Black forces Butterfly back to Butterfly's house, telling him he is going to search it. He wants to find the final, missing illustration. At the house, Butterfly turns the tables on Black, pinning him to the ground and threatening to kill him. Butterfly is worried that Stork and Olive are conspiring against him, and he convinces Black to accompany him to Olive's house. Olive is not at home.

In chapter 56, narrated by Stork, they arrive at Stork's house, ransack his possessions and quiz him about which miniaturist drew certain pictures for the storyteller in the coffeehouse. Eventually they all decide to join forces, since they are scared of Master Osman and the

tortures they may all face, and they find Olive at a dervish lodge. Chapter 57 is narrated by Olive, who claims he was not the one who drew the horse with the peculiar nostrils, but Black and Stork search his rooms anyway. Chapter 58 is then narrated by the murderer. The other miniaturists attack him, and Black thrusts a needle into his eyes. He finally confesses to the murders and reveals the missing illustration. It is not a portrait of the Sultan but of the murderer himself, who feels guilty about painting a self-portrait in the Venetian style. The murderer, now revealed as Olive, attempts to flee. He attacks and injures Black and then runs out and heads for the harbor. He is intercepted by Hasan, who beheads him with his sword.

The story is completed in Shekure's voice. She nurses the wounded Black back to health. He remains melancholy but retains his interest in painting. Enishte's book remains unfinished; Stork became Head Illuminator following Master Osman's death. Butterfly devotes his life to drawing ornamental designs for carpets and tents.

CHARACTERS

Black

Black is the nephew of Enishte. In Black's youth, Enishte enrolled him at the artisans' workshop, but he preferred a bureaucratic post. When he was twenty-four, Black fell in love with Shekure, but his uncle did not consider him a suitable match, and he was asked to leave the house. He then traveled extensively. While in Tabriz, he produced books for pashas and other wealthy patrons, dealing directly with the artists. He was also in the service of various pashas as clerk or treasurer's secretary. On his travels he witnessed many battles, and he has written a history of the Persian wars that he plans to present to the Sultan. Black is a cultured man who regards himself as a connoisseur of illustrating and decoration. He returns to Istanbul at the age of thirty-six at the request of Enishte. He is still in love with Shekure and wants to marry her. Black is tall, thin, and handsome, and Enishte regards him as a determined, mature, and respectful nephew.

Butterfly

Butterfly is one of the four master miniaturists selected to work on the secret book for the Sultan. Butterfly thinks he is the best artist since he makes the most money. He enjoys his work and has recently married a woman whom he regards as the most beautiful in the neighborhood. Enishte also thinks Butterfly is the most talented artist, and says Master Osman was in awe of him for years. Master Osman confirms this in his own reminiscences, saying that Butterfly was so handsome in his youth that people could hardly believe it and took a second look. As an artist, Butterfly's strength is in applying color, and according to Master Osman, he paints from the heart. But Osman also regards Butterfly as flighty and indecisive.

Elegant

Elegant was a master miniaturist who embellished books, coloring the borders with designs of leaves, branches, roses, flowers, and birds. When he was younger, he would decorate a plate or a ceiling, but he decided to work only on manuscript pages because the Sultan paid well for them. Elegant was murdered just before the story begins. He had been afraid that the illustrated book he and the others were working on was blasphemous, and it appears that he was murdered because of fears that he would denounce the entire project to the religious fundamentalists, thus endangering everyone who has worked on it. It also appears that Elegant was greedy for money; Shekure thinks he was ugly and spiritually impoverished.

Enishte

Enishte is Black's uncle. His wife and three sons are dead, and he lives with his daughter Shekure. Enishte aspires to be a venerable elder, and he has no objection to Shekure marrying a suitable man but insists that she should remain living in his house. However, Shekure fears that Enishte would not respect a son-in-law who was willing to live in his house and would soon start to belittle him.

Enishte is a former artist who has been commissioned by the Sultan to prepare a special book of illustrations, which are to be painted in the Western style, a style Enishte admires. This brings Enishte, who does not have the standing of a master illustrator, into conflict with Master Osman, who is a traditionalist. The two men dislike each other.

After the murder of Elegant, Enishte fears that he may also be murdered because of his involvement with the controversial book. At one point he decides to discontinue his involvement with it, but quickly reverses his decision. His fear of being murdered is justified, however, since this is to be his fate, killed by the same man who murdered Elegant.

Esther

Esther is an overweight Jewish woman who roams the streets of Istanbul selling clothing. She also acts as letter courier, mediator, and matchmaker. She has few principles, and thinks nothing of reading people's letters, even though she is illiterate and has to get someone else to read them for her. She allows Hasan, for example, to read the letters Black sends to Shekure. Esther is boisterous, good-natured, and lively, with a good understanding of human nature and the ways of the world. As a Jew in an Islamic city, she is forced to wear a pink dress.

Hasan

Hasan is Shekure's brother-in-law. He is in love with Shekure and seeks to force her to marry him. For a while after Shekure's husband went missing, he and Shekure lived together. But although Shekure liked his humble demeanor, and the fact that he played well with her children, he alienated her by forcing her to do housework, and this prevented her from loving him. Hasan, although he has an aggressive, belligerent element to his personality, lacks confidence and knows that Shekure will never love him. Because of this he tries to force her to return to live with him by getting a judicial order to this effect. When Shekure marries Black, Hasan accuses her of entering into an invalid marriage, but his protests lead nowhere, although for a brief time after Enishte's murder he does persuade her to live with him. At the end of the novel, it is Hasan who kills the murderer, believing that he is one of the men who took part in a raid on Hasan's house to abduct Shekure.

Hayrire

Hayrire is a slave girl in Enishte's house. She is also his mistress. Shekure suspects that she may have had a child by Enishte and that she is maneuvering to become mistress of the house.

Nusret Hoja

Nusret Hoja of Erzurum is a fundamentalist preacher who claims that recent disasters in Istanbul, such as plagues, fires, and wars with the Persians, happened because people have strayed from the path of Islam.

Olive

Olive is one of the four master miniaturists who are working on the illustrations for the secret book. In the chapters he relates, he reveals very little about himself, although he does let slip that he is conceited about his own abilities and thinks the other artists are jealous of him. Master Osman, who has known Olive since he was an apprentice, regards him as quiet and sensitive, but also proud and wily, and the most devious of the master artists. But Osman does not believe Olive is the murderer, and he has a high opinion of his talent, commenting that Olive comes from a long line of masters. Black believes that Olive is enthusiastic about the Frankish style favored by Enishte, although nothing Olive says confirms this, until the startling revelation at the end of the novel. Olive is ultimately exposed as the murderer.

Orhan

Orhan is the six-year-old son of Shekure. He is a mischievous boy who is constantly quarreling with his older brother. Black thinks he is sensitive and astute.

Master Osman

Master Osman is the ninety-two-year-old Head Illuminator. Regarded as a great master, he is half-blind. Gaunt and bony, he admits he is short-tempered and complains about everything. His virtue is that he has devoted his entire life to art, but Enishte despises him and calls him senile because of his allegiance to the old methods and his hatred of innovation. Master Osman has similar feelings about Enishte. Master Osman loathes the idea of imitating European artists and reveres the old masters. He claims that sixty years ago he met the great master Bizhad and kissed his hand. Master Osman's knowledge is vast and he identifies strongly with the dedication and the suffering of all the artists of the past, whose lifelong labors often ended in blindness. Eventually, realizing that the world he loves is coming to an end and there is nothing he can do to stop the advance of the Venetian style, he chooses to blind himself.

Shekure

Shekure is the daughter of Enishte, with whom she lives, along with her two young sons. Shekure is twenty-four years old; she is beautiful and intelligent and knows her own worth. However, she is in a dilemma. Her husband, a military man, has gone missing in the war, and she finds herself courted by two men, Hasan, her brother-in-law, and Black. She appears to put Black off, but really she is attracted to him. Shekure is a wily woman who does not always tell the whole truth, and she is often confused about her situation, wanting the best for her children, needing to please her father, and not sure of her own affections. After her husband disappeared, she fell upon hard times and had to go to live with Hasan, who sold their slave and made her do housework that she detested. So she is unwilling to marry him, fearing that she would become his slave rather than his wife. Eventually she agrees to marry Black, although she says he must solve the mystery of the murders and finish the Sultan's book before she will sleep with him.

Shevket

Shevket is the seven-year-old son of Shekure. His grandfather, Enishte, describes him as stubborn, but Black tells Shekure he thinks Shevket is strong, honest, intelligent, and decisive as well as stubborn.

Stork

Stork is one of the four master miniaturists who is working on the secret book for the Sultan. He was the first Muslim illustrator to go on a military campaign with the army and depict the scenes of battle. Stork also acquired a reputation as one who liked to depict gory scenes. When he talks about his craft, he says he commits everything he sees to memory, and Master Osman notes how Stork observes every obscure detail. Master Osman recalls how Stork committed to paper what no one before him had been able to do, but he also regards Stork as ambitious and conceited. He is a hard worker, and if left to himself, he would make all the illustrations in the workshop himself. Although according to Master Osman, Stork's approach resembles that of the Venetians, he did not depict people's faces as individual or distinct since he did not consider faces important. Master Osman believes, incorrectly, that Stork is the murderer.

The Sultan

The Sultan appears directly only once, when Master Osman and Black are in the palace. Black is almost overwhelmed by the sight of the man and throws himself at his feet. He is struck by the Sultan's dignity and handsome appearance. The Sultan takes an active interest in the illustrations for the book, and he orders that the murderer of Elegant and Enishte be quickly found.

THEMES

The Clash between East and West

At the heart of the novel is the clash between Eastern and Western methods of painting, which reflect different ways of seeing the world. The painter of Islamic miniatures followed tradition. He would imitate the work of previous masters; there was no question of cultivating originality, a personal style or an individual technique. He saw no need to sign his name somewhere in the picture. Individual creativity was frowned upon because creativity was considered the preserve not of man but of Allah.

The Islamic miniaturist attempted to represent the world from the point of view of Allah, from high above, so to speak, whereas the European painters of the Renaissance adopted a human point of view, developing the art of portraiture, in which every minute detail of an individual was represented. Islamic miniaturists depicted individuals in a more impersonal way. For example, Black sees an illustration at the artisans' workshop in which the Sultan's face is drawn adeptly, but "not so detailed as to permit one to distinguish Him from others by features alone." In contrast, in the Venetian style, individual portraits were clearly of one particular person and could not be mistaken for anyone else. Traditionalists such as Master Osman are appalled by this new method, which to them raises man to the center of the universe and therefore borders on the blasphemous. In the Venetian style, the painting exists for its own sake, whereas in traditional Islamic art, the miniaturists are only illustrating a story, not creating something that stands alone. The traditionalists fear that if they adopt the Venetian style, eventually the picture will become an object of worship in its own right. They are also alarmed by the use of perspective. Those who oppose the Venetian style regard it as a sin to draw a dog,

TOPICS FOR FURTHER STUDY

- Pick one of your favorite artists from any period in history and show how his or her paintings change the way you see the world. Make a class presentation in which you present images from your selected artist. Discuss the different aspects of the artist's work that you respond to.

- Find some examples of Renaissance art, such as paintings by Giovanni Bellini or Tiziano Vecellio (better known as Titian), and compare them in detail with some examples of Turkish miniature paintings. Make a list of all the differences you see. Is it fair to say, as it says in the novel, that one style is painted from the human point of view and the other is from the point of view of God? What do those terms mean to you? Write an essay in which you explore these issues.

- Lead a class discussion about the present-day conflict between East and West. In what way is the East-West culture clash a result of different ways of seeing the world? What might those differences be? Issues you might want to cover include human rights, religion, individuality and community, democracy and theocracy, and relations between church and state.

- Write an essay in which you discuss why Pamuk uses multiple narrators to tell his story. How does this technique relate to the issue of style presented in the novel? How does it relate to the differences between East and West presented in the novel? How would the novel have been different if it had been told by an omniscient narrator? If it were to be told by one single character, which character should that be, and how would the story have been different?

a horsefly and a mosque as if they were the same size, using the excuse that the mosque is in the background. In the traditionalist view, this is an inversion of true values because it sees from the human eye rather than the eye of God. In this novel, paintings raise important religious and spiritual issues because a painting influences the way a person sees the world.

The progressives among the artists want to make use of both Western and Eastern styles. The Sultan's purpose is political (although there may be individual pride involved as well). He wants to show that the Ottomans can use the Western style as well as the Europeans, thinking that such illustrations in a book about Islamic military strength and pride will awe the Venetians and increase Ottoman power. This turns out not to be the case, since Olive admits that his attempted self-portrait in the Frankish style is crude and unsuccessful. Despite his artistic talent, he failed in his task and says it will take the Islamicists centuries to attain the same proficiency as the Venetians. What the Sultan intended as a demonstration of Ottoman power becomes instead a symbol of its impotence.

Another character who wants to make use of both styles is Enishte. He argues that the coming together of two different styles is to be welcomed and has happened before in Islamic history. He says that Persian painting was a combination of Arabic illustrating and Mongol-Chinese sensibilities. This is confirmed by Stork, who attributes the renaissance of Islamic illustration hundreds of years ago to a man named Ibn Shakir who absorbed the techniques of the Chinese masters. Stork seems to endorse the new style in his argument with Butterfly in chapter 56. Stork is determined to illustrate battles the way he has actually seen them, "a tumult of armies, horses, armor-clad warriors and bloodied bodies." When Butterfly counters that the artist must draw what Allah sees, not a confused battle scene as it appears to human eyes, but two opposing armies in orderly array, Stork replies, "exalted Allah certainly sees everything we see," which neatly justifies the presentation of a subject from the human point of view, since such a view does not of itself invalidate the divine perspective.

The futility of much of the argument on both sides is made clear by Enishte after his death, when he confesses to Allah his attraction to the Venetian art. The answer Allah gives, which Enishte recalls in his thoughts, is "East and West belong to me," an all-encompassing viewpoint that makes the disputes that drive the novel seem small and petty by comparison. In this novel of fanaticism, in which people kill

over matters of art, Butterfly also reaches a sane conclusion with which the modern reader can concur: "An artist should never succumb to hubris of any kind ... he should simply paint the way he sees fit rather than troubling over East or West."

Blindness

The eventual blindness of the artist who labors all his life creating art is a recurring theme. But blindness is presented not as a tragedy but almost as a goal; instead of preventing the production of art, it actually enhances it. The idea in Islamic art is that the artist works within an established tradition, following the work of previous masters. He works not so much from direct observation of objects but from imitation of earlier works and repetition of the same methods. After many years of working in this way, the artists find that they are painting from memory, so they do not actually have to see in order to paint. Blindness also frees them from being influenced by other artistic styles and from the sensory realm and all the distractions that come with it. For example, Olive says to Black, "Blindness is a realm of bliss from which the Devil and guilt are barred." Blindness is not a disability or something to be feared; it is a reward offered by Allah after an artist has devoted his life to his work. Olive also remarks that some of the miniaturists who have become old without going blind are embarrassed by this fact and fear that it will be perceived as a lack of talent or skill. Some artists even pretend to be blind when they are not; they long to perceive the world the way a blind man does.

What an artist thinks about blindness is one of the three questions that Master Osman tells Black to put to the miniaturists. He says it will reveal how genuine a painter is. For Master Osman, blindness is "the farthest one can go in illustrating; it is seeing what appears out of Allah's own blackness." In other words, blindness helps the artist to present objects and scenes, not as they appear to men, but as they are viewed by Allah. When Master Osman spends the night poring over illustrations in the Treasury, he comes across many legends about blindness, which he refers to as "the ageless sorrow and secret desire of the genuine miniaturist." One illustration depicting a man being blinded by an arrow appears to him not as a tragedy but as a celebration. It is against this background that Master Osman's decision to

Skyline of Istanbul, Turkey (© Brand X Pictures / Alamy)

blind himself must be seen. It is a mystical desire to encounter the "blessed darkness" of Allah.

STYLE

Setting and Atmosphere

The novel creates a lively picture of late sixteenth-century Istanbul, a great imperial city that is going through troubled times. It has been shaken by fires and plague; military defeats against the Persians have disrupted the economy and led to runaway inflation, a situation made more unstable by the influx of counterfeit currency. The social disruption has allowed fiery conservative clerics to rise to prominence. They preach that the disasters that have afflicted Istanbul happened because people have strayed from the strict path laid out in the Koran. These preachers oppose tolerance to Christians, the sale of wine and the playing of music in the dervish houses. They also denounce the drinking of coffee as a sin that dulls the mind and causes

ulcers and hernias. They want the many coffeehouses in the city, which they see as the disreputable haunts of pleasure-seekers and the wealthy, to be closed. One of the coffeehouses is frequented by the miniaturists, and they enjoy listening to the irreverent stories told there by a storyteller who mocks the conservative preachers and undermines or questions traditional attitudes towards social and religious matters. This particular coffeehouse is located in the back streets of the slave market, a reminder that slavery existed in the Ottoman Empire at this time. Enishte keeps a slave, Hayrire, in his house.

The atmosphere of Istanbul is conveyed by characters such as Black, Enishte and the murderer as they walk through the streets of the city. Returning after a long absence, Black finds the city bigger and wealthier, but not as happy as he remembers it. It seems to be a city of extremes. He is astonished by the extravagant new houses that have been built, with expensive Venetian stained glass. But the streets seem narrow to him, and there are beggars on them, too. But despite the ominous aspects of the city, Black is entranced by its sights and sounds, which he captures in this passage as he looks down from a high vantage point:

> The cypress and the plane trees, the rooftops, the heartache of dusk, the sounds coming from the neighborhood below, the calls of hawkers and the cries of children playing in mosque courtyards mingled in my head and announced emphatically that, hereafter, I wouldn't be able to live anywhere but in their city.

Recurring Motifs

The title of the novel is a clue to the importance of the color red, a recurring motif (a motif is a recurring pattern, theme, symbol or image in a work of literature) that occurs in a number of contexts. Colors are vital to the painter and have a religious significance. Enishte speaks of "the mysteries of red ink," and the artists agree that if the Mongols had not brought "the secrets of red paint," they would not be able to produce their paintings. The Treasury itself, in which Black and Master Osman examine thousands of illustrations, is suffused with a dark red, caused by the cloth and dust in the peculiar light of the candles. Master Osman explains that the particular color red in one illustration belongs to the great master Mirza Baba Imami, who never disclosed his secret to anyone. "Allah never directly revealed this fine red except when He let the blood of his subjects flow," he says. It is only visible in the work of the greatest masters.

The connection between the painter's red pigment and human blood occurs in another context, too. When Black presents his uncle with a bronze three-hundred-year-old inkpot, he says "Purely for red." This is the same inkpot that Olive uses to kill him, which gives an ironic meaning to Black's earlier words, since the red color the inkpot produces is also the red blood of Enishte. As he dies, Enishte finds that red is the only color he sees: "What I thought was my blood was red ink; what I thought was ink on his hands was my flowing blood."

The color red also acquires a mystic significance. As Enishte's soul approaches Allah, he feels the presence of "an absolutely matchless red," and soon a beautiful red suffuses him and the whole universe:

> The red approaching me—the omnipresent red within which all the images of the universe played—was so magnificent and beautiful that it quickened my tears to think I would become part of it and be so close to Him.

HISTORICAL CONTEXT

The Ottoman Empire

The year 1591, in which the novel is set, was a significant date for Islam because it was the year before the thousandth anniversary of the Hegira, when the Prophet Muhammad emigrated from Mecca to Medina in 622. This date marked the beginning of the Muslim calendar. (The thousand years are lunar, not solar, years.) During this period the Ottoman Empire had just passed the zenith of its power and was beginning to face challenges from Europe (including, as the novel shows, the challenge of a new artistic style), that would eventually lead to its demise.

The Ottoman Empire had been growing in power since the Christian city of Constantinople was conquered by the Ottoman Sultan Mehmet the Conqueror in 1453. This event marked the end of the Byzantine Empire, and Constantinople, renamed Istanbul, became the capital of the Ottoman Empire. A century later, the reign of Ottoman Sultan Süleyman the Magnificent (1520–1566) ushered in what became known as the Golden Age of Ottoman Culture, in which architecture, art, and music flourished, as well as law-making and commerce. Süleyman expanded

the Ottoman Empire by military conquest. He set his sights on Central Europe, even laying siege to Vienna in 1529, although the siege was not successful.

In 1571, Ottoman power was checked by a huge naval battle in the Mediterranean, at Lepanto, in which combined European forces defeated the Ottomans. However, within two years, Venice made peace with the Ottoman Sultan Selim II (1566–1574) and agreed to give up Cyprus. But this would prove to be the last great Ottoman military success, even though for the next quarter century, between 1578 and 1606, the Ottomans continued to wage war against central Europe and the Persians.

Although much of his attention was occupied by war, Sultan Murat III (1574–1595), who appears briefly in the novel, was personally interested in books and miniatures, and it was at his request that many books, including the *Book of Victories* and the *Book of Festivities* (both mentioned in the novel) were produced. The characters Master Osman and Olive in the novel are based on real historical figures living in Istanbul during this period: Osman the Miniaturist and Velijan, respectively.

Despite this flowering of artistic excellence, however, during this period the Ottoman Empire was failing to counter the emerging power of a rapidly developing Europe. According to historian Halil Inalcik, "the fundamental institutions of the classical Ottoman Empire ... disintegrated under the impact of a new Europe and the Ottomans were unable to adapt themselves to the changed conditions." The Ottomans were inward-looking and did not feel the need to learn from European ideas and technology. During the reign of Sultan Ahmet I, for example, the large clock, a triumph of technology, which Elizabeth I of England had sent to the Sultan as a gift, was deliberately destroyed.

Istanbul

After its capture in 1453, Istanbul became the capital of the Ottoman Empire. The city grew rapidly in population as thousands of people were forcibly relocated there, and it was a cosmopolitan city, with Muslims, Greeks, and Jews comprising the three largest ethnic groups. By the late fifteenth century the population was nearly one hundred thousand people. Istanbul's buildings, including many mosques, schools and hospitals, were impressive. The Topkapi Palace,

COMPARE
&
CONTRAST

- **Late 1500s:** In Ottoman society, religious fanaticism is on the rise and has been since the early part of the century. Powerful conservative clerics known as *ulema*, who interpret and execute Islamic law, denounce mysticism, poetry, music, and dancing (among other things), as being against Islam. One such *ulema* is Mehmed of Birgi (1522–1573), whose followers continue to argue his point of view in Istanbul mosques in the 1590s, causing much social upheaval.

  Today: Turkey remains populated almost entirely by Muslims, but since 1923 it has been a secular state. Religious freedoms are respected, but the government restricts any signs of religious fundamentalism, such as the wearing of headscarves by women.

- **Late 1500s:** The powerful Ottoman Empire, with its capital city of Istanbul, is often at war with the rising powers in Europe. Indeed, the Ottomans acquire the island of Cyprus in 1593, but they face increasing challenges from the rapid development in Europe.

- **Today:** Turkey, with its capital city of Ankara, is negotiating to join the European Union. If all obstacles are overcome, the earliest date for Turkey's membership would be 2013. One such obstacle is Cyprus, which is divided into Greek and Turkish regions. Turkey refuses to acknowledge the Republic of Cyprus, which is a member of the European Union, as the sole authority on the island.

- **Late 1500s:** Istanbul is known as a relatively tolerant city, in which Muslims and Greek Orthodox Christians live together. Immigration of Jews from Europe is encouraged.

  Today: Because of rising nationalism in Turkey, some observers raise doubts about the nation's commitment to democracy and human rights. The issues of political and religious freedoms, freedom of speech, and the guaranteed rights of minorities, such as Kurds and Christians, are factors in Turkey's negotiations to join the European Union.

---

for example, built immediately after the Ottoman conquest and referred to in the novel simply as the palace, consisted of a number of buildings, gardens, courtyards and gates. The palace was the seat of government and included a throne room where the Sultan conducted official business.

The city continued to grow rapidly, reaching a population of four hundred thousand in the early part of the sixteenth century and rising possibly to around eight hundred thousand people by 1600. It was then the largest city in Europe, with excellent public services and flourishing trade. Centers of business, such as the Great Bazaar, were constructed around a bedestan, a central building with stone domes and iron doors where merchants could gather and goods could be securely stored. Shops and places of work grew up around the bedestans. Istanbul

was noted also for its coffeehouses, which, from the middle of the sixteenth century, were the centers of social life in the city. Istanbul was also noted for its public bathhouses (there were reportedly 150 of them) and its dervish monasteries or lodges, which were used for study and contemplation. (In the novel, Olive retreats to an abandoned dervish lodge where he is finally cornered by the other miniaturists.)

CRITICAL OVERVIEW

My Name Is Red met with unanimous praise from reviewers. A reviewer for *Publishers Weekly* admires the novel's "jeweled prose and alluring digressions, nesting stories within stories," and

Selim II, Sultan of Turkey, 1566–1574 (© *Mary Evans Picture Library / Alamy*)

concludes that Pamuk will gain many new readers with this "accessible, charming and intellectually satisfying, narrative." A *Kirkus Reviews* critic describes the novel as "a whimsical but provocative exploration of the nature of art in an Islamic society. ... A rich feast of ideas, images, and lore." Jonathan Levi, writing in the *Los Angeles Times Book Review*, comments that "it is Pamuk's rendering of the intense life of artists negotiating the devilishly sharp edge of Islam 1,000 years after its birth that elevates *My Name Is Red* to the rank of modern classic." Levi also notes, as other reviewers did, that the novel, although set four hundred years in the past, reflects societal tensions that can still be found in the world today. For this reason he refers to it as "a novel of our time." In the *New York Times*, Richard Eder describes Pamuk's intense interest in East-West interactions and explains some of the metaphysical ideas that permeate the novel. He also comments that the novel is not just

about ideas: "Eastern or Western, good or bad, ideas precipitate once they sink to human level, unleashing passions and violence. 'Red' is chockfull of sublimity and sin." Eder also has high praise for the characterization of Shekure, which he regards as the finest in the book. She is "elusive, changeable, enigmatic and immensely beguiling." Eder concludes with this comment about how readers are likely to experience the novel:

> They will ... be lofted by the paradoxical lightness and gaiety of the writing, by the wonderfully winding talk perpetually about to turn a corner, and by the stubborn humanity in the characters' maneuvers to survive. It is a humanity whose lies and silences emerge as endearing and oddly bracing individual truths.

CRITICISM

Bryan Aubrey

Aubrey holds a Ph.D. in English. In the following essay, he discusses the novel in terms of the clash between opposite values.

Istanbul in the 1590s, according to Orhan Pamuk's *My Name Is Red*, is a city which reverberates with the clashing opposites: not only the conflict between Eastern and Western approaches to art, but also between the highest ideals of art and a low commercialism in which the prime motivating factor is not the service of art or truth but the acquisition of money. At the root of the novel is the universal longing for immortality, for eternity, for timelessness, set against the stark facts of what it means to inhabit a human mind and body, with all its turbulent emotions, its anger, jealousy, and greed, and the despicable acts it is capable of.

It is the artists themselves who lay out, in their conversations with each other, the conditions and aspirations of their art, as well as their own human foibles and weaknesses. Believing in the surpassing beauty of their painting, they want to create illustrations that will last forever, that will somehow cheat or transcend time. The topic of time and timelessness is first raised by Master Osman in conversation with Black, and when Black asks Stork for his thoughts about time, the artist replies with three stories about painting and time, each of which suggests that the attempt to conquer time through art is likely to fail. The first describes the life of Ibn Shakir, a

WHAT DO I READ NEXT?

- Pamuk's nonfiction book, *Istanbul: Memories and the City* (2004), presents a portrait of the city in which he was raised and lived for decades. He describes the breakdown of his family and how he found his own way in the world; he captures the melancholy quality of the city and reflects on the history of the Ottoman Empire. The book contains 206 photographs.

- *The Name of the Rose*, by Italian philosopher and novelist Umberto Eco, is often mentioned as having similarities with *My Name Is Red*. The Everyman's edition (2006) contains Eco's own commentary on the novel. Like *My Name Is Red*, it is an erudite murder mystery, set in a period remote from modern times—in this case, a medieval monastery. It also includes much discussion and information about religion in the middle ages, including histories of the Catholic Church and of various sects within the Catholic Church.

- Readers intrigued by the philosophical and religious aspects of the novel might enjoy Mohammed Marmaduke Pickthall's *The Meaning of the Glorious Qur'an: Text and Explanatory Translation* (1996 edition). This is a classic, easy-to-read translation, made in the early twentieth century, of Islam's holy book, and this edition is edited in modern English by Dr. Arafat K. El-Ashi.

- Pamuk is sometimes compared to the Italian postmodern writer, Italo Calvino. In Calvino's novel *The Baron in the Trees* (1977), Cosimo, a young eighteenth-century Italian nobleman, decides, in a protest against society, to spend his entire life living in the trees. Calvino creates a convincing world in which this extraordinary act takes place, developing historical, philosophical and political themes as Cosimo's brother narrates the story of Cosimo's life.

> THE ARTISTS MAY ENGAGE IN ALMOST ENDLESS INTELLECTUAL DISCUSSION ABOUT THE NATURE OF THEIR ART, AND THERE IS NO DOUBT THAT THEY ARE DEDICATED TO IT, BUT THEY ALSO SUFFER FROM COMMON VICES SUCH AS GREED, VANITY, CONCEIT, LUST, AND JEALOUSY, AND THEY ARE ALSO MATERIALISTIC, AS MUCH IN SEARCH OF MONEY AS ARTISTIC EXCELLENCE."

renowned calligrapher who lived with a "deep and infinite notion of time," believing that the works he transcribed would last until the end of the world. He then had the misfortune to witness Mongol invaders destroy all these books. His response was to turn to painting, in which he created the godlike perspective that Islamic art would thereafter follow, and he believed once more in the notion of "endless time," manifested through painting, that would "survive forever in their revelation of Allah's worldly realm." The inevitable conclusion reached by the reader, although not, apparently, by Ibn Shakir or Stork, is that those paintings were equally liable to destruction as the books he had copied. Certainly, this is the conclusion reached by Enishte, who, just before he is murdered, makes a magnificent, two-page speech about how all their paintings will soon be lost ("Indifference, time and disaster will destroy our art")—a view that is so disturbing to the murderer that he promptly brings the inkpot crashing down on Enishte's head. Master Osman echoes the same sentiment in chapter 51, when he explains to Black that everything they value will soon be lost.

Stork's second story about time concerns the attempts of two warlords, one the conqueror of the other, to preserve their immortality through representing themselves in illustrations in manuscripts. Both attempts, for different reasons, fail. Stork's final story about time concerns an artist who so excelled at his craft that, when he was eighty, people thought he was so immersed in the legends he was illustrating that he was outside of time and would never grow old or die. But at the age of 119, he conceived a passion for a six-teen-year-old boy—the passion of older men for young boys is apparent many times in this novel and is apparently, as in ancient Greece, not con-demned—and as he tried to seduce him he gave in to lying and treachery. Cutting himself off from the eternal world of art and legend, he became ill, went blind, and died.

So if the notion of art lasting through an endless time, or an artist somehow defying time through art, proves impossible, what then might timelessness in art consist of? Rather different from the concept of something enduring through endless time is the idea that a painting itself can embody a kind of timelessness; the scene depicted may be of such beauty and perfection that it seems to step out of time and to partake of eternity—to belong, in a sense, to another world. One of the most beautiful passages in the entire novel is Master Osman's description of a paint-ing that depicts the romance between Hüsrev, a Persian prince, and Shirin, an Armenian prin-cess. The story of these lovers was a frequent subject for the sixteenth century miniaturists and is mentioned several times in the novel. As he praises the painting, Master Osman says, "It's as if the lovers are to remain here eternally within the light emanating from the painting's texture, skin and subtle colors. ... " The lovers are not depicted realistically; their faces are slightly turned towards each other but their bodies are half-turned towards the viewer, since they know they are in a painting. In this sense, "they've emerged from Allah's memory. This is why time has stopped for them within that picture." He continues, explaining that the lovers will:

> remain for all eternity there, like well-bred, polite, shy young maidens ... For them, every-thing within the navy-blue night is frozen. The bird flies through the darkness, among the stars, with a fluttering like the racing hearts of the lovers themselves, and at the same time, remains fixed for all eternity as if nailed to the sky in this matchless moment.

Readers will be reminded of John Keats's famous "Ode on a Grecian Urn," which expresses exactly the same idea: a single intense moment between lovers captured through art, which tran-scends time. Keats contrasts this ideal, eternal moment with the experience of love in the real world, which "leaves a heart high-sorrowful and cloy'd." However, in *My Name Is Red* there is one moment in which life seems to attain the perfection of art. It comes in the scene in which

Black and Shekure embrace for the first time, and Shekure feels as if "the whole world were engulfed in blissful light." Shekure, in a clear allusion to the love of Hüsrev and Shirin, imag-ines what that moment would be like it had it been depicted by a master miniaturist. She says that the observer would see in the technique, the perfectly applied colors, and the "mysterious light" that permeates the painting, the secret behind all such illustrations, which is that "they're created by love itself. It's as if a light were emanating from the lovers, from the very depths of the illustration." Shekure concludes that when she and Black embraced, "well-being flooded the world in the very same manner."

This pouring in of infinite love, of timeless-ness into time, is described on one other occasion in the novel. It occurs when Black and Master Osman are examining paintings in the Treasury. Black loses all track of time and comments, "It was as if the unchanging, frozen golden time revealed in the pictures and stories we viewed had thoroughly mingled with the damp and moldy time we experienced in the Treasury."

But such moments of grace, in which the heavenly and the earthly seem to be cut of one cloth, are few. For the most part, the ideal world revealed by art, with its perfection and timeless-ness, is in stark contrast to the swirling passions that dominate "this filthy and miserable world of ours"(as Olive puts it). To exist in the flesh is to be in time, and time is the world of opposites: joy and sorrow, kindness and cruelty, hope and despair, noble aspiration and petty selfishness. The artists may engage in almost endless intellec-tual discussion about the nature of their art, and there is no doubt that they are dedicated to it, but they also suffer from common vices such as greed, vanity, conceit, lust, and jealousy, and they are also materialistic, as much in search of money as artistic excellence. A number of characters com-ment on the fact that the murdered Elegant was greedy for money, and there is speculation that he was murdered for his wealth. Even when he is dead, one of the first things he informs the reader about is the exact salary he earned from his work, and he adds, "You know the value of money even when you're dead." Elegant had a habit (as we are informed by the gold coin that narrates chapter 19) of spending his evenings arranging his gold coins in various designs.

The otherwise high-minded Stork secretly makes obscene drawings for a pasha who pays well for them. Butterfly protests to Enishte about such practices: "Genuine miniaturists shouldn't loiter at the shops in the bazaar and paint any old thing, depictions of indecency, for a few extra kurush from anybody who happens by." But Butterfly himself, his protests notwithstanding, is not free of the lure of money, which he thinks he should have simply because he is talented. In this city, Black complains, value is placed not on painting itself but on the money that can be earned from it.

This curious mixing of the high and the low in terms of what motivates these miniaturists is part of their radically divided nature. They are pulled in opposite directions in so many ways; idealism and the service of art compete with greed and materialism, and although they are steeped in the artistic traditions of the East, they feel an irresistible pull towards the methods of the West, which they at once envy, fear, and long to emulate. So divided are they against themselves that all the time they are honored, elite members of their society, they are also subversives who regularly visit the coffeehouse where they make unusual drawings, in their own style and sometimes influenced by Venetian methods, as the people in the coffeehouse egg them on. They also whisper into the storyteller's ear the witty, irreverent stories he then tells to his audience. Unsure to whom or what they owe allegiance, it is not surprising that the miniaturists end up quarreling amongst themselves and either committing or falling prey to violence. They mirror the cracks that were beginning to show in the powerful Ottoman Empire, faced with a challenge from Europe that it did not know how to respond to, and that would eventually lead to its downfall.

Source: Bryan Aubrey, Critical Essay on *My Name Is Red*, in *Novels for Students*, Gale, Cengage Learning, 2008.

Sarah Coleman

In the following review, Coleman praises the ambitious, large-scale nature of the novel and the artistry and drama within it. However, she also faults it for a lack of balance. Though Coleman feels that My Name Is Red *is vivid, she also feels that it is overloaded with details.*

Anyone who's visited Turkey has probably been drawn to the charm of Turkish miniature paintings. These delicate, stylized images of battles and bathhouses, with their fine lines and flat colors, are exquisite examples of Eastern artistry. Looking at them is like peering into an exotic and radiant dollhouse.

In Orhan Pamuk's *My Name Is Red*, a 16th century Turkish illuminated manuscript is at the center of a historical murder mystery. Pamuk, a best-selling author in Turkey, uses the history of his country's art to examine intersections between religion, creativity and human desire.

The result is a huge and ambitious novel that is by turns charming and pedantic. Like Umberto Eco's *The Name of the Rose*, *My Name Is Red* combines down-and-dirty intrigue with scholarship and a postmodern sensibility. Written from multiple perspectives, it includes chapters narrated by recently murdered people, a dog, a tree and even the color red.

"I am nothing but a corpse now, a body at the bottom of a well," begins the compelling first chapter. The body belongs to Elegant Effendi, one of four master artists who has been commissioned, at the end of the 16th century, to illustrate a secret and controversial manuscript for Ottoman Sultan Murat III.

Unlike other Turkish illustrations, this one will incorporate the newest techniques from "Frankish," or Venetian painting, using perspective, shadows and—most daring of all—recognizable portraits of individuals.

To show how such artwork might threaten the social order, Pamuk sketches a lively Istanbul at the end of the 16th century. It is a time of plagues, fires and war, where religious repression coexists with decadent social and sexual behavior. Fundamentalism is gaining ground: A preacher called Nusret Hoja is making political capital by attributing Istanbul's corruption "to disregard for the strictures of the Glorious Koran, to the tolerance toward Christians, to the open sale of wine and to the playing of musical instruments in dervish houses."

According to Nusret's dogma, the individual expression in the new manuscript amounts to blasphemy against Allah. Its commission has thrown the community of illustrators into a panic, sowing division between the Islamists (who include the murdered Elegant) and the free-thinkers.

All of this allows Pamuk to explore the aesthetics of representation in great and sometimes exhausting detail. We learn about the significance of gilded borders, prescribed ways for drawing eyes and nostrils and the tension between innovation and imitation. "If the picture is to be perfect," says one illustrator, "it ought to have been drawn at least a thousand times before I attempt it." Others in the novel refuse to embrace such dictates. Enishte ("Uncle"), who is coordinating the secret manuscript, thinks that Western portraiture is the way of the future, though he acknowledges the danger of an art that glorifies individual humans.

Enishte charges his nephew Black with uncovering the identity of Elegant's murderer, knowing that Black will be motivated by his love for Enishte's daughter Shekure, a beautiful mother of two whose husband is missing in action in the Persian wars.

When Enishte is murdered, the stakes are raised, and the narrative becomes taut. The second murder scene is a wonderful set piece in which the color crimson dominates, as it overflows from the murder implement (a bottle of red ink) and in the blood that gushes from the victim's head.

In Shekure and Black, Pamuk has created compelling characters whose voices jump off the page. He also introduces another colorful narrator in the person of Esther, a Jewish fabric peddler who acts as an intermediary between the two lovers.

Unfortunately, the chapters related by these three only make up around a third of the book. Others, narrated by inanimate objects such as the drawn figures of horses and dogs, often lapse into dry art history seminars.

Perhaps Pamuk's greatest misstep, though, is that he fails to adequately characterize the three main murder suspects. These are Elegant's fellow illustrators, and although they are distinguished by the colorful nicknames of Stork, Butterfly and Olive, it's hard—up to the final chapters—to tell them apart. Instead of giving us scenes from their lives, the three men offer convoluted riddles about illustration. In his urge to make all of them viable suspects, Pamuk blurs the lines among them, thereby lessening the reader's involvement in the resolution of the murder case.

This is a shame, because at its best, *My Name Is Red* contains chapters of stunning artistry and drama, and it offers a fascinating view of life in a historic Istanbulite artist community.

Like Calvino, Borges, Kafka and Eco (to all of whom he's been previously compared) Pamuk is a writer who is able to combine avant-garde literary techniques with stories that capture the popular imagination.

Here, the ingredients are potent, but the balance is off. Like an overenthusiastic master illustrator, Pamuk paints a vivid picture, but loads it with so many details and symbols that the eye has nowhere calm to rest.

Source: Sarah Coleman, "A Detailed Tapestry of 16th Century Turkey," in *San Francisco Chronicle*, December 9, 2001, 2 pp.

Richard Eder

In the following review, Eder comments on the different concepts underlying Western and Eastern art that form the philosophical basis of My Name Is Red. *Eder also offers praise for the humanity of the characters and the skill of Pamuk's writing.*

Time's deletions, like a computer's, are not really deleted. A technician can restore what the keyboard has made to vanish, and the past is never quite gone. Historical change deteriorates and slides back; defeat hangs around, sometimes for centuries, awaiting the chance to become victory. Not only did the South rise again; it went Republican.

Proust was literature's foremost artificer at undeleting an individual's memory. The Turkish novelist Orhan Pamuk, whose intricate intrusions of past into present have been compared to Proust's, works on the memory of a nation and a civilization.

Kemal Ataturk obliterated every vestige of the once-powerful, long-tottering 600-year Ottoman Empire. He decreed Westernization: Islam was restricted, fezzes and veils were out, the grand accretions of Persian and Arabic in the Turkish language were annulled to the point where Turks today can find it hard to read poems only a century old.

Pamuk himself, now in his 40's, began as a literary Westernizer, though set against the oppressiveness and corruption of Ataturk's heirs. He gorged on European and American literature, studied at the Iowa Writers' Workshop and adopted a contemporary blend of modernist and postmodernist techniques. He wrote of the stagnation and backwardness that 80 years of modernization had not only failed to eradicate but, across

> " BUT *MY NAME IS RED* IS NOT JUST A NOVEL OF IDEAS. EASTERN OR WESTERN, GOOD OR BAD, IDEAS PRECIPITATE ONCE THEY SINK TO HUMAN LEVEL, UNLEASHING PASSIONS AND VIOLENCE. 'RED' IS CHOCKFUL OF SUBLIMITY AND SIN."

broad expanses of Turkish geography and society, had barely touched.

He is not an ideologue or a politician or a journalist. He is a novelist and a great one (nobody—other than a small committee of Swedes—could rule out a Nobel). His job is not to denounce reality, but to be haunted by it, as a medium is haunted.

The reality that possesses him is that Turkey's attempt to obliterate the Ottoman heritage in Turkey hacked away roots. It aimed not just at what was retrograde but at what was still stubbornly alive and perhaps precious. (It may have been futile, in any case, as the resurgence of Islamic fundamentalism could suggest.)

Not to denounce the reality that haunts you does not mean to praise it. It is more a matter of speaking in a medium's divided voices—a painful division and, in the case of Pamuk, both confusing and exhilarating. Three of his earlier dissonant-voiced novels have been published and critically praised here, but not widely read.

The new one, *My Name Is Red*, is by far the grandest and most astonishing contest in Pamuk's internal East-West war. Translated with fluid grace by Erdag M. Goknor, the novel is set in the late 16th century, during the reign of Sultan Murat III, a patron of the miniaturists whose art had come over from Persia in the course of the previous hundred years. It was a time when the Ottomans' confidence in unstoppable empire had begun to be shaken by the power of the West—their defeat at Lepanto had taken place only a few years earlier—as well as by its cultural vitality and seductiveness. (A chronology is given at the end; venturers into Pamuk should consult it at the start.)

The story, in a nutshell (containing multitudes), tells of two murders among Murat's court artists; one of Elegant, a master miniaturist, the other of Enishte, a cunningly complicated figure commissioned by the sultan to produce a book by his four finest artists, Elegant among them. The book is secret; the miniaturists only dimly suspect what it will amount to, and they barely admit to themselves the radically nontraditional nature of Enishte's commission.

Theirs is a secrecy of terror and shame: terror of being branded for heresy by the powerful Muslim clergy and punished by the sultan, whose dangerously elusive intentions are hidden from them. Shame, because they are imbued with the tradition they are violating, even as they both long and dread to violate it.

The art of classic miniature—implying here a much wider kind of order—depicts figures with great beauty and variety but ritually, impersonally and without individual characters or expressions. The paintings stand not as themselves but strictly as illustrations of text. The style the sultan's artists are surreptitiously instructed to adopt, on the other hand, is that of the Italian Renaissance. Figures are individual, portraits are of specific people, and even trees and dogs are particulars. These paintings are not illustrations; they stand as works of art in their own right.

Why should this be heresy? For one thing, Islam enjoined against figuration; if miniatures were allowed it was because they were generic, a decoration of the text and subordinate to it. To portray individuals or objects for their own sake and without cover of words was to give them iconic standing. What made it worse was the introduction of perspective. A mosque far off would be smaller than a man, or even his dog, close up. People and things, the objection went, "weren't depicted according to their importance in Allah's mind but as they appeared to the naked eye."

Noncommitally, Pamuk sets out these rock-hard orthodoxies. Clearly he has no use for fatwas or fundamentalist rage. Elsewhere, tough—his own civil war is fought on both sides with exquisite weapons—he sympathetically refines the implications. These, in fact, brush up against our own tradition's questioning of the place of art. Does it create its own order (or disorder) or does it discover, serve and bring out a larger, timeless order (or disorder)? One of the most beautiful passages in a book that abounds in them is the near-Rilkean discourse of Master Osman, the head miniaturist and a stubbornly mystical traditionalist. Lovingly, he evokes a classic miniature that illustrates the legend of the lovers Husrev and Shirin.

"It's as if the lovers are to remain here eternally within the light emanating from the painting's texture, skin and subtle colors which were applied lovingly by the miniaturist. You can see how their faces are turned ever so slightly toward one another while their bodies are half-turned toward us—for they know they're in a painting and thus visible to us. This is why they don't try to resemble exactly those figures which we see around us. Quite to the contrary, they signify that they've emerged from Allah's memory."

There are other engrossing elaborations of an "Eastern" concept of art, in which all painting is an act of memory and foreordained, and blindness is the ideal condition for creating pure art, being free of sensory distraction and temptation. But *My Name Is Red* is not just a novel of ideas. Eastern or Western, good or bad, ideas precipitate once they sink to human level, unleashing passions and violence. "Red" is chockful of sublimity and sin.

The story is told by each of a dozen characters, and now and then by a dog, a tree, a gold coin, several querulous corpses and the color crimson (*My Name Is Red*). It concerns investigation of the murders, the tales of the three master miniaturists who survive Elegant—one of them the killer—and Master Osman's long (considerably too long) perusal of the classic Persian miniatures in the sultan's library. Also myriad other incidents, scenes and characters gyrating wildly in an era of seismic shift.

Finally, and most precious, there is the passionate pursuit by Black, the murdered Enishte's deputy, of Enishte's daughter Sekure. Elusive, changeable, enigmatic and immensely beguiling, she is the finest portrait in the book. Not a portrait, in fact: a Persian miniature. Her body is half turned toward us, as if she were in a painting and not a flesh-and-blood figure.

It is Black, turbulent, striving, at times absurd, who is flesh and blood. Their marriage is the union, always unfathomable and unsettled, of flat miniature and Renaissance perspective, of stylized image and individual portrait, of Eastern art and Western.

To sum up, and each time the sums come out different: the ideas in "Red" give fascination and energy, and work to hold together its turbulent narrative. They work and they fail; and in a way, though not entirely, the failure is Pamuk's success. No story of the darker churnings of the Ottoman regime, its rule by secrets, lies, conspiracies and chaos, would be real if it were lucid. Readers will have spells of feeling lost and miserable in a deliberate unreliability that so mirrors its subject: a world governed by fog.

They will also be lofted by the paradoxical lightness and gaiety of the writing, by the wonderfully winding talk perpetually about to turn a corner, and by the stubborn humanity in the characters' maneuvers to survive. It is a humanity whose lies and silences emerge as endearing and oddly bracing individual truths.

Source: Richard Eder, "Heresies of the Paintbrush," in *New York Times Book Review*, September 2, 2001, 2 pp.

Maureen Freely

In the following review, Freely argues that in the novel's presentation of Istanbul, My Name Is Red *captures not only the contradictions, past and present, of the city, but also its timeless beauty.*

Istanbul is the only city in the world that sits on two continents. According to its travel posters, it is where east meets west. This suggests a happy exchange that leaves both parties energised and enriched. In Orhan Pamuk's Istanbul, the story is rather darker. His characters belong to neither camp, but are wooed and tantalised by both in equal measure. Their hearts are divided, and so are their minds. They are living proof that east and west meet only to invert each other—until the best man wins.

In *The White Castle*, Pamuk's first novel to be translated into English, the contest was between a 17th-century court astrologer and the Venetian astronomer he bought as his slave. He set his next two novels in contemporary Istanbul, but in *My Name is Red*, he returns to the resonant past. Going by our measurements, the year is 1591. According to the Islamic calendar, it's a year before the 1,000th anniversary of the Hegira, or the Prophet Mohammad's emigration from Mecca to Medina. The Ottoman empire is still strong, but its enemies no longer assume it to be invincible.

Ravaged by fires and plague, demoralised by military defeat and spiralling prices, the people of Istanbul have begun to pay attention to a fundamentalist cleric from Erzurum who claims they've brought it all on themselves by straying from the prophet and the strictures of the Koran. The sins he lists include the open sale of wine, the playing of wild music in dervish houses and the drinking of coffee. But another, even greater sacrilege is how the artists of the Ottoman court are succumbing to the temptations and innovations of Frankish painting. And not just the artists. The sultan himself has secretly commissioned a book of illustrations in the Frankish style, portraying his glorious empire not as Allah would see it, but as it appears to the human eye. His plan is to present the book as a gift to the Venetian court, hoping they will see that, even in art, the Ottomans can beat them at their own game. But among the small group of miniaturists involved with the project is one who is certain it will land them in hell.

As he reminds a colleague when they meet in secret, their traditional forms were mindful of the Koran's teachings: their aim was never to represent real life, but to illuminate stories in such a way as to make their moral meanings visible. Because they were in service to Allah, they did not sign their work. Any sign of individuality in the subject or the execution was a flaw. The best miniaturist was the one who could draw a horse or a tree or a woman in exactly the same way as the master who had trained him, and even then he would fall short of perfection. "A miniaturist would have to sketch horses unceasingly for 50 years to be able to truly depict the horse that Allah envisioned and desired." His best picture would be the one he drew out of memory in the dark as, 50 years on, the artist in question was sure to have gone blind. But when an artist followed Frankish fashions and started painting life as he saw it, he was dishonouring his faith.

When the story opens, the miniaturist who first gave voice to these doubts is lying dead at the bottom of a well. He retains the power of speech long enough to say what he stands for. His is the first of a series of monologues that work together to form a sort of verbal miniature, painting a picture not as Allah would see it, but as he might hear it. The form is a brilliant conceit: there is only one speaker who does not flaunt his identity in the manner of the Franks, and that is the murderer. We know this free-floating voice belongs to one of the central characters. But as Black, the artist charged with solving the crime, soon discovers, the murderer has left no trace of his movements in real life. The only clue to his true identity is hidden inside his work.

Time is not on Black's side—after the murderer claims his second victim, the sultan becomes impatient and threatens to torture all the suspects, Black included, unless he can solve the puzzle in three days. The interweaving of human and philosophical intrigue is very much as I remember it in *The Name of the Rose*, as is the slow, dense beginning and the relentless gathering of pace. The two titles are close enough to suggest that Pamuk is admitting his own debt to a Frankish innovator. But, in my view, his book is by far the better of the two. I would go so far as to say that Pamuk achieves the very thing his book implies is impossible. He has taken his inspiration from western modernist literature, but instead of destroying his 16th-century artists, he illuminates their world as no one has before. What matters in the end is not the identity of the murderer in their midst, but their devotion to an art they know is dying. As compelling and distinctive as they are, it is not "who" they are that counts. It is the loves and losses they have shared. The same can be said of the novel and indeed the city it illuminates between the lines. More than any other book I can think of, it captures not just its past and present contradictions, but also its terrible, timeless beauty. It's almost perfect, in other words. All it needs is the Nobel Prize.

Source: Maureen Freely, Review of *My Name Is Red*, in *New Statesman*, Vol. 130, No. 4552, August 27, 2001, p. 41.

Lynne Sharon Schwartz

In the following excerpt, Schwartz comments that My Name Is Red *is written on a grander scale than Pamuk's previous works. She notes that in the novel's plot and ideas, Pamuk alludes to current struggles between Islamic fundamentalists and advocates of freedom of expression in Turkey. She also argues that the love story of Black and Shekure is less successful than the presentation of aesthetics, politics, and religion, which she regards as the book's principal interest.*

Orhan Pamuk is not only a superb writer, he is a cultural phenomenon. Equally at home in the traditions of ancient Islamic literature and Western postmodernism, he's the first Turkish novelist to win spectacular success in Europe and the United States. His four novels published here, of which the best by far is *The White Castle* (1991), are curious variations on a handful of themes: Turkey's Ottoman past as a stage for the clash and cross-fertilization of East and West; the infinite, tortuous complications of individual and national identity; and above all, the magical properties of books. In every Pamuk novel a book, real or imaginary, is the source or trigger, virtually the protagonist, of the action.

"I read a book one day and my whole life was changed" is the first sentence of *A New Life* (1997). The narrator sets off on a picaresque road trip through a Turkey shaped by American incursions like Coca-Cola and Hollywood movies, to find the promised new life. Though the book turns out to be a hoax of sorts, the exhilaration and perplexity it causes are authentic and vivid. The lure of a new life—that is, of the old self given a new past along with a new future—is ubiquitous in Pamuk's work. In *The White Castle*, a 17th-century Venetian, sold into slavery by Turkish pirates, and his master spend years exchanging family histories and anecdotes until they change places and identities. By the end, both reader and characters are not quite sure who is who. The borders of the self, in Pamuk's world, are so porous and ambiguous that the lawyer-hero of *The Black Book* (1994) can move into his dead cousin's apartment and, without any great difficulty, take the deceased's phone calls and continue writing his idiosyncratic newspaper columns.

Pamuk's latest novel, *My Name Is Red* (Knopf, $25.95, 417 pp., translated by Erdağ Goknar), is conceived on a grander scale than his previous works. Its setting is late 16th-century Istanbul, in the ateliers of the Sultan's court painters and manuscript illustrators. In this milieu beset by religious fanaticism and strife, two artists working on a possibly heretical book are murdered weeks apart. (Readers may be reminded of Umberto Eco, but Pamuk has a lighter, playful touch, more in the vein of Italo Calvino or Jorge Luis Borges.) The opening chapter is told by the corpse of a miniaturist

recounting his brutal death, but only 400 pages later do we discover which of the three suspected master illustrators is the culprit.

The mystery moves along in first-person chapters narrated by the eight or so major characters, with intervening chapters contributed by a dog, a tree, Satan, Death, and similarly unexpected voices. We soon learn these voices are the improvisational riffs of a storyteller who entertains in a freewheeling coffee shop frequented by the illustrators and targeted by the repressive fundamentalists. Within the historical setting, Pamuk is obviously alluding to current political and religious struggles between Islamic zealots and advocates of free expression in Turkey and neighboring countries.

At the Sultan's request, the elderly master illustrator Enishte Effendi is supervising the creation of the dubious book whose artistic principles prove worth killing and dying for, intended to represent everything in the Sultan's world. The project is dubious because the Sultan and Enishte wish it to exhibit the intriguing new Venetian manner, with its cultivation of personal style and its use of perspective, portraiture and realistic depiction of the world, as opposed to the entrenched Persian tradition of painting as "the act of seeking out Allah's memories, seeing the world as He sees the world." (Enishte himself will be the second artist killed for reasons of esthetics.)

Attached to the murder mystery is a love story. Enishte's nephew, the former miniaturist Black, ends a 12-year exile to seek his early love, Shekure, Enishte's beautiful daughter. Shekure's soldier husband never came back from his last battle, and with her marital status in question, she has returned to her father's house to escape the advances of her volatile brother-in-law. When Black presents himself, the clever, pragmatic Shekure is utterly confounded. Should she wait faithfully but probably uselessly for her husband, or succumb to the persuasions of her wild yet attractive brother-in-law, or yield to Black, whose appeal is less frenetic? The two small quarreling sons she dotes on, Orhan and Shevket, complicate her choices. (In an interview, Pamuk said that he is the Orhan of the novel, who at the close is entrusted with telling the story, and that the family configuration mirrors his own childhood. Plus he has a brother named Shevket. "These are my essential subjects: rivalry, jealousy, problems of domination and influence, revenge"; they originate in sibling rivalry as well as in Turkey's ambivalent position between East and West.)

Despite the personal overtones, or perhaps because of them, the love story and family dilemma are the least successful parts of *My Name Is Red*. Shekure's arbitrariness is unconvincing, and the back-and-forth courtship ritual where Black is teased and manipulated and made to perform heroics in order to win his bride, becomes tiresome. The romance seems a distraction from Pamuk's genuine interest—the conjunction of esthetics, politics and religion. On this subject he can be brilliant at dramatizing subtle painterly distinctions and at offering an overview of Ottoman history and lore—battles, tales of passion, royal intrigue—as preserved in the ateliers of the master painters. The downside, unfortunately, is a great deal of repetition, and erudition often delivered in huge chunks that clearly fascinate the writer more than they will the reader.

The salient feature of Ottoman illustration, as Pamuk describes it, was close copying of the old masters; "style" as we know it was considered a flaw, a deviation. "Illustration," though, is the key word. "A beautiful illustration," according to an ancient Sultan, "elegantly completes the story. An illustration that does not complement a story in the end, will become but a false idol. Since we cannot possibly believe in an absent story, we will naturally begin believing in the picture itself. This would be no different than the worship of idols ..." Enishte's book has pictures but no text as yet— a risky departure from tradition. Black, besides courting Shekure, is enlisted to provide a text. The book's last page will show a realistic portrait of the Sultan, in perspective—"the same size as a dog ... Our Sultan's ... face in all its detail! Just like the idolators do!" This is what horrified the murdered painter, and what he threatened to tell the fanatics; this is why his colleague, eager to try the new methods, murdered him.

To portray life as Allah sees it, "the vision of the world from a minaret," means resisting the temptation of individual style: "No one ought to compete with Him ... claim to be as creative as He." But in the lengthy and sometimes violent arguments among the miniaturists, the opposite view is heard as well. Perhaps attempting to reproduce Allah's vision is the real presumption. Perhaps the Venetian artists, with their humanist perspective and distinctive styles, are more fittingly humble. As the artists take sides and the quest for the murderer heats up, Black and

Master Osman, who represents the old school of thought, spend three days in the Sultan's private library of old manuscripts, seeking clues to the murderer's identity in tiny stylistic quirks. Their research becomes Pamuk's elegiac tribute to the ancient Persian masters, who labored anonymously, for art's sake, to the point of blindness. In an ecstatic moment, Master Osman even blinds himself: blindness is supposedly Allah's gift to the faithful painter. Only when blind, after a lifetime of effort, can he see the world in memory, from an unending, Godlike darkness.

It doesn't much matter, finally, who the murderer is; in the tradition of Ottoman painting, the three suspects sound very much alike. Indeed, Pamuk's greatest tribute to his subject is his use of so many similar voices, in imitation of the technique of the ateliers, where several painters worked on the same pictures in a uniform, time-honored manner. The novel itself might well be the nonexistent text to accompany the daring illustrations, the rich book showing everything in the Sultan's world.

As Enishte approaches death—clobbered by the painter who kills for the right to his uniqueness—he sees "the presence of an absolutely matchless crimson. ... The beauty of this color suffused me and the whole universe." This is the "crimson within which all the images of the universe played." *My Name Is Red* takes no sides between Eastern and Western attitudes; it recognizes the need for both and the value of their mingling. "Nothing is pure," Enishte says. "To God belongs the East and the West."

That kind of inclusive vision makes the religious fanatics see red: In a climactic raid on the artists' coffeehouse, they kill the storyteller—the ultimate symbolic act. Though this novel wavers in places, it is the work of a master. But for an introduction to Pamuk at his most distilled, I would recommend starting with the incomparable *White Castle* ...

Source: Lynne Sharon Schwartz, "In the Beginning Was the Book," in *New Leader*, Vol. 84, No. 5, September 2001, p. 23.

SOURCES

Eder, Richard, "Heresies of the Paintbrush," in the *New York Times*, September 2, 2001.

Inalcik, Halil, *The Ottoman Empire: The Classical Age 1300–1600*, translated by Norman Itzkowitz and Colin Imber, 1973, p. 51.

Novels for Students, Volume 2 7

Keats, John, "Ode on a Grecian Urn," in *Keats: Poetical Works*, edited by H. W. Garrod, Oxford University Press, 1973, p. 210.

Levi, Jonathan, "The Plague," in the *Los Angeles Times Book Review*, October 7, 2001, p. 9.

Pamuk, Orhan, *My Name Is Red*, translated by Erdağ M. Göknar, Vintage International, 2002.

Review of *My Name Is Red*, in *Kirkus Reviews*, Vol. 69, No. 15, August 1, 2001, p. 1058.

Review of *My Name Is Red*, in *Publishers Weekly*, Vol. 248, No. 32, August 6, 2001 p. 58.

FURTHER READING

Cicekoglu, Feride, "Difference, Visual Narration, and 'Point of View' in *My Name is Red*," in the *Journal of Aesthetic Education*, Vol. 37, No. 4, Winter 2003, pp. 124–37.

This essay focuses on the difference between Eastern and Western ways of visual narration, taking *My Name is Red* as its frame of reference.

————, "A Pedagogy of Two Ways of Seeing: A Confrontation of 'Word and Image' in *My Name is Red*," in the *Journal of Aesthetic Education*, Vol. 37, No. 3, Fall 2003, pp. 1–20.

This essay explores the role that the confrontations between different traditions play in the resolution of the two aspects of the novel's plot, the love story and the murder mystery.

Ettinghausen, Richard, *Turkish Miniatures from the Thirteenth to the Eighteenth Century*, New American Library by arrangement with UNESCO, 1965.

This small, inexpensive book contains twenty-eight reproductions of Turkish miniatures from books such as *Album of the Conqueror*, *Book of Accomplishments*, *Book of the King of Kings*, and *Book of the Festival*.

Göknar, Erdağ, "Orhan Pamuk and the 'Ottoman' Theme," in *World Literature Today*, Vol. 80, No. 6, November-December 2006, pp. 34–38.

Göknar discusses Pamuk's writing as a whole, including *My Name Is Red*. Because the novel focuses on the Ottoman Empire in a European context, Pamuk is able to explore his frequent practice of presenting characters who question their identities and try to establish a new way of understanding themselves through painting or writing.

Gun, Ganeli, "Heresy in Miniature—Commissioned by the Sultan to Illustrate a Book in the European Manner, a Group of Artists Treads a Dangerous Path," in *World and I*, Vol. 17, No. 1, January 2002, p. 226.

In this review, Gun, who has translated two of Pamuk's books into English, argues that the effect of the novel is spoiled because the translation does not render the text into colloquial (everyday) English. She claims to have discovered numerous mistranslations and misreadings.

The Secret Life of Bees

SUE MONK KIDD

2002

The Secret Life of Bees, Sue Monk Kidd's first novel, was published in 2002 and has remained a bestseller since then. Kidd gave up professional nursing to begin her writing career in the form of short inspirational essays for newspapers and magazines. From there, she began writing longer nonfiction books on spiritual transformation and feminist theology. Encouraged by the continuous support of readers and publishers, she turned to writing fiction, combining the spiritual themes she had been exploring with her memories of the southern landscape in which she grew up.

In *The Secret Life of Bees*, the fourteen-year-old narrator, Lily Owens, runs away from home with her African-American nanny at a pivotal moment in southern history, 1964, the height of the Civil Rights movement. Kidd writes in the long tradition of other Southern Gothic storytellers who are known to focus on the elements of the South's decay and moral responsibility. The success of Kidd's first novel led to the publication of a second, *The Mermaid Chair* (2005), which handles the same theme of guilt and redemption. The heroines of both stories seek forgiveness and self-knowledge. In both novels, motifs of the divine feminine make Kidd's contribution to Southern Gothic fiction unique. She illuminates a path out of the harsh legacy of slavery and domination through a feminine viewpoint. *The Secret Life of Bees* is widely used in American classrooms, indicating its timely themes of tolerance and love over power and racism.

Sue Monk Kidd (AP Images)

AUTHOR BIOGRAPHY

Sue Monk Kidd was born Sue Monk on August 12, 1948, and raised in the small town of Sylvester, Georgia, which served as a model for Sylvan, South Carolina, in *The Secret Life of Bees*. As a girl, she listened to her father's stories and began writing stories of her own that were praised by her teachers. Kidd has been a life long journal writer, using the material for her stories and books. Nevertheless, she did not major in English but took a B.S. in nursing in 1970 from Texas Christian University. She worked as a registered nurse in pediatrics and surgery, eventually teaching nursing. She married Sanford Kidd, a theology student, and they had two children, Bob and Ann.

While living in South Carolina where her husband was teaching at a liberal arts college, she enrolled in writing classes in order to write fiction, but when a nonfiction essay of hers was published in *Guideposts*, she began to write personal inspirational pieces. She became a freelancer and editor at *Guideposts*, publishing many articles there and in other magazines and newspapers.

At this time, Kidd began to read widely in literature and spiritual classics, as well as mythology and psychology. Thomas Merton and Carl Jung are two writers who influenced her in these areas. Her first book, *God's Joyful Surprise*, was in the tradition of contemplative spirituality (1988). *When the Heart Waits*, describing her own spiritual transformation, followed in 1990, and was critically acclaimed. It is this kind of spiritual experience that is woven into her novels.

Her interests broadened to feminist theology and led her to write *The Dance of the Dissident Daughter* in 1996. From there, she took up her old dream of writing fiction and became an accomplished short story writer, studying at Emory and Sewanee and the Bread Loaf Writer's Conference. In 2002, Kidd published her first novel, *The Secret Life of Bees*, and it stayed on the bestseller lists for over two years. It has sold millions of copies and has been translated into twenty-three languages. Her second novel, *The Mermaid Chair*, was published in 2005, and was also a bestseller. In 2006, her early essays were collected and published under the title, *Firstlight: The Early Inspirational Writings of Sue Monk Kidd*. She has served on the board for Poets and Writers, Inc., to encourage emerging writers, and has been Writer-in-Residence at the Sophia Institute in Charleston.

Selected awards include the Book Sense Book of the Year in paperback, 2004, for *The Secret Life of Bees*; the inaugural Literature To Life award presented by The American Place Theatre, 2004; the Quill Award in General Fiction, 2005, for *The Mermaid Chair*; and the Southeastern Library Association Fiction Award in 2005, for *The Secret Life of Bees*.

PLOT SUMMARY

Chapter 1

Each chapter is headed by an excerpt from manuals on bees that parallel the action in the story. The quote preceding chapter 1 mentions the queen bee as the unifying force of the community. This sets the stage for the story of Lily Owens, age fourteen, and how the loss of her mother at age four fragmented her life.

MEDIA ADAPTATIONS

- *The Secret Life of Bees* was adapted as an unabridged audiobook (read by Jenna Lamia) by HighBridge Audio in 2002.
- *The Secret Life of Bees* was adapted and directed by Wynn Handman. This one-woman stage show was first performed by Denise Wilbanks in 2004.

The story is set in the summer of 1964 in Sylvan, South Carolina, where Lily is living on a peach farm with her abusive father, whom she calls T. Ray, and her African-American nanny, Rosaleen. She recalls the day her mother died in 1954, remembering few details—the suitcase on the floor, the fight her parents had, the gun that she picked up and accidentally set off. The police inquiry calls it a tragic accident.

Lily recounts her misery at school where she has few friends and only the encouragement of her English teacher, who tells her she is smart and should write. She thinks she is unattractive. Her father cannot help her with her adolescent issues, so she turns to Rosaleen, a surrogate mother.

Lily's longing for her mother is like a mystical religion. She has saved relics from her mother's things: a photograph, a pair of gloves, and a postcard of a Black Madonna (the Virgin Mary depicted as an African-American woman) with the place, Tiburon, South Carolina, written on the back. These are buried in a tin box in the orchard. When T. Ray catches her sleeping in the orchard with her box, he punishes her by making her kneel for hours on grits as sharp as ground glass.

That summer, President Johnson signs the Civil Rights Act into law, and Rosaleen walks to town with Lily to register to vote. Rosaleen gets in a fight with some Caucasian men hassling her and is beaten and thrown in jail for stealing fans from the local church.

Chapter 2

The head quote, concerning swarming bees, who leave the old nest and settle nearby to start a new colony, foreshadows Lily's running away from home. Lily and Rosaleen are put into jail, but Lily's father gets her out and leaves Rosaleen there. Lily begs T. Ray to get Rosaleen out too, but he says she is in big trouble, and the man she insulted might kill her. In an argument, T. Ray tells Lily that her mother didn't love her; she was leaving the day she was killed. Lily is in shock. When her father leaves the room, she stares at a jar she left open, hoping the captured bees would fly away. They are gone, and she hears a voice in her mind saying that her own jar is open too. She gathers her things and leaves quickly, catching a ride to town with the church minister. He is on his way to press charges against Rosaleen for stealing the church fans.

When Lily finds that Rosaleen is in the hospital because the Caucasian men came into the jail and beat her, she goes to the hospital and helps Rosaleen escape. The two hitchhike to Tiburon, South Carolina, chosen because it is the only hint Lily has about her mother. She has a mystical vision of Rosaleen as a kind of Black Madonna when they bathe naked in a creek in the moonlight.

Chapter 3

The bee headnote is the instruction for finding the queen bee: first locate her circle of attendants. Lily wakes up by the creek where she and Rosaleen have spent the night. She calls this day one of her new life. They walk to Tiburon and buy some food at the general store. Lily discovers her mother's picture of the Black Madonna on some jars of honey and asks about them, thinking it is an omen. The storekeeper tells her the honey is made by August Boatwright, a colored woman, and explains how to find her pink house. Walking through Tiburon, they see signs of the times: a sign about Goldwater for President and a bumper sticker supporting the war in Viet Nam. Lily buys a newspaper looking for news of their escape, but it is only full of news of Malcolm X, Saigon, and the Beatles.

Chapter 4

Each colony of bees is a family unit, explains the bee headnote. Lily and Rosaleen meet the Boatwright sisters, August, May, and June, African-American women who live on the edge of town on a bee farm. Everything in the large house is rubbed down with beeswax, including the black wooden figure in the corner whom Lily instinctively identifies as a Black Madonna. She feels a magnetic pull to it. Lily makes up lies about why Rosaleen has stitches in her head and what they are doing there. She says her parents are dead, and she is on her way to live with her aunt in Virginia. She asks if there is any work for them so they can earn some money. August says Rosaleen can help May in the house, and Lily can help with the bees.

When May starts to talk about her twin sister April who died, she begins to hum "Oh! Susanna," a distress signal to the other sisters that May is about to go on a crying jag. They send her outdoors to her wailing wall to calm down. The sisters make the refugees at home and give them sleeping cots in the honey house, a garage/factory. Even though Lily has never felt so white, surrounded as she is by African-American women, she feels she belongs in this house. Lily makes Rosaleen promise not to tell about the picture of the Black Madonna. The only strange thing is May's homemade wailing wall with its little bits of paper stuck in the stones, carrying names of the African Americans killed in civil rights demonstrations.

Chapter 5

The headnote speaks of the darkness of beehives. The first week at August's is a relief in Lily's life. August asks no questions but helps the visitors settle in. Lily is trained in beekeeping, as Rosaleen helps May with the cooking. May is oversensitive to suffering and will not even kill cockroaches. June is a history and English teacher at the African-American high school and plays the cello for dying people. Lily overhears June telling August that they should not have taken the strangers in; everyone is aware Lily is lying. June dislikes Lily because she is Caucasian, and this reverse racism surprises Lily. The soothing fatherly figure of Walter Cronkite giving the news on TV is the opposite of T. Ray in Lily's mind. When, however, Cronkite reports the racial violence that summer, May has a fit. Every night the family kneels before the Black Mary, called Our Lady of Chains.

One evening August tells Lily a story of the nun Beatrix who ran away from the convent. When Beatrix finally returned, humbled, she found the Virgin Mary had stood in for her all those years, so people wouldn't know she was gone. Lily realizes August is trying to tell her

something about her own situation, and after that, she begins asking the Virgin Mary for help. August teaches Lily bee etiquette and how to send them love so they won't sting. Lily wants August to love her, so she will keep her. August tells Lily about May's sensitivity stemming from her twin sister's suicide at fifteen when she discovered the suffering of African-American people. At night, Lily longs for her mother. She senses her mother has been here, but Rosaleen warns her, what if Lily finds out something she doesn't want to know?

Chapter 6

The queen bee produces queen substance that attracts the other bees, announces the headnote, introducing the chapter on Our Lady of Chains. Lily meets Neil, the principal of the African-American high school, who wants to marry June. She won't have him, because she was jilted once before at the altar. Lily and June have a private war. On Sunday the sisters host a religious meeting, called the Daughters of Mary. These are local African-American women who show up in colorful costumes that Lily loves to look at. They say Hail Marys, and August tells the story of Our Lady of Chains, as follows.

The statue was once a figurehead of a ship washed up and found by slaves. She looked like a Black Madonna with her fist raised. The slaves believed she had come to give them freedom and worshipped her. She was so powerful, the master hauled her off and chained her up, but she miraculously made her way back to the slaves fifty times without help, until the master gave in and let her stay there. One by one each Daughter of Mary touches the heart of the statue, and Lily longs to touch it too, but June stops playing the cello at that moment, as if to say, you aren't one of us. Lily faints. Walter Cronkite announces the plans for the first moon launch on TV, and August tells Lily this is the end of the moon's mystery. (The moon is where Our Lady lives.)

Chapter 7

The headnote wonders how bees ever became associated with sex. This introduces Lily's meeting with Zach, the teenage African-American boy who helps August with the bees. Zach surprises her by being smart and handsome. He becomes Lily's best friend. Her only problem continues to be June, who is constantly hinting it is time for Lily to be leaving. Lily tells Zach about her love of writing, and he explains he wants to be a lawyer. She has never heard of an African-American lawyer, but Zach tells her you have to imagine what has never been. Rosaleen teases Lily that she is living in a dream world, trying to make this their home. Lily wants to confess everything to August but is afraid she will be sent back to her father.

When Zach and Lily are out on the truck driving around to beehives, Lily begins to be attracted to him. This frightens her because of the racial difference. They visit Mr. Clayton Forrest in Tiburon, the Caucasian lawyer who has befriended Zach. Zach tells Lily about the famous local writer, Willifred Marchant, and Lily is defensive about her own desire to write. He comforts her when she starts to cry, and she puts her head on his shoulder. August tries to help Lily feel comfortable enough to open up, but Lily holds back. Neil and June have a fight and break up. Lily finds herself falling in love with Zach. When he gives her a notebook for her stories, they embrace and remark on how dangerous their affection is. Lily writes stories that feature Rosaleen and August and Zach as heroes.

Chapter 8

The bee headnote says that if a honeybee is isolated from her sisters she will die. Lily settles in to her new life with the Daughters of Mary. August becomes her teacher, showing her the beekeeping business. Lily imbibes a new culture that stems from the Black Madonna, the legacy of the Boatwright grandmother, Big Mama. August tells Lily that Mary is everywhere, inside everything. When Lily asks about her history, August says that both she and June graduated from a Negro college. When August could not get a job, she became a housekeeper in Virginia. Then she inherited the bee farm from her grandmother. She never married because she prefers her freedom.

August shows Lily the beehives and tells her bees have a secret life. If she doesn't want to get stung, she must give love to the bees. Lily has another of her mystical experiences with the bees. She feels they are greeting her as a sister, trying to comfort her. In Tiburon, the racial climate is tense as the movie star, Jack Palance, plans to come to town and integrate the theater by taking an African-American woman with him. Lily remembers the Northerners coming

down on a bus in her town to integrate the city pool. Lily wonders why God made different skin pigments. Lily goes with Zach to deliver honey in Tiburon to the lawyer's office. Lily makes a collect call from there to her father, hoping he has missed her. He begins yelling at her, and she hangs up. When Lily gets home, she writes a letter to T. Ray accusing him of being a bad father but tears it up. At night when everyone is asleep, Lily goes to Our Lady of Chains and prays to be fixed.

Chapter 9

The bee headnote mentions that the fabric of bee society depends on communication, implying a lack of it will be the theme of the chapter. Lily says that July 28 was a day for the record books. While Ranger 7 lands on the surface of the moon, and the police look for the bodies of dead civil rights workers, Lily and August water the bees with sugar water because the temperature will be over one hundred degrees that day. Lily gets stung on the wrist by a bee, a sort of initiation into beekeeping. May, Rosaleen, August, and Lily play in the water sprinkler, getting soaked. When June comes out, Lily soaks her with water, and they have a water fight, ending in laughter and forgiveness. Lily and June hug. Lily feels she should tell August about herself but is afraid to spoil the happiness she has found. When she sees May making a trail of graham cracker crumbs and marshmallows to get the roaches out of the house without killing them, Lily is startled, remembering her mother did a similar thing. She wonders if her mother had been here. She asks May if she knew a Deborah Fontenel. May says yes, she stayed in the honey house.

Just as Lily decides she needs to talk to August about her mother, Zach asks her to come to town with him. They see trouble happening between a group of colored boys and some white men. One of the black boys throws a bottle, and the glass cuts a white man. All of the boys are arrested, and no one will say who did it. Zach will have to stay in jail for at least five days before bail can be set. Everyone is angry and worried for Zach, and they decide to keep the news from May. August and Lily visit Zach in jail. Lily promises him that she will write all of these events in a story for him. A few days later, the phone rings and May answers it. It is Zach's mother, who tells May the boy is in jail. May collapses. Then she says she is going to the wailing wall. It is dusk. May takes a flashlight and goes out alone.

Chapter 10

The headnote concerns the shortness of a bee's life. When May is delayed returning from the wall, everyone sets out to find her. They comb the woods while June calls the police. August finds May in the river in two feet of water with a stone on her chest. Lily is nauseated and vomits in the wood. August tells the policeman that May was depressed. He questions Lily, and she lies about who she is and what she is doing there, saying she is an orphan. He does not understand why a Caucasian girl is staying with African-American women and tells her she had better not be there when he returns.

Lily dreams about Zach, but when she wakes, she remembers he is still in jail. The coffin with May in it, fixed up, comes home to the pink house, so May can be mourned properly by the Daughters of Mary. June plays the cello, and Lily feels May's presence in the room. She speaks to her, asking her to look up her mother in heaven with the message to send a sign to Lily that she loves her. Zach arrives, having been let out of jail, and Lily sees something in him has changed.

August, Lily, and Zach go out to drape the hives with black crepe. If the bees stay in the hive, it means the person will live again. August says there are pictures of bees scratched on the walls of catacombs as a symbol of resurrection. When the Daughters of Mary come for the vigil, they make Lily feel like one of them. Lily thinks African-American women are like hidden royalty and doesn't know how they had become so low on the totem pole. May's suicide note is found and she explains to her sisters that she is tired of carrying around the weight of the world. She is going to lay it down. She asks her sisters to live. August tells June it means she must marry Neil.

Chapter 11

The bee fact announced at the beginning of the chapter is that it takes millions of foraging trips to make one pound of honey. This chapter brings together the bits of happiness the characters have earned between them all summer. Now Lily is desperate to have her talk with August about her mother, but August is in her period of mourning and keeps to herself. Neil and June are courting, and Lily and Zach keep company. She wishes she were a Negro girl, but he says they can't change their skins, only the world. He still dreams of being a lawyer. Zach has an angry

edge to him now; he speaks of racial tensions and Malcolm X.

When the mourning is over, there is a celebration dinner and evening prayers, and Lily feels the world is back to normal. Lily prepares herself to talk to August about her mother, but she is afraid of being sent to prison for her crime of helping Rosaleen escape. The talk is put off once more, for it is Mary Day the next day, and everyone is baking and decorating. It is a day of thanks when the story of Our Lady of Chains is reenacted. Neil asks June to marry him again, and she says yes. They go off to buy her ring. The Daughters of Mary arrive in the evening and fuss over Lily. They form a circle of feeding and give each other a sort of communion of honey cakes. The statue of Mary is hauled in the wagon, and chained in the honey house for the night as part of the ritual.

Zach and Lily go for a walk by the river, and she asks him not to become mean in his anger at the world. He kisses her. He says he will do everything to become a lawyer, and Lily knows he will, because changes are coming, even to South Carolina. He promises after he makes something of himself, they will be together. He gives her his dog tag.

Chapter 12

The headnote explains the behavior of the queen bee, shy and skittish and perpetually in eternal night, the mother of the hive. This is a chapter about August and Lily's mother, Deborah, the mysterious queen bees of the story. Lily waits in August's room. When August enters, Lily lays out the picture of her mother and asks if they can talk now. August knows who her mother is and says Lily is the spitting image of Deborah. August tells her she worked for the Fontanel family in Virginia and took care of her mother when Deborah was a little girl.

Lily explains why she left home and cries in August's arms. August is like a sponge, absorbing her pain. Lily confesses how she accidentally killed her mother. August tells her that in spite of that, Lily is lovable, and that it seems she was meant to find them. August explains Deborah's background and painful marriage to her father, who was not always so mean. In the beginning, he worshipped her mother and was desolate when she left him. Deborah only married because she was pregnant, and when she felt trapped, she turned to August as a mother, the way Lily turns to Rosaleen. She fled to August's house in Tiburon when Lily was small, because she was falling apart.

Lily says she now hates her mother for leaving her behind. Lily had created a myth about her mother's love, and now she faces the bitter truth that she was an unwanted child. August defends Deborah, saying she had a nervous breakdown, but after three months, Deborah went back home to collect Lily and her things and move to Tiburon. The accident prevented that. August tucks Lily into bed and tells her that nothing is perfect; there is only life.

Chapter 13

A worker bee can fly with a heavier load than herself, explains the headnote. Lily carries the weight of her discovery about her mother in this chapter. The statue of Black Mary is still bound in chains in the honey house, but Lily approaches her for help. She wants someone to understand her devastation and anger at losing her mother. In a fit of anger she flings all the honey jars against the wall and smashes them. Emptied out, she falls asleep by the statue. Rosaleen finds her with blood on her arm, then cleans her up as Lily explains her anger. Lily realizes she could allow this bitterness to take over her life. Rosaleen and Lily clean the honey house before the Daughters of Mary come for the end of the Mary Day ceremony, celebrating Mary's Ascension to heaven.

Neil and Zach unchain the statue and put her on the ground in the sun. They take off her chains, read the Bible, and bathe the statue with honey. This ritual with the other Daughters has a healing effect on Lily. Lily thinks to herself if she could have one miracle from the Bible happen to her it would be to be raised from the dead. August brings Lily a box of her mother's belongings. Among the items is a photo of Deborah with her baby, Lily. Their noses are touching and her mother smiles radiantly. This is the sign of love from her mother that Lily had been looking for.

Chapter 14

The headnote announces that a queenless bee colony will die, but a new queen can be introduced to make great change. This comments on Lily's own healing and acceptance of her divine mother, Mary. Lily spends time by the river. She muses over all her hurts and is haunted by her mother. August says she is grieving. Meanwhile, June plans

her wedding to Neil, and Rosaleen goes to town to register to vote, to finish what she tried to do in Sylvan. Then Zach announces he is going to the Caucasian high school in the fall. Life goes on.

Lily cleans her room and makes an altar with her mother's things. She has finally made her peace. The next day she wears her mother's whale pin on her dress. Her mourning is finished, and she goes to the beehives with August. One of the hives is missing a queen. August explains they have to put in a new queen to save the hive. She also makes the connection to Lily's situation. If her own mother, Deborah, is missing, then Our Lady could be the stand in, she suggests. August says that Our Lady is not outside but inside of us. August takes Lily's hand and places it on her own heart.

T. Ray, who traced her from the collect call from Mr. Forrest's office, finds Lily at the Boatwrights. She is alone. T. Ray takes out his knife and stabs the chair in a threatening way, saying he will take Lily back. Then he sees the whale pin on her dress and is shocked, for he had given it to Deborah. Lily finally sees how much he must have loved Deborah. T. Ray hits Lily so hard, she falls into Our Lady. He starts calling her Deborah, as though temporarily mad, and she calls him Daddy to snap him out of it. Lily feels she has seen into the dark place in his soul that will never heal. She asserts that she will stay with August. August comes into the room and confirms they love Lily and want her to stay. The Daughters of Mary arrive to stand by Lily, and T. Ray leaves. As T. Ray is pulling out in his truck, Lily runs to ask him if she truly killed her mother. He says that she did, and that it was an accident. She doesn't know if he tells the truth, but she turns back to all the loving women on the porch waiting for her. Clayton Forrest has the charges dropped against Lily and Rosaleen. Lily becomes friends with Clayton's daughter, Becca, and they enroll in the same high school with Zach. Lily continues to write her stories and takes over May's wailing wall, feeding it with prayers. Often she feels Black Mary inside, rising up, filling up the holes life gouges out.

CHARACTERS

Big Mama

The grandmother of the Boatwright sisters passed on beekeeping and its lore to them when they spent summers on the farm with her as children. She also gave them the wisdom and worship of the Black Madonna, as well as the statue of Our Lady of Chains. Their grandfather then left the farm to August, who was able to stop being a servant and start her business as a beekeeper.

August Boatwright

The eldest Boatwright sister and leader of the Daughters of Mary is the owner of the bee farm and main beekeeper. She makes and sells her Black Madonna honey all over the county. She is tall and dignified, dressed in white like an African bride, when Lily first meets her. She has wire rim glasses and gray hair, is wise and reflective. Lily is surprised to find an African-American person who is so intelligent and well read. August was once a high school teacher like June but never married because she wants her independence. A storyteller and keeper of the myths about the secret life of bees and the Black Madonna, August is the mother figure to whom first Deborah, and then her daughter, Lily, turn in their need. Once the housekeeper for Lily's grandmother in Virginia, she is a respected business woman in Tiburon, South Carolina, with her Black Madonna honey in all the stores and delivered to customers in the truck. She believes in Lily and gives her a chance, making her an apprentice beekeeper. August's elevated status seems to be accepted in the county, for she is not challenged by the local authorities, especially when she harbors Lily. It is a time of fear in the south, but August is unafraid, clearly the queen bee and role model Lily is looking for. Lily feels as if her house is protected by the Black Madonna herself. August's spiritual equilibrium is demonstrated in her leadership of the Daughters of Mary, who rejoice when they are happy, and mourn when they are sad, but never harbor bitterness. August manifests the Madonna's wisdom and protection, balancing out June's excessive intellectual qualities and May's excessive emotional qualities.

June Boatwright

The intellectual and proud sister dislikes Lily at first. She teaches history and English at the colored high school and plays the cello for dying people and at the meetings of the Daughters of Mary. She dates Neil, the African-American principal of the high school who keeps proposing marriage to her, and she keeps refusing because she was once jilted at the altar. Her reverse racism shocks Lily, as she had no idea that African-American people could dislike Caucasians because they were Caucasian. June also dislikes Lily because she can cause trouble for them, and also because her sister August once had to be a servant for Lily's grandmother in Virginia. June is a little embittered, cautious, and does not like to embrace new things. After May's suicide, June marries Neil because May wanted her to live her life fully without fear.

May Boatwright

The emotionally disturbed and oversensitive sister of June and August commits suicide when she hears Zach is in jail. May's twin sister April similarly killed herself at fifteen when she first discovered racial injustice. May will not even kill cockroaches and has kept herself going by creating her wailing wall in the garden as a memorial to sufferers; she writes the names and dates of suffering on slips of paper, and inserts the papers in the cracks. She hums "Oh! Susanna" when she is upset. May is childlike, direct and intuitive and is the first to tell Lily that her mother was in their house. She has braids all over her head and likes to go barefoot. She teaches Lily the honey song, "Place a beehive on my grave" that is sung at her memorial vigil. May is the cook and housekeeper of the family. She is overly compassionate, compared to Mary, with her heart on the outside of her chest.

Rosaleen Daise

Lily's African-American nanny is a former peach orchard worker in Sylvan, whom T. Ray hires to take care of the house after Deborah's death. Rosaleen is Lily's surrogate mother, and they have a prickly but close relationship. Rosaleen does not go to church, but has made her own religion that is a mixture of nature and ancestor worship. She is rebellious, like Lily herself, and when Rosaleen goes into town to register to vote, gets into trouble with Caucasian men who hassle her. She spits her tobacco juice on their shoes and refuses to wipe it off. She is beaten and thrown in jail, and Lily rescues her and runs away to save her. Rosaleen is special friends with May Boatwright, helping her with cooking and housework. Rosaleen takes May's place after May dies.

Daughters of Mary

The Daughters of Mary include neighbors of the Boatwrights in the Tiburon area: Queenie and her daughter, Violet; Lunelle, who makes outrageous hats; Mabalee; Cressie; and one man, Otis Hill and his wife, Sugar-Girl. They are often joined by Neil and Zach. Colorful, cheerful, eccentric and loving, the Daughters are a circle of devotees that worship God as a woman, as Our Lady of Chains, an old slave legend of the Black Mary. They gather in the Boatwright parlor on Sundays and special holidays. Lily thinks they are special and feels honored to be accepted by them.

Clayton Forrest

The Caucasian lawyer in Tiburon wears red suspenders and a bow tie. He has sandy hair and blue eyes and a friendly smile. He is a good man, who is a friend of the Boatwrights and takes young Zach under his wing, encouraging him to be a lawyer. He helps out in legal matters, such as clearing Zach, Lily, and Rosaleen of possible legal charges against them. His daughter Becca becomes a friend of Lily and Zach's at the Caucasian high school in Tiburon. It is from making a collect call from Mr. Forrest's office that Lily's father is able to trace her.

Avery Gaston

Known as Shoe to the locals, he is the policeman in Sylvan, who appears nice and soft spoken but looks the other way when the Caucasian men come in to beat up Rosaleen in her jail cell. He has the ears of a child, says Lily.

Brother Gerald

The pastor of Ebenezer Baptist Church which Lily and T. Ray attend, is bigoted. Rosaleen and Lily rest there on their way to Sylvan when Rosaleen goes to register to vote. Rosaleen, being African-American, was not supposed to be in the church. Brother Gerald said, we love Negroes in the Lord, but they have their own place. It was so hot that Rosaleen stole the fans from the pew, and Brother Gerald was going to press charges against her, but Lily convinced him that Rosaleen was deaf and didn't know better.

Miss Lacy

The secretary of lawyer Clayton Forrest is about eighty years old and wears fire-red lipstick. It is clear she does not understand what a Caucasian girl like Lily is doing with the Boatwrights. Lily imagines her spreading the rumor all over town.

Willifred Marchant

The famous local author in Tiburon who, Zach says, has won three Pulitzer prizes for her books on deciduous trees of South Carolina. Her books are as esteemed by the Tiburons as the Bible, and every year the schools hold tree planting ceremonies in her name. Lily thinks Zach evokes her as a threat that she will never amount to anything as a writer and cries. Zach comforts Lily, telling her she will be a fine writer.

Neil

No last name is given in the book for the tall, African-American high school principal who is courting June. They work at the same school. He fixes things for the Boatwright sisters, such as their truck, and joins in the ceremonies of the Daughters of Mary. Eventually, June gives in and marries him, for this was May's wish before she died.

Our Lady of Chains

The old blackened ship's masthead in the parlor of the Boatwright house has the shape of a woman with her fist raised. She is thought to be a Black Madonna. According to legend, she was worshipped as the Virgin Mary by slaves. When taken away by the master and chained up, she miraculously returned to her people each time. She has a sacred heart painted on her chest that is touched during religious services held by the Daughters of Mary. The worship of the statue was passed down by August's grandmother, Big Mama. August, reading about the tradition of Black Mary, used the picture of the Black Madonna of Breznichar, the Bohemian portrait of the Black Virgin, on the honey jars that she sells. She is the Madonna who can release one from bondage, as she gave the slaves hope for freedom and, with her fist raised, represented redress of injustice.

Deborah Fontanel Owens

Lily's mother was the pretty daughter of the widow Sarah Fontanel, in Virginia, where August Boatwright was the housekeeper. Deborah was a somewhat dependent only child, and she clung to August as a mother figure. She moved to South Carolina to be near August when her mother died, and there she unhappily married T. Ray Owens when she became pregnant. She ran away from her husband and child when she was having a nervous breakdown and stayed for a time with the Boatwright sisters. She went back to Sylvan to pack and get Lily, but she was accidentally shot before she could return to the Boatwrights.

Lily Melissa Owens

The first person narrator and main character is a rebellious and spirited girl of fourteen in the summer of 1964, living with her abusive father, T. Ray, on a peach farm. She is implicated in the accidental shooting death of her mother, Deborah, when she was four years old and has been racked with guilt and longing for her mother ever since. Her birthday, July 4th, is the day her transformation begins, when her African-American nanny, Rosaleen, is arrested for insulting Caucasian men. Lily is likeable for her honest voice and passionate spiritual searching. Like May, she is unusually sensitive to the injustice around her, but she has strength and hope that May does not. Though Lily has inherited a bigoted way of life, she is willing to examine it in herself and change. She has a poetic and spiritual way of seeing the beauty around her. Something of an ugly duckling at home in Sylvan, South Carolina, she blossoms at the home of the Boatwright sisters in Tiburon where she runs away. She thinks she is unattractive but finds out she is pretty like her mother. Lily is smart; her English teacher encourages her to write and read. She keeps journals, making stories of her adventures. Imagination is not for escape for her, but is a means of bringing forth something better in life. As she discusses with Zach, one has to imagine what has never been. This ability is what keeps her from becoming bitter or depressed like her father and mother. Rosaleen tells Lily to quit pretending that the Boatwright home is their home, but because she projects so much of her imagination into living there, it does become their new home.

Lily is open to life and to change, and this keeps her moving in the right direction. Her courage is exhibited in the way she gets Rosaleen out of the hospital, and in the way she does not accept a false and cruel life with T. Ray. She refuses to live the hopeless life her mother chose. Though unworldly, she is resourceful and daring when it comes to running away, finding the Boatwrights through pluck and intelligence. Her quest is to find forgiveness and to find mother love, which she does through the Black Madonna. From the beginning, she is given to mystical experiences of places, events, and people. She thinks about God and questions why things are the way they are. Because of this, she receives answers and matures in the course of the novel.

Terrence Ray Owens

Lily calls him T. Ray. Lily's mean father was not always mean. Once loving, he became bitter when the wife he adored, Deborah, ran away and then was accidentally killed, leaving him with their young daughter. He takes his anger out on Lily, refusing to give her love or proper attention. He is bigoted, ignorant, and abuses his power as a white man to get his way. A peach farmer in rural South Carolina with little imagination or sympathy for others, he is moderately successful but an unreliable parent; Lily never knows if he is lying to her. She says he is the opposite of Walter Cronkite, who is her symbol for an honest and caring father figure. T. Ray goes after Lily when she runs away, using violence to try to make her return, but he backs down and leaves her alone when the Daughters of Mary stand by her.

Jack Palance

A movie star who plans to integrate the theater in Tiburon by showing his movie, accompanied by an African-American woman as his date. This upsets the bigots in town and causes the skirmish between the Caucasian men and Zach's friends.

Zachary Lincoln Taylor

Zach is a young African-American man (Lily's age) who works for August, tending the bees on the farm and delivering honey all over the county. He is intelligent and handsome and plans to become a lawyer, even though this was difficult for African Americans at this time. He attends the African-American high school, is an A student, a football player, and likes the jazz musician, Miles Davis, indicating his intellectual tastes. He transfers to a Caucasian high school in the new wave of desegregation. Befriended by Caucasian lawyer Clayton Forrest, who gives him law books and helps him when he is in trouble, Luke is unjustly thrown in jail for something he didn't do, and this injustice is what fuels May's suicide. He is Lily's first boy friend and he encourages her to write. Zach is a model of the young and ambitious African Americans who will emerge from the events of the sixties with new possibilities available to them.

THEMES

Racial Intolerance

The action takes place during the summer of 1964 after the signing of the Civil Rights Bill by President Johnson. There are references throughout

TOPICS FOR FURTHER STUDY

- Give a report to your class on how conditions have changed in the United States for African Americans since President Johnson signed the Civil Rights Act in 1964, especially in terms of voting, education, and segregation.

- Make a scrapbook with pictures and text about goddesses from different cultural traditions. Write down what you find in common with the religious practices and beliefs of the Daughters of Mary.

- Write an essay that compares and contrasts Lily's spiritual experiences of God to that of saints like Julian of Norwich or Hildegard of Bingen. In what way could Lily and August be thought of as contemplatives (those who find God through inner experience)?

- Compare and contrast the U.S. space program of 1964 with the space program today. How has the space race of the Cold War been replaced by a more cooperative approach? Use visual aids and historic photographs of space missions to illustrate your points in a class presentation.

- Highlight the achievements of African-American leaders in the cause of civil rights from 1955 to 1968. You might give an overview of the development of the Civil Rights movement or focus on some particular figure, like Rosa Parks, Martin Luther King Jr., or Malcolm X. Present your findings in a report.

- Read another story or novel in the Southern Gothic genre by a female writer (Harper Lee, Flannery O'Connor, Carson McCullers, etc.). In an essay, compare and contrast the settings, characters, and plot to *The Secret Life of Bees*.

the book to desegregation and racial violence, beginning with Rosaleen attempting to register to vote. When Rosaleen and Lily are hot, they go into the white Baptist church to cool off, and Brother Gerald, the minister, asks them to leave.

Brother Gerald's opinion is that Caucasians can love Negroes, but only in the Lord; they have their own place, not with Caucasians. When Rosaleen announces proudly to the Caucasian men she is going to register to vote, they hassle her, and she spits tobacco juice on their shoes. She is thrown in jail and charged with stealing fans from the church, then she is beat up because the policeman lets the Caucasian men into her cell.

May's wailing wall contains slips of paper with the names and dates of each racial atrocity, as she tries to live with so much injustice and suffering. Her twin sister, April, had killed herself at fifteen when she understood what was in store for her as an African American. The bee farm seems safe with the Black Madonna watching over Lily and her new African-American family, but even a clean cut boy like Zach, who has high aspirations, gets caught up in racial turmoil when his friend throws a bottle that cuts a Caucasian man. Though innocent, Zach stands with his friends in solidarity and goes to jail. The incident begins to make him angry and bitter, illustrating what happens to wound the souls of young African Americans, and how hatred perpetuates itself.

Lily has to confront racial prejudice in herself several times, such as, for instance, when she is surprised that August is intelligent and Zach is handsome. She feels ashamed when she watches the race riots on TV. Lily is completely shocked by her own attraction to an African-American boy. The policeman who tells Lily he doesn't want to see her at the Boatwrights when he comes back refers to a Jim Crow law in South Carolina indicating that no African American can be a guardian for a Caucasian child. In the end, the young people, Lily, Zach, and Becca Forrest, stand for the new trend of desegregation as they attend a Caucasian high school together in the fall as friends.

Need for Parental Love

Lily is starved for parental love and guidance. She confesses the tragedy of her life, the accidental shooting of her mother when she was four, and her constant prayer, "Mother, forgive." Lily is desperate for a mother's love and creates her own myth and worship of her mother, hoarding a few objects, such as a picture of her mother, and a postcard of the Black Madonna from Tiburon. Her impetus for running away is as much to find a sign that her mother loved her, as to save Rosaleen, who is a maternal surrogate.

Similarly, Lily is also missing a father, for though she lives with him, he ignores and abuses her. T. Ray is a bully, punishing Lily for the slightest offense, making her kneel for hours on grits as sharp as ground glass in order to humble and humiliate her. She sees the same sneer on her father's face as on the face of the racists who heckle Zach: "the sort of look conjured from power without benefit of love." He is a bigot, ignorant of the rights of others. In this way, the theme of parental love is widened to include a larger social scope as well. By contrast, Lily singles out Walter Cronkite on the evening news as a soft spoken and reliable father figure for the whole nation. Surely, Cronkite cares and tells the truth, unlike her father who lies to her. The Caucasian lawyer, Clayton Forrest, is a good father towards his own daughter, and Zach and Lily as well.

There is a hole in Lily's heart from not having parental love, especially mother love, but August teaches her that if one's earthly mother is not dependable, there is always a heavenly mother. Lily turns to the Black Madonna, through the circle of the Daughters of Mary, to be healed.

Guilt and Redemption

Lily has anger towards her parents, but she has guilt as well, especially towards her mother, as she feels responsible for her mother's death. There is no one in Lily's young world to help her bear or understand this kind of guilt. She uses her imagination to help her survive, imagining meeting her mother in heaven and writing stories, inventing her own myths about her mother and inventing secret ceremonies in the orchard with the buried mementos. Lily's guilt makes her both vulnerable and self-deprecating. She does not believe she is good or deserves much kindness because of her crime. At the same time, she is rebellious. She yearns for acceptance and forgiveness.

August becomes not only a mother, but a sort of spiritual teacher for Lily. She tells Lily about the secret life of bees, which includes the secrets of human life as well. The beekeeping lore and the lore of the Black Madonna give Lily new archetypes, a new religion of strength, love, and forgiveness. For instance, August tells Lily that she must give the bees love so she won't be stung:

"Every little thing wants to be loved." At first, the bees do not sting Lily when she loves them. She also has to learn that sometimes even when one gives love, bees sting anyway. Big Mama said that is why women make good beekeepers; they understand the stings from taking care of families.

Lily confesses killing her mother to August, who tells her it was a terrible accident and takes her in her arms and says she loves her. This confession and absolution start Lily's healing. In the beginning, it is Lily who must be forgiven for killing her mother. After she learns she was unwanted, she is angry, and it is she who must forgive her mother. August tells her, "There is nothing perfect ... There is only life."

Lily goes through a period of mourning once she learns the truth about her mother's temporary desertion. She is empty and drained out, ready to be filled again. During the Mary Day celebration the Daughters chant "We will rise." Lily desires to be miraculously brought back from the dead, as in the Bible. August finds a box of Deborah's belongings in which there is a picture of Deborah and Lily together. It is obvious from her mother's expression that Deborah loves her child. This is the sign Lily has looked for. People would rather die than forgive, because they come to love their wounds, Lily reflects. But not wanting to become bitter like her father, she chooses forgiveness. August tells her she must not only love, but persist in love. Lily, using her many religious epiphanies with the bees and Our Lady, is able to forgive herself and her mother, and even her father. August teaches her that she is divine, that God and forgiveness are inside.

God as Mother

Lily was raised a Baptist and had hardly ever heard of the Mother of God, who only appears at Christmas in the Protestant doctrine. By the end of the summer, she has experienced the truth August tells her: the divine Mother, the Black Madonna, goes into the holes life has gouged out of us. August teaches her to experience God as Mother in the religion of the Daughters of Mary. Lily has her own homemade mother religion before she even meets August, that includes the mysterious postcard of the Black Madonna her mother got in Tiburon. She makes a myth of how her mother loved her and imagines speaking to her in heaven. When they run away, she has a

Martin Luther King Jr. and his wife Coretta Scott King lead a civil rights march from Selma, Alabama, to the state capital in Montgomery (William Lovelace / Express / Getty Images)

vision of Rosaleen naked in the stream in moonlight, and it is a prefiguration of the Black Madonna she is about to discover in Tiburon.

On Sundays, the Boatwrights hold services so the congregation, the Daughters of Mary, can touch the sacred heart of Mary on the statue of Our Lady of Chains to receive grace. Mary Day, celebrating Mary's Ascension to heaven, is the main ceremony that allows Lily to rise from her spiritual death to a rebirth. It begins with the circle of feeding, a new sort of communion, where each one feeds the other honey cakes, symbolizing sharing and nurturing, both of which are maternal traits.

STYLE

Southern Gothic

The Gothic novel, or supernatural mystery story, that took its name from the spooky Gothic mansions of its settings, originated in eighteenth and nineteenth century Europe and was adapted to fiction that takes place in the Southern United States. The style may include old mansions, threats of violence, grotesque characters, death or a murder mystery, the theme of decay, an appeal to the supernatural, a haunting past with family secrets, omens and prophesies, and a spiritual or moral dimension. William Faulkner, Flannery O'Connor, Carson McCullers, Harper Lee, and Truman Capote are among writers of this genre. *The Secret Life of Bees* has some of these elements, such as the omens Lily sees around her: prophesies, such as bees swarming before a death; T. Ray's cruel character; May's suicide; the threat of racial violence; the mystery of Deborah's death; and the miraculous powers of Our Lady of Chains. The book is reminiscent of Scout's adventures in *To Kill a Mockingbird*, by Harper Lee. Scout confronts the evil in human nature the way Lily does, and both young heroines triumph, finding faith in life's continuance and renewal, despite cruelty and ignorance around them. Because of their own generosity and goodness, they see it in others, and receive it in turn. Like Scout's story, Lily's takes place in small southern towns full of bigoted characters. Atticus Finch, the liberal white lawyer in Harper Lee's story, is similar to Clayton Forrest in Kidd's novel.

Bildungsroman

The Secret Life of Bees is fashioned primarily as a bildungsroman, a coming of age novel, showing the emergence of a young person and their shift in views to see the world in a more adult perspective. In the bildungsroman, the main character's growth is chronicled, step by step, from innocence to experience. Usually, the hero or heroine must discover that life is not black and white, but mixed, and must learn to accept responsibility for his or her own life, rather than living a false, conventional life. This novel form became popular in the nineteenth century with such examples as *David Copperfield* by Charles Dickens and *Jane Eyre* by Charlotte Brontë. *Huckleberry Finn* by Mark Twain, for instance, has a similar innocent first person narrator whose perspective is more direct and truthful than an adult's, thus laying bare hypocrisy and injustice. Like Huck Finn, Lily is the young Caucasian person who runs away with an older African-American servant. Huck and Jim in Twain's novel, and Lily and Rosaleen in Kidd's novel, become friends in a treacherous and bigoted southern landscape. Both Huck and Lily have to overcome what they have been taught about the place of African Americans, using their own humane intuition and moral judgment. Their growth points to the larger moral growth needed in society.

Spiritual Memoir

One of Kidd's mentors was Henry David Thoreau, who wrote nonfictional spiritual memoir. *Walden* is assigned to Lily by Mrs. Henry, her English teacher. Like Thoreau, Lily does not just tell autobiographical incidents from her life but teases out the moral and spiritual implication of everything that happens to her. This is primarily achieved through paralleling the life of bees to human life, highlighted in the headnotes to each chapter. Thoreau had a similar habit of seeing spiritual laws in natural phenomena, such as a river rising in spring as a proof of the eternal resurrection of the spirit. Similarly, the secret life of bees contains the wisdom of life; for instance, the hive cannot survive without its mother or queen bee, symbolizing the search for mother. Lily ultimately must find the queen, or mother, within. Finding the spiritual truth within oneself is the message of many spiritual memoirs, a form popular today for its inspirational power.

HISTORICAL CONTEXT

Racial Tension

May's homemade wailing wall in the backyard of the Boatwright house in *The Secret Life of Bees* makes sense in terms of the historic context of the summer of 1964. This was the time when the efforts towards desegregation in the south were heating up, and there was much violence as protesters were thrown in jail or killed on the streets. The civil rights of African Americans were dearly bought, and May's heartbreaking notes stuck in her wall, memorialize the sacrifice. Racial tension in the United States is nothing new, but it is important to remember that, although African Americans had the legal right to vote, in the 1950s and early 1960s, when the Civil Rights movement began to take shape, African Americans were barred from registering to vote in the south and from running for office. At the same time, segregation made it impossible for African Americans to mingle with Caucasians in any public place. One must imagine separate restaurants, movie theaters, schools, churches, hotels, and parks. African-American citizens had little legal recourse for injustice. The federal court ruled segregation in schools unconstitutional in 1954, but it was still in practice. If African Americans were arrested and thrown in jail, it was common for them to be beaten and held without charges. Lily is like many Caucasians at this time, barely aware of the problem, for she lives on the privileged side of the fence. African Americans, like Rosaleen, and even August, were employed and taken for granted as nannies, housekeepers, cooks, and workers, much as in slave days. Zach's dream of becoming a lawyer is a revelation for Lily.

Demonstrations and the Civil Rights Act

In 1955, Rosa Parks in Montgomery, Alabama, broke the rule that African Americans had to sit in the back of the bus and she was arrested as a result. It was the spark that set off demonstrations and sit-ins by African Americans everywhere to win their civil rights. In 1962, when African-American James Meredith tried to attend the University of Mississippi by federal court order, two people were killed and twenty-nine marshalls shot trying to protect him. Zach's act of attending a Caucasian high school in Tiburon thus shows great courage. In 1963, the Children's Crusade, with thousands of African-

COMPARE & CONTRAST

- **1964:** Ranger 7 lands on the moon to send back pictures of the surface in the aggressive space race between the United States and Soviet Union during the Cold War.

  Today: U.S. astronauts take their spacewalk from the international space station, containing American and Soviet astronauts working together to create a permanent orbiting science institute in space.

- **1964:** Jim Crow laws in the south, proclaiming separate but equal status, prevent African-American students from attending white schools. During the Civil Rights Movement many Americans, African-American and Caucasian, are killed in demonstrations when African-American students try to integrate into Caucasian high schools and colleges.

  Today: African-American students are free to attend the schools of their choice, though inequities still exist, as for example, the low number of African-American faculty members in higher education.

- **1964:** Four years before his assassination, despite his arrests and time in jail, at the age of thirty-five, Martin Luther King Jr. is the youngest man to receive the Nobel Peace Prize.

  Today: Frequently compared to Lincoln in terms of his martyrdom, Martin Luther King Jr. is celebrated as one of the great patriots of his country. His birthday is a national holiday and is honored with as much importance as Lincoln's and Washington's birthdays.

- **1964:** Beekeeping is a local and ancient art. The usual beekeeping problems are stings, swarming hives, and regional weather patterns affecting honey production.

  Today: Beekeeping is commercialized, and the number of independent beekeepers has dropped. The first national bee crisis is reported and labeled as "Colony Collapse Disorder." Worker bees suddenly abandon the hive, possibly because of climate change, pesticides, or the stress of over production, thus threatening the pollination necessary for agriculture.

American high school student protesters, was attacked by fire hoses and police dogs in Birmingham. The violence roused public outrage. The 1963 march on Washington, DC, where Dr. Martin Luther King, Jr., delivered his famous "I Have a Dream" speech was attended by 200,000 people and made a huge impact on public awareness, yet it was not until July 2, 1964, that President Johnson was able to get the Civil Rights Act passed. This bill barred discrimination in public places, and mentioned voting rights, but voter's rights were addressed more fully in the Voting Rights Act of 1965, which suspended the poll taxes, literacy tests, and other measures that had kept African Americans from voting. Within months, a quarter of a million African Americans, like Rosaleen, registered to vote, and within four years, voter registration in the south doubled, as African Americans entered the political scene as a new force.

Violence

The Secret Life of Bees opens with the announcement of the Civil Rights Act of 1964, and that summer was a crucial one for the cause. Lily says, "Since Mr. Johnson signed that law, it was like somebody had ripped the side seams out of American life." It was Mississippi Freedom Summer where Caucasian college students from the north came in buses to help register African Americans to vote and to teach in Freedom Schools. The murder of four of those students is mentioned in the novel. Dr. Martin Luther King,

Jr., won the Nobel Peace Prize in 1964 for his nonviolent methods of creating change, but his future martyrdom in 1968 is referred to in Rosaleen's dream of the red spit in his mouth painting her toenails. It was a decade of assassinations: President John F. Kennedy in 1963, Malcolm X in 1965, Dr. King and Robert Kennedy in 1968. Meanwhile, there were race riots in northern cities like New York and Philadelphia and later in Watts, Los Angeles. African-American militancy was born in the Black Power groups and Malcolm X's ideas of African-American self-sufficiency appealed to many younger African Americans, who, like Zach, were impatient with slow change.

The Music of the 1960s

The reference to the Beatles, English pop stars, highlights mainstream music of the time, yet Zach listens to Miles Davis, one of the most influential African-American jazz musicians of the twentieth century, who pioneered cool jazz and jazz fusion. Zach signals his sophistication in admiring the intellectual Davis, who, though famous and respected throughout the world, still suffered the indignity of being beaten by a policeman in 1959 for appearing with a Caucasian woman in public—an event that made him bitter, as Zach becomes bitter after being arrested.

The Space Race

The space race, illustrated by the Ranger 7 flight in chapter 6, was a real political issue in the 1960s, as the United States and the Soviet Union competed to reach the moon first. Not only would such an achievement create prestige but it would display technical mastery in the Cold War. The Soviets seemed to be ahead in the early 1960s with their manned flights. The American Ranger 7 missile, launched the summer of 1964, was one of a series designed to explore the moon; it sent back 4,300 pictures showing the moon surface to be dominated by craters. These launches prepared for the actual moon landing in 1969. August Boatwright echoes a popular sentiment that the moon launches destroy the mystery of the moon, which she associates with Mary.

The Vietnam War

During the 1960s, the Vietnam conflict was in full force, another result, like the space race, of Cold War tension. The civil war in Vietnam between the Northern communist government in Hanoi and the Southern democracy of Saigon was taken as a proving ground between the Americans and Soviets. In 1964, the American involvement was escalating, and it was not until 1975 that Americans finally withdrew from their only military defeat. The anti-war movement at home is not mentioned in the novel, but Americans were furious at so much money and so many lives being wasted abroad when there was so much need at home. With these dramatic events, Kidd connects the events in Lily's life to the life of the country as a whole, as a moment of coming of age, in which the country must reflect on its priorities and aggressive methods, as well as its loss of mother consciousness.

CRITICAL OVERVIEW

From its first publication in 2002, the book was a bestseller and was critically acclaimed in reviews throughout the country. Adam Mazmanian's article in the *New York Times Book Review* is typical. "Lily is a wonderfully petulant and self-absorbed adolescent, and Kidd deftly portrays her sense of injustice as it expands to accommodate broader social evils," he states. Most readers agree with Mazmanian's assessment that the characters are "fully imagined." An article in the *Virginia Quarterly Review* describes the book as a "gem of a first novel" and mentions that the book is "rich in symbolism and feminine adaptations of devout religious practices ... a captivating story of self-discovery ..." A critique in the *Southern Literary Review* approves the plot and theme: "This well-written novel is a poetic coming-of-age story about mothers—the need for mothers, the need to know our mothers and the need to be mothers." Enthusiasm for the novel has spilled over to college and high school curriculums, many of which now list the novel as required reading for classes. A book review by Penny Stevens in *School Library Journal* gives a feel for why the novel is embraced by educators: "There is a wonderful sense of the strength of female friendship and love throughout the story."

Honey bees in a hive (© Juniors Bildarchiv / Alamy)

CRITICISM

Susan Andersen

Andersen is an associate professor of literature and composition. In the following essay, Andersen considers The Secret Life of Bees *in light of Kidd's ideas about the different stages of spiritual growth.*

Lily Owens, the fourteen-year-old heroine of *The Secret Life of Bees*, has a tragic personal story that includes accidentally shooting her mother and living with an abusive father. She runs away with her African-American nanny, Rosaleen, whose story is also heading towards tragedy. It is not until Lily stays with the Boatwrights that she learns any other alternative stories to the dead-end ones that she has grown up with. The book chronicles the way in which Lily, or any person, can change the tale of their lives.

In the tradition of the Southern women writers she keeps company with—Carson McCullers, Alice Walker, Harper Lee—Kidd reenvisions the female role, expanding it even as far as embracing a female image of God. Indeed, in her collection

of essays, *Firstlight*, Kidd has said, "Discovering our personal stories is a spiritual quest. Without such stories we cannot be fully human . . ." In order for Lily to find her own story, she has to hear the stories of other women, who have blazed the trail before her.

When Lily meets June's suitor, Neil, he asks where she comes from. Lily realizes this sort of introductory phrase comes from the desire all people have of fitting their stories together. To begin with, she has no way to connect her background to that of Neil or the Boatwright sisters because she is white and fourteen, and they are African-American and adult. August becomes a sort of mother and teacher who helps Lily resurrect herself by initiating her into a new culture, with new female stories about the secret life of bees and the Black Madonna. At Lily's first meeting of the Daughters of Mary, August retells the story of Our Lady of Chains, saying, "Stories have to be told or they die, and when they die, we can't remember who we are or why we're here."

When August asks Lily what her favorite things are, she mentions writing. She is seen

WHAT DO I READ NEXT?

- Clarissa Pinkola Estés, included in Kidd's own reading lists, is the author of a classic study of popular myths from European and native cultures that explain how woman's nature is either compromised or set free. *Women Who Run with the Wolves: Myths and Stories of the Wild Woman Archetype* was published in 1992.

- Sue Monk Kidd's *Firstlight: The Early Inspirational Writings of Sue Monk Kidd* contains short personal anecdotes of the spiritual significance of everyday occurrences, all held together by a new essay, "The Crucible of Story" that advocates storytelling as a method of spiritual growth. It was published in 2006.

- Kidd's second novel *The Mermaid Chair* contains similar themes to her first: a woman who thinks she caused a parent's death; forbidden love; and a mystery. The difference here is that the main character is a woman in her forties undergoing a midlife crisis. The book was published in 2005.

- *To Kill a Mockingbird* (1960), by Harper Lee, is an important predecessor to *The Secret Life of Bees*. Six-year-old tomboy Scout Finch is, like Lily, another innocent who faces the absurdities of Southern prejudice.

with paper and pen constantly, writing about her experience and making up exotic stories. Her facility with images and reflection is remarkable for a young girl; her English teacher has told her she should be a writer, and that is what she dreams of. When Zach is in jail, the only consolation she can think of is to tell him she will write it down and tell his story. She creates stories for her friends to star in, and August, in a way, allows Lily to change her own story.

What story needs changing? In *The History of Southern Women's Literature*, Ann Goodwyn Jones speaks of the limited roles for Southern

> IN ALL HER BOOKS, FICTION OR NONFICTION, KIDD MAPS OUT THE TERRITORY SURROUNDING THE TRANSFORMATION OF THE SOUL."

women that have always been the subject of Southern women writers—for Caucasians, "lady, belle, Christian yeowoman of the middle class, spinster, and trash; for blacks, mammy, mulatta, Christian yeowoman of the middle class, loud-mouth, and whore." The list is limited, but Harper Lee's heroine, Scout, manages to break free, as does Celie in *The Color Purple*, along with a host of Southern heroines, like Scarlett O'Hara. Sue Monk Kidd herself wanted to be a writer from an early age, like her character, Lily. But, she notes in *Firstlight*, that in a small Georgia town in the 1950s, she only knew of four careers: "teacher, nurse, secretary, and housewife." So she chose nursing and stayed in that profession through her twenties, though it wasn't what she wanted. The rest of her life, she continues, was a series of moves to undo the "Collective They," or the expectations of society that keep one from living an authentic life. Kidd says more in *Firstlight* about writing and storytelling as important tools of "soul-making," for when people share their stories, they come to find "we are all one story." In *The Secret Life of Bees* the reader identifies with Lily's story, sometimes in the particulars, but more importantly, in the stages of her spiritual growth. In all her books, fiction or nonfiction, Kidd maps out the territory surrounding the transformation of the soul. In *The Dance of the Dissident Daughter*, for instance, Kidd tells of an autobiographical journey from strict Southern Baptist to a religion that embraces feminist theology. In *When the Heart Waits*, she talks about the universal stages of growth as the three-fold cycle of waiting: separation, transformation, and emergence. The stages of waiting serve to illuminate Lily's growth from false to true story.

In the beginning, Lily doesn't know what it is to be female: "I felt half the time I was impersonating a girl instead of really being one." She bites her fingernails, wears Pentecostal dresses—dresses that look severely modest or religious rather than stylish—and cannot get into charm school because she has no mother to present her a rose at graduation. Neither her father nor Rosaleen can help her with her adolescent problems, and even the Baptist church has no female role model for her, except Mary at Christmas. When Lily finds the picture of the Black Madonna among her mother's possessions, she is intrigued by its mystery. August tells her later that all people need an image of God that looks like them, so they can feel divine. The Daughters of Mary connect with their black, female God. Lily, though not African-American, finally has a female image that can make her begin to feel both divine and loved.

The first step of transformation, according to Kidd in *When the Heart Waits*, is separation, often through crisis. Lily is forced to run away to save Rosaleen and herself from being abused. She runs to the only place she knows of, Tiburon, the place on the Black Madonna postcard. In this stage of separation, one leaves behind their false life. This may take some time, as it does for Lily; even though she arrives in a different place in one day, it takes her all summer to drop many of her false ideas—her inherited prejudices about African-American people, for instance, and her own belief that she is bad or will be further abused if she tells the truth.

According to Kidd, in the same book, the transformation stage is helped by withdrawing into a safe cocoon where one may let go. Lily says the first week at August's was "pure relief," a "time-out." Her first prayer to Our Lady of Chains is that she put a curtain of protection around the farm so no one can find them. Lily delays talking to August about her mother until the end of the summer. This appears to be a mistake on Lily's part, but although August knows who she is all the time, she never rushes Lily's confession. She tells her: "There's a fullness of time for things, Lily. You have to know when to prod and when to be quiet, when to let things take their course."

The time-out, spending time with the Daughters of Mary and working as a respected apprentice bee-keeper with August, gives Lily a chance to think deeply about her life, to discard the lies she has been told and to see the truth that her new friends show her. Kidd continues in *When the Heart Waits* to describe incubation as a time when one can hold tensions creatively, to live one's questions. Lily is alive because she asks countless questions about the way things are: Why did God make different

skin colors? Why do Baptists try to convert Catholics? Why don't white Christians accept African-American Christians? Why do Caucasians think African Americans are not intelligent or handsome when they are? Why are African-American women, who are so powerful, lowest on the social totem pole?

Kidd says of herself in *The Dance of the Dissident Daughter* that her own contemplative experiences put her at odds with her Baptist background, because contemplative religion favors the personal experience of God over dogma (accepted religious views). Kidd began to recognize that the ultimate religious authority was the divine voice in her own soul. The same realization happens to Lily, for from the beginning, her own spiritual insights mean more to her than what she learns from Brother Gerald's pulpit, for instance. She has mystical experiences with Our Lady of Chains and with the bees. In the Boatwright parlor, Lily first lays eyes on the Black Mary who is the Madonna of Slaves. Mary has the power to get out of the chains that bind—to take her followers to freedom. Lily is immediately attracted to her. Mary's smile speaks to her soul: "*Lily Owens, I know you down to the core.*"

The Dance of the Dissident Daughter asserts that a woman must trust her own feminine source and that it is a place inside that feels ancient. Lily calls the Black Mary in the parlor "older than old." Lily also experiences something ancient in beekeeping. August connects making honey to everything biblical and ancient, from fertility to death to resurrection. The fact that the queen bee runs the hive and that women make better beekeepers, according to Big Mama, connects it to the traditional power of women.

Kidd mentions in *When the Heart Waits* how knowing God as a mother in her own spiritual journey, allowed "the wedding of my soul with creation." Similarly, August shows Lily how to appreciate nature, how not to be afraid of bees, to give them love, so they won't sting. Lily does, and feels that she becomes one with the bees, floating, immune to everything. When May is buried, she feels the bees hum through the whole earth and souls flying away to heaven. Lily is consoled by the natural world, as when she goes to the river while she is mourning.

The stage of emergence, described in *When the Heart Waits*, has to do with forming a new relationship with others based on a renewed relationship with God. Knowing God as mother, says Kidd, brings us to greater intimacy with God, because it is an image of a caring and nourishing God rather than a punishing God. In her distress, Lily imagines a door in the Madonna's belly. She envisions crawling into a hidden room in Mary's abdomen, as though she is Mary's child. The reenactment of the legend of Mary's captivity in chains coincides with Lily's dark night of the soul when she smashes honey jars on the wall and falls asleep at Mary's feet. But "What is bound will be unbound," as the Mary Day ritual says. The climax of the festivity is bathing the statue in honey and taking off the Lady's chains. When Lily receives the picture of Deborah with herself as a baby, Lily begins to lose her own chains, for she finally realizes that her mother loved her. She forgives both herself and her mother. Lily's emerging intimacy with God leads her to experience intimacy with others.

Lily further exhibits this final stage of growth in her confrontation with T. Ray when he comes to get her. She is different, stands up for herself, and asserts her authority. The emergent stage is characterized by a new compassion, says Kidd. Lily sees her father in a new light, as someone who once loved and became cruel through disappointment. She calls him Daddy, thus acknowledging her connection to him. Once she makes it past the obstacle of forgiving her parents, she is ready for the final truth that August has to teach her: God, or Our Lady, is not outside, but inside. Lily affirms this: "I feel her in unexpected moments, her Assumption into heaven happening in places inside me."

Kidd says in her essay, "The Crucible of Story" in *Firstlight* that storytelling is soul-making, but it requires a risk of stepping into the shadows to find the angels there. Lily has demonstrated soul-making to us by reclaiming the shadows of her story and finding the angels within it at the same time. She would like to get her father to say that she didn't shoot her mother, but she accepts that even if she did, she can forgive herself and move on to better stories, because her mothers, both the human and the divine, know her true and best self.

Source: Susan Andersen, Critical Essay on *The Secret Life of Bees*, in *Novels for Students*, Gale, Cengage Learning, 2008.

Laura J. Bloxham

In the following review, Bloxham critiques the book from a theological angle, suggesting that fiction should serve as a guide for escaping evil. She confirms that the novel does this through its larger framework, with bees serving as a metaphor for human life.

A friend recently wrote to thank me for recommending. *The Secret Life of Bees.* "I finished it last night," she wrote, "finished the last third of the book bawling and laughing and feeling both full and empty at the same time when I put it down." Maybe my review should end there. What better recommendation than from one who has been moved across a spectrum of emotions all at the same time. But reading is not only about emotion. We read for different reasons, but a connection with characters is often a main reason. Often we identify with stages of our own development. Sometimes knowing someone else, even a character in a novel, has shared an experience, is enough to validate our experience. I studied with a professor one summer who said he looked for a vision of a way out in the novels he read. He said literature that merely confirmed the evil parts of the human condition did not go far enough. He said we already know what is wrong with life. It is the vision that we need.

Sue Monk Kidd, in *The Secret Life of Bees*, provides many of the elements that make for good reading. There is emotional connection, connection with characters, stages of development, shared experience, and vision. She also gives us a larger framework, both knowledge of and a metaphor for life, in the lore of bees. I'm not much of a scientist. When a friend asked if there were enough bee-knowledge in this book to use in a non-major science class, I was puzzled. I thought of the bees in this novel as angels, presences in the book that hovered and comforted. Sort of furry holy spirits. But then I read Kidd's interview at the back of the Penguin paperback edition where she talks about studying honey-making. And it came back. There is a lot of factual knowledge about the world of bees and that is a bonus in reading the book.

But, like Leif Enger's *Peace Like a River*, the captivating force in the novel is Lily, the young narrator. It is her voice and her plight that drive the novel. Of course the civil rights movement in 1964 makes for compelling reading too. Those of us who grew up outside the South want knowledge of what it was like to live in the midst of prejudice and change. We want the human story. Those who grew up in the South want to find a kind of redemption for their memories now digested so many years later (interview with Kidd). The story of Rosaleen, who spits on the shoes of white men, on her way to register to vote, deserves a novel of its own. The Boatwright sisters, who produce Black Madonna Honey, deserve their own novel. But, though they populate Lily's novel, this novel is Lily's story. It is the story of Lily's search for her mother, the truth about her mother, and her own rest in the forgiveness only a mother can give.

Perhaps what compels the reader most is Lily's need to tell her story. The poignant reason she reveals early on. That reason and the few relics she possesses from her mother frame the novel. While Lily's story is the journey to find answers, what she finds is "there is nothing but mystery in the world." The inner journey, however, has more answers than the outer journey. This inner quest begins with loneliness and the prayer, "fix me." Moves to confession and some sort of healing or, at least, acceptance.

The sources of healing are many. Lily has caused hurt, but she also avenges hurt when she springs Rosaleen from jail. Lily runs away from her father and finds a community of mothers. Lily needs love and finds that "Every little thing wants to be loved." Yet she learns that merely loving is not enough; the purpose of human life August Boatwright tells her is "to *persist* in love."

The medium for much of this learning is Our Lady of Chains, a figure of Mary, whose story mirrors the story of the community of women who surround her. Lily finds in Mary what she needs to face herself, her mother, the women who have nurtured her, and, finally, her father. This Mary is earthy, not ethereal. Lily wonders, in fact, "if Mary had been an outdoor type who preferred trees and insects over the churchy halo" she often wore. This Mary is not high in heaven, but a "Mary with a wide-open door and, inside, all these people tucked away in the secret world of consolation." This Mary is not a flat picture, but a wooden embodiment with a "thick arm jutting out." "This Mary," Lily knows, "is a muscle of love." More than that, for Lily, Mary enables Lily to live with herself, with the great sins she has committed, knowing that Mary "goes into the holes life has gouged out of us."

I know many Christians who get nervous around the thought of Mary, except as a vessel for Jesus' birth. Lily says her church "didn't really allow Mary ... except at Christmas."

And, while God and Jesus hover in the background of this novel, the discovery and recovery of Mary says much to these women on their spiritual journeys. My friend who was "bawling and laughing and feeling both full and empty" after reading *The Secret Life of Bees* goes on to say, "I don't know what I would do without good stories." There is no better recommendation than that.

Source: Laura J. Bloxham, Review of *The Secret Life of Bees*, in *Dialog: A Journal of Theology*, Vol. 44, No. 2. Summer 2005, pp. 197–98.

Rosellen Brown

In the following review, Brown offers a discussion of the characters and the form of the novel. Brown claims that everything in the book meshes a bit too neatly, citing examples such as the beekeeping head notes and their relation to the main action. The novel is "like honey," Brown claims, "nourishing but a touch cloying" on account of its fairytale resolutions.

Anyone who reads a great deal of fiction—for the purposes of reviewing, teaching, contest judging, "blurbing"—will tell you that authority announces itself immediately. Though it's impossible to know on page one whether a writer possesses depth, consistency, or even seriousness of purpose, we can usually tell whether we're in good hands by the end of a few sentences.

Sue Monk Kidd's fine first novel *The Secret Life of Bees* begins with a paragraph in which she establishes the voice that will carry us pleasurably through her story, and lays out, implicitly, the emotional terrain she will take us through. The narrator is lying in bed listening to the bees that have squeezed through the cracks in her bedroom wall. She describes their sound, the glint of their wings, "and felt the longing build in my chest. The way those bees flew, not even looking for a flower, just flying for the feel of the wind, split my heart down its seam."

By the end of that paragraph we know a lot—short of her name and age—about Lily Owens. If we're paying attention, we take note of the demographics: bees at large in her bedroom, cruising in not via door or window but through less than solid walls. And, of course, we notice the attentiveness to detail of a sensitive, empathetic observer. Finally, unavoidably, we hear the desperate sadness of someone with modest emotional expectations—"not even looking

> THERE ARE NO ROUGH EDGES, NO THREAT OF UNRESOLVABLE PAIN, THOUGH MANY ATROCIOUS THINGS HAPPEN, OR THREATEN TO HAPPEN, ALONG THE WAY."

for a flower"—that are not being met. This is solid writing, efficient, elegant and poignant.

It is 1964, in small-town Georgia peach country. Lily turns out to be the fourteen-year-old daughter of T. Ray, a man of implacable rage and vengefulness who in his bad moments, which are many, makes his daughter kneel on grits (a particularly Southern form of legal brutality). He mocks her, he beats her; his generally cruel behavior accounts for her envy of the freedom of honeybees. But, worse, the reason Lily has no one to stand between her and the tyranny of her father is that she herself, at the age of four, appears to have shot her mother accidentally when she picked up a gun in the course of a confrontation between her parents. Now, to turn the thumbscrews still tighter, T. Ray taunts his daughter by claiming that on the day of the shooting, her mother was about to flee and planned to leave her behind.

Abandoned twice over and accustomed to pain, it's no wonder that, in her futile attempts to conjure up her mother, Lily thinks, "Even her picking a switch off the forsythia bush and stinging my legs would have been welcome." Her mother, when they meet in heaven, will forgive her "for the first ten thousand years" and for the next ten thousand will fix Lily's hair, because "You can tell which girls lack mothers by the look of their hair."

The only care Lily has grown up with has been supplied by her black housekeeper, Rosaleen, who—in the tradition, pioneered by Dilsey, of indispensable servants who don't cut their charges much slack is a bracing combination of warmth and coolness, affection and correction. On the day of Lily's fourteenth birthday, which her father pointedly ignores, Lily and Rosaleen take a fateful walk into town so that Lily can buy herself a present and Rosaleen can register to vote.

So begin the complications, which become considerably tangled but emotionally simple: this is how two women, a female Huck and Jim, make a break for freedom and dignity. Like bees that seem to fly randomly, they will turn out to know exactly what they need and what will feed them.

Rosaleen, challenged, gets herself jailed for spitting on a white man's shoes, a provocation both brave and foolhardy; the feisty Lily springs her and, loosed from their assorted prisons, they take off. Lily is carrying one of her few mementoes of her mother, the "end-all mystery," a small wooden picture of a black Madonna on the back of which someone has written the words "Tiburon, N.C." There, not surprisingly, is where she heads, and there, aided by the kind of coincidence that under the circumstances is probably not as implausible as it seems, she encounters in the Tiburon general store the same strange painting of Mary on a bottle of locally made honey. As if to forestall scepticism, but quite in character, Lily insists that "there is nothing but mystery in the world, how it hides behind the fabric of our poor, browbeat days, shining brightly, and we don't even know it."

Suffice it to say, when Lily and Rosaleen follow their yellow brick road to the idiosyncratic compound of three black women beekeepers, May, June and August, they come upon a trio that embodies every form of maternal nurturance and emotional education Lily needs, and a comfortable nest for Rosaleen as well. In the Boatwright sisters, for whom the black Madonna is queen, Kidd has created a wonderful fantasy, a sort of beloved community, part Oz, part ashram, part center for racial reconciliation.

August, the oldest, is wise and patient, the kind of woman who knows every secret intuitively. May, the youngest, whose twin committed suicide years earlier, is now more sensitive than a tuning fork: whenever something disturbs her loving nature, she flees to her own private "wailing wall" to subdue her demons. The middle sister, June, gives Lily what appears to be the swat of a reverse racism that the humane, naïve young girl, as white as her name, cannot understand. And there is a boy, Zach, black and beautiful, who (rather too un-selfconsciously for Georgia in 1964) dares, without notable angst, to love Lily. Flies (rather than bees) in the ointment also land him in jail and compromise the peace of the farm. But all is well in the end, every uncertainty settled as surely as if this were a detective story. Lily even sees her way to a hedged sympathy for her father, who, she realizes, lost a wife the day she lost a mother.

Both the strength and the weakness of *The Secret Life of Bees* are exemplified by the presence at the head of every chapter of brief excerpts from books such as *Man and Insects*, *The Queen Must Die: And Other Affairs of Bees and Men*, *Exploring the World of Social Insects*, *Bees of the World*. Glosses for what's to come, they raise the engaging and unanswerable question of whether we're like the bees or the bees are like us. But though the quotations are undeniably intriguing, their smooth fit with the story is a touch too perfect, as if to point out conveniently snug connections we must not be allowed to miss. Kidd must have found them irresistible.

But this is, they confirm, a novel in which everything meshes smoothly. Though it is never frivolous, there is in it the sweetness and trust that things will work out in the end that one tends to see in comedy, not tragedy; or perhaps, more appropriately, in the comfort of fairy tales that put their characters through harsh trials so that, every demon slain, they can triumph reassuringly over danger. At tale's end, the princess-scullery maid, the cast-out wanderer through the dark wood, will be saved, even cherished. For all the volatility of its subjects violent death, child abuse both physical and emotional, suicide, racism and injustice—I had a hard time believing that anything truly terrible or irrevocable would be allowed to happen in these pages. There are no rough edges, no threat of unresolvable pain, though many atrocious things happen, or threaten to happen, along the way.

To be fair, whether that is cause for complaint or celebration will finally be a matter of taste. Lest this description seem to patronize an ingenious and generous book, let me add that Kidd scatters a good deal of wisdom like Hansel and Gretel's redemptive bread crumbs en route to the consoling denouement. "It was foolish to think some things were beyond happening," Lily thinks, dreaming about the flawless Zach, "even being attracted to Negroes. I'd honestly thought such a thing couldn't happen, the way water could not run uphill or salt could not taste sweet. A law of nature ... You gotta imagine what's never been, Zach had said." Taken in that

spirit, the world Kidd has imagined has the force of homespun myth.

Lily finds a good many of these perceptive, confiding discoveries planted along the road to a reconciliation not only with herself but with her history and her future; they make her endearing and her story a satisfying blend of salty sweetness. But there are those—clearly I vacillated—who will also find its lovingkindness like honey, nourishing but a touch cloying. Curmudgeonly, perhaps, but unless a book is meant for the very young we resist comfort that comes too readily. A consoling balm, *The Secret Life of Bees* has less sting in the end than its swarm of griefs would seem to promise.

Source: Rosellen Brown, "Honey Child," in *Women's Review of Books*, Vol. 19, No. 7, April 2002, p. 11.

SOURCES

Bloxham, Laura J., Review of *The Secret Life of Bees*, in *Dialog: A Journal of Theology*, Vol. 44, No. 2, Summer 2005, pp. 197–98.

Brown, Rosellen, "Honey Child," in the *Women's Review of Books*, Vol. 19, No. 7, April 2002, p. 11.

Jones, Ann Goodwyn, "Women Writers and the Myths of Southern Womanhood," in *The History of Southern Women's Literature*, edited by Carolyn Perry and Mary Louise Weaks, Louisiana State University Press, 2002, p. 280.

Kidd, Sue Monk, "A Conversation with Sue Monk Kidd," in *The Secret Life of Bees*, Penguin, 2003, Appendix, pp. 4–14.

———, *The Dance of the Dissident Daughter*, HarperCollins, 1996, pp. 16, 75–83.

———, *Firstlight: The Early Inspirational Writings of Sue Monk Kidd*, GuidepostsBooks, 2006, pp. 16, 20–21, 70.

———, *The Secret Life of Bees*, Penguin, 2003.

———, *When the Heart Waits: Spiritual Direction for Life's Sacred Questions*, HarperCollins, 1992, pp. 87, 102, 124, 158–63, 189.

Maryles, Daisy, "Kidd Kudos," in *Publishers Weekly*, April 18, 2005, http://www.publishersweekly.com.article/CA525302 (accessed July 27, 2007).

Mazmanian, Adam, Review of *The Secret Life of Bees*, in the *New York Times Book Review*, March 31, 2002, Vol. 151, No. 52074, p. 17.

Review of *The Secret Life of Bees*, in the *Southern Literary Review*, http://www.southernlitreview.com/reviews/the_secret_life.htm (accessed July 27, 2007).

Review of *The Secret Life of Bees*, in the *Virginia Quarterly Review*, Vol. 78, No. 3, Summer 2002, p. 91.

Stevens, Penny, Review of *The Secret Life of Bees*, in the *School Library Journal*, Vol. 48, No. 5, May 2002, p. 179.

FURTHER READING

Christ, Carol P., *Diving Deep and Surfacing: Women Writers on Spiritual Quest*, Beacon Press, 1980.
   Christ is one of Kidd's influences, and she insists that women tell their spiritual stories. She analyzes stages of awakening in the works of the authors Kate Chopin, Margaret Atwood, Doris Lessing, Adrienne Rich, and Ntozake Shange.

Thoreau, Henry David, *Walden, or Life in the Woods*, Princeton University Press, 1989.
   Thoreau's classic tale of finding his higher self at Walden pond was influential on Kidd and on her character, Lily. In it, Thoreau shares the spiritual lessons he has learned from nature.

Walker, Alice, *The Color Purple*, Washington Square Press, 1982.
   This is Walker's Pulitzer Prize winning novel about the life of African Americans in rural Georgia. Sometimes criticized for its explicit sex and violence, it is uplifting in its depiction of the spiritual triumph of a poor African-American woman, Celie.

X, Malcolm, and Alex Haley, *The Autobiography of Malcolm X*, Grove Press, 1965.
   Malcolm X, a Civil Rights leader, details his memories of the period in which Kidd's novel is set. The autobiography details Malcolm X's rise from drug dealer to African-American spiritual and political leader.

The Talented Mr. Ripley

PATRICIA HIGHSMITH

1955

The Talented Mr. Ripley is the first of five books in the Ripley series by Patricia Highsmith, an American writer who moved permanently to Europe in 1963. The series features her best-known character, Tom Ripley. Highsmith's suspense novel *The Talented Mr. Ripley* was first published in 1955 and was republished in 1999 by Vintage. The edition is out of print but second-hand copies are available. The book was also published in 1999 by Everyman in an anthology consisting of three of the Ripley novels, titled *The Talented Mr. Ripley, Ripley Under Ground, Ripley's Game*. As of June 2007, this book is still available.

The novel's themes include the nature of identity, the relationship of the real to the imagined, and homosexuality. Ripley literally gets away with murder and the innocent characters suffer in an amoral world that disconcerts the reader by subverting expectations. The novel exemplifies Highsmith's rejection of the honest, straight-talking hero of conventional crime fiction in favor of the morally compromised or criminal protagonist. The atmosphere of menace that Highsmith creates, with the relatively low level of actual violence, justify the English novelist Graham Greene's characterization of her in his Foreword to her short story collection *Eleven* as "the poet of apprehension rather than fear."

Patricia Highsmith (*Horst Tappe | Hulton Archive | Getty Images*)

AUTHOR BIOGRAPHY

Patricia Highsmith was born Mary Patricia Plangman in Fort Worth, Texas, on January 19, 1921, the only child of Jay Bernard Plangman, a graphic artist, and Mary Coates Highsmith, an illustrator and fashion designer. Highsmith's parents separated before she was born, and she was raised by her grandparents. At six years of age, Highsmith went to live with her mother and stepfather, Stanley Highsmith, in Greenwich Village, New York. She had an unhappy childhood and was not close to her mother. Highsmith was later to discover that when her mother was pregnant with her, she tried to abort the fetus by drinking turpentine.

The young Highsmith showed talent in painting and sculpting, but she made up her mind to be a writer. She attended Julia Richman High School, New York City, where she edited the school newspaper and read books by writers such as Leo Tolstoy, Fyodor Dostoyevsky, and Charles Dickens. She was particularly intrigued by Karl Menninger's book, *The Human Mind* (1930), which featured case studies of kleptomaniacs, pyromaniacs, and serial killers, because she realized that seemingly normal people could be hiding extreme mental pathology. Highsmith continued her education at Barnard College, University of Columbia, where she studied English, Latin, and Greek, and published short stories in the *Barnard Quarterly*.

After graduating in 1942, Highsmith lived in Manhattan and earned a living by writing text for comic strips. In 1944, she was admitted to Yaddo, the artists' colony in Saratoga Springs, New York, based on recommendations by the writer Truman Capote and others. While at Yaddo she got engaged to a fellow writer, Marc Brandel, but broke off the engagement shortly before the wedding, ostensibly because of her fear of being a mother.

Highsmith published her first novel, *Strangers on a Train*, a suspense thriller about a psychopath who commits what he hopes is the perfect murder, in 1950. The film director Alfred Hitchcock purchased the movie and stage rights for 6,800 dollars. The film was released in 1951. It proved a great success and Highsmith became famous overnight.

Highsmith's second novel, *The Price of Salt*, appeared in 1952 under the pseudonym Claire Morgan (other names under which Highsmith published are Mary Patricia Highsmith, Patricia Plangman, and Mary Patricia Plangman). The book was remarkable for its time in that it portrayed a lesbian relationship that ended happily. Highsmith admitted that she had fallen in love with the woman who had served as the model for the love object character in the novel, though she never publicly acknowledged her lesbianism. Highsmith went on to publish another novel about the quest for the perfect murder, *The Blunderer* (1954), which she followed in 1955 with *The Talented Mr. Ripley*. Highsmith wrote of the completed novel in her nonfiction work *Plotting and Writing Suspense Fiction* (1966), "No book was easier for me to write, and I often had the feeling Ripley was writing it and I was merely typing." The novel was given a special award by the Mystery Writers of America in 1956 and in 1957, it was awarded the Grand Prix de Littérature Policière and the Edgar Allan Poe Scroll of the Mystery Writers of America.

Highsmith's novel *The Two Faces of January* (1964) was awarded the Silver Dagger Award for best crime novel of the year by the Crime Writers Association of England in 1964. Other major novels include *People Who Knock on the Door*

(1983), and *Found in the Street* (1986). In her later novels, Highsmith began to address social issues. *A Dog's Ransom* (1972) comments on the ineffectualness of law enforcement agencies, while *Edith's Diary* (1977) explores the ways in which society forces women into subservient roles.

Highsmith also published short story collections. *Little Tales of Misogyny* (1974) contributed to the common criticism that she portrayed women negatively. In *The Animal-Lover's Book of Beastly Murder* (1975), animals take revenge on humans for their acts of cruelty towards animals. Highsmith famously preferred the company of animals to that of people, keeping pet cats and even snails.

Highsmith seems not to have formed long-term close relationships. In 1960, she shared a farmhouse outside New Hope, Pennsylvania, with the lesbian author Marijana Meaker. In 1963, she moved to the south of England to be with her lover, the wife of a London businessman. After the relationship ended she moved to France in 1967 and bought a house in Samois-sur-Seine, where she lived with her friend Elizabeth Lyne. In 1982, she moved to Switzerland, first settling in Aurigeno and then in Tegna, where she lived an increasingly reclusive life in a house that she had built to her own design.

In 1990, Highsmith was honored by the French government when she was named Officier dans l'Ordre des Arts et des Lettres (Officer of the Order of Arts and Letters). In 1991, she was nominated for the Nobel Prize in literature. She died of cancer in a hospital in Locarno, Switzerland, on February 4, 1995.

PLOT SUMMARY

Chapters 1–10

The Talented Mr. Ripley opens with the protagonist, Tom Ripley, walking along a street in New York and noticing that he is being followed. Tom fears that he is about to be arrested because he has been operating a scam involving the Internal Revenue Service.

The man following Tom introduces himself as Mr. Herbert Greenleaf, the father of Dickie Greenleaf, a wealthy young man whom Tom once accompanied to a party. Under the impression that Tom is a friend of Dickie's, Mr. Greenleaf explains that Dickie has been in Europe for two years. Mr.

MEDIA ADAPTATIONS

- *Plein Soleil*, or *Purple Noon* in the United States, is a French-language film adaptation of *The Talented Mr. Ripley*, starring Alain Delon (1960). It was directed by René Clément, produced by Raymond Hakim and Robert Hakim, and distributed by Titanus Distribuzione Spa. The film was released as a DVD by Miramax in 1996.

- *The Talented Mr. Ripley*, adapted as a film by Anthony Minghella and starring Matt Damon, Gwyneth Paltrow, and Jude Law, was produced by Mirage Enterprises/Paramount and distributed by Miramax/Paramount (1999). The film was released as a DVD by Paramount in 2000.

Greenleaf wants Dickie to come home because Mrs. Greenleaf has leukemia and may not live long, and because he wants him to take up his responsibilities in the family boatbuilding firm. Dickie prefers to stay in Mongibello, a village in Italy, sailing and painting. Mr. Greenleaf asks Tom to go to Europe at his expense and persuade Dickie to come home. Seeing a chance to escape his precarious existence in New York, Tom accepts.

Tom sails for Europe. He writes to his Aunt Dottie, who brought him up, telling her that he is leaving the country on business. Tom is relieved to have achieved independence from his aunt, who is in the habit of calling him and his late father "sissy." He feels he has wasted his life. He had come to New York wanting to be an actor, but had been rebuffed. As a child, he had fantasized about stabbing Aunt Dottie with her brooch and running away.

Tom arrives in Mongibello and finds Dickie on the beach with his friend Marge Sherwood. Dickie receives Tom without warmth. Tom broaches the subject of Mr. Greenleaf's wish for his son to return home. Dickie is dismissive. Neither Dickie nor Marge invites Tom to stay at their houses. Tom thinks that Marge is in love with Dickie but that Dickie is indifferent to her.

Tom watches Dickie and Marge go sailing in Dickie's boat as if he, Tom, did not exist. Tom is not surprised that Dickie does not want to give up his carefree life here. He badly wants to make Dickie like him, but Dickie treats Tom coldly until Tom tells him that Mr. Greenleaf employed Tom to go to Mongibello especially to persuade Dickie to go home. Dickie is amused, and warms to Tom. Tom tells Dickie that he has a talent for figures, can forge a signature, and can impersonate anyone. Tom does an impersonation, which Dickie enjoys, but Marge is unimpressed. Dickie shows Tom his paintings, which Tom knows are bad. Tom feels that Marge is in the way of his forming a bond with Dickie. Dickie invites Tom to stay at his house, and Tom moves in.

Tom and Dickie take a trip to Naples and Rome. As they are about to board the bus, Dickie recognizes an old friend, the American Freddie Miles. Dickie and Freddie arrange to meet at a ski resort called Cortina later that year. When Tom and Dickie return to Mongibello, Tom notes with satisfaction that Marge seems jealous of his closeness to Dickie.

Dickie is concerned that Marge is being pushed out. He leaves Tom to visit Marge. Tom follows Dickie to her house, where he sees them embracing. Tom runs back to Dickie's house in a hysterical state and throws Dickie's art tools around. He puts on one of Dickie's suits. Impersonating Dickie, he tells an imaginary Marge that he does not love her, and mimes strangling her. He accuses the imaginary Marge's corpse of "interfering between Tom and me—No, not that! But there *is* a bond between us!" Dickie enters and sees Tom dressed in his clothes. He angrily tells Tom that Marge thinks he (Tom) is homosexual, and that he (Dickie) wants to make clear that he himself is not. Tom insists that he is not, either. Tom asks Dickie if he is in love with Marge. Dickie says he is not, but he cares about her.

Chapters 11–20

Tom asks Dickie to accompany him to Paris as part of a drugs scheme operated by a local crook. To Tom's disappointment, Dickie says the plan is crazy and that Tom is under no obligation to do as he does. Tom realizes a terrible truth: he and Dickie are not friends, and neither do they know one another.

Tom receives a letter from Mr. Greenleaf terminating their agreement, as Tom has been unsuccessful with Dickie. Tom feels afraid and alone. Dickie declines to go to Paris with Tom. Also, Dickie and Marge have bought a refrigerator, which implies that Dickie plans to stay in Mongibello with Marge rather than going traveling with Tom.

Tom and Dickie go to San Remo. On the train, Dickie tells Tom that he wants to go to Cortina alone, with Marge. When they reach Cannes, they see two men sitting together. Dickie makes a contemptuous comment about homosexuals and looks at Tom with distaste. Tom is ashamed, remembering Aunt Dottie's taunts about sissies. Tom feels both hatred and affection for Dickie. He senses that Dickie has rejected his friendship. He has an impulse to kill him and works out a way to do it. He could become Dickie and steal his identity. He could keep an apartment in Rome or Paris and receive Dickie's allowance check every month. He resembles Dickie enough to use his passport.

At San Remo, Tom persuades Dickie to take out a boat. When they are far from land, Tom suggests a swim. As Dickie is taking off his trousers, Tom hits him over the head with an oar, in an act of premeditated murder. Tom steals Dickie's rings. He ties the anchor rope around Dickie's ankles and heaves the body, with the cement anchor to weigh it down, over the side of the boat. He loses his balance and falls into the water. He hauls himself back into the blood-stained boat. He fills the boat with stones and sinks it.

Thinking of his new life using Dickie's money, Tom is happier than he has ever been. On returning to Mongibello, he tells Marge that Dickie is staying in Rome and wants Tom to bring some of his belongings to Rome. He plans to ask a local man to act as agent for the sale of Dickie's house, boat, and furniture. Next day, Tom tells Marge he has had a letter saying that Dickie intends to stay in Rome indefinitely and will not go to Cortina. Marge feels shocked and hurt.

Back in Rome, Tom practices speaking in Dickie's voice. He forges Dickie's handwriting in a letter to Marge, telling her in his persona as Dickie that he wants to be alone. He adds that he is studying painting under a man called Di Massimo. In her reply, Marge expresses surprise that Dickie is staying in Rome, and advises him to get away from Tom, whom she dislikes.

Tom goes to Paris as Dickie. For the first time ever, he feels comfortable at a party. He feels reborn as a new person. After the party, he realizes that he has forgotten to tell Freddie that he was not going to his party at Cortina, which took place nearly a month ago. He picks up a letter from Marge to Dickie, in which she says that she is going back to the United States. She asks Dickie to go with her on the same boat. Tom does not reply, and the next letter she writes is resigned to the apparent truth that Dickie does not wish to see her. Later, she writes saying that Fausto, the Italian friend of Dickie's who taught Tom Italian in Mongibello, is coming to Rome and intends to visit Dickie.

In Rome, Tom rents an apartment, where he lives as Dickie. He feels poised and confident. Money begins to flow in from the sale of Dickie's furniture. Tom is alone, yet not lonely, and feels blameless and free.

Tom receives a surprise visit at his apartment from Freddie, who is wondering why Dickie did not come to Cortina. Tom tells him that Dickie has gone out to lunch and that he is leaving for Sicily soon. Tom sees Freddie staring at Dickie's silver identification bracelet on his wrist. He knows what Freddie is thinking: that Tom and Dickie are in a homosexual relationship, that they are living together in Dickie's apartment, and that Dickie is making Tom presents of his jewellery. As Freddie leaves, Tom overhears him talking with Signora Buffi, the landlady. She is telling Freddie that only Mr. Greenleaf lives upstairs and that he has not gone out today. Freddie comes back, and Tom realizes his cover is blown. Tom kills Freddie by hitting him over the head with an ashtray. He makes Freddie's death look like a robbery by stealing his wallet. He feels that Freddie's death was sad, but that he is a victim of his "own dirty mind."

Tom walks Freddie's body to his car in a way that looks like one drunk man supporting another. He drives to the Via Appia Antica, an ancient Roman road lined with tombs, and dumps the body. He leaves Freddie's car outside a nightclub with the keys in the ignition, throws his wallet in a sewer, and returns home. He wonders how Freddie found out where he lived, and concludes that someone must have followed him home and informed Freddie.

Tom receives a telephone call from Fausto for Dickie. Impersonating Dickie, Tom tells him he is leaving for Naples and arranges to see him

at the railway station, though inwardly, he has no intention of meeting him.

The police find Freddie's body. They know that he visited "Signor Greenleaf" yesterday and arrive to question Tom, or Dickie, as they think he is. Tom confirms that Freddie visited him. He says that Freddie was drunk when he left, but not too drunk to drive. Tom checks into a hotel to avoid any of Dickie's friends who might call on him. The newspapers report that Freddie was last seen at Dickie's house, but do not say that Dickie is a suspect. The same day, the bloodstained boat in which Tom killed Dickie is found near San Remo. Tom is terrified. He knows that if the police check the hotel registers for missing Americans, the name Richard Greenleaf would stand out, and Tom is now living as Dickie. In that case, it would be Tom Ripley who would be assumed missing and murdered, and Dickie would be suspected of murder. He falls asleep and dreams that Dickie is alive, having swum to safety.

The police call on Tom, thinking he is Dickie. They say that Tom Ripley is missing, perhaps dead. Tom says he believes he went back to the United States a month ago. The police are suspicious because Dickie Greenleaf has twice been near the scene of a murder (of Freddie and, as they believe, Tom).

Marge arrives at Tom's hotel room, looking for Dickie. Tom knows he has to keep Tom Ripley's clothes and passport for such emergencies as Marge turning up, but also because Dickie is a murder suspect and he may have to revert to being Tom. Tom tells Marge that Dickie is out being questioned by the police. To get rid of her, Tom arranges to meet her in five minutes at Angelo's bar, though he has no intention of going there.

Tom goes to Palermo, Sicily. Marge thinks that Tom and Dickie are having a homosexual relationship and writes a farewell letter to Dickie rebuking him for acting the coward in not telling her honestly. The Palermo police call, looking for Tom Ripley. Tom tells them that Tom Ripley is in Rome.

In Palermo, Tom feels lonely and sad. He had imagined acquiring a new circle of friends and a better life as Dickie, but he realizes that he will always have to keep a distance from people in order to avoid being found out. He receives a letter from Dickie's trust company suggesting that the signature acknowledging receipt of his allowance is forged. The company wants him to confirm that it is his (Dickie's). Panic-stricken,

Tom wonders if the company has been tipped off by the police as a result of their investigations, but he writes back confirming that the signature is his.

Chapters 21–30

Tom receives a threatening letter from the police ordering him to come to Rome to be questioned regarding Tom Ripley, who is still missing. Tom is frightened. He plans to get rid of Dickie's belongings. He reads a newspaper report saying that Dickie, a friend of the murdered Freddie, is missing after a Sicilian holiday.

Tom goes to Venice and, in his own persona, declares himself to the police as Tom Ripley. He feels that going back to being Tom is a great sadness. He tells the police that he last saw Dickie in Rome, before he went to Sicily. The police say that Dickie (actually Tom) was seen supporting a possibly dead Freddie beside Freddie's car, so they want to talk to Dickie. Tom says he does not know where he is. When they ask if Dickie and Freddie had quarreled, Tom says that Dickie did not go to Freddie's party in Cortina. The police suggest that they may have quarreled over Marge, and Tom encourages this belief. Dickie's apparent forgeries against himself and the murder of Freddie, combined with his disappearance, have made him a suspect. The police do not suspect Tom of anything, and dismiss him.

Tom, as himself, writes to Mr. Greenleaf and Marge saying that he thinks Dickie may have killed himself over the strain of being questioned for Freddie's murder. Marge thinks Dickie is merely hiding.

Tom now lives as Tom Ripley in a grand house in Venice, surrounded by antique pieces of art and furniture. He forges Dickie's will, leaving his income and estate to Tom, and seals it in an envelope, on which he writes that it is not to be opened until June. He is invited to parties by high society people who are fascinated by his association with the missing Dickie.

Marge comes to stay with Tom at his house. She chats with Tom about Dickie's disappearance, without suspecting him. Marge says that Mr. Greenleaf is in Rome, trying to find Dickie. Tom tells Marge that he failed to meet her at Angelo's in Rome because a man came to interview him for a job immediately after she left.

Mr. Greenleaf visits Tom and Marge in Venice. He has engaged an American private detective to try to find Dickie.

Tom receives a letter from Bob Delancey saying that the police have questioned him about an income tax fraud in which the culprit had used his house as the address to collect his checks.

Marge finds Dickie's rings in a box in Tom's house. Tom claims that Dickie gave them to him in Rome, in case anything happened to him, and that he had then forgotten about them. Instantly, Tom realizes he may have to kill Marge. He plans to hit her over the head with the shoe he is holding, dump her body in the canal, and claim she fell in. But Tom does not need to kill her, as she believes Tom's story. She thinks the rings prove that Dickie killed himself or changed his identity. Marge is grief-stricken, as for the first time, she believes that Dickie must be dead. Mr. Greenleaf also accepts this.

The detective, Alvin McCarron, arrives to question Tom. Tom adds to his previous story about the rings, saying that Dickie told Tom not to say anything about them. McCarron appears to conclude that Dickie may be hiding out after killing Freddie, and gives up the case.

Peter Smith-Kingsley, an English friend of Dickie's who lives in Venice, invites Tom to stay at his house in Ireland. Tom declines, as Peter reminds him of Dickie and "the same thing that had happened with Dickie could happen with Peter." Close to tears, Tom wishes that he had done things differently with Dickie, so that he could have lived with him for the rest of his life.

Tom writes to Mr. Greenleaf in the United States, saying that he has opened an envelope that Dickie gave him marked "Not to be opened until June." He says it has turned out to be Dickie's will, in which he leaves his entire estate to Tom.

Tom plans to sail for Athens, Greece, imagining himself as an ancient Greek hero returning home. He hears that the police have found Dickie's paintings, signed with his name, and other belongings, at the American Express office in Venice. (Tom deposited them there under a false name after murdering Dickie, in case he should ever need them.) Tom worries that the police may find his fingerprints on the belongings.

Tom is nervous during his trip to Greece, fearing he will be arrested over the fingerprints and the forgery of the will. When Tom disembarks at the port of Piraeus, the police are waiting, but they are not looking for him. Tom reads a newspaper report that says that the fingerprints on Dickie's belongings are the same as those found in his (really Tom's) abandoned apartment in Rome. Therefore, the police assume that Dickie deposited the belongings himself and that he then committed suicide, was murdered, or is living under the false name given (actually by Tom) to the American Express office. At the Athens American Express office, Tom picks up a letter from Mr. Greenleaf, who has been convinced by the will that Tom forged that his son has committed suicide. He gives his blessing to Tom's inheriting Dickie's estate. Tom realizes ecstatically that Dickie's money and freedom are his. He tells a taxi driver to take him to the best hotel in town.

CHARACTERS

Dickie

Dickie (formally named Richard) Greenleaf is a wealthy young man who is the heir to his father's boatbuilding firm. While Mr. Greenleaf wants Dickie to join the family firm, Dickie asserts his independence by going to live in Mongibello, Italy, where he sails, paints, and collects his monthly allowance check courtesy of the family fortune. Dickie's family wealth allows him to live a carefree life of refined hedonism and to have fine things about him. It is this lifestyle that Tom covets and this is one of the factors that leads him to murder Dickie.

Dickie is a relative innocent who is too naïve to see Tom's true agenda in time to save himself. His good-heartedness is shown in his affection for Marge and his desire not to hurt her, though his self-absorption is shown in the fact that he is happy to spend time with her in the full knowledge that she is in love with him but that he cannot return her feelings. Dickie only likes Tom for a short period in the novel, quickly tiring of his dependence and becoming suspicious that Tom harbors homosexual feelings for him.

To some extent, Dickie shares Tom's tendency to pretend to be something he is not. His paintings are, as Tom recognizes, without merit, but he takes them seriously. However, Dickie's self-delusion, in contrast with Tom's, is harmless.

Dickie's conventional and non-criminal outlook on life provide a foil for Tom's character. For example, when Tom suggests that they go to Paris in a coffin as part of a drug smuggling scheme, Dickie thinks that the plan is "crazy." His judgment highlights Tom's unbalanced addiction to risk. As another example, Dickie's affectionate relationship with Marge contrasts with Tom's friendless existence.

Aunt Dottie

Aunt Dottie does not appear in person in the novel, but she is an influential force in Tom's life and character. After Tom's parents die, she brings him up in Boston. She remorselessly belittles him and his late father, saying that each is (or was, in the case of Tom's father) a "sissy," and repeatedly reminding Tom how much he costs her to bring up. Even as a child, Tom fantasizes about stabbing her with her brooch and running away, one of the first hints of his mental instability.

One of the reasons why Tom seizes the opportunity to go to Europe in Mr. Greenleaf's employ is to escape his dependence on Aunt Dottie, who is in the habit of sending him checks for small amounts of money, gestures that Tom views as insults.

Fausto

Fausto is a young Italian man who lives in Mongibello and who teaches Tom to speak Italian. He poses a danger to Tom when he decides to visit Dickie in Rome. Tom has murdered Dickie and is living in an apartment as Dickie, so he avoids meeting Fausto. Fausto is the Italian form of the German name Faust. In German legend, Faust sold his soul to the devil in return for worldly glory. It is symbolically significant that Tom receives Fausto's call immediately after he has murdered Freddie and dumped his body. The moment is a chilling reminder of how far into the depths of evil Tom has sunk.

Mr. Herbert Greenleaf

Mr. Greenleaf, Dickie's father, is the powerful and wealthy head of the Greenleaf family boatbuilding firm. He evidently cares for his son, but his autocratic nature demands that Dickie follow him into the family firm. Under the impression that Tom is a good friend of Dickie's, he employs Tom to go to Europe to bring back his stubborn son. Mr. Greenleaf's mistaken assumption about the closeness of the two younger men, along with his unfortunate choice of a compulsive liar, psychopath, and potential murderer for the task, testify to his obtuse instincts with regard to other people. Mr. Greenleaf is, however, shrewd enough to realize quickly that Tom is not going to succeed in his task. It is, perhaps, Mr. Greenleaf's blindness to the finer points of human relationships that makes it easy for Tom to convince him that Dickie has died or willfully disappeared and that Dickie bequeathed his entire estate to Tom.

Mrs. Greenleaf

Mrs. Greenleaf, Dickie's mother, only briefly appears in the novel. She has leukemia, and according to her husband, does not have long to live.

Richard Greenleaf

See Dickie

Alvin McCarron

Alvin McCarron is the private detective whom Mr. Greenleaf hires to look for the missing Dickie. Though not unintelligent, he is no match for Tom, who manipulates him into suspecting Dickie of murdering Freddie. He gives up the case and returns to the United States.

Freddie Miles

Freddie is an old friend of Dickie's from the United States. He encounters Dickie and Tom as they are leaving for their trip to Rome and Naples, and arranges with Dickie to meet him at a ski resort, Cortina, later in the year. When Dickie does not turn up at Cortina (because he is dead), Freddie's suspicions are aroused. His search for Dickie at what he believes to be his apartment in Rome leads to his finding out that Tom is not what he pretends to be, and Tom kills Freddie to protect his secret. Freddie's role in the plot is thus to provide suspense by almost managing to reveal Tom as a fraud, and to solidify Tom's reputation as a cold-blooded murderer.

Tom Ripley

Tom Ripley is the protagonist and hero of the novel, which is narrated in the third person but from his point of view. Orphaned at an early age, Tom was brought up in Boston by his Aunt Dottie.

Tom is an unusual hero in that he is an amoral young man who starts the novel as a minor conman and ends it as a double murderer. At the novel's beginning, he lies constantly about the most trivial details of his life in an effort to make himself appear more important than he is. For example, he tells Mr. Greenleaf that he works in advertising and was educated at Princeton, when in fact he has had a series of humble jobs and the closest he got to Princeton was to pump a Princeton student for information, foreseeing a time when the information might come in useful. Tom's talent for lying proves crucial to his success in getting away with two murders, as he frequently has to concoct false stories to throw his victims' friends and the police off the scent. He has little conscience and has the potential to become a serial killer, which, in fact, he becomes in subsequent Ripley novels. At the time Highsmith wrote *The Talented Mr. Ripley*, the heroes of most suspense and crime novels were morally upright and straight-talking detectives, policemen, or victims of crime who were trying to solve the crime and bring the criminal to justice. Tom, on the other hand, is a force for dishonesty, immorality, and destructiveness. He brings chaos in his wake, first disrupting and taking away the hitherto contented lives of Dickie and Freddie, and bringing grief to Marge and sorrow to Dickie's parents, one of whom is terminally ill.

It is a critical commonplace to call Tom charming, but there is little evidence for this quality when Tom is being himself. Charming people are easily liked, whereas many characters react to Tom with distaste, dislike, and mistrust. What is more, the better they get to know him, they less they like him. This is true of Dickie, Marge, Freddie, and even, after his initial optimism has worn off, Mr. Greenleaf. Tom is sensitive enough to be highly aware of the effect he has on others, and this knowledge tortures him. Before he assumes Dickie's identity, he writhes and squirms in social situations, acutely conscious of what he sees as his inferiority. He is, however, a consummate opportunist, and he has the skill, when under pressure, of manipulating people to do what he wants. For example, he risks being dismissed by Dickie in his first few days in Mongibello, and determines to make Dickie like him. He has the idea of telling Dickie that Mr. Greenleaf employed him specifically to bring Dickie home to the United States. This amuses Dickie, who warms to Tom. This is not charm at work, but a desperate desire for approval and a calculated manipulation of others' emotions.

Similarly, Tom does not charm his way out of the many close scrapes he gets into with the police and Dickie's friends. Rather, he has the ability to impersonate sincerity and innocence, and the resourcefulness to think of a plausible answer to any probing question.

When Tom assumes Dickie's identity, he does acquire a charm that comes of being comfortable in his (or rather, Dickie's) skin for the first time in his life. He is confident and at ease at parties. Paradoxically, he is also lonely, because he dares not allow people to get to know him in case they discover his secret. Apart from his fear of getting caught, his positive motivations to keep up the pretence are first, because he enjoys having Dickie's money and influence, and second, because he thrives on the risk of being found out, and on the challenge of outwitting his pursuers every time with his ingenuity, talent, and luck.

Marge Sherwood

Marge is a young American woman who lives in Mongibello and who is in love with Dickie. She is an aspiring writer and appears to be more realistic about her talents than Dickie is about his—by the novel's end, she has a good chance of having her novel published.

Marge treats Dickie with loyalty and affection, attempting to remain on friendly terms with him even when he has apparently cast her off (after Tom has murdered him). She is immediately suspicious of Tom when he arrives in Mongibello, marking her out as the most perceptive character in the novel. It is not possible to know how much of her suspicions center on her perception of Tom as a rival for the attention and affection of Dickie, and how much is an instinctive realization that Tom's motives are not pure. Probably, both factors are at work.

Marge acts as the antagonist to Tom in the first part of the novel, since, as he sees it, she stands in the way of his relationship with Dickie. Tom thinks of her with a certain contempt and even disgust, and cannot bear to see her underwear around his apartment when she comes to stay. Sneering at her enthusiasm, friendliness, and cheerfulness, he dismisses her as a "typical Girl Scout." However, these qualities, standing in stark contrast to the moroseness and cynicism of Tom, make her a sympathetic character. The fact that she finally believes Tom's account of events and accepts his claimed honest motives at face value is both a testament to her generous nature and to his skill at persuasion.

Peter Smith-Kingsley

Peter Smith-Kingsley is an English friend of Dickie's who lives in Venice. Tom declines Peter's invitation to his country house in Ireland as Peter reminds him of Dickie and "the same thing that had happened with Dickie could happen with Peter." Tom then breaks down in tears, believing that if he had managed things differently, he might have been able to live with Dickie for the rest of his life. Peter is therefore a catalyst character whose resemblance to Dickie brings out the closest approximation to love, and a crisis of conscience, that Tom ever feels.

THEMES

Subversion of Conventional Morality

The Talented Mr. Ripley subverts conventional morality in several ways. First, the hero is a criminal. This contrasts with most literary heroes, who are fundamentally admirable, however flawed they may be. In particular, novels about crime often feature a hero who is morally upright and honest, who is trying to solve the crime and bring the criminal to justice.

Highsmith rejected these conventions with her criminal hero Tom Ripley, who not only gets away with murder, but is rewarded with the wealth of his victim, Dickie Greenleaf. This is partly an assertion by Highsmith of realism over the conventions of crime fiction. Highsmith said in a 1981 interview with Diana Cooper-Clark in *Armchair Detective*, "that only 11 percent of murders are solved."

Tom is even able to add happiness to the list of spoils he gains from murdering Dickie, contrary to the literary convention that the murderer is tortured by his deed until he receives his just deserts. After he kills Dickie, Tom has an "ecstatic moment", falling asleep "happy, content, and utterly confident, as he had never been before in his life." He feels happier impersonating Dickie than he did as himself, a sort of moral irony that gains its power from the reader's familiarity with the convention that people who live a lie must be unhappy.

Highsmith encourages her readers to collude in moral subversion by sympathizing with Tom, the criminal. While readers may not find Tom likable, he is more interesting than the conventionally virtuous characters, such as the Greenleafs, Marge, and Freddie. In addition, Highsmith's

TOPICS FOR FURTHER STUDY

- Consider some of the names of people or places that Highsmith uses in *The Talented Mr. Ripley*. Examples include Thomas Ripley, Dickie Greenleaf, Marge Sherwood, *Pipistrello* (the name of Dickie's boat), Otello's (a restaurant), and Fausto. What contribution to the story or characters do these names make by means of their associations? The first three examples require you only to think about simple word associations; the last three may require some research. Write a short paragraph on each name.

- Watch Anthony Minghella's movie version of *The Talented Mr. Ripley*. How accurate a depiction of the novel is it? What changes have been made, and what effect do they have on the characters, plot, moral tone, and the sympathies of the audience? Write an essay on your findings.

- Research the psychological definition of the term *psychopath*. To what extent does Tom Ripley fit this type? Give a class presentation on your findings using concrete examples from the novel.

- Research social attitudes toward homosexuality in the 1950s and compare them to social attitudes today. How have they changed, how have they stayed the same? Gather as much information as you can before presenting your findings to the class.

- Write a short story or screenplay about a murder from the point of view of either the murderer, or a person who is trying to solve the crime. Write a separate essay on how the point of view affects your plot, characters, moral tone and stance, and how it might affect the sympathies of your readers or audience.

---

sensitive examination of Tom's outsider status may encourage readers to sympathize with him on the emotional level even while they disapprove of or dislike him on the moral and intellectual levels. Consequently, readers may be pleased to see him walk free at the novel's end, thereby supporting the moral subversion that underlies the novel.

Reality and Unreality

The novel is narrated from Tom's point of view, and Tom has an elastic concept of the truth. To Tom, there is an atmosphere of unreality about New York, as if the city "was putting on a show just for him." Even before he arrives in Mongibello, he lies about many aspects of his life, generally with the aim of making himself appear more successful than he is, and also to protect himself. He tells Mr. Greenleaf he works in advertising, and constructs a fictional story about going to Princeton. An element of premeditation went into the latter lie: Tom pumped a Princeton student for information about his life because he felt it might come in useful one day. The only truth he tells Mr. Greenleaf is that he was brought up by his Aunt Dottie. Aunt Dottie's humiliations are a formative influence that Tom recalls just before he murders Dickie. Aunt Dottie represents the terrible truth about Tom's life, that he feels inferior and despised. Her taunt, "*Sissy! He's a sissy from the ground up. Just like his father!*" is the jumping-off point for Tom's life of crime and deception.

From the point when Tom murders Dickie, he begins to live the lies that he formerly told. He used to lie about being successful; now that he has taken on Dickie's identity, he is indeed successful, wealthy, and socially respected. Moreover, he comes actually to believe his own lies: "His stories were good because he imagined them intensely, so intensely that he came to believe them." Perhaps this is why others are convinced by his lies. Time and again after the murders, and frequently with the odds stacked against him, Tom is able to convince his victims' friends, and the police, that his fictional version of events is both plausible and correct. In this respect, he resembles an artist or writer who creates an act of the imagination and persuades people that it is the truth. There is an implied comparison between Marge, the conventional writer, whose achievement in getting interest from a publisher is modest, and Tom, who effectively writes his own new life and has it accepted as fact, and in the process gains a fortune and an impressive new persona.

The theme of reality and unreality extends to emphasize the malleable nature of identity. During the course of the novel, Tom lives first as himself, then steals Dickie's identity and lives as Dickie, and finally resumes his own identity, but with Dickie's wealth. These transformations are largely based on his manipulation of the means by which society defines identity: passports, handwriting, signatures, and wills. Such means are exposed by the events of the novel as superficial, fragile, and ultimately, unreal.

Homosexuality and Society

Homosexuality and society's attitudes to it are a constant underlying subtext in the novel. The theme is introduced in the first pages, with Tom wondering whether his pursuer is a "pervert." This was a common word in the 1950s for a homosexual, and its derogatory nature indicates the level of disapproval leveled against homosexuals by society in general.

In spite of Tom's apparent anxiety about homosexuals, his own feelings for Dickie have homoerotic undertones. In chapter 10, Tom sees Dickie embracing Marge and throws a violent tantrum. He throws Dickie's art tools around and removes Dickie's suit from the closet. It is possible that Highsmith introduced this incident in a tongue-in-cheek fashion to refer to Tom's feelings for Dickie, as the word *closet* meaning *secret* began to be applied to homosexuals in the mid-twentieth century. In removing Dickie's suit from the closet, is Tom figuratively enticing him into a homosexual relationship with himself, one that he assumes will be more rewarding than Dickie's relationship with Marge? In a chilling episode that prefigures events to come, Tom puts on Dickie's suit and, impersonating him, tells an imaginary Marge that he does not love her. Then he kills the imaginary Marge, accusing her of "interfering between Tom and me—No, not that! But there *is* a bond between us!"

Tom is denying any homosexual feelings for Dickie, but his denial is not convincing. He does not express or act on any homosexual feelings, but with good reason, as both Dickie and his friend Freddie express contempt and disgust for homosexual behavior. The shame that Tom feels at his sexuality is revealed in the incident that prompts him to murder Dickie. They see some men who may be homosexuals on a beach, and Dickie voices his contempt towards them, then looks at Tom with distaste, as if he is also homosexual. The episode recalls to Tom's mind Aunt Dottie's taunting of him as a sissy (an effeminate person). The homoerotic theme continues when

Fishing boats at a harbor in Amalfi, Italy
(© Medioimages / Alamy)

Dickie's final act, before Tom murders him, is to remove his trousers.

Tom comes closest to admitting the nature of his feelings for Dickie long after Dickie is dead. Reminded of Dickie by his friend Peter Smith-Kingsley, Tom gives way to genuine tears, reflecting that if he had done things differently, "he *could* have lived with Dickie for the rest of his life." This, like much of what Tom says and does, is a lie or self-delusion, as Dickie appears not to care about Tom.

Dickie and Freddie reflect the antagonistic attitude of 1950s society to homosexuality. While Tom does fall into the crime novel stereotype of the sinister homosexual who kills the object of his or her thwarted affections, he also expresses the more liberal and humane view: "Maybe Cannes was full of fairies. So what?"

STYLE

Suspense Novel

Suspense novels, sometimes called psychological suspense novels, are usually, though not always, crime or detective novels that have a misdeed at their center. They differ from crime or detective novels, however, in that they do not address the question of who did the crime. Suspense novels focus on the threat of violent physical action and danger, or the danger and action itself, while also offering lively entertainment.

All novels use suspense as a device to make the reader continue reading. The suspense question may be *Will the boy get the girl?* or *Will she succeed in becoming a Broadway star?*. In *The Talented Mr. Ripley*, the suspense question of the first part of the book is how the uneasy triangle between Tom, Dickie, and Marge will be worked out. The question changes after Dickie's murder to whether Tom will get away with it.

The difference between ordinary fiction containing suspense and a suspense novel lies in the way in which the suspense question is answered. A suspense novel seeks to engage the reader's intellect and emotions. The intellectual part of the answer lies in the detail of how the criminal perpetrates his crime, or how the detective solves it. The emotional part of the answer lies in the trajectory of the passions that led up to the crime, and the emotional consequences of the crime. It is noteworthy that in *The Talented Mr. Ripley*, Highsmith keeps up the suspense to the last page.

Irony

The Talented Mr. Ripley is a novel laden with irony of the type that arises from a discordance between acts and results. There is a perceived gap between an understanding or expectation of reality, and what actually happens. The fact that Tom feels so comfortable in his stolen identity as Dickie is ironic, as it might be expected that he would feel less comfortable when living a lie. There is also heavy irony in the fact that at the end of the novel, Tom expects to be arrested as a result of the fingerprints the police took from the belongings of Dickie that Tom deposited at the American Express office, whereas the fingerprints actually convince the police he is innocent. This is because the fingerprints on the belongings are the same as those found in the apartment in Rome that the police believe Dickie lived in, though in fact, Tom lived there disguised as Dickie.

Dramatic irony occurs when the reader or audience knows something that the character does not, adding a new level of meaning to the character's action or words of which the character is ignorant. An example is when Marge writes to

Dickie (in fact, Tom masquerading as Dickie) that she has told the police "that you and Tom are inseparable and how they could have found you and still missed *Tom*, I could not imagine." Unknown to Marge, Tom and Dickie are literally inseparable, as they are one and the same person.

The effect of such irony in the novel is twofold. First, it underlines Highsmith's purpose of moral subversion, in that morally wrong actions end up being rewarded. Second, it establishes a distance between the narrator and the events and characters, as if the narrator is viewing them with a certain wry humor.

Juxtaposition of the Macabre and the Banal

In the novel, macabre episodes such as Tom's murders of Dickie and Freddie are described in plain, everyday, non-descriptive prose, as if the events were no more remarkable than someone going to buy a carton of milk. The effect of this is to remind readers that the line between a psychopath like Tom and the rest of humanity is a fine one. It also shows readers that seemingly ordinary people such as Tom can be concealing shocking pathology. This is evident in scenes like the one in which Dickie catches Tom impersonating him in his suit, yet Tom is able to quickly resume an appearance of rationality.

Menace

Highsmith builds an atmosphere of menace leading up to Tom's murdering Dickie in two main ways. First, she shows evidence of Tom's mental pathology, which increases in seriousness as the novel progresses. He is shown fantasizing about murdering Aunt Dottie from eight years old, lying, and breaking the law. When his fascination with Dickie's lifestyle renders him part of a triangle of tension between him, Dickie, and Marge, it is obvious that at least one of these characters will suffer. The threat of Tom's unstable personality reaches its height in the scene in which Tom puts on Dickie's suit, impersonates him, and mimes murdering Marge on the grounds that she was "interfering between Tom and me." It is clear to the reader that something terrible is going to happen, but Dickie is too naïve to view the threat as seriously as he should.

Setting as Metaphor

Highsmith uses the European setting of *The Talented Mr. Ripley* in a similar way to the American author Henry James in his book *The*

COMPARE & CONTRAST

- **1950s:** In the United States, sexual acts between men are illegal in most states under sodomy laws. Homosexuals are stigmatized as being abnormal, diseased, or threats to national security.

  Today: While stigmatization continues in some regions, anti-homosexual laws are repealed or invalidated. In 2007, a bill outlawing discrimination against employees because of sexual orientation is introduced into Congress.

- **1950s:** Highsmith rejects the conventions of mainstream crime fiction by portraying the hero of *The Talented Mr. Ripley* as a criminal who gets away with murder.

  Today: Fictional figures such as the criminal hero and the morally compromised policeman

or detective, have become common in crime fiction, drama, and films. However, it is still unusual to find criminal heroes who are not punished in any way for their crimes.

- **1950s:** Fingerprinting is one of the few scientific means of identifying criminals available to the police. In *The Talented Mr. Ripley*, however, fingerprinting works in Tom's favor to clear him of a crime he really did commit.

  Today: DNA profiling, whereby genetic material in tissue residues found at a crime scene is analyzed to provide identification of an individual, is widely used in crime solving. If DNA profiling had been available to the police in *The Talented Mr. Ripley*, Tom would likely have been convicted.

Ambassadors. There is an implicit contrast between the innocence of the United States and the experience and corruption of the old European society. Europe is presented as a place where conventional morals and duties can be disregarded, and new roles taken on without accountability. It is significant that before Tom leaves the United States for Europe, Mr. Greenleaf asks him if he has read James' book.

HISTORICAL CONTEXT

Development of the Crime Novel

As well as belonging to the literary genre of the suspense novel, much of Highsmith's work, including *The Talented Mr. Ripley*, also belongs to the wider category of the crime novel. The rise of the crime novel as a genre occurred in late nineteenth- and early twentieth-century England, with the appearance of Sir Arthur Conan Doyle's Sherlock Holmes mysteries. From this time until Highsmith's *The Talented Mr. Ripley* appeared, most

crime novels featured an honest hero who brought the criminal to justice. This is particularly true of mainstream crime fiction written between World Wars I and II (1918–1939), which leaves no room for doubt that virtue lies with the forces of law and order and evil lies with the criminal, who ends up being punished.

During the 1920s and 1930s, a new type of morally compromised hero emerged with the appearance of a genre known as hardboiled crime fiction. Pioneered by writers such as Dashiell Hammett in the late 1920s and Raymond Chandler from the late 1930s, this genre featured detective heroes who were not averse to using violence and underhanded methods in solving crimes. Out of the hardboiled genre emerged a subgenre known as noir fiction. In noir fiction, the protagonist is usually not a detective, but a victim, suspect, or perpetrator of crime. Other features are that sexual relationships are used to advance the plot and the lead characters have self-destructive qualities. The American writer James M. Cain is considered to be one of the founders of noir fiction, with his novel *The Postman Always Rings Twice* (1934).

Beginning in the 1940s, noir tendencies found their way into Hollywood crime dramas, creating the genre known as *film noir*.

Highsmith's novel *The Talented Mr. Ripley* built on these trends to present a criminal hero who gets away with his crimes and appears not to suffer as a result. In her portrayal of Tom Ripley, Highsmith was able to draw upon the growing field of psychology to examine the roots and nature of his malaise. From the 1950s, crime and suspense novels contained a substantial complement of psychological insight and analysis. This is one of the factors that enabled Highsmith and other writers to thrust the criminal protagonist to center stage.

The Psychopath

Tom Ripley is frequently discussed in critical works as a type of mentally ill person known as a psychopath. Individuals who might now be classed as psychopaths were first described by the Frenchman Philippe Pinel (1745–1826), who is widely considered to be the father of modern psychiatry. He described patients who were insane in the sense that they seemed rational but lacked restraint and remorse for their harmful actions.

The next most influential work on psychopathy was carried out by the American psychiatrist Hervey Cleckley. In his book, *The Mask of Sanity* (1941), Cleckley lists the characteristics of the psychopath, including superficial charm and good intelligence, lack of remorse or shame, inadequately motivated social behavior, poor judgment and failure to learn by experience, unreliability, pathologic egocentricity and inability to love.

Although the term *psychopathy* is in widespread use, it is not listed as a mental condition in the *Diagnostic and Statistical Manual of Mental Disorders* published by the American Psychiatric Association, a handbook for mental health professionals that lists mental disorders and the criteria for diagnosing them. The closest correlate to psychopathy listed is antisocial personality disorder (ASPD), and the two terms are frequently used interchangeably by psychiatrists, many of whom consider that psychopathy differs from ASPD only in respect of its severity. This equation between ASPD and psychopathy is, however, disputed by some authorities, including a leading expert in the field, Robert D. Hare. Most psychopaths meet the criteria for ASPD, but not all people with ASPD are psychopaths.

According to the *Diagnostic and Statistical Manual of Mental Disorders*, ASPD is characterized by the individual's lack of empathy, disregard for the rights and feelings of others, superficial charm, inflated self-appraisal, deceitfulness and manipulation for his or her own ends, disregard for social and legal rules, irresponsibility, aggression, and sudden changes of jobs, residences, or relationships.

ASPD is called dissocial personality disorder by the World Health Organization. In its publication, *The ICD-10 Classification of Mental and Behavioural Disorders*, it lists the criteria for diagnosis of dissocial personality disorder as follows, stipulating that at least three of these criteria must be met:

- Callous unconcern for the feelings of others
- Gross and persistent attitude of irresponsibility and disregard for social norms, rules, and obligations
- Incapacity to maintain enduring relationships, though having no difficulty in establishing them
- Very low tolerance to frustration and a low threshold for discharge of aggression, including violence
- Incapacity to experience guilt or to profit from experience, particularly punishment
- Marked proneness to blame others, or to offer plausible rationalizations, for the behavior that has brought the patient into conflict with society

Attitudes about Homosexuality

In the United States and much of Europe in the 1950s, homosexuality was taboo. Homosexual men, in particular, could lose their jobs and official positions if their sexual orientation was revealed. Many politicians treated homosexuality as a sign of anti-American attitudes, marking out the homosexual as a threat to national security. This connection was also made by the Nazis during World War II, who exterminated homosexuals alongside Jews, gypsies, mentally and physically disabled people, and other minorities in the Holocaust. In the United States from the late 1940s to the late 1950s, Senator Joseph McCarthy used accusations of homosexuality as a smear tactic in his anti-communist crusade, combining the Red Scare against supposed communists with the so-called Lavender Scare against homosexuals.

Homosexuality has long been seen by some segments of the population as a disease or

Scene from the 1999 film version of The Talented Mr Ripley, *starring Matt Damon as Tom Ripley*
(Paramount / Miramax / The Kobal Collection / Bray, Phil / The Picture Desk Inc.)

disorder. Only as late as 1973 did the American Psychiatric Association vote to remove homosexuality from its *Diagnostic and Statistical Manual of Mental Disorders*. Some groups, particularly certain Christian groups, believe that homosexuality is a mental disease that can be cured by means of psychological conditioning programs.

Since the late twentieth century, a growth in the field of genetics has prompted the search for a homosexuality gene. This has raised fears among some homosexual rights groups that the purpose of such research is to modify or eliminate these genes (if any such genes exist).

As of 2007, many countries maintain laws that prohibit or regulate sexual activity between consenting adults of the same sex. In the United States, state sodomy laws, which made sexual acts between homosexual men illegal, were repealed in most states during the last half of the twentieth century, from the 1960s onwards. The remaining anti-homosexual laws were invalidated by the 2003 Supreme Court decision *Lawrence et al. v. Texas*, in which the court struck down the

prohibition of homosexual sodomy in Texas. On April 24, 2007, the Employment Non-Discrimination Act, was first proposed in Congress. This potential federal law would disallow discrimination based on gender identity or sexual orientation in the United States.

CRITICAL OVERVIEW

Highsmith's work was largely ignored in the United States during her lifetime. Possible reasons for this include her less-than-friendly personality and reputation for misanthropy (a dislike or distrust of all humankind). She was also unpopular for her public criticism of twentieth-century U.S. foreign policy. She did, however, enjoy great popularity in the United Kingdom, France, Spain, Germany, Switzerland, and Austria. Typical of the unenthusiastic critical response to her work in the United States at this time is a remark by Anthony Boucher in a 1956 *New York Times Book Review* article. Commenting on Highsmith's receipt of the

Edgar Allan Poe Scroll of the Mystery Writers of America award for *The Talented Mr. Ripley*, Boucher concedes that the novel is "good," but adds that it is "hard to envision in the year's best class."

Since Highsmith's death in 1995, however, her reputation has risen in the United States. Her Ripley novels were republished, and her increasing popularity was solidified by Anthony Minghella's 1999 film version of *The Talented Mr. Ripley*. One factor that may have contributed to the change in her reputation in the United States is the growing tendency to view society as an uncertain milieu in which evil is not always punished and good does not always prosper, a viewpoint that prevails in Highsmith's novels. Another factor is her sympathetic portrayal of homosexual and lesbian relationships, which has earned her an important place in gay and lesbian literature.

In the wake of Mingella's film, a new, and very different, range of reviews of the republished Ripley novels appeared. Writing in the *San Francisco Chronicle*, Oscar C. Villalon praises Highsmith as "one of the finest American writers of crime fiction." He adds, "she raised herself above genre with her unsettling view of who we are and how killing can be as unremorseful and easy as breathing."

In a review of the Everyman anthology, *The Talented Mr. Ripley, Ripley Under Ground, Ripley's Game* for the *New York Times*, Michiko Kakutani notes Highsmith's ability to create a "chilly, misanthropic world." This is a world, explains Kakutani, in which "murderers are rarely caught, much less brought to justice; a world in which identity is permeable and the macabre and the banal, the insane and the rational, live serenely side by side."

In Europe, Highsmith's popularity continues to grow. In 2000, the London *Times* named *The Talented Mr. Ripley* as one of its "100 Best Crime Novels of the 20th Century." The anonymous reviewer remarks on the charisma of the novel's protagonist, noting that "Tom Ripley is the sort of double murderer it's hard not to take a shine to," and adding: "you want him to get away with it—and he does." In her article for the London *Times*, Zoe Paxton draws attention to Highsmith's ability "to show the world through the eyes of her most despicable characters." Paxton points out that these people are not outside humanity: "They are everyday people doing unspeakable things in such an everyday way that you start, bit by bit, to realise that it could be

you." The details are so banal, Paxton notes, and the prose so neutral and direct, that the reader begins to identify with the person. This, says Paxton, is why Highsmith's stories are so haunting: "you realise that there is no way of escaping what humans are."

CRITICISM

Claire Robinson

Robinson has an M.A. in English. She is a former teacher of English literature and creative writing, and she is currently a freelance writer and editor. In the following essay, Robinson explores Patricia Highsmith's presentation of the criminal hero in The Talented Mr. Ripley *and examines how this affects moral tone, suspense, and possible reader responses to the novel.*

Whereas most literary heroes develop in the direction of becoming better people, Tom Ripley develops into a more amoral person and a more accomplished and calculating criminal. Thus *The Talented Mr. Ripley* can be seen as an inverted *bildungsroman* (a literary work showing the moral growth of the hero or protagonist) in that it attempts to subvert conventional morality.

At the beginning of the novel, Tom is a minor conman who lacks the nerve to make money out of his Internal Revenue scam, but his nerve strengthens with the success of each of his lies and schemes until by the novel's end, he has gotten away with two murders. By the time he kills Dickie, Tom is sufficiently confident and skilled in his criminal profession to succeed in hiding the murder, and killing Freddie seems almost easy for him. Only luck intervenes to save Marge from being his third victim. Not only does Tom get away with his crimes, but he enjoys a life of luxury, thanks to his appropriation of Dickie's wealth. Thus, whereas most works of literature, and notably crime novels, teach a variant on the Biblical dictum, "the wages of sin is death" (Romans 6:23), the message to be taken from this novel appears at first glance to be that the wages of sin can be wealth, influence, and a better life. Such an interpretation, however, would be simplistic in that it ignores the complexities of character and plot in the novel, as well as the complexities of reader response to Tom as hero.

WHAT DO I READ NEXT?

- The next novel in Highsmith's Ripley series after *The Talented Mr. Ripley* is *Ripley Under Ground* (1970). The novel shows Tom married and living a life of luxury in France. He collects art and sells fake paintings to supplement his income.

- *Mystery and Suspense Writers: The Literature of Crime, Detection, and Espionage*, edited by Robin W. Winks and Maureen Corrigan (1998), is a two-volume collection of over eighty articles on mystery, detective, and espionage fiction. The editors include biographies and criticism of writers such as Edgar Allen Poe, Patricia Highsmith, and Sarah Paretsky. There are also essays on subgenres such as the police procedural, the spy novel, and the whodunit.

- *The Postman Always Rings Twice* (1934), by James M. Cain, is a pioneering noir novel that set a precedent (or example) for the entire genre. It tells the story of a drifter who falls in love with the wife of the owner of a rural diner. The two begin a secret affair and plot to kill the woman's husband. The novel is a bleak, moody, and oddly compelling read.

- Highsmith once told an interviewer that the only suspense writing she read was by the Russian author Fyodor Dostoevsky. In her book *Plotting and Writing Suspense Fiction*, she wrote, "I think most of Dostoyevsky's books would be called suspense books, were they being published today for the first time." Dostoevksy's novel *The Brothers Karamazov* (1880) is a classic and prototypical suspense novel.

- Robert J. Corber's book *Homosexuality in Cold War America: Resistance and the Crisis of Masculinity* (1997) examines how homosexual men in the 1950s resisted pressure to remain in the closet. Corber argues that a gay male identity emerged in the 1950s that both drew on and transcended left-wing opposition to the cultural and political consensus of the Cold War. He explores novels, plays, and films of the period as well as social trends such as the national security state, the growth of the suburbs, and consumer culture to develop his ideas.

Highsmith's own writings suggest that one reason she made her hero amoral was to reflect her view that the universe in general is amoral. In *Plotting and Writing Suspense Fiction*, Highsmith writes, "I find the public passion for justice quite boring and artificial, for neither life nor nature cares if justice is ever done or not." Whether this view is true or not, the problem with it is that most readers do have a passion for seeing justice done. If a character escapes being punished for doing wrong within the novel, then readers may punish him with their own hatred or, worse, disengagement. If readers hate a character or cease to care what happens to him at the end of the novel, any moral subversion is undermined. This is because good is still affirmed and evil is still punished in the reader's own awareness, whatever the author intended.

Highsmith recognized that an important way of countering this problem of readers' sympathies is to make the criminal hero likable. In *Plotting and Writing Suspense Fiction*, she advises writers who wish to emulate her practice of constructing criminal heroes to give them "as many pleasant qualities as possible." As examples, she cites "generosity, kindness to some people, fondness for painting or music or cooking." In the light of this, it is worth asking to what extent she succeeds in making Tom likable and by what means.

Even the most flawed heroes of novels have qualities that mark them out as loveable, great, or deserving. The talent ascribed to Tom in the novel's title is used ironically to refer to his skill with figures, forgery, and impersonation. He perfects these qualities over time and turns them to good use in his criminal activities. They are not, however, qualities that make him likable. They are cold, inhuman, and even anti-human qualities. For the same reason, it is difficult to sympathize with his misogynistic squeamishness when faced with Marge's underwear in his apartment and the snobbishness that makes him unable to tolerate the company of "second-rate antique dealers."

Another problem with Tom as a hero is that while most heroes have a strong sense of self that makes them seem alive to readers, Tom lacks a sense of self. This lack is exacerbated by his habitual blurring of the line between reality and unreality. If a person is always acting (it is significant that Tom's early ambition is to be an actor), the real self disappears. When living as himself, Tom is something of a blank. This very characteristic, of course, makes him the consummate stealer of identities. Indeed, he appears to grow into himself when he takes on Dickie's identity, or perhaps it is more accurate to say that he grows into his interpretation of Dickie. Given the choice between spending time with Tom as himself, Tom as Dickie, or Tom with Dickie's wealth, most readers would certainly choose the last two. Tom is difficult to like because there is not much living, breathing humanity to grasp onto.

The question of moral subversion is not the only aspect of the novel affected by the question of Tom's likability. In order for the suspense aspect of the novel to work, the reader must care whether Tom is caught or not. Highsmith herself seems to have liked Tom, while conceding that others may not share her enthusiasm, if a general comment that she makes about her amoral heroes in her book *Plotting and Writing Suspense Fiction* can be applied to Tom. Highsmith writes: "Though I think all my criminal heroes are fairly likable, or at least not repugnant, I must admit I have failed to make some of my readers think so." Highsmith then cites one reader's hatred of Tom as a character.

Tom, then, has few, if any, likable qualities and a minimal sense of self, and his few remarkable talents are used to destructive ends. Yet many readers and critics surprise themselves in wanting Tom to escape his pursuers. Highsmith provides a masterly final scene in which Tom sails into Piraeus harbor in Greece filled with fear that he will be arrested over forging the will and leaving his fingerprints on Dickie's belongings at the

> IF READERS FEEL ANY RELIEF THAT TOM HAS GOT AWAY WITH IT YET AGAIN, EVEN IF THAT RELIEF IS MIXED WITH ANGER, HATRED, OR DISGUST AT TOM'S ACTIONS, THEN HIGHSMITH HAS SUCCEEDED IN CREATING A CRIMINAL HERO WHO HAS GAINED SYMPATHY ON SOME LEVEL."

American Express office. Tom sees police waiting on the harbor—but they are not waiting for him. If readers feel any relief that Tom has got away with it yet again, even if that relief is mixed with anger, hatred, or disgust at Tom's actions, then Highsmith has succeeded in creating a criminal hero who has gained sympathy on some level. What level might this be?

It is not Tom's exceptional but ill-used talents, or his refined taste in art and antiques that earn sympathy. It is necessary to look more deeply, at the effect that his aspirations and actions have on readers' emotions and instincts. With regard to his aspirations, at the beginning of the novel, Tom is eager to go to Europe in order to leave behind his old life, in which he thinks he has failed. At this point, he genuinely wants to do his best for Mr. Greenleaf and to succeed in his task of bringing Dickie home. He sees Dickie leading a carefree and luxurious life in an Italian village, and desires that life for himself: "Tom envied him with a heartbreaking surge of envy and self-pity." Cultivating a friendship with Dickie is one way to share in his beautiful life. But when he cannot make Dickie like him, Tom begins to grow desperate.

Indeed, in many social situations, Tom feels intense discomfort and inferiority. He frequently feels that people are laughing at him (for example, at the beginning of chapter 8). He physically writhes and squirms at the rejection, contempt, and disapproval he senses from others. When Dickie rejects his plan to go to Paris as part of a drug smuggling operation, Tom is struck with a feeling of isolation. He realizes "They were not friends. They didn't know each other. . . . He felt surrounded by strangeness, by hostility." Later, Dickie eyes him with disgust after seeing two supposed homosexuals, implying that Tom is homosexual too. Tom feels a "sharp thrust of shame" and "A crazy emotion of hate, of affection, of impatience and frustration" towards Dickie. Just as the eight-year-old Tom felt an impulse to kill his Aunt Dottie because of the many humiliations and rejections she heaped upon him, the adult Tom now feels an impulse to kill Dickie, for similar reasons. His instinct of defensiveness is so excessive that it tends towards aggression: even with the harmless Mr. Greenleaf, he feels "an impulse to attack him before he was attacked."

Tom's desire for a better life, his need for acceptance, and the shame, frustration, and anger he feels when he cannot get it, are universal human experiences. Many people will also admit (particularly during childhood) to having violent or murderous fantasies against those who deny them approval or love, and those who visit shame and contempt upon them. In these respects, Tom is an everyman; everyone can identify with these impulses to a greater or lesser degree. The difference between Tom and the majority of humankind is that he is willing to act out his hostile fantasies and kill those who humiliate him (Dickie) or threaten to expose him (Freddie, and very nearly, Marge).

This difference between the likes of Tom and the general populace is crucial. In *Plotting and Writing Suspense Fiction*, Highsmith writes, "Criminals are dramatically interesting, because for a time at least they are active, free in spirit, and they do not knuckle down to anyone." Most people are not free. They recognize that they must operate within accepted social mores or face negative consequences. They are conscious of some form of cause-and-effect, as expressed in the Biblical notion of "whatsoever a man soweth, that shall he also reap" (Galatians 6:7), that convinces them that if they do evil, then evil will rebound upon them. They resemble Tom far less than they resemble Highsmith herself, who wrote in *Plotting and Writing Suspense Fiction*, "I am so law-abiding, I can tremble before a customs inspector with nothing contraband in my suitcases." In short, they "knuckle down" daily. Because of this, it is hard to resist feeling a small, illicit thrill as Tom walks off the boat unchallenged at Piraeus.

There may be another process at work, too. While the difference between Tom and the rest of the populace is crucial, it is presented in the novel as slight. Tom does not go to Europe to

become a murderer. In common with many people, he would like to improve his life. He feels the same kinds of frustrations that most people feel, and even experiences the same impulses that most people experience. But whereas most people restrain their frustrations and impulses before they get to homicidal levels, Tom lacks that restraint. He concludes the thought that many people begin but abort. Perhaps, then, when Tom walks free at the novel's end, the reader is relieved that he is not the only one who escapes retribution.

Source: Claire Robinson, Critical Essay on *The Talented Mr. Ripley*, in *Novels for Students*, Gale, Cengage Learning, 2008.

Erlene Hubly

In the following excerpt, Hubly claims that Tom is Highsmith's portrayal of the "ultimate artist." As part of this discussion, Hubly explores the nature of identity and the creation of identity, positing that it is Tom's very creation of his identities that allows one to classify him as an artist.

… The effect of Europe upon Tom Ripley is immediate and lasting. Arriving in Mongibello, Italy, where Dickie Greenleaf has been living for the past few years, Ripley is at once charmed by all that he sees: the town; Dickie's house; the two original Picasso drawings that hang in Dickie's hallway; Dickie Greenleaf himself. But by far the most charming thing that Ripley sees is Dickie's way of life, Dickie pursuing the life of an artist, painting in the mornings, sailing in his boat at sundown, drinking aperitifs in the evening in one of the cafes on the beach, taking trips to such cities as Naples, Rome, Paris whenever the mood strikes, answerable to no one for the way he spends his time or money. Ripley, comparing his life to Dickie's, is overcome by feelings of envy and self-pity and vows that he will devote all his efforts to becoming Dickie's best friend and thus a part of his life.

If Europe offers the ideal way of life, it also provides the moral atmosphere in which to attain it. Non-Puritan, seemingly indifferent to questions of morality, thousands of miles from the United States, it can offer the American there—cut off from family and social ties and thus from moral accountability—liberation, release from inhibitions. Tom Ripley was, to be sure, a petty crook in America, but in Europe he is free, if he is so inclined, to become a killer. Successful with Dickie at first, Ripley's hopes for becoming his friend are shattered by Marge Sherwood, an American living in Mongibello and Dickie's best friend. Becoming suspicious of Ripley, warning Dickie that Tom may be a homosexual with designs on him—a charge to which there may be some truth—Marge effectively drives the two men apart. On a trip to San Remo with Dickie, Ripley, sensing Dickie's growing indifference to him, realizing that he has lost his friendship forever, feeling humiliated and rejected, kills Dickie while they are out in a boat together, hitting him in the head with an oar and then weighing his body down in the water with a cement anchor. Dickie's death, however, is not without its practical side. For if Ripley cannot share in Dickie's life, by becoming his friend, he can, once Dickie is dead, become Dickie himself, assuming his very identity.

Ripley is, of course, a man eminently qualified for such a task. Like Howard Ingham in *The Tremor of Forgery*, Tom Ripley is a man without a self. Having no clear identity, he is a man who has rejected himself and all that he is: his unhappy childhood; his upbringing by a cruel and somewhat sadistic aunt; his impoverished emotional life. And in finding Dickie Greenleaf he finds for the first time in his life an identity he can accept, that he would even like for his own.

This transformation, this process by which Ripley absorbs Dickie into his own being, begins slowly. At first it is on a superficial level, Ripley merely copying Dickie's bodily movements, the way he walks, the way he parts his lips when he is out of breath from swimming. Then his efforts become more serious and far more encompassing. Mastering Dickie's voice, the little growl in his throat at the end of phrases, he begins to impersonate the whole man Dickie and in one of the most striking scenes in the book, attempts for the first time literally to become Dickie. Standing in front of a mirror, his hair parted and fashioned as Dickie wears his, dressed in Dickie's clothes, even wearing Dickie's rings, Ripley acts out a scenario in which he, as Dickie, confronts an imaginary Marge Sherwood, first telling her that he, Dickie, does not love her and then strangling her with his bare hands because she threatens to come between Tom and himself. It is a chilling scene in itself, made all the more so because it reveals not only the depth of Ripley's feelings for Dickie, but also the nature of his madness. Identity has become a deadly game, one that he would kill for.

This is, of course, exactly what he does. Wanting a complete union with Dickie—in this sense Ripley is a homosexual—but unable to accomplish it physically—no one can *become* another person—Ripley accomplishes it, like the artist he is, through his imagination. Dickie's body, his physical substance, is, of course, the obstacle. But by removing that obstacle, by destroying Dickie's body, Ripley is then free to incorporate the *idea* of Dickie into his own being—through his mind. Murder, then, makes the process of attaining an identity complete and Ripley, with Dickie's physical presence removed, can become that which he thinks Dickie is.

There are, of course, several ironies here. For Dickie himself did not have much of an identity himself. Having rejected much of his own background, living off his father, refusing to do any kind of meaningful work, Dickie was a man who had yet to find himself. And Ripley, in modeling himself after Dickie, becomes that which had little substance to begin with. This irony underscores yet another one: Ripley, even after he thinks he has become Dickie, continues to act as Ripley, doing things, his murder of Dickie's friend, Freddie Miles, for example, when Freddie seems about to expose him, that Dickie himself would never have done. But in Ripley's world, where thinking something makes it so, Tom Ripley, thinking he is Dickie Greenleaf, becomes Dickie Greenleaf. Going to Paris, walking the streets, sightseeing, he delights in his new identity: "*Wonderful* to sit in a famous cafe and to think of tomorrow and tomorrow and tomorrow being Dickie Greenleaf! ... It was impossible ever to be lonely or bored, he thought, so long as he was Dickie Greenleaf!"

Ripley's joy at being Dickie is short-lived, however, for as Ripley, who is now Dickie, continues to act as Ripley, murdering Freddie Miles, for example, he begins to threaten Dickie's identity as well. Furthermore, the boat in which Ripley and Dickie had last been seen together in San Remo is found scuttled, blood stains on its bottom. And as the police cannot find Tom Ripley, who is now Dickie Greenleaf, they suspect Dickie of having murdered Ripley as well as Freddie Miles. Realizing that the time has come when it is more dangerous to be Dickie Greenleaf than to be Tom Ripley, that he must now kill Dickie again, this time for good, Ripley becomes despondent: "This was the end of Dickie Greenleaf, he knew. He hated becoming Thomas Ripley again, hated being nobody, hated putting on his old set of habits again. He hated going back to himself as he would have hated putting on a shabby suit of clothes." Ripley's confusion here—of identity with clothes—is characteristic and will provide the idea by which he gets rid of Dickie once and for all. Packing up Dickie's clothes, storing them in the American Express in Venice under the name of Robert Fanshaw, Ripley, in effect, kills Dickie for a second and final time. For if a person is the clothes he wears, then by disposing of Dickie's clothes, Ripley not only disposes of Dickie, but also makes it impossible for himself to become Dickie again.

If Ripley cannot be Dickie, he must become someone and it is at this point in the novel that Highsmith begins her deepest exploration into the question of identity. For as Tom Ripley begins to put together a new self, Highsmith lets the reader know what a genuine identity is not. For Tom Ripley, as artist, will base his ultimate creation, himself, on a lesson he has learned while posing as Dickie Greenleaf: that the important thing about an identity is not who you are, but who you think you are. Acting out something makes it so: "If you wanted to be cheerful, or melancholic, or wistful, or thoughtful, or courteous," all you had to do was "simply *act* those things with every gesture." Gestures then, have become personality; acting, being; appearance, reality. And Ripley, in creating a self based on such principles, will, like Highsmith's other artists, become a forger, passing off that which is false, a sham-self, for that which is real, a genuine identity.

The fact that he is an American in Europe again aids Ripley's enterprise. Without any family or friends nearby, without any job to define him, with the money to travel and thus the means to escape any fixed existence, he can make himself into anyone he wishes. In such a fluid world, geography can become character; a person, the sum of the places he has been[.] Going to Paris, Ripley begins to absorb that city into himself; walking the streets, he learns the names of its famous places; sitting in a well-known sidewalk cafe, he begins to have a new sense of who he is. It is a practice he will repeat in a number of cities—Rome, Venice, Athens—each place he's visiting adding further to his concept of himself. Sightseeing, then, literally becomes a way of life, the places one has been, the things one has seen, becoming one's self.

What one owns can also help to define one and Ripley sets out to associate himself with those things which best represent that which he would like to become. Ripley, of course, never owns anything; to own something would be to possess something of substance and value, an accomplishment he is at present incapable of. But he does rent. Moving to Venice, he leases a two-story house overlooking San Marco, with a garden "slightly run down," but with an interior which suggests all the splendor and wealth he would like for his own. There is a checkerboard black-and-white marble floor downstairs that extends from the foyer into each of the rooms, pink and white marble floors upstairs and carved wooden furniture so eloquent that it does not resemble furniture at all but rather "an embodiment of cinquecento music played on haut-boys, recorders and violas da gamba." He spends some time—Highsmith slyly points out "at least two weeks"—decorating the house and it reflects his growing good taste: "There was a sureness in his taste now that he had not felt in Rome, that his Rome apartment had not hinted at. "Indeed, Ripley's near-possessions, the house he rents, the way he has decorated it, all give him a new sense of himself: "He felt surer of himself now in every way."

If things can give one an identity, so can the media. The newspaper stories which begin to appear in the Italian press about the "sensational" Dickie Greenleaf case also help to define Ripley. In these stories he is described in some detail, as the friend of the now missing Dickie Greenleaf, as "a young well-to-do American" now living in a "Palazzo" in Venice. Ripley had never thought of his house as being a "palace" before, but seeing it called such in print must make it so and he immediately feels a new sense of pride. Going to a party, he becomes the center of attention. Recognized immediately, because of the newspaper stories, as being Tom Ripley, his identity is further confirmed; he must be someone because other people know who he is.

Slowly, then, Ripley puts together a self made up of the gestures he affects, the places he has been, the things he is associated with, the newspaper stories which confirm that he does, indeed, exist. A patchwork creation made possible by Dickie Greenleaf's money and held together by his own art—his ability to think up new plots, to act out new roles—Tom Ripley is, then, at the end of *The Talented Mr. Ripley,* the perfect hero for further adventures. Highsmith will, in the three Ripley novels which follow, *Ripley under Ground* (1970), *Ripley's Game* (1974) and *The Boy Who Followed Ripley* (1980), modify her concept of her hero somewhat, even suggest that as Ripley beings to lose his powers of invention—as he does in these novels—as he becomes, then, less of an artist, he becomes more of a human being, even moves toward acquiring a genuine self. But at the end of *The Talented Mr. Ripley*, Tom Ripley is Highsmith's ultimate artist, a man who because he has no real identity, can become all things.

Source: Erlene Hubly, "A Portrait of the Artist: The Novels of Patricia Highsmith," in *Clues: A Journal of Detection,* Vol. 5, No. 1, Spring–Summer 1984, pp. 115–30.

Anthony Channell Hilfer

In the following excerpt, Hilfer discusses the possible influences of latent homosexuality and/or schizophrenia on Tom's character. Hilfer ultimately concludes, however, that these factors are not as essential to Tom's actions if he is viewed as an example of protean man, or "a player with his own and others' destinies."

. . . It is not surprising that Tom "had wanted to be an actor" since the main thematic pattern in *The Talented Mr. Ripley* is Tom's confirmation in the belief that acting creates reality. At this point, a distinction is necessary. It is possible to construe a determinate identity for Tom in terms of two culturally talismanic terms: "Homosexual" and "Schizophrenic." The reader has doubtless picked up intimations of these identities simply in the quotes I've given, especially the one in which Tom, playing Dickie to the mirror, justifies himself to an imaginary Marge. "You were interfering between Tom and me—No, not that!" *That* obviously refers to homosexual attachment and we may suspect that Tom doth protest too much. Both earlier and later, Tom shows notable anxiety about being perceived as effeminate or homosexual and, in the scene where Dickie finds Tom

playacting in Dickie's clothes, Tom is accused to his face of being "queer." In what is so far the latest in the Ripley series, *The Boy Who Followed Ripley*, Tom dresses in drag partly as a disguise but more just for the experience. Most suggestive of all, Freddie Miles, before it dawns on him that Tom is impersonating Dickie Greenleaf, suspects that Tom's presence in what is supposedly Dickie's apartment wearing Dickie's cloths and jewelry must indicate a homosexual relation between them. After murdering Freddie, Tom thinks "how sad, stupid, clumsy, dangerous and unnecessary his death had been, and how brutally unfair to Freddie. Of course, one could loathe Freddie, too. A selfish, stupid bastard who had sneered at one of his best friends—Dickie certainly was one of his best friends—just because he suspected him of sexual deviation. Tom laughed at that phrase 'sexual deviation.' Where was the sex? Where was the deviation? He looked at Freddie and said low and bitterly: 'Freddie Miles, You're a victim of your own dirty mind.'"

The above passage also can be read as evincing Tom's schizophrenic tendencies. Tom's indignation at Freddie's suspicions seems curiously displaced. After all, Tom has *murdered* Dickie, surely rather more unfriendly an act than sneering, however unjustly, at supposedly deviant tendencies in him. Equally odd is that Tom, when he returns to his Ripley identity, feels free of guilt for Freddie's murder: "Being Tom Ripley had one compensation at least: it relieved his mind of guilt for the stupid, unnecessary murder of Freddie Miles." This is because Tom was being Dickie at that time. Later, when Marge asks Tom where he had been that winter—we know, of course, that he spent it playing Dickie—Tom suffers a slight identity slippage: "'Well not with Tom, I mean, not with Dickie,' he said laughing, flustered at his slip of the tongue."

But to anchor Tom's identity in latent homosexuality and schizophrenia is to read against the clear indications in Highsmith's novel that Tom's strength is in his indeterminacy of identity, in an emptiness of self that allows the superior performance of roles, eventuating in Tom's finest performance—the role of himself. So my answer to the question I raised at the beginning of this essay, the question of who Tom is, why we are interested in him and care about him is that we are interested in and care about Tom precisely because he is not anybody. It is this negative capability that exempts Tom from detection and exposure. Along, that is, with the author's sympathy for what Tom isn't.

HIGHSMITH DELIBERATELY AND SHAMELESSLY EVADES THE CONVENTIONAL MORALITY OF CRIME AND PUNISHMENT."

Ripley's non-essentiality, his lack of a determinate identity, is the making of him. It is his talent, his vocation, and we may recall that, as Falstaff pointed out, "'Tis no sin for a man to labour in his vocation." Ripley's interest is, in fact, paradigmatic; he refers back to the trickster archetype while traversing the narrow field of post-modern identity, beginning as a sleazy version of Riesman's other-directed man and developing into a sinister version of Lifton's protean man, a player with his own and others' destinies.

Tom's transformation begins with his other-directed need "to make Dickie like him," progresses to imitating Dickie, playing Dickie, and finally to the protean triumph of playing himself. The central feature of protean man, Robert Lifton notes [in "Protean Man," *History and Human Survival* (1971)], is the "repeated, autonomously willed death and rebirth of the self," associated with the theme of "fatherlessness." Tom, whose parents conveniently died in his early childhood, leaving him to the care of an aunt he detests, has carried the protean tendency to its logical extreme, reflecting at one point, "this was the real annihilation of his past and of himself, Tom Ripley, who was made up of that past, and his rebirth as a completely new person." Divested of past and parentage, Tom is remarkably free of the conventional constraints of superego, again matching Lifton's definition of protean man: "What has actually disappeared ... is the *classical* superego, the internalization of clearly defined criteria of right and wrong transmitted within a particular culture by parents to their children." Alisdair McIntyre, in a less sanguine view of protean man than Lifton, could have been describing Highsmith's creation [in *After Virtue* (1981)]: "The self thus conceived, utterly distinct on the one hand from its social embodiments and lacking on the other any rational history of its own, may seem to have a certain abstract and ghostly character." One recalls Iago, whose motto is "I am not what I am not what I am."

Tom's sexual anxieties, then, can be best explained as compounding a conventional enough shame at a socially derogatory label (the novel was published in 1956) with an emergent protean man's dislike of getting fixed in *any* identity. In accord with Diderot's paradox of the actor, Tom is able to be anyone or anything only by way of being detached from the acts and identities he performs. Marge may well be on the right track when she comments in a letter to Dickie—which Tom in his Dickie-role actually receives and reads—"All right, he may not be queer. He's just nothing, which is worse." In the later books, we find Tom happily married to a lady as amoral and as relatively passionless as himself. And though Tom's self-detachment may be taken as schizophrenic, it is questionable if he is any more so than other literary adumbrations or fulfillments of the protean self—say, for a short list, Gide's Lafcadio, Mann's Felix Krull, *Barth*'s Jacob Horner ("In a sense, I am Jacob Horner"), among others. In all these characters, as in Tom, indeterminacy of identity seems, as Lifton argues, less a dysfunction than a survival mechanism. Even when most absorbed in his role of Dickie, Tom never completely loses himself in his role: "He felt alone, yet not at all lonely. It was very much like the feeling on Christmas Eve in Paris, a feeling that everyone was watching him, as if he had an audience made up of the entire world, a feeling that kept him on his mettle, because to make a mistake would be catastrophic. Yet he felt absolutely confident he would not make a mistake. It gave his existence a peculiar, delicious atmosphere of purity, like that, Tom thought, which a fine actor probably feels when he plays an important role on a stage with the conviction that the role he is playing could not be played better by anyone else. He was himself and yet not himself. He felt blameless and free, despite the fact that he consciously controlled every move he made."

Finally, within the conventions of the suspense thriller, Tom's survival and triumph is an evident authorial endorsement. The structure of Highsmith's book is built on the tension between Tom's potential exposure and punishment and his actual evasion and exemption. The novel begins with Tom's fear of arrest and throughout the novel Tom varies between fear of "nemesis" and confidence in luck: "Something always turned up. That was Tom's philosophy." After his murder of Freddie, Tom imagines all the possibilities of disaster he must face in carrying a dead body down several flights of stairs; he "imagined it all with such intensity, writhing upstairs in his apartment, that to have descended all the stairs without a single one of his imaginings happening made him feel that he was gliding down under a magical protection of some kind, with ease in spite of the mass on his shoulder." His magical protector is, of course, Highsmith, a protection she extends on condition that Tom play his roles audaciously and with a kind of artistic lightness. Tom's initial blunder with Dickie is to have come on too seriously, heavily: "Tom cursed himself for having been so heavy-handed and so humorless today. Nothing he took desperately seriously ever worked out. He'd found that out years ago." (Note, again, the paradox of the actor.) Tom's virtŭ is his joy in risk taking: "Risks were what made the whole thing fun."

Highsmith deliberately and shamelessly evades the conventional morality of crime and punishment. Toward the end of the novel she presents us with a barrage of signs that Tom has pushed his luck too far, has risked too much, that nemesis is finally, if a bit belatedly, approaching. Tom "considered that he had been lucky beyond reason"; he speculates "something was going to happen now . . . and it couldn't be good. His luck had held just too long." Certainly this is the way it ought to be and in the film version of *The Talented Mr. Ripley*, Rene Clement's *Plein Soleil* (*Purple Noon* is the American title), Tom is exposed at the end as Dickie's body literally surfaces. In her how-to book on suspense fiction, Highsmith comments that it "makes a book altogether more eligible for television and movie sales if the criminal is caught, punished, and made to feel awful at the end." So Tom's exemption is a thoroughly calculated flouting of moral and literary expectations, a play against genre since even in the relatively subversive suspense genre a murderer-protagonist usually ends by being hoist on his own petard. Simone Trevanny in *Ripley's Game* stands in for readers shocked by any play with, evasion of, or undercutting of such expectation, though Highsmith rather unfairly characterizes Simone as hysterical and unreasonable for reacting with predictable shock and outrage to the bodies she keeps finding Tom stacking like cordwood. Highsmith can, however, turn back the accusation of immorality on more conventionally proper writers and readers: "The public wants to see the law triumph, or at least the general public does, though at the same time the public likes brutality. The brutality must be on the right side, however. Sleuth-heroes can be brutal, sexually unscrupulous, kickers of women, and still be popular heroes, because they are chasing something worse than themselves, presumably." Tom Ripley, it is true, has never achieved the popularity of Mike Hammer.

Still, he does all right for himself and Highsmith does all right by him. At the conclusion of *The Talented Mr. Ripley*, Tom has gotten off clear from two murders and found his forged will accepted with almost magical ease. It should not be too surprising that Highsmith's ending resembles that of Gide's *Lafcadio's Journey* (*Les Caves du Vatican*) where by a chain of extraordinary coincidences Lafcadio escapes the consequences of a gratuitous murder he has committed. Both endings imply a quasi-providential endorsement of the protagonists' actions with the respective authors in the role of *deus ex machina*. The deity is, of course, Proteus. Both these novels adumbrate a long reign for this usurper deity, an appropriate modern replacement for Zeus with his obsolescent baggage of nemesis and superego. In the last lines of *The Talented Mr. Ripley*, we see Tom instructing a taxi driver, "'To a hotel, please . . . Il meglio albergo. Il meglio, il meglio!'"

Source: Anthony Channell Hilfer, "'Not Really Such a Monster': Highsmith's Ripley as Thriller Protagonist and Protean Man," in *Midwest Quarterly*, Vol. 25, No. 4, Summer 1984, pp. 361–74.

SOURCES

Boucher, Anthony, "Criminals at Large," in the *New York Times Book Review*, May 6, 1956, p. 303.

Cleckley, Hervey, M.D., *The Mask of Sanity: An Attempt to Clarify Some Issues about the So-Called Psychopathic Personality*, Emily S. Cleckley, 1941, 5th edition, 1988, pp. 338–39.

Diagnostic and Statistical Manual of Mental Disorders DSM-IV-TR, American Psychiatric Association, 2000, pp. 701–03.

Greene, Graham, Foreword, in *Eleven*, by Patricia Highsmith, Atlantic Monthly Press, 1989, p. x.

Highsmith, Patricia, *Plotting and Writing Suspense Fiction*, St. Martin's Griffin, 1983.

———, *The Talented Mr. Ripley*, Vintage, 1999.

Highsmith, Patricia, and Diana Cooper-Clark, "An Interview with Patricia Highsmith," in *Armchair Detective*, Vol. 14, No. 4, Spring 1981, pp. 313–20.

The ICD-10 Classification of Mental and Behavioural Disorders: Clinical Descriptions and Diagnostic Guidelines, World Health Organization, 1993, p. 159.

Kakutani, Michiko, "Books of the Times: The Kinship of Macabre and Banal," in the *New York Times*, November 19, 1999.

King James Bible, Romans 6:23, Galatians 6:7, http://quod.lib.umich.edu/k/kjv (accessed July 30, 2007).

Lawrence et al. v. Texas, 539 U.S. 558 (2003), http://www.law.cornell.edu/supct/html/02-102.ZS.html (accessed July 30, 2007).

"100 Best Crime Novels of the 20th Century," in the *Times*, September 30, 2000, p. 4.

Paxton, Zoe, "Mistress of the Banality of Evil," in the *Times*, October 8, 2005, p. 15.

Villalon, Oscar C., "The Talented Ms. Highsmith: 'Ripley' Author Transcended Crime Genre with Unsettling Insights into Evil," in the *San Francisco Chronicle*, January 11, 2000, p. B-1.

FURTHER READING

Hare, Robert D., *Without Conscience: The Disturbing World of the Psychopaths among Us*, Guilford Press, 1999.
    Hare argues in this book that psychopaths are aware of the difference between right and wrong but ignore the distinction. In addition, they are egocentric and have no feelings of empathy, guilt, or remorse. While Hare draws on scientific research, he presents the material in a way that is accessible to the layperson.

Harrison, Russell, *Patricia Highsmith*, Twayne's United States Author Series, Twayne Publishers, 1997.
    Aimed at anyone from advanced high school students to university professors, this book is a critical introduction to the author and her work, setting it in the context of major literary trends.

Mawer, Noel, *Critical Study of the Fiction of Patricia Highsmith: From the Psychological to the Political*, Edwin Mellen Press, 2004.
    This book presents a thorough critical analysis of Highsmith's work. Mawer goes beyond the discussion of the author's suspense writing to explore her intense character studies.

Wilson, Andrew, *Beautiful Shadow: A Life of Patricia Highsmith*, Bloomsbury, 2003.
    This candid biography of Highsmith draws upon her journals, letters, and exclusive interviews with friends and associates. Wilson reveals her intelligence and frankness but does not attempt to gloss over the characteristics about her that others have criticized, including racial prejudice, anti-Semitism, cruelty, and insensitivity.

Through the Looking-Glass

LEWIS CARROLL

1871

In 1869, Lewis Carroll (the pseudonym for Charles Dodgson) began to write the sequel novel to his *Alice's Adventures in Wonderland*, which had been published four years earlier to mixed reviews. *Through the Looking-Glass* was published at Christmas in 1871 in an edition of nine thousand copies, with illustrations (as with the first book) by Sir John Tenniel (1820–1914). The second novel immediately found a more appreciative audience than its predecessor and has come to be considered a groundbreaking blend of playful (though sophisticated) logic, social satire, and exuberant fantasy that captures the imagination of children and adult readers alike. With its elaborate depictions of a world in which lives are manipulated like chess pieces and in which inverse relations become the norm, *Through the Looking-Glass* offers readers a chance to engage an imaginative dream world. For readers for whom the age of seven is a distant memory, the novel provides the chance to think about what has passed and, as the closing poem promises, to spend time "Dreaming as the days go by."

AUTHOR BIOGRAPHY

The writer who rose to prominence as Lewis Carroll was born Charles Lutwidge Dodgson on January 27, 1832, at Daresbury in Cheshire,

Lewis Carroll *(© Bettmann / Corbis)*

England. His father was a gifted mathematician (also named Charles) who had turned his back on a promising academic career in order to live his life in obscurity as a country parson. Young Charles was the third child (and eldest son) in a family that would eventually include eleven children. From all accounts, the childhood was a happy one, though young Dodgson suffered from a stammer, a condition that was shared by several of his siblings. He was also deaf in his right ear, which combined with his speech impediment may have stopped him from continuing the family tradition of taking orders in the Church of England.

In 1843, the elder Charles was made rector of Croft, north Yorkshire, a relatively lucrative position that meant moving the family into the local rectory, where they lived for the next twenty-five years. Dodgson's father provided his son a strong background in Latin, mathematics, and theology, which proved a solid foundation from which Dodgson could build when he entered the small Richmond School at the age of twelve. Life was more stressful and less happy when he moved to a larger school, Rugby, in 1845. Although he excelled in his studies, he was undoubtedly pleased to move on to his father's alma mater Christ Church, a college

within Oxford University, where he proved himself an above average student in mathematics. He remained at Oxford more than two decades, teaching mathematics and logic.

Always an avid storyteller and aspiring artist, Dodgson was especially drawn in the 1850s to the new art form of photography, which he mastered readily. He became especially well known as a portrait photographer, and a number of celebrities sat for him through the 1860s and 1870s. Among these subjects were: Crown Prince Frederick of Denmark (1808–1863); the writers John Ruskin (1819–1900), Dante Gabriel Rossetti (1828–1882), and Alfred, Lord Tennyson (1809–1982); and Lord Salisbury (1830–1903), the prime minister. Although he is notorious for his numerous photographic studies of children, it is significant that of the over three thousand photographs Dodgson took during his career, only about one-third have been recovered. Subjects in these pictures are diverse, ranging from dolls and statues to portraits of scientists and notable scholars.

Although he never married or fathered a child of his own, Dodgson doted on the children he came in contact with as a family friend and local artist. Intent on entertaining this youthful audience, and using the pseudonym Lewis Carroll, Dodgson produced an impressive body of writing aimed at children, including *Alice's Adventures in Wonderland* (1865), *Through the Looking-Glass* (1872), and *The Hunting of the Snark* (1876), as well as numerous books of word games and puzzles.

Following a colorful career as teacher, writer, and photographer, Dodgson died of pneumonia on January 14, 1898, while at his sister's home in Guildford, England. Despite the fact that he wrote a number of books explicating the principles of Euclidean geometry, he remains into the twenty-first century best known as Lewis Carroll, an important Victorian author of children's books.

PLOT SUMMARY

Chapter 1: Looking-Glass House

In sharp contrast with the earlier novel, *Alice's Adventures in Wonderland*, which opens outdoors on a mild spring afternoon, *Through the Looking-Glass* opens in a well furnished, Victorian drawing-room on a blustery midwinter day, with seven-and-a-half-year-old Alice

MEDIA ADAPTATIONS

- Although once considered a book that might never be adapted to other media, *Through the Looking-Glass* has appeared in many media versions. Film adaptations of *Through the Looking-Glass* have been especially numerous, beginning with a silent movie era version in 1928 followed by many feature-length live action and animated versions. Many film adaptations have blended elements of the two novels with little concern for the subtleties of context, for example, the 1933 release by Paramount Productions, in which W. C. Fields played Humpty Dumpty and Gary Cooper was the White Knight. Disney's treatment of *Alice's Adventures in Wonderlands* (1951) continued this pattern, incorporating renditions of "Jabberwocky" and "The Walrus and the Carpenter" into the first Alice framework.

- Over the decades, film and video adaptations included a figure-skating version (*Fairy Tales on Ice: Alice Through the Looking-Glass*, 1996), an anime lesbian adventure parody (*Miyuki-chan in Mirrorland*, 1995), and a number of *very* loosely based borrowings, including Terry Gilliam's *Jabberwocky*, 1977. In May 2005, the Lewis Carroll Film

Society hosted *Animating Alice*, a festival of films inspired by Carroll's writing.

- Television also has a longstanding relationship with Carroll's second Alice novel, beginning most notably with the 1966 version that starred Judi Rolin in the role of Alice, Jimmy Durante as Humpty Dumpty, the Smothers Brothers as the Tweedle twins, and Jack Palance as the Jabberwock. Subsequent small-screen adaptations appeared in 1973 (a BBC production), 1985 (with songs by Steve Allen), 1998 (with Kate Beckinsale in the role of Alice), and 1999, in a version heavily enhanced with computerized effects.

- Television cartoon adaptations of the Alice stories include the Walt Disney Productions *Thru the Mirror* (1936), a classic Mickey Mouse cartoon based on *Through the Looking-Glass*. Hanna-Barbera Productions added to this body of work with its 1966 *Alice in Wonderland, or What's a Nice Kid Like You Doing in a Place Like This?*, which reconfigured the two novels into a story about a young girl following her dog through a television tube.

sitting in her armchair watching her pet kitten, Kitty, unraveling a ball of string. An imaginative but lonely young girl, Alice takes Kitty into her lap and begins telling her about an imaginary world that exists on the other side of the mirror. The Looking-Glass House, as Alice explains to Kitty, is "just the same as [the] drawing-room, only the things go the other way." It is, in other words, a land in which everything is backward when compared to the world that Alice and Kitty inhabit.

As she wonders aloud to Kitty about what an adventure it would be to find a way to step through the mirror, Alice suddenly finds herself

standing on the mantelpiece in front of the mirror. More remarkably, the mirror itself seems "to melt away, just like a bright silvery mist." Alice quickly seizes the moment and steps through the mirror into the Looking-Glass room.

What Alice discovers on the other side of the mirror is a room very similar to the one that she had left, but with several dramatic and, to her at least, unexplainable differences. The first difference that Alice notices is that the chess pieces that she had been playing with earlier in the day have come alive and are moving about the room in various pairings. More upsetting to the always helpful Alice is the fact that one of the pieces, a

White Pawn, has rolled over and is kicking and protesting loudly. The Pawn, Alice discerns quickly, is named Lily and is the daughter of another chess piece, White Queen. Lifting the Queen in her hand, Alice places mother beside daughter in order that she can comfort the child. Only at this moment does Alice realize that she cannot be seen nor heard by the chess pieces moving about the room.

After a few moments, during which Alice moves other chess pieces, appearing in their world as a kind of mysterious force, her attention is captured by a book lying on a nearby table. An avid reader, she picks it up and discovers in it a strange poem written in a language that can only be read clearly when held up to a mirror. The poem she discovers in the mirror is "Jabberwocky," which leaves her frustrated and confused. Putting the poem aside, she sets off to explore the rest of the house.

Chapter 2: The Garden of Live Flowers

Attempting to go toward the garden, Alice is surprised to find that every time she sets out along the path she ends up back at the front door of the house. Trying to explain her confusion, she wonders aloud how to reach the garden, only to have a Tiger-lily answer her. Astonished at this turn of events, Alice is even more surprised when the other flowers begin insulting Alice. What Alice learns from the flowers is that the Red Queen is nearby, which prompts Alice to set off so that she might meet her. When they meet, the two engage in a conversation during which the Red Queen corrects Alice's etiquette.

The Red Queen also instructs Alice on the geography of the country Alice entered when she stepped through the looking glass. Looking around, Alice sees a landscape that is marked out like a large chessboard. Asking the Queen if she might take a place in the game, Alice is allowed to become a Pawn on the White Queen's side of the board, replacing Lily, who is too young to play. Explaining the rules of the game to Alice, the Red Queen articulates the goal of the adventure that is about to begin: "you're in the Second Square to begin with," the Red Queen states. "When you get to the Eighth Square you'll be a Queen." Suddenly and inexplicably, Alice finds herself running across the board, or at least she thinks she is running; oddly, the faster Alice runs the less she seems to move forward.

Pausing to catch her breath in preparation for her initial movement as part of the global chess game, Alice inexplicably finds herself aboard a train and confronting a Guard who is demanding that she produce a ticket. Looking around the train carriage she discovers that she is sharing her new space with an assortment of interesting characters, including a Goat, a Beetle, and a man dressed in white paper. Each takes a turn chiding Alice about one thing or another, until the train comes to a sudden halt. Reaching out to stop herself from falling over, Alice takes hold of the Goat's beard, only to have it dissolve in her hand as an indication that she has moved suddenly from the train to a wooded area.

Chapter 3: Looking-Glass Insects

Finding herself suddenly relocated from sitting in the train to sitting under a tree in the woods, Alice discovers a new companion, an extraordinarily large Gnat. The Gnat proves to be a knowledgeable though unhappy guide regarding the intricacies of life in the woods. Leaving the Gnat behind as she ventures deeper into the woods, Alice discovers that she has forgotten the names of the familiar things that she sees around her and has forgotten even her own name. Pushing forward into the shady woods, the now forgetful Alice meets a friendly Fawn who shares her memory loss. The short time that she spends with the Fawn is one of the few moments in the novel when Alice feels comfortable and cared for. When both Alice and the Fawn regain their memories, the Fawn remembers that she should be fearful of humans. Realizing that Alice is a human, she darts away and disappears from sight.

Chapter 4: Tweedledum and Tweedledee

Left to her own devices, Alice continues her journey until she meets Tweedledum and Tweedledee, a pair of rotund identical twins. When Alice asks for directions, the twins ignore her questions and choose instead to recite a poem called "The Walrus and the Carpenter." After a brief conversation about the poem, Alice hears an alarming noise nearby. The twins inform her that the noise is the snoring of the Red King, and, more importantly, that she is not really a little girl but is a character that exists only as a part of the King's dream. Initially upset by such an idea, Alice decides instead that the twins are nonsensical characters, an evaluation that seems to be proven out when they spontaneously erupt into an argument over a broken rattle. The argument ends as suddenly as it started when a giant crow appears, sending Tweedledum and Tweedledee running into the woods in fear.

Chapter 5: Wool and Water

Taking full advantage of this opportunity, Alice runs a little way into the woods where she comes across the White Queen, who explains that time moves backwards in the Looking-Glass world. After the Queen points out to Alice some of the liberties and problems associated with living backwards, as well as marking the fact that she used to practice the impossible on a daily basis, the White Queen is suddenly transformed into a Sheep in a shop. This shift leaves Alice disoriented, a feeling that is intensified when she realizes that the "shop seemed to be full of all manner of curious things—but the oddest part of it all was, that whenever she looked hard at any shelf, to make out exactly what it had on it, that particular shelf was always quite empty: though the others round it were crowded as full as they could hold."

The Sheep launches into a series of seemingly random questions, which culminates with an enquiry as to whether Alice can row. Answering that she can, Alice suddenly finds herself in a boat with the Sheep, rowing down a stream. Accidentally hitting herself with the handle of an oar, Alice finds herself back in the store, sitting with the Sheep, and negotiating the purchase of an egg that is sitting on a shelf at the end of the shop.

Chapter 6: Humpty Dumpty

The nearer to the egg that Alice moves the more she realizes that she is leaving the shop and returning to the woods. Next she comes to realize that the small egg has grown into Humpty Dumpty, a rude character who criticizes Alice for not understanding things and who boasts that he can change the meaning of any word at will. Their conversation turns more serious when Alice, confused and frustrated by Humpty Dumpty's arrogance, asks him to explain "Jabberwocky," the mirror poem she read earlier. Dissecting the first stanza of the poem through a series of equally nonsensical definitions, the giant egg ends the exercise abruptly in order that he might recite one of his own poems. He ends his recitation abruptly and bids an annoyed Alice goodbye. As she walks away quietly, the forest is

rocked by a resounding crash, and soldiers and horsemen suddenly rush past Alice, presumably to attempt to put the shattered Humpty Dumpty back together again.

Chapter 7: The Lion and the Unicorn

Meeting the White King, who has sent the men on their mission, Alice also meets his messenger, Haigha, who informs them that the Lion and the Unicorn have engaged in the battle in the middle of a nearby town. Heading off into town to watch the contest, Alice joins the King for refreshments during an intermission in the battle. Alice is asked to cut a cake but finds that in the backwards world of the Looking-Glass, she must first pass it around before it can be cut. The cake cutting affair is interrupted suddenly by a loud noise, and the sudden realization that she was all alone again.

Chapter 8: "It's My Own Invention"

Just as suddenly Alice finds herself as the prize in another battle, this time between the Red Knight (who wants to carry her away) and the White Knight (who protects her). As the threatening Red Knight is vanquished, Alice finds herself traveling with the benevolent though eccentric White Knight, who regales her with stories of his numerous inventions while delivering on his promise to bring her safely to the last square of the chessboard world. Crossing the final brook, Alice finds herself in the Eighth Square. Sitting on the bank of the brook, she is amazed when a gold crown appears magically on her lap.

Chapters 9–12: Queen Alice; Shaking; Walking; Which Dreamed It?

Placing the crown gingerly upon her head, Alice is no longer surprised when the Red and White Queens appear and begin to interrogate her about issues ranging from mathematics to the nature of truth itself. Just as suddenly as they have appeared, the two Queens decide to take a nap, and promptly fall asleep amidst a cacophony of snores. Alice inexplicably finds herself standing in front of the doorway of a massive castle. Written over the door are two words: Queen Alice. Knocking and waiting for some time, Alice is finally admitted by a very old Frog, who ushers her to a luxurious banquet set in her honor. Sitting down to enjoy the meal, Alice is forced instead to watch as the party quickly disintegrates into chaos.

Exasperated at the scene, Alice pulls away the tablecloth, sending plates, food, and gathered guests tumbling into a heap on the floor. Grabbing the Red Queen, who Alice sees as the cause of the commotion, Alice awakens gradually to the realization that she is shaking her beloved Kitty. The novel closes with Alice wondering aloud if her adventures were her own dream or, as Tweedledee and Tweedledum suggested, part of the Red King's dreams.

CHARACTERS

Alice

A returning character from Carroll's earlier *Alice's Adventures in Wonderland* (1865), Alice is the seven-and-a-half-year-old female protagonist of the novel. Raised in a wealthy Victorian household, the highly imaginative Alice wants to move out of childhood into young adulthood. As a necessary step in maturation, she determines to see the world as an ordered and controlled place within which her intelligence, decorum, and kindness are valued.

A vivid dream transports Alice to the Looking-Glass world, a random and chaotic world. The usually patient Alice feels frustrated and at times even confrontational as she attempts to make sense of this strange new land. She is lonely and isolated, and she realizes the Looking-Glass characters are unable to show her the true compassion that she wants from the family and community in which she lives.

Searching for companions, Alice confronts trials designed by such characters as Tweedledum and Tweedledee, Humpty Dumpty, and the overbearing Red Queen. These tests challenge her worldview and introduce her to what it means to be an autonomous young woman, living in a society that does not fulfill her hopes for kindness.

Fawn

One of Alice's woodland companions, Fawn is memorable for her beauty and for her propensity to forget names. She is a fearful creature who flees abruptly when she realizes that Alice is a human being.

Frog

Frog is the elderly footman at Alice's castle.

Gnat

One of the gentler characters of the Looking-Glass world and also one of the saddest, Gnat is Alice's helpful guide on the train and through the woods. During the course of their travels, Gnat grows to the size of a chicken. Gnat tells Alice about the potential pitfalls of puns and wordplay in this strange land.

Haigha and Hatta

Haigha and Hatta are recurring characters who make the trip from the antecedent novel, *Alice's Adventures in Wonderland*, in which they are known as the March Hare and the Mad Hatter. Whereas their frantic personalities and questionable connections with reality take control of the previous novel, they are very subdued in the Looking-Glass world. This shift is a commentary on the nature of the adventures that Alice embarks on in each of the novels as well as on her maturity in dealing with challenges.

Humpty Dumpty

Humpty Dumpty is an egg-shaped character that sits precariously on a narrow ledge and treats Alice with contempt. His attempt to explain the meaning of the nonsense poem "Jabberwocky" is marred both by his arrogance and his willingness to change the meaning of words to fit his interpretation of the poem. Humpty Dumpty undercuts Alice's (and the reader's) understanding of how language works, challenging, for instance, the relationship between her name and the type of person she is. The Humpty Dumpty episode, like those of Tweedledee and Tweedledum and the Lion and the Unicorn, takes its cue from the familiar nursery rhyme of the day.

Lily

White Queen's daughter, Lily is replaced by Alice as a white pawn on the chessboard because Lily is too young to play the game. At first a foil to Alice in her journey to reach a new level of maturity and autonomy, Lily is by novel's end a reminder that for every little girl there is an appropriate time to begin the journey toward adulthood.

Lion

The Unicorn's opponent in the town battle, the Lion acts in a way that reminds Alice of a nursery rhyme she was taught as a child. The image of the lion dominates the English coat of arms.

Red King

Red King, also known as the sleeping King, is first mentioned when Alice meets the twins Tweedledum and Tweedledee, who try to convince her that she exists only as part of the Red King's vivid dream. The twins' argument suggests that the Looking-Glass world is not a construction of Alice's dream at all but is a figment within the imagination of a more powerful dreamer, who might also be responsible for the seemingly random moves and sudden disappearances on the chessboard. The presence of the Red King, in this sense, raises questions about both the nature of reality and about the possibility that God exists as a kind of divine dreamer whose imagination brings the material world into existence.

Red Knight

Red Knight attempts to capture Alice during her time on the chessboard but is thwarted. He is eventually captured by the benevolent White Knight.

Red Queen

A domineering woman who brings Alice into the chess game, the Red Queen is obsessive about manners but unkind about her rules. Like many other Looking-Glass characters, she is often arbitrary and dictatorial. She is, as Alice points out to her, an illogical leader who justifies her management style by citing her rank. Alice's confrontations with the self-righteous Red Queen represents the young girl's growing awareness of the need to deal effectively and politely with people who might abuse their positions of power. In the end, it is the Red Queen who takes control of Alice's coronation feast, signaling the young girl's inability to negotiate the threshold from childhood to young adulthood.

Tweedledum and Tweedledee

Tweedledum and Tweedledee are identical twins, little heavy-set men dressed up as schoolboys who finish each other's thoughts and seem to be a peaceful duo until their relationship disintegrates during a nonsensical fight over a broken rattle. As mirror images of one another, the twins underscore the theme of inversion, which is further highlighted by Tweedledee's repetition of his favorite expression, "contrariwise," which means to take something that has already been said or done and move it in the opposite direction or toward the opposite side. Their names first

appeared in John Byrom's (1692–1793) poem "On the Feuds Between Handel and Bononcini."

Unicorn

A mythical horse-like animal with a long horn extending from its forehead, Unicorn believes that Alice is a monster in the Looking-Glass world. He attempts to negotiate a truce with her, agreeing to believe in her existence if she agrees to believe in his. The episode of the Unicorn and the Lion, like those of Tweedledee and Tweedledum and Humpty Dumpty, takes its cues from a familiar nursery rhyme of the day. Unicorn does battle with the Lion in one of the few episodes of the novel set in a town. The conflict can be interpreted as the political opposition on the Scottish coat of arms that depicts two crowned unicorns supporting a shield dominated by the image of a red lion (the symbol of Britain) on a yellow field. The two heraldic symbols in battle hints about intensifying tensions between England and Scotland.

White King

White King takes words literally. An ambiguous character, he is capable of both decisive actions (sending the horses to Humpty Dumpty after the great fall) as well as moments of fearful paralysis (as in his dealings with the Lion and the Unicorn).

White Knight

One of the kinder characters of the Looking-Glass world, the curious White Knight is an eccentric inventor with shaggy hair and pale blue eyes. He saves Alice from his counterpoint on the chessboard, the fearsome Red Knight, and leads her to the final square and, ultimately, to victory in the symbolic game of chess. Traditionally, many critics have interpreted the White Knight as a fictionalized representation of Carroll himself, based on the physical similarities between the two, the shared love of inventions (Carroll's puns and nonsense poems, for instance), and the fact that Carroll, like the White Knight, was a guide in the lives of children, forced to step aside as they matured.

White Queen

In one sense, the mirror image of the orderly Red Queen, the White Queen is disorderly to the point of being chaotic. She explains the Looking-Glass world, its reversal of time, and the need to believe that the impossible is always possible. One of the transformative characters in the novel, she moves backwards in time to become the Sheep, one of the many characters who is rude to Alice in order to test her good manners.

THEMES

The Nature of Reality

Through the Looking-Glass opens with young Alice imagining a world beyond the looking glass, and it ends with questions about whether Alice's dream might actually be a dream within a dream. In this way, the novel raises questions about the nature of reality. Carroll blurs the distinctions between being asleep and being awake so that it becomes difficult to tell where the conscious world ends and the world of dream begins. Sudden and apparently random movements from place to place may suggest shifts in waking reality or mark shifts in dream states. Alice seems to awaken into a backwards dream world, a place that exists as a kind of parallel universe which reminds readers, as the White Queen points out, that the impossible is available to them in the everyday.

But Carroll's examination of the nature of reality is more thorough than a dream sequence suggests. Alice's dream world seems embedded in the dream world of the Red King, and at the same time her dream world permits her to cross thresholds connecting one realm of reality to another. Her invisibility early in the novel, for instance, suggests an almost godlike power that derives from her ability to imagine the chess world. But when Alice suddenly becomes visible, she becomes a player in a different game, one that she cannot control.

Troubling, too, is the sense that Alice is trapped in a reality that cannot be proven to exist objectively. If she sets out to prove that she exists as a real little girl and *not* as part of the Red King's dream, Alice is forced to wake up the Red King by way of proving her point, an act which introduces two philosophical problems. If Alice is part of a dream, can her actions in the dream actually change the world outside the dream? In other words, can the dreamed Alice actually awaken the sleeping King who exists in a reality outside the dream? Then, too, what happens if Alice is a figment of the King's imagination? By waking him, Alice will end the dream and, in doing so, end her own existence; in order to prove

TOPICS FOR FURTHER STUDY

- Select an episode or character from *Through the Looking-Glass* that has not been illustrated by John Tenniel and create your own illustration. You might try to imitate Tenniel's original style or come up with something quite different, suggesting what a new edition might look like.

- Compile a collection of children's nonsense poetry by Carroll and Edward Lear. Write a brief introduction to your collection, explaining the importance of the poems and their relevance to a child's world. Provide illustrations for selected poems. Alternatively, do the same project using more familiar nursery rhymes, using your introduction to discuss their history and their place in the myth of childhood.

- Research the history of media adaptations of Carroll's Alice novels, creating a timeline graph or poster that shows the actors who played or gave voices to each of the central characters. Since the earliest adaptations, for instance, what actors have provided the voice of the Jabberwock?

- The chess game plays a prominent role in Carroll's imagining of the world on the other side of the looking glass, suggesting the presence of order amidst chaos and of an intelligent force controlling the moves of each of the individual pieces. Think about what game (board game, sports game, video game) best reflects the complexities of the world you live in. Write an essay in which you discuss a brief history of your selected game and explain the key points that make it relevant to your world.

her own existence, Alice must risk terminating that existence.

Carroll leaves unanswered questions about what is real and what is dreamed. He seems to invite readers to think about the question that he poses in the final line of the poem that concludes the novel: "Life, what is it but a dream?"

Childhood and Maturation

Like many Victorian novels, *Through the Looking-Glass* explores the hidden spaces and imagined worlds of childhood, as Alice steps through the looking glass into a backwards world of her own imagination. Unlike the fall (down the hole and from innocence) that opens the first Alice novel, this stepping through into a dreamscape of talking flowers and moving chess pieces represents a more mature and conscious gesture on Alice's part. It is a movement to escape the lonely drawing room world in search of community with guidance from characters such as the intelligent Gnat and the benevolent White Knight.

As Carroll's novels suggest, growing up was a well-organized affair in the nineteenth century, with guide books, moral conduct books, and didactic novels designed to guide children in their moral and physical development. With such titles as *The First Principles of Polite Behaviour* (1825), *Letters from a Mother to her Daughter* (1825), and *The Young Lady's Library of Useful and Entertaining Knowledge* (1829), these cautionary books included essays on morality, sermons, parables, and an assortment of exemplary tales complete with explanatory notes and commentary. Regardless of tone and content, however, these books shared a common assumption about childhood. It was seen as a vulnerable period in which uninitiated children required moral education and discipline.

Alice's imagined world provides release from this world of control, moving her into a backward, playful, and adventurous world. But the new location does not necessarily guarantee new understanding. In fact, Alice's maturity is realized during the course of the novel. Dreaming of a space in which her mature imagination might escape from the Victorian rules of civility and decorum, Alice finds herself in a world bound by arbitrary rules (chess) and by an implicit desire *not* to breach traditional boundaries and *not* to address directly the desire to become, metaphorically and literally, the queen of her own castle. Despite her own best efforts to create a world in which the crown of maturity is within reach, Alice wanders through a world in which solitude and frustration continue to weigh heavily upon her.

Tellingly, Alice seems to mature very little during her time in the Looking-Glass world, and her emotional and intellectual growth remains mostly unchanged. Opening her journey on a note of frustration (with "Jabberwocky," for instance), she ends it similarly, gathering the Red Queen into her fist and shaking her fiercely. But at the same time, Alice's willingness to venture into the other world and to find her way through encounters with rude flowers, combative Tweedle twins, and aggressive chess pieces, marks the beginning of a movement toward autonomy and a growing awareness of one's place in the world.

STYLE

Nonsense

In Chapter 6 of *Through the Looking-Glass*, Humpty Dumpty sets out to explain to Alice the meaning of the poem "Jabberwocky," arguably one of the most widely known nonsense poems in English literature. Perched precariously on a narrow ledge atop a high wall, he is the only character in the novel who speaks at length on the nature of language and meaning. "'Let's hear it'" says Humpty with the promise that he can "explain all the poems that ever were invented—and a good many that haven't been invented just yet."

Like his physical position, Humpty's critical stance is perilous, indeed, for in attempting to *explain* "Jabberwocky," he gets lost in a poem that not only emphasizes sound as a condition of meaning but is also loaded with puns, wordplay, and *portmanteau* (new words that pack together parts of other words and combine connotations as well). Despite the best attempts of Carroll's (un)balanced critic, "Jabberwocky" defies an easy explication and leaves both Alice and the reader a bit confused. The poem captured the interest of readers and scholars worldwide, and it was translated in more than fifty languages, including Latin, French (as "Le Jaseroque"), and German ("Der Jammerwoch").

Despite Humpty's arrogance, it is the seemingly confused Alice who gives the most insightful explanation of the workings of the nonsense poem. "'It seems very pretty,' she said when she had finished it, 'but it's *rather* hard to understand! . . . Somehow it seems to fill my head with ideas—only I don't exactly know what they are!'" Despite the continuing efforts of scholars to *translate* the

Alice meeting Tweedledum and Tweedledee, an illustration by John Tenniel. Tenniel created all the original illustrations for the Alice series (Rischgitz / Getty Images)

poem (as well as other instances of Carroll's radical wordplay) into a more comprehensible form, embracing the meaninglessness of the words remains one of the keys to understanding it. Carroll's strange words themselves have no familiar and precise meaning, but they do create a sense of meaning through their sounds. Such a word as "slithy," for instance, reminds a reader of a compound of two familiar words, *slimy* (covered with or having the semi-liquid consistency of slime) and *lithe* (flexible and supple). Other words, such a word as "mome," for instance, resists the efforts of scholars to trace lineage.

The nonsense of "Jabberwocky," coupled with Humpty Dumpty's equally nonsensical explication of the poem, points to the tenuous relationship between language and the real world. As Humpty Dumpty is quick to point out, language is a complex tool for negotiating between

individuals and groups, necessary in that it establishes some sense of shared reality. Alice and the Gnat agree, for instance, that one's name is generally seen to relate to one's physical presence as well as one's identity. But as Alice also explains during her travels with the chicken-sized insect, the tradition of naming is as much about classifying and organizing reality as it is about the person or thing being named: "'What's the use of their having names,' the Gnat said, 'if [the insects] won't answer to them?' 'No use to *them*,' said Alice; 'but it's useful to the people that name them, I suppose. If not, why do things have names at all?'" Humpty Dumpty later returns to the question of naming, when he challenges Alice on the relationship between her name and the *shape* that her name suggests she should take.

Both "Jabberwocky" and Humpty Dumpty serve to underscore the expectation that language will deliver meaning. As Humpty Dumpty begins to redefine words, he finds himself relying on other words to explain the new definitions that he offers. Humpty Dumpty does not understand that if the words that he uses to redefine words are as unstable, then his exercise in redefinition is futile. If language is as unstable as Humpty Dumpty suggests it is, reality is likely to come crashing down, as he does, and no words will be strong enough to put it back together again.

Metaphor

Through the Looking-Glass compares the world beyond the looking glass and the drawing-room world (the tenor of the metaphor) to a game of chess (the vehicle of the metaphor). The chess match is governed by a rigid set of rules that determine the movement of chess pieces, and Alice is similarly controlled by larger influences, both in the dream world of the chess game and in the waking world of the drawing room. Alice is, as she observes several times in her journey, a pawn in a larger game that she cannot control. She is at the mercy of strangers throughout her imagined journey, some of whom are rude and dismissive (the Talking Flowers and Humpty Dumpty) and some of whom are benevolent and caring (the Gnat, Fawn, and White Knight). In the Victorian world the waking Alice inhabits, she is controlled by social and moral rules.

This metaphoric comparison suggests a philosophic message to readers: free will and choice are illusions that hide the fact that individual lives in the real world are bound, like chess pieces, to predetermined paths. At the same time, though, Alice's successful dream transition from Pawn to Queen hints at the possibility or hope that a person can step beyond the predicted outcomes of their lives and achieve more.

HISTORICAL CONTEXT

The Expanding Empire

Between 1870 and 1900, the British Empire expanded to occupy an area of four million square miles. The expansion was motivated in part by the profit motive. Great Britain wanted to protect the financial interests of such companies as the British South Africa Company and the East India Company, the second of which became a kind of ruling government in India by the 1860s, when Carroll began writing the Alice novels. With imperial expansion, came new and lucrative markets for British goods, along with increased access to cheap raw materials and even cheaper labor, all of which made defense of these territories of particular importance. Trade improved, too, with technological advancements made during the Industrial Revolution, which included steam engine implementation, development of railway systems, and steam-fueled ships, inventions that facilitated exploration and transportation of goods.

At the same time, new international powers developed, both in Europe and in the antebellum United States, and these challenged British economic and imperial supremacy. Germany and France also developed, intent on competing in world markets with Great Britain. The underdeveloped world became very much a chess board, with territories serving as squares and various European countries as the players trying to occupy them, take control, and exploit natural resources. Even Alice describes the greater world as "a great huge game of chess being played—all over the world."

Alice is in some sense a prototypical imperialist, stepping into a foreign land with her preconceived notions of decorum and behavior only to find herself either at odds with local customs or bewildered when her own way of doing things proves less than useful in a world in which everything is done backwards. Alice's initial lack of knowledge about the Looking-Glass world leaves her feeling isolated and displaced, lodged between clashing cultures and frustrated expectations. As she learns to accept the advice and guidance of such locals as the Gnat and White Knight, however, Alice gradually adjusts to her new location and takes charge of it, however temporarily.

Victorian Crisis of Faith

If the historical context of the Alice novels was shaped, on the one hand, by the ideological confidences associated with imperial expansion, it was shaped on the other by the philosophical uncertainties caused by conflict between ideas promoted by science and religion. As the nineteenth century opened, the debate between the religion (faith) and science (empirical study) seemed oddly at peace. Traditional anxieties had been lessened, it seemed, by such an influential book as William Paley's *Natural Theology* (1802), which argued that the scientific study of the natural world reveals divine agency and intelligent design. Paley and others argued that evidence of design was wonderfully elastic, capable of being reconfigured to accommodate and explain new information brought forth from current scientific discoveries.

Paley's neutralizing influence lasted until about the 1830s, when a new generation of readers began to see in the new science both a suggestion of the limited scope of a designer's power and a potentially powerful means to radical political and theological ends. Geologists, for instances, were active in these early decades, and their examination of fossil records raised a very real threat to widespread belief in the creation as told in Genesis. Coming in a considerable line of thinkers who wrote and spoke about evolution, Charles Darwin published his *Origin of Species* in 1859, bringing the claims of scientific data head to head with the ancient biblical text.

In *Through the Looking-Glass*, Alice experiences moments that resonate with implications of this conflict, when what she believes about the world is undercut by the *reality* of a world in which everything seems to be done backwards. She faces moments, as did many Victorians, when her own faith is challenged by her experience. In the Looking-Glass world the impossible is always possible, as the White Queen tells Alice, and what a person believes can appear patently incorrect.

CRITICAL OVERVIEW

As Richard Kelly summarizes in his *Lewis Carroll* (1990), the earliest receptions of *Through the Looking-Glass* were very encouraging. Published in an initial edition of nine thousand copies (bound in red cloth gilt), the book sold so briskly that an additional printing of six thousand copies was ordered. By 1893, according to Kelly, "over sixty thousand copies had been sold." Kelly quotes a review that appeared in the *Athenaeum*: the reviewer claims that this book has 'the potentiality of [causing] happiness for countless children of all ages."

David L. Russell notes that Carroll's two Alice novels marked the apotheosis of what many critics consider the golden age of fantasy writing in English. "Abandon[ing] all the rules of writing for children," Carroll creates in these

novels an "extraordinary fantasy filled with a delightful mixture of satire and nonsense and almost devoid of instructional moralizing." Russell concludes that both novels "completely broke the bonds of didacticism" and have rightfully become "a part of childhood mythology."

Recent publications of Carroll's work attest to its continuing popularity. Gillian Engberg, writing for *Booklist* in 2005, compliments the 2005 Candlewick edition illustrated by Helen Oxenbury as a "splendid interpretation," noting its slightly different visual characterization of Alice: "Oxenbury's Alice . . . seems both old-fashioned and modern, and comfortable in worlds on both sides of the mirror." Carolyn Phelan, also in *Booklist*, remarks positively on a 2006 edition of *Alice's Adventures in Wonderland* illustrated by Alison Jay. Phelan commends "Jay's distinctive paintings" and urges that "Libraries with dozens of other Alices on the shelf will still want to make room for this handsome edition." Clearly, Carroll's novels about Alice are masterpieces that remain popular into the twenty-first century.

CRITICISM

Klay Dyer

Dyer holds a Ph.D. in English literature and has published extensively on fiction, poetry, film, and television. He is also a freelance university teacher, writer, and educational consultant. In the following essay, he discusses the feasting scene that closes Carroll's Through the Looking-Glass *as a symbol of the failure of Alice to cross the threshold from childhood to young adulthood.*

At the end of Alice's journey through the backwards world of Lewis Carroll's *Through the Looking-Glass*, the youthful protagonist steps through a castle door that bears her name, guided by an old Frog who serves as her footman. Passing over the threshold of the castle door, Alice finds a new place for herself amidst the noisy revelry of a royal feast held in her honor. It is an awkward process that involves acknowledging her inexperience with such occasions and her uncertainties about language and about her place in this world. Is she a Queen or a Pawn? Is she a girl dreaming or a girl being dreamed into existence by the snoring Red King? The final scene of Alice's adventures behind the looking-glass involves her finding her way around the food on the table. The feast

WHAT DO I READ NEXT?

- Martin Gardner's *The Universe in a Handkerchief: Lewis Carroll's Mathematical Recreations, Games, Puzzles, and Word Play* (2003) gives readers an exhilarating tour of Carroll's inventiveness with words, numbers, and logic, ranging from such games as arithmetical croquet to discussions of his speculations in symbolic logic.

- Poet Stephanie Bolster's *White Stone: The Alice Poems* (1998) takes its cues and images from the Alice novels as well as from Carroll's relationship (both real and imagined) with Alice Liddell.

- "Jabberwocky" has provided fertile ground for writers working in a variety of modes and genres. Frederic Brown's comic mystery novel *Night of the Jabberwock* (1951) tells the story of Doc Stoeger, editor of a small newspaper and an enthusiastic fan of the Alice novels who discovers that the books are not actually fiction but an elaborately coded report that leads readers into a new looking-glass world.

- For an engaging look at how "Jabberwocky" influenced various threads of art, literature, science, and law, readers may enjoy Joseph Brabant's *Some Observations on Jabberwocky* (1997).

- Readers interested in children's fantasy literature may enjoy L. Frank Baum's *The Wonderful Wizard of Oz* (1900), a story popularized by the 1930s color film with Judy Garland.

- Another fantasy children's story is Kenneth Grahame's *The Wind in the Willows* (1908).

> A CORONATION DINNER THAT MIGHT HAVE MARKED ALICE'S AWAKENING INTO A NEW WORLD OF MATURITY AND CONTROL DISINTEGRATES INTO CHAOS, LEAVING THE NEW QUEEN HUNGRY AND SPEECHLESS, EXASPERATED AT HER OWN FUTILE EFFORTS TO ENTER YOUNG ADULTHOOD."

leaves herself and all her guests hungry, cranky, and lost in chaos. Having reached both the head of the table and the seat of power in the chessboard land, Queen Alice proves herself ultimately unable to rule with the mature hand necessary to establish and maintain order.

When Alice enters the castle that bears her name, she is met with a clamor of "hundreds of voices" joining in chorus to mark that she has arrived late for her own celebration: "*To the Looking-Glass world it was Alice that said, / 'I've a scepter in hand, I've a crown on my head; / Let the Looking-Glass creatures, whatever they might be, / Come and dine with the Red Queen, the White Queen, and me!'*" The words of this rhythmic song are important, signifying Alice's table as one of the few places in the Looking-Glass world where *all* creatures, regardless of what they are and what their political role might be, can come together to share a meal. Alice's table is a symbol of equalizing the power struggles that characterized the chess board land; it brings together Red and White, human and nonhuman, sensible and nonsensical in one chorus. As Alice bursts through the door into a deafening silence, her first thought is to this new order of things: "Alice glanced nervously along the table, as she walked up the large hall, and noticed that there were about fifty guests, of all kinds: some were animals, some birds, and there were even a few flowers among them."

Uncomfortable in the silence and even more so with the composition of the gathering before her, she approaches her seat at the head of the table, admitting to herself that she could not have consciously organized such an open and welcoming affair. "'I'm glad they've come without waiting to be asked,'" she thinks to herself,

that ends the novel comes to represent the final breakdown of the Looking-Glass world and the final failure of Alice's imagined alternate universe to sustain anyone. With one dramatic pull of a tablecloth, Alice ends the dream, exits the world, and, both metaphorically and literally,

"'I should never have known who were the right people to invite!'" When she finally reaches her seat, located between the two other Queens of the chess board, Alice immediately relinquishes control of the whole affair. Instead of stepping forward to welcome her guests, she defers, "longing for some one [else] to speak." As both hostess and as a ruler who might serve as a harmonizing force, Alice misses an opportunity here.

Pointing out how tardy Alice is, the Red Queen steps in, setting the tone for the evening by reprimanding Alice: "At last the Red Queen began. 'You've missed the soup and fish,' she said." The silence is broken not with a welcoming speech from the host, as decorum dictates, but with the abrasive criticism of the Red Queen, who speaks for the status quo politics. The speech that breaks Alice's silence does little to ease the discomfort of the moment, for in response to the Red Queen's orders, the waiters place a leg of mutton before the newly arrived Alice. The first task of the new ruler and the hostess of the feast is to divide the food and share it among her welcomed guests, signaling community, equality, and a ruler's grace. The newest Queen fails miserably on all these counts; as "the waiters set a leg of mutton before Alice, [she] looked at it rather anxiously, as she had never had to carve a joint before."

As soon as Alice becomes Queen, she is required to demonstrate a mature understanding of the terms and conditions of the adult world that she hopes to enter. Again, however, it is the Red Queen who steps forward to fill the awkward silence and to explain to Alice the "etiquette" of the situation at hand, which leaves Alice even more confused than ever: "'You look a little shy'" the Red Queen begins, "'let me introduce you to that leg of mutton.'" Alice gives herself over to the Red Queen's directions, "not knowing whether to be frightened or amused." In the name of etiquette and good manners, the Red Queen will keep the community and the guest of honor from enjoying this meal.

Despite her usual confusion, Alice does *sense* that a feast must have food and that her gathered guests must eventually be fed. Not fully understanding "why the Red Queen should be the only one to give orders," Alice asserts her own will on the situation, calling out to the waiters to "[b]ring back the pudding" that the Red Queen has ordered taken away from the table. These words work magic and prove to be the beginning of a

new awareness in Alice. Conquering her shyness "by a great effort," Alice cuts "a slice" of the pudding and "hand[s] it to the Red Queen."

What Alice is not prepared for, however, is that the pudding talks back to her, resisting what Alice herself acknowledges is an "experiment" and a "conjuring-trick" in governance. The pudding will not submit quietly to the will of Queen Alice, but uses its one weapon (its own voice) to raise a challenge to her tenuous authority: "'What impertinence!' said the Pudding. 'I wonder how you'd like it, if I were to cut a slice out of *you*, you creature!'" Alice's inability to respond to such an impudent challenge underscores her social failure, marking her inability to become a true queen or offer a real alternative to the status quo politics of the Red and White Queens who flank her at the head table. Confronted with the "thick, suety sort of voice" of the pudding, Alice is once again speechless: "Alice hadn't a word in reply: she could only sit and look at it and gasp." Even the usually indecorous Red Queen sees the error of Alice's silence, chiding her to "[m]ake a remark" given that it is "ridiculous to leave all the conversation to the pudding!"

When Alice does speak, it is an act of avoidance rather than of leadership; she shifts focus from the challenges of the pudding to another topic totally, namely poetry and fish. Unable and unwilling to address the words of the pudding, Alice falls into the illogical patterns that define the Looking-Glass world. She engages verbal misdirection and *non sequitur* (irrelevance) in order to avoid settling her conflict with the pudding. In short, Alice becomes like the Queens on either side of her, attempting to rule without listening and to impose order rather than negotiate harmony.

When Alice finally does respond, raising a question about the local fondness for fish, she is cut off by the Red Queen, who retakes control of the table by asking her White counterpart to recite the riddle of the fishes. Unable to control even a rebellious pudding, Alice is silenced again, relegating control of a feast held in her honor and in her home to the Red Queen. Alice as a symbol of change and new order is returned to a role that she is accustomed to playing, the obedient child who believes, incorrectly, that she "can do quite well without" the support and guidance of her elders.

It is not surprising, then, when Alice later rises to give her coronation speech that she is interrupted one final time by the catastrophe of the tabletop. She must hold on for her life as place settings turn to birds, as guests change places with the leftover food on their plates, and as the soup ladle approaches the head table with more than a hint of threat. A coronation dinner that might have marked Alice's awakening into a new world of maturity and control disintegrates into chaos, leaving the new Queen hungry and speechless, exasperated at her own futile efforts to enter young adulthood. As the poem that closes the novel implies, Alice's dream of finding her own way into the world, of moving toward the autonomy of young adulthood remains a dream, lost amidst the scattering dishes and screaming guests of a dinner party spinning out of control.

Source: Klay Dyer, Critical Essay on *Through the Looking-Glass*, in *Novels for Students*, Gale, Cengage Learning, 2008.

Jennifer Geer

In the following excerpt, Geer discusses the tension between narrative frames (opening and closing) of Through the Looking Glass *and the representations of the domestic sphere within the novel. She connects this apparent incongruity to Carroll's interrogation of three familiar Victorian themes: the ideal of femininity, childhood as a paradise of innocence, and the convention of the benevolent storyteller. She concludes that Carroll's ironic treatment of these assumptions allows his novels to be read as satires and renders his tales of escape all the more necessary in a world whose youth are rapidly losing their innocence.*

The opening and closing sections of Lewis Carroll's two classic children's novels, *Alice's Adventures in Wonderland* and its sequel *Through the Looking-Glass*, have posed perennial difficulties for critics. The prefatory poem and final paragraphs of *Wonderland*, as well as the poems and drawing-room scenes that frame the central narrative in *Looking-Glass*, are nostalgic, gently teasing, and ostensibly serene—and they stand in sharp contrast to Alice's unsentimental, chaotic, and often violent adventures. Although this dichotomy has been interpreted in several ways, most critics agree that the framing sections give much more conventionally idealized picture of Alice and her dream-journeys than the adventures do. Such idealization is hardly surprising in light

> INSTEAD, CARROLL'S SPEAKER MAINTAINS THAT HIS 'FAIRY-TALE' WILL PRESERVE AN IDEALIZED, DOMESTIC CHILDHOOD WORLD THAT EXISTS IN COMFORTING OPPOSITION TO 'THE BLINDING SNOW' OUTSIDE."

of Carroll's legendary devotion to little girls, but in the context of Alice's adventures, the frames *do* surprise. Their portrayals of her journeys through Wonderland and Looking-glass country bear so little resemblance to the journeys themselves that it is difficult to take the frames quite seriously. The closing paragraph of *Wonderland* is lovely but absurd as it blithely affirms that the tale of Alice's adventures, in which mothers sing sadistic lullabies, babies turn into pigs, and little girls shout at queens, will lead Alice's older sister into reveries about delightful children and domestic bliss. From a logical perspective, this final scene is as nonsensical as anything in Wonderland. I would like to suggest that the contrast between frames and adventures in the *Alice* books implies that the frames' idealized visions of Alice are themselves constructed narratives, as fantastic in their own way as the dream-tales they so radically reinterpret.

The *Alice* frames encourage readers to interpret Alice's adventures as fairy tales, a category that in nineteenth-century usage includes literary and traditional tales, nonsense, and what we would now call fantasy fiction. In mid-Victorian discourse, fairy tales often exert a recognizably domestic influence on their readers or listeners. Contemporary periodical articles and reviews commonly portray the tales' virtues as analogous to an ideal home's: readers young and old will find their sympathies awakened and the corrosive effects of an amoral, competitive, and violent world lessened. *Wonderland* and *Looking-Glass*, like many Victorian texts, thus characterize the values inscribed in idealized childhood and its tales as domestic and feminine. The *Wonderland* frames suggest that the tale of Alice's dream fosters the happy, loving childhood that will enable her development into a good woman and mother, while the *Looking-Glass* frames anticipate that the tale will create a domestic space powerful enough to keep the stormy world at bay.

In both novels, the contrast between frames and adventures works to undermine such hopes and suggestions by foregrounding potential conflicts between adult and child figures. Adult and child characters in the *Alice* books, as well as the implied readers, often want rather different things from one another; tale-telling both fulfills and frustrates their desires. In *Wonderland* and *Looking-Glass*, Carroll ultimately suggests that both adults and children want power as well as comfort, and that the domestic world of little girls and fairy tales is the unlikely site of power struggles over the comforts of home and childhood. Still, Carroll does not reject the ideals of fairy tales and femininity he so deftly ironizes. He may delight in exposing their illogic, but he remains deeply committed to their emotional power. As Carroll's fellow Oxford don T. B. Strong noted, *Wonderland* and *Looking-Glass* draw heavily on mid-Victorian mores, often taking common words or phrases literally and pressing conventional assumptions to their logical conclusions. The books reveal "all sorts of pitfalls and surprises round the ordinary course of conversation" (Strong 306). Paradoxically, "pitfalls and surprises" can make conventional forms all the more alluring; by implying that the idyllic world of little girls and their fairy tales is really a narrative told by adults for self-interested purposes, the *Alice* books only intensify adult readers' desire for those idealized visions.

. . .

Although *Wonderland* offers the possibility that its antidomestic tale will foster Alice's development into a model of ideal womanhood, *Through the Looking-Glass* is far more skeptical about the tale's impact on her future. Much of this skepticism occurs because the later novel draws on rather different views of the relationships between adults, children's literature, and little girls. The *Wonderland* frames certainly idealize Alice, but their emphasis on the benefits she will reap from remembering the tale and retaining "the simple and loving heart of her childhood" assumes continuity between the child's experience and the woman's. The *Looking-Glass* frames, however, tend to follow another influential contemporary model of development, which portrays childhood as an innocent, feminized state vastly

different from the corrupt, sorrowful adult world. Childhood becomes a sort of secular Eden, a paradise "inviolably, savingly separate from the adult world of anxiety" (Gilead 283). Because this model perceives childhood as separate from and superior to adulthood, it holds that adults do not retain their childlike hearts. Adults can only recapture momentary glimpses of childhood's bliss by interacting with children or by reading, telling, or writing idealized forms of children's literature such as fairy tales. At the same time, childhood becomes the site of a deep sentimental regret that children must lose their innocence as they grow up.

Looking-Glass is thus more determined to idealize the child Alice and more pessimistic about her growth than *Wonderland* is. Whereas *Wonderland*'s prefatory poem gently teases the children who listen to the tale, its *Looking-Glass* counterpart does not. The *Looking-Glass* Alice is an ethereal "Child of the pure unclouded brow" rather than a pair of "little hands" steering the boat with "little skill." The *Looking-Glass* poem also assumes that Alice will lose her joyous innocence as she grows up. The simple, loving girl will develop all too quickly into a "melancholy maiden" subject to adulthood's "bitter tidings" and "unwelcome bed" of anxiety, sexuality and death. Although the poem's speaker wishes Alice to remember him and her happy girlhood, his sad prediction that "No thought of me shall find a place / In thy young life's hereafter" and his reference to "vanish'd summer glory" suggest that she will forget. These circumstances lessen the tale's value as a potentially formative influence on Alice. Instead, Carroll's speaker maintains that his "fairy-tale" will preserve an idealized, domestic childhood world that exists in comforting opposition to "the blinding snow" outside. The tale also will help delay Alice's departure into adulthood by weaving "magic words" to "hold [her] fast" in "childhood's nest gladness," if only for a moment.

Yet *Looking-Glass* indicates that this desire to see childhood as a domestic paradise separate from and superior to adulthood is problematic as well as alluring. In particular, the novel explores the conflicted relationships between Victorian ideals of femininity and a model of childhood that contrasts innocent, feminized children with corrupt, implicitly masculine adults. Although recent studies by U.C. Knoepflmacher and Catherine Robson have examined the ways in which idealizations of little girls play into Victorian narratives about middle-class men's development, these idealizations also interact—often in unsettling ways—with contemporary notions of adult womanhood. Robson correctly notes that domestic advice literature often upholds the girl as an "embodiment of the ideal home," whose "powerlessness in some ways makes [her] more 'feminine' than the grown woman." But this idealized girl is not merely a prepubescent, more charmingly dependent version of the adult angel in the house. She tends to undercut her adult counterpart; a model of girlhood which assumes that adults are anxious, sinful, and separated from their past implicitly contradicts the domestic ideal of a calm and cheerful woman who retains her childlike heart.

Mid-Victorian writers often try to avoid this contradiction by quietly omitting the figure of the woman; they portray the adult world in exclusively masculine terms and transfer the feminine powers of comfort and moral influences onto the child. *Looking-Glass*, however, takes the view of innocent child and corrupt adult to its logical conclusion, suggesting that adult womanhood is as competitive, individualistic, and disappointing as manhood. Such a move confirms adults' worst fears about children's growth, since it implies that all children, even girls, will lose their innocence and selfless affection as they mature. By undercutting the figure of the ideal woman, *Looking-Glass* increases adult readers' desire for an idealized girl who will perform the womanly functions of comfort and inspiration. The notion that childhood is precious yet fleeting also intensifies adults' desire for a tale that portrays the child and works to prolong her brief stay in paradise. Yet even as Carroll fosters these desires, he suggests that they are impossible to satisfy. Although the image of childhood as separate from and superior to adulthood may be inspiring, such a paradise is by definition inaccessible to adults. Furthermore, *Looking-Glass* indicates that the tale that might give adults a glimpse of childhood's bliss is at least as implicated in questions of power and self-interest as the *Wonderland* tale. The later novel assumes Alice will grow and indeed is eager to do so, but her eagerness only increases adults' futile wish that she remain young. Precisely because of its sentimentally nostalgic vision of girlhood, *Looking-Glass* present adults' and children's desire as mutually exclusive. Such conflict, in turn, places

enormous strain upon the tale: a story that satisfies adult readers' desire to fix Alice in her blissful childhood will hardly please child readers eager to grow up.

Although the prefatory poem's speaker may wish to fix Alice in an idealized childhood world, her adventures portray her as conspicuously uninterested in any such thing. As Knoepflmacher has pointed out, Alice's desire to play Looking-glass chess signifies her desire to grow up and gain an adult woman's powers ("Balancing" 511). In Looking-glass country, these desires are inseparable from ambition and competition; Alice is willing to enter the game as a Pawn, but she would "*like* to be a Queen, best.'" The speed and relative ease with which she wins the game and becomes a Queen has led Knoepflmacher to argues that *Looking-Glass* endorses Alice's desire to grow, at least until Carroll abruptly rescinds that endorsement in the final chapters (*Ventures* 197–200; 216–26). *Looking-Glass* certainly does depict Alice's progress and implicitly her growth as inevitable: she is a Pawn whose moves are mapped out for her even before she begins to play. But her smoothly overdetermined journey to the Eighth Square does not necessarily indicate acceptance of her growth. The contrast between her success and the coronation feast which literally overturns her triumph only intensifies the sense that maturity is no prize at all, but a profound disappointment. Alice herself, who calmly pretends to mother the black kitten once she returns to her own drawing-room in the final chapter, never quite grasps this implication, but it certainly is available to the adult reader.

Alice initially believes the Red Queen's assurance that "'in the Eighth Square we shall be Queens together, and it's all feasting and fun!'" Once Alice arrives at the Eighth Square, however, she discovers that her new role is hardly fun. The Red and White Queens are determined not to let her take her place with them as an equal. Instead, they assert their own superior status by treating her like a child, dismissing as ignorance and ill-temper all her attempts to establish her position as Queen. They even go so far as to invite themselves to her coronation dinner, justifying the breach of good manners by accusing Alice of not having "'had many lessons in manners yet'" The Queens' rudeness and Alice's bewildered resentment cast ironic doubt on adults' to place children in a world of youthful bliss. Alice's relationships with adult figures are no more blissful in Looking-glass country than they were in Wonderland. Her position during and immediately before her coronation feast may be childlike, but it is hardly the "nest of gladness" that the prefatory poem extols.

Alice's uncomfortable position as child-Queen suggests that the combination of a child's heart and a woman's offices might destroy domestic competence rather than create it. She fares no better at her coronation dinner than David Copperfield's "child-wife," Dora, does at housekeeping in Dickens's novel. Her title notwithstanding, Alice lacks the social experience to be an effective hostess, let alone a ruler. At first, she is even a little relieved when she discovers the feast has started without her; she remarks that she "'should never have known who were the right people to invite!'" All too soon, however, the order that should have characterized a combination of state dinner and Victorian dinner-party plunges into chaos in the face of her inexperience. As an untutored girl, Alice has neither a ruler's public authority nor a hostess's social and managerial skills. The polite compliance that an upper-middle-class girl such as Alice would have been taught in nursery and schoolroom only compounds the social reversals, as she bows to subjects who understand Looking-glass etiquette. And if chess pieces can exercise power over a human Queen at her own coronation dinner, the food and tableware might logically aspire to rule, also. The result is a sort of domestic coup: Alice looks up to find the leg of mutton in the White Queen's chair, the Queen herself in the soup-tureen, and the soup-ladle advancing purposefully toward her own chair, "beckoning to her impatiently to get out of its way."

Admittedly, the combination of a child's character and an adult's position serves Alice well in one respect. She manages to restore order by combining the traits of the mischievous child and the furious, domineering woman. Childishly, Alice demands attention by disrupting the already chaotic feast: "'I can't stand this any longer!' she cried, as she jumped up and seized the tablecloth with both hands: one good pull, and plates, dishes, quests, and candles came crashing down together in a heap on the floor." She then abandons the child's role for the furious woman's, asserting her own dominance by "turning fiercely upon the Red Queen, whom she considered as the cause of all the mischief." Since the scene is already a reversal of conventional order,

these additional reversals succeed in righting it. The Red Queen begins to turn into the harmless black kitten on the spot, and Alice soon wakes to find herself back in the snug comfort of a drawing-room armchair. With Alice and the Red Queen restored to their respective roles as child and kitten, the adult narrator can re-establish control over the scene and return to a peaceful vision of Alice in her drawing-room.

As it turns out, however, this return to order is even more tenuous than in *Wonderland*. On the surface, the end of Alice's dream satisfies child and adult readers' impulse to halt the feast's frightening chaos, as well as adult readers' desire that Alice return to a safe, enclosed childhood world. But although *Looking-Glass* applauds Alice's actions, is also ironizes them. The violence Alice herself does in restoring domestic order suggests that neither the ideal woman nor the ideal girl is fully recoverable: the furious woman underlies the former, while the mischievous child underlies the latter. Thus, even the scenes of Alice in her drawing-room question the figure of the loving, authoritative yet childlike woman more than the closing frame of *Wonderland* does. Because Alice is pretending to be a mother, these scenes imply that the ideal woman who can combine an adult's competence with a child's simplicity exists only in the imagination. Furthermore, Alice's games retain subtle forms of Looking-glass country's conflicts between child and adult figures. Alice mothers her kittens by imitating adult authority figures' treatment of herself, never quite forgetting that she remains under their control. Thus, when she is playfully telling the black kitten that she will punish it for its faults, she begins to wonder if the same technique could be applied to her: "'You know I'm saving up all your punishments for Wednesday week—Suppose they had saved up all *my* punishments? ... What *would* they do at the end of a year?'" The effect is to emphasize the scene's fictionality (readers know they are watching a child pretending to be a mother) and the possibility of conflict even in Alice's supposedly happy family.

Given *Looking-Glass*'s persistent sense of the ways in which adult figures bully child figures, the mischievous or rebellious child is never far from Alice's games, either. Alice may pretend to be a benevolent mother, but she does not pretend to be a compliant child. The narrator mentions that "once she had really frightened her old nurse by shouting suddenly in her ear, 'Nurse! Do let's pretend that I'm a hungry hyaena, and you're a bone!'" Even her dream-journey into Looking-glass House begins with Alice perched on the chimney-piece, which she almost certainly is not allowed to climb—especially when there is a fire burning. When Alice takes on a motherly role, she playfully recreates her own rebellious impulses in the figure of the black kitten, who is "'a little mischievous darling.'" To a large extent, these fantasies are charming to adult readers: they can recognize their own aggression in Alice's but rest assured that she herself is only "a little mischievous darling." On another level, however, Alice's games are slightly worrisome to adult devotees of idealized little girls. Because this dream-child happily pretends to be an adult and to resist adults, her games remind adults of childhood's transience and of potential conflicts between children's desires and their own.

These tensions between child and adult figures severely limit the possibility of creating a narrative that satisfies adults' longing for an idealized childhood paradise while also amusing child readers. The prefatory poem, for instance, suggests that the tale is as difficult to grasp as Alice's dream-rushes, which begin "to lose all their scent and beauty, from the very moment that she picked them." Like the White Queen's jam, the idealized "fairy-tale" of the *Looking-Glass* poem exists yesterday and tomorrow, but not today. The speaker promises that he will continue "[a] tale begun in other days," but that tale remains an elusive future pleasure. The tale of Looking-glass country as presented in Alice's adventures does not exactly live up to this promise; although it certainly resembles her adventures in Wonderland, it is hardly a vision of "childhood's nest of gladness." Moreover, even the delightfully nostalgic and sentimental tale the poem promises remains a product of adult fiat that may clash with the child's desires. The *Looking-Glass* poem's overtures may be flattering, but its consistent use of imperative verbs and negative constructions implies that it is as much a command as an invitation, and one Alice might choose not to heed.

Alice's adventures in Looking-glass country also question conventional notions of the benevolent tale-teller, the children who wish to be delighted, and the charming tale. Alice is usually

reluctant to listen to Looking-glass poetry and remains skeptical of the creatures' claims that their poems will comfort or amuse her. The creatures' poetry and conversations often have the effect of delaying Alice's progress in the chess game; like the prefatory poem's ideal tale, they work to arrest her symbolic journey toward adulthood. This tendency may satisfy adult readers, but it exasperates Alice, who only wants to advance to the next square and become a Queen. Thus, when Tweedledee asks her if she likes poetry, her response is hardly enthusiastic: "'Ye-es, pretty well—*some* poetry … Would you tell me which road leads out of the wood?'" The Tweedle brothers' determination to recite the longest poem they know dismays her still more. The poem they tell Alice, "The Walrus and the Carpenter," reveals that she has good reason to be wary. The Walrus and Carpenter lure the "young Oysters" out for what they claim will be "A pleasant walk, a pleasant talk / Along the briny beach," but the walk ends with their eating the young guests. The poem's nonsense exaggerates conflict between generations. Adult figures' benevolence is nothing more than a hypocritical cloak, and the desire to arrest children's growth is literalized as a desire to kill them. The same themes recur during Alice's encounter with Humpty Dumpty. His response to her remark that "'one can't help growing older'" reveals ominous undertones behind adults' desire that children not grow, as he takes the premise to its logical conclusion by asserting that "'*One* can't, perhaps … but *two* can. With proper assistance, you might have left off'" growing. Alice, understandably alarmed, hastens to change the subject.

Looking-Glass never comes to a definitive conclusion about the best ways to balance adult and child readers' desires. It simply gives—and undercuts—two possibilities for creating a tale that can amuse children while satisfying adults' wish for a nostalgic escape into a blissful childhood world. Alice's encounter with the White Knight implies that one way to create such a tale is to ask all parties to pretend. During this scene, Alice graciously submits to a deluded but well-meaning adult's determination to tell a tale, feigning interest in order to please him while giving her future adult self an opportunity to redefine the event in nostalgic, escapist terms. The White Knight casts himself as the ideal tale-teller, and according to the narrator, Alice eventually remembers him in such an idealized light. Admittedly, this memory of the Knight's "mild blue eyes and kindly smile ... and ... the melancholy music of the song" is a doubtful one. In typical Looking-glass fashion, it is a memory which has not yet happened to the Alice of the adventures, and as Knoepflmacher points out, it is by no means an accurate depiction of her experience in the narrative present (*Ventures* 221–23; "Balancing" 514–15). Although Alice may someday remember herself enjoying the beautiful picture the Knight makes with "the setting sun gleaming through his hair, and shining on his armour in a blaze of light," Carroll gives no indication that she has this reaction while listening to the Knight's song. In the narrative present she is somewhat bored and even critical; she remarks that "'the tune *isn't* his own invention'" and works hard at "trying to feel interested" in yet another piece of poetry. Yet even if Alice's fondness for the Knight and his tale is only an illusion created in retrospect, *Looking-Glass* ultimately presents it as both lovely and fulfilling. Alice's meeting with the Knight suggests that the conflicting desires behind Victorian ideals of girlhood and fairy tales can be well served by a deluded storyteller and a child's polite deception. Because he believes himself wise and benevolent, the Knight is one of the few characters in Wonderland or Looking-glass country who is courteous or helpful to Alice, and for all her impatience, Alice hides it well. Her actions form *Looking-Glass*'s closest approximation to the ideal little girl or to the ideal woman who retains her childlike heart. By exercising an adult's diplomatic tact, Alice manages to fulfill the ideal girl's role of delighting her elders, even if she is only feigning interest.

The closing poem also presents the child and her tales as a lovely yet satisfying illusion. It represents an ingenious, if tenuous, solution to the problem of creating an idealized childhood world. As *Wonderland* does, this poem validates storytelling—or in this case, poetry—as the best way to satisfy the desires behind mid-Victorian idealizations of childhood. The poem is an acrostic on Alice Pleasance Liddell's name; although the children who listened to the original tale of Wonderland have faded into memory and those who will hear the tale have yet to do so, the ideal child remains inscribed into the poem's present. And although Alice does not become and ideal woman who can delight her own children with her tales, this poem recreates the tale of Wonderland and Looking-glass country in a form that offers continuity across generations.

Recurring tales of "a Wonderland," told to successive groups of children, will ensure that the girl and her tales remain present, even though each telling's "[e]choes fade and memories die." The poem thus attempts to fix Carroll, the real Alice Liddell, the fictional Alice, and child-listeners in a perpetually available childhood world.

At the same time, however, the closing poem remains well aware of the irony in its depiction of a childhood paradise. After all, this idealized setting bears little resemblance to the Wonderland (or the Looking-glass country) of Alice's original adventures: the poem's inhabitants certainly do move "under skies / Never seen by waking eyes." Other children are present only as passive listeners, their desires carefully edited to correspond to those of the adult speaker, who creates the poem unilaterally and takes for granted his audience's "[e]ager eye and willing ear." The final stanzas wryly undercut the notion of an eternal tale even as they long for it. The idealized childhood world that tale and poem create may seem to exist in a timeless lyric present, but the double meanings of lines such as "Ever drifting down the stream" reveal that it does not. The final lines encourage readers to dream but remind them that they, too, are drifting steadily toward death and destruction, however they may wish to linger along the way:

> In a Wonderland they lie,
> Dreaming as the days go by,
> Dreaming as the summers die:
>
> Ever drifting down the stream—
> Lingering in the golden gleam—
> Life, what is it but a dream?

Images of idealized childhood and its tales can delight, but they are dreams, illusory and fleeting; furthermore, the adult tale-teller and imaginary child-listeners cannot escape the fact that "summers die." In *Looking-Glass*, however, the very transience and elusiveness of ideal childhood only increase adults' desire to tell lovely if delusive tales for and about little girls.

Source: Jennifer Geer, "'All Sorts of Pitfalls and Surprises': Competing Views of Idealized Girlhood in Lewis Carroll's *Alice* Books," in *Children's Literature*, Vol. 31, 2003, pp. 1–2, 12–21.

SOURCES

Carroll, Lewis, *Through the Looking-Glass*, in *Alice's Adventures in Wonderland and Through the Looking-Glass*, illustrated by John Tenniel, Penguin, 1997, pp. 144–311.

Engberg, Gillian, Review of *Alice through the Looking-Glass*, in *Booklist*, Vol. 102, No. 8, December 15, 2005, p. 46.

Kelly, Richard, *Lewis Carroll*, Twayne Publishers, 1990, pp. 21, 92.

Phelan, Carolyn, Review of *Alice's Adventures in Wonderland*, in *Booklist*, Vol. 103, No. 5, November 1, 2006, p. 52.

Russell, David R., *Literature for Children: A Short Introduction*, Longman, 2001, p. 13.

FURTHER READING

Gardner, Martin, ed., *The Annotated Alice: The Definitive Edition*, W. W. Norton, 2000.

Updating the earlier edition of this seminal text, this volume includes the complete collections of Tenniel's classic illustrations, recently discovered pencil sketches, as well as Gardner's trademark explanations of the puzzles, jokes, and wordplay that shape the worlds of the novels.

Jones, Jo Elwyn, and J. Francis Gladstone, *The Red King's Dream, or Lewis Carroll in Wonderland*, Pimlico, 1996.

This book provides an in-depth study of the complexities of Carroll's political attitudes towards empire and colonialism and how they find a place in his writing for children. Full of dates, details, and anecdotal bits of political history, this book provides a rich background for the novel.

Morris, Frankie, *Artist of Wonderland: The Life, Political Cartoons, and Illustrations of Tenniel*, University of Virginia Press, 2005.

This book takes a broad look at Tenniel's life and career, including his most famous work on Carroll's Alice novels. Morris relates in detail the disagreement between Carroll and Tenniel over the illustrations for each of the books, as well as Tenniel's role in the excision of "The Wasp in a Wig" chapter.

Parsons, Marnie, *Touch Monkeys: Nonsense Strategies for Reading Twentieth-Century Poetry*, University of Toronto Press, 1994.

Determined to reestablish nonsense writing as poetic exploration rather than simply child's play, Parsons presents an original approach to a generally misunderstood genre. Her goal is to re-envision nonsense language as the overlaying of several ways of making meaning within a verbal sense system, paying attention to Carroll's writing generally and "Jabberwocky" in particular.

Glossary of Literary Terms

A

Abstract: As an adjective applied to writing or literary works, abstract refers to words or phrases that name things not knowable through the five senses.

Aestheticism: A literary and artistic movement of the nineteenth century. Followers of the movement believed that art should not be mixed with social, political, or moral teaching. The statement "art for art's sake" is a good summary of aestheticism. The movement had its roots in France, but it gained widespread importance in England in the last half of the nineteenth century, where it helped change the Victorian practice of including moral lessons in literature.

Allegory: A narrative technique in which characters representing things or abstract ideas are used to convey a message or teach a lesson. Allegory is typically used to teach moral, ethical, or religious lessons but is sometimes used for satiric or political purposes.

Allusion: A reference to a familiar literary or historical person or event, used to make an idea more easily understood.

Analogy: A comparison of two things made to explain something unfamiliar through its similarities to something familiar, or to prove one point based on the acceptedness of another. Similes and metaphors are types of analogies.

Antagonist: The major character in a narrative or drama who works against the hero or protagonist.

Anthropomorphism: The presentation of animals or objects in human shape or with human characteristics. The term is derived from the Greek word for "human form."

Anti-hero: A central character in a work of literature who lacks traditional heroic qualities such as courage, physical prowess, and fortitude. Anti-heroes typically distrust conventional values and are unable to commit themselves to any ideals. They generally feel helpless in a world over which they have no control. Anti-heroes usually accept, and often celebrate, their positions as social outcasts.

Apprenticeship Novel: See *Bildungsroman*

Archetype: The word archetype is commonly used to describe an original pattern or model from which all other things of the same kind are made. This term was introduced to literary criticism from the psychology of Carl Jung. It expresses Jung's theory that behind every person's "unconscious," or repressed memories of the past, lies the "collective unconscious" of the human race: memories of the countless typical experiences of our ancestors. These memories are said to prompt illogical associations that trigger powerful emotions in the reader. Often, the emotional process is primitive, even primordial. Archetypes are the literary images that grow out of the "collective unconscious." They appear in literature as incidents and plots that repeat basic patterns of life. They may also appear as stereotyped characters.

Avant-garde: French term meaning "vanguard." It is used in literary criticism to describe new writing that rejects traditional approaches to literature in favor of innovations in style or content.

B

Beat Movement: A period featuring a group of American poets and novelists of the 1950s and 1960s—including Jack Kerouac, Allen Ginsberg, Gregory Corso, William S. Burroughs, and Lawrence Ferlinghetti—who rejected established social and literary values. Using such techniques as stream of consciousness writing and jazz-influenced free verse and focusing on unusual or abnormal states of mind—generated by religious ecstasy or the use of drugs—the Beat writers aimed to create works that were unconventional in both form and subject matter.

Bildungsroman: A German word meaning "novel of development." The *bildungsroman* is a study of the maturation of a youthful character, typically brought about through a series of social or sexual encounters that lead to self-awareness. *Bildungsroman* is used interchangeably with *erziehungsroman,* a novel of initiation and education. When a *bildungsroman* is concerned with the development of an artist (as in James Joyce's *A Portrait of the Artist as a Young Man*), it is often termed a *kunstlerroman.*

Black Aesthetic Movement: A period of artistic and literary development among African Americans in the 1960s and early 1970s. This was the first major African-American artistic movement since the Harlem Renaissance and was closely paralleled by the civil rights and black power movements. The black aesthetic writers attempted to produce works of art that would be meaningful to the black masses. Key figures in black aesthetics included one of its founders, poet and playwright Amiri Baraka, formerly known as LeRoi Jones; poet and essayist Haki R. Madhubuti, formerly Don L. Lee; poet and

playwright Sonia Sanchez; and dramatist Ed Bullins.

Black Humor: Writing that places grotesque elements side by side with humorous ones in an attempt to shock the reader, forcing him or her to laugh at the horrifying reality of a disordered world.

Burlesque: Any literary work that uses exaggeration to make its subject appear ridiculous, either by treating a trivial subject with profound seriousness or by treating a dignified subject frivolously. The word "burlesque" may also be used as an adjective, as in "burlesque show," to mean "striptease act."

C

Character: Broadly speaking, a person in a literary work. The actions of characters are what constitute the plot of a story, novel, or poem. There are numerous types of characters, ranging from simple, stereotypical figures to intricate, multifaceted ones. In the techniques of anthropomorphism and personification, animals—and even places or things—can assume aspects of character. "Characterization" is the process by which an author creates vivid, believable characters in a work of art. This may be done in a variety of ways, including (1) direct description of the character by the narrator; (2) the direct presentation of the speech, thoughts, or actions of the character; and (3) the responses of other characters to the character. The term "character" also refers to a form originated by the ancient Greek writer Theophrastus that later became popular in the seventeenth and eighteenth centuries. It is a short essay or sketch of a person who prominently displays a specific attribute or quality, such as miserliness or ambition.

Climax: The turning point in a narrative, the moment when the conflict is at its most intense. Typically, the structure of stories, novels, and plays is one of rising action, in which tension builds to the climax, followed by falling action, in which tension lessens as the story moves to its conclusion.

Colloquialism: A word, phrase, or form of pronunciation that is acceptable in casual conversation but not in formal, written communication. It is considered more acceptable than slang.

Coming of Age Novel: See *Bildungsroman*

Concrete: Concrete is the opposite of abstract, and refers to a thing that actually exists or a description that allows the reader to experience an object or concept with the senses.

Connotation: The impression that a word gives beyond its defined meaning. Connotations may be universally understood or may be significant only to a certain group.

Convention: Any widely accepted literary device, style, or form.

D

Denotation: The definition of a word, apart from the impressions or feelings it creates (connotations) in the reader.

Denouement: A French word meaning "the unknotting." In literary criticism, it denotes the resolution of conflict in fiction or drama. The *denouement* follows the climax and provides an outcome to the primary plot situation as well as an explanation of secondary plot complications. The *denouement* often involves a character's recognition of his or her state of mind or moral condition.

Description: Descriptive writing is intended to allow a reader to picture the scene or setting in which the action of a story takes place. The form this description takes often evokes an intended emotional response—a dark, spooky graveyard will evoke fear, and a peaceful, sunny meadow will evoke calmness.

Dialogue: In its widest sense, dialogue is simply conversation between people in a literary work; in its most restricted sense, it refers specifically to the speech of characters in a drama. As a specific literary genre, a "dialogue" is a composition in which characters debate an issue or idea.

Diction: The selection and arrangement of words in a literary work. Either or both may vary depending on the desired effect. There are four general types of diction: "formal," used in scholarly or lofty writing; "informal," used in relaxed but educated conversation; "colloquial," used in everyday speech; and "slang," containing newly coined words and other terms not accepted in formal usage.

Didactic: A term used to describe works of literature that aim to teach some moral, religious, political, or practical lesson. Although didactic elements are often found in artistically pleasing works, the term "didactic" usually refers to literature in which the message is more important than the form. The term may also be used to criticize a work that the critic finds "overly didactic," that is, heavy-handed in its delivery of a lesson.

Doppelganger: A literary technique by which a character is duplicated (usually in the form of an alter ego, though sometimes as a ghostly counterpart) or divided into two distinct, usually opposite personalities. The use of this character device is widespread in nineteenth- and twentieth-century literature, and indicates a growing awareness among authors that the "self" is really a composite of many "selves."

Double Entendre: A corruption of a French phrase meaning "double meaning." The term is used to indicate a word or phrase that is deliberately ambiguous, especially when one of the meanings is risqué or improper.

Dramatic Irony: Occurs when the audience of a play or the reader of a work of literature knows something that a character in the work itself does not know. The irony is in the contrast between the intended meaning of the statements or actions of a character and the additional information understood by the audience.

Dystopia: An imaginary place in a work of fiction where the characters lead dehumanized, fearful lives.

E

Edwardian: Describes cultural conventions identified with the period of the reign of Edward VII of England (1901-1910). Writers of the Edwardian Age typically displayed a strong reaction against the propriety and conservatism of the Victorian Age. Their work often exhibits distrust of authority in religion, politics, and art and expresses strong doubts about the soundness of conventional values.

Empathy: A sense of shared experience, including emotional and physical feelings, with someone or something other than oneself. Empathy is often used to describe the response of a reader to a literary character.

Enlightenment, The: An eighteenth-century philosophical movement. It began in France but had a wide impact throughout Europe and America. Thinkers of the Enlightenment valued reason and believed that both the individual and society could achieve a state of perfection. Corresponding to this essentially humanist vision was a resistance to religious authority.

Epigram: A saying that makes the speaker's point quickly and concisely. Often used to preface a novel.

Epilogue: A concluding statement or section of a literary work. In dramas, particularly those of the seventeenth and eighteenth centuries, the epilogue is a closing speech, often in verse, delivered by an actor at the end of a play and spoken directly to the audience.

Epiphany: A sudden revelation of truth inspired by a seemingly trivial incident.

Episode: An incident that forms part of a story and is significantly related to it. Episodes may be either self-contained narratives or events that depend on a larger context for their sense and importance.

Epistolary Novel: A novel in the form of letters. The form was particularly popular in the eighteenth century.

Epithet: A word or phrase, often disparaging or abusive, that expresses a character trait of someone or something.

Existentialism: A predominantly twentieth-century philosophy concerned with the nature and perception of human existence. There are two major strains of existentialist thought: atheistic and Christian. Followers of atheistic existentialism believe that the individual is alone in a godless universe and that the basic human condition is one of suffering and loneliness. Nevertheless, because there are no fixed values, individuals can create their own characters—indeed, they can shape themselves—through the exercise of free will. The atheistic strain culminates in and is popularly associated with the works of Jean-Paul Sartre. The Christian existentialists, on the other hand, believe that only in God may people find freedom from life's anguish. The two strains hold certain beliefs in common: that existence cannot be fully understood or described through empirical effort; that anguish is a universal element of life; that individuals must bear responsibility for their actions; and that there is no common standard of behavior or perception for religious and ethical matters.

Expatriates: See *Expatriatism*

Expatriatism: The practice of leaving one's country to live for an extended period in another country.

Exposition: Writing intended to explain the nature of an idea, thing, or theme. Expository writing is often combined with description, narration, or argument. In dramatic writing, the exposition is the introductory material which presents the characters, setting, and tone of the play.

Expressionism: An indistinct literary term, originally used to describe an early twentieth-century school of German painting. The term applies to almost any mode of unconventional, highly subjective writing that distorts reality in some way.

F

Fable: A prose or verse narrative intended to convey a moral. Animals or inanimate objects with human characteristics often serve as characters in fables.

Falling Action: See *Denouement*

Fantasy: A literary form related to mythology and folklore. Fantasy literature is typically set in non-existent realms and features supernatural beings.

Farce: A type of comedy characterized by broad humor, outlandish incidents, and often vulgar subject matter.

Femme fatale: A French phrase with the literal translation "fatal woman." A *femme fatale* is a sensuous, alluring woman who often leads men into danger or trouble.

Fiction: Any story that is the product of imagination rather than a documentation of fact. characters and events in such narratives may be based in real life but their ultimate form and configuration is a creation of the author.

Figurative Language: A technique in writing in which the author temporarily interrupts the order, construction, or meaning of the writing for a particular effect. This interruption takes the form of one or more figures of speech such as hyperbole, irony, or simile. Figurative language is the opposite of literal language, in which every word is truthful, accurate, and free of exaggeration or embellishment.

Figures of Speech: Writing that differs from customary conventions for construction, meaning, order, or significance for the purpose of a special meaning or effect. There are two major types of figures of speech: rhetorical figures, which do not make changes in the meaning of the words, and tropes, which do.

Fin de siecle: A French term meaning "end of the century." The term is used to denote the last decade of the nineteenth century, a transition period when writers and other artists abandoned old conventions and looked for new techniques and objectives.

First Person: See *Point of View*

Flashback: A device used in literature to present action that occurred before the beginning of the story. Flashbacks are often introduced as the dreams or recollections of one or more characters.

Foil: A character in a work of literature whose physical or psychological qualities contrast strongly with, and therefore highlight, the corresponding qualities of another character.

Folklore: Traditions and myths preserved in a culture or group of people. Typically, these are passed on by word of mouth in various forms—such as legends, songs, and proverbs—or preserved in customs and ceremonies. This term was first used by W. J. Thoms in 1846.

Folktale: A story originating in oral tradition. Folktales fall into a variety of categories, including legends, ghost stories, fairy tales, fables, and anecdotes based on historical figures and events.

Foreshadowing: A device used in literature to create expectation or to set up an explanation of later developments.

Form: The pattern or construction of a work which identifies its genre and distinguishes it from other genres.

G

Genre: A category of literary work. In critical theory, genre may refer to both the content of a given work—tragedy, comedy, pastoral—and to its form, such as poetry, novel, or drama.

Gilded Age: A period in American history during the 1870s characterized by political corruption and materialism. A number of important novels of social and political criticism were written during this time.

Gothicism: In literary criticism, works characterized by a taste for the medieval or morbidly attractive. A gothic novel prominently features elements of horror, the supernatural, gloom, and violence: clanking chains, terror, charnel houses, ghosts, medieval castles, and mysteriously slamming doors. The term "gothic novel" is also applied to novels that lack elements of the traditional Gothic setting but that create a similar atmosphere of terror or dread.

Grotesque: In literary criticism, the subject matter of a work or a style of expression characterized by exaggeration, deformity, freakishness, and disorder. The grotesque often includes an element of comic absurdity.

H

Harlem Renaissance: The Harlem Renaissance of the 1920s is generally considered the first significant movement of black writers and artists in the United States. During this period, new and established black writers published more fiction and poetry than ever before, the first influential black literary journals were established, and black authors and artists received their first widespread recognition and serious critical appraisal. Among the major writers associated with this period are Claude McKay, Jean Toomer, Countee Cullen, Langston Hughes, Arna Bontemps, Nella Larsen, and Zora Neale Hurston.

Hero/Heroine: The principal sympathetic character (male or female) in a literary work. Heroes and heroines typically exhibit admirable traits: idealism, courage, and integrity, for example.

Holocaust Literature: Literature influenced by or written about the Holocaust of World War II. Such literature includes true stories of survival in concentration camps, escape, and life after the war, as well as fictional works and poetry.

Humanism: A philosophy that places faith in the dignity of humankind and rejects the medieval perception of the individual as a weak, fallen creature. "Humanists" typically believe in the perfectibility of human nature and view reason and education as the means to that end.

Hyperbole: In literary criticism, deliberate exaggeration used to achieve an effect.

I

Idiom: A word construction or verbal expression closely associated with a given language.

Image: A concrete representation of an object or sensory experience. Typically, such a representation helps evoke the feelings associated with the object or experience itself. Images are either "literal" or "figurative." Literal images are especially concrete and involve little or no extension of the obvious meaning of the words used to express them. Figurative images do not follow the literal meaning of the words exactly. Images in literature are usually visual, but the term "image" can also refer to the representation of any sensory experience.

Imagery: The array of images in a literary work. Also, figurative language.

In medias res: A Latin term meaning "in the middle of things." It refers to the technique of beginning a story at its midpoint and then using various flashback devices to reveal previous action.

Interior Monologue: A narrative technique in which characters' thoughts are revealed in a way that appears to be uncontrolled by the author. The interior monologue typically aims to reveal the inner self of a character. It portrays emotional experiences as they occur at both a conscious and unconscious level. images are often used to represent sensations or emotions.

Irony: In literary criticism, the effect of language in which the intended meaning is the opposite of what is stated.

J

Jargon: Language that is used or understood only by a select group of people. Jargon may refer to terminology used in a certain profession, such as computer jargon, or it may refer to any nonsensical language that is not understood by most people.

L

Leitmotiv: See *Motif*

Literal Language: An author uses literal language when he or she writes without exaggerating or embellishing the subject matter and without any tools of figurative language.

Lost Generation: A term first used by Gertrude Stein to describe the post-World War I generation of American writers: men and women haunted by a sense of betrayal and emptiness brought about by the destructiveness of the war.

M

Mannerism: Exaggerated, artificial adherence to a literary manner or style. Also, a popular style of the visual arts of late sixteenth-century Europe that was marked by elongation of the human form and by intentional spatial distortion. Literary works that are self-consciously high-toned and artistic are often said to be "mannered."

Metaphor: A figure of speech that expresses an idea through the image of another object. Metaphors suggest the essence of the first object by identifying it with certain qualities of the second object.

Modernism: Modern literary practices. Also, the principles of a literary school that lasted from roughly the beginning of the twentieth century until the end of World War II. Modernism is defined by its rejection of the literary conventions of the nineteenth century and by its opposition to conventional morality, taste, traditions, and economic values.

Mood: The prevailing emotions of a work or of the author in his or her creation of the work. The mood of a work is not always what might be expected based on its subject matter.

Motif: A theme, character type, image, metaphor, or other verbal element that recurs throughout a single work of literature or occurs in a number of different works over a period of time.

Myth: An anonymous tale emerging from the traditional beliefs of a culture or social unit. Myths use supernatural explanations for natural phenomena. They may also explain cosmic issues like creation and death. Collections of myths, known as mythologies, are common to all cultures and nations, but the best-known myths belong to the Norse, Roman, and Greek mythologies.

N

Narration: The telling of a series of events, real or invented. A narration may be either a simple narrative, in which the events are recounted chronologically, or a narrative with a plot, in which the account is given in a style reflecting the author's artistic concept of the story. Narration is sometimes used as a synonym for "storyline."

Narrative: A verse or prose accounting of an event or sequence of events, real or invented. The term is also used as an adjective in the sense "method of narration." For example, in literary criticism, the expression "narrative technique" usually refers to the way the author structures and presents his or her story.

Narrator: The teller of a story. The narrator may be the author or a character in the story through whom the author speaks.

Naturalism: A literary movement of the late nineteenth and early twentieth centuries. The movement's major theorist, French novelist Emile Zola, envisioned a type of fiction that would examine human life with the objectivity of scientific inquiry. The Naturalists typically viewed human beings as either the products of "biological determinism," ruled by hereditary instincts and engaged in an endless struggle for survival, or as the products of "socioeconomic determinism," ruled by social and economic forces beyond their control. In their works, the Naturalists generally ignored the highest levels of society and focused on degradation: poverty, alcoholism, prostitution, insanity, and disease.

Noble Savage: The idea that primitive man is noble and good but becomes evil and corrupted as he becomes civilized. The concept of the noble savage originated in the Renaissance period but is more closely identified with such later writers as Jean-Jacques Rousseau and Aphra Behn.

Novel: A long fictional narrative written in prose, which developed from the novella and other early forms of narrative. A novel is usually organized under a plot or theme with a focus on character development and action.

Novel of Ideas: A novel in which the examination of intellectual issues and concepts takes precedence over characterization or a traditional storyline.

Novel of Manners: A novel that examines the customs and mores of a cultural group.

Novella: An Italian term meaning "story." This term has been especially used to describe fourteenth-century Italian tales, but it also refers to modern short novels.

O

Objective Correlative: An outward set of objects, a situation, or a chain of events corresponding to an inward experience and evoking this experience in the reader. The term frequently appears in modern criticism in discussions of authors' intended effects on the emotional responses of readers.

Objectivity: A quality in writing characterized by the absence of the author's opinion or feeling about the subject matter. Objectivity is an important factor in criticism.

Oedipus Complex: A son's amorous obsession with his mother. The phrase is derived from the story of the ancient Theban hero Oedipus, who unknowingly killed his father and married his mother.

Omniscience: See *Point of View*

Onomatopoeia: The use of words whose sounds express or suggest their meaning. In its simplest sense, onomatopoeia may be represented by words that mimic the sounds they denote such as "hiss" or "meow." At a more subtle level, the pattern and rhythm of sounds and rhymes of a line or poem may be onomatopoeic.

Oxymoron: A phrase combining two contradictory terms. Oxymorons may be intentional or unintentional.

P

Parable: A story intended to teach a moral lesson or answer an ethical question.

Paradox: A statement that appears illogical or contradictory at first, but may actually point to an underlying truth.

Parallelism: A method of comparison of two ideas in which each is developed in the same grammatical structure.

Parody: In literary criticism, this term refers to an imitation of a serious literary work or the signature style of a particular author in a ridiculous manner. A typical parody adopts the style of the original and applies it to an inappropriate subject for humorous effect. Parody is a form of satire and could be considered the literary equivalent of a caricature or cartoon.

Pastoral: A term derived from the Latin word "pastor," meaning shepherd. A pastoral is a literary composition on a rural theme. The conventions of the pastoral were originated by the third-century Greek poet Theocritus, who wrote about the experiences, love affairs, and pastimes of Sicilian shepherds. In a pastoral, characters and language of a courtly nature are often placed in a simple setting. The term pastoral is also used to classify dramas, elegies, and lyrics that exhibit the use of country settings and shepherd characters.

Pen Name: See *Pseudonym*

Persona: A Latin term meaning "mask." *Personae* are the characters in a fictional work of literature. The *persona* generally functions as a mask through which the author tells a story in a voice other than his or her own. A *persona* is usually either a character in a story who acts as a narrator or an "implied author," a voice created by the author to act as the narrator for himself or herself.

Personification: A figure of speech that gives human qualities to abstract ideas, animals, and inanimate objects.

Picaresque Novel: Episodic fiction depicting the adventures of a roguish central character ("picaro" is Spanish for "rogue"). The picaresque hero is commonly a low-born but clever individual who wanders into and out of various affairs of love, danger, and farcical intrigue. These involvements may take place at all social levels and typically present a humorous and wide-ranging satire of a given society.

Plagiarism: Claiming another person's written material as one's own. Plagiarism can take the form of direct, word-for- word copying or the theft of the substance or idea of the work.

Plot: In literary criticism, this term refers to the pattern of events in a narrative or drama. In its simplest sense, the plot guides the author in composing the work and helps the reader follow the work. Typically, plots exhibit causality and unity and have a beginning, a middle, and an end. Sometimes, however, a plot may consist of a series of disconnected events, in which case it is known as an "episodic plot."

Poetic Justice: An outcome in a literary work, not necessarily a poem, in which the good are rewarded and the evil are punished, especially in ways that particularly fit their virtues or crimes.

Poetic License: Distortions of fact and literary convention made by a writer—not always a poet—for the sake of the effect gained. Poetic license is closely related to the concept of "artistic freedom."

Poetics: This term has two closely related meanings. It denotes (1) an aesthetic theory in literary criticism about the essence of poetry or (2) rules prescribing the proper methods, content, style, or diction of poetry. The term poetics may also refer to theories about literature in general, not just poetry.

Point of View: The narrative perspective from which a literary work is presented to the reader. There are four traditional points of view. The "third person omniscient" gives the reader a "godlike" perspective, unrestricted by time or place, from which to see actions and look into the minds of characters. This allows the author to comment openly on characters and events in the work. The "third person" point of view presents the events of the story from outside of any single character's perception, much like the omniscient point of view, but the reader must understand the action as it takes place and without any special insight into characters' minds or motivations. The "first person" or "personal" point of view relates events as they are perceived by a single character. The main character "tells" the story and may offer opinions about the action and characters which differ from those of the author. Much less common than omniscient, third person, and first person is the "second person" point of view, wherein the author tells the story as if it is happening to the reader.

Polemic: A work in which the author takes a stand on a controversial subject, such as abortion or religion. Such works are often extremely argumentative or provocative.

Pornography: Writing intended to provoke feelings of lust in the reader. Such works are often condemned by critics and teachers, but those which can be shown to have literary value are viewed less harshly.

Post-Aesthetic Movement: An artistic response made by African Americans to the black aesthetic movement of the 1960s and early '70s. Writers since that time have adopted a somewhat different tone in their work, with less emphasis placed on the disparity between black and white in the United States. In the words of post-aesthetic authors such as Toni Morrison, John Edgar Wideman, and Kristin Hunter, African Americans are portrayed as looking inward for answers to their own questions, rather than always looking to the outside world.

Postmodernism: Writing from the 1960s forward characterized by experimentation and continuing to apply some of the fundamentals of modernism, which included existentialism and alienation. Postmodernists have gone a step further in the rejection of tradition begun with the modernists by also rejecting traditional forms, preferring the anti-novel over the novel and the anti-hero over the hero.

Primitivism: The belief that primitive peoples were nobler and less flawed than civilized peoples because they had not been subjected to the tainting influence of society.

Prologue: An introductory section of a literary work. It often contains information establishing the situation of the characters or presents information about the setting, time period, or action. In drama, the prologue is spoken by a chorus or by one of the principal characters.

Prose: A literary medium that attempts to mirror the language of everyday speech. It is distinguished from poetry by its use of unmetered, unrhymed language consisting of logically related sentences. Prose is usually grouped into paragraphs that form a cohesive whole such as an essay or a novel.

Prosopopoeia: See *Personification*

Protagonist: The central character of a story who serves as a focus for its themes and incidents and as the principal rationale for its development. The protagonist is sometimes referred to in discussions of modern literature as the hero or anti-hero.

Protest Fiction: Protest fiction has as its primary purpose the protesting of some social injustice, such as racism or discrimination.

Proverb: A brief, sage saying that expresses a truth about life in a striking manner.

Pseudonym: A name assumed by a writer, most often intended to prevent his or her identification as the author of a work. Two or more authors may work together under one pseudonym, or an author may use a different name for each genre he or she publishes in. Some publishing companies maintain "house pseudonyms," under which any number of authors may write installations in a series. Some authors also choose a pseudonym over their real names the way an actor may use a stage name.

Pun: A play on words that have similar sounds but different meanings.

R

Realism: A nineteenth-century European literary movement that sought to portray familiar characters, situations, and settings in a realistic manner. This was done primarily by using an objective narrative point of view and through the buildup of accurate detail. The standard for success of any realistic work depends on how faithfully it transfers common experience into fictional forms. The realistic method may be altered or extended, as in stream of consciousness writing, to record highly subjective experience.

Repartee: Conversation featuring snappy retorts and witticisms.

Resolution: The portion of a story following the climax, in which the conflict is resolved.

Rhetoric: In literary criticism, this term denotes the art of ethical persuasion. In its strictest sense, rhetoric adheres to various principles developed since classical times for arranging facts and ideas in a clear, persuasive, appealing manner. The term is also used to refer to effective prose in general and theories of or methods for composing effective prose.

Rhetorical Question: A question intended to provoke thought, but not an expressed answer, in the reader. It is most commonly used in oratory and other persuasive genres.

Rising Action: The part of a drama where the plot becomes increasingly complicated. Rising action leads up to the climax, or turning point, of a drama.

Roman à clef: A French phrase meaning "novel with a key." It refers to a narrative in which real persons are portrayed under fictitious names.

Romance: A broad term, usually denoting a narrative with exotic, exaggerated, often idealized characters, scenes, and themes.

Romanticism: This term has two widely accepted meanings. In historical criticism, it refers to a European intellectual and artistic movement of the late eighteenth and early nineteenth centuries that sought greater freedom of personal expression than that allowed by the strict rules of literary form and logic of the eighteenth-century neoclassicists. The Romantics preferred emotional and imaginative expression to rational analysis. They considered the individual to be at the center of all experience and so placed him or her at the center of their art. The Romantics believed that the creative imagination reveals nobler truths—unique feelings and attitudes—than those that could be discovered by logic or by scientific examination. Both the natural world and the state of childhood were important sources for revelations of "eternal truths." "Romanticism" is also used as a general term to refer to a type of sensibility found in all periods of literary history and usually considered to be in opposition to the principles of classicism. In this sense, Romanticism signifies any work or philosophy in which the exotic or dreamlike figure strongly, or that is devoted to individualistic expression, self-analysis, or a pursuit of a higher realm of knowledge than can be discovered by human reason.

Romantics: See *Romanticism*

S

Satire: A work that uses ridicule, humor, and wit to criticize and provoke change in human nature and institutions. There are two major types of satire: "formal" or "direct" satire speaks directly to the reader or to a character in the work; "indirect" satire relies upon the ridiculous behavior of its characters to make its point. Formal satire is further divided into two manners: the "Horatian," which ridicules gently, and the "Juvenalian," which derides its subjects harshly and bitterly.

Science Fiction: A type of narrative about or based upon real or imagined scientific theories and technology. Science fiction is often peopled with alien creatures and set on other planets or in different dimensions.

Second Person: See *Point of View*

Setting: The time, place, and culture in which the action of a narrative takes place. The elements of setting may include geographic location, characters' physical and mental environments, prevailing cultural attitudes, or the historical time in which the action takes place.

Simile: A comparison, usually using "like" or "as", of two essentially dissimilar things, as in "coffee as cold as ice" or "He sounded like a broken record."

Slang: A type of informal verbal communication that is generally unacceptable for formal writing. Slang words and phrases are often colorful exaggerations used to emphasize the speaker's point; they may also be shortened versions of an often-used word or phrase.

Slave Narrative: Autobiographical accounts of American slave life as told by escaped slaves. These works first appeared during the abolition movement of the 1830s through the 1850s.

Socialist Realism: The Socialist Realism school of literary theory was proposed by Maxim Gorky and established as a dogma by the first Soviet Congress of Writers. It demanded adherence to a communist worldview in works of literature. Its doctrines required an objective viewpoint comprehensible to the working classes and themes of social struggle featuring strong proletarian heroes.

Stereotype: A stereotype was originally the name for a duplication made during the printing process; this led to its modern definition as a person or thing that is (or is assumed to be) the same as all others of its type.

Stream of Consciousness: A narrative technique for rendering the inward experience of a character. This technique is designed to give the impression of an ever-changing series of thoughts, emotions, images, and memories in the spontaneous and seemingly illogical order that they occur in life.

Structure: The form taken by a piece of literature. The structure may be made obvious for ease of understanding, as in nonfiction works, or may obscured for artistic purposes, as in some poetry or seemingly "unstructured" prose.

Sturm und Drang: A German term meaning "storm and stress." It refers to a German literary movement of the 1770s and 1780s that reacted against the order and rationalism of the enlightenment, focusing instead on the intense experience of extraordinary individuals.

Style: A writer's distinctive manner of arranging words to suit his or her ideas and purpose in writing. The unique imprint of the author's personality upon his or her writing, style is the product of an author's way of arranging ideas and his or her use of diction, different sentence structures, rhythm, figures of speech, rhetorical principles, and other elements of composition.

Subjectivity: Writing that expresses the author's personal feelings about his subject, and which may or may not include factual information about the subject.

Subplot: A secondary story in a narrative. A subplot may serve as a motivating or complicating force for the main plot of the work, or it may provide emphasis for, or relief from, the main plot.

Surrealism: A term introduced to criticism by Guillaume Apollinaire and later adopted by Andre Breton. It refers to a French literary and artistic movement founded in the 1920s. The Surrealists sought to express unconscious thoughts and feelings in their works. The best-known technique used for achieving this aim was automatic writing—transcriptions of spontaneous outpourings from the unconscious. The Surrealists proposed to unify the contrary levels of conscious and unconscious, dream and reality, objectivity and subjectivity into a new level of "super-realism."

Suspense: A literary device in which the author maintains the audience's attention through the buildup of events, the outcome of which will soon be revealed.

Symbol: Something that suggests or stands for something else without losing its original identity. In literature, symbols combine their literal meaning with the suggestion of an abstract concept. Literary symbols are of two types: those that carry complex associations of meaning no matter what their contexts, and those that derive their suggestive meaning from their functions in specific literary works.

Symbolism: This term has two widely accepted meanings. In historical criticism, it denotes an early modernist literary movement initiated in France during the nineteenth century that reacted against the prevailing standards of realism. Writers in this movement aimed to evoke, indirectly and symbolically, an order of being beyond the material world of the five senses. Poetic expression of personal emotion figured strongly in the movement, typically by means of a private set of symbols uniquely identifiable with the individual poet. The principal aim of the Symbolists was to express in words the highly complex feelings that grew out of everyday contact with the world. In a broader sense, the term "symbolism" refers to the use of one object to represent another.

T

Tall Tale: A humorous tale told in a straightforward, credible tone but relating absolutely impossible events or feats of the characters. Such tales were commonly told of frontier adventures during the settlement of the west in the United States.

Theme: The main point of a work of literature. The term is used interchangeably with thesis.

Thesis: A thesis is both an essay and the point argued in the essay. Thesis novels and thesis plays share the quality of containing a thesis which is supported through the action of the story.

Third Person: See *Point of View*

Tone: The author's attitude toward his or her audience may be deduced from the tone of the work. A formal tone may create distance or convey politeness, while an informal tone may encourage a friendly, intimate, or intrusive feeling in the reader. The author's attitude toward his or her subject matter may also be deduced from the tone of the words he or she uses in discussing it.

Transcendentalism: An American philosophical and religious movement, based in New England from around 1835 until the Civil War. Transcendentalism was a form of American romanticism that had its roots abroad in the works of Thomas Carlyle, Samuel Coleridge, and Johann Wolfgang von Goethe. The Transcendentalists stressed the importance of intuition and subjective experience in communication with God. They rejected religious dogma and texts in favor of mysticism and scientific naturalism. They pursued truths that lie beyond the "colorless" realms perceived by reason and the senses and were active social reformers in public education, women's rights, and the abolition of slavery.

U

Urban Realism: A branch of realist writing that attempts to accurately reflect the often harsh facts of modern urban existence.

Utopia: A fictional perfect place, such as "paradise" or "heaven."

V

Verisimilitude: Literally, the appearance of truth. In literary criticism, the term refers to aspects of a work of literature that seem true to the reader.

Victorian: Refers broadly to the reign of Queen Victoria of England (1837-1901) and to anything with qualities typical of that era. For example, the qualities of smug narrowmindedness, bourgeois materialism, faith in social progress, and priggish morality are often considered Victorian. This stereotype is contradicted by such dramatic intellectual developments as the theories of Charles Darwin, Karl Marx, and Sigmund Freud (which stirred strong debates in England) and the critical attitudes of serious Victorian writers like Charles Dickens and George Eliot. In literature, the Victorian Period was the great age of the English novel, and the latter part of the era saw the rise of movements such as decadence and symbolism.

W

Weltanschauung: A German term referring to a person's worldview or philosophy.

Weltschmerz: A German term meaning "world pain." It describes a sense of anguish about the nature of existence, usually associated with a melancholy, pessimistic attitude.

Z

Zeitgeist: A German term meaning "spirit of the time." It refers to the moral and intellectual trends of a given era.

Cumulative Author/Title Index

Hammett, Dashiell
   The Maltese Falcon: V21
The Handmaid's Tale (Atwood): V4
Hard Times (Dickens): V20
Hardy, Thomas
   Far from the Madding Crowd: V19
   The Mayor of Casterbridge: V15
   The Return of the Native: V11
   Tess of the d'Urbervilles: V3
Harris, Marilyn
   Hatter Fox: V14
Hatter Fox (Harris): V14
Hawthorne, Nathaniel
   The House of the Seven Gables: V20
   The Scarlet Letter: V1
The Heart Is a Lonely Hunter
   (McCullers): V6
Heart of Darkness (Conrad): V2
Hegi, Ursula
   Stones from the River: V25
Heller, Joseph
   Catch-22: V1
Hemingway, Ernest
   A Farewell to Arms: V1
   For Whom the Bell Tolls: V14
   The Old Man and the Sea: V6
   The Sun Also Rises: V5
Herbert, Frank
   Soul Catcher: V17
Herzog (Bellow): V14
Hesse, Hermann
   Demian: V15
   Siddhartha: V6
   Steppenwolf: V24
Highsmith, Patricia
   The Talented Mr. Ripley: V27
Hijuelos, Oscar
   *The Mambo Kings Play Songs of
   Love:* V17
Hinton, S. E.
   The Outsiders: V5
   Rumble Fish: V15
   Tex: V9
   That Was Then, This Is Now: V16
The Hitchhiker's Guide to the Galaxy
   (Adams): V7
The Hobbit (Tolkien): V8
Høeg, Peter
   Smilla's Sense of Snow: V17
Hotel du Lac (Brookner): V23
The Hours (Cunningham): V23
House Made of Dawn (Momaday):
   V10
The House of Mirth (Wharton): V15
The House of the Seven Gables
   (Hawthorne): V20
The House of the Spirits (Allende):
   V6
The House on Mango Street
   (Cisneros): V2
*How the García Girls Lost Their
   Accents* (Alvarez): V5

Howards End (Forster): V10
Hughes, Langston
   Tambourines to Glory: V21
Hugo, Victor
   The Hunchback of Notre Dame: V20
   Les Misérables: V5
Hulme, Keri
   The Bone People: V24
Humboldt's Gift (Bellow): V26
The Hunchback of Notre Dame
   (Hugo): V20
Hurston, Zora Neale
   Their Eyes Were Watching God: V3
Huxley, Aldous
   Brave New World: V6

I

I Am the Cheese (Cormier): V18
I, Claudius (Graves): V21
I Know Why the Caged Bird Sings
   (Angelou): V2
I Never Promised You a Rose Garden
   (Greenberg): V23
Ida (Stein): V27
The Immoralist (Gide): V21
In Babylon (Möring): V25
In Country (Mason): V4
In the Castle of My Skin (Lamming):
   V15
In the Time of the Butterflies
   (Alvarez): V9
Independence Day (Ford): V25
Invisible Man (Ellison): V2
Irving, John
   A Prayer for Owen Meany: V14
   The World According to Garp: V12
Ishiguro, Kazuo
   The Remains of the Day: V13

J

James, Henry
   The Ambassadors: V12
   The Portrait of a Lady: V19
   The Turn of the Screw: V16
Jane Eyre (Brontë): V4
Japrisot, Sébastien
   A Very Long Engagement: V18
Jewett, Sarah Orne
   The Country of the Pointed Firs: V15
Jin, Ha
   Waiting: V25
Johnson, James Weldon
   *The Autobiography of an Ex-
   Coloured Man:* V22
Jones, Edward P.
   The Known World: V26
The Joy Luck Club (Tan): V1
Joyce, James
   *A Portrait of the Artist as a Young
   Man:* V7
   Ulysses: V26

July's People (Gordimer): V4
Juneteenth (Ellison): V21
The Jungle (Sinclair): V6

K

Kaddish for a Child Not Born
   (Kertész): V23
Kafka, Franz
   The Trial: V7
Keneally, Thomas
   Schindler's List: V17
Kerouac, Jack
   On the Road: V8
Kertész, Imre
   Kaddish for a Child Not Born:
   V23
Kesey, Ken
   One Flew Over the Cuckoo's Nest:
   V2
Keyes, Daniel
   Flowers for Algernon: V2
Kidd, Sue Monk
   The Secret Life of Bees: V27
The Killer Angels (Shaara): V26
Kim (Kipling): V21
Kincaid, Jamaica
   Annie John: V3
Kindred (Butler): V8
Kingsolver, Barbara
   Animal Dreams: V12
   The Bean Trees: V5
   Pigs in Heaven: V10
   Poisonwood Bible: V24
Kingston, Maxine Hong
   The Woman Warrior: V6
Kinsella, W. P.
   Shoeless Joe: V15
Kipling, Rudyard
   Kim: V21
Kitchen (Yoshimoto): V7
The Kitchen God's Wife (Tan): V13
Knowles, John
   A Separate Peace: V2
The Known World (Jones): V26
Koestler, Arthur
   Darkness at Noon: V19
Kogawa, Joy
   Obasan: V3
Kosinski, Jerzy
   The Painted Bird: V12
Kundera, Milan
   *The Book of Laughter and
   Forgetting:* V27
   *The Unbearable Lightness of
   Being:* V18

L

Lamming, George
   In the Castle of My Skin: V15
The Last King of Scotland (Foden):
   V15

Cumulative Author/Title Index

Cumulative
Nationality/Ethnicity Index

Cumulative Nationality/Ethnicity Index

Subject/Theme Index

Order
My Name Is Red: 220
Through the Looking Glass: 292
Ottoman Empire
My Name Is Red: 202, 213

P

Pain and suffering
The Assistant: 11, 15, 17–18, 22,
24–25
Blindness: 45, 47–48
Parental love
The Secret Life of Bees: 236–237
Patriarchy
The Golden Notebook: 94, 97,
104–105
Ida: 124–125, 127
Perception
Ida: 111–112, 116, 120
Life of Pi: 150–151
Personal growth
The Golden Notebook: 96
Politics and government
Blindness: 43
My Name Is Red: 224
Possibility
The Assistant: 7
Possibility of the Existence of God,
The
Life of Pi: 141–142
Postcolonialism
Life of Pi: 129, 145
Postmodernism
The Golden Notebook: 79, 98–100
Life of Pi: 146
Poverty
The Assistant: 1, 3, 17, 27
Lives of Girls and Women: 160
The Man Who Loved Children:
191–192
Power
The Book of Laughter and
Forgetting: 76
Lives of Girls and Women: 171
Through the Looking Glass: 281,
287, 290
Power of Storytelling, The
Life of Pi: 142–143
Prague Spring of 1968
The Book of Laughter and
Forgetting: 62–64
Predetermination
Through the Looking Glass: 285
Present
Ida: 124
Privacy
The Book of Laughter and
Forgetting: 69, 72

Q

Quest
The Assistant: 14, 20

R

Racial Intolerance
The Secret Life of Bees: 235–236
Racism and racial conflict
The Secret Life of Bees: 226, 228,
230, 233, 235–236, 239–241
Rape
The Assistant: 10, 19, 27
Blindness: 37
Re-creating the past
The Book of Laughter and
Forgetting: 68
Realism
Blindness: 47–48, 50
See also Magical realism
Reality
Lives of Girls and Women: 174
The Talented Mr. Ripley: 250,
259–260, 267, 270
Through the Looking Glass:
282–283, 286
Reality and Unreality
The Talented Mr. Ripley: 259–260
Rebirth
The Golden Notebook: 96
Redemption *See* Salvation
Redemption through Development of
Moral Awareness
The Assistant: 9–10
Reference code
Blindness: 47–48
Regret
The Assistant: 8
Religion
Blindness: 47–48, 50
Life of Pi: 132–133, 143, 146–154
Lives of Girls and Women: 160, 166
My Name Is Red: 211, 224
Through the Looking Glass: 285–286
Religion
Lives of Girls and Women: 166
Religious conversion
The Assistant: 24–25, 27–28
Remorse
The Book of Laughter and
Forgetting: 77
Renewal
The Assistant: 1
Repentance
The Assistant: 24
Repetition
Ida: 117
The Man Who Loved Children: 201
Repression
The Book of Laughter and
Forgetting: 75
Response to Crisis
Blindness: 38
Restlessness
Ida: 127
Revenge
The Book of Laughter and
Forgetting: 56

Revisionism
The Book of Laughter and
Forgetting: 76
Ritual
Life of Pi: 143
Rivalry
My Name Is Red: 223–224
Romanticism
The Assistant: 28

S

Salvation
The Assistant: 9–10, 15, 23–24, 27
Blindness: 44
The Secret Life of Bees: 226, 237
School life
Lives of Girls and Women: 161,
167–168
Science
Through the Looking Glass:
285–286
Search for self
The Assistant: 20–22
Selection
Ida: 117
Self realization
The Assistant: 27
The Secret Life of Bees: 226
The Talented Mr. Ripley: 267
Self-deprecation
The Golden Notebook: 101, 105
Self-punishment
The Golden Notebook: 105
Self-sacrifice
The Assistant: 10, 18
Selfishness
The Assistant: 11, 16, 19
Blindness: 44–45
Selflessness
Blindness: 45
Separation
The Secret Life of Bees: 243
Setting
Blindness: 42–43
The Talented Mr. Ripley:
261–262
Sex and sexuality
Lives of Girls and Women: 161,
165–166
Sex and Sexuality
Lives of Girls and Women: 166
Sexual abuse
The Book of Laughter and
Forgetting: 56
Shadows
Blindness: 46, 50–51
Shame
The Talented Mr. Ripley: 268,
272
Silence
The Book of Laughter and
Forgetting: 70